FORENSIC ANTHROPOLOGY

PUBLISHED AND FORTHCOMING TITLES IN THE *ADVANCED FORENSIC SCIENCE SERIES*

Published

Forensic Fingerprints
Firearm and Toolmark Examination and Identification
Forensic Biology
Forensic Chemistry
Professional Issues in Forensic Science
Materials Analysis in Forensic Science
Forensic Pathology

Forthcoming

Forensic Engineering
Behavioral Analysis
Digital and Documents
Forensic Toxicology and Drugs

FORENSIC ANTHROPOLOGY

Advanced Forensic Science Series

MAX M. HOUCK, PhD, FRSC

Managing Director, Forensic & Intelligence Services, LLC, St. Petersburg, FL, USA

Amsterdam • Boston • Heidelberg • London • New York • Oxford
Paris • San Diego • San Francisco • Singapore • Sydney • Tokyo

Academic Press is an imprint of Elsevier

Academic Press is an imprint of Elsevier
125 London Wall, London EC2Y 5AS, United Kingdom
525 B Street, Suite 1800, San Diego, CA 92101-4495, United States
50 Hampshire Street, 5th Floor, Cambridge, MA 02139, United States
The Boulevard, Langford Lane, Kidlington, Oxford OX5 1GB, United Kingdom

Library of Congress Cataloging-in-Publication Data
A catalog record for this book is available from the Library of Congress

British Library Cataloguing-in-Publication Data
A catalogue record for this book is available from the British Library

ISBN: 978-0-12-802214-6
ISSN : 2352-6238

For information on all Academic Press publications
visit our website at http://www.elsevier.com/

Working together
to grow libraries in
developing countries

www.elsevier.com • www.bookaid.org

Publisher: Sara Tenney
Acquisition Editor: Elizabeth Brown
Editorial Project Manager: Joslyn Chaiprasert-Paguio
Production Project Manager: Lisa Jones
Designer: Matthew Limbert

Typeset by TNQ Books and Journals

CONTENTS

SENIOR EDITOR: BIOGRAPHY

Max M. Houck is an internationally recognized forensic expert with research interests in anthropology, trace evidence, education, and the fundamentals of forensic science, both as a science and as an enterprise. He has worked in the private sector, the public sector (at the regional and federal levels), and in academia. Dr. Houck has published in a wide variety of areas in the field, in books, book chapters, and peer-reviewed journals. His casework includes the Branch Davidian Investigation, the September 11 attacks on the Pentagon, the D.B. Cooper case, the US Embassy bombings in Africa, and the West Memphis Three case. He served for 6 years as the Chair of the Forensic Science Educational Program Accreditation Commission. Dr. Houck is a founding coeditor of the journal Forensic Science Policy and Management, with Jay Siegel; he has also coauthored a major textbook with Siegel, *Fundamentals of Forensic Science*. In 2012, Dr. Houck was in the top 1% of connected professionals on LinkedIn. Dr. Houck is currently the Managing Director of Forensic & Intelligence Services, LLC, St. Petersburg, FL.

LIST OF CONTRIBUTORS

CGG Aitken
The University of Edinburgh, Edinburgh, United Kingdom

V Alunni
Université de Nice Sophia Antipolis, Nice, France

E Baccino
Hopital Lapeyronie, Montpellier, France

A Biedermann
The University of Lausanne, Lausanne-Dorigny, Switzerland

S Black
University of Dundee, Dundee, UK

J Brandi
National Institute of Forensic Science, ANZPAA, Melbourne, VIC, Australia

E Burton
Greater Manchester Police Forensic Services Branch, Manchester, UK

C Cattaneo
Università degli Studi di Milano, Milano, Italy

JG Clement
The University of Melbourne, Melbourne, VIC, Australia

SA Cole
University of California, Irvine, CA, USA

F Crispino
Université du Québec à Trois-Rivières, Trois-Rivières, QC, Canada

PA Cross
University of Central Lancashire, Preston, UK

E Cunha
University of Coimbra, Coimbra, Portugal

JM Curran
University of Auckland, Auckland, New Zealand

G Edmond
The University of New South Wales, Sydney, NSW, Australia

J Epstein
Widener University School of Law, Wilmington, DE, USA

TW Fenton
Michigan State University, East Lansing, MI, USA

D Franklin
The University of Western Australia, Crawley, WA, Australia

P Gabriel
University Clinic Düsseldorf, Düsseldorf, Germany

D Gibelli
Università degli Studi di Milano, Milano, Italy

WH Goodwin
University of Central Lancashire, Preston, UK

C Henderson
Stetson University College of Law, Gulfport, FL, USA

J Horswell
Approved Forensics Sendirian Berhad, Selangor, Malaysia

MM Houck
Consolidated Forensic Laboratory, Washington, DC, USA

W Huckenbeck
University Clinic Düsseldorf, Düsseldorf, Germany

JR Hunter
University of Birmingham, Birmingham, UK

CV Hurst
Michigan State University, East Lansing, MI, USA

RL Jantz
University of Tennessee, Knoxville, TN, USA

R Julian
University of Tasmania, Hobart, TAS, Australia

T Kanchan
Kasturba Medical College, Manipal University, Mangalore, India

SF Kelty
University of Tasmania, Hobart, TAS, Australia

G Kernbach-Wighton
University of Bonn, Bonn, Germany

K Krishan
Panjab University, Chandigarh, India

KW Lenz
Saint Petersburg, FL, USA

GB Leong
Center for Forensic Services, Western State Hospital, Tacoma, WA, USA

B Madea
University of Bonn, Bonn, Germany

P Margot
University of Lausanne, Lausanne, Switzerland

MK Marks
The University of Tennessee, Knoxville, TN, USA

P Millen
Paul Millen Associates, London, UK

JJ Miller
York Archaeological Trust for Excavation and Research Limited, York, UK

J Pinheiro
Instituto Nacional de Medicina Legal, Coimbra, Portugal

S Pollak
University of Freiburg, Freiburg, Germany

F Poole
Forensic Services Group, Parramatta, NSW, Australia

G Quatrehomme
Université de Nice Sophia Antipolis, Nice, France

K Ramsey
Greater Manchester Police Forensic Services Branch, Manchester, UK

O Ribaux
University of Lausanne, Lausanne, Switzerland

J Robertson
University of Canberra, Canberra, ACT, Australia

LR Rockwell
Forensic and Intelligence Services, LLC, Alexandria, VA, USA

C Roux
University of Technology, Sydney, NSW, Australia

P Saukko
University of Turku, Turku, Finland

B Saw
Australian Federal Police, Canberra, ACT, Australia

A Schmeling
Institute of Legal Medicine, Münster, Germany

U Schmidt
Freiburg University Medical Center, Freiburg, Germany

N Scudder
Australian Federal Police, Canberra, ACT, Australia

JA Silva
VA Outpatient Clinic, San Jose, CA, USA

T Simmons
University of Central Lancashire, Preston, UK

A Soler
Pima County Office of the Medical Examiner, Tucson, AZ, USA

CN Stephan
Central Identification Laboratory, HI, USA

M Steyn
University of Pretoria, Hatfield, South Africa

C Sturdy Colls
Forensic and Crime Science, Stoke-on-Trent, UK

F Taroni
The University of Lausanne, Lausanne-Dorigny, Switzerland

DSK Thurley
York Archaeological Trust for Excavation and Research Limited, York, UK

DH Ubelaker
Smithsonian Institution, NMNH, Washington, DC, USA

H Vogel
University Hospital Eppendorf, Hamburg, Germany

T Vosk
Criminal Defense Law Firm, Kirkland, WA, USA

R Weinstock
University of California, Los Angeles, CA, USA, West Los Angeles Veterans Affairs Medical Center, Los Angeles, CA, USA

DJ Wescott
Texas State University, San Marcos, TX, USA

L Wilson-Wilde
National Institute of Forensic Science, ANZPAA, Melbourne, VIC, Australia

FOREWORD

Forensic science has much to learn. The breadth of the discipline alone should render any reasonably learned person dizzy with expectations; insects, explosives, liver functions, DNA, firearms, textiles, adhesives, skeletons, and so on the list goes on forever. That is because anything, truly *anything*, can become evidence, from a single fiber to an entire ocean liner. Forensic science does not lack for specialized knowledge (some might stay too specialized), but what it is wanting is knowledge that is comprehensive, integrated, and foundational. Introductions to forensic science abound, and many highly specialized texts are also available, but a gap exists between the two: a bridge from novice to practitioner. As the 2009 NRC report noted:

Forensic science examiners need to understand the principles, practices, and contexts of scientific methodology, as well as the distinctive features of their specialty. Ideally, training should move beyond apprentice-like transmittal of practices to education based on scientifically valid principles. NRC (2009, pp. 26—27).

The *Advanced Forensic Science Series* seeks to fill that gap. It is a unique source, combining entries from the world's leading specialists who contributed to the second edition of the award-winning *Encyclopedia of Forensic Sciences* and organizing them by topic into a series of volumes that are philosophically grounded yet professionally specialized. The series is composed of 12 volumes that cover the breadth of forensic science:

1. Professional Issues
2. Biology
3. Chemistry
4. Fingerprints
5. Firearms
6. Materials Analysis
7. Pathology

8. Anthropology
9. Engineering
10. Behavioral
11. Digital and Documents
12. Toxicology and Drugs

Each volume contains sections common to all forensic sciences, such as professionalism, ethics, health and safety, and court testimony, and sections relevant to the topics in that particular subdiscipline. Pedagogy is included, providing review questions, discussion questions, the latest references in additional readings, and key words. Thus, each volume is suitable as a technical reference, an advanced textbook, or a training adjunct.

The *Advanced Forensic Science Series* provides expert information, useful teaching tools, and a ready source for instruction, research, and practice. I hope, like learning, it is the only thing for you.

M.M. Houck, PhD, FRSC
Series Editor

Reference

National Research Council, 2009. Strengthening Forensic Science in the U.S.: A Path Forward. National Academies of Science, Washington, DC.

PREFACE

"I am an invisible man. I am a man of substance, of flesh and bone, fiber and liquids—and I might even be said to possess a mind. I am invisible, understand, simply because people refuse to see me." Ralph Ellison, *Invisible Man*, prologue

There is an old joke about physical anthropologists, that they are either "wet," because they study living people, or "dry," because they study ancient bones. Based on that distinction, forensic anthropologists could be called "moist," because they work neither with the living nor with the ancient dead but the more-recently deceased. As unappealing as this may sound, the work of forensic anthropology is desperately needed in investigations as diverse as child abuse, missing persons, human trafficking, cold cases, and war crimes. Originating as many forensic disciplines have—an academic area of study that is begged or dragooned into the service of police—forensic anthropology has done well for itself by holding fast to its scholarly roots while ever branching into new areas of application and flowering new methods. Unlike other scientific methods that have been whittled down into exceedingly focused techniques (DNA analysis comes to mind), forensic anthropology has expanded itself and grown along with other related forensic areas, such as entomology and geosciences.

Like forensic pathologists, forensic anthropologists speak for those who cannot tell their tale. Even more so, they may speak for those whose tale was long ago and their remains may be the only pages left in that story. Medical doctors learn systems, like the circulatory system or the endocrine system, how they operate and what stops them from working. Anthropologists learn pieces and parts, identifying fragments and traces, translating minuscule bits of bone into biological realities. A medical doctor can identify a human femur (most of the time, anyway) but it takes a forensic anthropologist to recognize a piece of a lesser trochanter from a left femur. This ability to translate from traces to reality, inherited from archeology and the physical anthropology of decrepit osteological remains, is a key feature not only of forensic anthropology but all of forensic science. Thus, forensic anthropology lies at the very heart of what it means to be a forensic discipline.

More and more, forensic anthropologists do work with the living, identifying the stolen, the lost, and the abused. This expansion may seem to push the boundaries of the discipline too far from its skeletal origins but it falls cleanly within its purview: Expertise in humans, as a species, for legal or governmental purposes. The cases are heartbreaking but the work is necessary and, sadly, the application of forensic anthropology to identifying the living and describing the abuses they suffer will continue. Helping those who cannot help themselves, however, is what gives so much meaning to this profession.

Section 1. Overview

Forensic Anthropology: An Introduction

C Cattaneo, Università degli Studi di Milano, Milano, Italy

Today the adjective "forensic" seems to be applicable to almost any discipline. So in the past decades, the evolution of "saprophytic" disciplines (feeding on original ones such as pathology, entomology, botany, archeology, and many others) into forensic ones, that is, forensic pathology, forensic entomology, and so on has been seen. The same is true for anthropology, a very vast domain. Because it studies humans also in the context of culture and behavior, anthropology is sometimes classed as a social science. Traditionally, it has two main branches (according to some academic schools even more), which can be identified as cultural and physical anthropology: the first is related to the more social and artistic realms of man, whereas the second to the more physical ones. According to the American Association of Physical Anthropology, this discipline is defined as a biological science that deals with the adaptations, variability, and evolution of human beings and their living and fossil relatives. Physical anthropology is therefore the anthropology that has been adopted by forensics at the moment: but one can expect that in the future, many aspects of cultural anthropology may merge with criminal anthropology, and perhaps even criminology.

Forensic anthropology (FA) has been defined as the application of physical anthropology, generally intended as human osteology, to the forensic scenario. The following paragraphs therefore refer to what is traditionally known as FA and the new developing fields.

Before discussing what anthropologists do in the forensic scenario, it is worthwhile to spend a few words on who the anthropologist is. Certainly, the anthropologist is not superimposable to the pathologist. Even in cases of skeletal remains, a pathologist must always be involved as he or she is the only specialist (technically and bureaucratically) who can diagnose and certify the cause of death. Nonetheless, forensic pathologists usually have very little training in osteology and anthropology; therefore, the anthropologist is a fundamental figure for extrapolating from human remains information, which is written in the skeleton and needs specialized training to be deciphered appropriately (this goes beyond standard medical forensic training); for example, establishing age from the pubic symphysis or distinguishing a perimortem from a postmortem fracture. For what concerns training and certification, this is an even more difficult issue, as for many disciplines of the forensic realm. Some countries, such as the United States, have certified boards with specific prerequisites (an examination, a master's course, a PhD, and casework), others (most European countries) have none and FA is dealt with by both pathologists and physical anthropologists. Some countries have postgraduate training in FA (e.g., UK, Italy, and the United States) and, again, some do not. Therefore, depending on the country or even on the single situation, one may encounter different training—if at all—of the forensic anthropologist. Risks are that physical anthropologists with no experience in forensics will take on cases and that pathologists with no experience in osteology will deal with bones. Furthermore, the lack of certification or of some sort of "control" over who can actually practice this "profession" opens the field to many self-made men with inappropriate training. This, however, is a problem frequently occurring in other disciplines adopted by the forensic world, such as botany, geology, entomology, and so on.

Going back to the more technical discussion on FA, one can say that in the traditional scenario, the anthropologist comes in when "extreme" states of decomposition of the body are present (skeletonization and severe charring) and bone and teeth become the only tissues available (although this discipline can be useful also in cases of extremely putrefied cadavers where soft tissues are no longer informative and the study of the underlying calcified tissues may yield more information).

Though physical anthropology has always included the study of man and his diversity in toto, even with respect to skin pigmentation or blood type, for example, the forensic version has adopted the subsections closest to archeology, in other words, everything that implies the study of human skeletal remains. The discipline of anthropology, therefore, begins "on site," following the closest archeological tradition. Forensic archeology is a very close cousin, according to some subsection of FA, and contemplates the application of archeology to the forensic context for the search and proper recovery of human remains. The forensic anthropologist therefore usually has some competence in recovering human skeletal remains underground or on the surface.

Before studying the human remains themselves, these in fact have to be properly recovered and sometimes even need to be found. Mostly, searching for human remains is the scenario of the forensic archeologist: he or she must have the proper experience to know how to look for a criminal burial site—and know whether to use aerial photography, geophysics, or other means. When the remains, in particular, skeletal remains, are found, the scene of crime team should include an anthropologist who has appropriate training for recognizing and recovering bones, verifying if any are missing, and so on. Another example of the role of the anthropologist at the scene of crime is in the case of burnt and charred human remains, when all that is left of the entire body are small fragments of bone. In these cases, meticulous sieving through the remains (in a burnt car, for example) performed on behalf of an expert in osteology may help retrieve much more osseous material, and therefore, more information concerning identity, cause of death, and other precious data: it should always be kept in mind that in fact, in the case of human remains, the only lesion present may be on the smallest bone of the hand, such as a phalanx, and that it is therefore crucial to recover every single piece of bone.

Before dealing with the actual study of the bones as one or more individuals, in skeletonized cases, anthropology is the discipline with the tools for verifying whether a bunch of bones are of forensic interest, that is, if they are human, and, if so, recent. According to the morphological study of such remains (and at times histological), the anthropologist will verify whether the bones are human. Human bones, when intact, are generally distinguishable from nonhuman ones due to their specific morphology. However, in the case of small fragments or very degraded pieces of bone, shape and size are frequently of little help. DNA tests can of course be performed but quicker and less costly methods exist in anthropology which can easily lead to a diagnosis of human versus nonhuman. Once the anthropologist has decided for a human origin, another preliminary task to the actual study of human remains must be to verify whether they are ancient or recent and what the postmortem interval is. If such a diagnosis is relatively simple when soft tissues are still present, even though decomposed, through the study of the level of degradation (e.g., Accumulated Degree Days) or through entomological analyses, everything becomes more complicated with complete skeletonization. A clean skeleton may be 5, 10, or 100 years old and look the same—at times only sophisticated chemical tests can do the job when no macroscopic or microscopic method will give a reliable time since death estimation. Anthropologists have in fact recently become more and more acquainted with radiocarbon and other isotope tests and with the many laboratories across the United States and Europe who actually perform them.

The most traditional task of the anthropologist or osteologist is, however, what comes next—building the biological profile. For centuries, anthropologists (previously with calipers, nowadays also with more complex technology) have been experts at detecting and describing human diversity on bone, and therefore, at sexing, aging, determining ancestry, stature, and to a certain extent, pathology of the skeleton. Thus, the "identikit" of the skeleton of a victim will be built on the basis of bone morphology and metrics. In the end, a face can even be suggested if the anthropologist goes as far as performing what is known as facial reconstruction or approximation. This is a technique by which according to specific anatomical landmarks, soft tissues are applied step-by-step onto the cranium (or a cast) to provide a face, which may look like the person when he or she was alive. At this point, the anthropologist has set the basis for identifying the skeletonized victim of a murder or simply someone who died and whose body decomposed with no ID. The problem of unidentified human remains is becoming an increasing social, ethical, and juridical problem, particularly given the increase of illegal immigration in many countries; forensic anthropologists have the expertise to help solve such cases.

Once the biological profile is confronted with missing persons, a possible ID may come up; in other words, there is an idea of who the skeleton may have belonged to in life, then it is necessary to go on to the next step, personal identification. Personal or positive identification is usually performed by odontologists, fingerprint experts, and DNA specialists. It consists of comparing biological antemortem and postmortem data to verify whether a definite match can be made. However, sometimes, when such antemortem data is missing (e.g., no dental records exist, no family or DNA antemortem materials such as toothbrushes can be found, and the person does not have a criminal record, and therefore, no registered fingerprints), bone morphology may again be useful for identification, and therefore, anthropology (along with radiology) may provide positive identification. Every bone has a peculiar shape and has specific identification potential. Frontal sinus shape, for example, can be extremely useful for identifying remains when an antemortem X-ray of the cranium exists. The method of comparison of the antemortem and postmortem shapes of this part of the frontal bone has even been standardized but virtually all bones have sufficient identification potential. Sometimes no antemortem medical records at all exist, and all that is left is a photograph of the person whom one thinks the remains belong. In these cases, craniofacial comparison or superimposition can be attempted although it should be used with great caution, and according to some authors only to exclude identity.

As previously mentioned, the anthropologist can aid the pathologist in looking for and interpreting signs of bone trauma, especially in distinguishing genuine trauma from bone lesions deriving from weathering or postmortem artifacts, in other words from taphonomical events. This can be done only by experts properly trained in the effects of animals and environment on bone. An important issue is also that of identifying the correct timing of a bone fracture: was it produced at the time of death, before, or after? Anthropologists for these purposes have had to coin a new terminology. Contrary to pathologists who can usually tell from well-preserved soft tissues whether a lesion was produced before or after death, anthropologists are limited to antemortem, perimortem, and postmortem diagnoses, where antemortem represents a time necessary to visualize signs of bone healing (generally weeks before death), postmortem implies a time long enough after death to have allowed the bone to loose all elastic properties so that a break in the bone will appear "old," and perimortem includes any fracture produced at a point where the bone tissue still had elastic properties, which means, variably, some time before or after death. At this moment, there is no way of being certain, contrary to the situation with soft tissue, that a bone fracture was vital.

Anthropology usually also deals with the biomechanics of bone (how bone breaks) to extrapolate the dynamics behind a bone fracture and with the more frequent manifestations of trauma on bone, namely blunt force, sharp force, and gunshot injury. Anthropologists have started to concentrate not only on the appearance of these injuries on bone, but also on the survival of residues, which may help orient toward the type of instrument used. For other types of exogenous deaths, such as mechanical asphyxias (e.g., drowning and strangulation) and toxicological deaths, osteology collaborates with other subdisciplines: in the first case, for example, to verify the presence of minute microorganisms such as diatoms in bone to be able to verify if we are in front of a case of drowning; in the second, if there are actual toxicological substances surviving in the bone that can reveal something on cause of death, which, as previously mentioned, should be dealt with by the forensic pathologist.

Then there are the newer trends of FA. These consist of the extension of FA to the study of the morphology of body and face of the living—an area which has more of a tradition in Europe, particularly in Germany and in the East. Many more issues such as identification of individuals filmed by video surveillance systems from body shape and facial physiognomy are becoming important in the forensic scenario. For example, video surveillance has become extremely common in many public and private places across most developed countries, from banks to airports. Thus, a common question that judges are beginning to ask is whether it is possible to identify a suspect as someone committing a crime on a photograph or on a video. As a consequence, identification experts have to deal with determining stature and facial similarities from video home system or digital supports, a task which is extremely difficult also because of the lack of research in this area and of standards and tested protocols. The same can be said for

juvenile pornography. It has now been verified that the external appearance of genitals cannot be used for determining whether the objects of pornography are under age or not from photographs. Research is looking elsewhere for an answer, for example, toward facial morphology and proportions, another area of interest for anthropology in the forensic scenario. These and other new developments will probably require the integration of such topics in FA courses to prepare future scientists for novel fields of research and court work.

Regardless of what specific area of anthropology one is dealing with, the forensic expert, even in this field, must distinguish himself from anthropologists working in other contexts, thanks to a forensic mentality, a *forma mentis*, which encompasses sustaining scientific theory and facts according to specific prerequisites and regulations (in this day and age, Daubert and Kumho, for example, requesting that methods be accepted by the scientific community, that they have known errors, etc.). Anthropology cannot be conceived as forensic unless it is applied according to these rules which are fundamental to sustain results and hypotheses in court.

Finally FA has strong links with several disciplines related to the natural sciences which it cannot be separated from, especially in this period in which there is a growing conscience of how many subjects may be pertinent to a single scene of crime or a single body. For example, frequently the anthropologist deals with remains covered in soil, insects, and foliage. Before the osteologist even begins to clean the bone, the question must arise as to what should be saved—and how important it is—of all the "dirt" that needs to be washed off before the bone can be studied. Surely it contains elements of interest from a geological, botanical, and entomological point of view (to name but a few). Thus the osteologist needs to consult with the natural scientists before even beginning his or her work. During identification procedures, the anthropologists frequently need to compare notes with DNA and dental experts. For example, to complete the biological profile, sometimes dental work can give important clues, and tips on sex and race in difficult cases can be given by DNA.

In conclusion, FA cannot be easily and simply defined. It has, however, great relevance both in the study of human remains and of the living.

See also: **Anthropology/Odontology:** Aging the Dead and the Living; Ancestry; Animal Effects on Bones; Archeology; Biomechanics of Bone Trauma; Bone Pathology and Antemortem Trauma; Bone Trauma; Facial Approximation; Forensic Taphonomy; History of Forensic Anthropology; Identification of the Living; Personal Identification in Forensic Anthropology; Postmortem Interval; Sexing; Species: Human Versus Nonhuman; Stature and Build; **Forensic Medicine/ Clinical:** Identification.

Further Reading

Black, S., 2003. Forensic anthropology – regulation in the United Kingdom. Science and Justice 43, 187–192.

Blau, S., Ubelaker, D.H., 2009. Handbook of Forensic Anthropology and Archaeology. Left Coast Press, CA.

Brickley, M.B., Ferllini, R., 2007. Forensic Anthropology, Case Studies from Europe. CC Thomas, IL.

Cattaneo, C., 2007. Forensic anthropology: developments of a classical discipline in the new millennium. Forensic Science International 165, 185–193.

Cattaneo, C., Porta, D., De Angelis, D., Gibelli, D., Poppa, P., Grandi, M., 2010. Unidentified bodies and human remains: an Italian glimpse through a European problem. Forensic Science International 195, 1–3.

Christensen, A.M., 2004. The impact of Daubert: implications for testimony and research in forensic anthropology and the use of frontal sinuses in personal identification. Journal of Forensic Sciences 49 (3), 1–4.

Grivas, C.R., Komar, D.A., 2008. Kumho, Daubert and the nature of scientific enquiry: implications for forensic anthropology. Journal of Forensic Sciences 53, 771–776.

Komar, D.A., Buikstra, J.E., 2008. Forensic Anthropology: Contemporary Theory and Practice. Oxford University Press, Oxford.

Schmitt, A., Cunha, E., Pinheiro, J., 2006. Forensic Anthropology and Medicine. Humana Press, NJ, pp. 39–56.

History of Forensic Anthropology

S Black, University of Dundee, Dundee, UK

The history of a subject such as forensic anthropology can be relayed in many ways and with alternative focus depending upon where the narrator chooses to begin the story and which stream they choose to emphasize. For example, it may be told simply through a chronology of influential cases that illustrate the first of their kind, the most remarkable, biggest, most controversial, unsolved, or perhaps the most convoluted investigation. It may be told through a biography of the practitioners—characters who, for a variety of reasons, have shaped and molded the discipline (or indeed its precursors) and become its accredited pioneers or even blackguards. This definition holds equally true for an organization or an institution, where the combination of people, place, and time may result in advancements through leadership or event. These events may in themselves form the basis of a history, and they may relate not only to important physical phenomena such as mass disasters, but also to changes in approach and perception of the discipline, perhaps resulting in a change to legislation or accreditation. Indeed the event may even relate to a pivotal publication. The reality, of course, is that an accurate historical account of a discipline, such as forensic anthropology, combines and interweaves all of these, and it is how authors choose to relay those facts, in their own personal opinion, that lay down a series of narratives, all of which will have truth but will tell the story from a slightly different perspective. Such is the way with history; at the point of writing, it is merely a chronicle of a person's viewpoint based on how they interpret the evidence and how they choose it to be portrayed.

Perhaps, the easiest way to address a history is with consideration of "firsts"—the first case reported or the first person to do something, but this may rely on the definition one uses of the subject at a time when there was no such recognized or named discipline. Must one then define the discipline to be able to identify a time of its birth? Doing that opens up great debate, as it is well recognized that anatomy, anthropology, and, subsequently, physical anthropology are the natural predecessors of forensic anthropology. Yet, if one chooses a case that illustrates for the first time that the recognizable subject was used in a court of law (as is the true meaning of "forensic"), then the history starts quite late and takes little cognizance of the giants upon whose shoulders forensic anthropology truly stands.

Human anatomy has a history that dates back to the founders of modern medicine—Galen (AD 130–201) and Hippocrates (460–370 BC). But all anatomy prior to 1539 was superseded by a publication from Andreas Vesalius (1514–64), a Flemish anatomist, who challenged Galen and Hippocrates through his hugely influential *De humani corporis fabrica* 1539 (On the Workings of the Human Body). This text formed the basis of all modern studies in human anatomy and, one could argue, paved the way for anthropology and its successors. Physical anthropology as a science began to gain popularity during the sixteenth and nineteenth centuries with Johann Friedrich Blumenbach (1752–1840), a German physician, anatomist, and physiologist, who was widely regarded as the founder of the subject. His treatise on the racial classification of man was published more than 80 years before Darwin's *Origin of Species*. Paul Broca (1824–80), a French physician and anatomist of significant renown, was unquestionably one of the most influential supporters of the science of physical anthropology, and he founded the Anthropological Society of Paris in 1859. It was his understanding of anatomy, however, that led to his most well-known research into speech areas of the brain, comparative primate anatomy, and cranial anthropology.

If one is going to find the first fully documented case in which physical anthropology assisted the court (and hence turned it into forensic anthropology), then that is most likely to be attributed to anatomists at Harvard University in North America in 1849, although it is distinctly possible that anatomists will have assisted investigators prior to that time in matters pertaining to the human form. Dr John Webster was accused of the murder of George Packman following dispute over a bad debt. Burned remains were located in a vault under the office of Dr Webster and the identity of these was attributed to Packman following analysis by Prof. Jeffries Wyman (anatomist) and Oliver Wendell Homes (Dean of the Medical College). Webster was found guilty and hanged in 1850. There may well have been other legal cases in history prior to this which could carry the moniker of being the first time that anthropology or anatomy was used in the courts, but there is little merit in such debate as it serves only to set a start date for the recognition of the discipline recognized today; it is probably sufficient to accept that it can be traced to at least the 1850s. However, it is known for certain that the Harvard anatomists were the first to offer classes and training in physical anthropology in the 1890s.

A case of notoriety within the United Kingdom and the first to be attributed to the discipline in that country (although again it was via anatomists) was the murder of Isabella Ruxton and her housemaid Mary Jane Rogerson. Both were murdered by Isabella's common-law husband, Dr Buck Ruxton, who was a GP of Indian birth and worked in Lancaster in the north of England. He had dismembered the remains with expertise but had been careless in their distribution (a feature that was to be replicated over 70 years later with the murder, dismemberment, and deposition of the remains of Jeffrey Howe). A team led by Prof. John Glaister, a forensic pathologist at the University of Glasgow, and Prof. James Brash, an anatomist from the University of Edinburgh, pieced together the remains and, through superimposition of the skull onto photographs, confirmed the identities of the two individuals. Ruxton was found guilty and hanged in Manchester in 1936. The similarities between the Ruxton and Howe cases are worthy of consideration and confirm the well-understood principle that basic patterns of behavior can be learned from studying case histories, which can then be used to inform current investigations.

From the formative years of forensic anthropology, it is perhaps difficult to accredit single individuals as the undisputed pioneers of the discipline without causing offense, but undeniably one can include Blumenbach (1752–1840), Broca (1824–80), Virchow (1821–1902), Dwight (1843–1911), Bertillon (1853–1914), Boas (1858–1942), Dorsey (1868–1931), Hrdlicka (1869–1943), and Hooton (1887–1954). The start of the World War II saw a change in the discipline as it started to mature and become better recognized by law enforcement agencies for its capabilities. Throughout that time, reputations were made either through publications or single cases that would hit the headlines. In 1939, the modern era of forensic anthropology started to emerge with the publication of Wilton Krogman's *Guide to the Identification of Skeletal Material*, and he followed this sometime later in 1962 with the seminal text *The Human Skeleton in Forensic Medicine*. In the era up to the 1960s, the work of Trotter (1889–1991), Todd (1895–1938), Stewart (1901–97), Krogman (1903–87), Snow (1910–67), Angel (1915–96), McKern (1920–74), Kerley (1924–98), and many others too numerous to list should also be recognized. Snow, Trotter, Stewart, and McKern are renowned as pioneers in the identification of military war dead, both as a result of the World War II and following repatriation of personnel following the Korean War. This time saw a change in the utility of forensic anthropology, where the analysis of skeletal remains, in a time prior to DNA analysis, was the most reliable means of facilitating identification and repatriation of war dead.

There is little doubt that the United States has led the early stages of the recognizable discipline of forensic anthropology, and one of the clear indicators of this is the early recognition of the importance of professionalization of the discipline and the need to identify those who are competent to practice. In 1972, the Physical Anthropology section of the American Academy of Forensic Sciences met for the first time under the direction of Ellis Kerley and Clyde Snow. Five years later, the American Board of Forensic Anthropology was created, and, at the time of writing, this consisted of 88 certified diplomates, 65 of whom are current practitioners. The history of forensic anthropology within the United States is well documented, but the history of the discipline is also influenced by what goes on around the rest of the world.

Part one of the text *Handbook of Forensic Anthropology and Archaeology* edited by Blau and Ubelaker offers a summary of the history of the discipline from countries including the United Kingdom, Italy, France, Spain, South America, the United States, Canada, Australia, and Indonesia. Kranioti's paper adds some information from Ireland, Sweden, Norway, Denmark, Finland, Germany, Austria, Netherlands, Hungary, Russia, Portugal, the Balkan states, Turkey, Greece, and Cyprus. What is clear from these communications is the variety of origins, practitioner types, case type, and etiology of the discipline in each of these countries. The reasons that a detailed history of forensic anthropology outwith the United States has not really been attempted in any great depth are perhaps its complexity and nonconformity. Therefore, it is perhaps easier to look at temporal and geographical events rather than single cases or practitioners to establish what has occurred globally for this discipline.

Special mention is necessary for the development of forensic anthropology in Latin America. In 1984, Clyde Snow led a team from the American Association for the Advancement of Science into Argentina to assess the situation regarding the investigation of victims of political violence. With probably close to half a million missing from Guatemala, Argentina, El Salvador, Peru, Chile, and Colombia, it was clear that the value of forensic anthropology could be put to good use in the identification of those recovered from graves associated with these crimes. The Argentinean Forensic Team was set up in 1984, followed by a Chilean team in 1989, a Guatemalan team in 1992, and finally a Peruvian team in 2001. Not only did these highly experienced groups operate within their own territories, but it soon became clear that their experience and expertise would be called for all over the world, and nowhere more so than in the Balkan states during the wars of the 1980s and 1990s.

Figures vary but nearly 100 000 people lost their lives in the armed Bosnian conflict between 1992 and 1995. International forensic teams under the guidance of the United Nations collected evidence, exhumed remains, and undertook identification of the deceased in preparation for an anticipated International Criminal Tribunal. In 1994, the genocide of over 800 000 in the small East African country of Rwanda took the world by surprise, as it took place over the space of only

100 days. Forensic anthropologists were called to assist with the recovery and identification of the remains for the purposes of the International Criminal Tribunal for Rwanda. Then, several thousand more deaths were recorded in Kosovo, which terminated with the North Atlantic Treaty Organization (NATO) bombings between 24 March and 11 June, 1999. The experience of the forensic teams in Bosnia and Rwanda was critical but gratis teams from other countries were called to assist with Kosovo investigation as neither the Bosnian nor the Rwandan investigations were completed by the time forensic assistance was required in Kosovo.

So, while one could argue that throughout the 1990s, in particular, as forensic anthropology was at its height, there was an almost unprecedented demand for the expertise of these professionals, with the United States (and Latin America) as the only prime source of practitioners, it was not surprising that American anthropologists took a leading role in the collation and interpretation of evidence of war crimes. However, a protracted deployment that demands large number of practitioners faces a crisis when operations such as these begin to be wound up and services are no longer required. The wars with Iraq (Operation Desert Storm, 1990–91), particularly the second of those (Operation Iraqi Freedom, 2003–10), required investigation of mass graves identified following the killings of Sadam Hussein's regime but not on the same scale as had been seen in the Balkans and Rwanda.

Throughout the 1990s, academic institutions responded to the global demand for forensic anthropologists by offering degree courses at many credible, and perhaps not so credible, institutions. The media had latched onto the work of the discipline, and novels, television series, and movies started to portray the work in a light that encouraged more and more school leavers to study at institutions of further education. But it was clear that without the conflict and the demand, the likelihood of employment would be slim, and a large number of courses started to dwindle with the turn of the new millennium.

However, there was yet another turn of events that saw the discipline raise its profile not just in relation to single cases or war crime investigation but in response to disaster victim identification (DVI). The terrorist attacks on the World Trade Center in 2001, the Bali bombings in 2002 and 2005, the tsunami of 2004, London bombings of 2005, and the Australian bush fires of 2009 all required assistance from forensic anthropologists who became integral members of the DVI teams, and the discipline was incorporated into the DVI training programs and instructional texts. Particularly, those forensic anthropologists who were anatomically trained found that their services were in demand through their ability to identify not only the skeletal remains but also the soft tissue structures, and this made their involvement in early triage operations indispensable.

In 2003, forensic anthropologists in Europe set up the Forensic Anthropology Society of Europe as an official subdivision of the International Academy of Legal Medicine. One of the main objectives of this society was "to encourage the study of, to promote the practice of, to establish and enhance the standards for forensic anthropology and to promote training and create a board of trained professionals." According to its Web site, the society has 47 listed members and perhaps as many again who are not listed.

In 2010, the British Association for Forensic Anthropology was set up under the umbrella of the British Association for Human Identification. With over 80 people attending its inaugural meeting, this group aims to promote and develop the discipline within the United Kingdom and prepare practitioners for accreditation through processes agreed with the office of the Forensic Regulator, which is a part of the Home Office, and in alliance with the Royal Anthropological Institute as its professional and accrediting body.

Forensic anthropology has not yet fully matured as a discipline across the world. Some areas are clearly in advance of others, as they address standardization of practices, issues of competency among practitioners, and admissibility of evidence to the courts. It is clear though that the story has not yet come to a conclusion and indeed the discipline does not as yet seem to have reached its own zenith, as new and exciting avenues of investigation seem to be migrating to the discipline. For example, the science of taphonomy, evaluation of age in the living, and identification of individuals from images are all skills being offered by specializing anthropologists. Despite the almost increasing multiplicity of the discipline, it is clear that forensic anthropology is a recognized field of expert evidence that is highly relevant to the modern world and deserves its newly acquired seat at the table of decision-makers.

See also: **Anthropology/Odontology:** Aging the Dead and the Living; Identification of the Living; Personal Identification in Forensic Anthropology; **Biology/DNA:** Disaster Victim Identification; **Forensic Medicine/Clinical:** Identification.

Further Reading

Black, S., 2003. Forensic anthropology – regulation in the United Kingdom. Science and Justice 43, 187–192.

Black, S.M., Ferguson, E., 2011. Forensic Anthropology: 2000–2010. Taylor & Francis, London.

Black, S.M., Walker, G., Hackman, L., Brooks, C., 2010. DVI – A Practitioner's Guide. Dundee University Press, Dundee.

Blau, S., Ubelaker, D.H., 2009. Handbook of Forensic Anthropology and Archaeology. Left Coast Press, California.

Brickley, M.B., Ferllini, R., 2007. Forensic Anthropology: Case Studies from Europe. CC Thomas, Illinois.

Byers, S.N., 2010. Introduction to Forensic Anthropology. Pearson Education, Boston.

Cattaneo, C., 2007. Forensic anthropology: developments of a classical discipline in the new millennium. Forensic Science International 165, 185–193.

Kennedy, K.A.R., 2000. Forensic anthropology in the USA. In: Siegel, J., Knupfer, G., Saukko, P. (Eds.), Encyclopaedia of Forensic Sciences. Academic Press, London, pp. 786–791.

Komar, D.A., Buikstra, J.E., 2008. Forensic Anthropology: Contemporary Theory and Practice. Oxford University Press, Oxford.

Kranioti, E.F., Paine, R.R., 2010. Forensic anthropology in Europe: an assessment of current status and application. Journal of Anthropological Sciences 89, 71–92. http://dx.doi.org/10.4436/jass.89002.

Stewart, T.D., 1979. Essentials of Forensic Anthropology: Especially as Developed in the United States. CC Thomas, Springfield, IL.

Ubelaker, D., 1996. Skeletons testify: anthropology in forensic sciences. Yearbook of Physical Anthropology 39, 229–244.

Relevant Websites

http://docs.lib.purdue.edu—A History of Forensic Anthropology (last accessed 01.08.11.).

http://what-when-how.com—A History of Forensic Anthropology in the USA (last accessed 01.08.11.).

http://www2.fbi.gov—A History of Smithsonian–FBI Collaboration in Forensic Anthropology (last accessed 01.08.11.).

http://home.comcast.net—Biography of S L Washburn (last accessed 01.08.11.).

Principles of Forensic Science

F Crispino, Université du Québec à Trois-Rivières, Trois-Rivières, QC, Canada
MM Houck, Consolidated Forensic Laboratory, Washington, DC, USA

Glossary

Abduction Syllogism in which one premise is certain whereas the other one is only probable, generally presented as the best explanation to the former. Hence, abduction is a type of reasoning in which we know the law and the effect, and we attempt to infer the cause.

Deduction Process of reasoning which moves from the general to the specific, and in which a conclusion follows necessarily from the stated premises. Hence, deduction is a type of reasoning in which, knowing the cause and the law, we infer the effect.

Forensic intelligence Understanding on how traces can be collected from the scene, processed, and interpreted within a holistic intelligence-led policing strategy.

Heuristic Process of reasoning by rules that are only loosely defined, generally by trial and error.

Holistic Emphasizing the importance of the whole and the interdependence of its parts.

Induction Process of deriving general principles from particular facts or instances, i.e., of reasoning that moves from the specific to the general. Hence, induction is a type of reasoning in which, knowing the cause and the effect (or a series of causes and effects), we attempt to infer the law by which the effects follow the cause.

Linkage blindness Organizational or investigative failure to recognize a common pattern shared on different cases.

Science The intellectual and practical activity encompassing the systematic study of the structure and behavior of the physical and natural world through observation and experiment. It is also defined as a systematically organized body of knowledge on a particular subject.

Given that it identifies and collects objects at crime scenes and then treats them as evidence, forensic science could appear at first glance to be only a pragmatic set of various disciplines, with practitioners adapting and developing tools and technologies to help the triers of fact (juries or judges) interpret information gained from the people, places, and things involved in a crime. The view could be—and has been—held that forensic science has no philosophic or fundamental unity and is merely the application of knowledge generated by other sciences. Indeed, many working forensic scientists regard themselves mainly as chemists, biologists, scientists, or technicians, and rarely as practitioners of a homogeneous body of knowledge with common fundamental principles.

Even the 2009 National Academy of Sciences National Research Council Report failed to recognize such a concept, certainly blurred by a semantic gap in the terminology itself of field practitioners, who confuse words such as "forensic science(s)," "criminalistic(s)," "criminology," "technical police," "scientific police," and so on, and generally restrict the scientific debate on analytical techniques and methods. An independent definition of forensic science, apart from its legal aspects, would support its scientific status and return the expert to his domain as scientist and interpreter of his analyses and results to assist the lay person.

What Is Forensic Science?

In its broadest sense, forensic science describes the utility of the sciences as they pertain to legal matters, to include many disciplines, such as chemistry, biology, pathology, anthropology, toxicology, and engineering, among others. ("Forensic" comes from the Latin root *forum*, the central place of the city where disputes and debates were made public to be solved, hence, defining the law of the city. Forensic generally means of or applied to the law.) The word "criminalistics" was adopted to describe the discipline directed toward the "recognition, identification, individualization, and evaluation of physical evidence by application of the natural sciences to law-science matters." ("Kriminalistik" was coined in the late nineteenth century by Hans Gross, a researcher in criminal law and procedure, to define his methodology of classifying investigative, tactical, and evidential information to be learned by magistrates at law schools to solve crimes and help convict criminals.) In the scheme as it currently stands, criminalistics is part of forensic science; the word is a regionalism and is not universally applied as defined. Difficulties in differentiating the concepts certainly invited the definition of criminalistics as the "science of individualization," isolating this specific epistemologically problematic core from the other scientific disciplines. Individualization, the concept of determining the sole source of an item, enthroned a linear process—identification or classification on to individualization—losing sight of the holistic, variable contribution of all types of evidence. Assessing the circumstances surrounding a crime, where the challenge is to integrate and organize the data to reconstruct a case or propose alternative propositions for events under examination, requires multiple types of evidence, some of which may be quite nuanced in their interpretation. This is also true in the use of so-called forensic intelligence, which feeds investigative, police, or security needs, where one of the main reasons for failures is linkage blindness. Nevertheless, it seems that the essence of the forensic daily practice is hardly captured within the present definitions of both terms.

Forensic science reconstructs—in the broadest sense—past criminal events through the analysis of the physical remnants of those activities (evidence); the results of those analyses and their expert interpretation establish relationships between people, places, and objects relevant to those events. It produces these results and interpretations through logical inferences, induction, abduction, and deduction, all of which frame the hypothetico-deductive method; investigative heuristics also play a role. Translating scientific information into legal information is a particular domain of forensic science; other sciences must (or at least should) communicate their findings to the public, but forensic science is often required by law to communicate their findings to public courts. Indeed, as the Daubert Hearing stated, "[s]cientific conclusions are subject to perpetual revision as law must resolve disputes finally and quickly." This doubly difficult requirement of communicating to the public and to the law necessitates that forensic scientists should be better communicators of their work and their results. Scientific inferences are not necessarily legal proofs, and the forensic scientist must recognize that legal decisions based, in part, on their scientific work may not accord with their expert knowledge. Moreover, scientists must think in probabilities to explain evidence given possible causes, while jurists must deal in terms of belief beyond reasonable doubt. As Inman and Rudin state: "Because we [the scientists] provide results and information to parties who lack the expertise to independently understand their meaning and implications, it is up to us to furnish an accurate and complete interpretation of our results. If we do not do this, our conclusions are at best incomplete, at worst potentially misleading."

The Trace as the Basic Unit of Forensic Science

The basic unit of forensic science is the trace, the physical remnant of the past criminal activity. Traces are, by their very nature, semiotic: They represent something more than merely themselves; they are signifiers or signs for the items or events that are its source. A fiber is not the sweater it came from, a fingerprint is not the fingertip, soot in the trachea is not the victim choking from a fire, blood droplets are not the violence against the victim, but they all point to their origin (source and activity) to a greater or lesser degree of specificity. Thus, the trace is a type of proxy data, that is, an indicator of a related phenomenon but not the phenomenon itself. Traces come from the natural and manufactured items that surround us in our daily lives. Traces are, in essence, the raw material available at a crime scene which becomes forensic intelligence or knowledge. Everyday items and their traces become evidence through their involvement in criminal activities; the activities add meaning to their existing status as goods in the world; a fireplace poker is transformed into "the murder weapon" by its use as such. The meaning added should also take into account the context of the case, the circumstances under which the criminal activities occurred, boarding the trier of fact mandate.

Traces become evidence when they are recognized, accepted as relevant (if blurred) to the past event under investigation, and collected for forensic purposes. Confusing trace, sign, and evidence can obscure the very process of trace "discovery," which lies at the root of its interpretation. Evidence begins with detection by observation, which is possible because of the available knowledge of the investigator or scientist; unrecognized traces go undiscovered and do not become evidence. When the investigator's or scientist's senses are extended through instrumental sensitivity, either at the scene or in the laboratory, the amount of potential evidence considerably increased. Microscopes, alternate light sources, instrumental sensitivity, and detection limits create increases in the number of traces that can be recognized and collected. More evidence, and more evidence types, inevitably led to increases in the complexity not only of the search for traces but also to their interpretation. Feeding back into this system is the awareness of new (micro)traces that changed the search methods at scenes and in laboratories, with yet more evidence being potentially available.

Traces are ancillary to their originating process; they are a by-product of the source activity, an accidental vestige of their criminal creation. To be useful in the determination of associations, traces whose ultimate sources are unknown must be compared to samples from a known source. Comparison is the very heart of the forensic science process; the method is essentially a diagnostic one, beginning with Georges Cuvier and is employed by many science practitioners, including medical professionals. (Including, interestingly, Arthur Conan

Doyle, a medical doctor and author, whose Sherlock Holmes character references Cuvier's method in *The Five Orange Pips*.) Questioned traces, or items, may have a provenance (a known location at the time of their discovery) but this is not their originating source; a few examples may help.

Trace (questioned)	Source (known)
Fiber on victim	Sweater
Gunshot residue	Ammunition discharge
Blood droplet	Body
Tool marks in door jamb	Pry bar used to open door
Shoeprint in soil	Shoe from suspect
Fingerprint on glass	Finger from suspect

The collection of properly representative known samples is crucial to accurate forensic analyses and comparisons. Known samples can be selected through a variety of legitimate schemes, including random, portion, and judgment, and must be selected with great care. Thus, traces are accidental and known samples are intentional.

Some of the consequences of what has been discussed so far induce the capacities and limitations of a forensic investigation based on trace analysis. A micro- to nano-level existence allows forensic scientists to plan physical and chemical characteristics in their identifications and comparisons with other similar data. This allows forensic science to be as methodologically flexible as its objects of study require. Because time is asymmetric and each criminal action is unique, the forensic investigation and analysis in any one case is wedded, to a certain degree, to that case with no ambition to issue general laws about that event ("In all instances of John Davis being physically assaulted with a baseball bat …"). Inferences must be drawn with explicit uncertainty statements; the inferences should be revised when new data affect the traces' relevancy. Therefore, the search for traces is a recursive heuristic process taking into account the environment of the case at hand, appealing to the imagination, expertise, and competency of the investigator or scientist to propose explicative hypotheses.

Two Native Principles

With this framework, two principles can be thought of as the main native principles that support and frame philosophically forensic science. In this context, principles are understood as universal theoretical statements settled at the beginning of a deduction, which cannot be deduced from any other statement in the considered system and give coherence to the area of study. They provide the grounds from which other truths can be

derived and define a paradigm, that is, a general epistemological viewpoint, a new concept to see the natural world, issued from an empiricist corroborated tradition, accepted by the community of practitioners in the field. Ultimately, this paradigm can even pilot the perception itself.

Although similar but nonequivalent versions are used in other disciplines, Locard's exchange principle exists as the central tenant of forensic science. The principle that bears his name was never uttered as such by Locard, but its universal statement of "every contact leaves a trace" stands as a universally accepted short-hand phrasing. Locard's principle embraces all forms of contact, from biological to chemical to physical and even digital traces and extends the usual perception of forensic science beyond dealing only with physical vestiges.

One of its corollaries is that trace deposition is continual and not reversible. Increases in the number of contacts, the types of evidence involved, and cross-transfers (A–B and B–A) also increase the complexity of determining the relevance of traces in short duration and temporally close actions.

Even the potentially fallacious rubric of "absence of evidence is not evidence of absence" leads to extended discussions on the very nature of proof, or provable, that aims to be definitive, notwithstanding the explanations for the practical aspects of the concept (lack of sensitivity, obscuring of the relevant traces, human weakness, actual absence, etc.). Applying Locard's principle needs to address three levels. First, the physical level, which deals with ease of transfer, retention, persistence, and affinity of materials, which could better support the exchange of traces from one source to another. Second is the situational or contextual level, which is the knowledge of circumstances and environments surrounding criminal events and sets the matrix for detection, identification, and proximate significance of any evidence. Third, the intelligence level, which covers the knowledge about criminal behavior in single events or series, specific problems related to current trends in criminal behavior, and communication between relevant entities (police, scientists, attorneys, etc.); these components help the investigator in the field to focus on more meaningful traces that might otherwise go undetected.

The second, and more debated, principle is Kirk's individuality principle; again, Kirk did not state this as such beyond saying that criminalistics is the science of individualization. In its strongest form, it posits that each object in the universe can be placed demonstratively into a set with one and only one member: itself. It therefore asserts the universal statement, "every object in our universe is unique." Philosophers such as Wittgenstein have argued that without defined rules or limits, terms such as "the same" or "different" are essentially meaningless. There is little question that all things are unique—two identical things can still be numerically differentiated—but the core question is, can they be distinguished at the resolution of detection applied? Simply saying "all things are unique" is not useful forensically. For example, each fingerprint left by the same finger is unique, but to be useful, each print must also be able to be traced back to its source finger. Uniqueness is therefore necessary to claim individualization, but not sufficient. Thus, it is the degree of association that matters, how similar, how different these two things being compared are. Referring to Cole, "What distinguishes ... objects is not 'uniqueness'; it is their diagnosticity: our ability to assign traces of these objects to their correct source with a certain degree of specificity under certain parameters of detection and under certain rules governing such assignments," or as Osterburg stated, "to approach [individualization] as closely as the present state of science allows." Statistics, typically, is required to accurately communicate levels of comparison that are reproducible. In fact, Kirk noted that individualization was not absolute. ("On the witness stand, the criminalist must be willing to admit that *absolute identity is impossible to establish.* ... The inept or biased witness may readily testify to an identity, or to a type of identity, that does not actually exist. This can come about because of his confusion as to the nature of identity, his inability to evaluate the results of his observations, or because his general technical deficiencies preclude meaningful results" (Kirk, 1953; emphasis added).)

Nonnative Principles

Numerous guiding principles from other sciences apply centrally to forensic science, several of which come from geology, a cognate historical science to forensic science. That these principles come not from forensic science but from other sciences should not imply that they are somehow less important than Locard's or Kirk's notions. The first, and in many ways the most important, of the external principles is that of uniformitarianism. The principle, proposed by James Hutton, popularized by Charles Lyell, and coined by William Whewell, states that natural phenomena do not change in scope, intensity, or effect with time. Paraphrased as "the present is the key to the past," the principle implies that a volcano that erupts today acts in the same way as volcanoes did 200 or 200 million years ago and, thus, allows geologists to interpret proxy data from past events through current effects. Likewise, in forensic science, bullets test fired in the laboratory today do not change in scope, intensity, or effect from bullets fired during the commission of a crime 2 days, 2 weeks, or 2 years previously. The same is true of any analysis in forensic science that requires a replication or reconstruction of processes in play during the crime's commission. Uniformitarianism offers a level of objectivity to historical sciences by posing hypotheses or relationships generally and then developing tests with respect to particular cases.

Three additional principles from geology hold as applicable to forensic science. They are as follows:

- *Superposition*: In a physical distribution, older materials are below younger materials unless a subsequent action alters this arrangement.
- *Lateral continuity*: Disassociated but similar layers can be assumed to be from the same depositional period.
- *Chronology*: It refers to the notion of absolute dates in a quantitative mode (such as "10:12 a.m." or "1670–1702") and relative dates in a relational mode (i.e., older or younger).

These three principles are attributed to Nicolaus Steno but were also formalized and applied by William Smith. A forensic example of applying the principle of superposition would be the packing of different soils in a tire tread, the most recent being the outermost. A good case of lateral continuity would be the cross-transfer of fibers in an assault, given that the chances of independent transfer and persistence prior to the time of the incident would be improbable. An example of absolute chronology in forensic science would be the simple example of a purchase receipt from a retail store with a time/date stamp on it. Examples of relative chronology abound but could range from the *terminus post quem* of a product no longer made to something hotter or colder than it should be.

See also: **Foundations:** Forensic Intelligence; History of Forensic Sciences; Overview and Meaning of Identification/Individualization; Semiotics, Heuristics, and Inferences Used by Forensic Scientists; Statistical Interpretation of Evidence: Bayesian Analysis; The Frequentist Approach to Forensic Evidence Interpretation; **Foundations/Fundamentals:** Measurement Uncertainty; **Pattern Evidence/Fingerprints (Dactyloscopy):** Friction Ridge Print Examination – Interpretation and the Comparative Method.

Further Reading

Cole, S.A., 2009. Forensics without uniqueness, conclusions without individualization: the new epistemology of forensic identification. Law, Probability and Risk 8, 233–255.

Crispino, F., 2006. Le principe de Locard est-il scientifique? Ou analyse de la scientificité des principes fondamentaux de la criminalistique. Editions Universitaires Européennes No. 523, Sarrebrücken, Germany. ISBN:978-613-1-50482-2(2010).

Crispino, F., 2008. Nature and place of crime scene management within forensic sciences. Science and Justice 48 (1), 24–28.

Dulong, R., 2004. La rationalité spécifique de la police technique. Revue Internationale de Criminologie et de Police Technique 3 (4), 259–270.

Egger, S.A., 1984. A working definition of serial murder and the reduction of linkage blindness. Journal of Police Science and Administration 12, 348–355.

Giamalas, D.M., 2000. Criminalistics. In: Siegel, J.A., Saukko, P.J., Knupfer, G.C. (Eds.), Encyclopedia of Forensic Sciences. Academic Press, London, pp. 471–477.

Good, G. (Ed.), 1998. Sciences of the Earth, vol. 1. Garland Publishing, New York.

Houck, M.M., 2010. An Investigation into the Foundational Principles of Forensic Science (Ph.D. thesis). Curtin University of Technology, Perth.

Inman, N., Rudin, K., 2001. Principles and Practice of Criminalistics: The Profession of Forensic Science. CRC Press, Boca Raton, FL, pp. 269–270.

Kirk, P.L., 1953. Crime Investigation: Physical Evidence and the Police Laboratory. Interscience, New York, p. 10.

Kirk, P.L., 1963. The ontogeny of criminalistics. Journal of Criminal Law, Criminology and Police Science 54, 235–238.

Kuhn, T., 1970. La structure des révolutions scientifiques. Flammarion, Paris.

Kwan, Q.Y., 1976. Inference of Identity of Source (Ph.D. thesis). Berkeley University, Berkeley.

Mann, M., 2002. The value of multiple proxies. Science 297, 1481–1482.

Masterman, M., 1970. The nature of a paradigm. In: Lakatos, I., Musgrave, A. (Eds.), Criticism and the Growth of Experimental Knowledge. Cambridge University Press, Cambridge, pp. 59–86.

Moriarty, J.C., Saks, M.J., 2006. Forensic Science: Grand Goals, Tragic Flaws, and Judicial Gatekeeping. Research Paper No. 06-19. University of Akron Legal Studies.

National Research Council Committee, 2009. Identifying the Needs of the Forensic Science Community, Strengthening Forensic Science in the United States: A Path Forward. National Academy of Sciences Report. National Academy Press, Washington, DC.

Osterburg, J.W., 1968. What problems must criminalistics solve. Journal of Criminal Law, Criminology and Police Science 59 (3), 431.

Schuliar, Y., 2009. La coordination scientifique dans les investigations criminelles. Proposition d'organisation, aspects éthiques ou de la nécessité d'un nouveau métier (Ph.D. thesis). Université Paris Descartes, Paris. Université de Lausanne, Lausanne.

Sober, E., 2009. Absence of evidence and evidence of absence: evidential transitivity in connection with fossils, fishing, fine-tuning, and firing squads. Philosophical Studies 143, 63–90.

Stephens, C., 2011. A Bayesian approach to absent evidence reasoning. Informal Logic 31 (1), 56–65.

US Supreme Court No 92–102, 1993. William Daubert, et al., Petitioners v Merrell Dow Pharmaceuticals, Inc.. Certiorari to the US Court of Appeals for the Ninth Circuit. Argued 30 March 1993. Decided 28 June 1993.

Wittgenstein, L., 1922. Tractacus Logico-Philosophicus. Gallimard Tel 311, Paris.

Relevant Websites

http://www.all-about-forensic-science.com—Definition of Forensic Science.
http://www.forensic-evidence.com—Forensic Evidence.
http://library.thinkquest.org—Oracle ThinkQuest – What is Forensics?

Transfer

C Roux, University of Technology, Sydney, NSW, Australia
J Robertson, University of Canberra, Canberra, ACT, Australia

Glossary

Differential shedding A phenomenon by which fabrics composed of two or more fiber types that do not necessarily shed fibers proportionate to their representation in the donor fabric.

Primary transfer A direct fiber transfer from a donor item to a recipient item.
Secondary transfer (or *n* transfer) Fibers previously transferred on a recipient item are retransferred to another surface during a second contact (or subsequent contacts).

Introduction

Since the invention of textiles, the potential for the transfer of fibers has existed. The recognition that it may have forensic value was little recognized until the twentieth century. Although no one individual can actually be credited as the first to single out textiles as a source of trace evidence, the much-quoted Locard's exchange principle is generally accepted as the starting point of the modern era of criminalistics based on the ubiquitous nature of the transfer of trace materials. More generally, traces are increasingly seen as central to forensic science as they are remnants of the presence of one of several individuals and of an activity. As such, they can be considered as the most fundamental "physical" information about the crime itself. For this reason, it is important to the forensic fiber expert to understand fundamentals about fiber transfer and how this information impacts on the interpretation of fiber evidence.

Transfer

Studies since the 1970s by a number of key groups of workers including Pounds and Smalldon, Grieve, Robertson, and Roux have provided a sound basis for an understanding of the factors to be considered in the interpretation of the transfer and persistence of fibers in forensic investigations.

Textile fabrics used in upholstery, carpets, and clothing are manufactured using a wide variety of mechanisms and many different types of fibers. The transfer of fibers will be under the influence of the latter factors, fabric construction, and fiber type as well as the nature of the contact. Typically, contact will be between individuals wearing items of clothing or between an individual and an item such as a seat or a carpet.

Factors Affecting Transfer

In the general situation, the following factors have been shown to be important in determining the number of fibers which will transfer during a contact.

Fiber Type

This is important for both the "donor" item and the "recipient" item. Some fabrics can be expected to transfer more fibers than others. For example, fabrics made of wool and acrylic will shed more fibers than fabrics made of polyester fibers. Sometimes, the potential for a fabric to transfer fibers is called its "shedability." In a case situation, it may be useful to assess the shed potential of a donor item. Simple tape lifts may only provide a very rough guide to shed potential. Several authors have proposed the use of simulated contact devices. A rough order for shed potential would be wool $\geq$ acrylic $\geq$ cotton > viscose > polyester > nylon.

Shed potential does not depend solely on the fiber type. Construction and state of wear of fabrics are also key factors.

Fiber Morphology and Thickness

There is evidence that within one fiber type, finer fibers will transfer in greater numbers than coarser fibers. This probably relates to the greater fragmentation of finer fibers compared to their coarser counterparts. Studies have shown that fabrics constructed of microfibers can generate up to seven times more fibers than cotton under the same conditions (they are, however, more difficult to detect and collect than cotton, for example).

Fabric Texture and Construction

As a general rule for the same fiber type, more fibers will transfer from a coarse than from a smooth fabric. This is, however, a gross simplification. Fabric construction is also important. This involves a wide range of factors. As discussed above, the shed potential is determined by a complex interaction of fiber type, fabric construction, and the condition of an item, that is, how well it wears.

Area of Contact

As a general rule, the greater the area in contact, the more the fibers can be expected to transfer.

Number of Contacts

The number of fibers transferred increases with the number of contacts where the number of contacts is small. With increasing contacts, some fibers will transfer back to the donor item.

Force of Pressure or Contact

The number of fibers transferred increases with the force or pressure of contact until a plateau is reached beyond which increased force has no further effect. The force of contact also influences the size of fibers transferred, with higher pressure resulting in a greater proportion of short fibers.

Differential Shedding

Most studies have shown that with fabrics composed of two or more fiber types, they do not necessarily shed fibers proportionate to their representation in the donor fabric. A complicating factor which is sometimes forgotten is that a manufacturer's label may give proportions in terms of weight and not fiber or yarn numbers. The underlying reasons for differential shedding include fabric construction, in which only one fiber/yarn type is on the external, exposed surface of the fabric, and the shed potential of different fiber types. The need to consider differential shedding has been demonstrated in a number of published case studies. Where the proportion of recovered fibers in a case situation is clearly different from that found (by direct observation) in the putative donor, it is incumbent on the forensic scientist to explain this apparent discrepancy. This will usually involve simulation experiments. A further factor complicating the interpretation will be the influence of fiber persistence.

Primary and Secondary Transfer

In the discussion thus far, it has been assumed that the transfer is a primary transfer, that is, a direct transfer from a donor item to a recipient item. Primary, direct contacts can result in the transfer of hundreds and even thousands of fibers. It is well understood that it is then possible for these transferred fibers to be transferred "on" during subsequent contacts. A good example would be a person sitting in a cinema seat. The first person leaves behind thousands of fibers on the cinema seat, a second person then sits on the same seat and some of those fibers are transferred "on" to the clothing worn by the second person. This is a secondary transfer. At least in theory, tertiary and subsequent lower order transfers are a possibility. In a case scenario, the forensic scientist must remain alert to the possibility of such transfers. It is often the situation that a suspect will be part of an interconnected group of associates and may have been exposed to the potential for fibers to have arrived on their clothing through a nondirect contact. The interpretation of the location and the number of fibers require caution. A complicating factor is that there is no minimum number of fibers below which one can identify a secondary or subsequent transfer.

Special Cases

Most published studies have been conducted using garments. However, fibers may be transferred from any fibrous surface such as upholstery and carpets. The factors influencing fiber transfer from items such as blankets, bed sheets, and seat covers are no different from those outlined for the general case. Transfer from carpets has some different considerations, especially where the recipient surface is a shoe. Carpets are only a subcategory of any other fabric, although their construction is perhaps the major factor in determining their shed potential. Shoes are obviously a special case as a recipient surface. The composition and roughness of the sole are important parameters to consider. The mechanism of fiber transfer to a shoe surface is not identical to the mechanism of transfer between clothing fabrics. In some ways, fiber transfer to a shoe may be more comparable to transfer to any other physical object. **Figure 1** shows an example of results obtained by experiments reenacting the contact between shoe soles and a car carpet. These data were pivotal to solve a murder case. Fiber persistence on shoes is discussed elsewhere in this encyclopedia.

Another special case of fiber transfer is the transfer of fibers from a fabric to the individual wearing the item. The best example of this is from a mask or balaclava often worn in a robbery. Sometimes, a robber may discard other clothing. It may be possible through a study of fiber transfer to establish contact between the clothing and a suspect. Fiber recovery from the body of a deceased or an alleged victim and its potential to provide evidence is considered too infrequently.

Mechanism of Fiber Transfer

There has been considerable theorizing with regard to the underlying mechanisms of fiber transfer but only limited

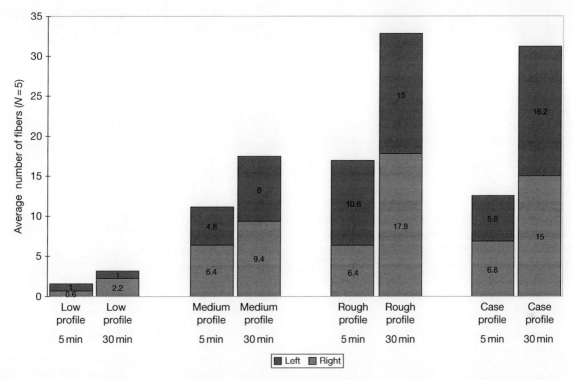

Figure 1 Typical example of comparison of case data with transfer experiments data (transfer of car carpet fibers on different shoe soles in this case).

attempts at providing experimental proof. It has been proposed that in the general fabric-to-fabric situation, three mechanisms may be involved:

- transfer of loose fragments already on the surface of the fabric;
- loose fibers being pulled out of the fabric by friction; and
- transfer of fiber fragments produced by the contact itself.

It is accepted that electrostatic attraction of fibers is not an important factor in the general case. However, electrostatic attraction may be a factor in special circumstances. This discussion has focused on the transfer of fiber fragments and not on the transfer of yarns or pieces of fabric torn or removed from a fabric by physical means.

Fiber Transfer: A Dynamic Process

It will often be the case that there will be a time gap between the commission of an offense and the apprehension of a suspect. There is evidence to show that the transfer properties of items can alter with the passage of time. This may be due to wear, washing, or other treatments. As a general rule, garments will

shed less through time. Caution should be exercised where there is a lengthy time gap between the commission of an offense and suspect items being submitted for examination. This factor also needs to be considered when making a decision as to whether or not to conduct simulation experiments.

Fiber Transfer Modeling

Knowledge of fiber transfer (along with other factors) is crucial to interpret fiber evidence correctly. In particular, such knowledge is necessary if one wishes to answer the question as to whether or not the number of fibers and the number of fiber types found in a given case are likely under the allegation of contact. In other words, knowledge on transfer (and persistence) assists to answer the typical competitive questions "what is the probability of finding the number of fibers and fiber types found in a given case if there was a contact?" and "what is the probability of finding the number of fibers and fiber types found in a given case if there was no contact?"

Since 1975, numerous transfer and persistence studies involving fibers have been undertaken. While it is still difficult to completely and accurately model the results, a wealth of information and data are available. General findings and information on how these assessments can be combined in a Bayesian framework are presented elsewhere in this encyclopedia.

Concluding Comments

Ultimately, the type of information that the forensic scientist seeks through fiber transfer should include the following:

- What is alleged to have taken place—who is involved and how?
- Where is the incident said to have taken place? If it was in a house or in a car, who was the occupier or owner?
- With a sexual assault, did it occur on a bed or on the floor? Is it possible to reconstruct the sequence of events? Were bed covers present and were they moved?
- When did the incident take place and was there any delay before the scene was examined?
- Did any person involved have legitimate access to the scene or legitimate contact with the other person or persons before the incident?
- Are reliable descriptions available of what was being worn by the offender?
- Were items of clothing removed during the incident?

This type of information is necessary if the scientist is to conduct meaningful experiments aimed at reconstructing the events of an alleged incident. There will rarely, if ever, be simple and easy answers to the interpretation of fiber evidence. This will also have to consider aspects described elsewhere in this encyclopedia.

> *See also:* **Chemistry/Trace/Fibers:** Fibers: Overview;
> Identification and Comparison; Interpretation of Fiber Evidence;
> Persistence and Recovery.

Further Reading

Bresee, R.R., Annis, P.A., 1991. Fibre transfer and the influence of fabric softener. Journal of Forensic Sciences 36 (6), 1699–1713.

Burch, H.J., 2008. The Transfer and Persistence of Fibres on Bare Skin. Thesis Submitted to Centre of Forensic Science. University of Strathclyde.

Cordiner, S.J., Stringer, P., Wilson, P.D., 1985. Fibre diameter and the transfer of wool fibres. Journal of the Forensic Science Society 25, 425–426.

Coxon, A., Grieve, M., Dunlop, J., 1992. A method of assessing the fibre shedding potential of fabrics. Journal of Forensic Sciences 32 (2), 151–158.

De Wael, K., Gason, F., 2008. Microfibre transfer experiments. Global Forensic Science Today 4, 31–37.

Grieve, M.C., Biermann, T.W., 1997. Wool fibres – transfer to vinyl and leather vehicle seats and some observations on their secondary transfer. Science & Justice 37 (1), 31–38.

Kidd, C.B.M., Robertson, J., 1982. The transfer of textile fibers during simulated contacts. Journal of Forensic Science Society 22, 301–308.

Merciani, P., Monard Sermier, F., Buzzini, P., Massonnet, G., Taroni, F., 2003. A study of the cross transfer of fibers. Forensic International 136 (1), 123.

Palmer, R., Burch, H.J., 2009. The population, transfer and persistence of fibres on the skin of living subjects. Science & Justice 49 (4), 259–264.

Parybyk, A.E., Lokan, R.J., 1986. A study of the numerical distribution of fibres transferred from blended products. Journal of the Forensic Science Society 26, 61–68.

Pounds, C.A., Smalldon, K.W., 1975a. The transfer of fibers between clothing materials during simulated contacts and their persistence during wear – Part 1: fibre transference. Journal of Forensic Science Society 15, 17–27.

Pounds, C.A., Smalldon, K.W., 1975b. The transfer of fibers between clothing materials during simulated contacts and their persistence during wear – Part 3: a preliminary investigation of mechanisms involved. Journal of Forensic Science Society 15, 197–207.

Robertson, J., Grieve, M.C. (Eds.), 1999. The Forensic Examination of Fibers. Taylor and Francis, London.

Robertson, J., Lim, M., 1987. Fibre transfer and persistence onto car seats and seatbelts. Canadian Society of Forensic Science Journal 20 (3), 140–141.

Roux, C., 1997. La Valeur Indiciale des Fibers Textiles Decouvertes sur un Siege de Voiture: Problemes et Solutions (Ph.D. thesis). University of Lausanne.

Roux, C., Chable, J., Margot, P., 1996. Fibre transfer experiments on to car seats. Science and Justice 36, 143–152.

Roux, C., Langdon, S., Waight, D., Robertson, J., 1998. The transfer and persistence of automotive carpet fibers on shoe soles. Science and Justice 39, 239–251.

Salter, M., Cook, R., 1996. Transfer of fibres to head hair, their persistence and retrieval. Forensic Science International 81, 211–221.

Salter, M.T., Cook, R., Jackson, A.R., 1984. Differential shedding from blended fabrics. Forensic Science International 33, 155–164.

Salter, M.T., Cook, R., Jackson, A.R., 1987. Differential shedding from blended fabrics. Forensic Science International 33 (3), 155–164.

Siegel, J.A., 1997. Evidential value of textile fibre – transfer and persistence of fibers. Forensic Science Review 9, 81–96.

Szewcow, R., Robertson, J., Roux, C.P., 2011. The influence of front-loading and top-loading washing machines on the persistence, redistribution and secondary transfer of textile fibres during laundering. Australian Journal of Forensic Sciences 43 (4), 263–273.

Technical Working Group for Materials Analysis, 1997. Forensic Fiber Examination Guidelines. Federal Bureau of Investigation, Washington, DC.

Interpretation/The Comparative Method

MM Houck, Consolidated Forensic Laboratory, Washington, DC, USA

Glossary

Alignable differences Differences that are connected to the hierarchical system of relatedness of two or more things.
Analogous trait A characteristic that is similar between two things that is not present in the last common ancestor or precedent of the group under comparison.
Analogy A cognitive process that transfers information or meaning from one subject (the analog or source) to another subject (the target).

Diagnosticity The degree to which traits classify an object.
Homologous trait A characteristic shared by a common ancestor or precedent.
Nonalignable differences Differences with no correspondence at all between the source and the target.

Introduction

Analogy, and its more specific relative comparison, is a central component of human cognition. Analogy is the process behind identification of places, objects, and people and plays a significant role in many human mental operations, such as problem solving, decisions, perception, memory, and communication. Some researchers, including Hofstadter, have even argued that cognition is analogy. Likewise, the cognitive process of analogy and the method of comparison lie at the heart of the forensic sciences. The ability to compare is predicated on some sort of classification (more properly, a taxonomy) that results in classes, groups, or sets.

Aristotle is considered the first to approach comparison as a way to arrange the world. His attempt to codify the process raised, however, an intractable problem that would only be addressed later: the classification of living things. Comparison, by itself, is a minimal technique, at best. A classification system—a taxonomy—is a prerequisite to a fuller comparative methodology. Comparative anatomy, one of the earliest formal applications of the method, goes beyond mere representation (mere comparison, that is) to explain the nature and properties of each animal.

The French naturalist Pierre Belon (1517–64) compared the skeletal structures of birds to humans in his book *L'Histoire de la Nature des Oiseaux* (*History of the Nature of Birds*, 1555; **Figure 1**), and, along with the Flemish naturalist Andreas Vesalius (1514–64), was one of the first naturalists to explicitly apply the comparative method in biology. Georges Cuvier (1769–1832) was the first to use comparative anatomy and taxonomy as a tool, not an end in itself, in his studies of animals and fossils. Cuvier was frustrated that biological phenomena could not be reconfigured into experimental conditions that would allow controlled testing, a difficulty common to many sciences (e.g., see Diamond). The intimate integration of a living organism's physiology with its anatomy created obstacles in teasing out and relating function to structure: Once an organism was dead and prepared for dissection, its function had ceased, thus confounding the relationship of form to function. Cuvier considered that careful examinations and the interrelating of structures between specimens might also prove to be useful in revealing principles of observation and comparison. Perhaps the original scientist-as-detective, Cuvier, used scattered, fractured bits of information to reconstruct the prehistory of the Earth and its animals. In a 1798 paper, Cuvier wrote on his realization of the form and function of bones as it relates to the overall identifiable anatomy of an animal, leading to the recognition of the creature from which the bone originated: "This assertion will not seem at all astonishing if one recalls that in the living state all the bones are assembled in a kind of framework; that the place occupied by each is easy to recognize; and that by the number and position of their articulating facets one can judge the number and direction of the bones that were attached to them. This is because the number, direction, and shape of the bones that compose each part of an animal's body are always in a necessary relation to all the other parts, in such a way that—up to a point—one can infer the whole from any one of them, and vice versa (Rudwick, 1998, p. 36)".

This has been called "Cuvier's Principle of Correlation of Parts" and is a central tenet in biology and paleontology. It is

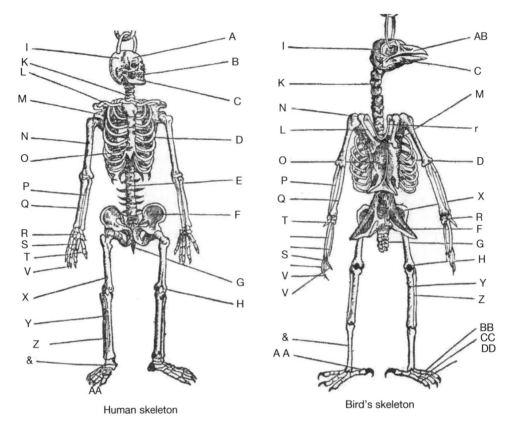

Human skeleton

Bird's skeleton

Figure 1   A drawing from Pierre Belon's 1555 book, *History of the Nature of Birds*, comparing the skeletal anatomy of birds to humans which is one of the first books using the science of comparative anatomy. Source: Wikimedia Commons, open source.

important to note that Cuvier claimed to be able to *identify* an animal taxonomically from a single bone, but not completely *reconstruct* it, as the above quote might imply. The reconstruction would only be possible with a sufficient number of bones representing the animal in question. The comparative method has been a successful cornerstone of science ever since, with new or emerging sciences, such as ecology, moving from the purely observational or descriptive approach to that of comparison through experimental or analytical methods.

A short discussion of terms in biology will help clarify concepts used in biological comparisons. The concept of homology, the same structure under every variety of form found in different animals, is the organizing foundation for comparative anatomy. Animals share homologous traits because they also share a common ancestor with the same or related trait. By contrast, analogous traits are similarities found in organisms that were not present in the last common ancestor of the group under comparison; that is, the traits evolved separately. The canonical example of the difference between homologous and analogous traits is the wings of birds and bats: They are homologous as forearms but analogous as wings;

the latter structures evolved their functions separately. A homologous trait is termed a homolog. In biology, evolution and natural selection formed the system within which these relationships developed and were maintained, homogenized, or differentiated.

In manufacturing, other external and internal constraints form the basis for homologous and analogous traits through design, function, form, and costs. Design follows from the product's intended end use, aesthetic concerns, and cost limitations. The function and form of an object tend to correlate and variances in design cluster around necessary and sufficient criteria. In **Figure 2**, for example, although the hammer heads, opposite sides, handles, materials, weight, shape, and components all vary, they are nonetheless identifiable as hammers. If **Figure 2** were finches, as Darwin studied in the Galapagos in his historic voyage with the *Beagle*, the base process of taxonomy would be the same but the criteria and foundations—the history and causes—would obviously vary because of the vastly different processes that produce hammers and finches.

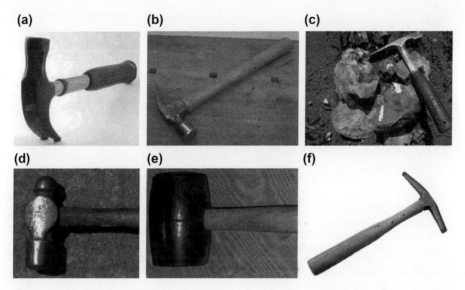

Figure 2 Hammers. All of the objects (a–f) are recognizable as hammers even though their components vary. (a) Claw hammer; (b) framing hammer; (c) geological hammer; (d) ball-peen hammer; (e) rubber mallet; and (f) upholstery hammer. Source: Wikimedia Commons, open source.

Broadly speaking, the supply chains and distribution networks of material goods are like the phylogenetic trees based on evolutionary descent. Regardless of whether the items are biological or manufactured, the independence of traits should not be assumed. Comparative studies that do not control for historical relationships through phylogeny or supply chains may imply spurious relationships (coincidences). Forensic science is unique in its use of the comparative method to reconstruct past criminal events and sourcing of evidence, either biological or manufactured (in essence, reverse engineering to a level of distribution or manufacturing resolution).

Analogy and Comparison Within a Forensic Process

Analogy is a cognitive process that transfers information or meaning from one subject (the analog or *source*) to another subject (the *target*); it thus implies at least two things: situations or events. The source is considered to be the more complete and more complex of the two and the target is thus less informative and incomplete in some way. The incompleteness may be due to any of several factors, alone or combined, such as damage, fracture, deterioration, or size. The elements or traits—including their relationships, such as evolutionary or supply chains—between the source and the target are mapped or aligned in a comparison. The mapping is done from what is usually the more familiar area of experience and more complete repository of information, the source, to the typically more problematic target.

Salience of the elements or traits is of prime importance: there are an innumerable number of arbitrary differences in either elements or relations that could be considered but are not useful given the question at hand ("Are both items smaller than the Empire State Building? Are they redder than a fire truck?"). Ultimately, analogy is a process to communicate that the two comparators (the source and the target) have *some* relationship in common despite any arbitrary differences. Some notion of possible or hypothetical connection must exist for the comparison to be made. As a forensic example, consider trace debris removed from the clothing of a suspect and the body of a victim: Although there may be no physical evidence (hairs, fibers, glass, soil, etc.) in common, the suspect's clothing and the victim's body have, at least prima facie, a common *relationship* (the victim is the victim and the suspect is a person of interest in the crime) until proven otherwise. Thus, common relations, not common objects, are essential to analogy and comparison.

The comparison process as a method makes several assumptions. First, the space in which the comparators are mapped is assumed to be Euclidean. Second, the method embeds the comparators in a "space of minimum dimensionality" (Tversky) based on all observed salient similarities. Each object, a, is detailed and described by a set of elements or traits, A. Any observed similarities between a and another object b, denoted as $s(a, b)$, are expressed as a function of the salient traits they are determined to have in common. The comparison and any observed familiarity can be expressed as a function of three arguments (**Figure 3**):

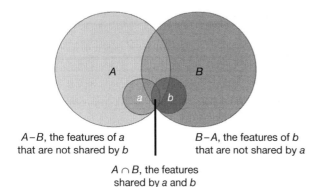

A−B, the features of a that are not shared by b

B−A, the features of b that are not shared by a

A ∩ B, the features shared by a and b

Figure 3 A comparison of observed familiarities can be expressed as a function of three arguments that are visualized here.

- $A \cap B$, the features shared by a and b
- $A - B$, the features of a that are not shared by b
- $B - A$, the features of b that are not shared by a

Psychological studies show that people tend to pay more attention to the target (the comparator with less information) than to the source. In forensic science, this means that analysts would pay more attention to the samples from the crime scene or actors than to the known samples collected. This is true even though the known has more salience, because arguably it has more information and a documented provenance than the questioned sample. For example, a toy ship is quite similar to a real ship because most of the main features of the real ship are expressed in the toy (otherwise it might not be recognized as a simulacrum of its referent). A real ship, however, is not as similar to the toy ship because many of the features of a real ship are not expressed in the toy (due to function, scale, or safety, among other factors). The reason for paying more attention to the target is, first and foremost, to determine if there is sufficiency of salient information in the target for the comparative process to occur (see Vanderkolk for a discussion on this).

The main determinant of feature salience for comparative purposes is the degree to which they classify an object, that is, their diagnosticity. A feature that serves as the basis to reassign an object from one class to another class with fewer members is more salient than one that does not. Salience is hierarchical and is based on how many members of a class share that feature; the goal is thus to place an object, by successive comparative features, into classes with increasingly fewer members. Salience of a feature, therefore, should increase inversely with the number of members of a class into which it places an object; $A \cap B$ increases and may be thought of as an expression of diagnosticity. A comparative process that does not maximize diagnosticity or exploit features that do so will have low forensic utility.

The Comparative Method Within Forensic Science

The comparative method involves the aligning of the relational structures between one or more targets (items of questioned source; Qs) and one or more sources (items of known provenance or source; Ks). This alignment, to work as a method, has three constraints or requirements:

- The alignment has to be *structurally consistent*, that is, it has to observe a one-to-one correspondence between the comparators in an argumentative structure that is the same between the comparisons (*parallel connectivity*). One point of comparison can be aligned with at most one other point of comparison in the target or source. Similarly, matching relationships must have matching arguments to support them (the reason for the proposed relationship cannot be based on an unrelated argument).
- The comparison has to involve *common relations* but does not have to involve common object descriptions. All the evidence that came from the crime scene, for example, need not have originated from only one source.
- Finally, comparisons are not made merely between the objects at hand but also include all of the higher order "constraining relations" that they may share (*systematicity*). In biology, this would relate to the evolutionary and genetic connections; for manufactured materials, this would be the design factors and the supply chain of raw materials and intermediate processes that lead to a finished consumer good. The deeper the relational history, the more higher order classes that two objects share, the stronger the relationship they share, and, therefore, the greater is the chance of a shared origin. This obviates the significance of coincidental matches between otherwise similar but unrelated objects: A series of coincidences between two objects are not a salient relationship, no matter how many of them exist. Type I and type II errors stem from these coincidences.

A comparison results in a type of cross-mapping of analogous traits or phenomena that have differential relational roles in two situations (e.g., victim's clothing and crime scene). A systematic mapping between source and target is a natural method for differentiating potentially ambiguous relationships. This relates to the classification of the target and source, the identification of traits or features each has that place them in one or more sets (classes) of items. The cross-mapping is of these traits within a class. Once a source has been aligned to a target, *candidate inferences*, based on the source, can be projected onto the target, such as a shared source or history. A handgun with blood on it, for example, can be compared to a bullet removed from a victim (through test firings of similar ammunition) and determined to have been the source (to some degree of certainty) of the bullet while the blood can be tested through DNA typing with the victim's known sample and be shown to have the victim as its source (again, to some degree of certainty); the fact that the victim's blood is on the handgun indicates a shared history of occurrence (lateral contemporaneity).

Comparison is selective. The requirement of systematicity is predicated on the idea that classes or sets are flexible and hierarchical. Higher order connections predict lower order relations, and commonalities that are not a part of the aligned system of relationships are considered inconsequential: A blue shoe and a blue car have little in common other than the stated color category; likewise, the fact that the source shoe and the target print might have the same kind of outsole design recedes in importance to the fact than none of the individual traits on the sole appears in the print. Differences that are connected to the hierarchical system of relatedness are called *alignable differences*; those differences with no correspondence at all between the source and the target are called *nonalignable differences*. Alignable differences are more meaningful and salient than nonalignable ones because they exist within the same relationship system making them more relevant to each other. The strange conclusion this observation leads to is that there should be more meaningful differences for comparators that are very similar (*toy train–real train*) than for ones that are less similar (*toy train–toy ship*) because the more similar comparators will have or be derived within more common systems of relationships and will have more alignable differences. As an example, consider all the possible differences for the pair *automobile–truck* and for the pair *duck–baseball*. More alignable differences could be found for the first pair than the second: After a few differences ("You don't play sports with a duck. You don't hunt baseballs."), the list seems pointless because the two are not aligned. The details that could be elicited by comparing *automobile* with *truck*, however, could go on for some time, depending on the level of detail desired. Most sets of comparators in the world are dissimilar (which is why forensic comparisons tend to be stronger in exclusion than inclusion) and this "nonconsideration" heuristic makes sense given humans' cognitive load: "Intuitively, it is when a pair of items is similar that their differences are likely to be important" (Genter and Markman). Psychological experiments support this statement and it seems to be an integral part of human cognition. Related to this idea is Wittgenstein's proposal 5.5303 in his work *Tractatus logico-philosophicus*: "Roughly speaking, to say of two things that they are identical is nonsense, and to say of one thing that it is identical with itself is to say nothing at all." This points to the need for a statistical evaluation of the *strength* of a comparison, either inclusive or exclusive.

See also: **Foundations:** Forensic Intelligence; Overview and Meaning of Identification/Individualization; Semiotics, Heuristics, and Inferences Used by Forensic Scientists.

Further Reading

Diamond, J., Robinson, J.A. (Eds.), 2010. Natural Experiments of History. Cambridge University Press, Cambridge, MA.

Gentner, D., Markman, A.B., 1997. Structure mapping in analogy and similarity. American Psychologist 52 (1), 45–56.

Hofstadter, D., 2001. Analogy as the core of cognition. In: Gentner, D., Holyoak, K., Kokinov, B. (Eds.), The Analogical Mind: Perspectives from Cognitive Science. MIT Press/Bradford Book, Cambridge, MA, pp. 499–538.

Markman, A.B., Genter, D., 2000. Structure mapping in the comparison process. American Journal of Psychology 113 (4), 501–538.

Pellegrin, P., 1986. Aristotle's Classification of Living Things. University of California Press, Berkeley, CA.

Rudwick, M., 1997. Georges Cuvier, Fossil Bones, and Geological Catastrophes. University of Chicago Press, Chicago.

Tversky, A., 1977. Features of similarity. Psychological Review 84, 327–352.

Vanderkolk, J., 2009. Forensic Comparative Science. Academic Press, New York.

Wittgenstein, L., 1922. Tractatus Logico-Philosophicus. Routledge, London (C.K. Ogden (1922), prepared with assistance from G.E. Moore, F.P. Ramsey, and Wittgenstein, Trans.).

Forensic Classification of Evidence

MM Houck, Consolidated Forensic Laboratory, Washington, DC, USA

Glossary

Set Any group of real or imagined objects.
Taxonomy The science of identifying and naming species with the intent of arranging them into a classification.

Taxon (plural taxa) A group of one or more organisms grouped and ranked according to a set of qualitative and quantitative characteristics; a type of set.

Introduction

Evidence is accidental: Items are transformed into evidence by their involvement in a crime regardless of their source or mode of production. By becoming evidence, their normal meaning is enhanced and expanded. Evidence is initially categorized much as the real world; that is, based on the taxonomy created by manufacturers. Forensic science adds to this classification to further enhance or clarify the meaning of evidence relevant to the goals and procedures of the discipline.

Methods of Classification

Set Theory

Any collection of objects, real or imagined, is a set; set theory is the branch of mathematics that studies these collections. Basic set theory involves categorization and organization of the objects, sometimes using diagrams, and involves elementary operations such as set union and set intersection. Advanced topics, including cardinality, are standard in undergraduate mathematics courses. All classification schemes are based on set theory, to a greater or lesser degree.

The notion of "set" is undefined; the objects described as constituting a set create the definition. The objects in a set are called the members or elements of that set. Objects belong to a set; sets consist of their members. The members of a set may be real or imagined; they do not need to be present to be a member of that set. Membership criteria for a set should be definite and accountable. The set, "All people in this room are over 5'5" tall," is a well-defined, if currently unknown, set—the height of the people in the room would have to be measured to accurately populate the set. If the definition is vague then that collection may not be considered a set. For example, is "q" the same as "Q"? If the set is "the 26 letters of the English alphabet," then they are the same member; if the set is, "the 52 upper-case and lower-case letters of the English alphabet," then they are two separate members.

Sets may be finite or infinite; a set with only one member is called a single or a singleton set. Two sets are identical if and only if they have exactly the same members. The cardinality of a set is the number of members within it, written |A| for set A. A set X is a subset of set Y if and only if every member of X is also a member of Y; for example, the set of all Philips head screwdrivers is a subset of the set of all screwdrivers. Forensic scientists would term this a "subclass" but that is a terminological and not a conceptual difference. Two more concepts are required for the remainder of our discussion. The union of X and Y is a set whose members are only the members of X, Y, or both. Thus, if X were (1, 2, 3) and Y were (2, 3, 4) then the union of X and Y, written $X \cup Y$, would contain (1, 2, 3, 4). Finally, the intersection of two sets contains only the members of both X and Y. In the previous example, the intersection of X and Y would be (2, 3), written $X \cap Y$.

Taxonomy

Natural items, such as animals, plants, or minerals, often occur as evidence. These items are classified according to schemes used in other sciences such as biology, botany, or geology. It is incumbent on the forensic scientist to be knowledgeable about the classification of naturally occurring items.

In biology, taxonomy, the practice and science of classification, refers to a formalized system for ordering and grouping things, typically living things using the Linnaean method. The taxa (the units of a taxonomic system; singular "taxon") are sufficiently fixed so as to provide a structure for classifying living things. Taxa are arranged typically in a hierarchical structure to show their relatedness (a phylogeny). In such a hierarchical relationship, the subtype has by definition the same constraints as the supertype plus one or more additional constraints. For example, "macaque" is a subtype of "monkey," so any macaque is also a monkey, but not every monkey is a macaque, and an animal needs to satisfy more constraints to be a macaque than to be a monkey. In the Linnaean method of classification, the scientific name of each species is formed by the combination of two words, the genus name ("generic" name), which is always capitalized, and a second word identifying the species within that genus. Species names (genus species) are either italicized or underlined, for example, *Homo sapiens* (humans), *Sus scrofus* (pigs), *Canis familiaris* (domesticated dogs), and *Rattus rattus* (rats).

The term "systematics" is sometimes used synonymously with "taxonomy" and may be confused with "scientific classification." However, taxonomy is properly the describing, identifying, classifying, and naming of organisms, while "classification" is focused on placing organisms within groups that show their relationships to other organisms. Systematics alone deals specifically with relationships through time, requiring recognition of the fossil record when dealing with the systematics of organisms. Systematics uses taxonomy as a primary tool in understanding organisms, as nothing about the organism's relationships with other living things can be understood without it first being properly studied and described in sufficient detail to identify and classify it correctly.

In geology, rocks are generally classified based on their chemical and mineral composition, the process by which they were formed, and by the texture of their particles. Rocks are classified as igneous (formed by cooled molten magma), sedimentary (formed by deposition and compaction of materials), or metamorphic (formed through intense changes in pressure and temperature). These three classes of rocks are further subdivided into many other sets; often, the categories' definitions are not rigid and the qualities of a rock may grade it from one class to another. The terminology of rocks and minerals, rather than describing a state, describes identifiable points along a gradient.

Manufacturing

Manufactured evidence is initially categorized by the in-house or market-specific system created by one or more manufacturers. Manufacturers of economic goods create their classifications through product identity or analytical methods. Set methods of production ensure a quality product fit for purpose and sale; the classification is based on the markets involved, the orientation of the company production methods, and the supply chain. Explicit rules exist on categories recognized by manufacturers and consumers, as either models or brands. Materials flow downstream, from raw material sources through to a manufacturing level. Raw materials are transformed into intermediate products, also referred to as components or parts. These are assembled on the next level to form products. The products are shipped to distribution centers and from there on to retailers and customers.

Forensic Approaches to Classification

The supply network of raw materials, intermediate steps, production methods, intended consumer end use, and actual end use all contribute to the characteristics available for forensic taxonomic classification. While the forensic taxonomies are unique to that discipline, they are based on the production taxonomies used in manufacturing. These characteristics form the basis for statements of significance, that is, the relative abundance or rarity of any one particular item in a criminal context. Some objects are common but have a short-entrance horizon (e.g., iPods), but are essentially identical at the outset while others are common with long-entrance horizons (denim blue jeans), but have a high variance (regular, stone washed, acid washed, etc.). It is in the best interest of forensic scientists to understand the fundamental manufacturing processes of the items that routinely become evidence. This understanding can form the basis for statistical significance statements in courts and may provide the foundations for a more quantitative approach to testimony.

Forensic analytical methods create augmented taxonomies because the discipline uses different sets of methods and forensic scientists have different goals. Their taxonomies are based on manufactured traits, but also aftermarket qualities, and intended end use, but also "as used." The "as-used" traits are those imparted to the item after purchase through either normal or criminal use. Forensic science has developed a set of rules through which the taxonomies are explicated. For example, forensic scientists are interested in the size, shape, and distribution of delustrants, microscopic grains of rutile titanium dioxide incorporated into a fiber to reduce its luster. The manufacturer has included delustrant in the fiber at a certain rate and percentage with no concern for shape or distribution (but size may be relevant). The forensic science taxonomy is based on manufacturing taxonomy but is extended by incidental characteristics that help us distinguish otherwise similar objects.

Natural, manufacturing, and forensic classifications lead to evidentiary significance because they break the world down into intelligible classes of objects related to criminal acts. Forensic science has developed an enhanced appreciation for discernment between otherwise similar objects but has yet to explicate these hierarchies to their benefit.

Class-Level Information

Identification is the examination of the chemical and physical properties of an object and using them to categorize it as a member of a set. What the object is made of, its color, mass, size, and many other characteristics are used to identify an object and help refine that object's identity. Analyzing a white powder and concluding that it is cocaine is an example of identification; determining that a small translucent chip is bottle glass or yellow fibrous material and determining that they are dog hairs are also examples of identification. Most identifications are inherently hierarchical, such as classification systems themselves: In the last example, the fibrous nature of the objects restricts the following possible categories:

● Hairs
● Animal hairs
● Guard hairs
● Dog hairs
● German shepherd hairs

As the process of identification of evidence becomes more specific, it permits the analyst to classify the evidence into successively smaller classes of objects. It may not be necessary to classify the evidence beyond dog hairs if human hairs are being looked for. Multiple items can be classified differently, depending on what questions are asked. For example, the objects in **Figure 1** could be classified into "fruit" and "nonfruit," "sports related" and "nonsports related," or "organic" and "inorganic."

Sharing a class identity may indicate two objects that come from a common source. Because forensic science reveals and describes the relationships among people, places, and things involved in criminal activities, this commonality of relationship may be critical to a successful investigation. Commonality can show interactions, limitations in points of origin, and increased significance of relationships. What is meant by a "common source" depends on the material in question, the mode of production, and the specificity of the examinations used to classify the object. For example, the "common source" for an automotive paint chip could be the following:

● the manufacturer (to distinguish it from other similar paints),

● the factory (to determine where it was made),
● the batch or lot of production (to distinguish it from other batches at the same factory),
● all the vehicles painted with that color paint, or
● the vehicle painted with that color paint involved in the crime in question.

All of these options, and they are not exhaustive, could be the goal in an investigation of determining whether two objects had a "common source."

Uniqueness and Individualization

If an object can be classified into a set with only one member (itself), it can be said to be unique. An individualized object is associated with one, and only one, source: It is unique. Uniqueness is based on two assumptions. The first assumption is that all things are unique in space and, thus, their properties are nonoverlapping. The assumption of uniqueness of space is considered axiomatic and, therefore, an inherently nonprovable proposition for numerous reasons. The population size of "all things that might be evidence" is simply too large to account. In addition, conclusive evidence is not readily available in typical forensic investigations. Because of this, as Schum notes, statistics are required:

> Such evidence, if existed, would make necessary a particular hypothesis or possible conclusion being entertained. In lieu of such perfection, we often make use of masses of inconclusive evidence having additional properties: The evidence is incomplete on matters relevant to our conclusions, and it comes to us from sources (including our own observations) that are, for various reasons, not completely credible. Thus, inferences from such evidence can only be probabilistic in nature (Schum, 1994, p. 2).

Figure 1 A range of objects may be classified in a variety of ways, depending on the question being asked. For example, given the objects in this figure, the sets would differ if the question was, "What is edible?" rather than "What is sporting equipment?".

A statistical analysis is therefore warranted when uncertainty, of either accounting or veracity, exists. If an absolutely certain answer to a problem could be reached, statistical methods would not be required. Most evidence exists at the class level, and although each item involved in a crime is considered unique, it still belongs to a larger class. In reality, the majority of forensic science works at a class level of resolution. Indeed, even DNA, the argued "gold standard" of forensic science, operates with classes and statistics.

It has been argued that the concept of uniqueness is necessary but not sufficient to support claims of individualization. If it is accepted that uniqueness is axiomatic, then

> What matters is whether we have analytical tools necessary to discern the characteristics that *distinguish* one object from all others or, in the forensic context, distinguish *traces* made by each object from traces made by every other object … Every object is presumably unique at the scale of manufacture. The question is whether objects are distinguishable at the scale of detection. Since all objects in the universe are in some respects "the same" and in other respects "different" from all other objects in the universe, according to Wittgenstein, what really matters is not uniqueness but rather what rules we articulate by which we will make determinations of "sameness" and "difference" (Cole, 2009, pp. 242–243).

Although things may be numerically unique at the point of *production*, this does not help to distinguish between otherwise similar objects at the point of *detection* or *interpretation*. This is where forensic science adds value to the investigative and legal processes.

Relationships and Context

The relationships between the people, places, and things involved in crimes are central to deciding what items to examine and how to interpret the results. For example, if a sexual assault occurs and the perpetrator and victim are strangers, more evidence may be relevant than if they live together or are sexual partners. Strangers are not expected to have ever met previously and, therefore, would have not transferred evidence before the crime. People who live together would have some opportunities to transfer certain types of evidence (e.g., head hairs and carpet fibers from the living room) but not others (semen or vaginal secretions). Spouses or sexual partners, being the most intimate relationship of the three examples, would share a good deal of more information (**Figure 2**).

Stranger-on-stranger crimes beg the question of coincidental associations, that is, two things that previously have never been in contact with each other have items on them, which are analytically indistinguishable at a certain class level. Attorneys in cross-examination may ask, "Yes, but could not [insert evidence type here] really have come from anywhere? Are not [generic class level evidence] very common?" It has been proven for a wide variety of evidence that coincidental matches are extremely rare. The enormous variety of mass-produced goods, consumer choices, economic factors, biological and natural diversity, and other traits create a nearly infinite combination of comparable characteristics for the items involved in any one situation.

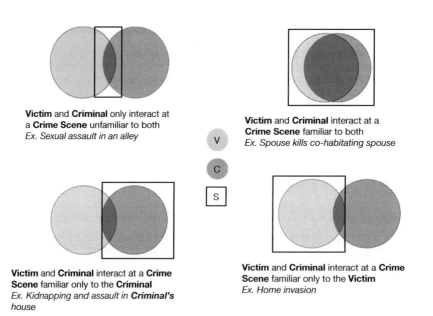

Victim and Criminal only interact at a Crime Scene unfamiliar to both
Ex. Sexual assault in an alley

Victim and Criminal interact at a Crime Scene familiar to both
Ex. Spouse kills co-habitating spouse

V

C

S

Victim and Criminal interact at a Crime Scene familiar only to the Criminal
Ex. Kidnapping and assault in Criminal's house

Victim and Criminal interact at a Crime Scene familiar only to the Victim
Ex. Home invasion

Figure 2   The relationship between suspect, victim, and scene influence, what evidence is collected, and what its significance is.

See also: **Foundations:** Evidence/Classification; Statistical Interpretation of Evidence: Bayesian Analysis; The Frequentist Approach to Forensic Evidence Interpretation.

Further Reading

Cole, S., 2009. Forensics without uniqueness, conclusion without individualization: the new epistemology of forensic identification. Law, Probability and Risk 8 (3), 233–255.
Devlin, K., 1993. The Joy of Sets. Springer, Berlin.

Haq, T., Roche, G., Parker, B., 1978. Theoretical field concepts in forensic science. 1. Application to recognition and retrieval of physical evidence. Journal of Forensic Sciences 23 (1), 212–217.
Houck, M.M., 2006. Production Taxonomies as the Foundation of Forensic Significance. European Academy of Forensic Sciences, Helsinki, Finland.
Johnson, P., 1972. A History of Set Theory. Weber & Schmidt, New York.
Kwan, Q.Y., 1977. Inference of identity of source (Ph.D. thesis), University of California.
Schum, D.A., 1994. Evidential Foundations of Probabilistic Reasoning. John Wiley & Sons, New York.
Thornton, J., 1986. Ensembles of class characteristics in physical evidence examination. Journal of Forensic Sciences 31 (2), 501–503.
Underhill, P., 2000. Why We Buy: The Science of Shopping. Simon & Schuster, New York.

Key Terms

Accreditation, Analogy, Classification, Comparison, Crime, Development, Epistemology, Evidence, Fabric construction, Fibers, Forensic, Forensic anthropology, History, Identification, Kirk, Locard, Method, Osteology, Paradigm, Science, Set, Skeletal remains, Taxon, Taxonomy, Trace evidence, Transfer, Trauma analysis

Review Questions

1. If the "basic unit of forensic science is the trace," how does this fit within forensic anthropology's conceptual framework? What would they be a "physical remnant" of?
2. What are the three levels that Locard's principle needs to address?
3. Besides Locard's principle, what else do Crispino and Houck consider to be a "native" forensic principle?
4. What are the nonnative principles that forensic sciences uses? Give an example of each one in action.
5. What is the difference between uniqueness and individualization?
6. How is forensic anthropology defined?
7. Why medical doctors do not have more training in osteology?
8. What are the major functions of a forensic anthropologist?
9. What other disciplines must forensic anthropology deal with?
10. Why is the need for identification of human remains increasing?
11. Who was Johann Blumenbach and why is he important to forensic anthropology?
12. What year was the Anthropological Society of Paris founded and by whom?
13. How did the Packman murder help establish the field of forensic anthropology in the United States?
14. What did the Ruxton case do for forensic anthropology in the United Kingdom?
15. What publication led to the emergence of forensic anthropology in the modern era?
16. Why were the Second World War and the Korean War pivotal points in the development of forensic anthropology?
17. In what year did forensic anthropology become a section of the American Academy of Forensic Sciences?
18. How is employment as a forensic anthropologist linked to war?
19. What kinds of transfer, a la Locard, occur in forensic anthropology?
20. What is the historic relationship between anatomy and forensic anthropology?

Discussion Questions

1. How is forensic anthropology like the rest of forensic science? How is it different? What aspects of nonforensic anthropology does it still embrace? Does forensic anthropology still "fit" within the wider discipline of anthropology?
2. Why was forensic anthropology founded by anatomists? When did it become its own discipline?
3. Forensic anthropology is a global discipline assisting not only in civilian criminal cases but also in mass disasters, war crimes, and war dead. How did this field develop from a handful of sensationalized murder cases to worldwide application?
4. How can forensic anthropology maintain itself as a discipline? If employment waxes and wanes with armed conflicts (with attendant efforts to identify the numerous dead), how can a professional have steady employment? What are the implications for educational programs?
5. What kind of "proxy data" do forensic anthropologists work with? How is their proxy data different from other forensic sciences?

Additional Readings

Black, S., Ferguson, E. (Eds.), 2016. Forensic Anthropology: 2000 to 2010. CRC Press.
Blau, J. (Ed.), 2016. Handbook of Forensic Anthropology and Archaeology. Routledge.
Steadman, D.W. (Ed.), 2015. Hard Evidence: Case Studies in Forensic Anthropology. Routledge.

Section 2. Taphonomy

Death is not the end. Organisms, once they die, continue to interact with other organisms that are still alive, the environment, and the physical laws of nature. The study of these complex processes is called taphonomy. Once the study of how organisms become fossilized (long-term taphonomy), it has broadened its scope to also look at the near-term interactions of the recently deceased with the rest of the world. In Martin's wonderful book, *Taphonomy: A Process Approach*,[1] offers an amended list of taphonomic rules:

1. Organisms are more likely to be preserved if they have hard parts
2. Preservation is greatly enhanced by a quick burial with little decay or scavenging
3. Information is lost due to dismemberment or decay (that is, entropy increases)
4. Remains consist of those from the immediate area, those transported to that area, and those derived from other remains
5. Taphonomic loss is greatest in shallow-water marine environments
6. Information loss is largely due to transport, disarticulation, sorting, and breakage by water and animals
7. Physical process that mix or move remains increase the diversity of remains found
8. The results of Rule 7 create errors of determining the extent of the assemblage
9. Information may be gained *because of* taphonomic agents and their processes
10. Catastrophic burial may result in "snapshots" of the dynamics of the event.

One can see how these can be readily applied to crime scenes and other forensic contexts. Martin goes on to note, sounding quite forensic, that although

> we must begin with the assumption of the uniformity of Nature, any application of principles or rules must be done in a *comparative* (case-by-case) manner because each historian entity bears the imprint of the unique (or nearly so) circumstances that led up to it.Martin (1999, p. 14); original emphasis.

Taphonomic processes are the start of the forensic application and a deep reading of these topics will enhance any forensic anthropologist's understanding of their work.

Animal Effects on Bones

C Cattaneo and D Gibelli, Università degli Studi di Milano, Milano, Italy

Glossary

Scattering Dispersion and dislocation of bone fragments in the environment due to animal activity.
Scavenging Modifications of bones due to animal chewing in the postmortem period.

Taphonomy The study of the phenomenon affecting the remains of biological organisms at the time of and after death. The term means "laws of burial" and was created by Efremov in 1940.

Introduction

The attack by animals is only one of the complex manifestations of the environment on the corpse, but undoubtedly brings about important modifications of the body or skeleton which may potentially hinder search and recovery as well as the assessment of lesions. Animals, in fact, are able to destroy bodies, produce postmortem artifacts, modify the site of deposition, and scatter human remains, with a consequent decrease in the success of research and in the number of bones which may be recovered.

---

[1] Martin, R., 1999. Taphonomy: A Process Approach. Cambridge University Press, Cambridge.

However, the scavenging activity has not yet been thoroughly studied experimentally. Several case studies exist but little research has been published. This is due to the difficulties which are obviously associated with this phenomenon. First of all, scavenging is a stochastic event, which occurs in specific geographical settings and concerns the behavior of animal species inhabiting the area of interest. Literature reports that almost every animal species under specific conditions can attack a corpse: a very limited inventory includes leopards, foxes, hyenas, dogs, wolves, deer, sheep, hogs, rodents (porcupines, mice, squirrels, rats), crabs, turtles, fish, birds, and even golden hamsters: scavenging is also reported by domestic dogs or other pets, particularly in cases where they have been forced to remain in the same environment with the cadaver. Every geographic region is often inhabited by different species, which give their specific contribution to the consumption of a corpse, often in cooperation with other species. For instance, in cases of buried corpses, vultures use the opening made by raccoons during their scavenging activity in order to attack soft tissue and detach bone segments. Such a "cooperation" is also characterized by different behavior: although animals usually scavenge corpses to feed on their soft tissues, other species are more interested in calcified tissues, such as rodents, who will gnaw on bones in order to reduce the length of their incisors. In addition, different species attack corpses at different times: vultures usually visit carcasses in the daylight whereas foxes, raccoons, opossums, and skunks act at night.

Experimental studies performed on pig carcasses have verified that bird scavenging tends to precede other scavenging activities, and is followed by canid activity, which initiates scattering. These few indications show that scavenging should be interpreted as a sign of the interaction between the corpse and a complex environment rather than the mere activity of animals producing different sets of lesions on bones; the phenomenon can only therefore be partially standardized, and the general profile of scavenging activity can hardly be anticipated, especially since most information concerning the environment is usually presumed indirectly: for example, the density of animal colonization in a specific area is usually estimated in correlation with the number of human inhabitants. However, the precise number of individuals and the specific species are often incompletely known. Another limit consists in the few existing geographical studies. Most of them deal with research conducted in specific geographic areas of North America, Europe, and Australia, and therefore their results are valid only for scavenging activity occurring within those areas and do not cover the entire geographical variability, which may be encountered in forensic practice.

At the moment, very few experimental studies deal with the scavenging and scattering phenomenon, and most of the information derives from empirical observations, which, however, have contributed to define initial general characteristics of animal attack and the effects on the different steps of anthropological analysis.

Search and Recovery

Scavenging is usually followed by scattering: animals disarticulate the bone segments and usually transport them far away from the deposition site, with consequent difficulties for the phases of search and recovery. This means that with time the number of bones which may be found progressively decreases, whereas the area which should be investigated increases. In addition, if operators presume that the remains have been scavenged, then the entire strategy of search should be adequately modified, in order to perform an efficient exploration of the area. Knowledge of precise patterns of scattering would therefore improve the manner of searching for dispersed human remains. For animals, the removal of bone segments is mainly aimed at reducing competition between different species and feeding the young: scattering is often coupled with the accumulation of remains, usually close to the dens of the specific scavenging animal; rodents, especially porcupines, are considered the most active accumulators. Every search procedure in case of scavenged remains should, therefore, also focus on dens and burrows of animals. Small bones and bone fragments may be eaten only to be later regurgitated or deposited with defecation. Hair, teeth, fingers, and small bones found in animal feces have been reported. Analysis of animal scat found in the area of scattering is important, since it may lead to the identification of the type of animal present in the area and to the detection of small bone or tooth fragments pertaining to the remains. For example, bone is more highly fragmented in small animals' scat, probably because of the limited dimension of their mouths. Felids have scats with a larger amount of bone mass, but contain fewer and greater fragments than dogs because of the bone-crushing profile of dogs' dentition. In addition, stomach digestion in dogs is more destructive, and this causes a deep modification of swallowed fragments. These are the first indications which may derive from the recent application of forensic scatology, and which show that the assessment of the scavenged and scattered body requires also a thorough analysis from a zoological point of view.

In addition, one should always consider that scavengers also come from above: vultures may attack corpses, and therefore spread human remains sometimes very far away from their point of origin. It is known that vultures can skeletonize a corpse in a short time, as seen during funeral rituals in different cultures which require the corpse to be exposed ("aerial burial"). Scattering distances of specific species are sometimes reported by authors, although there is a high variability due to the superimposition of other taphonomic factors such as the movement of skeletal remains due to sedimentation, rains, or other environmental or geological factors. In addition, scattering distance is related to weight and size of disarticulated remains, and to the strength of the scavenger as well.

Literature reports that the cranium is usually the most frequent anatomical area found in cases of scavenged remains;

however, this may be due to the fact that it is easier to find compared to smaller bones such as vertebrae or phalanges. Different authors report incomplete/broken skulls showing signs of tooth marks and destruction, especially in cases of extensive head trauma existing before death, and Rodriguez has shown that medium-sized dogs can transport human skulls.

Generally, bones of the upper extremity are recovered less frequently than those of the lower extremity (50% of recovery rate for scapula, to a low of 25% for the clavicle, while those of the lower extremity range from a high of 65% for the femur to a low of 42% for the tibia). Bones of the axial skeleton are recovered between 74% and 61% of the time.

The positioning of scattered remains may be useful for reconstructing the manner of scavenging: global positioning systems and other methods of mapping bone remains have a relevant role. These attempts may bring about relevant information for the reconstruction of a unique scattering profile, which may help in the differential diagnosis with other events that may have caused the spreading of bones, such as dismemberment.

Postmortem Interval Estimation

Scavenging is a natural phenomenon which has repercussions not only on the survival and consequent search and retrieval of human remains, but also on the stage of decomposition of the cadaver and, therefore, time since death evaluation; several authors state that a reliable estimation of postmortem interval (PMI) by evaluation of the decomposition process should always consider the possible scavenging activity by animals, since it may radically influence the trend of skeletonization of human remains. However, scavenging is not a physical effect such as temperature and weather, in general, which can be predicted, although with a large error; it has to do with animal behavior, which is hard to foresee. The first question concerns when exactly scavenging begins: relevant literature only gives partial information, since scavenged corpses are usually found after considerable time after death and the onset of scavenging cannot be reconstructed with precision. In cases of domestic pets, different authors state that the attack begins when food supplies are finished, although this indication is scarcely useful for predicting exactly when the scavenging lesions were produced. In addition, different case reports have shown that domestic pets may attack the corpse even when their food supplies are intact. In conclusion, the motivation of the animal is of the utmost importance, and although it is usually hunger, the precise dynamics concerning the decision to scavenge are not completely known.

The second question concerns how long scavenging lasts, and whether it is directly related with time. Different studies have observed that there is no precise correlation between scavenging and PMI, and that scavenging is not a linear process and does not

develop with a constant velocity. In addition, literature provides different indications concerning the general velocity with which each animal destroys a body: Willey and Snyder, for example, report that five adult wolves in an outdoor environment can consume a large deer weighing 55–73 kg in 4–7 days. This information gives a general idea concerning the velocity of the attack by a specific animal, but cannot be used to estimate PMI, since too many variables must be taken into account: for example, five wolves can consume a deer in 4–7 days, but what about one wolf? And are they likely to attack a human body in the same way as the deer? In addition, such general indications derived from case reports are not standardized and cannot be used as a reference for other conditions, or even for other animals: for instance, information concerning how wolves attack should not be used to evaluate scavenging by dogs.

Authors have also observed that several variables may influence the scavenging process, such as rigor and freezing, in the early postmortem period. Another variable which may influence the time of scavenging is body characteristics: for example, clothing has proved to limit the attack by rodents, but not by domestic dogs. In addition, probably the cause of death may have a large influence on scavenging, although very limited information is available: invasive trauma and a drug-related death may accelerate scavenging.

Finally, climatic variables are important as well; the few experimental studies performed show that scavenging may greatly influence decomposition during cold seasons, whereas in summer, when the body skeletonizes considerably earlier, the effects of scavenging are less pronounced.

PMI correlation with scavenging activity is an area of interest where information is still mainly anecdotal, and there is some disagreement among authors. This is further complicated by disagreement among authors: Wiley and Snyder, for example, suggest that it is difficult to correlate scavenging activity with time since death; on the other hand, Morse states that the amount of animal damage and the number of bones removed from the remains is directly correlated to the time of deposition. However, one should consider that not all bones are likely to be removed and transferred away from the original deposition site in the same manner. Ribs and vertebrae are likely to remain closest to the original place, as shown also by the few experimental studies actually available. In addition, degree of decomposition may produce relevant modifications of scattering, since it is usually more marked when the body is attacked early in the postmortem phase, when the soft tissues still hold together skeletal areas and relatively large segments of the skeleton can be easily removed, whereas when the corpse is skeletonized, bones around the specific one scavenged by the animal will be left in the original position. In addition, one should also consider that scavenging is often a discontinuous activity, which begins, may be abandoned, and initiated again according to the specific behavior of the animal and environmental variables.

Every attempt at standardizing a phenomenon must necessarily pass through a classification; Haglund suggests a classification for the evaluation of scattered remains called WDH (after William D. Haglund), where stage 0 represents the removal of soft tissue with no disarticulation; stage 1 the destruction of the ventral thorax characterized by absence of the sternum and damage to distal ribs, accompanied by evisceration and removal of one or both upper extremities, including scapulae and partial or complete removal of clavicles; stage 2 fully or partially separated and removed lower extremities; and stage 3 nearly complete disarticulation with only segments of vertebral column articulated. In stage 4, total disarticulation and scattering are usually observed, with only the cranium and assorted skeletal elements or fragments recovered. The original classification was made according to dog scavenging, but other animals disarticulate bodies in a similar manner, and this suggests that probably the dynamics of disarticulation are greatly influenced by anatomical factors also such as the intrinsic properties of bones and joint attachments.

If the dynamics of dismemberment of specific animals are similar, the same cannot be said for other parameters, such as the distance of scattering, which is strongly influenced by the size and strength of the involved species: Knight reports that foxes can drag body parts away to a distance of at least 3 km. In addition, the distance of scattering is influenced by ecological factors and soil characteristics.

Assessment of Lesions and Cause of Death

Animal scavenging usually occurs when bone surface is still covered with soft tissues; therefore, lesions due to animal scavenging usually display perimortem characteristics (though some authors automatically and erroneously classify them as postmortem-type lesions). This necessarily brings about relevant limits concerning the differential diagnosis between a lesion due to scavenging and one caused by some sort of trauma correlated to the cause of death. In addition, scavenging and trauma may be strictly related; for example, it has already been mentioned that crania affected by blunt trauma are more prone to be attacked by animals. Different authors report that scavenging may occur in areas affected by lesions, but that it is not more probable than in other areas. Blau and Ubelaker describe a case of a gunshot wound affected by scavenging signs. Quatrehomme and Iscan state that animal lesions may be confused with blunt and sharp force trauma or gunshot wounds, but postmortem activity usually does not result in beveling, or radiating or concentric fractures. Surprisingly, although literature extensively deals with scavenging dynamics, very little is known concerning whether its signs may actually disguise a lesion.

Literature has focused on specific characteristics of scavenging, especially those which concern rodents and carnivores.

Gnawing usually proceeds from the cancellous articular ends of long bones (e.g., subadult epiphyses are particularly vulnerable). Rodent tooth marks on bone surfaces have been described by different authors as channels or striae, straight parallel grooves which are flat bottomed. A characteristic of gnawed cross sections of long bone shafts is their uniform pitch, extending from the outer to inner surfaces, whereas damage from carnivores is less regular and often rounded without uniform pitch from the inner to the outer surface. However, distinct parallel striae are not always detectable, since the morphology of lesions depends on the general characteristics of the bone: in cancellous bone or small long bones such as metacarpals, metatarsals, and phalanges, where the cortical component is extremely thin, such striae may be absent. In addition, shape of the striae depends on the manner of gnawing, and therefore may be totally disorganized.

Haynes and Binford recognized four characteristic types of carnivore tooth marks: punctures, pits, scoring, and furrows. Punctures are produced when bone collapses under a tooth and are recognizable as oval penetrations through the cortex, usually where the bone surface is thinner; they may be caused both by canine and carnassial teeth. Pits are indentations caused by the tips of the teeth as the animal bites down and occur when the strength is insufficient to penetrate the bone. Scoring is caused by teeth slipping and dragging over the compact bone, usually oriented transversally to the long axis of the bone. Furrows are caused by repeated jaw action of either canine or carnassial teeth, and may lead to the removal of cancellous bone and licking out its content from open shafts (Figures 1–4).

In specific geographic contexts, the analysis of scavenging involves signs left by other less-common species: bears, for

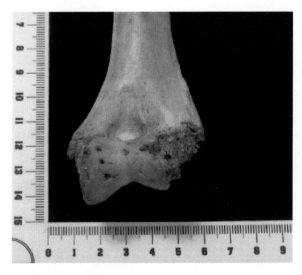

Figure 1   Example of gnawing.

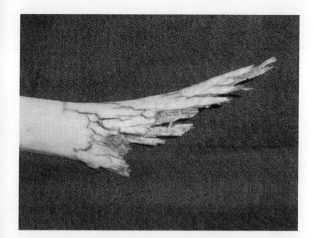

Figure 2   Crushing in a rib due to wild boar activity.

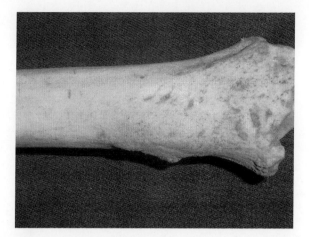

Figure 4   Furrows on the bone surface.

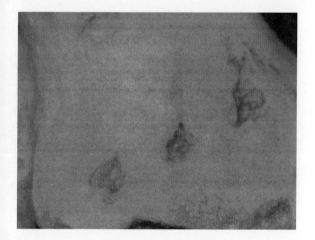

Figure 3   Punctures caused by teeth of carnivores.

example, are more likely to break open the shafts of long bones and carry off or consume portions of the upper limb and axillary skeleton, and leave bones of the lower extremities.

A relevant point of discussion concerns not only the differential diagnosis between traumatic lesions produced before death and animal activity, but also between lesions caused by different animals: for example, Miller states that the incisors of canids such as coyotes (*Canis* sp. *C. latrans*) and wolves (*Canis* sp. *C. lupus*) can cause hollow grooves that may mimic the gnawing marks of rodents when they gnaw with their incisors transverse to the longitudinal axis of long bones.

A classification of lesions according to different origins (rodent or carnivore) has been proposed as well: rodents usually produce tight and circumscribed defects, with relatively smooth or crenulated margins, without damage of the area beyond the margins; carnivores instead produce irregular lesions in shape and margins, and cause scratching of the area beyond the margins.

Another issue is whether scavenging may hide preexisting lesions. The few experimental studies actually performed on blunt trauma show that scavenging may cause a displacement of the bone fragments, with a decrease of the observer's ability to recognize the signs of trauma.

However, although animal activity is supposed to produce lesions, the lack of signs does not mean that the body was not scavenged: for example, vultures may leave very slight signs of their attack, which may be referred to other taphonomical causes (such as weather and environmental modifications), or even remain undetected.

Finally, one should consider that scavenging, though more frequently associated with a terrestrial environment, is a well-known phenomenon also in the aquatic context, were freshwater crustaceans are the main scavenging species; they cause limited and superficial skin lesions of variable shape. Large-sized animals, on the other hand, can produce relevant modifications, with loss of skin, muscle, and bone tissues.

See also: **Anthropology/Odontology:** Archeology; Biomechanics of Bone Trauma; Bone Pathology and Antemortem Trauma; Bone Trauma; Forensic Taphonomy; Postmortem Interval.

Forensic Taphonomy

T Simmons and PA Cross, University of Central Lancashire, Preston, UK

Glossary

Accumulated degree days (ADD) The sum of the average daily temperatures where the body was found from the time of death until the discovery of the body. ADD is used in conjunction with TBS to estimate the postmortem interval.

Commingling When body or skeletal parts of different individuals have become mixed together at the time of death or postmortem.

Postmortem interval (PMI) The time that has elapsed since the individual died. PMI estimation is important in identification of unknown individuals from missing person records as well as in establishing a range of dates when the individual likely died, which may be useful in eliminating or including suspects in a homicide investigation.

Total body score (TBS) An integer value assigned to a body by scoring three regions (head and neck, torso, and limbs) according to the appearance on a scale of decomposition. TBS is used in conjunction with ADD to estimate the postmortem interval.

Introduction

Forensic taphonomy is a rapidly developing field within forensic anthropology and forensic archeology. Research in forensic taphonomy encompasses refining estimates of time since death in various scenarios, differentiating peri- and postmortem trauma, identifying the effects of burning, understanding the directionality of impact in blunt force and projectile trauma in various skeletal elements, reassociating individuals commingled in secondary mass graves or explosions, weathering of bones and teeth, and an extended range of related topics.

Although taphonomy itself has a relatively long history in the paleontological and archeological literature, forensic taphonomy is a comparatively new discipline, developing in response to the demands of casework and to the various circumstances in which bodies are found.

History and Development of the Role of Taphonomy in Forensic Anthropology

Taphonomy roughly means the study of death assemblages and is said to refer to the laws of burial; the term itself was coined in 1940 by Efremov, who stated that taphonomy was the "study of the transition, in all details, of organics from the biosphere into the lithosphere of the geological record." Until relatively recently (the late 1980s), taphonomy was a term used predominantly within vertebrate paleontology, prehistoric archeozoology, and archeology. In 1997, Haglund and Sorg defined the goals of traditional taphonomy as the preservation, observation, or recovery of dead organisms; the reconstruction of their biology or ecology; and the reconstruction of the circumstances of their death. Taphonomy has featured prominently in paleontological and zooarcheological publications since the later three quarters of the twentieth century. In 1927, Johannes Weigelt's published *Rezente Wirbeltierleichen und ihre paläobiologische Bedeutung*, which was unfortunately not translated into English, as *Vertebrate Carcasses and their Paleobiological Implications*, until 1989. This prescient book detailed Weigelt's observations on the decomposition of animal carcasses on the coast of Texas and brought to light the role of insects, surface decomposition, carcass positioning in burial and partial burial contexts, sequences of disarticulation, and environmental significance among other topics. In 1981, Pat Shipman published an edited volume with a huge impact on prehistoric archeology and archeozoology entitled *Life History of a Fossil: an Introduction to Taphonomy and Paleoecology*, which introduced a wide variety of techniques for assessing taphonomic principles. Arguably, the first forensically relevant taphonomic publication in book format occurred in 1987 with Boddington, Garland, and Janaway's *Death, Decay and Reconstruction: Approaches to Archaeology and Forensic Science*; although it contained a chapter by W.M. Bass, it was primarily archeological in orientation and received little notice outside of the

United Kingdom. Lyman's *Vertebrate Taphonomy*, published in 1994, brought together the current knowledge in the field, ranging from skeletal assemblage accumulation and dispersal to the diagenesis of bone itself. The traditional goals of taphonomy were emphasized, including reconstructing pale-oenvironments, determining which factors cause differential destruction/attrition of bone, understanding selective transport of skeletal elements, discriminating human from nonhuman agents of bone modification, and reconstructing paleoenvironments.

Research in forensic taphonomy was spurred by the founding of the University of Tennessee, Knoxville's (UTK) Anthropological Research Facility (ARF), in 1981. Since 2000, the facility receives donations of approximately 100 bodies per year and the WM Bass Skeletal Collection, derived from the facility, now numbers around 700 skeletons. Although UTK staff and students have presented and published widely, the majority of publications emanating from the institution concern skeletal metrics rather than taphonomy itself. A paucity of publications from the ARF relating to decomposition have been forthcoming over the past 30 years of its existence; the best known are probably the earliest, for example, Rodriguez and Bass in 1987 and Mann et al. in 1990. Although the most recent publication by Vass in 2011 proposes formulae for calculating the postmortem interval (PMI), it presents no data from which these formulae are derived and no prior publications from the ARF provide these data. In the twenty-first century's recent years, at least three other human decomposition facilities have been founded: Texas State University at San Marcos, Western Carolina University, and Sam Houston State University, TX.

1997 saw the publication of Haglund and Sorg's landmark edited volume, *Forensic Taphonomy: The Postmortem Fate of Human Remains*. The volume consisted primarily of case studies and dealt with decomposition in different environments, bone modification (including fire, trauma, trophy skulls, and scavenging), and the fate of remains in water (lacustrine, riverine, and maritime). Haglund and Sorg stated the goals of forensic taphonomy to be estimating time and circumstances since death; distinguishing postmortem conditions, which may confound human identification; determining cause and manner of death; identifying factors relating to skeletal element survival; reconstruction of events following death; collecting and analyzing data about context; discriminating post- from perimortem modification; and estimating the PMI. The techniques of forensic taphonomy included involving the application of archeological search and recovery techniques, the laboratory analysis of remains, and the understanding of soft tissue and bone modification and distribution. The 1997 publication was followed in 2002 by a second edited volume, *Advances in Forensics Taphonomy: Method, Theory, and Archaeological Perspectives*, which presented more diverse and international case studies with a greater emphasis on context. Further publications in 2008 included Tibbett and Carter's *Soil analysis in Forensic Taphonomy: Chemical and Biological Effects of Buried Human Remains* and Adams and Byrd's *Recovery, Analysis and Identification of Commingled Human Remains*.

Forensic taphonomic literature and research are concerned with documenting the changes to the body that occur postmortem from the earliest signs of autolysis to skeletonization, as well as the fate of skeletalized remains in disarticulation, transport, weathering, and so on.

Decomposition and Postmortem Change

The cessation of oxygenated blood flow to body tissues initiates the start of autolysis or "self-digestion." Autolytic changes can be seen microscopically shortly after death. These include mitochondrial swelling and calcification, dilated endoplasmic reticulum, aggregated cytoskeletal elements, and membrane disruption. The cell nucleus and mitochondria also exhibit condensed chromatin as a result of the fall in pH. Autolysis begins in the most metabolically active cells, which are more sensitive to oxygen depletion, such as the brain and heart muscle and those that contain a large quantity and diverse array of hydrolytic enzymes, such as the liver, pancreas, stomach, and intestines.

Macroscopic autolytic changes result from the leakage of hydrolytic enzymes into the intercellular spaces where cell junctions facilitate cell-to-cell adhesion. The breakdown of this intercellular adhesion results in the gross appearance of tissue friability and eventual liquefaction, and some of the notable postmortem changes such as skin slippage.

Autolytic activity creates an increasingly anaerobic environment which favors the rapid growth of bacteria that normally inhabit the body. The release of large amounts of breakdown products provides nutrients for bacterial and fungal flora. The proliferation of microorganisms and their metabolic by-products results in the color, odor, and morphological changes characteristic of the putrefactive stage of decomposition.

Early Postmortem Changes

Early postmortem changes are often referred to as those that occur within 2 h of death. The changes include "pallor," a paleness of the skin on upper areas of the body seen in light-skinned individuals due to the loss of circulating oxygenated blood and the gravitational settling of blood to lower regions. Skeletal muscles relax during this period, including sphincter muscles, and this may cause early purging of fecal, urinary, or gastric contents.

Relaxation of the orbicularis oculi muscles may expose the cornea to drying, and this exhibits as a dark band running across the cornea, known as tache noir sclerotique. Postmortem autolytic changes within the retina, and to a lesser extent the lens, result in electrolytes diffusing into the vitreous body. Of particular interest, and the most studied, is the influx of potassium ions (K^+) into the vitreous humor. Owing to the isolation of the vitreous humor compared with blood or cerebrospinal fluid, levels of vitreous potassium are a favored area of study in estimating PMI.

Late Postmortem Changes

Late postmortem changes are often referred to as those that become observable from 2–4 h postmortem.

Livor mortis, also known as lividity or hypostasis, is the gravitational pooling of blood to lower dependant areas resulting in a red/purple coloration. Although livor mortis is commonly seen between 2 and 4 h postmortem, its onset may begin in the "early" period, as little as 30 min postmortem. In the early period of livor mortis, the coloration is not "fixed" and pressure of the skin can cause "blanching." During this period, changing the position of the body can result in resettling of the blood in newly dependant areas. After a period of time, the blood coagulates and livor mortis becomes fixed. Rigor mortis is a reversible postmortem stiffening of the muscles, beginning in the muscles of the face and jaw, and extending to the rest of the body as the postmortem period progresses. The onset of rigor mortis is dependent upon temperature and the metabolic status of the deceased and occurs concomitantly with early stage autolysis. The timing of the onset of rigor mortis is variable, but it normally begins 2–6 h postmortem and has extended over the body by 12 h postmortem. Rigidity can last for 24–82 h after which gradual resolution occurs, progressing in the same order as rigor mortis commenced. Algor mortis is the cooling of body after death as it equilibrates with ambient temperature. Normal body temperature (rectal) can vary between individuals, ranging from 34.2 to 37.6 °C with a mean of 36.9 °C. Rectal temperature is similar in value to that of the brain, lungs, and abdominal organs and is often referred to as "deep central temperature."

A number of factors can influence body temperature at time of death, including emotional stress, pathological febrile conditions, metabolic disorders, circulatory disorders, and exposure to extreme environmental temperatures. Further factors influence the rate of cooling. These include body posture, body size, body fat, and presence of clothing.

Skin slippage occurs as a result of autolytic release of hydrolytic enzymes at the junction of the epidermis and dermis. This results in loosening and sloughing of the epidermis. This may be seen initially as the formation of vesicles or blisters. Fluid-filled vesicles known as "bullae" can also form beneath the epidermis. Larger areas of skin may slough off, and this can occur on any area of the body. Hair and nails will also be lost with the skin, and when this occurs on the head, the whole scalp can slide off.

Color changes are indicative of putrefactive changes. They occur as a result of (1) the degradation of hemoglobin and (2) the formation of hydrogen sulfide (H_2S) within vessels and tissues by enteric bacteria. Greening of the lower abdomen may occur within a few hours of death. The cecum, in particular, has a large population of enteric bacteria and will produce a large quantity of hydrogen sulfide. This will react with hemoglobin and other heme-containing proteins (e.g., myoglobin) and produce a green coloration in the lower abdomen, which becomes widespread throughout body tissues. The greening of superficial blood vessels can give the appearance of "marbling," sometimes called suggillation.

Bloating occurs as a result of putrefactive gases becoming trapped within the body. In addition to hydrogen sulfide, a wide range of other gases are produced during the putrefactive stage. The trapped gases cause distension of the abdomen, and in males, the trapped gases can be forced into the scrotum via the inguinal canals, causing distension of the scrotum and penis. As gases build up within tissues, bloating can also be observed in the tissues of the face and neck.

Putrefaction results in a complex mixture of volatile gases produced from the breakdown of carbohydrates and proteins. Two notable products are putrescine and cadaverine, both products of protein breakdown. These products have the characteristic decompositional odor and are utilized by cadaver dogs in the search for human remains.

Insect Decomposers

The rate of autolysis and the rate of putrefaction resulting from microbiological activity are dependent primarily on temperature. Given time, autolytic and putrefactive changes will result in liquefaction of soft tissue.

The rate of decomposition of a body accessed by insects is rapidly increased, as larval masses can result in significant soft tissue loss in a short period of time. In a suitable environment, insects are attracted to a body within minutes, their activity being temperature-dependent also. The population of insects on a body will be particular to that specific environment, as well as to a given geographic area. Typically, blowflies (Diptera: Calliphoridae) will be attracted to the volatile gases emanating from the alimentary canal via natural orifices (e.g., mouth, nose, anus) and those produced by early stage putrefactive changes. Their larvae can form large masses feeding on soft tissue. Although beetles (Coleoptera) are commonly associated with remains in later stages of decomposition, some (e.g., Silphidae) are present on the body during early stage decomposition, as dipteral larval masses represent a food source for them.

Adipocere

Adipocere, also known as "grave wax," is a caseous material formed by the saponification of body fat. Adipocere may appear pastelike, be crumbly in texture, or may form a hard material depending upon the type of fatty acids involved and the chemical environment in which it is formed. Moist, anaerobic conditions favor the formation of adipocere but its appearance is not restricted to immersed remains. Any grave or terrestrial environment where adequate moisture is present can result in the formation of adipocere. In surface depositions, adipocere formation can occur in oxygen-deficient dependent areas where fat is in contact with moist ground. Adipocere is very persistent and may remain stable for many years, exerting a preservation effect on the body.

Drying and Mummification

Postmortem drying of remains is commonly seen in the early stages postmortem. This can frequently be seen in the extremities (e.g., fingers and toes, lips, and genitals).

In dry, low-humid environments, remains may become mummified. The skin becomes desiccated and takes on a dark leathery appearance. Putrefaction and insect activity may continue within the body, resulting in a skeleton within a shell of mummified skin. In extreme environments or where low temperatures inhibit microbial and insect activity, the entire remains may become desiccated, including internal organs and other soft tissues.

Animal Activity

The progression of decomposition may further be modified by the actions of carnivorous animals. In situations where death has occurred in a confined place in the presence of pet animals, it is not uncommon for dogs and cats to consume remains. The soft tissue from the face and extremities are commonly eaten in these circumstances.

In outside environments, remains may be exposed to wild carnivores and farm animals. In such cases, in addition to consumption, remains may become disarticulated and distributed over a wide area.

Decomposition of Hard Tissue and the Fate of Skeletal Remains

Skeletonized remains are less attractive to necrophagous insects and animal scavengers, and their decomposition takes place over a much longer time frame. Bacterial and plant activities continue to have a role in the breakdown of hard tissue, but other chemical and physical actions, such as weathering and abrasion, also influence this process.

Once remains are skeletalized, the substrate onto which or into which they have been deposited assumes greater importance than it did during decomposition itself. This soil pH is of critical importance, for instance, in determining skeletal element survival in burials. Unfortunately, little is known

about skeletal element weathering and damage and movement outside of the studies published by archeologists and vertebrate paleontologists. These are focused on the identification of stages of sun bleaching and drying, scavenging and transport within hyena dens, fluvial transport and stream bed accumulations, and the like—variables that are, generally speaking, somewhat more relevant to prehistoric assemblages and the African environments, which were the impetus for their formulation, than to the majority of modern forensic casework scenarios. Having said that, however, C.K. Brain's early research into the taphonomy of the karstic caves in which the bones of South African fauna and australopithecines accumulated has proved relevant to the interpretation, by Simmons in 2002, of contemporary execution site deposits of the victims of war crimes in Bosnia. The drawback to many of these studies is that the environment in the African Savannah, or Weldt, is quite dissimilar to, for example, temperate forests of North America, rain-soaked pastures in the United Kingdom and the like, and little if any research has been undertaken experimentally to catalog the progression of the processes in other environments from fresh bone through weathering. Several new studies have, however, examined color changes in bone and teeth as correlated to both UV radiation exposure and fluctuating humidity.

Diagenesis, also known as chemical weathering, is the exchange of ionic components between bone and the environment; in most cases, the soil. Once the collagen component of bone has been lost, chemical decomposition predominates and calcium ions leach into the soil in exchange for protons. Metal ions present in the soil (e.g., iron and aluminum) remove phosphate ions from the bone. The rate and degree of diagenesis are dependent on environmental factors, not least the chemical composition of the soil. Physical weathering constitutes the action of wind, sun, and wet/dry cycles. These physical forces create cracking and flaking of bone, thereby accelerating its destruction. Behrensmeyer defined six stages of bone weathering and their relationship to years since death.

Carnivore and rodent scavenging are also factors that affect bone over time. Haglund's research concerning disarticulation patterns commonly encountered in carnivore scavenging suggests that one of the last portions of the body to become separated is the thoracic vertebrae; therefore, it has been suggested that the location of articulated thoracic vertebrae may indicate the site of original body deposition. Likewise, Haglund also studied patterns of rodent scavenging on human remains in forensic contexts. Both rodent and carnivore scavenging can occur in urban as well as rural environments, indoors and outdoors.

Stages of Decomposition

Early stage postmortem changes are often described as being early (<2 h) or late (>2 h). A number of past studies have attempted to extend and refine postmortem stages to include the more advanced decomposition and skeletonization. Using a retrospective case study of human corpses, in 2005, Megyesi et al. introduced total body score (TBS), a standardized system for scoring decomposition in a human corpse. The system assigns a score to each of the three body areas (head and neck, trunk, and limbs), the score relating to observable changes on an advancing scale from fresh to skeletonized. The sum of the three scores is the TBS. This has become the chosen method of assessing decompositional stages by forensic anthropologists, and together with earlier work conducted by Vass et al. introducing the concept of accumulated degree days (ADD), has enabled more accurate estimation of PMI in cases of advanced decomposition.

Time Since Death Estimation

One of the fundamental questions arising in any forensic case is how long the remains have been where they are found and how long the individual has been dead. Similar to the most aspects of forensic anthropology, estimating the PMI is not an exact science, but in recent years (owing to the incorporation of two key concepts: ADD and TBS), the assessment of time since death has become, at least theoretically, more straightforward.

ADD was introduced into the anthropological literature in 1992 by Vass et al., although the concept of accumulated degree hours had been part of the entomological literature for some time. Vass et al.'s paper presented an experimental study based on volatile fatty acids in the soil under human cadavers. The critical concept of ADD as a measure of the variables of time and temperature combined allowed the calculation of PMI based on ADD and body mass. The concept operates on the same principle that water will boil at 100 °C no matter if you boil it on high heat for a short period of time or low heat for a longer period of time. Whenever the water accumulates enough temperature (100 °C), it will always boil. With ADD, the concept is that every corpse should display the same characteristics ("boil") once it has accumulated the same temperature. No matter where geographically or in what environment, once a corpse has accumulated a certain temperature (1285 ADD according to Vass et al.) the corpse will be skeletalized. Vass et al.'s data came from examining the volatile fatty acids leaching from the corpse into the soil and the time of skeletalization was when these were no longer detectable; this of course does not equate to the appearance of a dry skeleton, rather that the corpse is no longer undergoing active (wet) decomposition. Thus, above the developmental threshold for most insects (given as 5 °C), a corpse can reach 100 ADD in a myriad of different ways, for example, 5 days at 20 °C, 4 days at 25 °C, 10 days at 10 °C, and so on. All human remains will have a similar appearance at a particular ADD no matter how many days it has taken to accumulate that temperature.

The benefit of using ADD is that it allows researchers across a variety of geographic regions and environments (e.g., with differences in temperature) to compare the rate of decomposition data. When, in the past, researchers reported that it took X many days for a corpse to decompose (or to reach a particular stage), the results were rarely analogous to the same number of days elsewhere. It is unfortunate indeed that the Vass et al. article was largely ignored by taphonomists for over 12 years, quite likely because the article was published under the pathology biology section of the *Journal of Forensic Sciences* and contained complex equations and chemical analyses. It was never cited in either the 1997 or the 2002 volume of Haglund and Sorg at all. Only in 2005, when Megyesi et al. published a paper introducing the concept of TBS did the utility of ADD resurface for assessing PMI and come to the attention of researchers.

The use of TBS was based on Galloway's stages of decomposition published in 1997, but Megyesi et al. refined the descriptions associated with these stages and assigned numerical values to them, much as age-related changes in the pubic symphysis or sternal rib ends were assigned to successive phases. The underlying assumption to all of these methodologies is that one must pass through each successive stage to arrive at a subsequent one. Although mummification and adipocere may occur during decomposition, these are not ubiquitous features of the progression and thus may confound one's assessment of time since death. Megyesi conducted a retrospective study of cases where the dates of disappearance (death) and recovery were known; weather station data were used to calculate average daily temperatures and determine the ADD for the interval the person had been missing. She then examined the autopsy photographs and descriptions and scored the body's state of decomposition and assigned a TBS. A regression formula was calculated so that when TBS was known, the formula would predict the ADD. From the ADD, weather station data could be examined to subtract each average daily temperature backward from the date the corpse was found until the minimum and maximum dates for disappearance were computed.

As Vass et al. noted in 1992, body mass also affects the rate of decomposition and weight correction factors were provided for assessing ADD to skeletalization. Smaller corpses decompose at faster rates than larger ones, primarily due to the amount of tissue present for insects to consume. Additional studies indicated that the original categories provided (in increments of 50 lbs or 22.7 kg) were not accurate for predicting ADD from TBS, and further research is needed to refine this relationship. While Megyesi et al. indicated that they could find no difference between indoor and outdoor rates of decomposition in their study, the sample size of indoor bodies was quite small. Later research by Simmons et al. in 2010 indicted that there is a statistically significant difference between insect-mediated decomposition and decomposition when insects are excluded. There is no difference, however, in the rate of decomposition with regard to the environment in which the insects are excluded from the process; whether deposited in water, a burial, or indoors, a corpse will decompose at the same, slower rate. Furthermore, the rate of decomposition in carcasses where insects are excluded remains the same regardless of body size. A formula for predicting ADD for decomposed human bodies in the UK waterways was provided by Heaton et al. in 2010.

Trends in Current Research

The past 5–10 years have seen a great expansion in taphonomic research, although sadly, much of the research being conducted has still been poorly designed, for example, with sample sizes of only two to three individuals per "experiment," absence of controls and lack of standardized variable measurement (e.g., the continued use of "days" rather than ADD) and hence have produced little usable data. As in reports of case studies, these remain largely anecdotal in nature and thus would be inadmissible as the basis for evidence in a court of law. There is a great need for both the accumulation of more (standardized) data at the existing decomposition facilities and for the continued testing of a variety of variables that may affect the decomposition process, whether in rate or in pattern, but these must be conducted as replicable scientific experiments with sufficient numbers of experimental and control subjects, standardized variables, measureable data, and robust statistics.

There is a continuing debate concerning the value of animal-based research and whether it is applicable to human decomposition. There are certainly pros and cons to both animal- and human-based decomposition research. Decomposition research on human cadavers benefits from direct comparisons and applicability to forensic casework. However, it is limited by the availability of donated cadavers and refrigerated storage capacity that might facilitate conducting controlled experiments. Unfortunately, none of the human decomposition facilities has actually conducted and/or published any experiments involving sufficient numbers of experimental and control individuals, and in truth, very little published hard (more than purely descriptive) data have been forthcoming from these facilities. Although data for forensic casework should ideally be based on human analogs, what has been published on human decomposition cannot, thus far, provide a statistical basis for deriving a probability of occurrence, and hence, would not be acceptable in court given the new rules of evidence and expert testimony.

Decomposition research using animal models (namely, *Sus scrofa*, the domestic pig) obviously suffers from using subjects that are not directly analogous to human forensic cases and, though skin, an omnivorous diet and gut construction are

indeed similar to those of humans, the limb proportions, bone lengths, head shape, and so on, are not, thus making it hard to draw relevant conclusions with direct correspondence to the human form. On the other hand, animal models allow for the employment of a far greater sample size incorporating sufficient controls and experimental subjects from which to reach statistically sound conclusions. Using animals allows for the repetition, replication, and validation of results. One can also conduct studies on the animal subjects, which one might not receive permission to conduct on donated human cadavers (e.g., inflict and study a variety of traumatic insults—gunshots, burning, etc.—upon them). Both types of research are subject to similar, stringent ethical review, and in the case of animals, one must be compliant with the guiding principles of reduction, refinement, and replacement.

Trends in future research need to take taphonomic studies beyond observations and descriptions and the subjective. Taphonomic researchers should fully explore the decomposition "myths" regarding what does or does not influence decomposition rate and pattern, and researchers must do so using both standardized methods of scoring decomposition and ADD to allow the comparison of results over disparate chronology, geography, and environment. Further systematic experimental research regarding weathering and bone diagenesis is also warranted to extend and refine PMI estimates beyond decomposition and into taphonomic intervals where skeletal elements alone persist. Equipment such as weather stations, thermocouples and data loggers (internal), thermal imaging cameras, time-lapse photography, endoscopes to visualize decomposition internally, and so on, should also aid in elevating taphonomic research from the merely descriptive to higher scientific standard, reliability, and admissibility in court.

See also: **Anthropology/Odontology:** Animal Effects on Bones; Archeology; Biomechanics of Bone Trauma; Bone Trauma; Postmortem Interval; **Forensic Medicine/Pathology:** Early and Late Postmortem Changes; Estimation of the Time Since Death.

Further Reading

Adams, B.J., Byrd, J.E., 2008. Recovery, Analysis and Identification of Commingled Human Remains. Humana Press, Totowa, NJ.

Behrensmeyer, A.K., 1978. Taphonomic and ecologic information from bone weathering. Paleobiology 4, 150–162.

Boddington, A., Garland, A.N., Janaway's, R.C., 1987. Death, Decay and Reconstruction: Approaches to Archaeology and Forensic Science. Manchester University, Manchester.

Cross, P., Simmons, T., Cunliffe, R., Chatfield, L., 2009. Establishing a taphonomic research facility in the UK. Forensic Science Policy & Management: An International Journal 1 (4), 187–191.

Frund, H.C., Schoenen, D., 2009. Quantification of adipocere degradation with and without access to oxygen and to the living soil. Forensic Science International 188, 18–22.

Heaton, V., Lagden, A., Moffatt, C., Simmons, T., 2010. Predicting the post-mortem submersion interval for human remains recovered from UK waterways. Journal of Forensic Sciences 55 (2), 302–307.

Lyman, R.L., 1994. Vertebrate Taphonomy. Cambridge University Press, Cambridge.

Mann, R., Bass, W., Meadows, L., 1990. Time since death and decomposition on the human body: variables and observations in case and field studies. Journal of Forensic Science 35 (1), 103–111.

Megyesi, M.S., Nawrocki, S.P., Haskell, N.H., 2005. Using accumulated degree-days to estimate the post-mortem interval from decomposed human remains. Journal of Forensic Science 50 (3), 1–9.

Rodriguez, W.C., Bass, W.M., 1985. Decomposition of buried bodies and methods that may aid in their location. Journal of Forensic Science 30, 836–852.

Shipman, P., 1981. Life History of a Fossil: An Introduction to Taphonomy and Paleoecology. Harvard University Press, Cambridge, MA.

Simmons, T., Cunliffe, R., Moffatt, C., 2010. Debugging decomposition data – Comparative taphonomic studies and the influence of insects and carcass size on decomposition rate. Journal of Forensic Sciences 55 (1), 8–13.

Tibbett, M., Carter, D.O., 2008. Soil Analysis in Forensic Taphonomy: Chemical and Biological Effects of Buried Human Remains. CRC Press, Boca Raton.

Vass, A.A., Bass, W.M., Wolt, J.D., Foss, J.E., Ammons, J.T., 1992. Time since death determinations of human cadavers using soil solution. Journal of Forensic Science 37 (5), 1236–1253.

Weigelt, J., 1989. Vertebrate Carcasses and Their Paleobiological Implications. University of Chicago Press, Chicago.

Postmortem Interval

DH Ubelaker, Smithsonian Institution, NMNH, Washington, DC, USA

Glossary

Arthropods Invertebrate organisms of the phylum Arthropoda (includes insects, crustaceans, arachnids, and myriapods).
Barnacle Marine crustaceans.

Entomology The scientific study of insects.
Sphagnum A type of moss.

Estimation of the postmortem interval of relatively recently deceased individuals in early stages of postmortem change generally falls within the discipline of forensic pathology. Such estimations depend on observations of the condition of the soft tissues of the cadaver but often are supplemented with information from the context of the recovery site, as well as what is known regarding the deceased individual's activities during life. Accuracy is strongly correlated with time since death. As the postmortem period increases, the time range and difficulty of estimation increase as well.

In the immediate postmortem period, body temperature (algor mortis), the extent of body muscular relaxation, body stiffening (rigor mortis), skin discoloration (livor mortis), and the stages of decomposition all provide valuable clues. The early stages of decomposition include both autolysis (break down of tissues by digestive enzymes) and putrefaction (impact of bacterial activity). However, research and casework experience have revealed that many factors can influence these processes and complicate interpretation. Such factors include climatic conditions, clothing, body temperature at time of death, postmortem environmental context, and antemortem conditions of the individual (body size, muscular development, pathological conditions, and age at death).

With advanced decomposition and/or alteration of human remains by thermal events or fragmentation, the need for anthropological perspective becomes enhanced. This perspective relies extensively on observations of the conditions of both soft and hard tissues but is supplemented by expertise in entomology, botany, and other fields.

Entomology

Forensic entomology plays an especially important role in assessing the early stages of decomposition. Although this represents a field distinct from forensic anthropology, anthropologists frequently are involved in the recovery of entomological evidence and/or recognize the need for evaluation by entomologists. Although many different kinds of arthropods can be involved in human decomposition, the two most important groups are flies (Diptera) and beetles (Coleoptera). The flies are attracted to moist tissue and thus are early arrivals to remains. The fly larvae are responsible for considerable reduction of soft tissue. In the chain of arthropod succession, beetles generally arrive later, being attracted by more desiccated tissue. Other arthropods may also arrive to consume feeding insects. A forensic entomologist may collect adults, eggs, and larvae; identify the type of arthropod present; and use that information to assess time since death.

Blow flies (a large family of flies including the secondary screwworm fly (*Cochliomyia macellaria*), the Arctic blow fly (*Protophormia terraenovae*), green bottle fly (*Lucilia* sp.), blue bottle fly (*Calliphora vomitoria*), and bronze bottle fly (*Lucilia cuprina*)) are of particular entomological interest. Adult flies deposit large numbers of eggs that rapidly hatch. The larvae (maggots) molt into multiple instars before the formation of the puparia and the emergence of the adult. The timing of each of these growth stages has been researched enabling this information to be used to estimate time since death. Interpretation also considers temperature and other relative information.

Botany

A variety of botanical evidence also can provide useful information if properly recovered and documented. Roots from plants growing nearby can penetrate human remains and their immediate surroundings. If properly sampled, identified, and assessed, roots can reveal a minimum time since death. In such studies, the association with the remains must be clearly established. Leaves, branches, and a variety of other plant materials also can prove useful depending upon the circumstances of the case.

Other Animal and Cultural Indicators

Anthropological assessment of postmortem interval can also be aided through many other biological materials that might be associated with human remains. Examples can include barnacle formation in marine environments and the presence of the nests of flying insects. Evaluation by the appropriate specialist may reveal the minimum time required for the evidence to have been associated with the remains.

Observations of cultural practices also may provide vital clues. Patterns of dental alteration, skull deformation, or even trephination (surgical-type alterations in crania) may suggest an ancient origin of human remains. Extreme dental wear (attrition) suggesting a very rapid rate of wear was common in ancient times but rare among modern populations. Certain types of surgical practices and orthopedic devices also can be dated linking remains to particular periods of the past.

Tissue Morphology

Traditionally, forensic anthropologists have evaluated time since death utilizing observations on the extent of preservation of soft and hard tissues. However, casework and experimental research have revealed the complex taphonomic factors that affect soft-tissue decomposition and hard-tissue alteration complicating this assessment. Primary influencing factors include temperature, environmental pH, amount of moisture, and oxygen availability. Other related factors include age and constitution of the individual, body treatment after death, extent and type of injury to the individual, extent of exposure to scavenging animals, protection by clothing or other materials, climate, seasonality, burial type, burial depth, and local vegetation patterns.

The timing and pattern of postmortem change demonstrate regional variation and even differences in microenvironments within regions. Dry environments can induce rapid bloating followed by extensive mummification. In contrast, a body exposed above ground in a tropical environment can be reduced to a skeleton within 2 weeks. The decomposition process can be influenced by mechanical injury as well as extensive freezing and thawing.

Although the exceptions are impressive and extensively influenced by the factors discussed above, a general sequence of postmortem alteration has been noted in temperate climates. This sequence begins with fresh remains with no discoloration and then proceeds through early decomposition and advanced decomposition and culminates in skeletonization. In their

research, Megyesi et al. noted that the manifestation of these stages varies in different areas of the body. Their research indicates that, for the head and neck, early decomposition begins with a pink-white appearance with some skin slippage and hair loss. The process then proceeds to include gray to green discoloration with some retained fresh-appearing flesh. This is followed by desiccation of the nose, ears, and lips with brownish discoloration at the margins. Later, fluid is purged from the eyes, ears, nose, and mouth with some bloating of the neck and face. This stage culminates in brown to black flesh discoloration.

Advanced decomposition in the head and neck begins with a caving in of the tissues of the eyes and throat. This stage is followed by some moisture retention but less than 50% bone exposure. The remaining soft tissue then becomes desiccated.

The skeletonized stage begins with bone exposure progressing to more than 50% of the area with the presence of greasy material and some decomposing tissue. Desiccated tissue is then recognized followed by dryness of the bones themselves but with some grease retention. The final stage is represented by dry bones.

For the trunk, Megyesi et al. recognize a slightly different sequence. The early decomposition process begins with a pink-white appearance with some marbling and skin slippage. This proceeds to a gray/green discoloration with some retained fresh-appearing flesh. Bloating then occurs with green discoloration and fluid loss. A postbloating phase then involves gas release and black discoloration.

Advanced decomposition of the trunk begins with caving in of the abdominal cavity and general sagging of flesh areas followed by moist-tissue retention but less than 50% bone exposure. The remaining tissue then becomes desiccated.

The final skeletonization stage of the trunk is marked by retention of some body fluids and grease. Retained desiccated tissue then covers less than 50% of the area. This is followed by largely dry bones but with some grease retention. The final stage is dry bones.

For the limbs, Megyesi et al. note that early decomposition begins with a pink-white appearance with some skin slippage of the hands and/or feet. A gray/green discoloration then occurs with some marbling and fresh flesh retention. Desiccation of the fingers, toes, and other areas is then noted with some brown discoloration. The skin then takes on a leathery appearance with brown/black discoloration.

Advanced decomposition in the limbs begins with the presence of some moist tissue and less than 50% bone exposure. The tissue then becomes desiccated.

The skeletonization phase begins with more than 50% bone exposure with retention of some body fluids. The bones then become largely dry but with some grease retention. The final stage is dry bone.

Megyesi et al. produced not only the above detailed description of the general sequence of skeletonization of human remains, but also a method to estimate the postmortem interval. Their approach considers not only the stage of decomposition/skeletonization of the remains but also a calculation of degree days in recognition of the key role of temperature in the rate of decomposition.

In 2011, Vass proposed a more complex approach to estimate the postmortem interval. Based largely on research conducted at the University of Tennessee, Vass differentiates processes involved in remains recovered from surface context versus those from the subsurface. The Vass approach also considers temperature, but in addition, moisture and oxygen partial pressure.

Mummification

Mummification represents a variant of the postmortem process usually involving extreme desiccation. Although mummification can occur within dry microenvironments in most locations, it is most commonly associated with arid regions of the world. Since mummified/desiccated tissue is extremely resistant to further alteration as long as low humidity is maintained, its presence can complicate estimates of postmortem interval. In dry regions of the world, naturally mummified remains have been dated to hundreds of years ago. Mummification can also result from thermal factors, chemical factors, anaerobiasis (anaerobic conditions), excarnation (defleshing), and other conditions.

Preservation by cooling represents the primary thermal factor resulting in mummification. While cool temperatures can slow the decomposition process, freezing of course prolongs preservation as long as low temperatures are maintained. Maintenance of low temperature, either accidentally, naturally, or purposefully, can complicate interpretations of postmortem interval. High temperatures also can promote rapid desiccation and mummification.

Chemical factors can include the presence of heavy metals and chelation. Mercury, copper, and arsenic have all been implicated in unusual soft-tissue preservation. Prolonged soft-tissue preservation in the vicinity of copper artifacts represents a well-known phenomenon in remains from both archeological and forensic contexts. Arsenic also represents a well-known preservative of soft tissue and historically has been used by embalmers. Chelation refers to chemical agents that combine with other materials reducing their availability to the bacteria of decomposition. Peat bogs are well-known sources of chelating agents that facilitate long-term preservation of soft tissues. The sphagnum in peat bogs also can generate a tanning process.

Other factors that can contribute to the mummification process and long-term preservation include certain resins and spice, lime, lye, salt, and even bat guano. In ancient times, encasement of remains in plasterlike material succeeded in producing long-term preservation of soft tissue.

Adipocere

Adipocere represents a special form of mummification variously referred to as corpse wax or grave wax. Although definitions vary considerably, most recognize its tenacious nature that it can present a waxy, greasy, or crumbly appearance and can vary in consistency from soft to hard and in coloration from gray to white. It represents a form of arrested decomposition of soft tissue involving saponification of fat/adipose tissue that can preserve aspects of original morphology. The term is derived from the Latin words "adeps" (fat) and "cere" (wax), and its use can be traced back to as early as 1789 in France. Chemical analysis has detected the saturated fatty acids of palmitic, myristic, stearic, and 10-hydroxy stearic acid. Unsaturated fatty acids present include oleic, palmitoleic, and linoleic.

Although formation is usually associated with prolonged exposure of human remains to damp environments, adipocere can form in dry environments, water submersion, and cold sea water. Although adipocere most commonly forms in individuals with high body fat and in body areas with an elevated fat component, formation can occur in individuals of all ages, both sexes, and in both embalmed and unembalmed remains. Moisture presence is an important factor, but it can originate from the environment of the remains or from the body itself. Burial in soils that retain moisture can promote adipocere formation but a variety of soils may be involved. The presence of clothing that can retain moisture favors formation. Adipocere formation can be slowed or prevented if the body is protected by plastic. Although climatic conditions of the general environment are important, factors in the microenvironment of the remains are most critical. Factors favorable to adipocere formation include mildly alkaline pH, warm temperature, anaerobic conditions, and moisture. Cold temperature, lime, and aerobic conditions are limiting factors. Clearly, many factors other than postmortem interval are involved in adipocere formation.

Although early indications of adipocere formation have been detected only a few hours after death, clearly visible expressions usually require weeks. Formation of morphologically apparent adipocere has been reported between 5 weeks and 3 months.

Once formed, adipocere can remain extremely resistant to alteration as long as appropriate environmental conditions are maintained. Adipocere can be retained in remains dating back hundreds of years. However, if environmental conditions are altered, adipocere may degrade. Conditions favorable to the degradation of formed adipocere include air exposure, increased environmental moisture, fungal growth, and the presence of Gram-positive bacteria. Clearly, adipocere formation complicates estimation of the postmortem interval.

Chemical Approaches

A variety of chemical approaches have been attempted to estimate the postmortem interval. Those involving analysis of bone include carbonate analysis, fluorescence, specific gravity, superconductivity, nitrogen content, quantification of amino acids, analysis of neurotransmitters, decomposition of by-products, benzidine testing of bone surfaces, luminal testing, odor analysis, and X-ray diffraction studies of bone crystalline structure. Although these approaches have shown some promise, lack of definition of influencing taphonomic factors has limited their application.

In 1992, Vass et al. reported research on volatile fatty acids resulting from soft-tissue decomposition that could be detected from soil associated with human remains. Experimental research revealed that patterns of volatile fatty acids could be detected in associated soils during soft-tissue decomposition and of specific anions and cations in the skeletal phase. In consideration of degree days, this information offered useful perspective on time since death.

Some research attention also has focused on immunological approaches to evaluating time since death, the fat content of bone, and histological techniques. Immunological approaches document the effect of time since death on properties of bone protein but existing approaches are limited by soil contamination and other factors. Research has documented the decrease in bone fat content over time, especially within histological structures, but measures lack the precision necessary to reliably determine postmortem interval.

Radiocarbon Analysis

In the traditional application, radiocarbon dating provides a widely used approach to estimating the antiquity of relatively ancient remains. Used primarily for remains found in archeological contexts, radiocarbon analysis can provide absolute dating for remains likely of considerable antiquity. This approach recognizes that the isotope carbon-14 is mildly radioactive and decays at a predictable rate. The half-life of carbon-14 is about 5730 years. The extent of degradation is measured from the standard present in 1950. After about 50 000–60 000 years, most decay has taken place and the amount of carbon-14 is too small to accurately measure. Thus, while radiocarbon dating (using isotopic degradation) has proven useful for analysis of relatively ancient remains, it generally is not applicable to modern forensic cases, other than to document when cases thought perhaps to be of modern origin are actually of great antiquity.

In recent years, radiocarbon isotope analysis (distinct from radiocarbon dating as described above) has emerged as a very useful approach to evaluating the postmortem interval in modern remains. Atmospheric testing of thermonuclear devices during the 1950s and early 1960s unleashed large amounts of radiocarbon (carbon-14) into the atmosphere. The quantity increased sharply until 1963, when, following cessation of testing, atmospheric levels began a gradual descent.

However, in 2011, the atmospheric levels remain above those documented prior to the bomb-pulse period. Through the food chain, these modern elevated levels of radiocarbon have been incorporated into the tissues of all living organisms, including humans. For this reason, elevated levels of radiocarbon represent an isotopic marker of the modern period and can distinguish tissues formed during this period from those that formed earlier. Using this knowledge in regard to recovered human remains, samples can be collected and analyzed for radiocarbon content. If elevated levels are detected, the analysis clearly indicates that the individual was alive during the bomb-curve period. Since the bomb-curve period corresponds generally to the period of forensic interest in human remains, the technique has emerged as a key contributor to postmortem interval evaluation.

Analysis basically reveals average values within the samples submitted and must consider the nature of the tissue analyzed. Dental enamel forms during the preadult years and does not remodel. Thus, even in mature adults, the radiocarbon content of dental enamel reflects dietary radiocarbon levels at the age when the dental crown formed. Bone does remodel but at different rates depending on the type of bone tissue. Cancellous bone, especially that associated with blood-forming tissue (e.g., bodies of vertebrae), remodels more rapidly than compact bone (such as that found in the outer layer of long bone diaphyses). Most soft tissues of the body, especially internal organs, remodel at much faster rates. Thus, analysis of the different tissues presents varying radiocarbon values that document different life stages of an individual. Interpretation of these values with recognition of their formation times allows proper placement on the bomb curve (older ascending portion, apex, or more recent descending portion). This information, considered with the estimated age at death of the individual, may reveal important aspects of the postmortem interval, the approximate date of death, and even the approximate birth date.

See also: **Anthropology/Odontology:** Animal Effects on Bones; Forensic Taphonomy; **Forensic Medicine/Pathology:** Early and Late Postmortem Changes; Estimation of the Time Since Death.

Further Reading

Aufderheide, A.C., 2003. The Scientific Study of Mummies. Cambridge University Press, Cambridge, UK.

Coyle, H.M. (Ed.), 2005. Forensic Botany: Principles and Applications to Criminal Casework. CRC Press, Boca Raton, FL.

Forbes, S., Nugent, K., 2009. Dating of anthropological skeletal remains of forensic interest. In: Blau, S., Ubelaker, D.H. (Eds.), Handbook of Forensic Anthropology and Archaeology. Left Coast Press, Walnut Creek, CA, pp. 164–173.

Haglund, W.D., Sorg, M.H. (Eds.), 2006. Forensic Taphonomy: The Postmortem Fate of Human Remains. CRC Press, Boca Raton, FL.

Haskell, N.H., Williams, R.E. (Eds.), 2008. Entomology and Death: A Procedural Guide, second ed. Forensic Entomology Partners, Clemson, SC.

Megyesi, M.S., Nawrocki, S.P., Haskell, N.H., 2005. Using accumulated degree-days to estimate the postmortem interval from decomposed human remains. Journal of Forensic Sciences 50, 618–626.

Ubelaker, D.H., 2001. Artificial radiocarbon as an indicator of recent origin of organic remains in forensic cases. Journal of Forensic Sciences 46, 1285–1287.

Ubelaker, D.H., Buchholz, B.A., 2006. Complexities in the use of the bomb-curve radiocarbon to determine time since death of human skeletal remains. Forensic Science Communications 8 (2), 1–9.

Ubelaker, D.H., Buchholz, B.A., Stewart, J.E.B., 2006. Analysis of artificial radiocarbon in different skeletal and dental tissue types to evaluate date of death. Journal of Forensic Sciences 51, 484–488.

Ubelaker, D.H., Zarenko, K., 2011. Adipocere: what is known after over two centuries of research. Forensic Science International 208 (1–3), 167–172.

Vass, A.A., 2011. The elusive universal post-mortem interval formula. Forensic Science International 204, 34–40.

Vass, A.A., Barshick, S., Sega, G., et al., 2002. Decomposition chemistry of human remains: a new methodology for determining the postmortem interval. Journal of Forensic Sciences 47, 542–553.

Vass, A.A., Bass, W.W., Wolt, J.D., Foss, J.E., Ammons, J.T., 1992. Time since death determinations of human cadavers using soil solution. Journal of Forensic Sciences 37, 1236–1253.

Vass, A.A., Smith, R.R., Thompson, C.V., Burnett, M.N., Dulgerian, N., Eckenrode, B.A., 2008. Odor analysis of decomposing buried human remains. Journal of Forensic Sciences 53, 384–391.

Early and Late Postmortem Changes

B Madea and G Kernbach-Wighton, University of Bonn, Bonn, Germany

Introduction

Dying and death are continuous final biological processes that have been undefined for a long time. In his work on contemporary Roman law, the well-respected nineteenth-century jurist Friedrich Carl von Savigny wrote that death represents such an elementary and natural event that has no need for closer definitions of its elements. It was not until the introduction of machines to take over circulatory or respiratory functions that the need for a legal definition of death arose, such as would protect a physician from judicial prosecution (e.g., turning off of life-support systems). Today, the accepted criteria for death are irreversible cessation of respiratory or circulatory functions, or determination of brain death following serious primary or secondary brain damage, where, in the case of brain death, functioning of the cerebrum, cerebellum, and medulla oblongata has ceased.

Supravitality

Irreversible circulatory or respiratory arrest is the main criterion for death, followed by early postmortem changes, lividity, and rigor mortis. However, metabolism of tissues does not cease immediately after death but continues for some hours. Supravitality is the survival of tissues under global ischemia. Supravital reactions are reactions of tissue on excitation which are much like those during life. The supravital period is specific for each tissue, depending on specific metabolisms (enzymes, substrates) and local temperature. The main energy-producing metabolic processes in the early postmortem period are the creatine kinase reaction and anaerobic glycolysis. Studies on global ischemia in various organs focus mainly on organ preservation and organ transplantation. The latency period is defined as an undisturbed time interval characterized by continuing aerobic energy production. The survival period is the interval to the point following which every aspect of life ceases. During the survival period, there may be spontaneous activity of organs (e.g., instantaneous but decreasing myocardial contractility), and also reagibility (e.g., response of muscles to stimulation). The resuscitation period is defined as the duration of global ischemia after which the ability to recover expires. The resuscitation period mainly comprises the interval when complete recovery of morphological, functional, and biochemical parameters in the postischemic period is still possible. Some supravital reactions are of great practical importance in forensic medicine as they can easily be examined at the scene of crime and provide immediate results on the time elapsed since death: these are mechanical and electrical excitability of skeletal muscles and the pharmacological excitability of the iris.

Mechanical Excitability of the Muscle

The mechanical excitability of skeletal muscle is examined by rigorously hitting a muscle with the back of a knife or a chisel, for example, the biceps brachii muscle, in a perpendicular direction; other muscles can be examined as well but reference figures for estimating the time since death are available for the biceps brachii muscle only.

Electrical Excitability of the Skeletal Muscle

In the early postmortem interval, excitation causes strong contraction of muscles including those distant from the electrodes, while with increasing postmortem interval, contraction will become weaker and muscular response will be confined to the excitation location, a reaction pattern intensely involving more or less all muscles. Finally, only fascicular twitching or movement of the electrodes will be visible. The most extensive investigations have been carried out on orbicularis oculi muscles as its movements are easy to identify. For the orbicularis oculi muscle, needle electrodes are inserted in 15–20 mm distance into the nasal part of the upper eyelid at 5–7 mm depth. The muscular response is graded into six stages (**Figure 1**). In the very early postmortem stage (degree VI), the whole ipsilateral muscle will contract, whereas in degree V, only the upper and lower eyelid and forehead will respond. With increasing postmortem interval, reactions will be confined to the excitation location.

For stimulation, a small square wave generator producing constant current rectangular impulses of 300 mA at 10 ms duration is used at a repetition rate of 50 ms (producer and supplier: Peschke J, http://home.t-online.de/home/j-peschke/rztg1.htm).

Pharmacological Excitability of the Iris

Compared to skeletal muscles, the smooth iris muscle is irritable by electrical and pharmacological stimulation for a much longer period of time. In some cases, excitability by

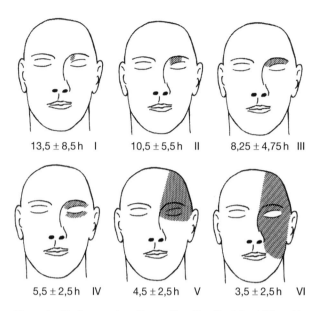

13,5 ± 8,5 h   I   10,5 ± 5,5 h   II   8,25 ± 4,75 h   III

5,5 ± 2,5 h   IV   4,5 ± 2,5 h   V   3,5 ± 2,5 h   VI

Figure 1   Six degrees of positive reaction after stimulation of the orbicularis oculi muscle (see also **Table 1**).

subconjunctival injection of noradrenaline or acetylcholine may persist up to 46 hpm.

Postmortem Lividity

After irreversible circulatory arrest, postmortem lividity develops as the earliest postmortem change. Following circulatory arrest, hydrostatic pressure becomes the leading force within the parallelogram of forces comprising blood pressure, structural barriers, tissue turgor, and pressure from underlying surfaces. Hypostasis means the movement of body fluids according to gravity. All compartments are involved in hypostasis, not only intravascular but transcellular fluids as well. Influenced by gravity, blood moves to the lowest parts within the vascular system; in a supine position, it flows to the back, buttocks, thighs, calves, and back of the neck. Irregular facial pink patches, especially over the cheeks in the agonal period, are caused by local stasis. Postmortem cutaneous lividity is a consequence of movement of blood into capillaries of the corium. It may appear 20–30 min postmortem, still as pink patches in the early stages becoming gradually confluent with increasing postmortem time. Due to consumption of oxygen, the color changes from pink to dark pink or bluish.

In areas of intense hypostasis, cutaneous petechial hemorrhages due to capillary ruptures, called vibices, may develop. It is not only the development of lividity or of color that is of diagnostic and criminalistic relevance, but also its distribution, as well as the phenomena of fixation (disappearance after turning the body) and disappearance (blanching) on blunt/thumb pressure.

In case of carbon monoxide poisoning and cyanide toxicity, the color of hypostasis is typically cherry pinkish, while methemoglobin intoxication is brownish. Due to lack of dissociation of oxygen from hemoglobin, a bright pink color may be seen in hypothermia as well. In a body transferred from a cold environment into normal room temperature, typical zonal segmentation of hypostasis may be seen with a dark bluish color in the rewarmed areas.

Of predominant criminalistic significance are the phenomena of disappearance on pressure and disappearance of lividity after turning the body. In the early stages, lividity will completely disappear on soft thumb pressure, but with ongoing postmortem interval, the pressure also has to increase. Later, lividity will disappear only incompletely on pressure and finally it will not disappear at all.

If the body is turned in the early postmortem interval, some or all of the hypostasis may move to different areas. In a comparatively later postmortem interval, only some of the hypostasis will migrate down to new areas and only slight blanching will be noted in the original region.

With increasing postmortem time, disappearance of lividity on thumb pressure and relocation after shifting decreases, and then ceases completely.

The best statistical data available for the different criteria of lividity were summarized by Mallach, who calculated mean values, standard deviations, and 95% limits of confidence based on textbook reports (**Table 1**). As better data are still missing, these data are still undisputed. However, it should be kept in mind that these data do not represent absolute thresholds. Investigations based on quantitative measurements of livor mortis have not yet gained practical importance.

Rigor Mortis

The second postmortem change and sign of death, developing in normal ambient temperature about 3–4 h postmortem after primary flaccidity, is rigor mortis, which was misinterpreted as the sign of death until the nineteenth century although Shakespeare (Romeo and Juliet, Act. IV, Scene 1) described all elements of rigor mortis very well:

> Each part, deprived of supple government, shall, stiff and stark and cold, appear like death.

With irreversible circulatory arrest, all muscles will become completely flaccid due to loss of tone. In the early postmortem interval, adenosine triphosphate (ATP), the biochemical source of energy, can be resynthesized via the creatin kinase reaction and anaerobic glycolysis. Once the ATP level has fallen below 85% of the initial value, actin and myosin filaments form a complex which is not split so that the muscle remains inextensible. Development and state of rigor mortis are proven subjectively by bending a joint: either the muscles are flaccid or

Table 1 Time course of different criteria of lividity

	$\overline{X}$	s	2s Lower limit	2s Upper limit	Range of scatter Lower limit	Range of scatter Upper limit	Number of quotations
Development	¾	1/2	–	2	1/4	3	17
Confluence	2(1/2)	1	3/4	4(1/4)	1	4	5
Greatest distension and intensity	9(1/2)	4(1/2)	1/2	18(1/4)	3	16	7
Displacement							
1. Complete on thumb pressure	5(1/2)	6	–	17(1/2)	1	20	5
2. Incomplete on sharp pressure (forceps)	17	10(1/2)	–	37(1/2)	10	36	4
Displacement after turning the body							
1. Complete	3(3/4)	1	2	5(1/2)	2	6	11
2. Incomplete	11	4(1/2)	2(1/4)	20	4	24	11
3. Only little pallor	18(1/2)	8	2(1/2)	34(1/2)	10	30	7

Statistical calculations by Mallach based on textbook reports. The statistical calculations are not based on cross-sectional or longitudinal studies but on empiric knowledge quoted in textbooks. $\overline{X}$ = mean value; s = standard deviation.

during development of rigor mortis some resistance may be noted. If rigor is fully developed, even a strong examiner cannot flex or stretch a joint.

Rigor must not be mixed up with cold stiffening. When rigor is present, hypostasis must be present as well, whereas in cases of cold stiffening (body core temperature 30–33 °C), hypostasis is absent.

The development and state of rigor should be examined in several joints (mandibular joint, finger, knee, elbow) to assess whether it is still in progress or has already reached its maximum.

Rigor mortis does not commence in all muscles simultaneously. Nysten's rule (1881) that rigor starts in the mandibular joint, muscles of the trunk, then in the lower, and lastly in the upper extremities applies to most cases with dying in a supine position. However, in cases with glycogen depletion during agony in the lower extremities, rigor will commence there.

Dissolution of rigor mortis is due to protein degradation (increase of ammonia, NH_3).

As in different fibers of a muscle, rigor does not start simultaneously but successively; this phenomenon can be used for a rough estimation of the time since death as well. If some of the fibers have already become stiff, this stiffness can be broken by bending a joint; rigor may now develop in other, not yet stiffened fibers. Depending on the time when stiffness has been broken, rigor may develop again on a higher or lower level unless it was already fully developed (**Figure 2**). This phenomenon of reestablishment of rigor mortis may be seen up to 6–8 h postmortem and in very low ambient temperatures up to 12 h postmortem.

Secondary flaccidity of muscles may become apparent in normal ambient temperature after 2 days. In low ambient temperatures, fully developed rigor mortis may linger for 2 weeks and longer.

Cadaveric rigidity, cataleptic spasm, or instantaneous rigor are names for a phenomenon that is always mentioned in textbooks but nonexistent in practice. Not a single case reported in the literature withstands criticism.

Rigor mortis can be found not only in skeletal muscles but also in smooth muscles, for example, the skin. Rigidity of the smooth musculi arrectores pilorum can be seen as goose pimples (cutis anserina).

Development, duration, and dissolution of rigor mortis depend on the amount of glycogen in the muscle at the moment of death, ambient temperature, and other factors.

Therefore, rigor may develop very fast in persons who die close to exhaustion due to physical exertion or from electrocution. All of the criteria of rigor mortis mentioned earlier (e.g., development, reestablishment, full development, duration, resolution) are time dependent. This was already evident from one of the rare studies from the nineteenth century on rigor mortis. Niderkorn, who determined the time necessary for the completion of rigor mortis in 113 bodies, found it fully established after 4–7 h in 76 corpses (67%). In two cases, rigidity was complete within 2 h postmortem, and in two others, within 13 h postmortem.

However, interindividual variability from endogenous and exogenous factors covers a wide range. Longitudinal studies on large random samples are missing; however, a number of animal experiments taking into account various factors influencing the time course of rigor mortis have been published. Devices for objective measurement of rigor mortis have been developed but have not yet gained practical importance.

The best available data despite all justifiable criticism originate again from Mallach, based on the compilation of literature (1811–1969) with statistical analyses (**Table 2**). These figures again cannot claim to be absolute limit values. Like lividity, rigor mortis can give only a rough estimate and no high accuracy can be expected. It never should be examined isolated.

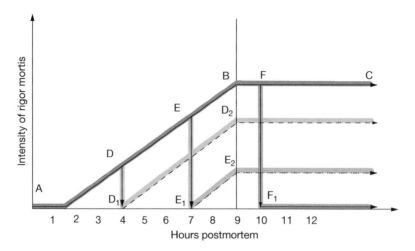

Figure 2   Reestablishment of rigor mortis after breaking. The later rigor during development of rigor mortis is broken, the lower will be the level after reestablishment. If rigor is broken after it has already been fully developed (F), it will not be reestablished at all.

Table 2   Time course of different criteria of rigor mortis according to the calculations by Mallach based on textbook reports

| Rigor state | Average hours postmortem and standard deviation | Range of scatter in hours (2s) | | |
		Lower limit	Upper limit	Number of quotations
Beginning	3 ± 2	–	7	26
Maximum	8 ± 1	6	10	28
Duration	57 ± 14	29	85	27
Complete resolution	76 ± 32	12	140	27

Algor Mortis, Postmortem Body Cooling

If the ambient temperature is lower than the body core temperature (normally 37.2 °C), the body temperature will decrease postmortem. The postmortem drop of the body temperature results from four factors: convection, conduction, radiation, and evaporation, the first two being the leading causes.

Postmortem heat production is low as anaerobic glycolysis ceases within a few hours postmortem. Convective heat transport within the body stops with circulatory arrest. Heat exchange is then mainly based on conduction. The conductive heat transport within the body is mainly due to temperature differences of neighboring tissue layers. As the heat conductivity of body tissues is rather low, conductive heat transport within the body proceeds slowly.

The rate of cooling depends on various conditions and varies with several factors:

- ambient conditions (temperature, wind, rain, humidity)
- weight of the body, mass/surface area ratio
- posture of the body (extended or thighs flexed on the abdomen)
- clothing/covering

In case of temperature differences between body center and surface or body surface and surrounding temperature, heat transport basically takes place radially, from the axial center of the body to the surroundings. Postmortem cooling of core temperatures (e.g., rectal temperature) is best represented by a sigmoid curve comprising the following three phases (**Figure 3**):

- initial phase, the so-called temperature plateau or lag period during which the body temperature remains relatively constant
- intermediate phase, with a rapid drop of the body temperature
- terminal phase, in which the drop slows down continuously as the core temperature approaches that of the environment

The postmortem temperature plateau is mainly determined by physical preconditions as it is due to the fact that central axial temperatures cannot begin to decrease until a heat gradient is set up between the core of the body and its surface. This delay is variable and may last for some hours.

Its duration depends on the same influencing factors as the exponential cooling curve following the plateau (radius, radial position of measuring site, cooling conditions). The shorter the temperature plateau, the steeper the curve drops away.

The postmortem temperature plateau causes a sigmoid shape of the cooling curves at any site of measurement far from the surface. It is a combined effect of the postmortem

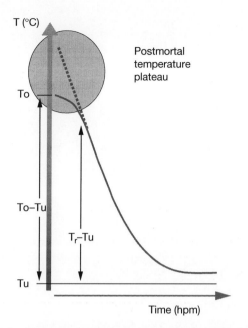

T (°C)

Postmortal
temperature
plateau

T_o

T_o-T_u

T_r-T_u

T_u

Time (hpm)

Figure 3 Sigmoid shape of the cooling curve, which is best described by Marshall and Hoare's two-exponential term. The quotient (T_r-T_a/ T_o-T_a) is a good measure of the progress of cooling. If this quotient Q is <0.3, only a minimum interval of the time since death should be given. T_o, rectal temperature at death ($T=0$); T_r, rectal temperature at any time, and T_a, ambient temperature.

temperature plateau followed by single exponential cooling according to Newton's law.

Different temperature probe sites were used (surface skin temperature, axilla, liver, rectum, brain temperatures); for practical purposes, only central core temperature. Authors in the nineteenth century, using rectal temperatures, described a lag time, the postmortem temperature plateau, before exponential body cooling according to Newton's law commences (**Figure 3**).

A mathematical expression of rectal cooling after death was published by Marshall and Hoare, taking into account the sigmoid shape of the cooling curve. They performed experiments under "standard conditions of cooling" which were defined as "naked body with dry surfaces, lying extended on a thermally indifferent base, in still air." Their mathematical model was expressed in a two-exponential term:

$$Q = \frac{T_r - T_a}{T_o - T_a}$$

$$A \exp(Bt) + (1 - A) \exp\frac{(AB)}{A-1} t$$

where Q = standardized temperature; T_r = rectal temperature at any time t; T_o = rectal temperature at death ($t = 0$); T_a = ambient temperature; A = constant; B = constant; t = time of death.

The second exponential term is subtracted from Newton's exponential term taking into account that temperature plateau is from zero, increasing temperature decrease.

This mathematical expression is valid for all central axial temperatures and represents the ultimate success in modeling body cooling for the purposes of estimating the time since death.

The exponential form with the constant B expresses the exponential drop of temperature following the plateau according to Newton's law of cooling; the term with the constant A as part of the exponent describes the postmortem temperature plateau.

The experimental work which led to an identification of these constants is outlined in several original papers and two monographs, which are referred to here.

With this empirical solution of Marshall and Hoare's formula, the time since death can be computed either according to

$$Q = \frac{T_r - T_a}{37.2 - T_a} = 1.25 \exp(Bt) - 0.25 \exp(5Bt)$$

(for ambient temperatures up to 23 °C) or

$$Q = \frac{T_r - T_a}{37.2 - T_a} = 1.11 \exp(Bt) - 0.11 \exp(10Bt)$$

(for ambient temperatures over 23 °C)

Using computer programs developed by Henssge or using a nomogram (**Figure 4**).

The nomogram is valid for the chosen standard conditions of cooling (naked body with dry surfaces, lying extended on a thermally indifferent base, in still air). Conditions which accelerate or delay body cooling compared to standard conditions (e.g., deposition in water, wind on the one hand, clothing, covering on the other) theoretically reduce or increase the real body weight. Extensive cooling experiments under varying cooling conditions led to empiric corrective factors for the body weight (**Table 3**). With these the nomogram can also be used for nonstandard cases. The corrective factors themselves depend on the body weight in case of low and/or high body weights under higher thermic insulation conditions. Higher body weights need lower factors and, vice versa, lower weights require higher factors. The nomogram can also be used in cases of sudden changes of ambient temperatures.

From all methods developed to estimate the time since death, the nomogram method based on the double exponential term by Marshall and Hoare is by far the most successful and reliable one because:

● Actual cooling conditions can be taken into consideration quantitatively.
● Data on the precision of the method are available.
● Field studies have confirmed the accuracy and reliability of the method.

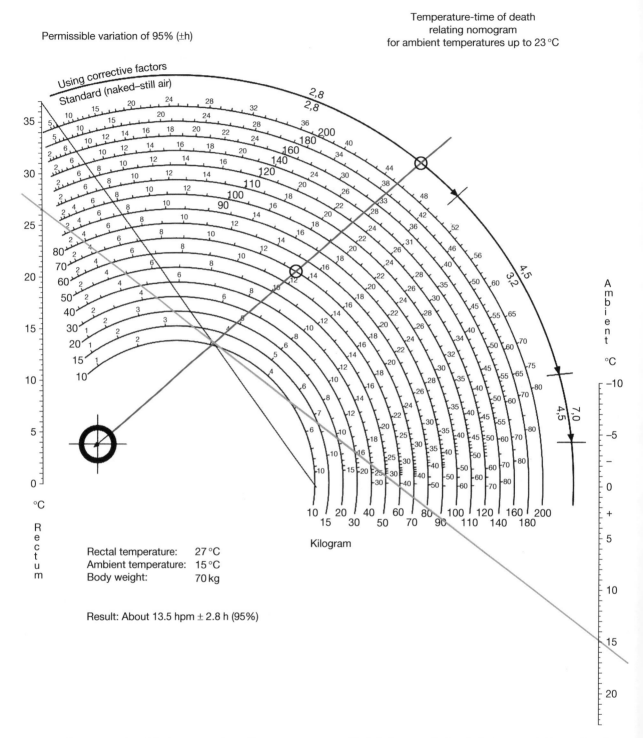

Permissible variation of 95% (±h)

Temperature-time of death
relating nomogram
for ambient temperatures up to 23 °C

Using corrective factors
Standard (naked–still air)

Rectal temperature: 27 °C
Ambient temperature: 15 °C
Body weight: 70 kg

Result: About 13.5 hpm ± 2.8 h (95%)

Kilogram

Figure 4 Temperature–time of death nomogram for ambient temperatures up to 23 °C. At the scene of crime, for instance, a rectal temperature of 27 °C at an ambient temperature of 15 °C were measured. At first, the point of the scale of the measured rectal temperature and ambient temperature have to be joined by a straight line [yellow (light gray in print versions)] which crosses the diagonal of the nomogram at a specific point. For the second

Table 3 Empiric corrective factors (c.f.) for body weights. The listed values of c.f. apply to bodies of average weight (reference: 70 kg, see Table 10) in an extended position on a thermally indifferent supporting base

Dry clothing/covering	Air	Corrective factor	Wet through clothing/covering wet body surface	In air	In water
		0.35	Naked		Flowing
		0.5	Naked		Still
		0.7	Naked	Moving	
		0.7	1–2 thin layers	Moving	
Naked	Moving	0.75			
1–2 thin layers	Moving	0.9	Two or more thicker layers	Moving	
Naked	Still	1.0			
1–2 thin layers	Still	1.1	Two thicker layers	Still	
2–3 thin layers		1.2	More than two thicker layers	Still	
1–2 thicker layers	Moving or still	1.2			
3–4 thin layers		1.3			
More thin/thicker layers	Without influence	1.4			
		–			
Thick blanket		1.8			
		–			
+		2.4			
		–			
Clothing combined		2.8			

"Thermally indifferent" supporting bases are, for example, usual floors of rooms, dry soil, lawn, asphalt. In comparison, bases which appear more thermally insulating heat than conducting should additionally be taken into account. (a) Excessively thick upholstered bases require c.f. of 1.3 for naked bodies. In cases of clothed bodies, c.f. should be increased by 0.1 units (thickly clothed) to 0.3 units (very thickly clothed). (b) Insulating but not excessively thick upholstered bases such as a mattress (bed) or thick carpet require c.f. of 1.1–1.2 for naked bodies. (c) Bases that accelerate cooling, for example, concrete, stony, or tiled bases on ground, require c.f. up to 0.75 for naked bodies. (d) In cases of clothed bodies lying on bases, c.f. should be reduced by 0.1 units (thicker clothes) or by 0.2 units (very thin clothes).

Postmortem Changes

Due to their time sequence, the early signs of death in a cadaver (rigor mortis and livor mortis), along with the supravital reactions, are today instrumental in accurately determining the postmortem interval (i.e., the time elapsed since onset of death). Immediately following the early signs of decay, the later stages begin. These cannot be separated strictly chronologically. They lead not only to decomposition of the cadaver, but in some cases also to its preservation. Different exogenous and endogenous factors contribute to destruction and decomposition of a corpse. Among endogenous factors are autolysis, putrefaction, and decay, while exogenous factors include animal predation, exposure to the elements, and mechanical injury.

Onset and extent of postmortem changes are influenced by many extrinsic and intrinsic factors (**Table 4**).

Various dissimilar signs of advanced decay may appear simultaneously in a cadaver resulting from changes to the surrounding conditions. If a corpse is exposed due to its

Table 4 Intrinsic and extrinsic factors influencing onset and extent of postmortem changes

Acceleration of onset and extent of postmortem changes
Death occurring in a hot, moist environment/under high ambient temperatures
Body surface insulation by warm clothing or other covering
Considerable time interval elapsed after death until artifactual cooling of the body was started
Subject was overweight/had a high fat content
Subject suffered/died from underlying infection or sepsis
Subject was intoxicated (e.g., with illicit drugs such as heroin)
Subject suffered/died from open wounds (perforating/penetrating traumatic injuries such as stab wounds, gunshot wounds, impalement injuries) or during surgical procedures
Deceleration of onset and extent of postmortem changes[a]
Death occurred in a cold, dry environment/under low ambient temperatures
Subject was scantily dressed/naked/undressed shortly after death
Subject was stored in a cooling device shortly after death

[a]These factors decelerate the rate of postmortem changes but do not in general alter the underlying postmortem biological processes.
According to Tsokos (2005).

step, a second straight line has to be drawn passing through the center of the circle (lower left of the nomogram) and the intersection of the first line and the diagonal [red line (dark gray in print versions)]. The second line crosses the semicircles for different body weights. The time since death (in this case, for 70 kg body weight) can be read off at the intersection of the semicircle of the given body weight. The intersection gives the mean time since death, and the intersection with the outer circle, the 95% limits of confidence, which may be higher if corrective factors have to be used.

Figure 5 Venous marbling over an arm.

Table 5 Morphological changes in the putrefaction phase. Aboveground exposure at 20–24 °C (68–75 °F) without insect infestation

Indication	Interval after death
Initial greenish discoloration of the abdominal skin	1–2 days
Cutaneous venous marbling	2–4 days
Beginning of filmlike slippage of the epidermis	5–6 days
Loss of pigmentation in the *stratum germinativum*	6–8 days
Putrefactive blisters and putrefactive transudates in the body cavities	8–14 days
Putrefactive emphysema in the *subcutis*	8–14 days
Bloating of abdominal cavities	8–14 days
Diffusion of all fluids, collapse of organs	Usually not until months later
Beginning of mummifying	Usually not until months later
Dehydration of soft tissues	

Please note that this table gives only rough indications for the sequence of putrefaction in cadavers exposed aboveground at a relatively narrow range of temperature. Numerous deviations are possible, depending on the body's built, the underlying surface, coverings, and terminal illness.
According to Berg.

position to different environmental conditions (such as lying in a roadside ditch, half-submerged in water, half-exposed to air), varying processes of decay may occur simultaneously.

Autolysis (Self-Digestion)

Autolysis is defined as the destruction of an organ's structures by its own enzymes. Organs, such as the pancreas, which are already rich in enzymes in life, are thus subject to very quick self-digestion after death. Under convenient circumstances, for example, when a cadaver is stored at high temperatures, only a few hours are required to render a histological diagnosis of the organ itself impossible. Due to the effects of gastric acid, autolysis of the stomach lining occurs relatively quickly, possibly leading to complete softening. The adrenal medulla is also destroyed quite rapidly.

Putrefaction

Contrary to autolysis, putrefaction described as a "heterolytic" alkaline colliquative process on a reductive basis caused by bacteria, displays typical characteristics while progressing, both visual (bloating) and olfactory (foul ammoniacal odors), due to the production of gases (hydrogen sulfide, hydrocarbons) and the release of ammonia. Body parts particularly affected by bloating from gas accumulation are all tissues with a low turgor ("liquid" pressure from within), such as eyelids, mouth, and tongue, which may become monstrously swollen. The abdomen may also become extremely swollen due to gas accumulation. Gas production is the main reason for drowned bodies soon floating at the water surface. The abdominal wall shows a greenish discoloration, resulting from production of sulfhemoglobin as oxygen is used up by intestinal bacteria. As this process requires oxygen, the green discoloration caused by sulfhemoglobin accumulation first appears over those parts of the body where the intestines lie closest to the abdominal wall, such as the lower right abdomen. Discoloration may then, however, gradually extend to the entire body surface. The spread of bacteria within the veins in subcutaneous fatty tissue and hemolysis of red blood cells causes the venous "marbling" of the skin (**Figure 5**). A further feature of putrefaction is the formation of putrefaction transudates (accumulations of putrefied fluids) leaking out of the dermis and causing the

epidermis to detach from the dermis. Such putrefactive blisters may grow to large sizes, finally even tearing apart the epidermis, causing it to come off in shreds and exposing the dermis, which can very quickly dry out and change to brown. In addition, during putrefaction, hair and nails loosen and can then easily be pulled out. This looseness of finger and toenails and hair found in drowned bodies is an important criterion for determining the length of time of their deposition in water. In the course of putrefaction, there is finally liquefaction of fatty tissues. Liquid fat may then leak out of the body like butter or margarine when there are skin defects, and there might be decomposition of the body's proteins (proteolysis), during which there is accumulation of biogenic amines (putrescine, cadaverine, histamine, choline, etc.) as well as cadaveric alkaloids, referred to as ptomaines (cadaveric poisoning). Even though these ptomaines have shown muscarinic atropine-like effects in tests on animals, we cannot use the term ptomaine/cadaveric poisoning to indicate that it makes the area around a putrescent corpse "toxic." Health risks from corpses, similar to those from living people, originate from infectious pathogens (tuberculosis, hepatitis, human immunodeficiency virus), as these pathogens are able to survive the death of their host (the deceased person) (**Table 5**).

During bacterial proteolysis, certain amino acids such as delta-aminovaleric acid or gamma-aminobutyric acid can be found in brain and liver, which can be used to make a rough estimate of the time elapsed since death. Further symptoms arising from gas accumulation and gas bloating are the

Table 6   Criteria used in estimating the age of inhumed bones, average indications for neutral to alkaline, calcareous soil subject to weather conditions

| | *Interval in years* | | | | | | |
Indication	0–5	5–10	10–20	30–50	50–100	100–1000	>1000
Odor activity	+	–	–	–	–	–	–
Impregnation of fat at the epiphyses	+	+	–	–	–	–	–
Remnants of soft tissue	+	+	(+)	–	–	–	–
Adipocere efflorescence on the surface	+	+	+	–	–	–	–
Filling of the medullary cavity	+	+	+	(+)	–	–	–
Presence of adipocere, histological	+	+	+	+	(+)		–
Presence of collagen, histological	+	+	+	+	+	+	(+)
UV fluorescence	+	+	+	+	+	+	(+)
Hardness, heaviness	+	+	+	+	+	+	(+)

Reproduced from Berg, S., 2004. Todeszeitbestimmung in der spätpostmortalen Phase. In: Brinkmann, B., Madea, B. (Eds.), Handbuch Gerichtliche Medizin Band 1. Springer, Berlin, Heidelberg, New York, pp. 191–204.

formation of so-called foam organs—organs permeated with gas and macroscopically detectable cavities—as well as the leaking of putrefactive fluids from mouth, nose, anus, and genitalia. In pregnant women, the pressure arising from putrefactive gas may cause the fetus to be expelled through the genitalia, a phenomenon described by the macabre term "coffin birth." While early signs of decomposition can be used for a rough estimate of the time of death, the sequence of symptoms of decay depending on previous organ disease, duration of agony, environmental conditions, especially the ambient temperature, bacterial infestation, and other factors are so variable that one cannot draw conclusions regarding the time of death (**Table 6**), but make very gross estimates only. A rule of thumb going back to the Berlin forensic physician Johann Ludwig Casper (1796–1864), named Casper's Law, after him, says that 1 week in air equals 2 weeks in water equals 8 weeks buried in the ground. Casper's Law thus highlights the decomposition process under different environmental conditions (air, water, earth) but does not allow precise determination of time of death.

Preservation of Decomposing Bodies

Regarding the skin, the essential signs of putrefaction are hemolysis, transudation, and accumulation of gas. It is possible to prevent signs of putrefaction for a longer period of time by special storage conditions, for which it is of utmost importance that packaging of the body or body parts is extremely airtight.

Experimental investigation of the influence of vinyl materials on postmortem alterations in rabbit and mice cadavers kept in plastic bags of different air volumes (3 l/five pints, 1 l/13/4 pints, no air) at room temperature revealed a clearly delayed decomposition by storage in plastic materials. The volume of air in the bag is obviously of great

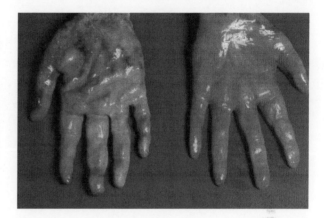

Figure 6   Body parts found in garbage bags.

importance for the progression of decay. In one particular case of a body which had been dismembered to hide evidence with the parts wrapped in plastic bags, an extremely good state of preservation after a period of 2 years allowed even positive dactyloscopic identification, despite epidermolysis (**Figure 6**). Along with the inhumation of the body parts in winter time, one factor for preservation in this case was considered to be the very airtight packing into plastic bags, together with physical covering clearly contributing to delayed decomposition processes.

Destruction of Corpses by Maggots

Maggots may contribute significantly to the destruction of a corpse (**Figure 7**). Flies may begin to lay eggs on a body even in the period preceding death. Depending on the ambient conditions, egg deposits can often be seen in the nostrils and in the

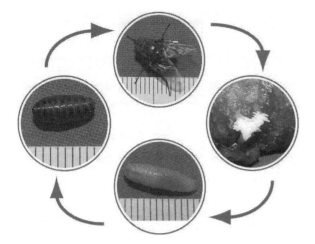

Figure 7 Development cycle of the fly: egg mass, maggots, pupae, and adult flies. Original Dr. Marco Strehler, Institute of Forensic Medicine, University of Bonn.

angles of mouth and eyes. Egg deposits develop into maggots, then pupae, followed by empty pupal shells and adult flies. The development cycle lasts between 3 and 5 weeks, depending on species and temperatures. Maggots produce enzymes which can break down proteins and feed on disintegrated soft tissues. In summer, it is possible for maggots to reduce an aboveground cadaver nearly completely to a skeleton within a few weeks time. For the coroner, an additional problem is that eggs are frequently deposited in wounds to the skin while the subject is still alive, resulting in extensive destruction to the wounds with loss of evidence regarding the cause of death.

Decomposition

Decomposition, as distinct from putrefaction, is a dry, acidic process on an oxidative basis, leading to the splitting off of acids (H_2CO_3, H_3PO_4, and H_2SO_4). Decomposition is accompanied by a rancid odor described as a musty or rotting smell. Very often colonies of mold can be found (**Figure 8**).

The Chemistry of Decomposition

While putrefaction is mainly an anaerobic bacterial reduction process, decomposition is dominated by aerobic microbiological processes, which may create pungent, rotten odors originating from the metabolic products of oxidation.

Period up to Skeletonization

The period up to skeletonization varies widely, depending on the storage conditions of the body; this has already been expressed by Casper's Law, saying that a corpse on the ground decomposes more quickly than one in water or underground, although the ratios Casper has defined are certainly also subject to numerous variations. Bodies lying on the surface of the ground are as a rule skeletonized within 1 year, and after 2 years the bones are almost completely free from soft tissues. Considerable proportions of soft part reduction during summer result from maggot infestation and animal predation.

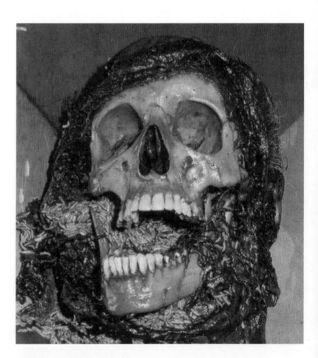

Figure 9 A cadaver partially skeletonized by maggot infestation. Postmortem interval of about 2 weeks in an apartment in summer.

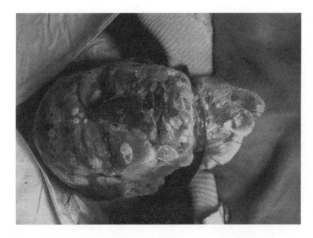

Figure 8 Mold colonizing over a cadaver.

Such conditions may make a body completely skeletonized within a few weeks (**Figure 9**). If a body is stored underground, the time required for skeletonization depends essentially on the composition of the surrounding soil. Under normal conditions, with usually water-permeable, aerated soil at a depth between 1 and 2 m (3 ft 3 in. to 6 ft 6 in.), about 5–7 years are needed for complete skeletonization, although considerably longer periods have been recorded. In warmer climate, skeletonization normally happens in clearly shorter periods. Results of exhumations indicate, however, that even after burial times of 5–7 years, some bodies plus clothing were often found well preserved. In some cases, even the inner organs with the gastrointestinal tract were still intact. This is of particular importance as, among other issues, toxic substances and their routes of ingestion have to be determined. Bodies

interred in crypts or sarcophagi may undergo mummification (see later). A form of interment particularly in warmer countries is the mausoleum, usually a marble-clad building with up to five aboveground rows of sealed cells. Depending on ventilation and time of interment (summer or winter), mummification or putrefaction, larval infestation, and gangrenous decay occur. The rate of decomposition is considered between that of aboveground exposure and burial in soil. Finally, special conditions apply to burials in mass graves. Even if bodies are buried together simultaneously, they may display quite different degrees of decomposition. Bodies lying at the periphery are usually extensively decomposed, while bodies at the center may still have good preservation of soft tissues (see later) with pronounced grave wax formation (see later). The bones of bodies lying aboveground are, as a rule, completely skeletonized after 1–2 years, showing no remnants of soft tissues, and no traces of cartilage or tendons. In inhumed bodies, remnants of soft tissues may still be found up to the second decade after burial, but more rarely after the third or fourth decade. Remains of clothing can be preserved for longer. With ongoing time, the originally smooth surfaces of buried bones show signs of wear. Deterioration of the bone surfaces strongly depends on the composition of the surrounding soil (**Figure 10(a)**). Bones may lie intact in graves and crypts for centuries, and several criteria allow for rough estimates of their ages (**Table 6**). Therefore, the medullary cavities of relatively recently living bones still show adipocere, whereas centuries-old bones are free of adipocere (**Figure 10(b)**). Even after soft tissues, particularly muscles and inner organs, have largely been consumed during the advanced stages of putrefaction and decomposition, there are often portions of more decay-resistant skin still present covering the bones.

(a)

(b)

Figure 10 (a) A several-hundred-year-old bone with deterioration of the bone surface. (b) Left: Centuries-old bone (cross section) with empty medullary cavity. Right: The medullary cavity of a bone from a recently living individual, filled with adipocere.

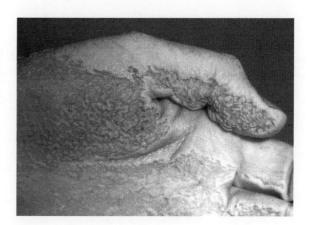

Figure 11 Characteristic mice gnaw markings on the epidermis of the left hand.

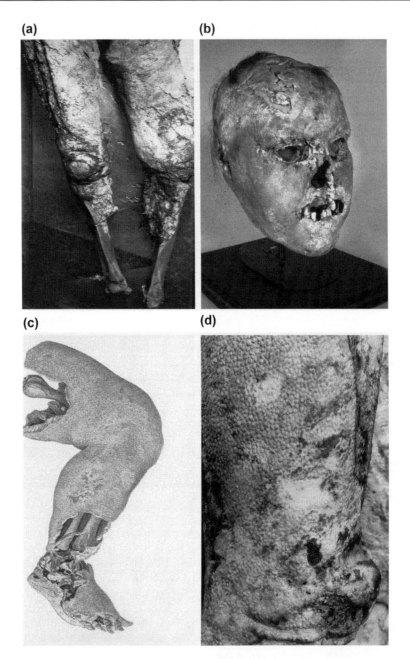

Figure 12   (a) Soft tissues of the thighs were converted into hard shells of adipocere, with the long bones hanging loosely. (b) Saponification of the head. (c) The leg of a newborn child, with saponification, after lying in flowing water for several months. The outer shape of the leg was preserved; the chalk-like brittle mass, which looks like a stiff tube, contains loose bones. The muscles are missing. (d) The texture of the fat nodules in the subcutaneous fatty tissue was fixed by adipocere formation (*état mammelloné*).

Animal Predation

Even in the early postmortem interval, there may already be traces of animal predation, not only from rats or mice, or—in water—crabs and fish, but also from pets (dogs and cats). Mice

will typically gnaw away the epidermis, leaving characteristic gnaw marks (**Figure 11**).

Extensive damage by a dog to soft tissues immediately after death can be explained by the dog's wish to obtain a reaction from its lifeless owner, first licking the face, and then, without result, behaving instinctively, biting, and mutilating.

Preservation Processes in Cadavers

While natural processes described so far (autolysis, putrefaction, and decomposition) cause dissolution and disintegration of the cadaver down to bones and tendons, special environmental conditions may preserve the body. Preservation processes include mummification and adipocere formation, which are also found in bog and permafrost corpses.

Mummification

Mummification usually takes place when the water in the body's tissues evaporates due to dryness and good ventilation. Mummification from natural processes may occur in bodies buried in churches or crypts (e.g., the lead cellar of Bremen cathedral), but it can also be seen in bodies lain at home or indoors for some time. Mummification dries the skin into a hard leathery state, dehydration sometimes causing the body to be fixed in the position it had assumed at the time of death. Furthermore, there is substantial weight loss, due to desiccation and shrinking of tissues. Rapid loss of water contributes to mummification, caused by storage in dry drafty air on a warm and dry ground. Mummification leading to leathery, hard stiffening of the skin may, under appropriate environmental conditions, begin relatively quickly (already after 2–3 days), starting at the limbs (fingers, toes, tips of the nose and chin, ears, skin over the cheekbones). Pronounced mummification, however, as a rule, is not detectable until after several weeks.

Decomposition of the Body in the Grave—Saponification

A body buried in soil should be reduced to a skeleton after 15–20 years, at the most. It is well recognized that skeletons may remain preserved much longer (e.g., several centuries). Whether a corpse largely decomposes within this period, however, also depends mainly on properties of the soil—mineral composition and aeration—and on groundwater conditions.

Grounds where the coffins actually lie in groundwater are unsuitable for burials, or where the area of decay constantly or temporarily contains groundwater, or even areas subject to flooding used for the production of water for public use. Nevertheless, under such conditions, preservation processes such as saponification—formation of adipocere or grave wax—may occur. Saponification can be observed in bodies having lain in a completely or partially hermetic damp environment (e.g., water corpses and damp graves). During formation of adipocere, unsaturated fats (oleic acids) are converted into saturated fats (palmitic and stearic acids).

Saponification begins in the skin after about 6 weeks and in muscles after 3–4 months. Entire extremities may be converted into adipocere, although this requires several months to years (**Figure 12(a)–(d)**). The term adipocere (adeps = fat, cera = wax) goes back to Fourcroy (1789) and Thouret (1792) who, during the closure of a cemetery in Paris, noticed that the bodies buried there, some in groups, had not "wasted away," but had been preserved in the same characteristic way.

Permafrost Bodies

Extensive body preservation may also occur in permanently frozen ground. Permafrost bodies were found in northern Canada, for example, in the early 1980s. The bodies were of members of the Franklin expedition in the 1840s. The cadaver found in the Hauslabjoch area of the Italian Alps ("Ötzi") is a famous frozen body from central Europe.

Bog Bodies

In bog bodies, the effects of humic acid include bone demineralization, tanning of soft tissues, and typical reddening of the hair. Due to preservation of the body surfaces, it is possible to collect significant evidence on circumstances and cause of death. Along with the presence of tannin and humic acid, a third factor is the oxygen-poor peaty soil suppressing putrefaction processes, which thus contributes to good preservation. Along with tanning of skin and hair, some of the internal organs remain preserved, but muscle and fatty tissue usually disintegrate. The high acid content of the soil softens bones. Bog bodies are of special value, not only archeologically, but also forensically, as evidence of injury relating to the cause of death has been saved by preservation of the body.

Livor mortis, rigor mortis, algor mortis, other factors.

See also: **Forensic Medicine/Pathology:** Autopsy; Estimation of the Time Since Death; External Postmortem Examination.

Further Reading

Aufderheide, A.C., 2003. The Scientific Study of Mummies. Cambridge University Press, Cambridge.

Beattie, O., Geiger, J., 1992. Der eisige Schlaf. Das Schicksal der Franklin-Expedition. München Zürich: Piper (Originally Published 1987 as: Frozen in Time: The fate of the Franklin Expedition by Bloomsburry Publishing Ltd., London).

Berg, S., 2004. Todeszeitbestimmung in der spätpostmortalen Phase. In: Brinkmann, B., Madea, B. (Eds.), Handbuch Gerichtliche Medizin Band 1. Springer, Berlin, Heidelberg, New York, pp. 191–204.

Doberentz, E., Madea, B., 2010. Estimating the time of immersion of bodies found in water – an evaluation of a common method to estimate the minimum time interval of immersion. Revista Española de Medicina Legal 36 (2), 40–50.

Dotzauer, G., 1958. Idiomuskulärer Wulst und postmortale Blutung. Dtsch Z Gesamte Gerichtl Medical Journal 46, 761–771.

Haglund, W.D., Sorg, M.H., 1997. Forensic Taphonomy. CRC Press, Boca Raton.

Henssge, C., 1988. Death time estimation in case work I. The rectal temperature time of death nomogram. Forensic Science International 38, 209–236.

Henssge, C., 1992. Rectal temperature time of death nomogram: dependence of corrective factors on the body weight under stronger thermic insulation conditions. Forensic Science International 54, 51–56.

Henssge, C., 2002. Temperature based methods II. In: Henssge, C., Knight, B., Krompecher, T., Madea, B., Nokes, L. (Eds.), The Estimation of the Time Since Death in the Early Postmortem Period, second ed. Edward Arnold, London.

Henssge, C., Knight, B., Krompecher, T., Madea, B., Nokes, L., 2002. The Estimation of the Time Since Death in the Early Postmortem Period, second ed. Edward Arnold, London.

Henssge, C., Madea, B., 1988. Methoden zur Bestimmung der Todeszeit an Leichen. Schmidt-Römhild-Verlag, Lübeck.

Henssge, C., Madea, B., 2004. Estimation of the time since death in the early postmortem period. Forensic Science International 144, 167–175.

Henssge, C., Madea, B., 2004. Leichenerscheinungen und Todeszeitbestimmung. In: Brinkmann, B., Madea, B. (Eds.), Handbuch Gerichtliche Medizin Bd. I. Springer, Berlin, Heidelberg, New York, pp. 79–150.

Henssge, C., Madea, B., 2007. Estimation of time since death. Forensic Science International 165, 182–184.

Klein, A., Klein, S., 1978. Todeszeitbestimmung Am Menschlichen Auge Dresden (MD thesis). Dresden University.

Krause, D., 2004. Späte Leichenveränderungen. In: Brinkmann, B., Madea, B. (Eds.), Handbuch Gerichtliche Medizin Band 1. Springer, Berlin, Heidelberg, New York, pp. 150–170.

Krompecher, T., 2002. Rigor mortis: estimation of the time since death by the evaluation of the cadaveric rigidity. In: Henssge, C., Knight, B., Krompecher, T., Madea, B., Nokes, L. (Eds.), The Estimation of the Time Since Death in the Early Postmortem Period, second ed. Edward Arnold, London, pp. 144–160.

Madea, B., 1994. Importance of supravitality in forensic medicine. Forensic Science International 69, 221–241.

Madea, B., 2002. Muscle and tissue changes after death. In: Henssge, C., Knight, B., Krompecher, T., Madea, B., Nokes, L. (Eds.), The Estimation of the Time Since Death in the Early Postmortem Period. Edward Arnold, London, pp. 134–208.

Madea, B., 2005. Is there recent progress in the estimation of the postmortem interval by means of thanatochemistry? Forensic Science International 151, 139–149.

Madea, B., 2009. Death: time of. In: Jamieson, A., Moenssens, A. (Eds.), Wiley Encyclopaedia of Forensic Sciences, vol. 2. John Wiley and Sons Ltd, Chichester, pp. 697–716.

Madea, B., 2009. Time of death determination. In: Jamieson, A., Moenssens, A. (Eds.), Wiley Encyclopaedia of Forensic Sciences, vol. 5. John Wiley and Sons Ltd., Chichester, pp. 2466–2479.

Madea, B., Henssge, C., 2003. Timing of death. In: Payne-James, J., Busuttil, A., Smock, W. (Eds.), Forensic Medicine: Clinical and Pathological Aspects. Greenwich Medical Media Limited, London, pp. 91–114.

Madea, B., Preuss, J., Musshoff, F., 2010. From flourishing life to dust – the natural cycle of growth and decay. In: Wieczorek, A., Rosendahl, W. (Eds.), Mummies of the World. Prestel, Munich, Berlin, London, New York, pp. 14–29.

Mallach, H.J., 1964. Zur Frage der Todeszeitbestimmung. Berliner Medizin 18, 577–582.

Marshall, T.K., Hoare, F.E., 1962. I Estimating the time of death. The rectal cooling after death and its mathematical expression. II the use of the cooling formula in the study of postmortem body cooling. III the use of the body temperature in estimating the time of death. Journal of Forest Science 7 (56–81), 189–210, 211–221.

Pounder, J., 2000. Postmortem interval. In: Siegel, J.A., Saukko, P.J., Knupfer, G.C. (Eds.), Encyclopaedia of Forensic Sciences, vol. 3. Academic Press, San Diego, pp. 1167–1172.

Spindler, K., Wilfing, H., Rastbichler-Zissernig, E., Zurnedden, D., Nothdurfter, H., 1996. Human Mummies. A Global Survey for the Status and the Techniques of Conservation. Springer, Wien, New York.

Tsokos, M., 2005. Postmortem changes and artefacts occurring during the early postmortem interval. In: Tsokos, M. (Ed.), Forensic Pathology Reviews, vol. 3. Humana Press, Totowa, pp. 183–237.

Wieczorek, A., Rosendahl, W. (Eds.), 2010. Mummies of the World. Prestel, Munich, Berlin, London, New York.

Estimation of the Time Since Death

B Madea, University of Bonn, Bonn, Germany

Introduction

Estimation of the time since death is a practical task in daily forensic casework. The main objective is to give the police a first estimation on the time since death already at the place where the body was found. Methods of estimating the time since death should be of course as precise as possible but even more important is reliability. The main principle of determining the time since death is the calculation of a measurable date along a time-dependent curve back to the start point. Characteristics of the curve (e.g., the slope) and the starting point are influenced by internal and external and antemortem and postmortem conditions. Therefore, the estimation of the time since death will never reveal a time point but an interval.

Methods of estimating the time since death are based on two different approaches:

- Which antemortem changes, either physiological or pathological, can be detected and allow, together with police investigations, a conclusion on the time since death (survival time)?
  Methods such as wound age estimation and gastric emptying when time and volume of the last meal are known follow this approach.
- Which postmortem changes allow a conclusion to be made on the time since death?
  Most methods which are used in practice follow this second approach.

There is a huge literature on methods proposed for estimating the time since death. However, most of them have never gained practical importance.

The methods proposed for estimating the time since death are completely different in nature:

- Predominant physical processes such as body cooling and hypostasis
- Metabolic processes, for example, concentration changes of metabolites, substrates, activity of enzymes
- Autolysis (loss of selective membrane permeability, diffusion according to Fick's law with increase or decrease of analytes in various body fluids, morphological changes)
- Physicochemical processes (supravital reagibility, rigor mortis, immunological reactivity)
- Bacterial processes (putrefaction)

Furthermore, the methods for estimating the time since death are not only different in nature, but have a widely differing scientific value concerning the underlying scientific background, the mode of investigation, and the validation of the method.

The highest scientific value is of course attributed to methods with a quantitative measurement of the postmortem changes, with a mathematical description which takes into account influencing factors quantitatively. Clear data on the precision of the method are available and these data have been proved on independent material and in field studies.

On the other hand, the lowest scientific evidence for death time estimation is acquired by methods that provide just a subjective description of the postmortem change. The progression of postmortem change is entirely dependent on ambient factors. However, these ambient factors cannot be taken into account quantitatively.

For estimating the postmortem interval (PMI) during criminal investigations, different sources are used (Pounder):

1. Evidence on the body of the deceased (postmortem changes)
2. Information from the environment in the vicinity of the body (date of the newspaper, open TV program)
3. Anamnestic factors concerning the deceased's habits (leaving the apartment, arriving at work, day-to-day activity)

For the forensic investigation of the time since death, all sources of information on the time since death should always be used, though the focus of the forensic pathologist is of course the postmortem changes.

Temperature of Corpses

From all methods of death time estimation, postmortem body cooling has been studied most extensively, and some of the investigations that fulfill the criteria for high-quality research are quantitative measurement, mathematical description, taking into account influencing factors quantitatively, declaration of precision, and proof of precision on independent material.

The cooling of bodies is mainly a physical process, and the factors affecting the rate at which a body cools after death were identified long ago.

For estimation of the time since death only central core temperatures such as rectal temperature or brain temperature should be taken, as a surface can cool down already during life (**Figure 11.1**). The Glasgow professor, Henry Rainy, was one of the first to realize that Newton's law of cooling does not describe the decrease of rectal temperature due to the postmortem temperature plateau. Rainy transferred Newton's rule of cooling to the cooling of bodies and, thus, he considered the environmental temperature. By measuring the temperature several times, he could even determine experimentally the individual steepness of temperature decrease. Furthermore, he had already identified the postmortem temperature plateau as the declination of the single-exponential model, and he consequently identified the estimated time since death using Newton's law as minimum time. By multiplication with 1.5, he revealed also a maximum time.

It was not before the two-exponential model of Marshall and Hoare in 1962 that a real breakthrough could be noticed: The exponential term with exponent p stands for the postmortem temperature plateau and that with exponent Z for the Newton-part of cooling after the plateau:

$$\frac{T - T_u}{T_0 - T_u} = e^{-Zt} - e^{-pt} = \frac{P}{p - Z} e^{-Zt} - \frac{Z}{Z - p} e^{-pt}$$

where T is the deep rectal temperature (°C); T_0 is the rectal temperature at death, fixed at 37.2 °C; T_U is the ambient temperature (°C), t is the time of death (h); $Z = 0.059 - 0.00059$ $(0.8 \, AM^{-1})$ with body surface, A, according to DuBois and body weight, M; $P = -0.4$.

In 1974, Brown and Marshall demonstrated that more than two-exponential terms complicated the model without leading to more precise results. With this model, Marshall could individually determine time of death by a single measurement of the rectal temperature considering body proportions and (constant) ambient temperature under standardized conditions of cooling (unclothed, not covered, standing air, stretched supine position). Surprisingly, this breakthrough in death time determination did not meet with great response. The new model was only described in a general application report and included in one textbook.

Rectal Temperature Time of Death Nomogram

A further breakthrough was achieved with the investigations by Henssge who presented a simplified method to determine the Newton cooling coefficient. He determined statistical figures for the deviation between calculated and real death times for cooling under standardized conditions. These data on the precision were at first valid for standard conditions of body cooling, which include the following:

- Naked body with dry surfaces
- Lying extended on the back
- On a thermally indifferent base
- In still air
- In surroundings without any source of strong heat radiation
- In constant ambient temperature

Furthermore, Henssge extended the application spectrum of the double-exponential formula to different cooling conditions by using empirical body weight correction factors and published nomograms for reading the time since death instead of calculating it.

From all methods of estimating the time since death, the nomogram method by Henssge based on body cooling after death is the most intensively investigated, most precise, and reliable procedure. For the application of the nomogram method in casework, the following points have to be taken into consideration:

Inspection of the body posture, clothing, covering, sunshine on the body, windows (closes, opened: when?), radiators, floor (thermally indifferent?) on the scene of crime.

Measurement of ambient temperature (air) close to the body and at the same level (10–20 cm above the base); measurement of the temperature of the underlying surface as well. Have any changes of thermic conditions been made since the body was found?

Single measurement of deep rectal temperature at the scene using an officially calibrated electronic thermometer with probes for measuring air, surface, and rectal temperature.

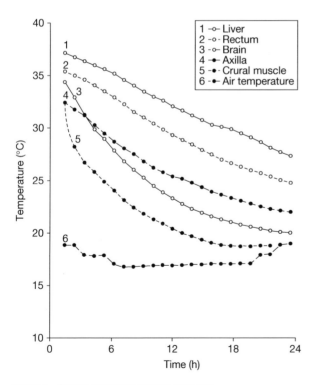

Figure 1   Cooling curve from different body sites.

Table 1   Empiric corrective factors for body weight

Dry clothing/covering	Air	Corrective factor	Wet through clothing/covering wet body surface	In air	In water
		0.35	Naked		Flowing
		0.5	Naked		Still
		0.7	Naked	Moving	
		0.7	1–2 thin layers	Moving	
Naked	Moving	0.75			
1–2 thin layers	Moving	0.9	Two or more thicker layers	Moving	
Naked	Still	1.0			
1–2 thin layers	Still	1.1	Two thicker layers	Still	
2–3 thin layers		1.2	More than two thicker layers	Still	
1–2 thicker layers	Moving	1.2			
3–4 thin layers	or	1.3			
More thin/thicker layers	Still	1.4			
	Without influence	–			
Thick blanket		1.8			
+		–			
Clothing combined		2.4			
		2.8			

The deep rectal temperature must at least be measured 8 cm within the anal sphincter.

Estimation of the body weight. At autopsy control to check whether the estimation was correct.

Evaluation of the corrective factor. Are there any conditions which accelerate or delay cooling compared to standard conditions?

For rectal temperature, the following thermic conditions of the lower trunk only are relevant:

- Clothing/covering
- Resting or moving air
- Kind of supporting base
- In cases of strong insulation conditions and very high or low body weight, the corrective factor must be adapted to the body weight
- Use of the nomogram

Requirements for use include the following:

No strong radiation (e.g., sun, heater, cooling system)
- No strong fever or general hypothermia
- Place of death must be the scene where the body was found
- No uncertain severe changes of the cooling conditions in the period between death and examination
- No high thermal conductivity of the surface beneath the body
- Longer agonal period after fatal injury (time since death may be inconsistent with the time of assault)

Connect the points on the scales for rectal and ambient temperature by a straight line. This line crosses the diagonal at a particular point. Draw a second straight line going through the center of the circle below left of the nomogram and the intersection of the first line and the diagonal. The second line crosses the semicircles which represent the body weight. At the intersection of the semicircle with the body weight, the time of death can be read. The second line touches a segment of the outmost semicircle. Here the permissible variation of 95% can be seen for standard cases or cases using corrective factors.

The nomogram was at first constructed for chosen standard conditions of cooling (naked body with dry surfaces, lying extended on a thermally indifferent base in still air). Conditions with improved or delayed body cooling compared to standard conditions reduce or increase the real body weight. Extensive cooling experiments under varying cooling conditions led to empirically found corrective factors for body weight (**Table 11.1**). With these corrective factors, the nomogram can be used for nonstandard cases as well. Systematic examination revealed that higher correction factors (e.g., for clothes and/or blankets) have to be used for lower body weights. That means that corrective factors themselves are dependent on the body weight. Higher body weights need lower factors and lower weights need higher factors. Furthermore, the nomogram can also be used in cases of sudden change of ambient temperature and in cases with ranges of the ambient temperature and the corrective factor. This nomogram was developed for ambient temperatures below 23 °C. For ambient temperatures above 23 °C, another nomogram was developed based on the published material of De Saram et al.

Table 2   Table for estimation of the time since death based on supravital reactions and postmortem changes

		Time after death (hpm)
Electrical excitability		
Musculus orbicularis oculi	VI upper and lower eyelid + forehead + cheek	1–6
	V upper and lower eyelid + forehead	2–7
	IV upper and lower eyelid	3–8
	III whole upper eyelid	3.5–13
	II 1/3 to 2/3 of the upper eyelid	5–16
	I upper eyelid local around the puncture electrodes	5–22
Musculus orbicularis oris		3–11
Thenar muscle		Up to 12
Hypo thenar muscle		Up to 12
Pharmacological excitability of the iris		
Mydriatica	Noradrenalin/adrenalin	14–46
	Tropicamide	5–30
	Atropine/cyclopent	3–10
Miotica	Acetylcholine	14–46
Drop of body core temperature (rectal temperature)	At first temperature plateau of 2–3 h, thereafter approximately 0.5–1.5 °C h^{-1}, depending on ambient temperature, clothing, covering, body proportions, weather conditions (wind, rain)	
Drying of the cornea (open eyes)	After 45 min	
Drying of the cornea (closed eyes)	After 24 min	
Postmortem lividity		
Beginning	After 15–20 min	
Confluence	~1–2 h	
Maximum	After a few hours (~6–8)	
Complete displacement on thumb pressure	~10 h (10–20 hpm)	
Displacement after turning the body	~10 h	
Rigor mortis (jaw)	After 2–4 h	
Complete rigidity	After 6–8 h	
Beginning of resolution	After 2–3 days depending on the ambient temperature	
Reestablishment possible	Up to 8–12 hpm	
Complete resolution	After 3–4 days, in deep ambient temperatures, rigor mortis may be preserved much longer	

Brain Temperature Time of Death Nomogram

The two-exponential model by Marshall and Hoare was also suitable for the mathematical description of the brain temperature drop curve:

$$\frac{T_{\text{Brain}} - T_{\text{U}}}{37.2 - Y_{\text{U}}} = 1.135e^{-0.127t} - 0.135e^{-1.07t}$$

According to the rectal temperature time of death nomogram, a brain temperature time of death nomogram was constructed. Up to 6.5 h postmortem, the most precise computation of time of death was achieved by the exclusive application of brain temperature, which gave a time of death within ±1.5 h (95% confidence limits). Between 6.5 and 10.5 h postmortem, the brain/rectum-combined computation of time of death balanced in the ratio of 6:4 was the most precise one, at ±2.4 h. Beyond 10.5 h postmortem, the most precise computation of time of death was achieved by exclusive application of rectal temperature, which gave a time of death within ±3.2 h.

Field Studies

Meanwhile, both a single center and a multicenter study on the accuracy of the nomogram method compared to the investigations of the police were carried out. Both studies covered a wide range of ambient temperatures, body weights, and corrective

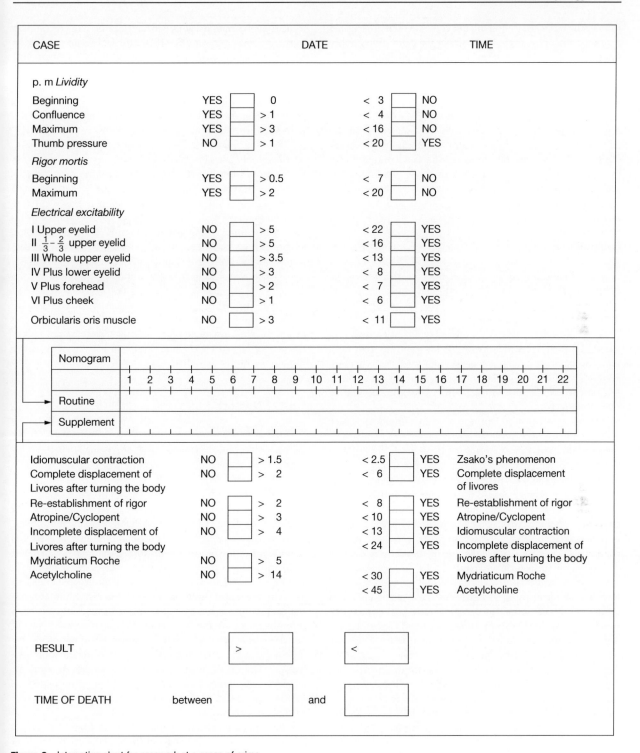

Figure 2 Integrating chart for casework at a scene of crime.

factors. The estimated period did not contradict the investigated period in any of the cases. Especially in the early stages, police investigations can be greatly supported by this method.

Cooling Dummy

More than 20 years ago, a cooling dummy which reproduces almost exactly the cooling of corpses was developed. With this dummy, cooling can be simulated in any condition, for example, even at the location where the body was found. The cooling dummy is an essential help in cases when body cooling under rare cooling conditions has to be evaluated.

Compound Method

From all methods of death time estimation, the nomogram method is the most intensively investigated, most precise, and reliable procedure. However, in the best case, a precision of ±2.8 h around the mean value (95% confidence limits) can be achieved. Therefore, other methods of death time estimation should be used to narrow down this range further (electrical and mechanical excitability of skeletal muscles; chemical excitability of the iris; lividity and rigor mortis) (**Table 11.2**). But how to use the different data on various time-dependent postmortem changes?

Mean values do not represent the time frame in which a special degree of postmortem changes may be positive. For instance, the mean value of degree IV of electrical excitability of the orbicularis oculi muscle is 5.5 h; however, it may be positive between 3 and 8 h. Therefore, not the mean values but the upper and lower range should be used for death time estimation. For casework, the data of the described times of death and supravital reactions were, together with the signs of death estimation, based on the nomogram rearranged into a special chart which facilitates the choice of the subsequent helpful criteria in an actual case (**Figure 11.2**). In casework, the examination begins with taking rectal and ambient temperatures and choosing the appropriate corrective factor and a first estimation of the time since death using the nomogram. Concerning temperature measurements and choosing the appropriate corrective factor, see the chapter on early and late postmortem changes. Then the further criteria are examined. Especially those criteria are of interest which can narrow down the time frame by the nomogram method further. Using this chart at the scene of crime or a computer program, it is guaranteed that nothing will be forgotten and the inspection and examination of the body is efficient and complete concerning death time estimation. For instance, at the scene of crime, the nomogram method reveals a death time between 4.5 h (lower limit) and 10.5 h (upper limit) (**Figure 11.3**). The lower limit can be confirmed or improved only by a criterion with a higher value than 4.5 h, and the upper limit can be reduced only by a criterion with a lower value than 10.1 h. The electrical excitability of facial muscles (musculus orbicularis oculi) showed a positive reaction according to degree IV; that means time since death was below 8 h. Therefore, the upper limit of death time estimation (10.1 h) could be reduced to 8 h. In the early postmortem period especially, the combined application of the nomogram method and electrical excitability of facial muscles increases the precision of death time estimation from body cooling alone. Even if the result of the nomogram method is not improved but just confirmed, this confirms also the self-confidence of the investigator in his opinion and statement of the time since death as his estimation is based on two independent criteria. If the nomogram method must not be used, for example, in cases of hypothermia or fire in the setting where the body was found, the other methods may give reliable results on the death time estimation.

A recent field study on the compound method on 72 consecutive cases over a long-lasting PMI revealed that in 49 cases the limits of the period since death by the temperature methods were improved by the nontemperature methods. The degree of electrical excitability was the most valuable additional method, but the classical signs of death may improve the nomogram results as well.

Further Methods

Vitreous Potassium

There is huge literature especially on chemical methods of death time estimation. Among these are many in vitro methods. Most chemical methods of death time estimation have a factor in common that they are of no value in practice. While the earlier studies were mainly carried out on blood and cerebrospinal fluid (CFS), for more than 60 years, most investigations have been performed on vitreous humor (VH). This is mainly due to the fact that VH is topographically isolated and well protected and, thus, autolytic changes proceed slower compared to blood and CSF. The most studied parameter in VH is potassium. Postmortem rise of the potassium concentration (K^+) in VH has been known for 50 years and has been recommended for the estimation of the time since death. However, the practical application has been hampered by different results concerning the accuracy of death time estimation. Optimistic results of early investigations with an accuracy of death time estimation of ±9.4 h in a time period up to 104 h postmortem could not have been confirmed by succeeding investigations.

The correlation and the strength of correlation between K^+ and the time since death depend on different factors such as cause of death, duration of agonal period, ambient temperature, etc. These factors influencing the accuracy of death time estimation can partly be taken into consideration by using

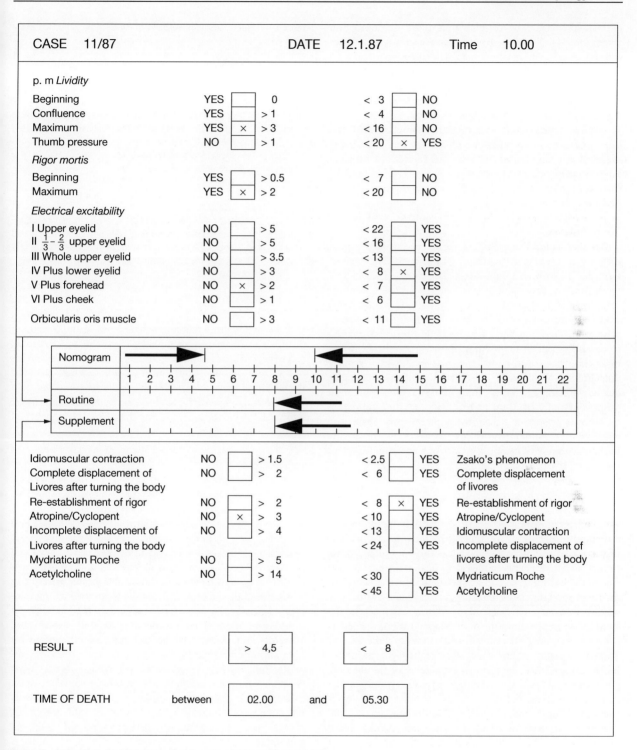

CASE 11/87			DATE 12.1.87			Time 10.00	

p. m *Lividity*

Beginning	YES	☐	0	< 3	☐	NO
Confluence	YES	☐	> 1	< 4	☐	NO
Maximum	YES	☒	> 3	< 16	☐	NO
Thumb pressure	NO	☐	> 1	< 20	☒	YES

Rigor mortis

Beginning	YES	☐	> 0.5	< 7	☐	NO
Maximum	YES	☒	> 2	< 20	☐	NO

Electrical excitability

I Upper eyelid	NO	☐	> 5	< 22	☐	YES
II $\frac{1}{3} - \frac{2}{3}$ upper eyelid	NO	☐	> 5	< 16	☐	YES
III Whole upper eyelid	NO	☐	> 3.5	< 13	☐	YES
IV Plus lower eyelid	NO	☐	> 3	< 8	☒	YES
V Plus forehead	NO	☒	> 2	< 7	☐	YES
VI Plus cheek	NO	☐	> 1	< 6	☐	YES
Orbicularis oris muscle	NO	☐	> 3	< 11	☐	YES

Nomogram

1 2 3 4 5 6 7 8 9 10 11 12 13 14 15 16 17 18 19 20 21 22

Routine

Supplement

Idiomuscular contraction	NO	☐	> 1.5	< 2.5	☐	YES	Zsako's phenomenon
Complete displacement of Livores after turning the body	NO	☐	> 2	< 6	☐	YES	Complete displacement of livores
Re-establishment of rigor	NO	☐	> 2	< 8	☒	YES	Re-establishment of rigor
Atropine/Cyclopent	NO	☒	> 3	< 10	☐	YES	Atropine/Cyclopent
Incomplete displacement of Livores after turning the body	NO	☐	> 4	< 13	☐	YES	Idiomuscular contraction
				< 24	☐	YES	Incomplete displacement of livores after turning the body
Mydriaticum Roche	NO	☐	> 5	< 30	☐	YES	Mydriaticum Roche
Acetylcholine	NO	☐	> 14	< 45	☐	YES	Acetylcholine

RESULT	> 4,5		< 8
TIME OF DEATH	between	02.00	and 05.30

Figure 3 Integrating chart for casework at a scene of crime with an example.

internal standards (urea concentration as an indicator of an antemortem electrolyte dysregulation). For example, in cases with electrolyte dysregulation due to impaired renal function, the precision of death time estimation by vitreous potassium is lower than in cases with normal renal function. However, even in the most favorable case, precision of death time estimation is ±22 h up to 5–6 days postmortem.

In most investigations on vitreous potassium, the PMI has been used as the independent and K^+ as the dependent variable in linear regression analysis between PMI and K^+. According to a recommendation of Munoz et al., however, K^+ should be used as the independent variable for regression analysis. According to the authors, this approach leads to a higher accuracy of death time estimation. This could be confirmed by own calculations.

Another statistical approach has reevaluated six large studies on the rise of vitreous K^+ using a local regression analysis (Loess procedure). Based on this reevaluation, an accuracy of death time estimation has been recommended (95% limits of confidence of ±1 h in the early PMI and ±10 h postmortem) which has surpassed even optimistic results of earlier investigations. This recommended accuracy of death time estimation has been checked on a random sample of 492 cases. Only 153 cases have been within the predicted PMI, while 339 lay outside with a systematic overestimation of the time since death. Furthermore, the accuracy of death time estimation cannot be confirmed. As the precision of death time estimation by vitreous potassium is low, the author knows of no case worldwide where this method has been used as evidence for the PMI. The amount of literature on vitreous potassium is reciprocal to its practical importance.

Gastric Contents and Time Since Death

Although examination of gastric contents is mentioned as a method to determine the time since death nearly in every textbooks, gastric content alone allows only a rough estimation of the interval between the last meal and death. Time and size of the last meal have to be known to derive conclusions on the survival time between last food intake and death. State of digestion and the distribution of the last meal in the stomach and upper intestine have far long been proposed as a method to estimate the time since death. Even if the volume of the last meal is not known, the type of the meal (breakfast, lunch, dinner) may allow rough estimation of the daytime when death occurred. Gastric emptying has been studied and quantified in the last decades using different methods (radiologic, intubation, aspiration, radioisotopes, ultrasound, absorption kinetics of orally administered solutes, pheromagnetic traces). Liquids leave the stomach much faster than solids. While gastric emptying obviously follows an exponential function for liquids, solids show a linear emptying pattern. The following gastric emptying times are given in the

Table 3 Progression of putrefaction of bodies in air, temperature of about 20 °C

Progression of putrefaction of bodies in air, temperature of about 20° C	
After 1–2 days	Green discoloration of abdominal wall, softening of eyeballs.
After 3–5 days	Dark green discoloration of great parts of the abdominal wall. Some patchy green discolorations of the skin of other body regions. Bloody fluid leaking out from mouth and nostrils. Marbling.
After 8–12 days	Whole body surface dark green. Face, neck, and thoracic wall partly reddish green. Bloating of abdomen, scrotum, and face. Fingernails still fixed. Hair loose, begins to peel.
After 4–20 days	Whole body green or reddish brown. Bloating of the whole body. Blisters, partly filled with putrefactive fluid, partly burst with desiccation of the dermis. Eyes (iris, pupil, sclera) reddish brown discolored. Fingernails peeling.

literature: 1–3 h for a light small-volume meal; 3–5 h for a medium-sized meal; 5–8 h for a large meal. However, it must be kept in mind that different anatomical and functional disorders cause delayed or rapid gastric emptying. According to a review by Horowitz and Pounder, only solid components of a mixed solid and liquid meal should be considered and the weight of the stomach content should be compared with an estimated weight of the last meal and reference made to the known 50% emptying times for the solid components of meals of various sizes.

Putrefaction

Putrefaction is a bacterial process, predominantly influenced by environmental factors, mainly ambient temperature, but by underlying diseases and body proportions as well. Medical treatment with antibiotics in the terminal phase may delay putrefactive changes. Otherwise, in cases of sepsis, advanced putrefaction may be seen soon after death. Advanced stages of putrefaction may be seen within a few hours after death which, in moderate or cold climate, are not seen after weeks. Even in relatively constant ambient temperatures, the progression of putrefaction varies considerably (**Table 11.3**). Therefore, putrefactive changes are not a sound method for estimation of the PMI.

Recently, there seems to have been a change, since methods developed in radiology such as H magnetic resonance spectroscopy (MRS) have been applied for the identification of metabolites emerging during decomposition of brain tissue as a step toward quantitative determination of PMIs in putrefaction.

Brain decomposition resulted in reproducible concentration changes of known metabolites and the appearance of decay products that had to be characterized first.

The investigations on postmortem decompositions by H MRS may represent a real progress in research for the following reasons:

- A noninvasive chemical analysis in situ is possible with quantitation of analytes.
- Longitudinal studies of postmortem changes with reproducible results are possible.
- The sheep model seems to be valid for human brains as well.
- With this model, influencing factors such as temperature can be easily studied.
- The definition of analytical functions for the time courses of 10 metabolites up to 400 h postmortem was successful.
- Prediction of PMI based on the combination of five metabolites correlates very well with true time postmortem up to 250 h postmortem.
- These metabolic changes cover a PMI where no other method allows a quantitative calculation of the time since death with any acceptable degree of certainty.

Putrefaction in Water

For bodies recovered from water, quite a good and reliable method for estimating the minimum and maximum water time has been developed based on putrefactive changes which are visible at external examination or at the dissection of the body.

This is mainly due to the fact that water temperature is relatively constant over a longer period of time and during day and night, while air temperature differs not only from day to night but from one day to the other. Morphological findings which are taken into consideration for the estimation of duration of immersion in immersed bodies include the following:

External findings

1. Rigor mortis
2. Lividity
3. Marbling
4. Bloating of face, scrotum, subcutaneous tissue
5. Discoloration of skin (green, black, reddish)
6. Loss of epidermis
7. Loss of hairs
8. Hands
   a. washerwomen's skin
   b. loosening of nails
   c. peeling of skin
   d. loss of nails
9. Feet
   a. washerwomen's skin
   b. loosening of nails

Table 4 Chart to estimate the minimal time interval of immersion

	Month	Jan	Feb	Mar	April	May	June	July	Aug	Sept	Oct	Nov	Dec
Ø	Median water temperature (°C)	3.5	3.9	5.8	9.9	13.0	17.4	18.6	18.6	17.3	13.2	8.8	4.7
1.	Marbling	32	25	16 (23)	9–10	4–5	2	1–2	2	3	4–5	10	17
2.	Distension of tissues by gas	35	25	16 (23)	10	4–5	2–3	2	3	3–4	7	10	17
3.	Discoloration of the body	35	25	16 (23)	(14)	4–5	2	2	3	3–4	7	10	17
4.	Peeling of the epidermis	35	25	16 (23)	(16)	4–5	3	2	3	3–4	7	10	17
5.	Hair lost	35	25	16 (23)	10–12	4–5	2–3	2–3	3	3–4	7	10	17
6.	Hands: beginning of wrinkling	(1)	(1) 28–30	(12 h)			(6 h)			2 h		2 h	(1)
7.	Nails become loose	Over 35	(40) 30–32	23	16	5	2–3	3	3	3–4	11	17	28
8.	Peeling of skin in glove form	35	(45)	23	16	10	3	3	3–4	4	7	20	28
9.	Nails lost	Over 53	45	30 (40)	21	14	8	3	4	10	Over 11	20	Over 35
10.	Feet: beginning of wrinkling	(1)	(1)	(12 h)	(1)		(6 h)	0.5 h		2 h		2 h	(1)
11.	Nails become loose	Over 53	40	26 (35)	17	10	5	3	4	8	12	17	28
12.	Peeling of skin	Over 53	60	35	16	10	5	3	5–6	8–9	Over 11 (14)	20	28
13.	Nails lost	Over 53	Over 60	53	Over 35	Over 28	Over 10	3		Over 10	Over 10	Over 11	Over 20	Over 35
14.	Transudate in pleural cavity[a]	35	25 (40)	18 (35)	10	5	3–4	3	3	11	5	Over 20	
15.	Heart without blood	Over 39	32–34 (40)	23	14–15	9	4	3	3	5	11	20	28
16.	Brain liquefied	35	30 (40)	(23)	14–16	5	3–4	3	3	6	10	17	28

[a]Volume over 500 ml.

First line: months; second line: median water temperature for the month; left column: signs of putrefaction and maceration; following columns: minimal time interval in days. If, for example, in July marbling, distension of tissues by gas, discoloration of the body, peeling of the epidermis, loosening of finger and feet nails, peeling of the skin of hands and feet, and a liquefied brain are observed, the minimum time interval of immersion would be about 2–3 days.

c. peeling of skin

d. loss of nail

Internal findings

1. Volume of transudate in pleural cavity
2. Heart without blood
3. Liquefaction of brain

The warmer the water, the sooner a definite stage of putrefaction is achieved. From the mean water temperature for each month and the stages of decomposition, the German forensic pathologist Reh developed a chart with the minimum time intervals of immersion. Considering all 16 parameters for estimating the minimum time of immersion, the chart provided in **Table 11.4** can be used. On the left side are the useful criteria: in the first line the months, in the second line the mean water temperature, and in the following line the minimum time interval in days.

As many criteria as possible should be used for estimating the minimum time interval since death. With more than only one or two criteria, the result will become more reliable. For estimating the minimum time interval, the mean water temperature which is nearest to the actual water temperature at the time of recovery should be used. With this chart, not only the minimum time interval of immersion can be estimated but also the maximal interval by considering those criteria which have not yet developed. If in June marbling, bloating, and discoloration of the body have developed, and the nails are loose but not lost, it may be concluded that the interval of immersion is over 3 days but below 8 days. Our personal experience with this chart is quite good as it is much better than the old rules of thumb because it takes the actual temperature for the progression of putrefaction into consideration.

A recent evaluation of own cases revealed that the actual water temperatures (of the river Rhine) have risen during the last 40 years. Especially in summer, reliable results can only be expected when the actual water temperature is similar to the temperatures in the table. Therefore, for higher water temperatures, the time interval of immersion may be underestimated when using the table since systematic observations on the progression of putrefaction in correlation to the elevated water temperature are missing. Therefore, the table should be adapted to the elevated water temperatures.

Immunohistochemical Detection of Insulin, Thyroglobulin, and Calcitonin

Although morphological methods on death time estimation are of no practical value in forensic practice, there seems to be some change by the application of immunohistochemistry methods. Wehner et al. studied whether a positive immunoreaction to various antigens such as insulin, thyroglobulin, or

calcitonin is correlated with the time since death. The philosophy of these investigations is that with increasing PMI the tertiary structure of the antigen undergoes postmortem changes and due to protein denaturation stainings become negative.

Meanwhile, a chart was developed to give a rough estimation on the time since death by immunohistochemical methods.

> *See also:* **Forensic Medicine/Pathology:** Autopsy; Early and Late Postmortem Changes; External Postmortem Examination.

Further Reading

De Saram, G.S.W., Webster, G., Kathirgamatamby, N., 1955. Post-mortem temperature and the time of death. The Journal of Criminal Law and Criminology 46, 562–577.

Henssge, C., 1988. Death time estimation in case work I the rectal temperature time of death nomogram. Forensic Science International 38, 209–236.

Henssge, C., 1992. Rectal temperature time of death nomogram: dependence of corrective factors on the body weight under stronger thermic insulation conditions. Forensic Science International 54, 51–56.

Henssge, C., 2002. Temperature based methods II. In: Henssge, C., Knight, B., Krompecher, T., Madea, B., Nokes, L. (Eds.), The Estimation of the Time Since Death in the Early Post-mortem Period, second ed. Edward Arnold, London.

Henssge, C., Althaus, L., Bolt, J., et al., 2000. Experiences with a compound method for estimating the time since death. I. Rectal temperature nomogram for time since death. II. Integration of non-temperature-based methods. International Journal of Legal Medicine 6, 303–319, 320–331.

Henssge, C., Beckmann, E.R., Wischhusen, F., Brinkmann, B., 1984. A determination of time of death by measuring central brain temperature. Zeitschrift für Rechtsmedizin 93, 1–22.

Henssge, C., Knight, B., Krompecher, T., Madea, B., Nokes, L. (Eds.), 2002. The Estimation of the Time Since Death in the Early Postmortem Period, second ed. Edward Arnold, London.

Henssge, C., Madea, B., 1988. Methoden zur Bestimmung der Todeszeit an Leichen. Schmidt-Römhild-Verlag, Lübeck.

Henssge, C., Madea, B., 2004a. Estimation of the time since death in the early postmortem period. Forensic Science International 144 (2–3), 167–175.

Henssge, C., Madea, B., 2004b. Frühe Leichenerscheinungen und Todeszeitbestimmung im frühpostmortalen Intervall. In: Brinkmann, B., Madea, B. (Eds.), Handbuch Rechtsmedizin Bd. I. Springer, Berlin/Heidelberg/New York, pp. 79–150.

Horowitz, M., Maddern, G.J., Chatterton, B.E., Collins, P.J., Harding, P.E., Sherman, D.J.C., 1984. Changes in gastric emptying rates with age. Clinical Science 67, 213–218.

Horowitz, M., Pounder, D.J., 1985. Gastric emptying – forensic implications of current concepts. Medicine, Science, and the Law 25, 201–214.

Ith, M., Bigler, P., Scheurer, E., et al., 2002a. Observation and identification of metabolites emerging during postmortem decomposition of brain tissue by means of in situ ^{1}H-magnetic resonance spectroscopy. Magnetic Resonances in Medicine 48, 915–920.

Ith, M., Bigler, P., Scheurer, E., et al., 2002b. Identification of metabolites emerging during autolysis and bacterial heterolysis of decomposing brain tissue by 1H-MRS in situ and in vitro. Proceedings of the International Society for Magnetic Resonance in Medicine 10, 580.

Knight, B., 2002. The use of gastric contents in estimating time since death. In: Henssge, C., Knight, B., Krompecher, T., Madea, B., Nokes, L. (Eds.), The Estimation of the Time Since Death in the Early Postmortem Period, second ed. Edward Arnold, London, pp. 209–215.

Madea, B., 1992. Estimating time of death from measurement of electrical excitability of skeletal muscle. Journal of the Forensic Science Society 32, 117–129.

Madea, B., 1994. Importance of supravitality in forensic medicine. Forensic Science International 69, 221–241.

Madea, B., 2002. Gastric contents and time since death. In: Henssge, C., Knight, B., Krompecher, T., Madea, B., Nokes, L. (Eds.), The Estimation of the Time Since Death in the Early Postmortem Period, second ed. Edward Arnold, London, pp. 215–225.

Madea, B., 2005. Is there recent progress in the estimation of the postmortem interval by means of thanatochemistry? Forensic Science International 151, 139–149.

Madea, B., 2009a. Death: time of. In: Jamieson, A., Moenssens, A. (Eds.), Wiley Encyclopaedia of Forensic Sciences, vol. 2. John Wiley and Sons Ltd, Chichester, pp. 697–716.

Madea, B., 2009b. Time of death determination. In: Jamieson, A., Moenssens, A. (Eds.), Wiley Encyclopaedia of Forensic Sciences, vol. 5. John Wiley and Sons Ltd, Chichester, pp. 2466–2479.

Madea, B., Henssge, C., 1990. Electrical excitability of skeletal muscle postmortem in casework. Forensic Science International 47, 207–227.

Madea, B., Henssge, C., 2002. Eye changes after death. In: Henssge, C., Knight, B., Krompecher, T., Madea, B., Nokes, L. (Eds.), The Estimation of the Time Since Death in the Early Postmortem Period, second ed. Edward Arnold, London.

Madea, B., Henssge, C., 2003. Timing of death. In: Payne-James, J., Busuttil, A. (Eds.), Forensic Medicine: Clinical and Pathological Aspects. Greenwich Medical Media Limited, London, pp. 91–114.

Madea, B., Herrmann, N., Henssge, C., 1990. Precision of estimating the time since death by vitreous potassium – comparison of two different equations. Forensic Science International 46, 277–284.

Madea, B., Käferstein, H., Herrmann, N., Sticht, G., 1994. Hypoxanthine in vitreous humour and cerebrospinal fluid – a marker of postmortem interval and prolonged (vital) hypoxia? Remarks also on hypoxanthine in SIDS. Forensic Science International 65, 19–31.

Madea, B., Rödig, A., 2006. Time of death dependent criteria in vitreous humor – precision of estimating the time since death. Forensic Science International 164, 87–92.

Mallach, H.J., Mittmeyer, H.J., 1971. Totenstarre und Totenflecke. Zeitschrift für Rechtsmedizin 69, 70–78.

Musshoff, F., Klotzbach, H., Block, W., Traeber, F., Schild, H., Madea, B., 2010. Comparison of post-mortem metabolic changes in sheep brain tissue in isolated heads and whole animals using ^{1}H-MR spectroscopy – preliminary results. International Journal of Legal Medicine. http://dx.doi.org/10.1007/s00414-010-0463-3. published online May 07, 2010.

Pounder, J., 2000. Postmortem interval. In: Siegel, J.A., Saukko, P.J., Knupfer, G.C. (Eds.), Encyclopaedia of Forensic Sciences, vol. 3. Academic Press, San Diego, pp. 1167–1172.

Prokop, O., 1975. Supravitale Erscheinungen. In: Prokop, O., Göhler, W. (Eds.), Forensische Medizin. Volk und Gesundheit, Berlin, pp. 16–27.

Scheurer, E., Ith, M., Dietrich, R., et al., 2003. Statistical evaluation of ^{1}H-MR spectra of the brain in situ for quantitative determination of postmortem intervals (PMI). Proceedings of the International Society for Magnetic Resonance in Medicine 11, 569.

Scheurer, E., Ith, M., Dietrich, D., et al., 2005. Statistical evaluation of time-dependent metabolite concentrations: estimation of postmortem intervals based on in situ ^{1}H MRS of the brain. NMR in Biomedicine 18 (3), 163–172.

Tröger, H.D., Baur, C., Spann, K.W., 1987. Mageninhalt und Todeszeitbestimmung. Schmidt-Römhild, Lübeck.

Tsokos, M., 2005. Potmortem changes and artefacts occurring during the early postmortem interval. Forensic Pathology Reviews 3, 183–237.

Wehner, F., Wehner, H.D., Schieffer, M.C., Subke, J., 1999. Delimitation of the time of death by immunohistochemical detection of insulin in pancreatic b-cells. Forensic Science International 105, 161–169.

Wehner, F., Wehner, H.D., Schieffer, M.C., Subke, J., 2000. Delimitation of the time of death by immunohistochemical detection of calcitonin. Forensic Science International 122, 89–94.

Wehner, F., Wehner, H.D., Subke, J., 2001. Delimitation of the time of death by immunohistochemical detection of thyroglobulin. Forensic Science International 110, 199–206.

Relevant Websites

http://www.rechtsmedizin.uni-bonn.de—For the Practical Application of Henssge's Nomogram No Photocopies From the Nomogram of Textbooks Should Be Used since There Might Be Photocopier/Scanner Distortions. The Nomograms Can Be Downloaded From the Homepage of the Institute of Forensic Medicine, University of Bonn.

http://shadow.pohn.kom—Those Who Use an Iphone or Blackberry "App" Should Look This Web site.

http://home.t-online.de—Square Wave Generators Can Be Purchased Online.

Key Terms

Accumulated degree days, Adipocere, Animal activity, Animal predation, Autolysis, Bodies recovered from water, Body cooling, Bog bodies, Bones, Circumstances of death, Commingling, Corrective factors, Death and dying, Decay, Decomposition, Desiccation, Electrical excitability of facial muscles, Entomology, Forensic anthropology, Gastric content and time since death, Mechanical and electrical excitability of skeletal muscles, Mechanical excitability, Mummification, Nomogram method, Paleontology, Permafrost bodies, Pharmacological excitability of the iris, Postmortem body cooling, Postmortem lividity, Postmortem changes, Postmortem interval, Postmortem, Preservation of decomposing bodies, Putrefaction, Preservation, Radiocarbon analysis, Rigor mortis, Scattering, Scavenging, Skeleton, Supravital reactions, Supravitality, Taphonomy, Time since death, Total body score, Trauma analysis, Volatile fatty acids.

Review Questions

1. What effects can animal scavenging have on bones? How does this hinder the forensic anthropologist's work?
2. Why is researching animal scavenging difficult?
3. Scavenging is followed by what? Why?
4. What kinds of animals are scavengers?
5. What is taphonomy? Where did the term originate?
6. Who is Bass and what did he contribute to the study of taphonomy?

7. What is diagenesis?
8. What does "PMI" stand for? How is it determined?
9. Why are pigs considered to be research analogs for taphonomic study?
10. Can hard tissue decompose? Why or why not?
11. How does climate affect estimating postmortem interval?
12. What is mummification? When does it occur?
13. What is adipocere? Where does it come from?
14. How can radiocarbon dating help in a forensic case?
15. How do insects assist a forensic anthropologist in assessing postmortem interval?
16. What are supravital reactions?
17. What is postmortem lividity?
18. What is rigor mortis?
19. What is the difference between autolysis and putrefaction?
20. What is saponification?

Discussion Questions

1. Forensic anthropology developed from physical anthropology and archaeological methods. How did the study of taphonomy evolve from archeology to forensic science?
2. When Ubelaker states, "Certain types of surgical practices and orthopedic devices also can be dated, linking remains to particular periods," what does he mean? Give two historic examples and two current ones.
3. How does research in physical anthropology and archeology assist forensic anthropology? Does forensic research inform traditional anthropology? How?
4. Do the early stages of decomposition matter to the forensic anthropologist? If all they look at are the bones, then what difference would it make knowing about the early stages of postmortem activity?
5. Discuss how the environment matters to decomposition, taphonomy, and animal scavenging, both from the larger climate view and from the local context of body placement and positioning.

Additional Readings

Bates, L.N., Wescott, D.J., 2016. Comparison of decomposition rates between autopsied and non-autopsied human remains. Forensic Science International 261, 93–100.
Colard, T., Delannoy, Y., Naji, S., Gosset, D., Hartnett, K., Bécart, A., 2015. Specific patterns of canine scavenging in indoor settings. Journal of Forensic Sciences 60 (2), 495–500.
Forbes, S.L., Carter, D.O., 2015. Processes and Mechanisms of Death and Decomposition of Vertebrate Carrion. Carrion Ecology, Evolution and Their Applications. Taylor and Francis, Surrey, UK, pp. 13–30.
Pokines, J.T., 2015. Taphonomic alterations by the rodent species woodland vole (*Microtus pinetorum*) upon human skeletal remains. Forensic Science International 257, e16–e19.

Section 3. Recovery

Crime scenes are a very different thing for forensic anthropologists, if for no other reason than they may have to excavate their scene. In many settings, Nature will have her way with the deceased and her numerous "little helpers," such as scavengers and insects, hurry the remains through the taphonomic process. Surface recovery and excavation are skills from archeology and any forensic anthropologist who wants to be successful in their field needs to spent some time in "the field." Well-honed archeological skills, as well as traditional crime scene techniques, pay dividends to those working in body recovery or forensic anthropology scenes.

Archeology

JR Hunter, University of Birmingham, Birmingham, UK
C Sturdy Colls, Forensic and Crime Science, Stoke-on-Trent, UK

Background

Forensic archeology first emerged in the United States in the later 1970s as part of a broader recognition of the role of anthropology in medicolegal matters. There the development of forensic anthropology has been well charted, with professional competency being recognized by the American Academy of Forensic Sciences. However, in Britain, where archeology was traditionally seen as a free-standing discipline with roots embedded more strongly in excavation and field skills, forensic archeology developed somewhat later. Furthermore, differences in medicolegal practice at scenes of crime between the two countries also serve to confine the role of forensic archeology in Britain to one more specifically concerned with field activities than with postmortem study. Elsewhere, forensic archeology plays a less prominent role in criminal investigation, although with formal interest now developing in other parts of northern Europe, in particular, the Netherlands and Australasia. In addition, the excavation of mass civil or war graves relating to both recent and sociohistoric conflicts in places such as Argentina, Rwanda, Bosnia, South Africa, Spain, and Eastern Europe has widened the application of archeological recovery techniques to other parts of the world.

Archeological input to criminal investigation reflects the skill base of modern archeology and its role in society. In Europe and the United States, archeologists are now extensively employed on behalf of central and regional government in order to identify and assess archeological remains ahead of planning and redevelopment schemes. The archeologist's interest is almost exclusively concerned with understanding the past from buried material remains; this can be expressed in general terms of finding evidence, recovering evidence in a manner that will maximize its value, and interrogating evidence in order to reconstruct sequences of past events. As a process, this has much in common with law enforcement detection and is now widely recognized as having a role in modern forensic investigation when buried remains are encountered. This skill base provides a collective expertise in landscape analysis, knowledge of resources (photographic and cartographic), geology, land use, site location methods, and excavation techniques.

In addition, archeology is a process that has access to a range of associated areas of specialisms, many of which also have forensic application. These include, for example, aerial photographic interpretation, identification of pollen assemblages, soil analysis, animal/human bone differentiation, and recognition of cremated human materials. Archeologists have also developed some techniques that are peculiarly suited for forensic purpose, for example, geophysical survey for the detection of shallow subsurface remains. Archeology, such as forensic science, is also concerned with scientific analysis across a broad range of material types.

The main areas of interest common to both archeology and criminal investigation might be listed as follows:

- skeletal analysis (physical anthropology),
- scientific analysis,
- field search, and
- excavation and recovery.

The first two of these are completely discussed elsewhere in this volume and are not detailed here other than for cross-reference purposes. Skeletal analysis, for example, is a major section in its own right with a recognized modern history in criminal matters as well as in military and disaster scenarios in the United States, Europe, and Asia. Equally, the application of both physical and life sciences is now a fundamental part of modern archeology and much analytical science is dedicated to matters of provenance or dating. Provenance—the ascribing of a finished product (e.g., pottery) to the location of a source, place, or company of manufacture—is a well-attested method of evaluating the trade, transport, and social economics of earlier societies. Like forensic science and the Locard's principle, it ascribes a material to a parent source. The methods used are also common to forensic science, as indeed are many of the materials under study (e.g., silicates, soils, metals, and pigments). There are many cross-reference points throughout this volume, although interplay between the two disciplines of forensic science and archeological science, respectively, is curiously exclusive.

Absolute dating methods also have some relevance here. Although archeological and forensic timescales have little in common, radiocarbon dating has some application in demonstrating whether human remains pre- or post-date 1952 (the era of atomic weapon testing, which generated high atmospheric radiation levels). This is particularly important in providing coarse dating in instances of stray or displaced human bone, and also for determining if remains are of "forensic significance," particularly in countries where a 70-year rule for the pursuit of prosecutions applies. More relevant, perhaps, is the observation of taphomomic (decay) processes in buried environments and the determination of interval since deposition. There has been considerable interest in recent years in the degradation of both human and associated modern materials buried over short timescales.

The number of homicide victims who are ultimately buried to avoid detection is relatively small in relation to the total of homicide victims, although several of these have been multiple or serial killings and have been of high profile. A greater percentage involves concealment in one form or another. Recent history has emphasized a number of cases that have demonstrated a potential role for archeology: in the United States, these have been highlighted by one of the pioneers of forensic archeology, Dan Morse, from cases in Illinois and Texas; in Britain notably from the Moors Murder enquiry in the early 1960s; and the later investigation of the north London garden of Dennis Nilsen in 1984. All these situations were effectively archeological scenarios, which would have been approached and handled in very different ways if taken on a straight archeological basis. However, since the late 1980s, but with some notable setbacks, such cases have been fewer and awareness of the potential value of using archeological techniques has increased among law enforcement agencies. Indeed, many so-called "cold cases," where the time since deposition may range from 2 to 70 years, are being revisited utilizing archeological techniques in light of this. It is, nonetheless, not simply

a straightforward matter of creating awareness or applying appropriate techniques. The process is two-way: archeologists also need to recognize the protocols and processes of crime scene work; the timescales involved; and, most importantly, the judicial constraints that surround forensic work. The philosophy and practice of forensic archeology is very different from that of its parent. Also, different are the objectives and the means to achieving those objectives (see Recovery section).

Archeology is based on the principles of stratigraphy, namely, that the ground subsurface comprises discrete layers of earth, which differ in texture, color, and physical properties reflecting the effects of both natural and artificial activity over time. These layers can be generated by natural processes of soil formation or, in areas of habitation, by building, farming, and general development caused by a wide range of activities. In rural areas, these layers can be of relatively shallow depth above bedrock (i.e., a few centimeters) or in urban areas up to several meters deep reflecting centuries of activity and use. Archeologists try and interpret what each layer represented in past time and also how the various layers relate to each other chronologically. The order of their formation can usually be determined quite easily. Many modern layers, particularly those relating to building activity, may be able to be dated by modern records.

In effect, the profile of layers in a given area of the subsurface makes a type of statement about the history of that place. It also presents a "snapshot" in time, in that all the layers have a broad chronological relationship in which one layer that overlies another is clearly of later date (**Figure 1**). If a grave is dug into the ground, the existing layers in that place become disturbed; a relationship occurs between these layers and the grave; and the timeframe of the overall stratigraphy becomes extended. Archeology involves identifying and interpreting changes of this type.

A grave identified within these layers will have a contextual integrity, no matter how few layers are involved. Recovering or excavating a victim without awareness of related layers (i.e., the layers that are earlier than the grave, the layers that are later than the grave, and the grave itself) will stand to lose much of the evidence that may be available. Questions that the pathologist or medical examiner will try to answer pertaining to interval since death, identity, or the cause/manner of death may be more readily resolved if the edge and sides of the grave can be defined in three dimensions; this effectively identifies the physical boundaries within which the human remains and associated materials will be found. The presence of the associated layers may assist in dating the event.

Human remains often appear during building or development work when bones become unearthed during machine excavation. In such instances, it is particularly important that remains are retained in situ in order that the relationship of the grave within its buried environment can be retained as much as possible.

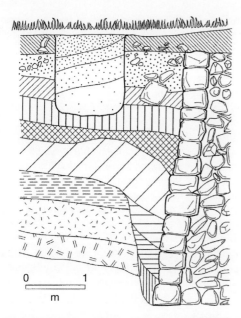

Figure 1 Example of local stratigraphy showing development of layers through time, including wall (right) and later pit or grave (top left). Drawing by H. Buglass.

Search

Locating buried materials can involve a range of target types, although the most common are human remains. Other targets can include firearms, drugs, or stolen goods covering all shapes, sizes, and materials of organic, inorganic, ferrous, or nonferrous type. In nearly all instances, the method of search involves the identification of the disturbance caused by the burial in the first instance, rather than the item buried. Even with homicide victims (for which this entry is primarily intended), the target characteristics can vary according to stature, age, clothing, or dismemberment.

The initial phase of search usually involves targeting the most likely locations in a given area using factors of feasibility (i.e., geological suitability, soil cover, land use, etc.) in combination with a suspect's movement, psychological profiling, and other intelligence. "Dump-site" analysis, as it is known, has been the subject of valuable research in both Britain and the United States: it enables factors such as the relationship between victim and suspect, location of last sighting, or likely distance traveled to be fed into the search equation. The use of geological maps and existing aerial photographs (vertical and oblique) can facilitate this. Often, the process can be carried out as a "desktop" study, sometimes using geographical information systems, and the target areas are located accordingly. This is highly desirable, as it neither arouses suspicion, runs the risk of damaging evidence on the ground nor necessarily incurs great expense. It also allows what are known as site histories to be devised, which details any landscape change (natural or man-made) that may have affected the burial environment or caused disturbance to the remains.

Once the area can be narrowed down, a more detailed approach can be taken. When a victim, or for that matter any object, is buried, the subsurface is disturbed in relation to the surrounding environment. This disturbance can have a number of effects on (1) the subsequent ground vegetation, (2) the immediate topography, and (3) the geophysical signature of the disturbed area.

The original digging of a grave is likely to create a looser, damper, more aerobic area of ground when the grave is filled in. This will almost certainly affect the height or density (or even species) of the resulting vegetation on the ground surface (**Figure 2**)—an effect that may become more pronounced as the human decay process provides nutrients to an already moistened soil medium. The converse might apply if the grave was filled in with stones and the vegetational growth inhibited accordingly. These changes will have a long-term effect. There will also be a shorter term effect on the surrounding ground

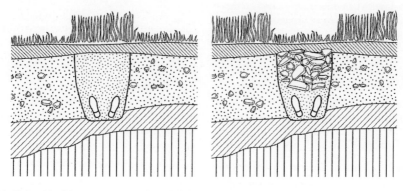

Figure 2 Some potential effects of burial on surface vegetation. Drawing by H. Buglass.

surface, where the excavated soil was dumped when the grave was first dug. There may also be excess soil providing a low mound over the grave, which in time may sink to form a depression as the grave infill consolidates. A secondary depression may occur as the body cavity collapses, and cracking may take place at the grave edges during dry weather. In addition, the infilling of the grave may contain obvious traces of deep disturbance, such as soil or bedrock of different color (e.g., clay or chalk) brought to the surface in an otherwise undisturbed area.

Although many of these features of vegetation, topographic, or soil change might be seen at ground level, they are often at their optimum when viewed from the air, some features being particularly prominent through the use of shadows at appropriate times of the day. Aerial reconnaissance is an ideal nonintrusive primary method of search, but its effectiveness may be seasonally specific given that light and land use are variable components. The value of historic aerial imagery in criminal investigations involving buried remains has also recently been realized. Any photography, however, may be supported by imagery analysis for which there is now highly developed military and archeological expertise is available.

There are a number of methods that can be used to detect buried remains; some of the most commonly used are listed below on a scale that runs from the noninvasive (i.e., those least likely to destroy buried evidence) to the invasive (i.e., those most likely to destroy buried evidence). The list is not comprehensive and is presented only as a general guide; it also tends to reflect the selective narrowing down of the target area. The deployment of these techniques, and their complementary or sequential use, depends on a range of factors including the local environment, the geology, the nature of the target, and the interval since burial. Some techniques, particularly geophysical methods, are only suited to certain types of environment or situation (e.g., indoors, outdoors, concrete, soil, and clay) and are wholly ineffective in other environments. It is not possible to outline the complex range of variables in the space available here; search is a specialist area of expertise for which advice should be sought (see below). The primary use of one method may completely negate the effectiveness of another or may be wholly wasteful of resources. A routine list of techniques might be as follows:

- Aerial photography and reconnaissance for the detection of disturbances identified from the vegetation or topography (shadow or color change) or by soil marks (color).
- Field craft for the detection of discrete areas of vegetation, topography, or soil difference; for the presence of ground cracking; and for the identification of burial locations by using prominent local landmarks or features, which may have been used as guide points by the offender (sometimes known as "winthroping").
- Body scent dogs for the identification of buried remains by virtue of characteristic odor, which may be released from the ground by systematic or selective probing.
- Geophysical survey for the detection of shallow subsurface features, typically by using electrical resistance (to detect disturbance that has affected local moisture content of soils), magnetometry (to detect disturbance caused by changes to a local magnetic field), ground penetrating radar (to detect responses to changes in ground density using an electromagnetic pulse), and metal detector (to detect both ferrous and nonferrous items associated with buried individual).
- Probing/sampling for the identification of subsurface disturbance, emission of methane, or thermal change.
- Excavation for the identification of soil disturbance (color, texture, and physical properties) and changes consistent with a grave (see Background section).

The principle on which all of these methods are based is the ability to detect a disturbance or change within an otherwise undisturbed environment. Also to be considered are effects brought about by the decay process of the body itself. This may not only generate heat (and allow the target to be identified using thermal imaging during the decay activity) but also affect the geophysical properties of the grave and inhibit or enhance the likelihood of detection depending on the survey technique used. Variables that might accelerate or delay this decay process include factors of depth, climate, soil pH, wrapping or clothing, water content, and presence of oxygen. Optimum methods of search rely on knowledge of as many of these variables as possible.

In light of the closure of the Council for the Registration of Forensic Practitioners in 2009, under which practitioners could become registered as competent, the Forensic Archeology Special Interest Group and Expert Panel was created in 2011 in the United Kingdom under auspice of the Institute for Archeologists. The Special Interest Group aims to raise awareness of the discipline and developing a training network for students. The Expert Panel consists of a group of specialists who have undergone proficiency testing and were deemed competent based on their experience in criminal investigations as "reporting" practitioners (i.e., those who have given evidence in court). Members adhere to a code of practice and are responsible for designing operational standards. Most are employed by universities and fewer by private firms or as independent consultants, but they are all actively engaged in both casework and research concerning search and recovery.

Recovery

Although recovering buried remains can occur in a variety of different situations and environments, the process of recovery follows a well-established routine in order to maximize the evidence available. This is based on the awareness that archeology is a destructive process and that each recovery operation is seen as a nonrepeatable exercise.

When the burial of a victim takes place, three main activities are undertaken: the physical removal of earth from the ground, the deposition of the body on the grave, and the infilling of the grave. Proper forensic investigation of the grave follows this process in the reverse order: the body is exposed in order to show the manner in which it was disposed, the body is lifted, and subsequently the manner in which the grave was dug is identified.

Once the outline of a disturbance has been identified, it is normally half-sectioned (i.e., half of the infill should be excavated), usually by bisecting the long axis at around the midway point leaving an exposed vertical profile of the unexcavated part of the disturbance. This has two main benefits: first, it serves to identify whether the disturbance is in fact a grave or not without excavating (and destroying) the whole disturbance, and second, it provides visible evidence in the exposed profile as to how the disturbance was infilled and how it might most effectively be excavated to resolve questions pertinent to the particular case.

Sometimes, because of depth or other constraints, it becomes necessary to extend the working area available by excavating additional space adjacent to the grave itself (having first suitably recorded the grave sides). This allows lateral access to the grave/body and facilitates proper excavation. In situations where this is impossible, it may be necessary to construct struts or planking to wedge across the grave as a working platform. This ensures that the weight of the excavator is taken by the planking rather than the underlying victim (at whatever depth), thus minimizing unnecessary damage to the victim and to any associated materials. Although no two scenes are ever the same, and each has a different situation and timescale, a number of general elements need to be addressed during the recovery process. These are outlined below and should only be seen in general terms, given the great variability of situations and constraints of individual scenes.

- *Preserving the integrity of the grave.* It is critical that the integrity of the grave (i.e., the boundaries and area of disturbance) is maintained throughout, in order to preserve the exact situation that occurred when the victim was buried. This not only allows the original scene of crime to be recreated but also ensures the absolute recovery of the individual and any associated materials. Furthermore, determination of the parameters of the grave is also necessary in order to eliminate the possibility of contamination.

- *Emptying the grave.* The grave infill is normally removed by trowel in layers, which reflect the manner in which the grave was infilled by the perpetrator. This also enables the nature of the grave infill to be identified. If there are no observable layers, the grave infill is excavated in a series of "spits" typically 10 cm deep in order to provide a controlled removal of the grave deposits.

- *Objects found within the grave.* Exhibits discovered within the grave are normally recorded in three dimensions within the layers or "spits" in which they occur. Recording of this type is now a standard practice on archeological sites and is carried out using an electronic distance measurer, which is both accurate and rapid. This ensures that individual objects are properly associated with any layers in which they occurred and that the contents of the grave can be recreated spatially. These exhibits can include items belonging to the individuals, such as clothes, buttons, jewelry, the contents of pockets; items associated with the burial event, such as a weapon, papers, clothing, and wrapping; or materials introduced to the grave infill in an attempt to minimize discovery, such as rubble or lengths of wood.

- *Recording.* Because archeology is a destructive exercise, the recording process is comprehensive and wherever possible is undertaken in three dimensions. The outline of the grave is normally planned with reference to permanent base points at ground level in order that it can be relocated in the future; the base and the profile of the grave are planned using graphic conventions such as contours or hachures and a vertical record of the infill from the half section (above; also **Figure 3**). This section is drawn as a part of the basic recording methodology and is essential in demonstrating the dimensional properties of the grave. In addition, the

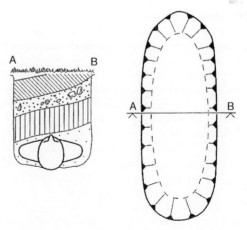

Figure 3 (Left) Vertical profile of grave infill taken at approximately half-way point across disturbance. (Right) Hachure plan of overall grave profile on completion of excavation and removal of victim. Cross-reference provided by section line A–B. Drawing by H. Buglass.

development of laser scanning technologies offers the potential in the future for the digital recording of grave sites.

On archeological sites, human skeletal remains are drawn to scale as a part of the recording process; this may not be possible at a scene of crime, but the disposition of the body and the location of any associated features are usually subject to detailed photographic record. The body is normally revealed entirely before lifting. The lifting process itself is a delicate operation, which takes place bearing in mind that footprints may have survived in the floor of the grave. The method of lifting varies depending on factors such as depth, condition, and wrapping but is often most satisfactorily carried out by sliding a board or metal sheet under the body, although this may have implications for the survival of any foot impression.

Photography occurs throughout the recovery process, ideally taken from a fixed point at one end of the grave (normally the foot end) and identifies specific rather than arbitrary points during the recovery process, for example, before excavation, at changes in layers or "spits" in the grave infill, at the point where significant exhibits occur, when the body is exposed and when the body has been lifted. These photographs will not only record the main sequences of events but, viewed in reverse order, also recreate the offense in exactly the way it occurred.

Excavation and record along these lines may be able to answer several important questions about the original crime:

- How was the grave dug and with what implement? This may be resolved by examination of the sides of the grave, which exhibits mechanical grab, shovel (curved edge), spade (straight edge), or pick (short blade) markings. In exceptional instances, it may be possible to identify a specific implement that bears characteristic markings or nicks on the blade. This is especially the case in soils that sustain impressions such as heavy clays.
- Was the grave dug in a hurry or was it carried out carefully in a prepared way? The professional opinion of the archeologist may be canvassed in an attempt to determine whether a grave site was premeditated on the basis of its profile and depth (or even of its primary silted deposits if the grave had been open for some time before burial). This clearly has implications for manslaughter or murder charges.
- Did the grave contain any evidence of cause or manner of death? The infill of the grave may bear traces of toxins, blood, or firearms discharge and the excavator will be prepared for these within the grave deposits. Toxins will normally be the subject of a sampling strategy by the scene of crime personnel. The location of bullets/pellets may be determined by the use of a metal detector. Bullets may, for example, have passed through the base of the grave into the subsoils if the victim was shot in the grave itself.
- Was there transfer of materials from offender to grave infill? Locard's principle points to the natural transfer of materials

(e.g., fibers, hair, sweat, or footwear impressions) into the grave infill. These are often extremely hard to identify or recover but should be borne in mind during the recovery operation.
- Was there foreign material in the infill or layer matrices, and if so where did it come from? During the excavation, the descriptions of individual layers or "spits" are recorded using accepted soil definitions and terminology. Soils or materials that are unlikely to have been dug out from the area of the grave can provide additional evidence. Their provenance may have considerable bearing on convicting the offender.

Summary

Forensic archeology is now an acknowledged area of expertise in field search and recovery and has been legally recognized in prosecution and defense areas during the late 1980s and 1990s in both the United States and Britain, as well as being actively developed in other European countries. It has been recognized as a subdiscipline in its own right and is offered within university degree programs on both sides of the Atlantic. Forensic archeology also features in postexperience and validated postgraduate courses and seminars intended for both archeologists and law enforcement personnel, forensic scientists, and associated professionals. Despite its academic origins, its familiarity with sampling, three-dimensional study, and recording processes lends itself naturally to scene of crime investigation. Furthermore, its extensive repertoire of associated disciplines provides a valuable range of distinctive forensic skills.

See also: **Anthropology/Odontology:** History of Forensic Anthropology; **Chemistry/Trace/Forensic Geosciences:** Crime Scene Considerations; Forensic Geoscience; Soils; **Forensic Medicine/Pathology:** Estimation of the Time Since Death; **Investigations:** Crime Scene Analysis and Reconstruction; Recovery of Human Remains.

Further Reading

Blau, S., Ubelaker, D.H., 2009. Handbook of Archaeology and Anthropology. Left Coast Press, Walnut Creek.

Boddington, A., Garland, A.N., Janaway, R.C. (Eds.), 1987. Death, Decay and Reconstruction: Approaches to Archaeology and Forensic Science. Manchester University Press, Manchester.

Clark, A., 1996. Seeing Beneath the Soil: Prospecting Methods in Archaeology. Batsford, London.

France, D.L., Griffin, T.J., Swanburg, J.G., et al., 1992. A multidisciplinary approach to the detection of clandestine graves. Journal of Forensic Sciences 37 (6), 1435–1750.

Haglund, W.D., Sorg, M. (Eds.), 2002. Advances in Forensic Taphonomy: Method, Theory, and Archaeological Perspectives. CRC Press, Boca Raton.

Hunter, J.R., 1998. The excavation of modern murder. In: Downes, J., Pollard, A. (Eds.), The Loved Body's Corruption. Cruithene Press, Glasgow, pp. 197–211.

Hunter, J.R., Cox, M., 2005. Forensic Archaeology: Advances in Theory and Practice. Routledge, London.

Hunter, J.R., Roberts, C.A., Martin, A. (Eds.), 1995. Studies in Crime: An Introduction to Forensic Archaeology. Seaby/Batsford, London.

Iscan, M.Y., 1988. Rise of forensic anthropology. Yearbook of Physical Anthropology 31, 203–230.

Killam, E.W., 1990. The Detection of Human Remains. Charles C. Thomas, Springfield.

Morse, D., Dailey, R.C., Stoutamire, J., Duncan, J., 1984. Forensic archaeology. In: Rathbun, T.A., Buikstra, J. (Eds.), Human Indentification: Case Studies in Forensic Anthropology. Charles C. Thomas, Springfield, pp. 53–63.

Morse, D., Duncan, J., Stoutamire, J. (Eds.), 1983. Handbook of Forensic Archaeology and Anthropology. Rose Printing, Tallahassee, FL.

Pye, K., Croft, D.J., 2005. Forensic Geoscience: Principles, Techniques and Applications. Geological Society of London, London.

Rodriguez, W.C., Bass, W.M., 1983. Insect activity and its relationship to decay rates of human cadavers in East Tennessee. Journal of Forensic Sciences 28 (2), 423–432.

Snow, C.C., 1982. Forensic anthropology. Annual Review of Anthropology 11, 97–131.

Stevens, J.A., 1997. Standard investigatory tools and offender profiling. In: Jackson, J.L., Bekerian, D.A. (Eds.), Offender Profiling: Theory. Research and Practice, Chichester, pp. 77–91.

Ubelaker, D.H., 2008. Human Skeletal Remains. Aldine, Chicago.

Ubelaker, D.H., Houck, M.M., 2002. Utilization of radiocarbon dating and paleontological extraction techniques in the analysis of a human skull in an unusual context. Forensic Science Communications 4. Available at: www.fbi.gov.

Packaging

J Horswell, Approved Forensics Sendirian Berhad, Selangor, Malaysia

Background

The ideal method of collecting and subsequent packaging of items for transport to the forensic science laboratory will vary considerably, depending on the nature of the item concerned. Likewise, the material from which a package is fabricated will also vary considerably.

Paper as a Packaging Medium

Generally, the use of paper in the form of bags of various sizes is recommended. Paper bags are fabricated in various sizes and should be readily available. If using envelopes, A4 white bond paper should be employed in the first instance for smaller items such as hairs, fibers, glass, or paint. Place the item onto a previously folded piece of paper, a bindle, or what is referred to as a "pharmacist's fold," and then place this into an envelope or plastic zipper bag. This will prevent the loss of items from envelope corners or through the zipper of a plastic bag, and the use of folded paper will simplify the subsequent examination under a low-powered microscope.

The placement of clothing and biological material in paper allows the item to breathe; placement in a plastic bag, on the other hand, may result in bacterial action and encourage the growth of mold. All items should be air dried prior to packaging in paper.

Extensively blood-stained or semen-stained items recovered from crime scenes should be first placed into paper and then protected by a plastic bag with the top left open to allow it to breath; however, the item must be removed from the packaging material on arrival at the forensic science laboratory and thoroughly air dried.

Items wet with volatile substances should be placed in nylon bags or new, clean, paint cans. Normal polyethylene bags are not suitable for the retention of volatiles.

Infested Material

In some instances, material recovered from crime scenes or mortuaries, which is to be returned to the forensic science laboratory or to be stored as property for long term, may be infested with pests, such as fleas, lice, maggots, or coffin beetles. Care must be taken when examining this material by wearing protective clothing, which includes overalls/laboratory coats, face mask, gloves, and protective eye wear. If possible, always use a large open search bench.

If insect infestation is present within the item, there are at least two methods available for killing them:

- Place the material and container in a large plastic bag and seal it. Place the bag into a deep freeze for approximately 3 h or until the insects are dead.
- Add a few drops of ethyl formate to the plastic bag containing the item and its container. Seal the bag and leave for approximately 1 h or until the insects are dead.

Where blood or semen stains are present, samples from stains must be collected prior to freezing. Consideration should also be given to entomological aspects of the case: both live and dead insect specimens may be required for examination.

Collection of Items

It is better to collect excess material than to have an examination fail because there is insufficient material for examination and/or analysis. Where difficulty may be encountered in collecting minute traces of substances, specialist collection techniques should be employed. If, however, traces of evidence are on small items and there is a chance of loss, the traces subsample should be recovered and placed into a separate package; if circumstances do not permit this, the entire item should be packaged and secured as soon as possible. If the trace is a stain, then the stain should remain on the item for assessment and examination in the forensic science laboratory. This is particularly relevant where the item as a whole is vitally relevant, for example, a blood-stained knife.

In many cases involving stained material, for example, fire debris, it is necessary to submit unstained material for analysis to determine if the material itself interferes with the analytical procedures.

In any comparison of the constituents of two substances, sufficient reference sample material should be provided. For example, if dust on clothing is suspected of being ballast from a particular money safe, a sufficient amount should be collected from the money safe itself, packaged, and submitted together with the items of clothing in order that a satisfactory comparison may be performed. The reference sample should be representative of the source from which the test sample originated. For example, it is useless attempting to compare a body hair found at the crime scene with a head hair from the suspect; like can only be compared with like. Similarly, the comparison of soil from a shoe with soil from the crime scene may be unsuccessful if the sources of the two samples are separated by only a few meters.

Labeling

- The purpose of a label is twofold: to identify the nature and source of the item and to establish a chain of custody.

Ideally, a label should have the following information recorded on it:

- Nature of contents
- Source (where found or from whom recovered)
- Date and time
- Signature and printed name of the collector (or person initiating the chain of custody)
- Sequential collection number
- Unique case identifying number

Additionally, room should be available on the label to record the movement of the item (from hand to hand—person's name and signature, date, and time).

The label should be completed at the time of collection or receipt of the item. If an item is collected from a person, use that person's name, for example, "Trousers from John Smith." Do not mark the item with the word "Suspect" as this wording on exhibit labels can lead and has led to the item being excluded from being tendered as an exhibit in a trial. Some courts are of the view that to mark items in this way is "unnecessary" and "objectionable" because whenever such an item is mentioned in evidence during the trial, the jury is being told that the accused has been a "suspect." This perhaps gives the impression that she/he was a suspect early in the investigation as well as indicating that the investigating officer and/or his delegate/s may have a fixed view or preconceived ideas regarding the status of the person answering the charges, which may be a view not held by all on the investigating team. The court may also wrongly hold the view that there may be more to know about the accused, which could be prejudicial, particularly in jurisdictions that still have the jury trail system. Obviously, the words "offender" and/or "perpetrator" should never be used as this is a presumption of guilt.

The sequential number used should relate to the collectors item list and could be JH1, JH2, JH3, and so on or items 1, 2, 3, and so on. When making a subsequent examination of the items collected, any material removed should be given a number that relates to the original item. For example, a pair of trousers is marked JH1 and hair is recovered from the trousers; this item should be marked JH1.1. Alternatively, if the trousers

are number 31 then the hair would be 31.1; if DNA is extracted from the hair then those derivatives would be 31.1.1, 31.1.2, and so on. In this way, each subsample can be easily traced back to the original source item.

If the item is something substantial, for example, a knife or clothing, then the item itself should be marked as well as the container. It may be appropriate to tie a label with a piece of string to the item. If this is done then there can be no doubt about later identifying the item in the witness box if it becomes separated from its container.

When using plastic pots or vials, ensure that there is a corresponding mark on both the lid and the container to avoid any mixing up of containers. The sequential number and unique case identifying number are normally used for this purpose.

Collection

The proper collection of items and trace material is essential in obtaining the greatest evidential value from an examination. Special clothing should be worn during all scene and laboratory examinations. Scene suites, white cotton overalls, or laboratory coats should always be worn as white cotton has the least evidential value as a fiber and is, therefore, suitable in preventing contamination of crime scenes or clothing with fibers from the examiner's clothing. Disposable protective clothing is preferable, as it protects the wearer as well as prevents contamination through reuse. There is also an occupational health and safety dimension to the use of appropriate clothing.

Collection Case

Collection cases must be kept clean, with equipment stored in an orderly manner. The principal collection items and their uses are listed in **Table 1**.

Collection Techniques

A variety of techniques have been developed for the collection of trace material and other potential evidential material. Each technique is designed to prevent damage to, and contamination of, the material. The main collection techniques can be described as:

- Handpicking
- Tapelifting
- Swabbing
- Sweeping
- Vacuuming

Handpicking

Whenever examining the crime scene, garments, bodies, or other articles, the initial emphasis should be directed toward the

Table 1   Principal items of collection equipment and their uses

Item	Collection use
Scalpel	Paint smears, visible fibers, vegetation, and dried blood
Probe	Paint, fibers, residues, oils, greases, manipulation of microscopic particles
Brush	Trace particles: paint, metals, vegetation, glass
Swab (dry)	Small particles, which will be caught in the coarse fibers of the swab
Paint brush	Sweeping localized and constricted areas
Spatula	Soil samples, whole- or party-congealed blood, mixing casting compound
Tweezers (metal)	Trace material, such as fibers, hair, and vegetation
Tweezers (plastic)	Items that may be damaged if metal tweezers are used; recovery of projectiles and fragments during postmortem examinations and for use when recovering blood stains using small pieces of moistened cotton. Each pair of tweezers are inexpensive; therefore, they can be destroyed after each use
Cotton	Linen moistened with distilled water for the recovery of dried blood stains
Magnet	Recovery of particles of iron and steel after covering the magnet with plastic

collection of gross and macroscopic items that can be recovered by hand or by the use of tweezers. Items large enough to see with the naked eye should be collected by handpicking. Material such as hairs, large paint and glass fragments, and pieces of vegetation should be collected before the application of other collection techniques, such as tapelifting, sweeping, and vacuuming.

Handpicking has the advantage of establishing the position of the material on the item and requires no further time in searching, whereas tapelifts, sweepings, and vacuuming have to be further searched to isolate small particulate matter of interest.

When collecting items by hand, disposable gloves should be worn and changed whenever there is chance of contamination between items or locations. Various types of tweezers are available to cope with small particulate matter and a moistened fine brush will recover paint particles. It is essential that each item of collection equipment is cleaned between individual collections.

Tapelifting

Tapelifting is a reliable method for collecting trace microscopic material from a variety of surfaces, in particular, garments and motor vehicle seats. Transparent adhesive tape no more than 7.5 cm in length is applied to the surface of the object. At the completion of the application, the tape is placed over a clean piece of glass or rigid plastic and then placed into a clean labeled plastic bag. Garments and other larger objects should be examined in segments, for example, the front and rear of a shirt as two discrete areas. The tape should only be used while the adhesive qualities remain.

Too much material should not be placed on one tape. The collection of material in this manner facilitates the examination of trace material using a microscope and, in particular, assists in sorting material of interest from a myriad of other insignificant material. When using adhesive tape from a dispenser, the first 5 cm should be discarded to prevent contamination. The method of tapelifting is used more widely in the forensic science laboratory, although it does have its uses in the field, for example, when processing the interior of automobiles.

Sweeping

This method is particularly useful in collecting material from a variety of areas, including inaccessible sites or those where there is a mass of material. Sweeping is also a useful collection technique for the examination of motor vehicles where large amounts of debris can be present on vehicle floor surfaces or in boots.

It is essential that the brush is clean and that separate brushes are used whenever contamination or cross-transfer is a consideration, for example, examining a scene and a suspect's vehicle. New paint brushes approximately 25-mm wide with nonpainted handles, along with new pans from dustpan and broom sets, should be used on each occasion where sweeping is employed.

Vacuuming

The collection of microscopic material, from garments, motor vehicles, and other large objects, by vacuuming is another means of collecting trace material. However, the circumstances in which it should be employed need to be considered carefully, as the vacuuming collected is difficult to handle, involving the expenditure of a great deal of time in searching them in the laboratory. Vacuuming can be too effective, in that it can lead to the collection of a great deal of "ancient history."

This method requires a specialized nozzle for the vacuum cleaner. Nozzles are made from plastic where you can place a filter paper to trap and retain material vacuumed from items. In earlier years, nozzles were custom made from stainless steel and connected to heavy duty vacuum cleaners. **Figure 1** depicts two portable vacuum cleaners that are suitable for crime scene and forensic science laboratory vacuuming.

Material is collected by suction on to a clean filter paper that is placed inside the trap. Traps must be cleaned before use, between vacuuming separate items or particular localized areas on an object, vehicle, or scene. The complete nozzle should be washed in warm soapy water, rinsed with clean water, and dried. Bottle brushes are ideal for cleaning nozzle pipes and the trap itself. When in the field that is away from the ability to clean the nozzle, it must be brushed clean between each use, run without filter paper, and then run a "blank" with filter paper to ensure that the trap and its nozzle are clean.

A blank/control vacuuming should be run before each sampling run, using a clean filter paper in place inside the trap.

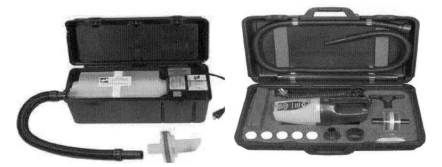

Figure 1   Two examples of portable vacuum cleaners for trace evidence retrieval. "3M" Trace Evidence Vacuum, "Sirchie" Trace Evidence Vacuum.

This is then removed and bagged separately for later examination. Each sample run must also have a clean piece of filter paper. Once set up and ready for a sample run, the nozzle is applied to the surface, for example, with a garment with a series of strokes. Each area of the garment will be a discrete searching area in its own right, for example, pockets, back, and front of the garment. When not in use, the nozzle/trap should be thoroughly cleaned and stored in a sealed plastic bag.

Preservation

Items must be preserved, so that they remain, as far as possible, in their original state and may be produced in court in the condition in which they were found. In some cases, it is not possible to retain the exhibit intact, for example, in analytical procedures, the items may have to be altered or it may be totally consumed in the procedure.

The crime scene investigator should take all necessary steps to protect items collected from the following problems:

Loss: Small items such as hairs, fibers, and paint flakes may be lost from packages that are not properly sealed. Envelopes on their own are unsuitable for small samples as the particulate matter may be lost through corners of the envelope. Volatile liquids from fire scene may evaporate from the containers that are not airtight and impermeable.

Deterioration or damage: Biological material such as blood or seminal stains may deteriorate rapidly. Valuable shoe impressions and blood stains in outdoor scenes must be protected and/or collected before wind and rain may destroy them.

Contamination: Items that are not properly packaged may become contaminated by the introduction of foreign matter into the packaging.

Tampering: Items should be packaged and sealed securely and should not be left unattended at crime scenes. The crime scene investigator should guard against innocent tampering as well as that intended to destroy potential evidence, for example, a firearm left unattended with a fired cartridge case in the breech may arrive at the forensic science laboratory with several impressions on the firing pin if the firearm is not packaged appropriately and secured.

Sealing Containers

The sealing of containers is necessary to keep items from being lost, contaminated, or tampered with. The container should be sealed with sealing tape and then with evidence tape. The evidence tape should be signed by the crime scene investigator/collector.

Chain of Custody

The chain of custody refers to the documentation of possession of items from their recovery collection through examinations to their tendering in court as potential items of evidence. This allows interested parties to trace who has had custody of the item at a given time, as well as being able to account for where the item has been while it has been in an individual's or organization's custody.

Proximal containers and, if applicable, items should be labeled with a movement record of the container/item, and the case file and/or the exhibit movement log should also record the movement of the item.

Hazard Labeling

It will be necessary to mark containers with appropriate hazard labels. Those that contain items that are stained with body fluids should be marked with a biological hazard label, and those that contain items that have been treated with chemicals to enhance fingerprints should be marked with a chemical hazard label. This should go some way in encouraging court staff to resist the temptation to open all packages and dispense with containers before the item is tendered as an exhibit in court.

Summary

This chapter has discussed packaging material and how to deal with infested material, along with the techniques employed and the sequence of collecting items.

Chain of custody has also been discussed, as has the use of appropriate labeling and sealing. Appendix 1 outlines the collection of specific items normally encountered in crime scene investigation, pointing out the most appropriate packaging and collection technique and the significance of each specific item.

Appendix 1 Collection and Packaging

The following is offered as a guide to the collection and packaging of commonly encountered items of physical evidence.

Ammunition

This includes projectiles, live and expended cartridges, shot, and wads.

1. Undamaged material can be wrapped with tissue paper and placed into a rigid plastic container. In the case of distorted projectile fragments, place in a small plastic bag and place each item in separate plastic or cardboard container/s. Never mark ammunition—label the proximal container instead.
2. Wash projectiles and air dry if removed from a deceased person during an autopsy before packaging.

Packaging: Placed the item into a plastic bag and then place into a rigid plastic container. Do not use cotton wool or tissue paper for fragmented and distorted projectiles.
Significance: Determine type of ammunition and its origin.

Bite Marks

On Skin

1. Photograph using a digital camera using Polilight® to provide a variety of wavelengths to obtain best contrast.
2. Wipe area around bite mark with a sterile dry swab or piece of cotton and then place in container and label.
3. Cast mark if possible.

Packaging: Place swab and cast in separate small rigid plastic containers.
Significance: In consultation with an odontologist, comparison of the bite mark may be made with any suspect's teeth and possible DNA analysis.

On Perishable Items

1. Photograph in the studio to get the best result.
2. Cast mark.

Packaging: Place cast into rigid plastic container.
Significance: In consultation with an odontologist, comparison of the bite mark may be made with any suspect's teeth and possible DNA analysis.

Suspect

1. Photograph teeth recording all teeth from a variety of positions.
2. Obtain a saliva sample using sterile cotton gauze, air dry, and package.
3. Cast teeth of suspect. Casts are taken and usually remain with the odontologist.

Packaging: Place 2 once air died into a small rigid plastic container. Place 3 into a small cardboard box.
Significance: 1 and 3 are for use by the consulting odontologist for comparison work with bite marks and suspect's teeth; 2 for DNA analysis.

Blood

On Absorbent Material

1. Cut material, air dry, and package separately.
2. Cut out a control sample.

Packaging: Large blood-stained items should be packaged in paper; small samples that have been dried should be placed in rigid plastic containers or wrapped in A4 paper, folded, and placed in paper envelopes.
Significance: DNA analysis. Comparison with reference samples.

On Nonabsorbent Material

Wet: For large volumes of liquid blood, suck up with a spoon or disposable pipette and package in a small glass container. For smaller stains, rub a piece of cotton through the stain, air dry, and package in a small rigid plastic container.
Dry: For large volumes, use a scalpel blade to scrape dried "peeling" into a small rigid plastic container. For small volumes, rub a piece of previously moistened (with distilled water) cotton through the stain and transfer the stain onto the cotton. Air dry and package in a rigid plastic container.
Packaging: Plastic and glass phials.
Significance: DNA analysis. Comparison with reference samples.

Whole Blood

1. Obtained by a doctor or nursing staff. Consideration may have to be given to relevant local Acts and Regulations when taking intimate body samples. Three samples are required.
2. One straight without any additional material.
3. One with anticoagulant.
4. One with preservative.

Packaging: One sample is placed in a pink top-seeded small rigid plastic container with EDTA, one sample placed in a brown top-seeded small rigid plastic container with sodium oxalate; one sample in a plain small rigid plastic container.

Significance: Blood alcohol determination of contents of brown-topped plastic container. DNA analysis with the remainder and then comparison of results with crime scene stains.

Bloodstain Pattern Interpretation

1. Photograph the entire scene using digital photography.
2. Take overview photographs of stains at 90° from each stain section.
3. Take close-up views including a measuring tape.
4. Take blood samples from different types of stain as stains may have a different origin.

Packaging: As mentioned above.
Significance: Aid in the reconstruction of events and using DNA analysis may assist in identifying the donor of the blood stains.

Cigarette Butts

1. Collect with plastic tweezers, air dry if wet, and package.

Packaging: Place each butt in separate rigid plastic containers or glass phials.
Significance: Identify cigarettes. Is there more than one person smoking? DNA analysis on residue saliva, examine for fingerprints and lipstick.

Clothing

1. Photograph, note, and describe.
2. Remove any obvious trace material and package separately.
3. Remove clothing from suspects over clean white paper, air dry wet clothing, and package separately.

Packaging: Place each item separately in a paper bag.
Significance: Search for any trace material for comparison with any reference material. DNA analysis on different blood stains to identify suspects and proof of contact.

Documents

1. Wearing white cotton gloves, collect with tweezers, and package separately.

Packaging: Place in a prelabeled plastic document sheet or envelope already containing a piece of cardboard.
Significance: Indented writing, obliterations or additions, signature verification, ink comparison and analysis, photocopier identification, and original/overtyped letters or as material for comparison in handwriting analysis in an attempt to identify the writer.

Fibers

1. Collect fibers with tweezers or submit the whole item containing fibers.
2. Using the tapelifting collection technique, tape the area of interest using clear transparent adhesive tape and place tape, adhesive side down, on a clear plastic sheet.

Packaging: Small plastic phial for loose fibers and plastic bags for plastic sheets.
Significance: Identify possible source. Comparison with other known fibers in fiber transfer issues in crimes of violence.

Fire Debris

1. Collect debris from suspect point or points of fire origin. Collect charcoal or burnt wood as this material absorbs minute traces of ignitable liquid residues.

Packaging: Clean new paint cans, nylon bags, or polyvinylidene chloride bags. When using bags, be careful of sharp debris, which may penetrate the bag.
Significance: Determine the presence or absence and type of ignitable liquid residues.

Firearms Discharge Residue

On Hands

1. Photograph and visible evidence.
2. Photograph using various wavelengths using Polilight®.
3. Collect from the web of the hand using prepared adhesive SEM stubs.
4. Take control samples from other skin area where Firearm Discharge Residue (FDR) has not been deposited.

Packaging: Use a commercially or laboratory-fabricated SEM FDR collection kit.
Significance: Determine if a firearm has been discharged by the person being tested.

On Clothing

1. Photograph visible evidence.
2. Photograph using various wavelengths with Polilight®.
3. Package.

Packaging: Paper bags.
Significance: Determine if a firearm has been discharged by the person who was suspected of wearing the clothing.

Projectile Hole in Clothing

1. Photograph visible evidence, location photograph, close-up photograph with tape measure.

2. Protect the projectile by pinning paper over it.
3. Place cardboard behind area to prevent bending.
4. Do not bend clothing at the projectile hole if it can be avoided.
5. Package.
6. During laboratory examinations, photograph using various wavelengths with Polilight®.

Packaging: Paper bags.

Significance: Determine distance from target. Analysis of residue at projectile hole may reveal the identity of the projectile and, therefore, the ammunition.

Projectile Hole in Dead Skin

1. Photograph visible evidence, location photograph, close-up photograph with tape measure.
2. Cut beyond the blackened area, surrounding the bullet hole and identify the "12 o'clock position" with a suture.
3. While fresh, conduct laboratory examination on the projectile hole.
4. Photograph visible evidence, location photograph, close-up photograph with tape measure.
5. During laboratory examinations, photograph using various wavelengths with Polilight®.
6. Swab around hole, dry, and place in rigid plastic container for SEM EDX analysis.

Packaging: Rigid plastic container when fresh. After laboratory examination, place in a small glass jar with 10% formalin.

Significance: Firing distance and angle of entry and identification of ammunition by chemical analysis.

Glass

At the scene in general area,

1. Photograph both sides of glass before removing it from the frame.
2. Collect fragile fragments first.
3. Wrap each separately to protect edges.
4. Place fragments in a suitable rigid plastic container or cardboard.
5. Collect all pieces if possible.

Packaging: For small fragments, for analysis, use a rigid plastic phial. For larger pieces (direction of breaking and mechanical fit examinations), use cardboard boxes—self-made or commercially available.

Significance: Small pieces as control or reference samples for refractive index measurements; identification of source by mechanical fit examinations and direction of force by examining hackle marks on edge of broken pieces of window.

On Clothing

1. Collect fragile fragments first.
2. Collect clothing and package separately.

Packaging: Plastic phials, larger plastic containers, and cardboard boxes.

Significance: Identify possible source by physical and/or chemical analysis; identify possible source by mechanical fit; and identify direction of force by examining the glass edges.

Hairs

On Moveable Objects

1. Collect and protect the complete item.
2. If there is a need to collect before moving and packaging the garment, then collect.

On Fixed Objects

1. Using a pair of plastic tweezers, collect hairs and package.

Suspect's Head Hair

In cases where during the offense (e.g., armed robbery and rape), a balaclava or other covering has been worn over the head or in breaking case where the suspect could have been in close proximity to breaking glass then a sample of what may be in the hair should be taken. This is undertaken using a moistened seeded comb. The comb is seeded with white cotton wool, moistened with distilled water, and then the head of the suspect is combed. This must be done quickly after the offense has been committed as any foreign material in the hair maybe lost in time. This is not intimate and may be done with the consent of the suspect or in some jurisdictions, a senior police officer.

In rape cases, a seeded combing should also be done where the suspect has come to notice quickly. Both the head and the pubic hair regions should be combed.

Control Samples

Head: Pluck 30–40 hairs from various areas.
Pubic: Pluck 20–30 hairs.
Others: Pluck 10–20 hairs.
Packaging: Folded white paper inserted into an envelope or plastic bag.
Significance: Human or animal; determine color, sex, and race of person; identification of areas of the body the hair originated from; was the hair pulled or shed; and mitochondrial DNA to identify the person who shed the hair.

Insects: Flies

There are four stages in the life cycle of flies: eggs, maggots, pupae, and adults (flies). Collect across the life cycle.

1. Collect 60–80 individuals from each position, on, under, and approximately 90–150 cm from the decomposing body.
2. Collect from hidden areas, beneath leaves, and floorboards.

Note: Pupae may be found in the form of brown capsules under the body or in the soil under the body.

Packaging: Glass container. Place specimens in 70% V/V ethyl alcohol of 10% formalin in distilled water. Place an equal amount of specimens in a plastic phial and freeze. Place an equal amount of specimens in a plastic container with some flesh.

Significance: Estimation of time of death.

Maggots

Packaging: Glass container. Place specimens in 70% V/V ethyl alcohol of 10% formalin in distilled water. Place an equal amount of specimens in a plastic phial and freeze. Place an equal amount of specimens in a plastic container with some flesh.

Significance: Estimation of time of death.

Submit all to the entomologist urgently for examination and identification.

Paint

On Tools or Vehicles

1. If possible collect the item (tool or vehicle) containing the evidence.
2. Collect paint chips separately.
3. Care should be taken not to fragment paint chips.
4. Take reference samples of each color, ensuring that they are scraped down to the base color.

Packaging: Folded white paper inserted into an envelope or a plastic bag or rigid plastic container.

Significance: Determine possible source: color, model, and type of vehicle. Identify the vehicle when it comes to notice.

On Clothing

1. Collect fragile evidence first.
2. Collect clothing and package individually.

Packaging: Folded paper inserted into an envelope or plastic bag followed by its insertion into a rigid plastic container.

Significance: Determine possible source: color, model, and type of vehicle. Identify the vehicle when it comes to notice.

Postmortem Samples

Alcohol

1. Obtain 10 ml clean arterial blood.
2. Obtain 10 ml bladder urine.
3. Obtain 10 ml vitreous humor.

Packaging: Plastic tube seeded with a preservative (oxalate or fluoride).

Significance: Indicates state of intoxication at the time of death.

Blood for DNA and/or Serology

1. Obtain 10 ml of clean arterial blood for each phial.
2. Place one 10 ml lot in a plain plastic phial.
3. Please a second 10 ml lot in a seeded plastic tube containing EDTA.

Packaging: Plain phials and EDTA-seeded phials.

Significance: Reference sample for DNA analysis and any other serology requirements for comparison with scene and other unknown stains on suspect or in those found in the suspect's environment.

Drugs

1. Obtain 10 ml clean arterial blood.
2. Obtain 10 ml bladder urine.

Packaging: Plain glass phials without anticoagulant or preservative.

Significance: Indicates if the decadent was under the influence of drugs at the time of death, a chronic drug user, and met his/her death through drug overuse.

Toxicology

1. Obtain 10 ml clean arterial blood.
2. Obtain a 100 g portion of liver.
3. Obtain all the stomach contents.
4. Obtain 10 ml vitreous humor.

Packaging: Glass containers of various sizes.

Significance: Identify the presence of any poison present in the body of the deceased.

Diatoms

1. Obtain a portion of the femur bone.

Packaging: Glass container containing absolute alcohol.

Significance: To establish location of suspected drowning, in salt water or fresh water.

Safe Insulation and Safe Surface Paint

From Suspect's Clothing and/or Environment

1. Collect clothing and package separately.
2. Tapelift and/or vacuum items from suspect's environment.

Packaging: Paper bags for clothing. Plastic bags for vacuum residues and tapelift plastic sheets.

Significance: Comparison of any safe ballast and/or paint found on clothing or in the suspect's environment with a reference sample of safe insulation.

From Safe

1. Collect reference samples of paint and safe insulation from the safe at the burglary site.

Packaging: Small rigid plastic container for safe material and small plastic bags for paint.

Significance: For comparison with any trace material found on the suspect or in his/her environment and, therefore, linking the suspect with the scene.

Saliva

Collect saliva, ensuring that it is saliva and not mucus, on clean white gauze or using a DNA database collection kit.

Air dry and package.

Packaging: Rigid plastic container or DNA database collection kit (jurisdictional specific).

Significance: DNA analysis.

Seminal Stains

Photograph stains for location and distribution.

Photograph using various wavelengths using Polilight®.

Collect items exhibiting stains wearing gloves.

Air dry and package.

Packaging: Paper bags.

Significance: Identification of donor by DNA analysis.

Soil from Scene and Suspect's Clothing and/or Environment

Collect sample from suspect vehicle or footwear.

Collect clothing from suspect.

Collect several 50-g samples from the scene and surrounding area as reference samples.

Packaging: Rigid plastic containers for the soil samples and paper bags for the clothing.

Significance: Geographical origin of samples and a possible link between suspect and scene.

Tools

Photograph where located.

Protect working ends.

Packaging: Plastic bags.

Significance: Location of paint on cutting edge that may match paint at the scene and to link the tool to a particular toolmark.

Toolmark(s)

Photograph (overview, midrange, and close-up with scale).

Make a cast.

Take paint sample if the area is painted.

Recover complete item for further examination if possible.

Packaging: Rigid plastic container or plastic bag. Plain white paper in envelope for paint sample/s.

Significance: Link toolmark to a particular tool.

Vegetation

Photograph various types of vegetation.

Collect samples consisting of complete plants and roots.

Packaging: Paper bags with cardboard stiffening to prevent damage to items.

Significance: Identify species and growth patterns and compare with trace material found on suspect or in his/her environment.

Wires

Photograph site and location of wire.

Protect ends of wire.

Label ends cut on site.

Packaging: Plastic bags.

Significance: Identify tool type and compare with tools submitted for examination for a possible identification of the tool.

Notes

Potential evidence should be recovered and submitted to the forensic science laboratory as soon as possible, and the examination of individual items at the scene should be kept to minimum. *Do not do at the scene what can be done in the laboratory*!

The above are *general* guidelines. Different jurisdictions may advocate some variation on these procedures based on their own SOPs within their relevant quality systems and also in accordance local legislation.

See also: **Investigations:** Collection and Chain of Evidence; Contamination; Preservation.

Further Reading

Fisher, B.A.J., 2000. Techniques of Crime Scene Investigation, sixth ed. CRC Press, Boca Raton, FL.

Horswell, J. (Ed.), 2004. The Practice of Crime Scene Investigation. CRC Press, Boca Raton, FL.

Houck, M.M., Siegel, J.A., 2010. Fundamentals of Forensic Science, second ed. Elsevier, Amsterdam.

Kim, W. (Ed.), 2007. Handbook of Forensic Services. Federal Bureau of Investigation Laboratory Division, Quantico, VA.

Lee Henry, C., Palmbach Timothy, M., Miller, M.T., 2001. Henry Lee's Crime Scene Handbook. Academic Press, London.

Saferstein, R., 2001. Criminalistics: An Introduction to Forensic Science, seventh ed. Prentice-Hall, Upper Saddle River, NJ.

White, P.C., 2010. Crime Scene to Court the Essentials of Forensic Science, third ed. Royal Society of Chemistry, Cambridge.

Preservation

F Crispino, Université du Québec à Trois-Rivières, Trois-Rivières, QC, Canada

Forensic evidence, which typically begins as a trace, defined as a vestige of a past action or presence, is generally fragile and can be composed of a variety of materials. Evidence is best understood as a specimen instead of as a sample, as the materials that become evidence can hardly be seen as a random representative sample from a so-called population limited to the crime under study. The value of evidence as proof at trial depends on a complex set of inferences, one of which is admissibility. Admissibility requires two things: the trace should be legally accepted as evidence, and the evidence should be analytically reliable. Both these things depend greatly on proper preservation of the evidence.

Preservation: A Time Frame Process

Preservation addresses the need to limit or, when possible, eliminate potential alteration, decay, or destruction of evidence. Hence, it covers two domains: crime scene management and evidence management. Proper crime scene management requires securement, protection, and documentation of the scene, and proper evidence management requires adoption of correct sampling and storing processes. Engaging in both these activities will provide the conditions necessary to protect evidence, as well as documentation of the preservation of the evidence to both the analytical and judicial chains of custody. This, in turn, will help prove the evidence's admissibility in court.

This chapter focuses primarily on how the crime scene environment can endanger crime scene management in the first few minutes after the crime has been committed, how to document the scene, and how to identify, and thus provide countermeasures to, conditions that may jeopardize the collected evidence. Taking chronological notes (preparing crime scene and evidence logs) is a safe activity throughout the process. This critical task could be accomplished by a dedicated officer, whose activity could be supplemented by a voice recorder used to register all the crime scene examiners' remarks. Written records should be produced immediately after the end of the crime scene management.

Preservation of the Crime Scene

Locard said that as time elapses, truth evades us. Indeed, as soon as a crime is committed, the crime scene is already modified through the action of the perpetrator, the reaction of the victim, the legitimate intervention of a number of persons (such as witnesses, SWAT officers, medical personnel, patrol officers, and detectives), or natural conditions (such as weather conditions, rain, snow, wind, heat, and cold; and the effects of time, temperature loss, evaporation, microtrace release, etc.).

Recording the scene with film and video on arrival, registering any person who enters or exits the scene, and making notes of first responders' observations could build a foundation of relevant data that can be used to make sense of traces discovered later, or of traces that are modified. This record may also provide relevant information for the case at hand. For instance, noticing the colors and smell of flames in the case of an arson attack can provide relevant information to investigators and crime scene examiners regarding evidence preservation inside the crime scene.

As traces and evidence are fragile and subject to alteration and destruction, patrol officers should use the abovementioned procedures to immediately "cast a protective net on," or "freeze," the immediate scene of the crime. This can be later reassessed by the crime scene examiner. Access to this area should be forbidden, and any person (or cars) on site or around should be identified, including SWAT and rescue team members. As this task is generally performed by patrol officers, the crime scene examiner should verify that it has been completed correctly.

On arrival at the scene, the crime scene examiner should identify himself or herself to all persons on the scene and create a personnel log to record their identifying information. This will allow investigators to obtain relevant information—such as shoeprints, fingerprints, and DNA swabs—from the policemen, firemen, witnesses, etc., who were present at the crime scene. During evidence search and collection, this personnel log will allow the immediate exclusion of traces made by legitimate personnel (such as the bloody imprint of a paramedic's shoe). These personnel logs should contain the names of patrol officers, first responders, firemen, paramedics, the coroner, detectives, the attorney in charge, witnesses—anyone who was in the crime scene before or during its processing. Obtaining DNA swabs, fingerprints, shoeprints, or other comparison materials from these persons could be done later, although photographs of these persons should be taken at the crime scene to create a record of the clothing or shoes they were wearing at the scene.

Crime scene examiners should consult first responders, who can generally provide an understanding of the nature of the site (public, private, commercial; type of activity; size; access points; etc.), to better assess the dimension of the crime scene. This knowledge is necessary to determine the dimension of the area to be preserved. If the crime scene examiner finds that too much or too little area has been protected by the patrol officers, he or she must make immediate corrections to enlarge or decrease the dimensions of the crime scene. Speaking to first responders will also allow crime scene officers to better understand the actions taken by the first responders (the rooms they visited, the objects they touched, and what medical assistance was rendered, etc.), so that they may better appraise the relevant areas and search more efficiently for evidence. As far as possible, pathways used by first responders should be identified and new pathways created, if necessary, to avoid further contamination of the scene. Barrier tapes or barricades should be positioned to denote these pathways and protect the scene.

Once this primary area of interest has been identified and before its management commences, roads and tracks leading to it should be secured to determine the second area of interest, where partial "freezes" and evidence searches need to be conducted in the same way. As the scene of crime grows, additional officers may be required to secure the perimeter of each of the separate areas that are beyond the scene. Once these additional areas of the crime scene have been identified, all persons—including onlookers, patrol officers, and first responders—should be removed from those areas. The only persons on the crime scene should now be the few crime scene examiners who are authorized to work on the crime scene, and they should be wearing full protective suits.

Preservation of Evidence

Temporary evidence—such as shoeprints in snow, blood on concrete on a sunny day, impressions in mud in the rain, or even the temperature of water in which a cadaver lies—should be secured before any other evidence is collected or preserved. Securing this evidence may be done by any available means, including but not limited to covering and protecting the site, taking photographs or notes, or measuring the temperature. Although the patrol officers who arrive at the scene often conduct these tasks, it is the responsibility of the crime scene examiner to ensure that all evidence has been properly secured. The crime scene personnel can then begin the physical and chemical collection of evidence following known, standardized—if not accredited—processes.

Collection of evidence at the crime scene should anticipate the need for the preservation of evidence through the use of procedures reducing its alteration. These include visualization with the naked eye, use of a forensic light source, and, occasionally, chemical or physical processing; all these methods should be documented with photographs taken at each stage of the process as well as written accounts of the procedure. Appropriate packaging should be used to prevent damage to the evidence, be it the item itself or traces on the item (such as to-be-developed fingermarks and biological materials). Evidence collection procedures should also be designed to protect the health and safety of the examiner and experts, who may come across hazardous material, including contaminated material and sharps, while processing the crime scene.

To ensure that the proper packing materials are available at the crime scene, the crime scene examiner should assess beforehand not only the items that may need to be analyzed but also the environment that the packaged evidence will be in. Biological evidence (such as blood, semen, DNA, and plant materials) should be allowed to breathe by being stored in packaging that will inhibit putrefaction. These materials should not be stored in packing that might, on the article's movement, wipe off latent traces. Paper envelopes are an excellent container for storage of biological evidence; brown paper bags are better for wet—let them dry, if possible—and soiled clothes. Chemically active products (such as illicit drugs or accelerants) should be stored in airtight containers, such as nylon 6 × 6 bags or hermetic paint cans.

When collecting evidence from cadavers, tapings from exposed skin and clothing can be done with low-impact fingerprint tape, or even Scotch tape, to secure traces before moving the body. Each tape lift is then pressed down upon a clear, appropriately labeled acetate sheet. Cotton swabs moistened with distilled water should be gently passed over any visible stain or bruise on the body. Hands and feet should be sealed in paper bags.

Further evidence collection can be undertaken after body removal, such as pupae or maggot sampling. Half of them will be dipped in a 50% alcoholic solution, the other half packed in a holey box with a few nutrients, and all of it sent immediately to the entomological lab.

Evidence should also be transported in a manner that secures it. Biological or putrescent evidence should be moved in a temperature-controlled (4 °C) container or vehicle. Underwater evidence is best transported in a container filled with the water in which it was found in order to avoid further destruction (such as physical dismantling) or rusting in the outside air.

Judicial requirements for admissibility of evidence can be satisfied by sealing evidence containers with tamper-evident tape and identifying the person who packed it (with the packer's signature, initials, or right thumb fingerprint on the tape).

Threats to Evidence

An additional approach to preserving evidence is to analyze the risks to the evidence from its detection to its final storage—such as physical damage, deterioration, contamination, infection, decomposition, loss, and tampering—then propose solutions to preserve it.

Physical Damage

Physical damage is mainly due to human mishandling and can be easily countered with the following measures:

- Clearly indicating both the pathway to be used to enter and move within the crime scene and the locations of evidence with flags, marks, protective covers, etc. Evidence locations should be marked as soon as the evidence is discovered.
- Protecting any detected trace and stain, particularly if such traces are situated outdoors. Wind, rain, and sometimes sun can damage trace integrity.
- Transporting evidence in a way that prevents breaking and avoids the effects of friction. This can be done by adapting the container to the shape of the item and fixing the item (e.g., with plastic binders) to avoid movement.

Deterioration

Biological materials are very fragile in a hot, wet atmosphere. Chemical materials can also lose some of their properties under these conditions and may also pollute the environment if the seal on their packaging is not airtight. Hastening the collection and submission process is helpful when securing these kinds of traces.

A questioned document or comparison document should never be marked, defaced, or altered. Documents should never be folded, except along their original folds. Documents should not be exposed to sticky materials.

Underwater evidence should be submitted to the laboratory immersed in the water in which it was found. The container in which the water and evidence are shipped should be sealed and sent to the laboratory, where stabilization processes (such as barometric depression, osmosis equilibrium) will be carried out before the evidence is retrieved.

Contamination

Contamination of evidence begins immediately after its deposit. Crime scene examiners reduce the risk of contaminating evidence while collecting it by following protective measures on the crime scene, such as wearing white coats and using other protective equipment such as gloves, masks, and goggles. The more latent, microscopic, and invisible the trace is, the greater the risk of contamination. The more sensitive the analysis to come—that is, the smaller the trace input—the greater the care and precautions that must be taken. Interpretation of the evidence should take contamination into account.

Unfortunately, the proper collection, packaging, and sealing of evidence cannot completely prevent contamination: properly handled evidence can be contaminated by improperly handled evidence stored on nearby shelves at the evidence depository or laboratory. Hence, the log officer should also assess the vicinity where the evidence and comparison materials under his or her responsibility will be stored, plan different vehicles to transport evidence and any suspected person, and take measures to prevent a suspect from polluting the crime scene (or polluting himself or herself with diffused traces of the crime scene). This can be done by requiring identified suspects to wear the white protective coats worn by crime scene examiners. This should be done as soon as the suspect is identified. Should there be a need for a suspect to enter the crime scene, he or she must wear the protective clothing worn by the crime scene examiners.

Infection

Biological materials collected from the crime scene can be infected by insects, fungi, parasites, etc. Crime scene examiners should take measures to protect themselves when handling these pieces of evidence (such as wearing protective clothing) and to limit the damage that could be caused by these infectious agents. Materials used to collect biological exhibits should be washed once a month with bleach.

Apart from the sampling for entomological purpose (see *supra*), insects can be killed after the evidence has been collected through two techniques: either through a deep freeze of the material or by placing several drops of ethyl formate inside a sealed, airtight container with the material until all the insects have died. Use of the freezing technique would require prior collections of biological stains (blood, semen, saliva, etc.). Removing other infestations requires specialized knowledge. Fully infested clothing may need to be examined as quickly as possible (without ending the infestation) and then discarded.

Decomposition

Biological material can decompose in heat. This process is hastened in wet conditions, as bacterial action supports the growth of mold, and when biological materials are stored in plastic containers. Hence, such evidence should be air dried before being packaged, preferably in paper wraps or envelopes.

Refrigeration at 4 °C (but not freezing) is required for the preservation of biological evidence. In France, -18 °C freezers are used for long-term preservation of unidentified stains and comparison swabs of jailed suspects.

Charred documents should be protected from decomposition by placing them on top of loose cotton in a dedicated cardboard container. Care should be taken during their transportation.

Loss

The small size of many pieces of evidence must be taken into account when choosing their containers. Small items—such as hairs, fibers, paint chips, soils, pollen, and pupae—can be easily lost through the corners of envelopes, which typically are not sealed. Similarly, vapors can leak out of non-airtight containers.

Tampering

As soon as evidence is collected, it is the responsibility of the crime scene officer to safeguard its integrity against unintentional or purposeful tampering. Until the evidence is sealed in appropriate containers, items of evidence should be clearly marked and not left unattended. An officer can be assigned to guard the evidence at the scene of the crime if many days will be needed to manage it.

Once collected and sealed, evidence can generally be examined by experts working on behalf of both the prosecution and defense throughout the investigation and trial. Such counterexpertise is possible because forensic analyses are generally nondestructive. Destruction of evidence, or modification of its integrity, should be noted, and the appropriate judicial authorities should be notified.

Only two techniques can preserve evidence during transportation from the crime scene to the laboratory and beyond: packaging and labeling.

Packaging

As noted previously, paper is the primary method used to package solid and physical evidence, including dried stain swabs, single traces, powders, macroscopic objects (such as firearms and tools), and inorganic exhibits. Paper containers come in many forms, such as envelopes, bags, and cardboard boxes, and in many sizes. In the case that evidence does not fit into or would be harmed by preexisting containers (such as through friction), crime scene examiners may be required to fashion relevant containers out of available paper materials.

All supports that contain traces (marks, stains, etc.) should be specifically protected, for example, by wrapping them in paper. For instance, the barrel of a gun should be covered with paper and that paper fixed in place with tape or a rubber band to prevent the loss of organic residue (polycyclic aromatic hydrocarbons) in the barrel, which would indicate whether the weapon had been recently used.

Paper containers will allow damp fabrics and biological material to dry and breathe, decreasing the risk of deterioration and decomposition. Air drying of such evidence is recommended prior to packaging. If the evidence and support are too wet to package in paper and air drying is impossible prior to leaving the scene, a plastic bag, pot, or bucket can be used temporarily to transport the exhibit to a safe place (such as the

laboratory) where it can be dried. Exhibits that release vapors should never be placed in paper containers. In order to preserve the vapors for analysis, these exhibits (which include low-carbonate compounds, such as solvents that are found in paints, explosives, and accelerants) should be packaged in sealed nylon bags or new paint cans.

A folded piece of paper can be used to collect scraped or tweezered microtraces such as paint chips, fibers, hairs, pieces of glass, and soil. Once the paper is folded in such a way that the collected item cannot escape, the paper should be stored inside a sealed envelope. This manner of collection will make it easier to examine the collected item in the laboratory under a macro- or microscope.

Regardless of the type of container used to collect evidence, the seal on the container must ensure that the evidence cannot be lost, contaminated, or tampered with. Seals may be made of sealing tape and covered by evidence tape to mark the judicial nature of the container. In France, wax seals bearing the police service stamp prevent tampering and clearly mark that the material is under judicial control.

Labeling

Proper labeling of evidence is vital to evidence management and to preserving the chain of custody. The label for each exhibit should be prepared prior to the collection of the trace. The label should include designated space to be used later to track the chain of custody during forensic analysis, when the evidence may be handled by personnel at several law enforcement agencies, storage facilities, and forensic laboratories. The crime scene examiner should also be aware of the judicial requirement attached to such labeling, to avoid prejudicial judgment and possible rejection of evidence at trial. When labeling pots, cans, bottles, and vials, both the lid and the container should be labeled to prevent inadvertent mixing of caps and containers, which increases the risk of contamination. Relevant information that should be included on each label includes the following.

- the nature and place of discovery of the exhibit;
- the identity of the collector;
- the hazards (if any, such as chemical, biological) posed by the evidence, which can be marked with standardized hazard stickers applied to the containers and lids;
- the date and time of collection;
- the case the evidence relates to; and
- the exhibit's serial number.

The purpose of the serial number is to uniquely identify each piece of evidence. The serial numbers are recorded in the crime scene examiner's log book. For example, items of evidence, such as a jacket and weapon that had been identified as belonging to Frank Crispino, may be labeled "Jacket of FC" and "Firearm owed by Frank Crispino," with the serial numbers FC1 and FC2. These numbers provide the ability to identify evidence that originated from these supports. For instance, using the example above, question and comparison fibers could be collected and sampled from the jacket, which would be labeled FC1.1 and FC1.2, respectively. In the same manner, a fingermark found on the weapon would be labeled FC2.1. After securing the fingerprint, a final swab (which would be labeled FC2.1.1) could be done probably leading to a DNA profile. Hence, the numbers make it apparent that FC2.1.1 was derived from the DNA profile in the fingermark (FC2.1), which was in turn derived from the firearm (FC2) found in Frank Crispino's possession.

See also: **Investigations:** Collection and Chain of Evidence; Contamination; Packaging; Recording.

Further Reading

Baldwin, H.B., Puskarich, M.C., 2000. Preservation. In: Siegel, J., Knupfer, G., Saukko, P. (Eds.), Encyclopedia of Forensic Sciences, 3 vols., pp. 440–443.

Green, M.A., 2000. Preservation of evidence. In: Siegel, J., Knupfer, G., Saukko, P. (Eds.), Encyclopedia of Forensic Sciences, 3 vols., pp. 1172–1177.

Horswell, J., 2000. Packaging. In: Siegel, J., Knupfer, G., Saukko, P. (Eds.), Encyclopedia of Forensic Sciences, 3 vols., pp. 432–440.

Horswell, J., 2004. Crime scene investigation. In: Robertson, J. (Ed.), The Practice of Crime Scene Investigation. CRC0-748-40609-3, Boca Raton, FL, pp. 2–45.

Recording

J Horswell, Approved Forensics Sendirian Berhad, Selangor, Malaysia

Background

The accurate recording of details of a crime scene, incident scene, or any subsequent examination of potential evidentiary material is important for several reasons. It is important for the crime scene investigator as it will provide the basis for the statement and report that the crime scene investigator must prepare at a later date and it will provide investigators with information of which they may not otherwise have knowledge. It will also assist the court in reconstructing the scene and may provide the most reliable facts regarding potential physical evidence, critical measurements as well as its positioning within the scene. Finally, it may provide the court with best evidence available.

Notes

Experience has demonstrated that crime scene investigators can never make too many notes during a scene investigation and subsequent examination of potential evidentiary material. Notes should always be compiled during the course of the investigation, be it onsite or later when examining potential physical evidence. Notes should not be done later; however, if it is not possible to do so then details should be recorded as soon as possible after the examination/s.

There are obvious and very good reasons for compiling contemporaneous and accurate notes:

- Notes made at the time of an examination are likely to be more reliable and accurate than notes made some time later.
- By making notes as she/he is conducting the examination, the crime scene investigator is less likely to overlook minor details committed to memory.
- An accurate record of times and dates will be maintained. This will avoid discrepancies with the records of other investigators involved in the investigation.
- An accurate record is available for later reference during the investigation and when compiling reports.
- An accurate record is available for later reference during the finalization of the investigation when compiling a witness statement for court.
- When giving evidence in court, the crime scene investigator may be permitted by the court to refresh his or her memory by referring to the notes taken during the investigation and while conducting any specific examination/s.

Obviously, if notes are made during the conduct and at each stage of an investigation and/or examination of potential evidentiary material, then there should be no dispute as to their accuracy.

The main aim therefore for writing comprehensive notes is to provide an accurate and comprehensive record of events and observations which will be meaningful months later. For this reason, it is preferable to write detailed notes at the time rather than attempting to save time by using abbreviations, which, although readily understood at the time of writing, might be insufficient to refresh the crime scene investigator's memory after several months have lapsed.

On arrival at a scene, the following should be noted:

- Day, date, and time of arrival
- Names of persons present at the scene on arrival
- Weather conditions
- Lighting conditions at night
- What has happened—the incident?
- What has taken place—activity at the scene since the primary incident?
- Officer-in-charge of the case
- Scene guard
- Assistance provided at the scene
- Other resources already requested

The sequence of the crime scene investigator's actions following arrival at a scene will vary depending upon the situation with which she/he is faced. If there is no requirement to start a particular examination immediately, it is advantageous to spend some time studying the crime scene, noting all observations. Any movement through the crime scene, noting observations, can only be done if there is no risk of contaminating or damaging possible evidence. A pathway should be identified, which is used as a common approach path into and out of the critical areas of the crime scene.

Photographs

Photographs can provide a detailed record of the condition of a scene, illustrating the items present and their relative locations. For this reason, photographs should be taken before items are moved or interfered with, and they should be taken from various angles.

There may be items shown in the photographs which were not mentioned in the written notes taken at the time, and the photographs may help to refresh the crime scene investigator's memory on some aspect of the scene or examination. On the other hand, during court hearings, defense counsel may cross-examine the crime scene investigator about objects shown in the photographs, and if there are no notes made about the issue under examination it may prove embarrassing. It is therefore important not to rely too heavily on photographs alone without the assistance of supporting documented notes.

A general survey, where the scene is inspected before photographs are taken, will help determine what photographs will be required and the sequence in which they are to be taken. As a general rule, the scene should be photographed after the general survey and before further examination/s are conducted, without reconstructing the scene in any way. The crime scene investigator should be able to demonstrate photographically how the scene was before the start of the scene examination.

It is not the intent of this chapter to provide a short course on photography; however, the points raised will ensure that there is adequate coverage of the scene by the crime scene investigator.

Before commencing the photographic aspect of the crime scene investigation, it must be remembered that photographs should not include items introduced by the crime scene investigator and other investigators. Brief cases, clipboards, photographic equipment bags, crime scene kits, or the photographer's feet should not feature in any of the photographs.

Each crime scene will be different but the following should be considered:

- The photographic record should be comprehensive and should include the general layout of premises or features of an area.
- The photographic record should illustrate the relative positions of room, the state of those rooms, and the position of houses in streets in relation to the crime scene.
- Footprints, tire tracks, and toolmarks should be photographed with a scale before casting. A close-up and positioning photograph should also be taken.
- Photographs should be taken from a number of angles or positions, including those described by witnesses, if known. These maybe taken later if not known and are required.
- A series of photographs should be taken from the point of entry to the point of exit.
- Detailed photographs should be taken of potential evidentiary material, such as the body, injuries, weapons, trace material, cartridge case/s, damage, and other relevant items.
- As the scene examination progresses, further photographs should include new potential evidentiary material found, or areas of importance which were previously concealed.

Before taking any photographs, the crime scene investigator must reflect on the following:

- What am I going to photograph?
- Why should it be photographed?
- What do I want to demonstrate using photography?
- How can I record it as I see it?

Having made these comments, it is necessary to cover all pertinent material. It is wiser to take too many photographs than too few. It must, however, be remembered that it is not necessary to have all the images printed. This should create no problem in court as long as the investigating officer is aware of the situation and it may be necessary in some jurisdictions to advise the defense of their existence. One way to cover this point is to have the investigating officer involved in the selection of the photographs for presentation in the crime scene investigators court statement. This issue will certainly be addressed if the defense obtains a court order to "produce all documents." The crime scene investigator should be prepared to defend the selection of photographs in the witness box.

Digital Photography

Digital photography is now being used widely in policing including the capture of images at crime and incident scenes. It is not my intention to go into this medium in any detail except to say that the increase in memory available for each image has given this media abilities which far surpass silver halide or traditional photography. Crime scene investigators can now:

- See instant results and know they have what they want to record, recorded.
- Use the magnifying component to look at detail in the image.
- Move images between investigators as attachments to email messages.
- Move images instantly over long distances in the course of the investigation.

Images can be easily manipulated but they can easily be checked for alteration if required which now makes this media ideal for use at crime and incident scenes. The crime scene investigator must remember that when giving evidence he/she should be prepared to state that the picture clearly represents what she/he saw at the time when she/he took the photograph. This should negate interference with the image after all the issue will then become one of credibility of the witness.

Video Recording

It is useful to video the crime scene; a recording may be an invaluable briefing tool for investigators and others to view later, as well as to introduce as potential evidence in court.

The recording of a crime scene by video be undertaken in each serious and major crime. Experience has shown that the video of any crime scene should be taken without sound. The subsequent audiences that view the video should be guided through it by the crime scene investigator or investigating officer, either in person or by means of a "voice over."

The video recording of what is called a "reenactment" should be attempted only after the suspect has been interviewed and the crime scene has been processed, and only after an invitation to participate is accepted by the suspect, with the video being taken with full sound while the suspect is under caution. Such videos have been shown to be a very successful tool in presenting the prosecution case at court. The court will also be able to see if the suspect is under stress or duress at the time of the reenactment video, along with his or her general demeanor and that of the interviewing officer. Experience has shown that powerful evidence can be gained from this recording technique.

The video recording of a crime scene and any subsequent reenactment video should be done under the direct control and guidance of the crime scene investigator or crime scene manager, as it is only these individuals who are aware of the current position regarding the processing, recording, search, and recovery of potential evidentiary material at the crime scene.

Plans

There are two types of plan: a sketch drawn by the crime scene investigator and a scale plan, which can be drawn by an experienced crime scene investigator or a draftsman. These complement written notes and photographs, and these are notes recorded of the crime scene examination. They may provide perspective and will provide distances between objects within the scene. Computer programs and photogrammetry are tools that can assist in producing professional scale drawings.

Computer-Aided Design

Computer-aided design (CAD), also known as computer-aided design and drafting (CADD), is the use of computer technology for the process of design and design documentation. Computer-aided drafting describes the process of drafting with a computer. CADD software, or environments, provides the user with input tools for the purpose of streamlining design processes; drafting, documentation, and manufacturing processes. CADD output is often in the form of electronic files for print or machining operations. CADD environments often involve more than just shapes. CAD is used in crime scene drafting producing professional results.

Photogrammetry

Photogrammetry, as its name implies, is a three-dimensional coordinate measuring technique that uses photographs as the fundamental medium for metrology or measurement. The fundamental principle used in photogrammetry is triangulation. By taking photographs from at least two different locations, so-called "lines of sight" can be developed from each camera to points on the object. These lines of sight, sometimes called rays owing to their optical nature, are mathematically intersected to produce the three-dimensional coordinates of the points of interest.

Triangulation is also the principle used by theodolites for coordinate measurement. Crime scene investigators familiar with these instruments will find many similarities and some differences between photogrammetry and theodolites. Triangulation is also the way the two human eyes work together to gauge distance which is called depth perception.

The choice of equipment to draw crime scenes is one of "practice" and "procedure" of crime scene investigators within a given jurisdiction.

I will now, however, go back to the basics for crime scene sketching.

Sketch Plan

A sketch enables the crime scene investigator to show the location of items and their relationship to other items. A sketch only needs to be freehand; it must be neat enough for the crime scene investigator or draftsman to accurately interpret the data at a later date in order to produce a scale drawing.

There are several basic types of drawing that are commonly encountered in sketching crime scenes. The floor plan view is the most common and is the easiest to complete. It depicts the location of items looking down from above. This should be used for both indoor and outdoor scenes. The exploded view or cross-projection method is similar to the floor plan view and differs only in that the walls fold out to reveal items of evidence found on or in the walls. Isometric projection of walls as stand-alone drawings may be used to indicate items of evidence, such as bloodstain patters found on walls at a crime scene, recording extreme violence. Three-dimensional drawings, virtual reality, and animated computer programs are now being used more and more in crime scene investigation.

Coordinate and Triangulation Methods of Measuring Crime Scenes

The following two basic methods are suitable for measuring crime scene:

- *Coordinate method*: This method uses the principles of measuring the distance of an object, such as a body, from two fixed points. One form of the coordinate method involves the use of a baseline, which is drawn between the two known points. The baseline may also be a wall or drawn as a mathematical center of a room, the exact dimensions of which are known. The measurement of a given item is then taken from left to right along the baseline to a point at right angles to the item which is to be plotted.
- *Triangulation method*: The triangulation method requires three measurements:
  - Base
  - Shortest side of the triangle
  - Longest side of the triangle

An established base may be used, for example, the side of a house. Two measurements are then taken, from the corners of that side of the house to the item to be plotted. When a crime scene is in an open area, such as a beach, paddock, or park, the triangulation method is usually employed but it is necessary to establish a base. This can be achieved with the aid of a magnetic compass to determine true north, the taking of coordinates using a global positioning system reader, and the placement of a peg in the ground or the use of an electricity pole or something that is fixed and may have a serial number fixed to it.

Procedure for Measuring Crime Scenes

- Accurately determine north with a compass and place it at the top of the plan.
- Determine the crime scene position coordinates using a global positioning system reader.
- Determine what is to be included in the plan and the method of recording it.
- Draw a rough sketch on which the items will be plotted and the measurements recorded.
- Work systematically throughout the scene, recording dimensions, in the case of a room, and the location of important items within it.
- It is ideal that the person responsible for both the sketch plan and the scale drawing be the person who records the measurements on the sketch plan.
- Use the progressive system of measurement where possible; for example, corner of a room to the nearest point of window 0.3–3.5 m to the other side of the window frame.
- In order to locate items within a room or open area, use either the coordinate or triangulation method or a combination of both.
- The position of bodies and important items should be plotted prior to removal or collection; however, the position of "fixed" objects may be recorded at a subsequent time and date, thus enabling a quicker examination of the scene.
- If objects must be moved prior to plotting then mark their location before moving them, for example, with chalk, felt marking pen, crayon, or spray paint. Remember photographs must be taken before anything is moved.
- Add the crime scene investigator's name, the case, date, time, and location. If anyone assisted, his or her name should also be included on the sketch.

Scale Plan

Scale plans are used to convey accurately the size, shape, and position of important potential evidence and other features of the crime scene. They are a valuable adjunct to scene photographs. Scale plans are also an aid in reviewing a crime scene with investigators.

The use of modern surveying equipment at the scene overcomes many of the problems encountered in preparing crime scene plans. These tools along with those mentioned above are now being put to good effect by many practitioners.

Computers

The use of computer technology has also advanced and recorded material that was provided to courts in hard copy can now be shown to judges, juries, prosecutors, and defense council simultaneously through linked computers. The paperless office has at long last arrived in the court room!

Summary

The fundamental reason for recording crime scenes is to take a crime scene and reproduce what has occurred for the information of the investigation team and, ultimately, the court.

See also: **Investigations:** Major Incident Scene Management; Packaging; **Digital Evidence:** Digital Imaging: Enhancement and Authentication.

Further Reading

Fisher, B.A.J., 2004. Techniques of Crime Scene Investigation, seventh ed. CRC Press, Boca Raton, FL.
Horswell, J. (Ed.), 2004. The Practice of Crime Scene Investigation. CRC Press, Boca Raton, FL.

Recovery of Human Remains

JJ Miller and DSK Thurley, York Archaeological Trust for Excavation and Research Limited, York, UK

This article is a revision of the previous edition article by H.B. Baldwin and C. Puskarich May, volume 1, pp. 447–457, © 2000, Elsevier Ltd.

Glossary

Cordon A defined area around a body recovery site into which access is only granted with permission and which is recorded.

Ossification The name given to the process by which cartilage in a juvenile is replaced by bone during maturation growth.

Spit A thin lens of soil taken over a certain area from a thicker layer of similar soil to enable accurate recovery and interpretation of items within it.

Stratigraphy Layering of soil that has accumulated over time from the oldest layers at the bottom to the youngest at the top.

Introduction

Fundamentally similar techniques are utilized in every problematic human remains recovery. Search and recovery must withstand scrutiny in court, so careful scene examination is vital, helping to determine whether a crime has been committed, by whom and how. Selection of the correct experts may further determine whether or not an investigation has a satisfactory conclusion. You know what you find but may never know what was missed.

Good communication between forensic specialists and law enforcement officials is vital in problematic body recovery. The responsibilities of law enforcement officials may impact upon specialists, while one specialist's intervention may be contra-indicatory to another. Determining the recovery strategy ahead of any intervention, followed by good scene control, helps minimize this risk. Each case is assumed suspicious until proven otherwise.

First Officers on the Scene

The first officers protect the scene with inner and outer cordons. Witnesses will be detained separately and notes taken as the scene changes. Senior officers are informed and a crime scene manager (CSM) requested.

Crime Scene Manager

The CSM is responsible for the health and safety and the security of evidence at the scene, using common approach paths (CAPs), cordons, and scene entry (log) books to document everyone entering the scene. They inform the senior investigating officer (SIO), instruct photographic record, and determine personnel and equipment requirements.

Senior Investigating Officer

The SIO directs the police investigation, liaises with media and public prosecutor, informs the pathologist, and invites relevant experts including scene examiners, forensic scientists, and prosecutors to a forensic strategy meeting ahead of the recovery. The SIO reports to the public prosecutor who ultimately prosecutes the case.

Forensic Scientist

Scientists locate, recover, and interpret various categories of physical evidence; interpret blood spatter, cast tire, and tool marks; and recover fragile trace evidence including blood, hair, semen, accelerants, or firearms discharge residue.

Crime Scene Examiner/Photographer

Either one or two operatives depending on local procedure, scene examiners locate and seize physical evidence, take photographic record at the locus and postmortem, and recover items for fingerprint examination and lift fingerprints.

Production/Exhibit Officer

Exhibit officers seize, package, record, and store evidence to ensure a secure chain of custody and submission to the correct experts for further examination.

Forensic Pathologist/Medical Examiner

The pathologist/medical examiner views and swabs the body at the scene and does a postmortem to establish the cause of death. They may confer with a forensic anthropologist regarding bone trauma.

Forensic Entomologist

Forensic entomologists use the life cycle of invertebrates including flies (eggs, maggots, pupa, and adults) and beetles to refine time of death in problematic cases. Human DNA may also be recovered from larvae/puparia.

Forensic Anthropologist

Forensic anthropologists examine human bones to determine trauma, sex, stature, age at death, ancestry, and health to ascertain identity and cause of death.

Forensic Archeology

A forensic archeologist undertakes body recovery and trace evidence gathering for courts. Working with forensic botanists, they locate clandestine graves; excavate; record and lift the remains; search the area around and below for evidence; and take soil samples to help link tools, weapons, vehicles, clothing, or a suspect to a deposition site.

Forensic Botany

Forensic botanists use vegetation changes to find concealed bodies; date the deposition; explain events at the scene; and interpret plant trace evidence to link a perpetrator, tool, vehicle, or weapon to a scene. Some may do pollen analysis (palynology), although palynologists are often geographers.

Police Search Team

Highly trained in an extensive range of search environments including sewers, river beds, cliff tops, or quarries, these officers search large areas rigorously. Their methods may destroy fragile trace evidence so they stop after finding the remains, returning to sweep the area once the scientists are finished and the body recovered.

Scene Processing

Securing the scene and wearing full protective clothing, gloves, and face mask to prevent DNA and other transfer helps minimize cross-contamination. Eye protection may also be required.

Search Techniques

Discovery of decomposed human remains can be intelligence led following informant information or during a structured search. Others are discovered accidentally. Protocol demands that informant information is verified and bones confirmed as human before searches begin. Police search advisors then assimilate information regarding landscape boundaries including quarries, rivers, housing, and woodland to define search strategies, identifying hazards that require specialist equipment or personnel.

Standard search methods are adapted to suit the terrain, dividing the total area into smaller, manageable sectors with unique identifier codes. Methods include:

- Grid: large grid "squares" (sectors) are searched methodically, individually, and consecutively. Sectors may be further subdivided. When remains are found, close grid search across the actual deposition spot ensures rigorous, accountable evidence recovery.
- Line: a line of personnel walk at arm's length to look for a body, weapon, etc. Closer scale searchers shoulder width apart on hands and knees will find small evidence such as ammunition casings.
- Zone: a grid-type method for smaller, irregularly shaped areas.

Methods utilized depend on the terrain; number of searchers; and the purpose of the search, whether a missing person, phone, or shotgun casing. A combination of some or all methods may be used. Whenever anything potentially relevant is found, it is photographed, recorded, and either collected or flagged before the search continues.

Dogs

Trained dogs can find evidence, bodies, or trapped live individuals. Training for different functions varies, so dogs taught to find cadavers may not find live victims and vice versa. Dogs can be cross-trained for various searches, such as blood and drugs, arsons or explosives, but are less effective than specifically trained cadaver dogs.

Buried Remains

The time of year, terrain, duration of burial, and exposure to weather will affect what is visible to find. Dismembered body parts may have multiple, small burials rather than one, grave-sized plot. Disturbed vegetation and soil, compaction, differential drying, and random piles of mixed soils are indicators of burial sites that may or may not be seen.

Disturbed Vegetation

Grave digging disturbs overlying vegetation. Recent cases may have upturned roots, broken stems, or wilted stems. A flattened area may be obvious within the undergrowth. Bare soil gradually becomes revegetated, the young shoots highlighting the grave until indistinguishable from the surrounding vegetation.

A body within vegetation becomes better concealed over time. However, a long established burial hidden by tall summer growth may be revealed over winter as a sunken hollow when vegetation dies back. A deep, substantial grave with vegetation carefully removed and replanted may be concealed within weeks, while a shallow, hurried grave may remain obvious for months or years. This is because the decomposing body releases toxic volumes of nutrients that inhibit growth over shallow graves until remains decompose and soil nutrient levels benefit rather than inhibit vegetation. The time for this depends on season, temperature, and invertebrate activity.

Soil Compaction and Disturbance

Soil accumulates naturally in layers (strata) over time. Impoverished glacial subsoils have high clay and gravel content while fertile plow soil is organic and sandy. Glacial events, bedrock weathering, organic accumulation, and human intervention contribute to the "stratigraphy" (layering) of soils. Once disturbed, natural stratigraphy is changed and may be identifiable.

Graves retain water since the fill is less compacted than surrounding soils, which may assist or hinder vegetation recovery in different environments. The body within means less soil fits back in, leaving a mound that gradually sinks as soil settles into the decomposing body cavity. Conversely, if the grave surface is flattened, leftover soils and stones may be nearby, a depression becoming very noticeable as grave soil collapses into the body cavity. In warm weather, grave margins may crack since the fill is wetter than the surrounding soil. This is often emphasized by collapse of grave soil into the body cavity.

Infrared Photography

Used in darkness to detect temperature differentials, infrared photography has best application in aircraft-led wide area searches for recent cases. A large maggot biomass that raises the body temperature can boost success rates.

Methane Detection

Methane escaping from a body can indicate a burial, although all decomposing organics produce methane gas and detection rates decline considerably over time, so this technique is only used to investigate small suspicious areas using dogs.

Aerial Photography and Maps

Preexisting and new aerial images can be compared to identify suspicious areas. Photographs are examined in conjunction with maps to exclude nonsuspicious events such as pipelines, natural features, or archeology. Aerial photographs also highlight new construction within the period under investigation.

Geophysical Survey

Geophysical survey techniques identify underground anomalies when surface examination is not practicable. Techniques include:

- Resistivity: Measures speed of electrical current underground between two electrodes, giving a peak with loose, wet soil, including graves and archeological features. Works with agricultural soils but not waterlogged or arid landscapes.
- Magnetometry: Detects anomalies in the soil's natural magnetic signal caused by infilling the grave with mixed soils with different magnetic signals. Works in wet or dry landscapes but is affected by underground/overhead cables and metal on clothing.
- Ground-penetrating radar: A common technique for urban environments, detecting voids to 3 m below concrete or hard standings. Avoids excavating such areas during wider searches.

Construction Equipment

Although a last resort, a backhoe and bulldozer operator guided by an experienced archeologist can remove 5–30 cm of soil at a time to expose disturbance or a grave cut. The potential for damage to the deceased is considerable.

Recovery of Human Remains
Surface Recovery

Inner and outer cordons established across the body deposition site and surrounding area will restrict access and protect evidence. All personnel entering the outer cordon are logged by a designated cordon control officer. A CAP through the inner cordon to the body that avoids routes likely to be taken by a perpetrator is established, defined with tapes, and searched before use. The site is photographed and a strategy meeting set up with specialists to plan the methodology of recovery. Video images facilitate decision-making. A command/control post may be set up at the outer cordon for personnel to gather for briefings.

Photographic record is taken throughout the recovery process. Fragile biological evidence is of paramount importance and must always be first priority, especially if recent, where the body will be sampled in situ. Observed by the biologist, the botanist and archeologist record, clear, and examine overhanging vegetation and debris, recording indicators of duration, trauma, or scavengers. The botanist notes vegetation overlying and growing through the remains to determine the duration of deposition. During and following the body recovery, the entomologist collects invertebrate evidence to corroborate this. A grid is set up across the site, the size reflecting natural boundaries including walls or logs, but with a minimum perimeter of one grid sector surrounding the remains that is free of visible evidence. The size of grid sectors used is situation dependent, but 0.5 or 1 m^2 are normal. The grid is labeled alphanumerically with markers to give each sector a unique identifier. The grid facilitates accurate, relative spatial recording of items recovered and ensures rigorous search. Spatial patterning of evidence and remains can be reproduced diagrammatically for the court to explain even complicated sequences of events at the scene. Prior to evidence recovery, a metal detector will highlight any hidden weapons, needles, or armament.

Items located are marked with a flag or stake and plotted on a scale drawing of the grid. When reproduced by an illustrator for the court, this sanitizes the image for explanation to a jury, ensuring they focus on the specialist interpretation of evidence without the distraction of distressing images. The grid is photographed to show the distribution of flags, then individual close-up images of items are taken, scales and markers denoting their original grid square and size. Evidence is packaged and recorded by the exhibits/evidence recovery officer. Dry evidence is generally packaged in paper products (paper fold, bag, or box), and wet items within plastic bags. Wet items are dried subsequently in a forensic drying cabinet. Liquids can be recovered in glass or polythene vials. Evidence at fires must be packaged in special acetate bags that will not give false positive results if tested subsequently for accelerants.

The methodology of surface body recovery varies with circumstances. The location of each bone from a single disarticulated skeleton within the grid should be recorded, with bones packaged and then placed together within a body bag. Bones separate from the rest of the body should be wrapped individually but those within clothing may be retained together. Separate body parts may retain other evidence upon them and should be packaged individually with grid locations noted, although they may still be placed within the same body bag. In an intact or almost intact cadaver, the hands, feet, and head are protected by bags before moving. Clothing on a fresh body is carefully removed to prevent semen or leakage from wounds contaminating fabrics and distorting the interpretation of events. This is not generally relevant for decomposed remains and may increase disarticulation.

With the body and superficial evidence removed, the area may be checked again with a metal detector prior to the recovery and search of soil within the gridded area. The archeologist recovers soil down to an undisturbed layer to confirm that nothing was hidden below the body or has sunk into the substrate over time. Soil is recovered per grid sector down to an undisturbed level and either removed for washing

and subsequent examination for fibers, hairs, etc. for a recent investigation, or sieved on site for teeth, missing bones, fingernails, projectiles, or small jewelry for skeletonized remains where recovery of fragile biological trace evidence is no longer viable. A sieve of maximum 3- to 6-mm diameter should be used for sieving of soil on site but finer gauge sieves or 1-mm mesh supported within a sieve are appropriate when washing soil for very small items, in the laboratory or at the locus. The entomologist observes the soil recovery process and collects invertebrates throughout.

Poisons, drugs, or accelerants can be retained in soil beneath the remains, so samples should be collected for analysis. Representative samples of soil within the locus and likely offender access paths are also recovered to enable cross-comparison with sediment found on any footwear, tools, weapons, clothing, or vehicles recovered subsequently, to help link them to the scene. This is crucial since soil from the locus will not remain representative once disturbed by the excavation team.

With the gridded recovery of the main deposition complete, the team moves on to recover evidence or body parts elsewhere. If the skull has detached from the neck bones, it may be some distance from the main decomposition, especially on sloping ground or if scavengers are active. Consequently, the ground between must be searched for additional evidence. Items moved by scavengers may or may not require a grid search, although rigorous recording and packaging remain standard practice. If bones are missing from a body on banking above or on the flood plain of a river, search of the river bed downstream is required. Depending upon the current, heavy long bones may not travel as far as vertebrae or ribs, but some may never be found. Remains settle in river bends or snag in submerged debris, so water searches will require divers and appropriate health and safety guidance.

The total time needed to recover scattered human remains and related evidence, then search for bones missing at postmortem may be days or weeks, so weather, comfort, and health and safety must be considered accordingly.

Excavation of Buried Remains

Three common methods of excavation are utilized to maximize evidence recovery potential in graves. Gridding the grave helps define locations of soil and evidence recovered during the process. Standard archeological practices including detailed recording, drawing, planning, and photographic record apply in all circumstances. Methods include:

● Within feature: grave soil is gradually removed to reveal the remains. Excavating half at a time shows the processes of concealment. Careful excavation up to the grave cut may reveal tool marks on the four grave walls. It is difficult to remove remains from deep graves using this method.

- Trench: a trench is dug adjacent to the grave, at least 0.5 m deeper than the body surface. The trench must be longer than the body and wide enough to provide sufficient room to work in to collect evidence and the remains. Three of the four walls of the grave can be defined and the grave infilling processes revealed.
- Table: a table is dug by trenching all around the grave cut, approximately 1.25-m wide by 2-m long, extending 0.5 m beyond it, leaving all four grave walls intact and providing sufficient room to work around the body. It provides ease and comfort while working but one wall must be dug through for recovery from deeper graves.

A combination of any or all three methods may provide the optimum evidence recovery potential in problematic circumstances.

Prior to excavation, the body position is estimated, based on visible indicators and extent of the disturbed area. Soil is recovered in layers (spits) of approximate 5- to 10-cm depth, respecting the overlying grid and any grave soil stratigraphy. Numbering spits makes each layer uniquely identifiable and enables three-dimensional spatial patterning of evidence. Each spit can be sieved for missing bones and small evidence, the locations of which can be illustrated diagrammatically to help interpret the sequence of events. Coins, jewelry, projectiles, paint, fabrics, ID cards, imported vegetation, SIM cards, and more have been recovered from sieved grave soils.

The hands, feet, and head of an intact body are protected by bags. The easiest way to remove an intact body is to slide it onto plastic over a body bag on a wooden backer board and wrapping before lifting it. This helps prevent disarticulation of decomposing remains. Skeletons should be recovered like a surface recovery. Soil below the body is recovered to an undisturbed layer, checking first for any footwear imprints left by the grave digger(s). Soil below the body should be sieved for additional evidence including bones, projectiles, and teeth.

Forensic Anthropology

The forensic anthropologist reconstructs the skeleton when a decomposed body is recovered, including shattered bones. Identification of pre- and postmortem skeletal trauma in relation to preexisting disease or injury helps determine cause and/or manner of death. Analysis of the skull, pelvis, and long bones confirms gender, height, age range, and possible ethnic origin in addition to trauma and illness. Ribs and vertebrae are also useful sources of data.

Depending on counting methods, the adult human skeleton has 206–211 bones. Juveniles have more since many bones have independent parts in the infant that fuse at different stages during growth and maturation. This facilitates age determination in juveniles. Unfused parts are contained by cartilage that gradually ossifies, enabling bones to increase in length and diameter as the child grows, develops, and matures. Gender and ethnic origin of prepubescent juveniles cannot be determined confidently. Juvenile epiphyses (joint ends) resemble amorphous clay, so soil from a juvenile recovery should be sieved with a forensic anthropologist in attendance. Growth and bone fusion is usually complete by the age of 25, after which age can only be related to degenerative change, with correspondingly wider estimation parameters.

Teeth and Odontology

A forensic odontologist compares dental radiographs/records of a suspected victim to any teeth or mandible recovered at a locus to confirm identify. Absolute identification requires the entire dentition, but unique variations of even a single tooth may help the process. If a tooth is lost during life, the tooth socket and the edges of it are not clearly discernible. By contrast, if teeth are lost after or around death (post- or perimortem), the socket walls remain identifiable and may be empty or dirt filled. There is no need to search further for teeth lost during life, although partial or total premortem tooth loss may suggest that a dental plate should be found. Teeth dislodged after death may be found by a systematic search of the soil between the skull and main decomposition site.

Trauma

Flies lay eggs in orifices, such as the eyes and mouth, anus, and wounds. Consequently, initial maggot activity is concentrated in these areas. Large maggot masses away from natural orifices can indicate wounds on a partially decomposed body with no damage to underlying bones. The forensic anthropologist will assess the skeleton for trauma, including potentially defleshing a decomposed body, and localized maggot activity noted during recovery helps guide observations. Comparison to medical history of a suspected victim may assist in identification, while perimortem trauma may help determine cause and manner of death. Trauma that affects only soft tissues may not survive decomposition, with even violent deaths retaining no indication of attack on the skeleton.

To avoid inadvertent damage to bones during transportation from locus to the mortuary, separate long bones, the pelvis, skull, and mandible should be packaged separately, ensuring that the skull is especially well protected. Containers remain within the same body bag as the rest of the remains to ensure continuity of evidence.

Exhumations

Exhumation (disinterment) of a body legally buried in consecrated ground may be undertaken for an investigation of that individual's death initiated after burial; for an enquiry into another, potentially connected death that requires examination of that body; or if misidentification of the individual is alleged. Warrants require proof that examination of the body is important for the investigation. Separate permissions are needed for the exhumation and the removal of the headstone 3 days prior to the event. Further considerations are necessary if the plot is one having multiple occupancy. Information about the alleged deceased must be available, including name, age, weight, height, sex, and cause of death. A positive identification will be required, whether through DNA, fingerprints or from visual identification if possible. The grave must be photographed before, during, and after the exhumation. As with any body recovery, exhumations require close adherence to health and safety, and personal protective clothing must be worn.

Soil is removed to just above the level of the coffin. Thereafter, screening helps avoid media attention and maintains the dignity of the deceased. Best practice is to excavate around the coffin, allowing side access. As the ground settles over time, coffins move and neighboring graves may merge into each other. Once the body is exposed to the air, it must be transported to the mortuary quickly since decomposition accelerates on exposure to air. Security is maintained at the grave site until reburial. A body transported from abroad may be embalmed, potentially affecting toxicological analysis of tissue, so chemicals used and methods employed should be reported. Common embalming chemicals include formaldehyde, methanol, monopropyleneglycol, and mineral salts.

Soil from above and around the coffin, clothing, shroud, fluids, and sawdust from the coffin interior might be sampled, plus fragments of the coffin itself and any sealant used. An intact coffin should not be opened at the locus unless absolutely necessary due to the potential for disease transfer and evidence contamination.

Other Considerations at the Crime Scene

Legal Permissions

Valuable evidence can be excluded from court by paperwork errors or gaps in the chain of custody. The correct warrants, permissions, and protocols are needed before remains are recovered, searches made, or evidence seized.

Health and Safety

Personnel should wear latex or nitrile gloves (double gloved), liquid repellent disposable coveralls, protective shoe covers, particle mask/respirator, and goggles or face shield. Evidence seized should be packaged in the appropriate containers, properly labeled, and bags signed by witnesses. It is unacceptable to eat, drink, or smoke at crime scenes. Nondisposable equipment used should be decontaminated afterward with a 10% bleach solution. Regular comfort breaks should be taken outside the scene to prevent dehydration and overtiredness.

Additional Information

The area around the deposition site must be searched for tools, clothing, tire tracks, footprints, or other evidence. Consideration must be given to underground cables and pipes. If media, weather, or circumstances dictate, the deposition site should be tented, although this increases temperature and reduces natural light for excavation and botanical interpretations, so cases must be considered individually.

See also: **Anthropology/Odontology:** Odontology; **Biology/DNA:** Disaster Victim Identification; Future Analytical Techniques: DNA Mass Spectrometry; **Chemistry/Trace/Forensic Geosciences:** Botany; Forensic Geoscience; Soils; **Investigations:** Major Incident Scene Management.

Further Reading

Bass, W.M. (Ed.), 1998. Human Osteology: A Laboratory and Field Manual of the Human Skeleton, fourth ed. Missouri Archeological Society, Columbia, MO.

Catts, E.P., Haskell, N.H., 1990. Entomology and Death: A Procedural Guide. Joyce's Print Shop, Clemson, SC.

Fisher, B.A.J. (Ed.), 2000. Techniques of Crime Scene Investigation, sixth ed. CRC Press, Boca Raton, FL.

Geberth, V.J. (Ed.), 1990. Practical Homicide Investigation, third ed. Elsevier, New York.

Haglund, W.D., Sorg, M.H., 1997. Forensic Taphonomy: The Post-Mortem Fate of Human Remains. CRC Press, New York.

Hunter, J., Cox, M., 2005. Forensic Archaeology: Advances in Theory and Practice. Routledge, London.

Hunter, J., Roberts, C., Martin, A., 1996. Studies in Crime: An Introduction to Forensic Archaeology. Batsford Ltd, London.

Killam, E.W., 1990. The Detection of Human Remains. Thomas, Springfield, IL.

Miller Coyle, H., 2005. Forensic Botany: Principles and Applications to Criminal Casework. CRC Press, London.

Morse, D., Duncan, J., Stoutamire, J., 1983. Handbook of Forensic Archaeology and Anthropology. Bill's Book Store, Tallahassee.

Sansone, S.J. (Ed.), 1998. Police Photography, fourth ed. Anderson, Cincinnati.

Skinner, M., Lazenby, R., 1983. Found! Human Remains. Archaeology Press, Burnaby, BC.

Spitz, W.V., Fisher, R.S. (Eds.), 1993. Medicolegal Investigation of Death, second ed. Thomas, Springfield, IL.

White, T.D., Folkens, P.A., 2005. The Human Bone Manual. Elsevier, London.

Relevant Websites

http://www.northlight-heritage.co.uk—Northlight Heritage.
http://www.yorkarchaeology.co.uk—York Archaelogical Trust.

Collection and Chain of Evidence

F Poole, Forensic Services Group, Parramatta, NSW, Australia

Glossary

Denaturing of DNA The process by which double-stranded DNA unwinds and separates into single-stranded strands through the breaking of hydrogen bonds between the bases.

DNA amplification A process called polymerase chain reaction; a DNA testing procedure that mimics the cell's ability to replicate DNA, essentially copying it a million-fold.

Electrostatic lifting device A device consisting of a high-voltage supply used with a special conductive lifting film to transfer a dry origin footwear impression electrostatically from a surface to a film.

Latent evidence Evidence at a crime scene that cannot be seen with the naked eye. Examples might be a blood stain that was bleached out, semen stains that cannot be seen without special lighting, or a fingerprint that cannot be seen without powdering.

Probative value Evidence which is sufficiently useful to prove something important in a trial.

Trace evidence Evidence such as hairs, fibers, and residue as well as other microscopic evidence that may not be visible to the naked eye.

Introduction

The role of crime scene investigators at major scenes and incidents is to identify and recover physical and trace evidence that has some probative value in the crime. Crime scenes may involve single or multiple locations and these are referred to as the primary and secondary scenes. For example, the primary scene may be where a person has been killed; however, secondary scenes may result when the body has been moved to a different location, and/or the weapon is found at another location. All locations involved form part of the overall crime scene and the evidence collected from each scene helps solve the puzzle piece by piece.

Forensic evidence collected must be relevant to the crime, not be at risk of being misplaced, lost, or tampered with, not be at risk of contamination from other sources, and remain intact throughout the process of collection and analysis. For this reason, the preservation of forensic evidence commences at the time of arrival of the first police responder at the crime scene. At this time, an immediate assessment must be made and action taken to protect any fragile evidence at risk of loss or damage. From this point on, crime scene investigators must be meticulous in their approach to the collection of evidence and maintain an unbroken chain of custody from the time of collection, to the laboratory for analysis, and through to the presentation of the evidence in a court of law.

Scene Examination

Forensic evidence can appear in many forms, including physical, trace, and latent evidence. In the twentieth century, forensic scientist Edmond Locard advanced the theory on which most forensic science is founded today, and that is that "every contact leaves a trace." Locard's principle of exchange is based on the theory that any contact made between two objects will result in transfer of material from one to the other. Therefore, using this principle, items of evidence that have probative value can be determined by assessing areas where the offender, victim, and items within the scene have potentially come into contact with one another.

Initial information received upon arrival at the scene and updates from investigating police will help indicate what is, or could be, potential evidence. The following are considered at the scene or during subsequent investigations: the area the offender used to enter and exit the scene; areas within the scene that have been disturbed; anything that the offender has potentially handled or come into contact with; anything that has been left behind by the offender, that is, a weapon.

Successful identification, recovery, and collection of evidence are dependent upon a methodical and diligent approach to scene examinations. The analysis of any evidence should take into consideration the possible destruction of other trace evidence. The development of a crime scene plan ensures that systematic searches are conducted, and appropriate light sources and chemical enhancement techniques are used by applying least destructive to most destructive methodology. Sequencing the order in which the examinations and/or analysis is conducted is paramount to preserving the integrity of all available evidence types.

Evidence Collection

Once all identified evidence has been recorded in situ by way of notes, sketch plans, photography, etc., appropriate techniques are used to collect the evidence. To prevent damage or contamination of the sample, systematic collection/sampling techniques are used. By following a collection sequence, the potential evidence on the item is maximized while providing the highest level of protection to that evidence. For example, a gun used in the commission of a crime would first need to be fingerprinted, then swabbed for DNA, then submitted for test firing. If this sequence is not followed, one or more evidence types would be lost.

Collection techniques are many and varied and include methods such as swabbing, swatching, lifting, vacuum sweeping, picking, and casting. These techniques are selected according to the type of evidence, the substrate the evidence is located upon, and the physical properties of the evidence itself.

For example, swabbing is the preferred sampling method for biological stains, for example, blood, semen, and saliva; however, if a confirmatory test indicates either semen or saliva on an item of clothing, the preferred method of collection is to cut out a swatch of the stained fabric. Trace or contact DNA can be collected using either a swab or a tape lift. Swabbing involves rubbing a moistened swab over the stain, which rehydrates the cells attached to the area, making them easier to retrieve through the rubbing action of the swab. Tape lifting removes trace or contact DNA from the item using sterile or ultraviolet (UV)-treated sticky tape. Both techniques allow a large surface area to be sampled, which concentrates any DNA present to a smaller, analyzable sample.

Tape lifts may be used to collect not only trace material such as fingerprints and trace DNA but also macroscopic material such as hairs and fibers. The adhesive side of the tape is repeatedly and firmly patted or rolled over the item causing loosely adhering trace evidence to stick to the tape. The collected lifts are placed onto a transparent backing such as clear plastic sheeting or glass slides which protects the evidence against contamination and permits samples to be easily viewed and removed for further examination or comparison. Hand-picking of hairs, fibers, vegetation on clothing, etc., is another acceptable method of recovery using disposable tweezers. Gel lifts are useful for collecting shoeprints in dust. Similarly, electrostatic dust-lifting kits are also commonly used for lifting shoe marks off many surfaces.

Vacuuming is another technique used to collect material from inaccessible areas or where there is a large amount of scattered material. There are several different types of vacuum cleaners used for this purpose. One such vacuum cleaner has a one-use only attachment head that the material is collected into. Once collected, the attachment is removed and sealed in an evidence bag and the contents are later examined in the laboratory. Another type of vacuum cleaner has changeable filters; however, the filter and catchment area of the vacuum cleaner must be changed and rigorously cleaned between each vacuuming to avoid contamination. This method of collection should be used subsequent to other collection techniques as it is indiscriminate and may result in the collection of a large amount of extraneous material.

Casting is a technique used for collection of three-dimensional impressions such as shoe marks in soil or a jemmy mark in a doorframe. This technique involves filling of a three-dimensional footwear impression with material such as Dental Stone that sets, capturing the characteristics that were left in that impression by the footwear. Mikrosil is a casting material used to capture three-dimensional tool mark impressions.

When collecting forensic evidence, it is absolutely essential to properly preserve each item so that the evidence on the item is not damaged or degraded in any way, which would limit its potential evidentiary value. For example, all bloodstained clothing items need to be air dried before packaging. When the garment is fully dried, it should be packaged in a paper bag, as paper allows for the circulation of air. If the garment is packaged in plastic, the garment would become moldy, which may result in the denaturing of the DNA.

All items of evidence need to be handled with the utmost care to prevent contamination. Contamination of evidence can occur in many ways such as handling of evidence without gloves and coughing or sneezing near evidence items destined for DNA analysis. Control measures are put in place to minimize potential contamination including the wearing of personal protection equipment (PPE) such as disposable overalls, gloves, masks, overshoes, and goggles. PPE also provides investigators with a means of self-protection from body fluids that may cause hepatitis or human immunodeficiency virus-related diseases. Another control measure is to regularly change disposable gloves between the collection of evidence items which will reduce the potential for cross-contamination from item to item.

Control Samples

When samples are collected from a crime scene, it is also necessary to collect a control sample of the same material. This control sample is a portion of undamaged material from the same general area as where the crime scene sample is collected.

A comparative analysis is conducted between the control sample and the crime scene sample which determines the original components of the material allowing for any introduced substances in the crime scene sample to be identified. For example, during arson investigations, control carpet samples are often collected from preserved areas such as underneath wardrobes for comparison against carpet samples collected from suspected areas of fire origin. Once the composition of the carpet samples are established, any flammable liquid that may have been used to accelerate the fire, such as petrol, can be identified.

An infamous forensic case in the 1970s involved the conviction and subsequent exoneration of Edward Charles Splatt for the murder of a woman in her home. Among other trace evidence, fibers were recovered from the bedsheet on the victim's bed. The three fibers collected were gray in color, like those on Splatt's trousers. Years later, a Royal Commission into the case concluded that the fibers found on the bedsheet had been selectively collected to include only gray fibers and were not representative of Splatt's trousers. This evidence, in part, led to the exoneration of Splatt some 13 years later.

This case demonstrates the criticality of collecting a representative sample of all evidence found at a crime scene, just as it is equally important to collect a control sample that is completely representative of every component it comprises. Materials such as patterned fabrics may appear to be homogeneous in composition but may actually be heterogeneous and contain different colored fibers, or in the case of a blended fabric, different fiber types such as polyester and cotton. It is essential that the complete range of both dyed fibers and fiber types are captured in the control sample to ensure accurate comparison with crime scene samples.

Chain of Custody

Evidence management is critical to the outcome of criminal prosecutions. Chain of custody is the process of validating how any piece of evidence has been gathered, tracked, and protected on its way to a court of law. Proving chain of custody is necessary to affirm that the evidence has not been tampered with, changed, or substituted. It is essential for police, scientists, and other specialists involved in the case, to demonstrate that a chain of custody exists on every occasion the item is transferred from one person to the next to show with absolute confidence that there is no possibility of misidentification or adulteration of the evidence. Should the defense counsel question the chain of custody for any piece of evidence, a documented path of continuity can prove that the item presented at court is in fact the same item collected from the crime scene. Where there is any discrepancy about where an item has gone to or who has had possession of the item throughout the process, the judge may rule that the chain of custody has been broken and the item may not be admitted into evidence.

Chain of custody requires three different questions to be answered to verify the accuracy and reliability of court testimony by police and forensic scientists: First, that the piece of evidence in question is actually what it is reported to be; second, that a continuous trail of possession by each individual handling the item can be demonstrated from the time it was collected until the time it was presented in Court; and third, that each person who had possession of the item can state that it essentially remained in the same condition from the moment he or she received it, to the moment he or she released it.

Key factors in proving a chain of custody need to commence at the crime scene itself. When items of evidence are located at a scene by the crime scene investigator, an identification marker displaying a unique number or letter is placed next to each item of evidence and recorded in situ by way of photographs, notes, and sketch plans. This procedure of marking the items for identification and accurately recording the details of each item is the first step in the chain of custody tracking process.

After the evidence has been recorded, appropriate packaging is essential to preserve the integrity of the evidence. All evidence bags or containers must be sealed with tamper-evident tape and appropriately labeled. Tamper-evident tape is designed to pull apart or shatter when the seal of the packaging is broken and is very difficult, if not impossible, to remove all telltale signs of this tape from the packaging. If the sealing tape is not tamper-evident tape, a signature and date across the tape and the bag is required as another control measure of tampering. Details of the evidence item and its collection are recorded on either preprinted label templates on the evidence bags or on adhesive labels, which are affixed to the front of the bag or container. The label information includes the description of the item, the location, date, time of collection, name of the person collecting it, and a unique forensic case number. These labels, whether preprinted templates or affixed as adhesive labels, also have a chain of custody section that must be signed and dated whenever the evidence bag or container is handed by one person to another.

In some jurisdictions, once all the items of evidence have been packaged and sealed, a forensic exhibit list is compiled by the crime scene investigator that comprises an itemized list of all evidence to be handed over to the officer in charge (OIC) of the case. The OIC will sign the bottom of the exhibit list providing continuity that he or she has taken possession of the forensic evidence items.

Once the items of evidence are transported from a crime scene to a police station or laboratory, the chain of custody procedures must be strictly adhered to. Continuity, storage, and security of the evidence are of utmost importance in the chain of custody process. All evidence items must be entered into an exhibit book or electronic case management system and secured in a locked exhibit room while awaiting further analysis. It is imperative that exhibit storage areas have restricted access that is regularly monitored and audited. Access to searching suites, examination areas, and drying cabinets within laboratories often have security controls in place limiting access to authorized personnel only.

When evidence items are removed from exhibit rooms, the items must be either manually signed out of the exhibit book or electronically transferred using a computerized case management system. Electronic transfers can be completed manually on the system or via a bar code label, where the bar code is scanned and movement of the item is confirmed with a personal pin number. This technology has improved the accountability and accuracy of tracking evidence movements within laboratories.

When a sealed evidence bag is opened for further examination or laboratory analysis, the person doing so must sign the chain of custody details that form part of the label. The crime scene investigator or laboratory analyst will thoroughly document their examination or analysis for each evidence item and record any findings or results. Upon completion of the examination or analysis, the evidence item must be resealed inside the evidence bag or container and the chain of custody details on the label must be updated to reflect that the bag or container has been resealed by that person.

When external laboratories receive evidence for analysis, another unique laboratory number will be allocated, first to track the items through that laboratory system and, second, to ensure that each item of evidence can be identifiable by the laboratory analyst in court.

By following the chain of custody rule to the letter, the case can proceed with the knowledge and confidence that the movement of all forensic evidence can be precisely tracked from crime scene to courtroom. This rigorous process ensures that forensic evidence critical to the case is admissible into judicial proceedings allowing a judge and jury to impartially reach a fair and just conclusion based on the forensic evidence before them.

See also: **Investigations:** Contamination; Evidence Collection at Fire Scenes; Major Incident Scene Management; Packaging; Preservation; Recording.

Further Reading

Brown, M., Wilson, P., Whelan, J., 1992. Justice and Nightmares: Successes and Failures of Forensic Science in Australia and New Zealand. New South Wales University Press, Sydney.

Fisher, B.A.J., 2004. Techniques in Crime Scene Investigation, seventh ed. CRC Press, Taylor & Francis Group, Boca Raton, FL.

Geberth, V.J., 2006. Practical Homicide Investigation – Tactics, Procedures, and Forensic Techniques, fourth ed. CRC Press, Taylor & Francis Group, Boca Raton, FL.

Saferstein, R., 2003. Criminalistics: An Introduction to Forensic Science, eighth ed. Prentice Hall, Upper Saddle River, NJ.

Saferstein, R., 2008. Forensic Science: From the Crime Scene to the Crime Lab. Prentice Hall, Upper Saddle River, NJ.

Stauffer, E., Bonfanti, M.S., 2006. Forensic Investigation of Stolen-Recovered and Other Crime-Related Vehicles. Elsevier, Burlington, MA.

Swanson, C.R., Chamelin, N.C., Territo, L., Taylor, R.W., 2009. Criminal Investigation, tenth ed. McGraw Hill, New York.

Relevant Website

http://www.crime-scene-investigator.net—Crime-Scene-Investigation.

Contamination

P Millen, Paul Millen Associates, London, UK

Glossary

Blank sample A random sample of unused consumable.
Contamination The (accidental, deliberate, or neglectful) introduction of material into a location which is likely to undermine the integrity of inferences that may be drawn of any examination or investigation made of it.

Control sample A sample of background material close to the item or material being recovered.

Definition

Contamination is the (accidental, deliberate, or neglectful) introduction of material into a location which is likely to undermine the integrity of inferences that may be drawn of any examination or investigation made of it.

Background

Forensic science evidence is founded on the outcome of contact and transfer of material. Contamination is a natural but unwanted reality. Therefore, contamination by contact of material between objects or places, which one would later want to associate, must be avoided if at all possible. The nature of the evidence type, whether it is a mark, impression, or contact trace will determine the degree of likely transfer and therefore the risk of contamination. The nature of forensic science evidence must also consider not only association and contamination between two specific objects, but also between generic materials of a similar or the same type.

Contamination should be at the forefront of the mind of any person conducting examinations in forensic science. All those involved in the process have a responsibility to identify potential contamination risks, record, and address them. The issue should be considered a threat within the knowledge and remit of investigators as they assess the potential of the investigation. The risk of contamination should be considered an integral part of their scene investigation planning.

Contamination, or the suggestion of it, may undermine any examination and the evidence from material recovered within an investigation. Laboratory-based scientists may have a particular advantage in conducting their examinations within controlled laboratory conditions which are subject to organizational or national protocols. This is not normally necessarily the case with crime scene investigators. They are sometimes faced with multiple challenges: numerous scenes, dealing with victims, suspects which may be time critical.

The avoidance of contamination is paramount. The total elimination of sources contamination is desired but not feasible. Demonstration (by the taking of actions, additional samples, and recording them) is the only safeguard that an examination is safe, or not if that proves to be the case.

Demonstrating that contamination has occurred may be seen by some as professional neglect. That could not be further from the truth. Practice which has led to contamination occurring may be disappointing and regrettable even if with better practice it was avoidable. However, identifying contamination and communicating the fact when it has occurred is the higher professional ideal. The discovery and disclosure of this information is wholly professional.

Steps to Avoid Contamination

Control of the crime scene is obviously important. This can be done by establishing the boundary of the scene (be it a location, item, or person) and protecting it. The establishment of a cordon at a major crime scene, marking it with incident tape, and protecting it with police officers is common practice. The same principles apply if the examination is that of a person (a suspect, victim, or witness), recovered vehicle, or any other item. The recording of the names of those who enter and leave the defined scene (or comes into contact with it) and at what time, maintains the integrity of the scene management process. The scene or investigation also extends to persons removed from the scene and those who may be potentially connected with it. The availability of trained crime scene investigators to examine such scenes may not always be adequate. It is a long-established principle that all areas such as scene, victim, vehicle, and suspect should be dealt with by separate scene investigators. But at some stage, most often in the laboratory, items will be examined and compared by the same scientist, where systems are also required to ensure that there is no contamination.

Separation (by time, location, and of examiners), does however, have its drawbacks. It discourages or impedes the subconscious and intuitive linking of observations and evidence by investigators, which is an important part of any investigation. The limited availability of suitably experienced personnel may result in the examination of certain areas being delayed or examined in priority order where the risk of contamination remains an issue.

Contamination continues to be a consideration long after the initial scene examinations have been completed. So the packaging and storage of any material collected must be thought through in advance. This is not simply an issue of continuity of exhibits (sometime referred to as the chain of custody) but more importantly integrity of material within the investigation itself. This is particularly so in a protracted enquiry. If further examinations are conducted by the same person, then the passage of time itself should not be the only separation.

With sound practice it is possible for the same person to examine areas of a crime scene which may be desired to link. Ultimately, items may be examined by a single scientist within the forensic science laboratory albeit at different times and in different locations within the laboratory. So too in the field then it is necessary to prepare and plan clean and clear areas of separation in time, place, and the equipment used. The ideal conditions we have already established. It is possible to seriously aim to totally eliminate field contamination and be seen to do so to the satisfaction of the courts.

It is necessary to consider the actions of others before the preservation of the scene areas in the event that contamination has already taken place. It is then that the previous actions of the scene examiner, whether they are in relation to that enquiry or not, along with the equipment used and the added safeguard of adequate controls can be developed.

The nature of the crime investigation may often lead to unintended exposure of the various aspects under investigation at an early stage. This can be done by members of the public prior to the arrival of police and possibly by the first officer attending the scene who may be pursuing other areas without full regard for forensic evidence. This is never an insurmountable issue providing that it is immediately identified so that areas that are still relevant may be targeted. The availability of verbal or written statements of those involved must be secured.

Case Example: Two youths are seen in a car that has previously been reported stolen after an unsuccessful robbery. Following a car chase, the youths abandon the vehicle. Some considerable distance from the vehicle and following a search of the area, a person matching description of one of the youths is detained following a struggle. The arresting officers take the arrested person to the vehicle and one of the same arresting officers searches it in the arrested person's presence.

The total denial of involvement by the suspect and the absence of other evidence may result in a request for the examination of the vehicle by a crime scene investigator. Clearly, the subject of transfer of trace evidence such as fibers may not be appropriate due to the actions of the unsuspecting officers who arrested and then took the suspect back to the vehicle while it was searched. The search of a vehicle by a first responder normally has the purpose of recovery of property (stolen goods, drugs, or weapons) and is not for contact or trace evidence. When a suspect is arrested from within a vehicle this is a common practice. That is not the case here, the suspect was arrested away from the vehicle. The exact action of the arresting officers, what they touched and recovered, and any steps they took needs to be known and recorded. The early identification of this problem is paramount. A refusal on the part of the crime scene investigator to conduct a further detailed examination of the vehicle due to possible, previous contamination may also be inappropriate. Any suggestion that the arresting officer had sat or crawled over the seats to search the vehicle would mean that a subsequent examination to locate fibers on the seats from the suspect's clothing would be highly questionable. However, it is still possible for a crime scene investigator to examine the vehicle for material that could not have been accidentally contaminated. This includes finger marks in particular and marks in general. In the event that those involved may have discarded gloves and masks in the car, consideration may be given to the simultaneous examination of the suspect's hair for fibers by a different crime scene investigator. The persistence of fibers in head hair in numbers beyond those considered by the scientist to be the result of contamination may give the court clear direction. It may be suggested that one fiber could be within the realms of contamination. A large number of fibers in such a specific area (such as the suspect's hair) perhaps would not be. This is a matter of consideration and interpretation by the scientist who later conducts the laboratory examination. The examination of papers in the foot wells of the vehicle may reveal shoe marks in dust. This is a potentially strong form of evidence which it would not be possible to contaminate without the suspect actually sitting in the vehicle.

Contamination is not necessarily the highest priority for first responders, nor should it be. They should not, however, return to a crime scene with an arrested person whom they may later wish to associate with the scene using forensic science evidence. Arresting officers are rarely if ever in a position to search a suspect or vehicle using anticontamination techniques and clothing available to crime scene investigators and scientists. Once the actions of first responders are known, a detailed examination may reveal potential evidence which is beyond the suggestion and risk contamination.

Choosing Who Should Examine the Scene (Location, Person, or Item)

Once the scene investigator has considered the events prior to their arrival, they must now consider what actions are then required. It is at this point that they assess whether they are the suitable candidate for examining the required areas. Direct contact with the suspect may prevent the attendance and examination of the scene itself. In relation to material that would be easily transferred such as fibers, paint, glass, or DNA-rich material, then it must be avoided.

Further thought is also necessary as although not previously involved in that particular enquiry the scene examiner may have previously examined an area in another scene that may contaminate their next examination. If a scene investigator is asked to examine a person suspected of firing a gun, then the recent handling by the investigator of a firearm in another case would make this latter examination totally inappropriate without taking vigorous steps to decontaminate first. It may be possible to pursue this examination safely with certainty when appropriate safeguards in place as will be discussed later. There is, however, a risk that contamination may occur which will undermine the examination. So if there is a better candidate for conducting the examination available, then that should be pursued.

It may not always be possible to take into account at the time matters that only become relevant later. Although contamination may occur, the properties of a particular type of material and whether it can be transferred accidentally are particularly relevant. Directional blood staining is a clear example of this as it cannot be transferred by wiping after the event as the shape of the deposited material has evidential value itself. So too, a mark or impression of an object without direct contact of the items. This is not so with trace DNA-rich material. Potential contamination of material may only occur in one direction. For example, a scene investigator may take and seal the clothing of a person suspected of breaking a glass window. They then go to the scene where they also take control samples of the glass from the window frame. No contamination of the clothing by glass could have occurred. This is not the case if they go to the scene first and later personally obtain the suspect's clothing. The clear recording of the actions of the scene examiner at the time of the original and subsequent examinations is obviously important. This is also the case in protracted inquiries where proper control must be kept of all potential evidence.

Actions Within the Examination

The need to use disposable overshoes, overalls, and gloves at every opportunity is good practice. These items must be discarded after use in a way that cannot lead to contamination.

The composition of personal protective clothing such as overalls must be suitable for the purpose (white paper, for example) and free from any contamination. Every effort must be made by the scene investigator not to contaminate one suspect with material from another similar scene. The example of potential contamination of firearm residues from another firearm is relevant here.

Contamination between unrelated scenes and suspects can be minimized by the use of separate cases or bags of equipment and consumables for the examination of scenes, vehicles, and suspects. So a case for crime scene examinations and a separate one for the examination of persons is a sound first step. There should under no circumstances be a movement of any material (even the most trivial such as labels of sealing tape) between the two. Carefully considered control samples (as will be described later) should be taken to demonstrate if any contamination has occurred. Where there is any doubt then control samples should be taken. Many forensic science laboratories or their suppliers provide kits with control safeguards included. This does not relinquish the responsibility of the examiner to consider the location, equipment, and personnel issues before sampling. A properly taken but positive control although unwanted in any enquiry is there to safeguard the suspect against matters outside the control of the scene examiner.

The Use of Blanks and Controls

Control samples are taken to determine if there is any background contamination. Properly taken they may include non-disposable equipment being used, samples of the environment of the examination (in the case of the examination of an individual) or the area around suspected material (without touching the suspect material itself). Blank samples may include a sample of the types of consumables used (an unused bag from the same stock) again to monitor and demonstrate that they are free of any material which may be important in the examination. Blank samples include materials such as bags, containers, and tape. Blanks and then control samples should always be taken prior to the sampling of the suspect material as to do so after may contaminate the blank or control itself.

Blanks and controls are equally important to within scene contamination issues, that is, relating to movement within the same scene. If steps are not taken to change personal protective clothing and take blanks and controls within a single scene, it may be possible to contaminate trace material from one area to another within the scene. The significance of this may only occur later when the statements of witnesses and the interview record of suspects show that a particular point needs to be proved or disproved. The consequence of this may be that it is not possible to determine if a witness, suspect, or scene examiner moved material within the scene. The change of personal protective clothing between zones (such as rooms within a scene) at natural breaks or when then examiner even momentarily leaves and reenters the scene cordon, limits the risk of contamination within the scene as a whole and as the examination progresses.

Many forensic science laboratories or their associated consumable suppliers prepare and monitor sampling kits for examinations such as DNA, firearm discharge residues, or metal traces. If the kit itself is not laboratory prepared and monitored, then blank materials should also be obtained before obtaining controls. When two suspects have already been detained at the same location and sampling is required from both, then the same trained operator can be used provided that consideration has been given to again discard disposable material such as gloves and the appropriate areas are cleaned and that the blank and control samples are obtained. This is certainly the case when obtaining hair combings from two persons suspected of previously wearing discarded woolen masks from a scene. Best practice suggests that two examiners should be used, one sampling each suspect. But what if there is only one individual available and the only additional person available is inexperienced or unwilling to take the sample? However well briefed that person is (by the scene examiner), this apparent option may be ruled out in favor of the trained examiner sampling both suspects while taking appropriate and disclosed safeguards. The established method of combing vigorously the subject's head hair with a seeded comb over a sheet of paper may not contaminate the gloved hands or forearms of the operator. But the words "may not contaminate" are not good enough. There needs to be some proof that the safeguards have been successful and the procedure is sound. Before sampling each suspect, the scene examiner should wash their own hands and forearms only then obtain a blank tape and then a control taping of their own hands and forearms before sampling the suspect. Finally, if the suspect is wearing a woolly sweater, it may be prudent to take this after the combing or obtain a sample of it in order to eliminate it from any material found in the head hair.

Thought must also be given to contamination from unrelated scene to scene, where the common denominator is the scene examiner or investigators. Although this may not be as important as that from scene to suspect, it is still contamination. In general, where material is being obtained, then new packaging must be used and all disposable equipment such as overalls, overshoes, or even scalpel blades discarded. The mere wearing of disposable protective and clean clothing should not solely satisfy contamination considerations. What it will do is reduce at worst and prevent at best, a transfer of material between operator and scene and removal of material from the scene by the examiner. Where equipment is reused such as brushes, tools, and heavy duty protective safety clothing, then they must be thoroughly cleaned after use. The taking of control samples from them at the time of next use will

determine if the cleaning process has been thorough and successful. Where material may become easily contaminated by accelerants such as a bag taken into an arson scene, but not used, then they should be discarded and destroyed so that they cannot be reused.

Case Example: Bad Practice

A supply of nylon bags for the preservation of accelerants (from either petrol bombs or the clothing of suspects) is retained within the custody area of a police station.

On one occasion, an officer recovers a large petrol container and uses one of the bags to package the item, realizing that the bag is too small, he chooses a larger bag and puts the first back into the stock cupboard.

A short time later an officer arrests a suspect for a different petrol bomb offense, bringing him to the custody area. On seizing the suspect's gloves, they place them in the contaminated bag obtained from the stock cupboard.

On examination of the gloves in a laboratory environment, the discovery of trace accelerant within the bag (particularly in the absence of a suitable control from the crime scene) may suggest contact with accelerants, which may not be the case.

The lessons from this are as follows:

1. Packaging materials should never be reused.
2. The supply of packaging materials should only be handled and controlled by trained individuals who maintain their integrity.

The consequences of contamination are a real problem that must be fully considered particularly in field situations. Careful consideration must be given to the actions of others prior to the commencement of any crime scene examination. If an area has been contaminated, then the direction of the contamination may result that only a one-way transfer could have occurred. The examination for a transfer in the opposite direction or material that cannot be easily contaminated may still be appropriate and safe. The discovery and disclosure of this information is wholly professional.

Demonstrating the Integrity of Items and Investigations

Demonstrating that an item is free from contamination is as important as minimizing it.

The recording of accurate notes relating to the integrity of the scene and its examinations can support this by the following:

- statement and oral accounts of witnesses
- actions of the first officers
- containment of the scene
- setting of a scene cordon
- maintenance of a log detailing who entered and left the scene and when

- continual taking of photographs of the scene as it is examined
- notes of any briefing given to those entering the scene
- scene examination/investigation plan
- record of sources and control of consumables
- details of search and examination
- details of protective clothing worn, by whom and when it was changed
- details of the retention and/or destruction of personal protective clothing
- details of the retention and/or destruction of consumables
- taking and retention of any blanks and controls
- list of all items recovered and retained
- steps taken to preserve, protect, and package items
- storage of recovered items
- movement of items
- details of any examinations made of recovered items
- final disposal of recovered items

Conclusion

The risk of contamination is specific to each evidence type and the circumstances of the scene and its examination. Separation from any outside source of the material under investigation and the ability to demonstrate that this has taken place are essential to maintain the integrity of the investigation and any interpretation or conclusions gained from it.

See also: **Foundations:** Forensic Intelligence; **Investigations:** Collection and Chain of Evidence; Fingerprints; Forensic Intelligence Analysis; Preservation.

Relevant Website

http://www.paulmillen.co.uk—Paul Millen Associates: Homepage.

Principles for the Organization of Forensic Support

J Robertson, University of Canberra, Canberra, ACT, Australia

Scope of Forensic Support

The word "forensic" can include anything which could end up in a civil or criminal tribunal or court. Hence, the potential scope of forensic support is enormous. Forensic support can be provided at the level of the individual all the way up to a very large organization. Organizations may exist in the private or the government sector. They may have forensic science as their primary business or forensic work may only be a minor part of the activities of a particular organization.

For the purposes of this chapter, the scope will focus on the organization of forensic support to include field-based and laboratory-based applications of science, medicine, or technology for a forensic end purpose.

An Ideal Organizational Model?

At an international level, forensic support will usually include at least some of the "field" forensic support being provided by a policing or law enforcement body or agency. "Field" forensic support will always include crime scene examination but typically some (or all) aspects of fingerprint examination (and often fingerprint identification), firearms and ballistics, and photography or imaging will be included.

In some countries, forensic medicine and pathology support may also be a unit within a law enforcement agency.

The laboratory component of the forensic sciences may or may not be a unit within a law enforcement agency. In many instances, the laboratory will be either a stand-alone unit, or, more typically, part of a "parent" government department. In some countries, a forensic laboratory may even be part of an academic institution.

Hence, there is no unifying or ideal organizational model for the provision of forensic support. The organization of forensic support will generally reflect how it has evolved within a particular country, influenced by historical, cultural, and political factors and sometimes simply chance and opportunity. There will be examples of carefully thought out strategic decisions in how forensic support has evolved, but it is perhaps more the norm that the evolution of a particular model has been more ad hoc.

Organizational Theory

Consideration of the principles for the organization of forensic science requires some discussion of broader organizational theory and, specifically, what may be different about the types of "parent" organizations from which forensic support is provided.

Organizational theory includes many aspects of management and leadership, and it is outside of the scope of this chapter to deal with these in depth.

An important focus of organizational theory in more recent times has been on change management and an increased emphasis on demonstrating accountability and effectiveness and "doing more with less" through greater efficiency. It is widely accepted that the modern organization needs to be adaptive and capable of relatively rapid change to meet future challenges.

Academic and classical views of organizations emphasize their multidisciplinary nature with three main aspects influencing organizations. These are the social system or sociology, the personality system or psychology, and the cultural system or anthropology. The economic and political environment impacts on all organizations regardless of the "behavioral" characteristics of the organization.

The goal of behavioral science is to understand the sometimes conflicting needs of the organization for maximum productivity, with the needs of the individual and their development. Behavioral science also attempts to provide a greater understanding of what motivates the individual. However, the individual is usually part of a larger team or work group and, as such, is influenced by that environment. Sometimes, individuals and groups are defined in terms of age groups such as the so-called baby boomers, generation X, and generation Y along with somewhat clichéd broad-brush analysis of the primary motivation for each group. As far as there is some truth in these high-level motivations, there are some implications for the leadership and management of staff and how to encourage a motivated workforce. For example, the last two decades have seen the forensic industry move from a largely male-dominated occupation to a female-dominated occupation, especially in the laboratory. Rapid increases in staffing levels in some aspects of forensic work have also resulted in a younger, more independent workforce with middle-aged managers.

Management can be defined as the process through which the work of individuals is coordinated and directed to achieve the goals and objectives of the organization. The role of management as an integrating activity can be summarized as shown in **Figure 1**.

Management practices have of course changed with the passage of time from almost all organizations being hierarchical with decision-making held closely by senior

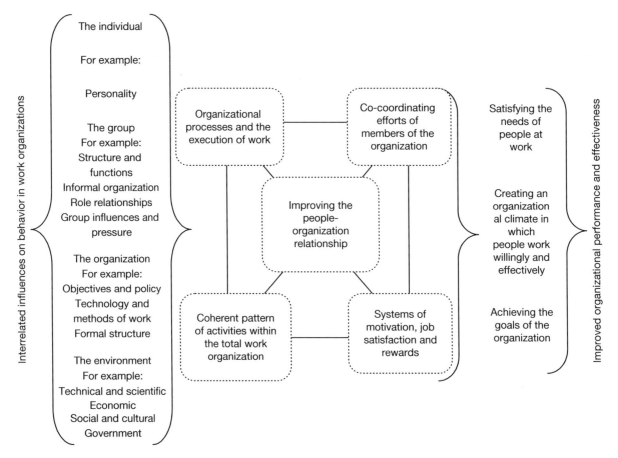

Figure 1   The role of management in integrating organizational performance. From Mullins, 2010–reproduced with permission etc.

management, to the "modern" organization in which knowledge and information is more widely held and shared and management is less hierarchical and is shared.

The latter has been achieved by decentralization with flatter organizational structures and increased empowerment of teams and individuals. For this approach to be successful, spans of control still need to be defined. A balanced approach would suggest that most organizations still require some level of bureaucratic structure. In particular, in government and public sector organizations, there is a need to balance an increasing need to demonstrate accountability, fair and uniform treatment of individuals, and the cost of the systems used to produce regularity and adherence to rules and procedures.

Forensic Organizations—A Special Case?

Against this very brief background of organizational theory, the question needs to be asked as to whether or not the forensic organization has any special or unique aspects which require special consideration.

Clearly, it would be highly desirable that all organizations delivering forensic support operate in an ethical, effective, and efficient manner with a goal of meeting suitable practice standards. It is given that such organizations must meet the highest levels of integrity and ethical behavior and many forensic practitioner groups have published specific ethical guidelines for forensic science. For many forensic providers, this is measured to some extent by seeking to meet the relevant ISO body of standards. Providers may then seek to be tested against compliance with these standards. For testing and calibration laboratories, the relevant standard is ISO/IEC 17025.

With respect to management, this standard requires the following:

Management Requirements
4.1 Organization
    4.1.1 The laboratory or the organization of which it is part shall be an entity that can be held legally responsible.
    4.1.2 It is the responsibility of the laboratory to carry out its testing and calibration activities in such a way as

to meet the requirements of this international standard and to satisfy the needs of the customer, the regulatory authorities, or organizations providing recognition.

4.1.3 The management system shall cover work carried out in the laboratory's permanent facilities, at sites away from its permanent facilities, or in associated temporary or mobile facilities.

4.1.4 If the laboratory is part of an organization performing activities other than testing and/or calibration, the responsibilities of key personnel in the organization that have an involvement or influence on the testing and/or calibration activities of the laboratory shall be defined in order to identify potential conflicts of interest.

4.1.5 The laboratory shall

a. have managerial and technical personnel who, irrespective of other responsibilities, have the authority and resources needed to carry out their duties including the implementation, maintenance, and improvement of the management system and to identify the occurrence of departures from the management system or from the procedures for performing tests and/or calibrations, and to initiate actions to prevent or minimize such departures;

b. have arrangements to ensure that its management and personnel are free from any undue internal and external commercial, financial, and other pressures and influences that may adversely affect the quality of their work;

c. have policies and procedures to ensure the protection of its customers' confidential information and proprietary rights, including procedures for protecting the electronic storage and transmission of results;

d. have policies and procedures to avoid involvement in any activities that would diminish confidence in its competence, impartiality, judgment, or operational integrity;

e. define the organization and management structure of the laboratory, its place in any parent organization, and the relationships among quality management, technical operations, and support services;

f. specify the responsibility, authority, and interrelationships of all personnel who manage, perform, or verify work affecting the quality of the tests and/or calibrations;

g. provide adequate supervision of testing and calibration staff, including trainees, by persons familiar with methods and procedures, purpose

of each test and/or calibration, and with the assessment of the test or calibration results;

h. have technical management which has overall responsibility for the technical operations and the provision of the resources needed to ensure the required quality of laboratory operations;

i. appoint a member of staff as quality manager (however named) who, irrespective of other duties and responsibilities, shall have defined responsibility and authority for ensuring that the management system related to quality is implemented and followed at all times; the quality manager shall have direct access to the highest level of management at which decisions are made of laboratory policy or resources;

j. appoint deputies for key managerial personnel (see Note);

k. ensure that its personnel are aware of the relevance and importance of their activities and how they contribute to the achievement of the objectives of the management system.

Note: Individuals may have more than one function and it may be impractical to appoint deputies for every function.

4.1.6 Top management shall ensure that appropriate communication processes are established within the laboratory and that communication takes place regarding the effectiveness or the management system.

4.2 Management system

4.2.1 The laboratory shall establish, implement, and maintain a management system appropriate to the scope of its activities. The laboratory shall document its policies, systems, programs, procedures, and instructions to the extent necessary to assure the quality of the test and/or calibration results. The system's documentation shall be communicated to, understood by, available to, and implemented by the appropriate personnel.

4.2.2 The laboratory's management system policies related to quality, including a quality policy statement, shall be defined in a quality manual (however named). The overall objectives shall be established and shall be reviewed during management review. The quality policy statement shall be issued under the authority of top management.

A key element of ISO/IEC 17025, with respect to organizational management, is an emphasis on impartiality and that staff are free from any pressures which might influence their technical judgment.

Further, the requirements are explicit in saying that where a laboratory is part of a larger organization, the organizational arrangements should be such that departments having conflicting interests must not adversely influence the laboratory's compliance (see Management Requirements).

An example of potentially conflicting interests could be the police investigators' view of what forensic support is required and the role of the forensic provider in this decision-making process.

Finally, the requirements also emphasize that managerial and technical personnel have the "authority" and "resources" to carry out their duties.

In addition to these general requirements, the Australian (National Association of Testing Authorities, NATA) application document has supplementary requirements (SRs) for accreditation in the field of forensic science.

These requirements again emphasize that the laboratory director's authority must be well defined, with sufficient authority commensurate with his/her responsibilities. There must be sufficient delegation of authority to managerial/supervisory staff, supervisors must be commensurate with their responsibilities, each subordinate should be accountable to only one immediate supervisor per function, and performance expectations must be established and understood by laboratory personnel.

Management must have a business plan and manage budgets to provide services to meet customer requirements, and the laboratory must have and use a management information system which provides information which will assist it in accomplishing its objectives.

This document is more specific than the general ISO/IEC requirement in that it spells out in greater detail the authority and responsibilities of the laboratory director. It is also explicit in saying that there shall be a business plan and a budget suitable for the laboratory to meet its objectives.

An interesting requirement is 4.1.5.a., where it states that "the organizational structure must group the work and personnel in a manner that allows for efficiency of operation, taking into account the interrelation of various forensic disciplines."

The SRs recognize that there is no single perfect organization for a forensic laboratory.

The SRs also have quite a lot to say about the responsibilities of supervisors, channels for communication, and input from staff including human resource policies.

Hence, while there are some nuances, which may be forensic specific, the guiding principles from an organizational management perspective are largely common irrespective of the nature of the business. Forensic science providers should seek to meet the levels of service and other characteristics as described in ISO 17025.

For nonlaboratory providers, the same management principles should be met irrespective of any alternative technical standard such as ISO 17020, which has been proposed in some parts of the world as a suitable standard for crime scene operatives.

Public versus Private Providers

As many forensic support groups are within law enforcement agencies, the issue of forensic management having appropriate authority, control of adequate budget, and management structures to demonstrate appropriate independence from undue influence are critical to enhance public perception of the impartiality expected of forensic science. While the same observations are equally applicable regardless of parent organization, there is a greater perceived chance that forensic decisions could be subject to inappropriate influence when the parent organization is within law enforcement.

Forensic science support is largely based in the public sector. As stated earlier, this does not mean that improved and more efficient services are not expected. However, it has been argued that as a government function the need to provide a large number of activities and the exposure to political initiatives come at a real cost which affects any assessment of how private sector techniques can be applied. A private sector model for laboratory forensic support has been introduced in England and Wales and in New Zealand. In the former country, commercial pressures have led to the Forensic Science Service (FSS) being dismantled with the government aim being to have no state interest in a forensic provider. However, the state will of course retain a major interest through "ownership" of their police services and "in-house" forensic support. In New Zealand, the model has been described as at best "pseudo-commercial." Under this model the provider is a Crown Research Institute (CRI) and is required to:

- undertake research,
- pursue excellence in all its activities,
- comply with applicable ethical standards,
- promote and facilitate the application of the results of research and technological developments,
- be a good employer, and
- exhibit a sense of social responsibility by having regard to the interests of the community.

As a CRI, unlike a State-Owned Enterprise (SOE), a CRI is not required to "enhance commercial returns to government."

It is not the purpose of this chapter to promote one service delivery model over another but to recognize that, regardless of the provider model, an unavoidable requirement of any organization today is to be accountable and to demonstrate it is running in a cost-efficient manner. The challenge for any organization is how to demonstrate a balance of effectiveness (and define what this means) and efficiency (lowest acceptable trade-off of unit service cost).

People Are Our Most Valuable Asset!

Are there any specific aspects relevant to the management of scientists and technicians in a forensic environment, and will the change in balance of employees have implications for organizations?

In a general sense, there has been a move away from hierarchical management structures toward flatter structures and from classical team organization to an expert team or cross-functional team mode. For example, see **Figures 2 and 3**.

These models may suit the "modern" employee as they devolve decision-making and encourage elements of self-run teams; however, they have implications for organizations with more traditional management structures. Whichever model of team environment is used a key element to success is staff motivation. There are a number of well-regarded theories of motivation including Maslow's needs model and

modifications (simplifications) of this model such as Alderber's ERG theory where E stands for "existence," R for "relatedness," and G for "growth." These, and other theoretical treatments, suggest that for specialists there is a greater need for a higher degree of independence, challenging tasks, open and honest communication, and recognition of job status.

Finally, these motivators need to be considered against an age matrix for individuals as motivation changes according to age. As forensic science requires job and life experience and knowledge acquisition, forensic scientists are likely to experience increased motivation as their abilities increase and results in enhanced self-image.

However, this may decline in older employees as they believe they enter a period of biological decline and cognitive

Figure 2   Expert team organization. Adapted from Laegaard, J., Bindslev, M., 2011. Organisational Theory. Ventus Publishing ApS. (Available as a free book on Bookboon.com).

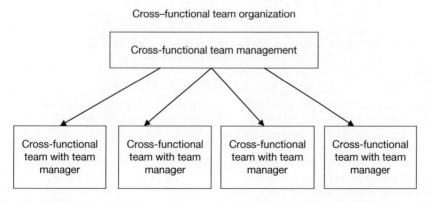

Figure 3   Cross-functional team organization. Adapted from Laegaard, J., Bindslev, M., 2011. Organisational Theory. Ventus Publishing ApS. (Available as a free book on Bookboon.com).

ability. Initially, they may compensate for this by simply working longer hours.

In conclusion, human resource management is complex without simple easy-to-follow guidelines. Forensic scientists are only "different" in the same sense as many specialist professionals and good management practices should recognize the factors likely to motivate specialists. In so far as organizational structures can be modified a more empowering model is likely to achieve the best outcomes when managing knowledge workers.

Conclusions

From an organizational management perspective, the forensic science "industry" is not unique but it has some individual elements which require careful consideration and management. The "workforce" is dominated by knowledge workers or science specialists. While there is still significant disparity of the level of academic qualifications across the industry, professional development is recognized as essential. Typically, forensic science providers will be part of a larger parent organization with a different mix of staff which may present some culture issues for managers of the forensic component.

Important organizational-level issues include a focus on appropriate levels of impartiality of service and some quite specific requirements if formal accreditation is sought at ISO level.

Finally, forensic providers are not immune from broader management issues including a change in culture and environment and the desire for greater accountability and demonstrated efficiency.

Further Reading

Becker, W.S., Dall, W.M., Pavur, E.J., 2010. Forensic science in transition: critical leadership challenges. Forensic Science Policy and Management 1, 214–223.

Bedford, K., 2012. Forensic science service models – is there a 'best' option? Australian Journal of Forensic Sciences 43, 147–156.

Heames, J.T., Heames, J.T., 2010. Forensic science staffing: creating a working formula. Forensic Science Policy & Management 2 (1), 5–10.

Houck, M.M., 2009. Is forensic science a gateway for women into science? Forensic Science Policy and Management 1 (1), 65–69.

Kobus, H., Houck, M., Speaker, P., Riley, R., Witt, T., 2011. Managing performance in the forensic sciences: expectations in light of limited budgets. Forensic Science Policy & Management 2 (1), 36–43.

Laegaard, J., Bindslev, M., 2011. Organisational Theory. Ventus Publishing ApS (Available as a free book on Bookboon.com).

Mullins, L.J., 2010. Management and Organisational Behaviour, ninth ed. Pearson Education Ltd, Essex.

Speaker, P.J., 2009. Key performance indicators and managerial analysis for forensic laboratories. Forensic Science Policy and Management 1, 32–42.

Relevant Websites

www.ascld-lab.org—American Society of Crime Laboratory Directors Laboratory Accreditation Board (ASCLD/LAB).

www.european-accreditation.org—European Co-operation for Accreditation.

www.iso.org—International Organization for Standardisation (ISO).

www.nata.asn.au—National Association of Testing Authorities (NATA).

www.ukas.com—United Kingdom Accreditation Service (UKAS).

Key Terms

Accreditation, Admissibility, Aerial photography, Anthropology, Archeology, Blank sample, Bone, Botany, Burial, Casting, Chain of custody, Chain of evidence, Collection and packaging of items routinely found in casework, Collection of items, Collection techniques, Computer-aided design, Contamination, Continuity, Control sample, Control, Crime scene, Crime scene investigator, DNA, Effectiveness, Efficiency, Entomology, Evidence, Examination, Excavation, Geophysical survey, Grave, Hazard labeling, Human resources, Infested material, Integrity, Interpretation, Investigation, ISO 17025, Knowledge workers, Labeling, Landscape analysis, Layer, Leadership, Management, Motivation, Odontology, Organizational theory, Packaging, Paper as a packaging medium, Photogrammetry, Possession, Preservation, Recording, Recovery, Sample, Sealing containers, Search, Sequence, Sketch, Soil, Stratigraphy, Tape lift, Targeting, Theodolites, Trace evidence, Transportation.

Review Questions

1. What are the archeologist's main interests and how do those help forensic applications?
2. How does the original digging of a grave help an investigation? What traces can be left behind?
3. Why is preserving the integrity of the grave of forensic importance?
4. Why would paper be a preferred method of packaging skeletal remains? Based on those characteristics, what else would work?
5. How would you remove infestations from recovered remains?
6. When should remains be packaged together? When should they *not* be?
7. Should human remains be labeled as "biohazards"? Why or why not?

8. What is the goal of preserving evidence?
9. What does Crispino mean when he mentions Locard's phrase, "as time elapses, truth evades us"?
10. What "temporary evidence" would a forensic anthropologist encounter?
11. How could human remains become contaminated from a forensic perspective?
12. With digital photography so prevalent and cheap, why should field notes and sketches still be taken at a crime scene?
13. What kinds of photographs should be taken at a crime scene? What kind should be taken during an excavation?
14. What is the triangulation method? How would it apply to a forensic anthropology recovery scene?
15. How could aerial photography help with recovery of remains?
16. What does it mean to "table" remains?
17. What is an exhumation?
18. What health and safety considerations are important during body recoveries?
19. What is a chain of custody? Why is it important?
20. What should be collected from the surface of a body recovery? Why do things like vegetation matter?

Discussion Questions

1. Compare and contrast the foundational principles of forensic science (Houck and Crispino) with those of archeology (Hunter and Colls). Can forensic science rightly be called "short-term archeology"?
2. How is an excavation of a grave like a crime scene? What is the same and what is different?
3. Is forensic archeology distinct from forensic anthropology? Why or why not?
4. As technology advances, so should field methods. How do things like remote sensing, field detection instrumentation, and drones change how bodies (surface and buried) are located?
5. Does the process of an exhumation differ from the criminal burial of a body? If so, how?

Additional Readings

Dick, H.C., Pringle, J.K., Sloane, B., Carver, J., Wisniewski, K.D., Haffenden, A., Porter, S., Roberts, D., Cassidy, N.J., 2015. Detection and characterisation of Black Death burials by multi-proxy geophysical methods. Journal of Archaeological Science 59, 132–141.
Fibiger, L., Ubelaker, D.H., 2016. Forensic Archaeology. Routledge.
McCullagh, N.A., Knupfer, G.C., 2015. Forensic archaeology and the independent commission for the location of victims' remains. Forensic Archaeology: A Global Perspective 407.
Pringle, J.K., Giubertoni, M., Cassidy, N.J., Wisniewski, K.D., Hansen, J.D., Linford, N.T., Daniels, R.M., 2015. The use of magnetic susceptibility as a forensic search tool. Forensic Science International 246, 31–42.
Ralebitso-Senior, T.K., Thompson, T.J.U., Carney, H.E., 2016. Microbial ecogenomics and forensic archaeology: new methods for investigating clandestine gravesites. Human Remains and Violence: An Interdisciplinary Journal 2 (1), 41–57.

Section 4. Analysis

The hubbub and disorder of scene work is replaced by the almost calming and Zen-like approach in the laboratory for the forensic anthropologist. Sorting, categorizing, cleaning, and record-keeping cannot be hurried. Likewise, the analysis itself, the careful measuring, recording, and calculating of the osseous landmarks and features, sets a careful, methodical pace. The puzzles to be solved can be many, from what bone or part thereof is this to minimum number of individuals to which metrics will provide the best estimate. The painstaking work and the many numbers yield features that help bring the victim back to life—sex, age, height, ancestry.

Species: Human versus Nonhuman

D Franklin, The University of Western Australia, Crawley, WA, Australia
MK Marks, The University of Tennessee, Knoxville, TN, USA

This chapter is reproduced from the previous edition, volume 3, pp. 1894–1907, © 2000, Elsevier Ltd.

Glossary

Alveolus Socket (or pit) in which the root(s) of a tooth is located.

Antemortem Preceding death.

Calcination Process of high-temperature heating.

Commingled Mixture of bones from more than one individual and/or species.

Cortical bone Dense highly calcified bone primarily found in the shafts of the limb bones (also known as compact bone).

Dentine Yellowish body of the tooth underlying the crown and surrounding the pulp.

Dentinoenamel junction Interface of the enamel and dentine of the crown of a tooth.

Diagenesis Postmortem physical and chemical changes to bone.

Diaphysis The shaft of a long bone between its proximal (toward point of articulation) and distal (away from point of articulation) ends.

Enamel prism Basic structural unit of the enamel extending from the dentinoenamel junction to the surface of the tooth.

Fetal Embryo from the eighth prenatal week to birth.

In situ Original place of deposition.

Osseous Bone tissue.

Osteon The primary cellular unit of cortical bone.

Perimortem At (or around) the time of death.

Perinate Around the time of birth; 24 weeks gestation to 7 postnatal days.

Plexiform bone Horizontal regular layers of cells in mammalian cortical bone.

Postmortem Following death.

Subadult Age range encompassing nonadult (nonskeletally mature) individuals (also known as juvenile).

Taphonomy The study of postmortem processes affecting a body after death.

Trabecular bone Light and porous bone with a honeycombed or spongy appearance creating a latticework that is filled with bone marrow (also known as cancellous bone).

Trochanter Points of muscle attachment on the upper femur.

Vertebrate An animal that has a backbone or spinal column.

Introduction

Distinguishing human from nonhuman bone is a critical initial step in the forensic investigation of remains, and confirmation or exclusion will direct the investigation. If human, analyses may include, but is not limited to, formulating a biological profile, that is, sex, age, stature, and ancestry, estimation of postmortem time, and contributing to the pathologist's determination of a possible cause and manner of death via the interpretation of perimortem skeletal pathology.

Preferably, a forensic anthropologist will process the discovery scene. This provides an in situ opportunity to examine context, estimate whether the remains are actual bones, and evaluate origins. An array of nonosseous objects including rocks, roots, and plastics can mimic bone in a variety of contexts. An onsite diagnosis of human or nonhuman prevents further time and financial investment. If skulls and/or teeth are present, then confirming or refuting human origin is not usually very difficult. There are, however, instances in forensic cases where recovered skeletal material includes only postcranial bones (either whole or fragmentary) and identification is required as to whether they are human, nonhuman, a mixture of both, or nonanimal. Postcranial bones of humans are similar in number to those of other mammals and even other vertebrates; the differences are in overall and relative sizes and in the presence of some structures (e.g., third trochanter in some nonhuman primates).

Forensic anthropologists draw upon their knowledge of human anatomy and osteology in conjunction with vertebrate osteology of species common to specific geography to help determine human from nonhuman. This relatively straightforward, noninvasive, macroscopic approach to bone and tooth assessment may not always confirm or refute species origins, especially if it involves bone reduced by burning, fragmentation, cortical loss, and, typically characteristic of such specimens, a combination of these effects. Hence, histological or molecular methods, though destructive, may be necessary.

We discuss how skeletal remains are commonly referred to the forensic investigator and how some biofunctional differences account for human and nonhuman skeletal variations. We also explore the key concepts underlying selection of the most appropriate method, given the condition of the remains, for example, degree of completeness and available resources. The main focus of this chapter, however, is to provide exposure to the methods available to the forensic anthropologist for diagnosing human from nonhuman bone.

Discovery of Skeletal Remains

Unidentified bones and objects are eventually transferred to the forensic investigator via the medical examiner, coroner, or other medicolegal official specific to a given jurisdiction. The exact proportion of human to nonhuman material discovered annually is highly variable and influenced by numerous extrinsic factors, for example, size of the jurisdiction, urban or rural setting, local geography and fauna, and public sensitivity to such discoveries. In Knox and Anderson Counties in East Tennessee, ~30% of the cases examined are nonhuman remains. This frequency has steadily grown during the past quarter century, given heightened public awareness of the forensic significance of skeletal remains from media bombardment.

There is a diverse array of situations bringing remains to the attention of a forensic anthropologist. Nonhuman "animal" habitation areas are frequently discovered by hunters, hikers, bushwalkers, and spelunkers and even during search and rescue operations for missing persons. This is common during the cooler months of the year when these activities are performed in areas not traveled during the warmer months. When hunted animals are butchered outdoors, parts become treats apportioned to dogs. Parts lacking meat or cleaned of muscle after butchering include long bones, joints, hooves, and paws.

To the untrained, the bones of bear (*Ursus*) paws are strikingly similar to human hand bones. In Australia, the bones of various kangaroo (*Macropus*) and sheep species (*Ovis*), among others, can be introduced in a similar manner. Only a fraction of the people making these discoveries would possess the knowledge to distinguish between human and nonhuman origin. Beyond skulls, the accuracy of the untrained observer drops significantly with postcranial bones and becomes virtually impossible when bones are fragmented.

Other potential scenes with human and nonhuman remains include motor vehicle and aircraft accidents, residential and commercial fires, and natural disasters. Here, it is not uncommon for pets and wildlife to become commingled, fragmented, and/or calcined alongside the human skeletal assemblage. Also, it is not uncommon for bones to be uncovered during earthmoving operations while digging foundations at utility and industrial sites. In Western Australia, urban renewal, in addition to residential expansions, has resulted in the discovery of nonhuman skeletal remains as food refuse.

Bone Morphology and Function

A well-established axiom in vertebrate paleontology points out that bone form is intimate with biomechanical function. This relationship intertwines form with the most fundamental movement, that is, locomotion, feeding behavior, etc. Alongside rote morphological species recognition, the principles of form and function underlie many of the methods that anthropologists and zoologists apply to distinguish isolated and fragmentary human and nonhuman mammalian vertebrate specimens. The uniquely human pattern of bipedalism is mentioned in regions of the skeleton, making it distinct when compared to skeletons of nonhuman quadrupeds.

Human locomotion is plantigrade, meaning the entire sole of the foot contacts the ground with each stride. Balance and support of the body's weight requires robust, irregularly shaped tarsal bones and elongated metatarsal bones. This tarsal–metatarsal arrangement forms the longitudinal and transverse arches of the foot which, along with select joints, provide foot strength and mobility and also act as a lever. Dogs, pigs, and other four-legged critters have digitigrade locomotion, walking with only toes contacting the ground. This movement requires elongated tarsal and metatarsal bones, termed metapodials, which, compared to humans, are reduced in number and have functionally become the limb bone, lengthening it for increased stride length during running. These behavioral distinctions are not only reflected in the size and shape of the gross bone anatomy but also in the histological and molecular structure of the tissue. Hence, the relationship of form to function is an elementary characteristic that enables the anthropologist to diagnose human from nonhuman remains.

Method Selection

The majority of evaluations are successful through examination of gross morphological features, attainable with complete or substantial portions of diagnostic surface bone. The loss of diagnostic features and degree of fragmentation or cortical damage, loss, or weathering will determine the appropriate analytical method, for example, histological or molecular. Very often, method choice is linked to the cause and/or manner of death and/or postmortem taphonomy.

Another crucial aspect during gross evaluation is the biological age of the victim. Subadult bones, especially fetal and perinate, often bear faint resemblance to their adult counterparts and are frequently dismissed as nonhuman. Hence, it is imperative that the observer has a thorough and comprehensive understanding of the structural appearance of human skeletal and dental elements at all stages of growth. Such knowledge is assimilated after years of training and "hands-on" experience, and although textbooks on juvenile osteology are an invaluable source, in isolation they do not provide sufficient demonstrations of the morphological complexities of nonadult bone.

For secure identifications when isolated fragments or calcined or cremated remains are discovered, assessing human or nonhuman origin will require either a histological approach in quantifying patterned cellular differences or immunological tests and DNA analysis at the molecular level. These methods too have their inherent shortcomings that limit their widespread utilization, including young age with the appearance of plexiform bone, sex, pathology, for example, osteoporosis

affecting cortical bone, diagenesis obliterating structural arrangement, contamination, and diverse results from sampling design. Irrespective of all this, these non-morphological methods require appropriate expertise and specialized laboratory equipment. To this end, there need to be some a priori inference that human remains are potentially involved.

Methodologies

Gross Skeletal Morphology—Macroscopic

An experienced osteologist can expeditiously ascertain human from nonhuman complete adult or subadult bones based on size and shape. Similar recognition applies to portions and fragments if they contain familiar diagnostic features such as joint articulations and muscle attachment sites (see **Figure 1**). The osteologist recognizes surface landmarks that relate to biomechanical function. Diagnosing an unidentified specimen involves deciding whether the bone(s) lies outside the range of human morphology while taking into account age, sex, ancestry, and antemortem pathology. Whole skulls and post-cranial bones are not problematic to identify. However, fragmentary specimens from any region of the skeleton present challenges.

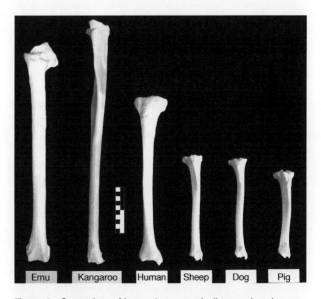

Figure 1 Comparison of human to commonly discovered nonhuman right anterior tibiae. All specimens are adult with the exception of the kangaroo being adolescent. Besides representing commonly discovered vertebrate species in forensic contexts, these bones demonstrate the relative variation in gross features between the species, including size, shape, joint articulations, and muscle markings (centimeter scale).

While law enforcement may be slightly embarrassed, though relieved when a "nonhuman" diagnosis is achieved, species recognition of the nonhuman bones may be desirable. Not all osteologists performing forensic identifications have training and access to comparative faunal collections of multiple vertebrate species, particularly those outside their geographic range. Such skeletal collections are a valuable resource for differentiating human from nonhuman bone. These collections are accessible in museums or vertebrate osteology collections in university anthropology and/or zoology departments. Quality reproductions of numerous extant species are available through France Casting® and Bone Clones®.

Where comparative bone is unavailable, bound atlases and CD versions of vertebrate skeletal anatomy are valuable. These were initially developed for archeologists and zooarcheologists examining archeological bone, but recent editions are styled for forensic applications. Recent atlases provide images and descriptions of juvenile and adult nonhuman bones commonly encountered. Standard views of most bones highlight the most relevant distinguishing features and describe potential variations related to sex, age, and pathology. Most of these recent atlases focus primarily on North American fauna. Forensic practitioners examining unique indigenous fauna from other continents should consult regional published sources and zoological journals.

The teeth reveal more about life than any other vertebrate tissue. At both gross and histological levels, mammalian teeth are species specific, and one does not have to be a dentist or a dental anthropologist to immediately recognize an unfamiliar whole tooth (see **Figures 2 and 3**). Current paleoanthropological research assesses speciation and dietary trends in cuspal gross morphology and the microstructural nuances of enamel prism and dentine patterning. At the forensic level of morphological interpretation, there are several atlases which provide an appreciation of teeth in the comparative format.

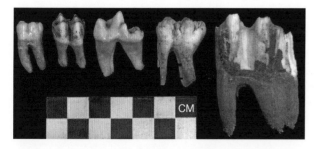

Figure 2   Buccal view of the mandibular left first molars among commonly discovered vertebrate species from forensic contexts. Note the crown and root size and contour differences between, starting at left, human, deer, dog, pig, and cow (centimeter scale).

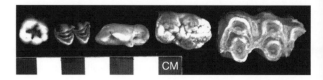

Figure 3   Occlusal view of the mandibular left first molars among commonly discovered vertebrate species from forensic contexts. Note the differences in cusp size, shape, and arrangement between, starting at left, human, deer, dog, pig, and cow (centimeter scale).

The orofacial structures are particularly vulnerable to blunt force impacts and breakage with fragmentation and dissociation from the body. Fracture with separation and distancing may be enhanced in an extended postmortem interval between death and discovery and result in skeletonization. Hence, the forensic anthropologist, with adequate training, immediately recognizes whole teeth as human or nonhuman and similar to pieces and fragments of bone, there is an inverse relationship between tooth fragment size and species recognition. Yet, like vertebrate bone, mineralized tissues from the orofacial region, including the alveolus, root dentine, and enamel, are histologically distinct from one another and between species (see **Figures 4 and 5**). The smaller the specimen, the more problematic the identification and the more necessary a histological approach. Histology is a remedy for troublesome pieces and fortunately, dental fragments typically contain alveolar bone with roots and crown parts attached.

Gross Morphology—Radiographic

Comparative osteological collections and/or atlases are helpful in the identification of whole bones or fragments with macroscopic diagnostic features. Diaphyseal fragments alone, especially the midshaft, are less reliably identified macroscopically, although morphometric methods are being developed. With fragments, differentiation between human and nonhuman animals is possible by evaluation of cortical thickness and internal trabecular patterning.

Cortical bone thickness is greater in nonhuman animals, which can be recognized. Radiographic features are common in the nonhuman diaphysis, including nutrient canals with medullary extensions, more dense and homogenous trabecular bone, and a sharp transition between cortical and trabecular regions. Some of these features may be observable in larger fragments not requiring radiography. However, if nondiagnostic, fragments require specialized destructive methods.

Histology

In bone fragments lacking species-specific macroscopic surface features or radiographic specifics, a histological evaluation is

Figure 4 Light micrograph of human dental enamel × 100 showing simple enamel prism structure. The dentoenamel junction is at the upper left of the image.

required. Visual and quantifiable metric analyses can discern pattern differences in the microscopic arrangement of human and nonhuman bone (see **Figures 6 and 7**). The most obvious differences are in limb cortices which are directly related to the aforementioned functioning. Plexiform cortical bone is commonly found in nonhuman mammals, characterized by osteons arranged in regular horizontal layers. This rectangular pattern is rare in humans, with the possible exception of developing fetal and younger subadult bone.

Microscopically, human bone is termed osteonal or Haversian, and has a central canal surrounded by concentric rings. This arrangement allows vascular and nervous nourishment of the cortices. Human osteons have a true circular appearance and are arranged in randomly overlapping configurations. Osteons in nonhuman animals also have a uniform circular shape, though with more regularity. In humans, replacement or "secondary" osteons develop during modeling and remodeling; also, the dimensions of the osteon, its Haversian canal, and other features of the tissue are significantly larger than those in cow, pig, sheep, horse, dog, and rabbit.

After proper orientation of the convex cortex and concave medullary surface of an unidentified midshaft, the fragment is embedded in an epoxy medium and cross-sectioned at ~100 μm. The most consistent results are obtained from adult long bones as opposed to irregular or flat bones or newborn and subadult specimens. Undecalcified ground sections are the simplest to manufacture and diagnostic success is equal to more difficult sectioning protocols.

After grinding and polishing, sections are examined at 40–200× magnifications using a compound light microscope. And while light microscopy adequately performs the diagnostic identification work, scanning electron microscopy, though cost-prohibitive, more clearly elucidates pathological and/or diagenetic alterations. The structural characteristics can be qualitatively assessed with confirmation or refutation of human origin.

Quantitative visual inspection affords a degree of statistical confidence in assessments. Depending upon the level of jurisdiction, for example, state or federal, this may be mandatory for admissibility in court. Osteonal measurements can be obtained using a variety of methods. Thin sections, generally visualized at around 200×, are captured and imported into a software package, allowing direct measurement. Those measurements can be compared to species means or used in specific two-group (in this case human and nonhuman) or multiple-group discriminant functions. The former is designed to discriminate between human and nonhuman origin, while the latter provides species identification. Smaller osteonal dimensions are generally found in smaller animals. Data taken from published literature show that the mean maximum diameter of a human femoral secondary osteon is approximately 264 μm; corresponding figures for rabbit, sheep, pig, and cow are 131, 206, 211, and 270 μm, respectively.

When evaluating forensic human or nonhuman bone(s), it is unlikely that species identification beyond those two groups is necessary. However, the ability to make a species-level estimation is valuable to the database of forensic standards. The degree of expected classification accuracy for histomorphometric discriminant analyses is between 76% and 83%. One factor that has not received due research attention is the degree of intra- and interobserver error in osteon measurements; this has potential ramifications for evidence under legal scrutiny. Importantly however, the degree of uncertainty in the final determination is quantified.

Molecular—DNA

The development of DNA profiling technology has revolutionized forensic practice, and its applications are widespread and clearly cross-disciplinary. With respect to the identification of unknown human skeletal remains, DNA profiling is a core method of obtaining a positive identity, especially in the absence of antemortem dental and medical records. There are numerous other applications of DNA technology relevant to the forensic anthropologist, including sex estimation, ancestry informative markers, and familial relationships. It is also possible to distinguish human from nonhuman bone on the basis of DNA sequences. It is important to note that the feasibility of undertaking such analyses may be restricted in routine forensic anthropological casework given the expense, equipment, and expertise required, not to mention the destructive sampling technique. Regardless, it is possible to analyze DNA markers for species identification.

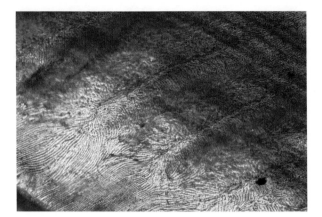

Figure 5   Light micrograph of domestic horse dental enamel × 100 showing exuberant, though a patterned, enamel prism structure. The dentoenamel junction is at the lower left of the image.

The species to which an unidentified bone sample belongs can be determined through the analysis of species-specific DNA sequences. Hence, by determining species origin, this technique provides insight beyond answering whether the remains are human or nonhuman. These distinctions may be crucial in cases involving poaching of endangered species or ritual animal sacrifice. In distinguishing human from nonhuman tissue, the analysis of mitochondrial DNA is generally preferred compared to examination of nucleic DNA. Mitochondrial DNA contains a high copy number within cells, so it is more likely to yield a useable profile from degraded bone.

To avoid contamination, a bone specimen for DNA analysis needs cleaning and decontamination. Several protocols are popular. After decontamination and preparation, the sample is drilled or sectioned, depending on the amount of destructive sampling allowed. The bone is then decalcified in an ethylenediaminetetraacetic acid (EDTA) or Chelex® suspension, and protein digestion is performed using extraction buffers. Following DNA extraction, PCR amplification, DNA sequencing, and analysis are performed. Human DNA is distinguished from nonhuman on the basis of species-specific base changes. If nonhuman animal species identification is sought, species-specific primers that only produce a PCR product with the animal species for which they are designed are commercially available. It is important to note that it may not be possible to extract and amplify DNA from highly degraded, burnt, and/or contaminated specimens, and in these instances an immunological approach may be more feasible.

Molecular—Radioimmunoassay

There are instances when both histological and DNA analyses of nonmorphologically distinct bone fragments is unable to resolve the human origin. This may occur because the microscopic arrangement of all regions of human bone is not mutually exclusive to all vertebrate species or it could be due to burning and extreme fragmentation. Solid-phase radioimmunoassay (pRIA) techniques offer a promising alternative approach toward confirming or refuting the human origin of even the smallest fragments of bone on the basis of protein collagen detection. The development of pRIA techniques took place in the field of molecular evolution to examine relationships of fossil species. Recently, its forensic applicability has

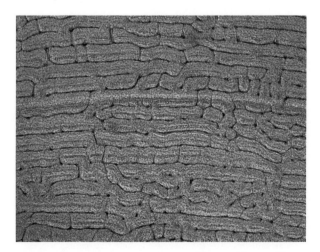

Figure 6   Nonhuman (deer) plexiform bone at 50×. Note the rectangular block pattern and distinct structure different from human bone at the same magnification.

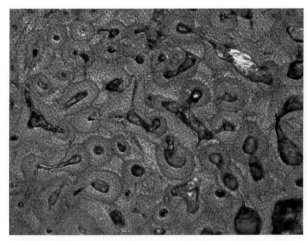

Figure 7   Human osteonal bone at 50×. Note the random overlapping circular pattern.

been championed through robust collaborative research by a select group of anthropologists and molecular biologists.

Sample preparation involves removing surface contaminants and, depending on the bone type, drilling to a depth of 2 mm to acquire noncontaminated material. An EDTA solution is typically used for dissolution of the bone powder to isolate protein. Following dissolution, the protein in the EDTA solution is bound to plastic discs, which is termed the "solid-phase" aspect of the technique. The remainder of the process, taking at least 48 h, involves the addition of species-specific polyclonal antisera and other radioactive antibodies. The antisera are produced specifically for human and many nonhuman species, including sheep, dog, bear, and chicken. The binding of specific antisera to specific antigens is quantified to determine the species.

Blind tests of radioimmunoassay approaches have yielded 100% accuracy in discriminating human from nonhuman origin. Only a very small amount of bone, in the order of ≤ 200 mg to 1 g is required. It is important to note that some immunological techniques, such as inhibition ELISA to detect human albumin, may still be viable in cases where DNA is poorly preserved but the associated protein epitopes have maintained their informative characteristics. Histomorphometric approaches, however, can be effectively applied to calcined bones lacking quantifiable DNA. The inclusion of radioimmunoassay methods in mainstream forensic anthropology is limited due to the advanced expertise and costs involved.

These results are limited in independent testing of the method for forensic remains in corroboration to the excellent results received in the original research. Validation of the power and utility of this technique has been established pertaining to evolutionary relationships of various fossil species. On these grounds, this should be considered a method of choice in situations involving extreme fragmentation and/or especially where bones are burned or altered to the point where quantifiable DNA cannot be retrieved.

Summary and Conclusions

Accurate identification of the human origin of even the smallest of bone fragments is a crucial initial step in a forensic investigation involving skeletal remains. As discussed, the appropriate method is related to many factors, which include the degree of representation, preservation, and whether destructive sampling is permitted. A variety of methods are available and although all potentially offer positive identification, their utility is not without specific limitations. They include expertise, specialized equipment, and the cost and time necessary to employ the technique. The exceptions are instances in which assessment is performed through the examination of gross morphological features and obviously this is the preferred method for the confirmation or exclusion of the human origin of unidentified skeletal remains.

See also: **Anthropology/Odontology:** Ancestry; Bone Trauma; Sexing; Stature and Build.

Further Reading

Adams, B.J., Crabtree, P.J., 2008. Comparative Skeletal Anatomy: A Photographic Atlas for Medical Examiners, Coroners, Forensic Anthropologists, and Archaeologists. Humana Press, New Jersey.

Cattaneo, C., DiMartino, S., Scali, S., Craig, O.E., Grandi, M., Sokol, R.J., 1999. Determining the human origin of fragments of burnt bone: a comparative study of histological, immunological and DNA techniques. Forensic Science International 102, 181–191.

Cattaneo, C., Porta, D., Gibelli, D., Gamba, C., 2009. Histological determination of the human origin of bone fragments. Journal of Forensic Sciences 54 (3), 531–533.

Chilvarquer, I., Katz, J.O., Glassman, D.M., Prihoda, T.J., Cottone, J.A., 1987. Comparative radiographic study of human and animal long bone patterns. Journal of Forensic Sciences 32, 1645–1654.

Croker, S.L., Clement, J.G., Dolon, D., 2009. A comparison of cortical bone thickness in the femoral midshaft of humans and two non-human mammals. Homo 60, 551–565.

France, D., 2009. Human and Non-human Bone Identification: A Color Atlas. CRC Press, Boca Raton, FL.

Guglich, E.A., Wilson, P.J., White, B.N., 1994. Forensic application of repetitive DNA markers to the species identification of animal tissues. Journal of Forensic Sciences 39, 353–361.

Hillier, M.L., Bell, L.S., 2007. Differentiating human from animal bone: a review of histological methods. Journal of Forensic Sciences 52, 249–262.

Komar, D.A., Buikstra, J.E., 2008. Forensic Anthropology: Contemporary Theory and Practice. Oxford University Press, New York.

Lowenstein, J.M., Reuther, J.D., Hood, D.G., Scheuenstuhl, G., Gerlach, S.C., Ubelaker, D.H., 2006. Identification of animal species by protein radioimmunoassay of bone fragments and bloodstained stone tools. Forensic Science International 159, 182–188.

Martiniakova, M., Grosskopf, B., Omelka, R., Vondrakove, M., Bauerova, M., 2006. Differences among species in compact bone tissue microstructure of mammalian skeleton: use of a discriminant function analysis for species identification. Journal of Forensic Sciences 51, 1235–1239.

Mulhern, D.M., Ubelaker, D.H., 2001. Differences in osteon banding between human and nonhuman bone. Journal of Forensic Sciences 46, 220–222.

Murray, B.W., McClymont, R.A., Strobeck, C., 1995. Forensic identification of ungulate species using restriction digests of PCR-amplified mitochondrial DNA. Journal of Forensic Sciences 40, 943–951.

Ubelaker, D.H., Lowenstein, J.M., Hood, D.G., 2004. Use of solid-phase double-antibody radioimmunoassay to identify species from small skeletal fragments. Journal of Forensic Sciences 49, 924–929.

Whyte, T.R., 2001. Distinguishing remains of human cremations from burned animal bones. Journal of Field Archaeology 28, 437–448.

Sexing

M Steyn, University of Pretoria, Hatfield, South Africa

This chapter is a revision of the previous edition chapter by S.R. Loth, M.Y. Işcan, volume 1, pp. 252–260, © 2000, Elsevier Ltd.

Glossary

Discriminant functions Algebraic expressions used to determine which continuous variables/characteristics discriminate between two or more naturally occurring groups/populations.

Geometric morphometrics A technique that is used to study the mathematical and statistical properties of shape, based on three-dimensional landmark data.

Gonial eversion The outward flaring of the gonial region of the mandible, which is said to be often present in males.

Greater sciatic notch The deep indentation on the posterior border of the pelvic bone that occurs at the union of the ilium and ischium.

Morphology The study of the shape and structure of an object or organism, in this case a skeletal element.

Osteometry Anthropometric measurement of the bones belonging to the human skeleton.

Preauricular sulcus The groove on the surface of the ilium, lateral to the auricular surface that is often more pronounced in females than in males.

Robusticity The degree of robustness expressed through the diameter or circumference of a bone in relation to its length.

Sectioning point A statistical line that provides insulation between adjacent sections without disrupting the current continuous collection.

Sexual dimorphism Morphological differences between males and females of the same species.

Univariate discriminant The distribution of a single variable/characteristic in a population or species.

Introduction

Assessment of sex is extremely important when it is necessary to establish identity from skeletal remains. In the first place, this classification effectively cuts the number of possible matches in half, and proper identification could never be made if officials were told to look for a male when the remains were actually those of a female. Moreover, other analyses such as estimation of stature cannot be correctly done as the sex of the individual must be known in order to select the correct formula. Thus, isolating, interpreting, and quantifying the manifestations of sex are an essential part of all skeletal analyses. Unfortunately, this is often not a simple process as male and female attributes span a continuum of morphological configurations and metric measures in the skeleton. Although some bones are better indicators than others, there is no skeletal feature that rivals the definitiveness of differences between fleshed individuals.

In some cases, remains of clothing, hair, jewelry, and other artifacts may be helpful to corroborate a skeletal assessment and indeed lead to a positive identification of the items in question, but they may also be misleading. One must be particularly careful in mass disasters where both bones and personal items may be commingled. Therefore any identification should always be corroborated by an assessment of the skeletal remains.

Sexual Dimorphism

In normal, living humans, sex is a discrete trait determined by the genotype and diagnosed by observing one of only two possible morphological features. These differences (e.g., external genitalia) are apparent at birth and clearly recognizable even during the prenatal period. In the skeleton, however, the most effective sex indicators do not begin to develop until adolescence, and some are not fully expressed until adulthood. Therefore sex estimation in children remains problematic, and even with a complete adult skeleton available for assessment, it may not always be possible to arrive at the correct estimate in all cases.

There are two methodological approaches to sexing skeletal remains: morphological and metric. Morphological techniques focus on shape—the bony configurations that are macroscopically visible and differ between males and females. There are important advantages to this approach, especially when a particular form is recognizable despite temporal and population variation. Obvious morphological differences such as those observed in the pelvis of an adult may allow optimal separation of the sexes (approaching 95% accuracy). The main drawback of the morphological approach in general (especially when judgment of size is involved) is that it is based on "eye balling," so if the formation in question is not patently obvious, experience becomes an essential component. The observer must develop a sense of what is relatively large or small, angled or curved, or wide or narrow. Intra- and inter-observer repeatability and statistical analyses of these features are also problematical, and it is difficult to assign a degree of confidence with which the estimate has been made.

In the past few years, geometric morphometrics has become a popular method with which to confirm and quantify observed shape differences. Using this method it is possible to observe in more detail exactly where the variations in shape occur, and what their magnitude is. Several software packages are available for this purpose, and all provide statistical data such as classification accuracies and level of significance of observed differences. It works well at the population level to assess and quantify differences, but remains difficult to apply to an individual forensic case, when sex estimation for only that specific individual is needed.

Not all skeletal components have consistent and discernible morphological evidence of sexual dimorphism. Problems arise when differences are only size based and there is no clear male or female shape, or where the remains are incomplete and the observer has to rely on less dimorphic bones. In these cases, a metric (size based) approach is followed. The advantages of these methods are that they are easy to use and provide indications of the accuracy with which the estimation can be made. However, the overlap between the sexes, along with significant population variation, creates some problems. These metric analyses are based on bone dimensions and are the methods of choice for skeletal parts like long bones that do not exhibit clearly definable shape variants. Often a combination of measurements is selected from each bone to maximize sex diagnosis using discriminant function statistics. The major problem with this technique is that standards are temporally sensitive and population specific (both between and within groups)—a formula for African Americans may not work on black individuals from southern Africa. This approach draws heavily on the fact that males tend to be more robust because normal testosterone levels produce greater muscle mass, but cultural variation in functional demands may lead to both differences in the expression of sexual dimorphism and its magnitude. This is of concern in bones where dimorphism is not primarily developmental, that is, those that reflect weight-bearing and labor-intensive stress.

The diagnosis of sex from the skeleton is further complicated by a number of diverse factors ranging from environmental influences and pathological conditions to secular trend, diet, and occupational stress. All skeletal sites and traits are not equally effective at distinguishing one sex from the other. So the question arises—why bother with the less definitive parts? The answer is simple—skeletal remains are rarely complete and undamaged, even in recent forensic cases. Therefore, the investigator must be able to glean as much information as possible from any bone or fragment. This chapter presents an overview of current methods and their accuracy for sex determination from the human skeleton.

Sex Estimation in Subadults

Because sex differences in the immature skeleton are not readily observable before puberty, the few attempts that have been made to look for dimorphic indicators have met with limited success, especially for individuals in the first few years of life. This problem is confounded by the fact that very few well-documented skeletal collections with large numbers of juvenile skeletons are available, making it very difficult to develop and test methodology.

A number of differences in the pelvis have been studied, among them the elevation of the auricular surface, angle of the greater sciatic notch, depth of the sciatic notch, curvature of the iliac crest, and the "arch criteria" at the auricular surface. In general, the association of these traits with a specific sex becomes more pronounced with age, and relatively poor results are found in individuals below 2 years of age. Using these criteria, some researchers have reported success rates around 80% in slightly older children, whereas others caution against their use in a forensic setting.

Several studies have also been done on the development of sexual dimorphism in the mandible, and aspects such as the shape of the inferior symphyseal border and corpus, gonial eversion, mandibular protrusion, mentum shape, and mandibular arcade shape have been assessed. Once again, conflicting success rates have been reported. It seems that the expression of these traits may vary throughout the childhood years and may also vary between populations. The same can be said for differences in orbit shapes, robusticity of long bones and the basicranium. These methods may all be used in an attempt to estimate the sex of an unidentified subadult, but should be used with caution and only by a trained individual who has experience with the specific method. It should also only be used in a population for which that method has been tested.

Attempts to capitalize on sex differences in the size of both the deciduous and permanent dentition have been somewhat more successful. Tooth dimensions (length and breadth) do vary between the sexes, but a large degree of overlap exists so that it is difficult to use this in individual cases. Formulae developed on the basis of permanent teeth of adults may also not necessarily be valid for juveniles, as selective mortality or cultural bias may increase or decrease the level of sexual dimorphism closer to adulthood. Tooth size varies between populations, but discriminant function formulae are available for a number of populations and may be of use in those specific regions.

In a recent study, the nonmetric characteristics of the distal humerus were used to estimate sex in adolescents. The four characteristics used were trochlear constriction, trochlear symmetry, olecranon fossa shape, and angle of the medial epicondyle. The expected male/female differences are shown in **Figure 1**. This method has been tested in adults as well. In a study of 42 adolescent distal humeri, an average accuracy of 81% was obtained. These results look promising but still need to be repeated by other researchers.

The Adult Skeleton: Morphology

When the morphological expressions of sexual dimorphism in the adult skeleton are easily distinguishable, they provide a reliable means of diagnosing sex. Traditionally the pelvis and skull have been used for this purpose, whereas other bones such as the humerus, scapula, and proximal femur may also show some shape differences.

The Pelvis

The pelvic girdle is composed of three bones: two coxal (or hip) bones and the sacrum (**Figure 2**). Each hip bone is in turn the product of the fusion of three bones: the ilium, ischium, and pubis. The female pelvis is designed to accommodate childbirth whereas the only requirements for males are support and locomotion. These differences manifest in various parts of this complex structure. **Table 1** summarizes the morphologic differences in the pelvis.

The most easily assessable morphological feature is the subpubic angle formed by the ventral articulation of the pubic bones at the symphysis (**Figure 2**). The male pelvis is characterized by roughly triangular pubic bones that form a narrow subpubic angle. Pubertal growth modifications in females are centered on the facilitation of childbirth. Elongation of the pubic bones creates a more rectangular shape and results in a much wider subpubic angle and larger outlet. Further enlargement of the pelvic outlet is accomplished by widening of the greater sciatic notch in females, but this feature may show considerable variability and is sometimes difficult to assess. It also shows some variations in expression between different populations. If the sacrum can be articulated, it gives a much clearer picture of the width of the notch by completing the dorsal portion. Other female adaptations which can be used in sex determination include a rounded (as opposed to the heart-shaped male) inlet, a dorsally orientated tilt of the sacrum, and a small and everted ischial spine. The upper section or "false pelvis" is broader and deeper in males, whereas the lower portion or "true pelvis" is wider in females.

The ischial tuberosity is positioned more dorsally in males and laterally in females. A uniquely male trait is the rough everted area of the medial border of the ischiopubic ramus for the attachment of the crus (corpus cavernosum) of the penis. This ramus is more gracile in females and narrows as it approaches the symphysis. In the sacrum, females show a proportionally smaller superior articular surface relative to the total width of the wings.

If a well-developed preauricular sulcus is present, this also indicates a female individual. This sulcus usually develops after a pregnancy and is caused by stress on the sacroiliac ligament. Extensive scarring on the posterior (dorsal) side of the pubis, such as dorsal pitting, may also be the result of pregnancy and labor.

As in all skeletal remains, the most diagnostic parts are not always available, especially following extended periods of exposure to the elements or years of burial. Since spongy bones are more prone to destruction, highly dimorphic bones like the pubis may not be available for diagnosis.

The Skull

Sex differences have been investigated in nearly every feature of the skull. **Table 2** contains a list of dimorphic cranial characteristics (**Figure 3**). In general, the male skull is expected to have more rugged sites of muscle attachments, a prominent glabellar region, and thicker bones. A large, pronounced supraorbital torus and rugged occipital protuberance can be considered reliable male characteristics. When viewed laterally, the sloping male forehead gives the vault a more rounded outline than that of the relatively vertical female forehead. Males have larger mastoid processes. Both frontal and parietal eminences tend to be better developed in females. Some differences in the cranium are of a proportional nature such as the orbits. Because eyes are of similar size in both sexes, the orbits appear to take up a larger portion of the face in females. Females also tend to have round or square orbits with sharp superior orbital margins, in contrast to the more rectangular orbits with rounded margins in males.

One of the most dimorphic parts of the skull is the mandible. If only the symphyseal region of the mandible is present, a squared or undercut base is often associated with males and a round or pointed inferior outline with females. Initial research on the ramus of the mandible indicated that flexure in this area is associated with males; however, subsequent research yielded conflicting results. Geometric morphometrics, in particular, has shown that this is not a consistent shape difference that can be used with a high level of accuracy to distinguish between the sexes, although other independent morphological studies have shown some success with this method. The same can be said for gonial eversion, which seems to be unreliable for sex estimation. In general, the male

(a) Trochlear constriction: less pinched in males, more pinched in females

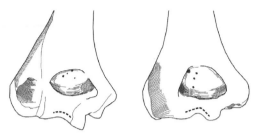

(b) Trochlear symmetry: assymetrical in males, symmetrical in females

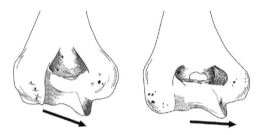

(c) Olecranon fossa shape: triangular in males, oval in females

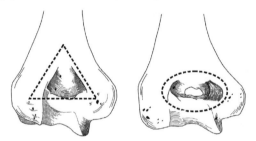

(d) Angle of medial epicondyle: horizontal in males, angled in females

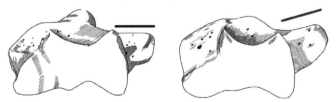

Figure 1   Morphological differences in the distal humerus (Male, left; female, right).

mandible is more robust, with a broad ramus and well-developed chin area.

In all skeletal assessments, it is important to remember that humans vary both temporally and spatially. To this one may add variation arising from growth factors, environmental stress, and pathology or trauma. Therefore, small or absent brow ridges or prominent eminences are not necessarily female indicators. The same can be said of a rounded chin and a less rugged occipital region, both of which are not uncommonly seen in males. In this regard, population differences are a major cause of variability in the expression of sexual dimorphism.

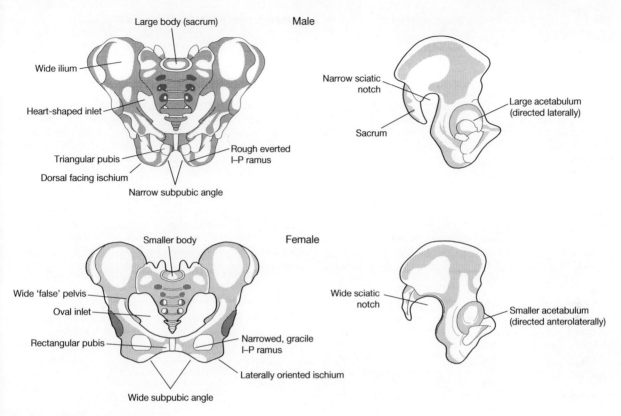

Figure 2 Sex differences in the pelvis.

Other Postcranial Indicators

A number of papers have been published outlining differences in the morphology of especially the distal part of the humerus. Sexual dimorphism in this area is said to be due to differences in the carrying angle of the articulated humerus, radius, and ulna. In adults, accuracies ranging from 74% to 94% have been reported for various populations when combinations of characteristics demonstrated in **Figure 1** are used. These differences have also been elucidated by means of geometric morphometrics.

Similarly, geometric morphometrics has been used to outline differences in the shape of scapulae and orbits between males and females, with high rates of accuracy in separating the sexes. These results need to be tested in various populations, also making them practically applicable when assessing single skeletons.

The Adult Skeleton: Metric Analysis

Osteometric analysis generally yields high levels of accuracy for the diagnosis of sex. Techniques range from the calculation of a simple sectioning point derived from a single measurement to complex multivariate discriminant function analysis. Indices formed by the relationship of one dimension to another, such as that of the ischiopubic index, allow male/female comparisons while eliminating size as a factor.

Discriminant function analysis is one of the most commonly used techniques to develop sex determination formulae using one or more measurements from the skeleton. Discriminant function formulae have been developed for almost all bones of the postcranial skeleton, for a wide range of populations across the world. Generally, the formulae for the larger long bones such as the femur and humerus provide the best results, whereas those for smaller bones such as the bones of the hands and feet perform less well. Usually tables are published with unstandardized coefficients, which should be multiplied with the measured values of the specific bone. Within one specific formula these should be added together, along with the constant. Values higher than the sectioning point usually indicate a male individual and vice versa, and percentages are given to indicate the accuracy with which the individuals from the original population were classified.

Table 1   Morphological sex differences in the pelvis

Trait	Male	Female
Pubic symphysis	Higher	Lower
Pubic bone shape	Triangular	Square or rectangular
Ventral arc on pubis	Absent	Present
Subpubic angle	Narrow, V-shaped	Wide, U-shaped
Acetabulum	Large, laterally directed	Smaller, anterolaterally directed
Greater sciatic notch	Narrow, deep	Wide, shallow
Ischiopubic rami	Rough everted margin	Gracile, narrows near symphysis
	Broad medial surface	Ridge on medial aspect
Sacroiliac joint	Large	Small, oblique
Postauricular space	Narrow	Wide
Preauricular sulcus	Rarely present	Often present
Iliac tuberosity	Large, not pointed	Small or absent, pointed or varied
Sacrum	Long, narrow, and straighter	Short, broad, marked curvatures
Pelvic inlet	Heart shaped	Circular, elliptical

Table 2   Morphological sex differences in the skull

Trait	Male	Female
General appearance	Rugged	Smooth
Supraorbital ridges	Medium to large	Small to absent
Mastoid processes	Medium to large	Small to medium
Occipital area	Prominent muscle lines and protuberance	Muscle lines and protuberance not prominent
Frontal eminences	Small	More prominent
Parietal eminences	Small	More prominent
Orbits	Rectangular, relatively smaller	Round, relatively larger
Orbital margins	Rounded	Sharp
Forehead	Sloped	Vertical
Palate	Large, broad, U-shaped	Small, parabolic
Mandible	Robust, broad ramus	Gracile, narrower ramus
Mental eminence	Large	Smooth, small eminence
Teeth	Large, lower M1 more often five-cusped	Smaller, molars often four-cusped

In general, selection of dimensions for a formula depends on levels of intercorrelation as well as the degree of difference between the sexes. It is, for example, very likely that femoral distal breadth is significantly correlated with tibial proximal breadth and therefore one of these may suffice to provide the best result. In the major long bones, it has been observed that epiphyseal measurements are better indicators of sex than length or diaphyseal dimensions, and accuracies are fairly high. With this in mind, univariate discriminant functions were calculated using eight single dimensions from the humerus, femur, and tibia (**Table 3**). Although most of the dimensions used are standard measurements (clearly defined in major reference books) these dimensions were also selected because these segments of the skeleton are commonly recovered, even when the skeleton is badly fragmented. In order to make this methodology applicable to diverse populations, osteometric analyses of modern (twentieth century) skeletal samples have been conducted on US whites and blacks, South African whites and blacks, and Asians, including mainland Chinese and Japanese. **Table 3** lists descriptive statistics for males and females along with the average of the two sexes (sectioning point) and percentage accuracy. In all samples, males were significantly larger than females. Using this technique,

determination of sex is accomplished by comparing the dimension of an unidentified bone with the sectioning point for that population. For example, if the humeral head diameter of an unidentified American white is 47 mm, classification would be "male" (any value larger than 45.6 mm classifies a person as male in this group). Although overall accuracy is 84.8% (**Table 3**), the farther the measurement is from the sectioning point, the greater the likelihood of correct sexing. Moreover, if the humeral head diameter is greater than the male mean (48.6 mm) or less than the female mean (42.6 mm), the probability of correct determination would be much higher. It must be emphasized, however, that it is necessary to know ancestry in such cases, unless the values of the unidentified specimen are extreme.

As noted earlier, metrics are group specific, except probably for the pelvis. As is evident from **Table 3**, populations differ from each other in the degree and range of dimorphism exhibited by various dimensions. This reflects differences in both size and proportions. In general, South African whites are the largest of the groups assessed, whereas South African blacks are among the smallest, with a mean closer to that of the Chinese and Japanese. **Table 3** also reveals population differences in the locus of dimorphism. For example, femoral distal

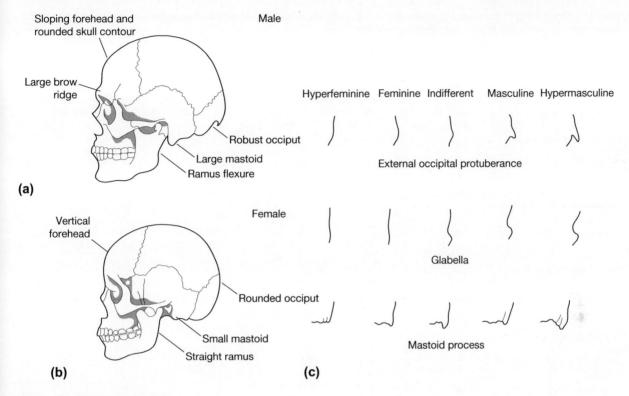

Male

Sloping forehead and rounded skull contour

Large brow ridge

Robust occiput
Large mastoid
Ramus flexure

(a)

Vertical forehead

Rounded occiput

Small mastoid
Straight ramus

(b)

Hyperfeminine Feminine Indifferent Masculine Hypermasculine

External occipital protuberance

Female

Glabella

Mastoid process

(c)

Figure 3   Sex differences in the skull.

breadth is the most diagnostic measurement in South African whites, whereas maximum dimorphism in the Japanese is found in the epicondylar breadth of the humerus.

FORDISC 3.0 (FD3), which is distributed by the University of Tennessee, is an example of an analytic program that employs discriminant function analysis to assist in assessing sex, ancestry, and stature from unidentified skeletal remains. With the measurements entered from the crania or postcranial remains, discriminant function formulae are created on the fly. Statistical output includes group membership, cross-validated classification accuracy, posterior probabilities, and typicalities. Posterior probabilities are calculated to provide information on group membership, based on the distance of a group to each of the other groups, whereas typicality (F, Chi, and R) probabilities represent the likelihood that an unidentified part belongs to the group to which it has been assigned. Authors of the program strongly caution against using the software if the population that one is examining is not represented in the database.

Summary and Conclusions

Although there are many techniques to determine sex from practically every part of the skeleton, there are a number of

caveats. The accuracy of both morphological and osteometric sex assessment depends on rigorous training and firsthand experience in observing skeletal remains. The overlap between the sexes implies that structures show gradations of differences within and between sexes and populations. This gradation must be carefully evaluated by studying large documented skeletal collections from different regions of the world. Bone measurement is a tedious process and requires consistency and standardization. The technique has a long history and although there is international agreement among scientists on how measurements are taken (to allow comparability), individual variation in measuring and interobserver error are always troublesome factors.

Even though decades of research have resulted in a plethora of methods and standards of assessment, many factors complicate the determination of sex from the skeleton. Age must be considered because the skeleton does not exhibit maximum dimorphism until sexual maturation and growth are complete. It has also been shown that the degree of sexual dimorphism may change with advancing age and that especially osteoporotic females may show an increase in robusticity in old age. Problems also arise when one has only a partial or fragmented skeleton. It is not always easy to distinguish certain bones of a male of 17 from one in his 20s and as growth can continue into the latter decade, sex differences may be clear

Table 3   Metric determination of sex and classification accuracy from single long bone dimensions (mm) in American whites and blacks, South African whites and blacks, and Chinese and Japanese populations

	Terry Whites		Terry Blacks		South African Whites		South African Blacks		Chinese		Japanese	
Dimensions	Mean	SD	Mean	SD	Mean	SD	Mean	SD	Mean	SD	Mean	SD
n	Male: 46 Female: 45		Male: 45 Female: 44		Male: 44 Female: 42		Male: 37 Female: 44		Male: 33 Female: 29		Male: 39 Female: 32	
Humeral head diameter												
Males	48.6	4.18	48	3.17	49	3.28	43.8	2.23	45.1	2.56	44	1.72
Females	42.4	2.33	42.8	2.29	43	2.28	37.7	2.08	39.3	2.2	39.1	2.67
Average	45.6	4.6	45.4	3.81	46.1	4.13	40.5	3.73	42.4	3.76	41.8	3.27
% Accuracy	84.8		86.8		84.6		90.9		80.5		87.3	
Humeral epicondylar breadth												
Males	63.9	4.35	64.5	4.42	63.6	3.67	61.3	6.43	58.5	3.87	59.9	2.11
Females	56.3	3.52	57.5	3.02	55.7	2.69	53.5	3.62	52.2	2.75	52.2	3.95
Average	60.2	5.5	61	5.13	59.7	5.1	57	10.05	55.6	4.62	56.4	4.91
% Accuracy	83.7		86.8		88.4		88.6		84.4		91.1	
Femoral head diameter												
Males	48.9	3.14	48.1	3.23	48.4	2.76	45.3	2.33	46.2	2.6	46	1.86
Females	42.8	2.39	42.6	2.03	43.1	2.13	39.2	2.6	41	2.31	40.8	2.54
Average	45.9	4.13	45.4	3.86	45.8	3.64	42	3.94	43.8	3.58	43.6	3.4
% Accuracy	82.6		88		85.9		91.9		83.1		88.6	
Femoral midshaft circumference												
Males	91.5	4.82	92.7	5.65	92	5.47	90	5.16	85.3	6.37	85.4	4.16
Females	82.8	5.67	84	5.73	84.5	5.14	78.8	4.74	75.3	4.66	78.3	6.4
Average	87.2	6.8	88.4	7.16	88.3	6.48	84	7.45	80.6	7.53	82.2	6.32
% Accuracy	79.1		79.1		74.3		89.9		81.7		78.5	
Femoral distal breadth												
Males	83.1	4.44	82.8	4.68	84	4.61	79.2	4.24	80.2	4.47	81.1	2.73
Females	75.3	3.58	74.7	3.66	75.2	3.27	69.6	4.78	69.8	3	72.4	4.31
Average	79.2	5.62	78.8	5.85	79.7	5.98	74	6.6	75.3	6.5	77.1	5.58
% Accuracy	79.4		87		90.5		86.4		92.3		85.5	
Tibial proximal breadth												
Males	76	3.68	77.1	4.14	78.2	4.43	74.9	3.72	72.8	3.74	73.5	2.87
Females	68.6	3.69	68.3	3	69.8	2.96	64.9	7.37	63.6	3.36	66.2	4.42
Average	72.3	5.25	72.8	5.68	74.1	5.63	69.5	7.8	68.5	5.81	70.2	5.16
% Accuracy	85.9		89.1		87.7		86.5		89.5		88.6	
Tibial circumference at nutrient foramen												
Males	96.2	5.76	100.1	6.91	97.3	6.13	98.4	6.35	93.1	6.52	91.6	4.9
Females	86.7	7.9	90	6.2	87.2	6.13	85.1	5.2	76.4	5.77	82.5	8.56
Average	91.5	8.36	95.1	8.28	92.4	7.94	91.2	8.78	85.3	10.41	87.5	8.13
% Accuracy	76.1		80.4		82.1		83.5		90.4		80	
Tibial distal breadth												
Males	47.7	3.15	47.6	3.76	46.8	2.62	45.4	2.56	45.1	2.38	45.3	2.18
Females	43.3	2.86	47.6	2.7	41.9	2.5	39.9	2.23	39	2.34	40.7	2.41
Average	45.5	3.71	45.4	3.98	44.4	3.53	42.4	3.63	42.2	3.87	43.3	3.24
% Accuracy	78.3		80.4		80.7		87.5		90.1		82.5	

neither metrically nor morphologically. This is further complicated by the fact that there is significant variation between populations who inhabit different geographic regions and constitute established gene pools.

Finally, since anything that affects the growth, development, maintenance, and remodeling of the skeleton can modify the expression of sexual dimorphism, trauma and disease can result in missexing. Some conditions cause abnormal bony enlargement whereas others result in atrophy or obliterate normally clear morphological differences. The intimate relationship between bone and muscle means that even in the absence of obvious damage to a skeletal component, muscular impairment can lead to inappropriate remodeling. All of these factors, above and beyond the normally occurring variability, subtleness, and overlap of features in the human skeleton, make it essential that only properly trained and experienced forensic anthropologists be consulted in every case involving the medicolegal system.

See also: **Anthropology/Odontology:** Aging the Dead and the Living; Ancestry; Forensic Anthropology: An Introduction; History of Forensic Anthropology; Personal Identification in Forensic Anthropology; **Biology/DNA:** X-Chromosome Markers; **Forensic Medicine/Clinical:** Identification.

Further Reading

Buikstra, J.E., Ubelaker, D.H., 1994. Standards for data collection from human skeletal remains. Arkansas Archaeological Survey Research Series No. 44.

Franklin, D., Oxnard, C.E., O'Higgins, P., Dadour, I., 2007. Sexual dimorphism in the subadult mandible: quantification using geometric morphometrics. Journal of Forensic Sciences 52 (2), 6–10.

İÇşcan, M.Y., Loth, S.R., King, C.A., Ding, S., Yoshino, M., 1998. Sexual dimorphism in the humerus: a comparative analysis of Chinese, Japanese and Thais. Forensic Science International 98, 17–30.

Krogman, W.M., İÇşcan, M.Y., 1986. The Human Skeleton in Forensic Medicine. Charles C Thomas, Springfield.

Pretorius, E., Steyn, M., Scholtz, Y., 2006. Investigation into the usability of geometric morphometric analysis in assessment of sexual dimorphism. American Journal of Physical Anthropology 129 (1), 64–70.

Rogers, T.L., 2009. Sex determination of adolescent skeletons using the distal humerus. American Journal of Physical Anthropology 140, 143–148.

Rosing, F.W., 1983. Sexing immature skeletons. Journal of Human Evolution 12, 149–155.

Schutkowski, H., 1987. Sex determination of fetal and neonatal skeletons by means of discriminant analysis. International Journal of Anthropology 2, 347–352.

Spradley, M.K., Jantz, R.L., 2011. Sex estimation in forensic anthropology: skull versus postcranial elements. Journal of Forensic Sciences 56 (2), 289–296.

Steyn, M., İÇşcan, M.Y., 1997. Sex determination from the femur and tibia in South African whites. Forensic Science International 90, 111–119.

Sutter, R.C., 2003. Nonmetric subadult skeletal sexing traits: 1. A blind test of the accuracy of eight previously proposed methods using prehistoric known-sex mummies from Northern Chile. Journal of Forensic Sciences 48 (5), 927–935.

Walker, P.L., 2008. Sexing skulls using discriminant function analysis of visually assessed traits. American Journal of Physical Anthropology 136, 39–50.

Workshop of European Anthropologists, 1980. Recommendations for age and sex diagnoses of skeletons. Journal of Human Evolution 9, 517–549.

Aging the Dead and the Living

E Baccino, Hopital Lapeyronie, Montpellier, France
E Cunha, University of Coimbra, Coimbra, Portugal
C Cattaneo, Università degli Studi di Milano, Milano, Italy

Introduction

In the forensic context, aging the dead and aging the living have different goals. For the dead, it is identification: determining the age of a decedent helps create a biological profile, which can be compared to that of a missing person. For the living, it is to solve judicial problems: for example, aging a living person can help in cases of suspected pedopornography and when determining criminal responsibility and pensionable age for adults lacking documents.

Dental and skeletal methods are most commonly used for aging. There is no one aging method that is applicable and reliable for all individuals and for all ages, from neonates to the elderly, living and dead, although there are a variety of methods and combinations of methods available in the literature. There are several reasons for this.

- Very few methods are reliable in both the living and the dead.
- Different methods typically use different statistical procedures, which make results incomparable.
- The reference samples, on which the methods have been developed, are often too specific, making the method results dependent on the demographic and chronological profiles of the series.
- Many published methods have not been tested on diverse populations or in a variety of contexts and, therefore, cannot be used in forensic practice.

For both the living and the dead, the goal of aging is to determine physiological age, which might be quite different from chronological age. Consequently, the older the person is, the larger is the discrepancy between physiological and chronological ages, and the less accurate the methods are. As a result, aging a person (living or dead) is never a simple procedure and always needs a multistep approach, such as the one described below.

- First, determine the age category (or stage or phase) the person belongs to: subadult (0–20 years), transition phase (20–30 years), young and mature adult (30–55 years), or elderly (>55 years).
- Second, choose the method that provides the best results within the age category, taking into account the characteristics of the case (sex and ethnicity) and the practical conditions (state of the body for the dead and the available technologies for the living).
- The so-called reality principle, which takes into account the time required to provide an age and the cost of the method used to provide the estimation, must also be considered.

This chapter provides the reader with practical advice on choosing the right strategy for each type of aging case.

The Dead

Literature Review

This section does not review the literature in the archeological context, as this literature is almost useless for forensic purposes because the material it covers (different states of preservation, taphonomic effects, etc.) and its goals are very far from the judicial requirements (time, cost, and precision of evaluation). However, the chapter on aging in Ubelaker's classic textbook is widely used as the successive editions have moved from archeological to forensic concerns.

Determining Age Categories

Well-preserved remains
In well-preserved bodies, a simple visual external examination will allow the examiner to classify the decedent into a subadult, young adult, mature adult, or elderly adult.

Partially decomposed remains
In the autopsy room, basic X-rays (and the increasingly available CT scan) can provide valuable information about epiphyseal fusion and tooth eruption stages, as well as degenerative changes in bone and joints, all of which can help examiners identify an appropriate age category. X-rays of the third molar, the sternal end of the clavicle, the hand, and the wrist can provide particularly valuable information.

Skeletonized remains
In skeletal cases, the size of the bones (especially the long bones) and the general appearance of the skeleton can provide enough information to allow the examiner to properly

categorize the case. In fragmented remains, a more precise osteological study with measurements of length, width, and diameters of bones is necessary.

Methods by Age Category

Subadults (0–20 years)

Classically, subadults are divided as follows: fetus, newborn, infant (0–6 years), child (7–12 years), and adolescent (13–20 years). Whatever the method used, having a reference population with which the sample can be compared is of utmost importance.

1. *Fetuses.* As dentition is more reliable in aging fetal remains than skeletal development, one must first verify dental, and then skeletal, development. If crowns are present inside the crypts, X-rays should be performed and the Schour and Massler method, as processed by Logan and Kronfeld, should be used. When examining skeletal remains, the data provided by Fazekas and Kosa on long bone development are largely used; Scheuer and Black's method is based on this method. Recent literature is attempting to validate these methods with updated radiographic data.

2. *Newborns.* In order to verify whether the fetus is full-term, one must check the following elements: the greater fontanel has to be open and the smaller ones should be in the process of closing or should be closed; the ossification of the distal epiphysis of the femur should be present; and mineralization of the tip of the cusp of the first permanent molar should be visible on X-ray. Diaphyseal length of long bones is not determinant (because of variation in body size), but one should measure tibia, femur, or humerus as a general indicator. Scheuer and Black's method can be used as well.

3. *Infants (0–6 years) and children (7–12 years).* Tooth calcification and eruption are the methods of choice for aging the remains of infants and children and have been calibrated extensively on mandibular and maxillary teeth. Several tables and charts, including the Schour and Massler charts and the Demirjian charts, exist. The Willems revisited method has shown the most reliable results, followed by the Demirjian method.

   Skeletal development should also be assessed when aging the remains of infants and children. A comparison between dental and skeletal ages is always necessary in order to corroborate results (and verify possible discrepancies), as well as to look for indications of sex, as males have a delay in skeletal growth when compared with females. In infants, the examiner must check for the ossification of skull bones, mainly temporal, occipital, and frontal bones, as well as the mandible. In children, the examiner should consider long bone diaphysis, appearance of ossification centers, and the fusion of epiphyses. In these cases, the age estimation

cannot be assessed without a comparison with tables from the correct reference population in order to reduce impact from racial and environmental factors.

4. *Adolescents (13–20 years).* Demirjian's method can be used to age adolescent remains. The same general rules apply as for children; however, more specific and accurate information can be obtained by applying methods, which were devised for aging the living. For example, age estimation in adolescents can be assessed by evaluation of skeletal development of hand and wrist bones, by X-ray examination, and by comparison with the Greulich and Pyle atlas (GPA), Tanner–Whitehouse (TW) score, and FELS method. All methods have proved to give similar results and to be influenced by the racial characteristics and medical and economical development of the country to which the samples belong.

Transition phase (between 20 and 30 years)

This period spans adolescence to early adulthood. From an anthropological point of view, adulthood can be defined as the time when epiphyses are fused, indicating the end of bone growth. As a general indication, the end of adolescence can be checked through the fusion of thoracic and lumbar vertebral rings, and iliac crest with X-ray examination by Risser staging. The iliac crest of the ilium begins to fuse with the ilium between 14 and 23 years of age, with complete union at 24 years for both sexes. However, as there are differences between populations, it is recommended to use the proper population standard. The union of the medial clavicle begins at different ages, depending on the population studied. The other indicators are third molar development evaluation according to Mincer classification, and obliteration degree of spheno-occipital suture. In the case of fresh and putrefied bodies, which cannot be immediately classed as clear adults or subadults, it is necessary to perform these methods (**Table 1**).

Table 1   Recommendations concerning age estimation methods for remains of adolescents and subjects in transition phase; standard errors go from 0.5 to 2 years

Adolescents
Dental development (and Demirjian)
Long bone development
Maturation of hand and wrist (Greulich and Pyle, Tanner–Whitehouse (TW))
Subjects in transition
Third molar development (Mincer)
Fusion of spheno-occipital/basilar synchondrosis, iliac crest, and vertebral ring
Maturation of hand and wrist (Greulich and Pyle, TW)
Fusion of clavicle sternal end

Adults

Age estimation is more difficult in adults than in subadults because skeletal and dental developments are already complete, creating a consequent increase in the error range. Assessing age in adults must, therefore, be based on physiological degeneration of skeletal and dental structures with age. However, articular degeneration is modified by pathological and occupational factors, which may radically modify the degeneration process, overcoming the importance of aging. The same limits are observed in dental wear, where physiological and pathological elements both contribute to dental structure degeneration with aging. The first step in aging adult remains is choosing one or more methods that will be the most appropriate to the state of body preservation.

Well-preserved remains

This group includes well-preserved bodies that are visually recognizable but remain unclaimed and unidentified. In these cases, apparent age can be estimated by simply examining the corpse; however, this method is unscientific and subjective. A two-step procedure, consisting of combining the pubic symphysis Suchey-Brooks (SB) system with the dental Lamendin method, can provide a scientific estimation of age. For SB phases I, II, and III, the age estimate is given using chronological interval corresponding to each phase. If the SB phase is 4, 5, or 6, the Lamendin method is applied. In case of lack of pubic symphysis, the fourth rib can be used for age determination of the first four stages, the last four stages being assessed by the Lamendin method. Dental pulp chamber can be used if there are no monoradicular teeth. The Lamendin method is considered the most accurate method of age estimation for decedents over 45 years of age, although it is problematic in subjects over 65 years of age and in cases of periodontal disease. The advantages of this method are that it is very easy to use and there is minimal impact of population variation on the accuracy of age estimation. If there are no teeth available, in substitution of Lamendin, examiners can use osteon count analysis by the Kerley–Ubelaker and Ahlqvist–Damsten methods. These methods are based on a microscopic analysis of bone section from a long bone diaphysis in order to assess an osteon count evaluation. X-rays should be performed on these bodies to check for the presence of dental or osseous elements, which may still be in formation or fusion. In a growing number of institutes, CT scans are available and allow the evaluations of areas, such as the pubic symphysis and the auricular surface, that are difficult to reach anatomically in less time; however, applicability still needs to be tested.

Decomposed remains

1. The second group will be called "decomposed bodies," which includes putrefied, mummified, and saponified bodies. Slightly burnt bodies will also be added to this category, which entails all states of preservation that severely alter physiognomy.

In these cases, not even apparent age can be given; therefore, biological methods are even more important. The same procedure as discussed elsewhere in this encyclopedia is proposed.

Skeletonized remains

As all parts useful for aging are exposed, the examiner must choose using between one preferred method and many methods with a multifactorial approach. Although the literature is still unclear in relation to this issue, the authors suggest using the two-step procedure described in the well-preserved bodies paragraph above. If teeth are missing or the pubic symphysis and ribs are damaged, then some methods—such as suture closure—should be avoided. The auricular (Meindl–Lovejoy–Mensforth) method may be a better option, even if intraobserver error is significant, leading sometimes to inaccurate results. This method should be used in association with evaluation of the acetabulum, a more recent method that—although it requires more testing—is especially promising for 60-year-old, or older, individuals. In all these cases, if any bone indicator suggests a very young adult, it is advisable to confirm the state of epiphyseal union of the sternal end of the clavicle and of the iliac crest (see section "Transition phase (between 20 and 30 years)").

Calcined remains

In cases of calcined remains, such as those found in burnt cars, the choice of the method depends on the preservation of anatomical sites and how badly they are burnt. X-rays should always be performed on burnt bodies to check for dental and osseous developments, in case the person is an adolescent or subadult. If the remains consist only of burnt bones, a possible method could be osteon counts as heat may not significantly alter osteon shape or disposition for these purposes. One should, however, use such methods cautiously when the anatomical site of the bone is not determined, when the histological structure can no longer be identified, or when the bones are too fragmented. None of the dental methods for adults should be used for aging burnt remains apart from, perhaps, pulp chamber methods, which, however, need further testing.

Body parts
Skull with teeth

- If all teeth are present, the authors recommend the use of Lamendin if post-mortem interval (PMI) can reasonably point to a recent case. The Lamendin method has not been tested on historical samples or even samples that have been buried in soil for several decades. Therefore, in these situations, the authors recommend the use of the pulp chamber method, which considers the ratio between pulp chamber and total dental area in upper and lower canines because it has greater possibilities of not being affected by taphonomy and is simpler to run than cementum annulation techniques.

- If no monoradicular tooth is present, the available methods are pulp chamber and amino acid racemization. Although the latter seems to be more precise than all other methods, it should be kept in mind that very few labs in the world perform this difficult technique and have prepared calibration curves for this purpose; that this technique is much more expensive than any other method; and that the method has only been tested on recent material, and never been compared to other methods on the same sample.
- Spalding et al. and Ubelaker et al. have pointed out that radioisotope concentration analysis in dental enamel provides a method of aging. Between 1950 and 1963, the increase in carbon-14 by the thermonuclear device allows one to verify that childhood and consequent teeth development have occurred before that time threshold, with reconstruction of date of birth.

Skull with no teeth

- Little should be assumed when teeth are not present. Loss of teeth may occur at any stage of life and can be caused by social habits, drugs, infections, and diseases. Edentulous mouths do not necessarily belong to an old individual although it is more probable.
- Suture closure methods have extremely large intervals/ standard deviations for forensic purposes and are affected by a wide inter- and intraindividual variability in case of maxillary suture and cranial sutures (ecto- and endocranial). Moreover, sutures in the same individual may show different degrees of fusion.
- For osteons, some published methods seem to allow one to place age, depending on the number and the maturity of osteons, into gross "young-middle" and "old" categories. However, no equations exist as for long bones; thus, the accuracy is very poor. Amino acid racemization on bone, on the other hand, is much less accurate than on teeth because of bone remodeling and, therefore, cannot be recommended.

Entire postcranium (no skull)

- The authors recommend using pubic symphysis to age a subject when no skull is available. If the result is within the first three stages of Suchey–Brooks, it should be left at that. If it belongs to the last three stages, a method that is more accurate and precise for older individuals should be used, such as osteon analysis. The examiner can always confirm age estimation by pubic symphysis by the fourth rib and auricular surface or can perform an analysis of the acetabulum.

Torso only

- The Iscan method has proven to be reliable, especially in females and in subjects 60 years of age and older. In males, the recent literature has shown a morphological variability between the articular surfaces of different ribs.

Upper limbs

- RX examination and assessment of humeral bone structure in the Acsadi and Nemeskeri combined method.

Lower limbs

- Osteon counts with adequate equations by the Kerley–Ubelaker method.

In conclusion, as regards aging adults, it should be mentioned that there are virtually no methods useful for the estimation of age at death after 60 years of age: it is impossible to discriminate between 70 and 80 or 90. A summary of all the recommended methods, including the literature references, is shown in **Table 2**.

The Living

Age estimation of the living has become more and more common. The main issues of age estimation in the living concern "imputability" with regard to criminal activities, asylum seekers, illegal immigrants, and unaccompanied minors: the age limit might be 14, 16, 18, or 21 years, depending on the country. Aging the living is also important in

Table 2 Recommendations concerning age estimation methods in case of well-preserved, decomposed, skeletonized, and calcined remains; standard errors are between 7 and 15 years

Methods	Remarks
Well preserved and decomposed	
Suchey–Brooks	More reliable between 20 and 40 years
Iscan	Higher reliability after 60 years
Lamendin (in TSP protocol)	Periodontal disease influence; high reliability between 40 and 60 years
Microscopic analysis of osteons	More time consuming
Skeletonized	
Suchey–Brooks	
Iscan	
Lamendin (in TSP protocol)	
Auricular surface	Interindividual and intraindividual variations
Calcined remains	
Microscopic analysis of osteons	With great caution

issues surrounding adoption and old-age pensions (50, 55, 60, or 65 years of age, again depending on the country). Aging the living requires the use of noninvasive methods as well as higher levels of accuracy and precision than the dead, due to specific legal requirements. In agreement with the recent work of the Study Group on Forensic Age Diagnostic, the authors believe that a correct assessment of age estimation in the living should consist of three steps: a physical (or clinical) examination, an estimation of bone development, and an estimation of dental development.

Clinical Examination

1. For nonadults or young adults, the first step in age estimation is the collection of medical information through a complete anamnesis. Physiological and pathological factors, as well as social and economic contexts, influence body development and sexual development; this physical examination will verify growth and particularly sexual development. First, height and weight must be accurately measured, and the measurements should be compared with the specific percentiles concerning the standard growth of children provided by WHO and CDC. These percentiles are commonly used in clinical practice. Pediatricians commonly use the Tanner stages, an analysis of sexual traits in males and females. The Tanner method considers breast and pubic hair development in females, while in males, increase in testicular volume and pubic hair is taken into account. Important limits concerning racial and interindividual variability have been pointed out, and Tanner himself has stressed that the method should not be used for chronological age—thus forensic—purposes.
2. For adults, although bodily and sexual growth have terminated, a complete physical examination should not be excluded. In females, menopause (also affected by ethnic and interindividual variability) in addition to physical modifications can be confirmed by hormonal dosage.

Dental Assessment

Adults

Age assessment is more difficult in living adults than in living subadults; at present, there is no recommendation concerning the most appropriate method to use. Root methods may provide a useful tool for age estimation in adults if future literature will offer further population data confirming their reliability. The aforementioned amino acid racemization in dentine has also been suggested; however, this method involves destruction or damage of the individual's tooth. Very recently, DNA alterations linked with aging—such as age-dependent accumulation of the 4977 bp deletion of mitochondrial DNA and the attrition of telomeres—have

shown promise. These are currently very preliminary results, however, and must be confirmed and standardized.

Children and young adults

Among the numerous dental methods, Demirjian and Mincer (for the third molar) are the most commonly suggested by the literature; Demirjian is based on the growth assessment of several teeth (usually half a dental arch). It is considered a reliable method that is easy to use and offers well-defined morphological stages. Several studies have shown the high dependence on the specific characteristics of the population. Moreover, where the original method was applied with specific calibration curves, the results showed an increase in accuracy. This confirms that the high ethnic variability requires particular caution in the discussion of the final result. The Mincer et al. method also is a good option for using the third molar to age older adolescents. This method has been tested on various populations with a high variability in age threshold: every Mincer stage has been verified with different mean ages. A recent study showed that the best methods as regards bias (average difference) and median absolute difference between the estimated and chronological ages were Willems's (with a bias of 0.12 years and a difference of 0.52 years) and Liversidge's flat distribution (with a bias of 0.03 years and a difference of 0.69 years) in a sample of 946 children. Although the literature suggests the use of classical methods, other methods should not be disregarded. Pathological factors have not been considered so far, but they should be among the exclusion criteria of subjects from the studies, and the dental age estimation methods should be applied to subjects who have a healthy dental profile.

Skeletal Assessment

1. For adults, see the section titled "Dental Assessment."
2. When the legal age limit is around 18 years, the method of choice for aging subadults is an X-ray on the hand–wrist area (generally the left hand, but when the person is left-handed, the right hand may be preferable) to evaluate the degree of fusion of the cartilage in this area. The most popular is the GPA, which provides a series of X-ray standards for the hand and wrist from birth to 17/18 years of age for females and 19 years of age for males. This method is comparative and consists of the evaluation of the X-ray examination from the proband and the standards from the atlas. The final result includes mean age estimation and an error range. The TW method is based on a scoring system that evaluates the ossification degree and morphological appearance of the ossification nuclei and bones in the hand and wrist. A maturity score is then given, with the indication of mean age and error range. There is a majority consensus that both methods reliably assess age, though GPA is quicker and more user-friendly. The FELS computerized

method provides an evaluation concerning concordance between the wrist and hand X-ray pattern and the age declared. It is, however, more complex and less user-friendly than the other two methods.

3. Ethnic, pathological, and socioeconomic statuses affect skeletal development; therefore, the issue of the applicability of methods to different populations has been questioned. A study of GPA on 1390 males and females ranging from 1 day to 18 years of age showed that the bone age was overestimated in Asian and Hispanic children, who seemed to mature sooner than their African-American and white peers. Thus, population data are extremely important and are beginning to appear for the GPA and TW methods. As shown in a recent meta-analysis, however, age estimation in living individuals cannot be considered accurate when only X-ray methods on the left hand and wrist area are used; exhaustive combinations of various procedures (i.e., physical examination, dental, and skeletal methods) must also be used.

4. In countries where the age of 21 years may be of some legal interest, the fusion degree of the clavicle sternal end may provide relevant information because it occurs in the useful age range for imputability assessment. Use of NMR, although the first results have yet to be confirmed, may overcome the limitations of the use of X-ray examination.

5. Use of X-rays on the living can endanger health. Established doses for X-ray examinations in forensic age estimations are low and vary from less than 0.1 mSv (left-hand X-ray) to up to more than 800 mSv (CT), and despite the higher sensibility of children to radiation, hand radiographs are harmless. Computed tomography on children is, however, a relatively high-dose procedure. Ultrasonography and NMR technology may provide a healthy alternative to X-rays. Ultrasonography has been mainly aimed at the assessment of ossification of clavicular sternal extremity and an ultrasonographic version of the GPA was developed. At the moment, however, the use of the ultrasonography and NMR technique for forensic purposes needs adequate standardization (**Table 3**).

Age Estimation in Juvenile Pornography Images

The crime of pedopornography is based on the specific ages that each country considers relevant for this crime (usually 14, 16, or 18 years, depending on the country). In these cases, judges require age estimation of possible victims who may not be physically present, requiring examiners to create age estimates based only on two-dimensional (2D) images in photos or videos, which may be of poor quality. The sexual characteristics of possible victims, as seen in pictures or videos, are often deceiving; a new approach for age estimation from 2D pictures is needed. A research field, which may hold some answers, could be the morphological and metrical analysis of

Table 3   Recommendations concerning age estimation methods in the living

Methods	Remarks
Subadults	
Physical assessment and Tanner sexual classification	High racial and interindividual variability; strong criticism concerning its use for forensic purposes
Bone development (radiological)	
Greulich and Pyle atlas and Tanner–Whitehouse	Greulich and Pyle user-friendly, quick; some population data available
Clavicle sternal end fusion (radiological)	Still being tested
Dental development (radiological)	
Demirjian method	Some population data available
Mincer method	Asset: gives probability of having reached 18 years; disadvantage: high frequency of third molar agenesia (up to 8% in Caucasoids)
Adults	
Physical assessment and hormonal dosage for women	High racial and interindividual variability
Pulp chamber-based methods	High error range; need for further experimental data

the face, which may have a relationship with chronological age. In the videos in which possible victims smile or open their mouths, it may be possible to evaluate dental eruption and development in order to provide a rough age range estimate. Thus, in general, physical and sexual maturation stages should be used with great caution for forensic purposes, particularly in regard to photographic material.

In Court

Judges are often required to make decisions based on whether or not an individual has reached a specific age threshold, and therefore, they may require precise and definite age evaluations in which explanation of error is crucial. Most methods give standard errors or standard deviations, allowing examiners to provide a judge with an age range; for example, 17.5–18.5 years. Giving the probability of that person actually having reached the threshold (e.g., 18 years) might also be helpful to the judge. In this perspective, methods such as the Mincer's, which, along with the mean age and error, give the probability of the subject having reached the limit of 18 years, could be more useful to the judge.

In a study performed on 47 judicial immigration cases, skeletal and dental methods provided borderline results that—by making it difficult to determine whether the defendant was an adult or a juvenile—would have severely complicated the sentencing portion of the proceedings. An examination of the final sentences showed that when the Mincer method was applied, therefore allowing the judges to know the probability of the individual having reached the age of 18, the judges were appreciative. Knowing the age of the defendant with some degree of confidence allowed the judges to better carry out sentencing: when the probability of the individual of being 18 or over was over 70%, the judges felt "confident" in taking the risk of sentencing the individual as an adult.

Conclusions

This chapter makes the case that despite the enormous literature on this issue—perhaps one of the most common topics in anthropological publications—age estimation for the dead or the living, and particularly for adults, can provide only large age ranges. Although new methods may be tempting, for forensic purposes, it is safer to use traditional, standardized, and tested methods. When using a combination of methods, the simple pooling of data cannot be performed because every method expresses its error range in different ways (mean error, standard deviation, etc.) and some do not even provide an error indication. Interpolating results from different methods, however, is possible provided a rough age indication is given. This can be performed by principal component analysis, which has proven to be reliable. The consequent issue concerns how to present results to investigating authorities: an age estimation report must include indications about the methods performed, information about specific limits, and the mode of processing data. Finally, it is necessary to point out that age estimation concerns biology, where variability is the rule; even considering population data, every individual may show different aging patterns. Correct age estimation must consider this unavoidable limit, in order to define the precision and accuracy of the results provided. At the moment, the most challenging field of aging is for the population above 65 years of age as no method, so far, has been found suitable for this purpose. When considering that this population is the fastest growing in most parts of the world, it must be considered a major concern. More research is thus needed and here as well, similar to other fields of forensic sciences, the future might be in DNA studies.

See also: **Anthropology/Odontology:** Ancestry; Identification of the Living.

Further Reading

Ahlqvist, J., Damsten, O., 1969. A modification of Kerley's method for the microscopic determination of age in human bone. Journal of Forensic Sciences 14 (2), 205–212.

Anderson, D.L., Thompson, G.W., Popovich, F., 1976. Age of attainment of mineralization stages of the permanent dentition. Journal of Forensic Sciences 21 (1), 191–200.

Baccino, E., Schmitt, A., 2006. Determination of adult age at death in the forensic context. In: Schmitt, A., Cunha, E., Pinheiro, J. (Eds.), Forensic Anthropology and Medicine. Complementary Sciences from the Recovery to Cause of Death. Humana Press, Totowa, NJ, pp. 259–280.

Blankenship, J.A., Mincer, H.H., Anderson, K.M., Woods, M.A., Burton, E.L., 2007. Third molar development in the estimation of chronologic age in American blacks compared with whites. Journal of Forensic Sciences 52 (2), 428–433.

Bradtmiler, B., Builstra, J.E., 1984. Effects of burning bone microstructure: a preliminary study. Journal of Forensic Sciences 29 (2), 535–540.

Brooks, S., Suchey, J., 1990. Skeletal age determination base on the os pubis: a comparison of the Acsádi-Nemeskéri and Suchey-Brooks methods. Human Evolution 5, 227–238.

Cameriere, R., Brogi, G., Ferrante, L., et al., 2006. Reliability in age determination by pulp/tooth ratio in upper canines in skeletal remains. Journal of Forensic Sciences 51 (4), 861–864.

Cunha, E., Baccino, E., Martrille, L., et al., 2009. The problem of aging human remains and living individuals: a review. Forensic Science International 193, 1–13.

Greulich, W., Pyle, S.I., 1959. Radiographic Atlas of Skeletal Development of the Hand and Wrist, second ed. Stanford University Press, Stanford, CA.

Hummel, S., Schutkowski, H., 1993. Approaches to the histological age determination of cremated human remains. In: Grupe, G., Garland, A.N. (Eds.), Histology of Ancient Human Bone: Methods and Diagnosis. Springer, Berlin, pp. 112–123.

Işcan, M.Y., Loth, S.R., Wright, R.K., 1984. Age estimation from the rib by phase analysis: white males. Journal of Forensic Sciences 29 (4), 1094–1104.

Işcan, M.Y., Loth, S.R., Wright, R.K., 1985. Age estimation from the rib by phase analysis: white females. Journal of Forensic Sciences 30 (3), 853–863.

Iscan, M.Y., Loth, S.R., Wright, R.K., 1987. Racial variation in the sternal extremity of the rib and its effect on age determination. Journal of Forensic Sciences 32 (2), 452–466.

Kerley, E.R., Ubelaker, D.H., 1978. Revisions in the microscopic method of estimating age at death in human cortical bone. American Journal of Physical Anthropology 49 (4), 545–546.

Kósa, F., Fazekas, I.G., 1978. Forensic Fetal Osteology. Akademiai Kiadò, Budapest.

Kvaal, S.I., Kolltveit, K.M., Thomsen, I.O., Solheim, T., 1995. Age estimation of adults from dental radiographs. Forensic Science International 74 (3), 175–185.

Lamendin, H., 1973. Observations on teeth roots in the estimation of age. International Journal of Forensic Dentistry 1, 4–7.

Lamendin, H., Baccino, E., Humbert, J.F., Tavernier, J.C., Nossintchouk, R., Zerilli, A., 1992. A simple technique for age estimation in adult corpses: the two criteria dental method. Journal of Forensic Science 37, 1373–1379.

Lovejoy, C.O., Meindl, R.S., Pryzbeck, T.R., Mensforth, R.P., 1985. Chronological metamorphosis of the auricular surface of the ilium: a new method for the determination of adult skeletal age at death. American Journal of Physical Anthropology 68 (1), 15–28.

Martrille, L., Ubelaker, D.H., Cattaneo, C., Seguret, F., Tremblay, M., Baccino, E., 2007. Comparison of four skeletal methods for the estimation of age at death on white and black adults. Journal of Forensic Sciences 52 (2), 302–307.

Meijerman, L., Maat, G.J., Schulz, R., Schmeling, A., 2007. Variables affecting the probability of complete fusion of the medial clavicular epiphysis. International Journal of Legal Medicine 121 (6), 463–468.

Rissech, C., Estabrook, J.F., Cunha, E., Malgosa, A., 2006. Using the acetabulum to estimate age at death of adult males. Journal of Forensic Sciences 51 (2), 213–229.

Ritz-Timme, S., Cattaneo, C., Collins, M.J., et al., 2000. Age estimation: the state of the art in relation to the specific demands of forensic practise. International Journal of Legal Medicine 113 (3), 129–136.

Ritz-Timme, S., Rochholz, G., Schütz, H.W., et al., 2000. Quality assurance in age estimation based on aspartic acid racemisation. International Journal of Legal Medicine 114 (1–2), 83–86.

Roche, A.F., Chumlea, C., Thissen, D., 1988. Assessing the Skeletal Maturity of the Hand-Wrist: FELS Method. Charles C. Thomas, Springfield, IL.

Rösing, F.W., Graw, M., Marré, B., et al., 2007. Recommendations for the forensic diagnosis of sex and age from skeletons. Homo 58 (1), 75–89.

Scheuer, L., Black, S., 2000. Developmental Juvenile Osteology. Academic Press, San Diego, CA.

Schmeling, A., Olze, A., Reisinger, W., Rösing, F.W., Geserick, G., 2003. Forensic age diagnostics of living individuals in criminal proceedings. Homo 54 (2), 162–169.

Schmidt, S., Mühler, M., Schmeling, A., Reisinger, W., Schulz, R., 2007. Magnetic resonance imaging of the clavicular ossification. International Journal of Legal Medicine 121 (4), 321–324.

Schmitt, A., Murail, P., Cunha, E., Rougé, D., 2002. Variability of the pattern of aging on the human skeleton: evidence from bone indicators and implications on age at death estimation. Journal of Forensic Sciences 47 (6), 1203–1209.

Schour, I., Massler, M., 1937. Rate and gradient of grown in human deciduous teeth with special reference to neonatal ring. Journal of Dental Research 16, 349–350.

Schour, I., Massler, M., 1941. The development of the human dentition. Journal of the American Dental Association 28, 1153–1160.

Schulz, R., Mühler, M., Mutze, S., Schmidt, S., Reisinger, W., Schmeling, A., 2005. Studies on the time frame for ossification of the medial epiphysis of the clavicle as revealed by CT scans. International Journal of Legal Medicine 119 (3), 142–145.

Tanner, J.M., Whitehouse, R.H., Marshall, W.A., Healy, M.J.R., Goldstein, H., 1975. Assessment of Skeletal Maturity and Prediction of Adult Height (TW2 Method). Academic Press, London.

Ubelaker, D.H., 1987. Estimating age at death from immature human skeletons: an overview. Journal of Forensic Sciences 32, 1254–1263.

Stature and Build

K Krishan, Panjab University, Chandigarh, India
T Kanchan, Kasturba Medical College, Manipal University, Mangalore, India

Introduction

Stature and body build are quantitative measures of physique that are indicative of individuals' physical growth and development, and reflect the health, nutrition, and genetics of a population. Stature is the linear dimension of the skull, vertebral column, pelvis, and bones of the lower limbs. Estimation of stature is fundamental to the evaluation of skeletal remains and is therefore an important aspect of forensic identification. Stature—along with age, sex, and ethnicity—is one of the "Big Four" identifying factors in forensic anthropology. This baseline biological information, known as the biological profile, helps forensic scientists identify victims by narrowing down the pool of possible victim matches. Age, sex, and ethnicity should be taken into account when estimating stature in forensic examinations. Stature estimation is a major domain of medicolegal investigation in establishing the biological profile of unknown, fragmentary, and mutilated remains. Body build is a measure of overall body size of an individual and includes both stature and body mass.

Individuals' stature is influenced by genetic and environmental factors such as health, disease, nutrition, and physical activity. Physical activity, in addition to good health and proper nutrition, encourages bone growth and development. The extent of physical activity during the growth period determines whether an individuals' genetic potential for stature is achieved.

The body proportions of different ethnic groups may also vary because of selective adaptation to different climate zones characteristic of each endogamous group. It is therefore desirable to derive stature estimation formulae for different ethnic groups. This is difficult, however, because of the practical difficulties in deriving these formulae for each ethnic and caste group, particularly in countries such as India and many African countries, where hundreds of such groups exist. Because of this, researchers' opinions on the need to derive regression models for each ethnic group are divided. The issue, however, is simplified in regions inhabited by homogeneous population groups where a single regression formula represents the region.

Measures of Body Build and Body Size

Estimation of body build and body size has received much less attention than stature estimation in forensic anthropology, but is nonetheless important in the evaluation of skeletal remains. Among scientists, it is generally agreed that the postcranial features have a more direct relationship to overall body size than cranial dimensions and can therefore produce the most accurate estimates of body mass. Two methods can be used to estimate body mass from postcranial skeletal remains: mechanical method and morphometric method. Mechanical method relies on the functional association between weight-bearing skeletal elements and body mass. Mechanical methods may employ articular surface dimensions or use diaphyseal breadths and cross-sectional dimensions of the bones for the estimation of body mass. Articular surface dimensions are less influenced by the differences in the activity level or muscular loadings during life than diaphyseal dimensions. Morphometric methods of estimating body mass reconstruct body size and/or shape from the available bones. Morphometric methods for reconstructing body mass based on stature estimation alone have been developed by researchers. On the basis of a worldwide sampling of modern humans of diverse body shape, Ruff derived a morphometric method—which is a combination of stature and body breadth (bi-iliac or maximum pelvic breadth)—that provides relatively accurate estimates of body mass. According to Ruff, articular surface dimensions are less influenced by differences in activity levels and muscular loadings during life when compared to diaphyseal dimensions and thus are more important. In addition, attempts have also been made to estimate body mass from metatarsal dimensions, pelvic bi-iliac breadth, long bone lengths, and femoral head diameter.

Methods of Stature Estimation

The two basic methods of stature estimation in forensic examinations are the anatomical method and the mathematical method. The anatomical method of stature estimation was introduced by Fully. Fully's method estimates individuals' stature by summing the measurements of all the skeletal elements that contribute to the stature and adding a correction factor for the soft tissues. The skeletal elements essential for the estimation of stature are skull, vertebrae, femur, tibia, talus, and calcaneus. Lundy later devised a correction index to account for the thickness of the scalp, intervertebral disks, and soft tissue of the sole.

A revision of Fully's method by Raxter and colleagues is considered the best and the most accurate method of stature estimation in spite of its drawbacks: it is intricate, laborious, time-consuming, and requires the essential components of the skeleton to be present. Fully's original method does not provide explicit directions for taking all of the necessary measurements. Raxter and colleagues revised Fully's anatomical method for reconstruction of stature by testing, then clarifying, the measurement procedures. Raxter et al. tested Fully's process on 119 adult black and white male and female cadavers of known stature from the Terry Collection. The cadaveric statures were adjusted to living statures, according to the recommendations of Trotter and Gleser. Raxter and colleagues found that statures derived using the Fully's original technique underestimated the living stature by an average of about 2.4 cm and that the correction factors applied by Fully to convert summed skeletal height to living stature was too small. Fully's technique did not take into consideration the size of cartilage and other soft tissues that might affect proper spacing. Hence, Raxter and colleagues derived new formulae to calculate living stature from skeletal height.

The mathematical method of stature estimation is based on the standard of deriving a formula that can be applied directly to estimate stature from a given bone or body part in forensic examinations. Estimation of stature using mathematical formulae is based on the principle of a definite biological relationship that exists between stature and the body parts, especially those which contribute directly to individuals' stature such as the head, trunk, vertebral column, pelvis, lower extremity, and feet. The well-defined relationship between these parts allows a forensic scientist to estimate stature from various bones and body parts. The mathematical method of stature estimation includes two submethods: the multiplication method and the regression analysis method. Many earlier studies have utilized either or both of these methods of stature

estimation; however, studies have shown that the regression method of stature estimation is more accurate and reliable than the multiplication factor method. The studies on the extent of variability in estimated and actual stature using both these submethods, however, are limited in literature.

Anatomical method is considered advantageous over the mathematical method of stature estimation as the former gives more reliable stature estimates. However, all bones required for stature estimation using Fully's method may not be available in routine forensic practice, thus limiting its utility. Therefore, the mathematical method remains a more popularly used method of stature estimation in forensic and medicolegal investigations.

Stature Estimation from Long Bones

Regression analysis is based on the linear relationship between dimensions of bones, body parts, and stature. Various regression formulae have been derived for estimation of stature from long bones in different population groups worldwide (**Table 1**). Trotter and Gleser conducted a major on stature estimation using humerus, radius, ulna, femur, tibia, and fibula bones from black and white Americans. Samples were taken from the Terry Collection and from remains of World War II American military personnel. Trotter and Gleser used these measurements to formulate sex—and population—specific regression equations. Later, they revised these formulae using a large number of skeletons of black and white American service members who were killed between 1950 and 1953 while serving in the Korean War. They also devised regression formulae for Americans of Mexican, Puerto Rican, and Asian origin. Following these major studies on stature estimation, a variety of authors worked in different regions of the world to generate standards for stature estimation. Additional regression

Table 1   Regression models derived for stature (cm) estimation from various bones in different populations

Population/origin	Males	Females
Caucasoids (cm) (Trotter and Gleser)	$2.38 \times$ femur length $+ 61.41 \pm 3.27$	$2.47 \times$ femur length $+ 54.10 \pm 3.72$
Negroids (cm) (Trotter and Gleser)	$2.11 \times$ femur length $+ 70.35 \pm 3.94$	$2.28 \times$ femur length $+ 59.76 \pm 3.41$
Mongoloids (cm) (Trotter and Gleser)	$2.15 \times$ femur length $+ 72.57 \pm 3.80$	–
Chileans (cm) (Ross and Manneschi)	$2.53 \times$ humerus length $+ 820.36 \pm 36.7$	$1.91 \times$ humerus length $+ 989.28 \pm 41.5$
Chileans (cm) (Ross and Manneschi)	$2.26 \times$ tibia length $+ 356.48 \pm 31.0$	$1.41 \times$ tibia length $+ 1026.97 \pm 41.1$
South Indians (cm) (Nagesh and Pradeep Kumar)	$1.882 \times$ vertebral length $+ 60.699 \pm 4.38$	$1.899 \times$ vertebral length $+ 55.361 \pm 4.16$
Portuguese population (mm) (Cordeiro and coworkers)	$11.678 \times$ first metatarsal $+ 963.949 \pm 57.0$	$12.006 \times$ first metatarsal $+ 919.146 \pm 43.5$
South africans whites (cm) (Bidmos)	$0.87 \times$ calcaneus length $+ 84.65 \pm 4.56$	$1.25 \times$ calcaneus length $+ 52.51 \pm 4.59$
South africans blacks (cm) (Bidmos and asala)	$0.63 \times$ calcaneus length $+ 100.87 \pm 5.34$	$0.82 \times$ calcaneus length $+ 82.49 \pm 4.98$
Portuguese population (cm) (de Mendonca)	$0.3269 \times$ humerus length $+ 59.41 \pm 8.44$	$0.2663 \times$ humerus length $+ 47.18 \pm 6.90$
Portuguese population (cm) (de Mendonca)	$0.3065 \times$ femur length $+ 64.26 \pm 7.70$	$10.2428 \times$ femur length $+ 55.63 \pm 5.92$
Thai population (cm) (Mahakkanukrauh and coworkers)	$2.722 \times$ femur length $+ 45.534 \pm 5.06$	$2.778 \times$ femur length $+ 40.602 \pm 5.21$
Thai population (cm) (Mahakkanukrauh and coworkers)	$3.015 \times$ tibia length $+ 52.964 \pm 5.15$	$2.620 \times$ tibia length $+ 63.089 \pm 5.94$

formulae were developed by Allbrook, for British and East Africans, in 1961; by Olivier, for French men and women, in 1963; by Yunghao and colleagues, for Chinese, in 1979; and by Černý and Komenda, for the Czechs, in 1982. Dupertuis and Hadden later provided bone/stature ratios and regression formulae for Americans from femur, tibia, humerus, and radius measurements using materials from the Hamann–Todd Collection. They also recommended that a combination of two or more bones be used to provide better estimations of stature.

Jantz modified the Trotter and Gleser formulae in view of the secular trends in modern population. Jantz tested the Trotter and Gleser formulae for femur and tibia using the data from the Forensic Data Bank at the University of Tennessee and observed that stature estimates differed from one another by about 3 cm. Jantz and his colleagues observed that Trotter and Gleser's study inappropriately measured tibia length, resulting in tibia measurements that were 10–12 mm shorter than the actual measurements. These faulty measurements were responsible for the overestimation of stature (averaging 2.5–3.0 cm) when the regression formulae were used on the appropriately measured tibia.

Ross and Konigsberg provided stature estimation formulae for Balkans by measuring long bones from a sample of 177 Eastern European males, including Bosnian and Croatian victims of war. They compared the estimated stature from the East European sample with a reference sample of 545 white American males—Trotter and Gleser's data from World War II—and observed that Trotter and Gleser's formulae systematically underestimated the stature of Balkans. Ross and Konigsberg concluded that the stature prediction formulae developed for white Americans may be inappropriate for European population because Eastern Europeans are typically taller than white Americans.

Auerbach and Ruff calculated regression formulae for indigenous North Americans using femur and tibia lengths. They used 967 skeletons from 75 archeological sites and estimated stature using revised Fully anatomical technique. After comparing the new stature estimation equations with previously available equations using several archeological test samples, they observed that the new stature estimation equations were more precise than those previously available and recommended the use of derived formulae throughout most of the North America.

Stature Estimation from Percutaneous Bone Measurements and Body Parts

The identification of mutilated and isolated body remains has remained a challenging task for forensic scientists. Body parts such as the head, trunk, upper and lower limbs, and feet and hands display a definite biological relationship with an individuals' stature. While forensic anthropologists typically estimate stature from length of the bones, they also examine

human remains at mass fatality sites where analysis of the fleshed bodies or body parts is more common. For stature estimation at mass disaster sites where only parts of bodies or mutilated remains are found, the presence of soft tissue on the human remains would usually necessitate dissection to expose skeletal elements to derive metric data for stature estimation; however, it is possible to estimate stature from various parts of the body using anthropometric techniques. In such a scenario, standard anthropometric soft tissue or percutaneous measurements can be used instead of skeletal measurements. Stature estimates derived from anthropometric data are reasonably accurate and eliminate the necessity for dissection when working with fleshed body portions.

Adams and Herrmann compared the results of skeletal measurements and the anthropometric measurements from two studies (National Health and Nutrition Examination Survey and US Army Anthropometric Survey) and found that the US Army Anthropometric Survey models were similar to the skeletal models. The National Health and Nutrition Examination Survey models, however, exhibited weaker correlation coefficients and higher standard errors for the same.

Researchers have successfully estimated stature from measurements on percutaneous bones of living individuals as well as cadavers in different populations worldwide. This has allowed the development of regression formulae for estimation of stature from head, face, and upper extremity measurements in North Indian ethnic groups and the Turkish population; from hand dimensions in the Punjabi Indian, North Indian, South Indian, Mauritian, and Egyptian populations; and from lower extremity dimensions (including foot dimensions) in American, Turkish, North Indian, Mauritian, and Nigerian populations, as well as the Rajbanshis of North Bengal in India.

Stature Estimation from Radiographically Determined Long Bone Length

Scientists have shown that radiographically determined bone lengths can provide stature estimates using regression formulae. While conducting the X-ray examination, however, the specific position of the subject must be taken into consideration. Size standards of the positives are obtained and landmarks are located on the positives and precise measurements are taken. Researchers have made use of various radiographic methods, such as dual-energy X-ray absorptiometry, computed radiography, and digital radiography, for this purpose.

- Munoz and colleagues estimated stature from radiographically determined lengths of the long bones in a Spanish population. They reported femur and tibia as the most accurate predictors of stature in the population.
- Patil and Mody devised regression formulae for estimation of stature from various measurements of lateral cephalograms in a central Indian population.

- Sarajlic and coworkers measured long bones from the X-rays obtained from the cadavers in a Bosnian population and derived regression formulae for stature estimation.
- Sagir successfully estimated stature from various measurements on radiographs of metacarpals in a Turkish population.
- Petrovecki and colleagues calculated relationship of stature with all the six long bone lengths measured from the radiographs of the cadavers in a Croatian population. Petrovecki and colleagues concluded that the best prediction of stature can be made from the humerus in females and the tibia in males.
- Fan and colleagues measured fibulae and tibiae of living Han subjects of China using computed radiographs and successfully derived regression formulae to estimate stature.
- Hasegawa and colleagues took measurements on radiographically determined lengths of femur, tibia, and humerus in living Japanese subjects and calculated multiple regression models for estimation of stature.
- Kieffer demonstrated the feasibility of creating bone lengths and stature databases of significant size for modern living human population from digital radiographic archives and medical records. He measured the lengths of tibia and fibula from the digital radiograph images and stature measurements were obtained from medical records. Kieffer observed that the bone lengths obtained from radiographic images were almost 3 cm longer than those obtained from skeletalized collections; consequently, the stature estimation formulae produce ranges up to 10 cm lower than the currently available formulae. Kieffer suggested that accuracy of stature estimation can be improved by making corrections for the small magnification produced by digital images.

Thus, estimating stature from the radiographic measurement of the length of the long bones of the upper and lower extremity seems to be a simple and practical approach to estimate stature in forensic practice.

Stature Estimation from Small Bones and Other Bones of the Body

Although stature estimation from long bones is more reliable and accurate than from any other bone or part of the body, in some cases, other bones need to be used for stature estimation. A fair amount of accuracy has been achieved by researchers using foot bones such as calcaneum, talus, and metatarsal bones for stature estimation in various populations. Metacarpals have also been used effectively in stature estimation, and regression equations have been derived. Similarly, the vertebral column and its parts, pelvic dimensions, scapular measurements, sternal measurements, and clavicle dimensions have been utilized for stature estimation in some population

groups. Stature estimation from these bones is quite valuable when the long bones are not available for examination.

Estimation of Stature from Fragments of Bones

In a number of forensic and archeological cases, only bone fragments or parts of long bones are available for examination. In such cases, stature estimation from parts of the bone can help in identification of the victim. Studies have shown that stature can be estimated from fragmentary bones by either a direct method or an indirect method. Direct method involves estimation of stature directly from the individual measurements or combination of measurements of fragments of the bone. The indirect method involves the calculation of maximum length of the bone from the measurements of its fragments that is followed by stature estimation from the estimated maximum length of the long bone. Indirect method is considered more useful and accurate than the direct method of stature estimation from fragmentary bones. However, Bidmos has observed that the direct method of stature estimation is more accurate and reliable than the indirect method and is less complicated when the direct measurements are involved in stature estimation.

Most of the studies on stature estimation from fragmentary remains have been conducted on femur fragments from various population groups. Chiba and Bidmos derived regression equations from fragments of tibia that allow estimation of full-length tibia measurements and stature. These studies show that in the absence of intact long bones, the equations derived from the fragments of the bones can provide a reliable estimate of skeletal height and living stature.

Secular Change and Variation in Limb Proportions in Relation to Stature in Different Populations

Secular change is the increase or decrease in size over a period of time in a population, and allometry is the proportional relationship of anatomical structures in humans and other biological organisms. Studies on secular change and allometry have observed differential limb proportionality between sexes and among populations, which could affect the accuracy of stature equations depending on the skeletal elements used to calculate such estimates. In other words, the long bone lengths and body proportions of one population do not necessarily correlate with the stature in another population. This may be attributed to the genetics and environmental factors—such as nutrition and disease—of a population, which result in variations in body and limb proportions among population groups. The environmental conditions appear to be the primary controlling factors in an individual achieving the fixed genetic potential for stature. These factors account for the necessity of population-specific regression formulae, which were discussed previously.

Allometric secular changes in black and white Americans has shown that stature formulae based on dated measurements—such as Trotter and Gleser's nineteenth-century samples from the Terry Collection—are inappropriate for use in modern forensic cases. It is, therefore, recommended that the regression equations should be derived at opportune intervals to take account of secular trends in a population.

Factors Affecting Stature Estimation in Forensic Examinations and Making Population Standards and Databases

Factors such as aging, limb asymmetry, diurnal variations, gender, and measurement error can also affect the stature estimation of victims. The effect of aging on stature estimation is well known. Stature alters as an individual goes through the life cycle, increasing during youthful growth and development, leveling off for several decades after maturity, and decreasing in later adulthood. The effective loss of stature begins at about 40 years of age and continues rapidly thereafter. Thus, it is recommended that age group categorization of the subjects should be done for making stature estimation standards and databases in a population.

Another factor that can affect stature estimation is the presence of limb asymmetry in individuals and a population as a whole. Limb asymmetry is considered as a general and natural phenomenon in the human body. Bilateral asymmetry in the human body exists because of genetic as well as environmental causes and is a good indicator of developmental stability in an organism. Thus, different formulae need to be derived for estimation of stature from the right and left sides. While examining human remains, forensic anthropologists should take asymmetry into consideration and apply an appropriate formula for estimation of stature for that side of the body.

Stature is subject to diurnal variations, and the time of the day when an individual's stature is measured can affect the measurements. Individuals have maximum stature shortly after waking (whether from nighttime sleep or an afternoon nap) and are shorter later in the day due to the gradual compression of the intervertebral disks that occurs during walking, standing, and sitting. Taller and heavier individuals have a greater potential for diurnal variations than lighter or smaller persons. Significant diurnal variation is known to affect the stature database in forensic examinations. It is, therefore, recommended that individuals' height be measured at a defined time in a day to avoid variations in stature that may affect the generated standards and formulae derived for estimation of stature.

Technical or personal errors inherent in measuring stature of individuals or measuring bones can substantially affect stature estimation and, therefore, must be considered in forensic casework. Anthropometric measurements are taken using standardized instruments and techniques. Height measurements are typically taken with an anthropometer or a stadiometer; osteometric boards, Flower's calipers, and sliding calipers are used to take measurements of long bones and skeletal material. These measurement techniques must include calculations of measurement error in terms of inter- and intraobserver bias. A minimal error can affect the reliability and precision of analysis, leading to erroneous conclusions. The precision, reliability, and reproducibility of the measurements are essential. Individuals' posture (such as a slouch, which may occur because of aging or ill health) or the effects of footwear may also substantially alter stature measurements.

Gender also has an effect on stature estimation. It is customary to derive regression formulae separately for males and females because of statistically significant differences in stature and dimensions of male and female bodies. Estimation of sex thus becomes a critical requirement in applicability of sex-specific regression models in stature estimation. It may not always be possible to estimate sex with reasonable accuracy, and hence, there is a need to derive universal regression formulae for estimation of stature that can be applied in remains with unknown sex.

See also: **Anthropology/Odontology:** Aging the Dead and the Living; History of Forensic Anthropology; Identification of the Living; Personal Identification in Forensic Anthropology; **Investigations:** Recovery of Human Remains.

Further Reading

Adams, B.J., Herrmann, N.P., 2009. Estimation of living stature from selected anthropometric (soft tissue) measurements: applications for forensic anthropology. Journal of Forensic Sciences 54, 753–760.

Auerbach, B.M., Ruff, C.B., 2004. Human body mass estimation: a comparison of morphometric and mechanical methods. American Journal of Physical Anthropology 125, 331–342.

Auerbach, B.M., Ruff, C.B., 2010. Stature estimation formulae for indigenous North American populations. American Journal of Physical Anthropology 141, 190–207.

Bidmos, M.A., 2008. Estimation of stature using fragmentary femora in indigenous South Africans. International Journal of Legal Medicine 122, 293–299.

Cattaneo, C., 2007. Forensic anthropology: developments of a classical discipline in the new millennium. Forensic Science International 165, 185–193.

Fully, G., 1956. Une nouvelle méthode de détermination de la taille. Annales de Medecine Legale 35, 266–273.

Groote, I.D., Humphrey, L.T., 2011. Body mass and stature estimation based on the first metatarsal in humans. American Journal of Physical Anthropology 144, 625–632.

Jantz, R.L., Ousley, S.D., 1993–2005. FORDISC 1.0–3.0: Personal Computerized Forensic Discriminant Functions. Forensic Anthropology Center, The University of Tennessee, Knoxville.

Jantz, R.L., Hunt, D.R., Meadows, L., 1995. The measure and mismeasure of the tibia: implications for stature estimation. Journal of Forensic Sciences 40, 758–761.

Jantz, R.L., 1992. Modification of the Trotter and Gleser female stature estimation formulae. Journal of Forensic Sciences 37, 1230–1235.

Jason, D.R., Taylor, K., 1995. Estimation of stature from the length of the cervical, thoracic, and lumbar segments of the spine in American whites and blacks. Journal of Forensic Sciences 40, 59–62.

Kanchan, T., Menezes, R.G., Moudgil, R., Kaur, R., Kotian, M.S., Garg, R.K., 2010. Stature estimation from foot length using universal regression formula in a north Indian population. Journal of Forensic Sciences 55, 163–166.

Kieffer, C.L., 2010. Tibia and fibula stature formulae for modern female populations based on digital radiographic measurements. Journal of Forensic Sciences 55, 695–700.

Klepinger, L.L., 2001. Stature, maturation variation and secular trends in forensic anthropology. Journal of Forensic Sciences 46, 788–790.

Krishan, K., Kanchan, T., DiMaggio, J.A., 2010. A study of limb asymmetry and its effect on estimation of stature in forensic case work. Forensic Science International 200, 181 e1–5.

Krishan, K., 2008. Determination of stature from foot and its segments in a north Indian population. The American Journal of Forensic Medicine and Pathology 29, 297–303.

Muñoz, J.I., Liñares-Iglesias, M., Suárez-Peñaranda, J.M., Mayo, M., Miguéns, X., Rodríguez-Calvo, M.S., Concheiro, L., 2001. Stature estimation from radiographically determined long bone length in a Spanish population sample. Journal of Forensic Sciences 46, 363–366.

Ousley, S.D., 1995. Should we estimate biological or forensic stature? Journal of Forensic Sciences 40, 768–773.

Raxter, M.H., Auerbach, B.M., Ruff, C.B., 2006. Revision of the fully technique for estimating statures. American Journal of Physical Anthropology 130, 374–384.

Ross, A.H., Konigsberg, L.W., 2002. New formulae for estimating stature in the Balkans. Journal of Forensic Sciences 47, 165–167.

Ruff, C., 2007. Body size prediction from juvenile skeletal remains. American Journal of Physical Anthropology 133, 698–716.

Trotter, M., Gleser, G.C., 1952. Estimation of stature from long bones of American whites and negroes. American Journal of Physical Anthropology 10, 463–514.

Trotter, M., Gleser, G.C., 1958. A re-evaluation of estimation of stature based on measurements of stature taken during life and of long bones after death. American Journal of Physical Anthropology 16, 79–123.

Wilson, R.J., Herrmann, N.P., Jantz, L.M., 2010. Evaluation of stature estimation from the database for forensic anthropology. Journal of Forensic Sciences 55, 684–689.

Ancestry

RL Jantz, University of Tennessee, Knoxville, TN, USA

Glossary

Fisher's linear discriminant Developed by R.A. Fisher, the linear discriminant finds a set of weights, or coefficients corresponding to each variable, which maximize the differences between groups. This means that variables exhibiting greater differences between groups receive more weight than those with smaller differences. The linear discriminant maximizes the correct classification of individuals.

Geometric morphometry Evaluation of morphology using Cartesian coordinates, which may be two or three dimensional. It provides more information about where differences occur than ordinary morphometry.

Mahalanobis Generalized distance. A statistic developed by P.C. Mahalanobis which produces a multivariate assessment of the difference between two population samples, expressed as a single number. It takes into account variation and covariation. It is a summed distance, so in general, more measurements mean larger distances.

Morphometric Evaluation of morphology by measurement.

Morphoscopic Evaluation of morphology by observation. It usually means scoring the traits as present or absent, or ranking them, in contrast to measuring them.

Introduction

Ancestry is one of the components that go into the biological profile. The biological profile is a description of a person estimated from the skeleton, including, along with ancestry, sex, height, and age. The biological profile is the initial stage in identifying unidentified skeletal remains, and ancestry is arguably the most difficult. Sex, height, and age are relatively fixed attributes and not subject to interpretation. Not so with ancestry. Ancestry pertains to the individuals in one's genealogy, but in forensic anthropology, it has the further implication of identifying the region of the world from which those ancestors originally came. The rise of hybrid groups in the past few hundred years, for example, many Latin American populations and African Americans, has resulted in many whose ancestors came from widely different parts of the world. To make matters more difficult, ancestry is connected to the highly controversial concept of race and has come into use largely to avoid that term, often regarded as emotionally charged. Regardless of what it is called, forensic anthropologists have been criticized for using the terms and for including them in their biological profiles. The basis of the criticism is that ancestry is a social construct with little or no biological meaning, and therefore forensic anthropologists are unable to reliably estimate it and risk providing faulty information to law enforcement. Tests designed to demonstrate that ancestry estimation is unreliable are often not grounded in modern concepts of human variation and are set up with unrealistic expectations, ensuring that they will fail, thereby supporting the preordained conclusions that race/ancestry is a flawed concept and that attempts to assign individuals to ancestry groups cannot be successful. Critics also argue that use of a priori-defined groups biases results, but recent work in statistical modeling has shown that human crania sort themselves into geographic groups without prior definition.

Forensic anthropology is rapidly incorporating what we know about human variation and population structure into its ancestry assessments and is also contributing new knowledge to those disciplines. It is also important to understand growth and secular changes for making ancestry assessments. Secular changes in skeletal morphology have been documented in many groups in different parts of the world, which necessitates the use of appropriate modern reference samples. Availability of such samples is one of the most critical needs to put ancestry estimation on a sound footing.

Resources

Criteria for ancestry estimation, such as those for sex, height, and age, require documented skeletons from which to derive them. In the early days of forensic anthropology, this purpose was served by anatomical collections, such as the Terry and

Todd Collections from St Louis and Cleveland, respectively. These collections contain skeletons belonging to people primarily born in the latter half of the nineteenth century. These collections may still serve useful purposes, but for ancestry estimation, the large changes in the skeleton and particularly the cranium have made them inappropriate. The problem has been addressed in two ways. (1) Development of a database of modern skeletal measurements obtained from forensic cases. This database is known as the forensic anthropology database and is maintained at the University of Tennessee, Knoxville. Measurements are taken while the skeleton is in a forensic laboratory, and information about the person becomes available when a positive identification is made. Ancestry, along with sex, height, weight, and any other information, is then attached to the record. Ancestry is obtained from records such as missing persons' reports, police, or medical records. As such, it is essentially self-reported. (2) Development of modern collections of donated bodies, specifically donated for that purpose. The University of Tennessee's William M. Bass collection is the largest such collection, numbering around 1000 skeletons at the time of this writing. The donated collection at the University of New Mexico also contains significant numbers of skeletons. The University of Tennessee's program relies heavily on predonors, that is, individuals who make arrangements to donate their bodies prior to death. This in turn provides the opportunity to obtain information, including self-reported ancestry, from them.

The Bass-donated collection contains mainly Whites, some Blacks, and a few Hispanics, Asians, and other ethnicities. The database of cranial measurements collected by W.W. Howells contains world samples, but nearly all are composed of individuals born in the nineteenth century or earlier, some several thousand years old. Nevertheless, it is often useful in assessing the part of the world from which an unknown cranium may originate.

There are hundreds of skeletal collections held in institutions around the world, although their suitability to serve as training samples for forensic identification criteria, ancestry in particular, varies considerably. They are too numerous to mention specifically, although two in South Africa are particularly noteworthy: the Raymond Dart Collection and the Pretoria Bone Collection. The Dart Collection in Witwatersrand, apparently inspired by the R.J. Terry collection, contains remains of individuals of both African and European ancestry, mostly with nineteenth-century birth years. The Pretoria bone collection has the added advantage of containing remains of individuals mainly born in the twentieth century. Both individuals of African and European ancestry are represented. The Pretoria collection has considerable potential in understanding skeletal variation in recent South Africans and in developing ancestry criteria for that country.

Why Do Ancestry Estimation?

Ancestry estimation is most commonly conducted in medicolegal situations as part of the biological profile, as the first step in identifying unknown skeletal remains. Ancestry is normally included on missing persons' reports so the ancestry estimate provided by the forensic report helps narrow the field of candidates. There are other contexts in which ancestry estimation can be important. The passage of the Native American Graves Protection and Repatriation Act in 1990 and the National Museum of the American Indian Act allows the return of Native American remains to their lineal descendents, provided cultural affiliation can be established. Ancestry estimation is often a component of establishing cultural affiliation. This normally involves comparing the remains in question to documented series representing tribal claimants. Questions may also arise because museum records are not always accurate. Sometimes remains said to be Native American are actually White or Black. Internationally, repatriation has also become an issue. Indigenous Australians have been the most successful in obtaining remains from institutions in Europe and America. As is the case of Native Americans, it is often necessary to confirm by ancestry estimation that remains are actually of Australian origin.

Estimation from the Cranium

Historical

Cranial morphology has long been the choice for estimating ancestry. The historical development of ancestry estimation can be conveniently divided into three stages.

The first stage involves assessing ancestry visually using traits, often referred to as morphoscopic traits. This approach dominated the first half of the twentieth century, but continues to the present in a modified form. It is derived from attempts to organize the world's human populations into racial types based on suites of features each race was said to have. The most influential figure in establishing these lists was E.A. Hooton of Harvard University. Although Hooton's trait list was never published and he did not use it to specifically estimate ancestry, it had a major impact on traits used by forensic anthropologists through his students and their students who were the early forensic practitioners. These traits continue to be included in introductory texts in forensic anthropology. An example of commonly used traits and their association with racial groups is shown in **Table 1**.

Effective use of visual assessment is experience based. Forensic anthropologists who have broad experience in crania from diverse populations can often do well in estimating ancestry through visual appraisal. The problem is that this experience cannot readily be communicated to students and it is difficult to know error rates. The second stage in ancestry estimation attempted to deal with these problems through measurement and statistical analysis. This stage required the appropriate statistical techniques and computer data-processing capability to handle the laborious computations.

Table 1 Example of traits traditionally used by forensic anthropologists to assess ancestry

Trait	White	Black	Native American
Inferior nasal border	Sharp	Guttered, no sill	Indistinct
Palate shape	Triangular	Rectangular	Parabolic
Nasal bones	Tower	Quonset hut	Tented
Cranial sutures	Simple	Simple	Complex
Nasal aperture	Narrow	Wide	Medium, rounded
Postbregmatic depression	Absent	Present	Absent
Orbit shape	Sloping	Square	Rounded

The statistical techniques rely mainly on Mahalanobis generalized distances and linear discriminant analysis, both of which were developed early in the twentieth century, but were little used because of the heavy computational burden. These techniques were introduced into forensic anthropology for sex and ancestry in the late 1950s and early 1960s. They are some of the earliest uses of computer technology in anthropology.

The well-known Giles and Elliot discriminant functions allowed a skull to be classified as Black, White, or American Indian. The reference or training samples were the Terry and Todd collections for Blacks and Whites, and Indian Knoll, an Archaic site, for American Indians. The Giles and Elliot discriminant functions were widely used by forensic anthropologists for 30 years. Giles and Elliot and other early functions provided the discriminant coefficients, or weights, which were multiplied by the measurements and summed, to obtain a discriminant score, which could then be compared to a sectioning point to obtain the classification. Giles and Elliot also provided a graph on which the unknown skull could be plotted to obtain a visual picture of its relationship to the reference samples and which could also be included in the forensic report.

These early functions required that all the measurements be present in order to use them. This presents a serious liability because fragmentary crania are not uncommon in forensic work, often making complete measurement sets impossible.

The third stage in ancestry estimation depended on the confluence of personal computers and the availability of more appropriate databases. This has allowed relatively easy computation of discriminant functions, and many have been published. Most importantly, new databases and more powerful personal computers allowed the development of software with the flexibility to allow users to choose groups and variables based on the needs of a particular case or set of remains. This development occurred with the release of Fordisc, which presents the user with a wide range of variable and training sample choices, classifying the unknown specimen anew each time.

Current Status

Forensic anthropologists are dealing with forensic cases drawn from increasingly complex populations, making ancestry the most difficult component of the biological profile to estimate. In the United States in particular, the influx of immigrants from Latin America, especially Mexico, has increased ethnic diversity. Hispanics are of mixed ancestry, primarily Spanish and Native American. Estimates of Hispanic ancestry normally assess it at around 50% contribution from each group. African Americans too are a mixed group, with up to 20% of their ancestry derived from European sources in some populations. In cranial morphology, as in genetic markers, mixed populations assume intermediate positions between ancestral populations. **Figure 1** using data from the forensic anthropology data bank illustrates this with respect to Hispanics, African Americans, and groups representing parent populations from which they were derived. Intermediate positions of mixed populations are obvious, as is the overlap in distributions, not only with parent populations, but with each other as well.

Most of the intermixture resulting in these hybrid groups occurred in the colonial period. In the United States, many states enacted antimiscegenation laws, some of which were not repealed until the 1960s. The United States census data indicate that, even now, the vast majority of marriages are within race, despite recent increases in interracial marriage. Biracial individuals pose difficult problems for ancestry estimation.

Unfortunately ancestry estimation has been drawn into controversies concerning whether race should be considered a real taxonomic subdivision of the species. If biological race means anything, it must refer to the inhabitants of the major geographic regions of the world, which are sometimes called

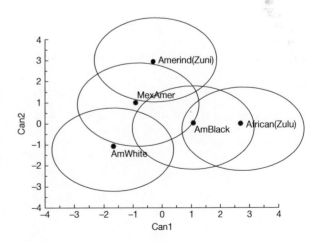

Figure 1 Canonical plot showing cranial relationships of genetically mixed populations, African Americans and Mexican American, to their parent populations. Ellipses enclose an area including 95% of the variation within groups.

geographical races. There has not, of course, ever been any agreement about the number of races that exist because, as was pointed out long ago, the distribution of genes and traits is clinal in nature and there are few abrupt changes as one moves through geographical space. Fortunately, it really does not matter to forensic anthropologists whether race is a valid taxon or not. What we know exists are populations, and populations, even local ones, are often sufficiently differentiated so that their individual members can be discriminated with reasonable accuracy. **Table 2** illustrates this with respect to several different situations. It illustrates that groups that would not be considered different races, such as North and South Japanese, or Arikara and Sioux Native Americans, can nevertheless be assigned to their correct group with high accuracy. It also shows that even groups that can be considered belonging to the same population at different points in time, such as nineteenth- and twentieth-century Whites, can also be discriminated accurately. The results in **Table 2** illustrate that populations are the relevant units and stress the importance of having reference samples appropriate to the situation at hand.

On a global level, the geographical patterning of craniometric variation has been shown in many instances. Recent analyses have shown that 75% of crania can be correctly classified into their correct population, and 90% classify into a population in the same region. Even on a global scale, the local population is the important unit, but the geographical patterning of local populations is evident.

The task of ancestry assessment in forensic anthropology is to identify the race/ethnic group the person would most likely

Table 2   Examples of ability to discriminate among populations at different scales, ranging from broad geographic groups to local populations

Comparison	Number of variables	% correct	Reason
BM vs WM	19	97	Biological race
BM vs WM vs CHM vs NAM	25	96	Biological race
BM vs WM vs JM vs NAM	25	84	Biological race
JM vs CHM vs VM	25	80	Ethnicity/language
Arikara vs Sioux females	7	87	Ethnicity/language
N Japan vs S Japan males	18	89	Geography
WM born 1840–90 vs WM born 1930–80	10	96	Time

BM, American Black males; CHM, Chinese males; JM, Japanese males; NAM, Native American males; VM, Vietnamese males; WM, American White males.
Source: Ousley, S.D., Jantz, R.L., Freid, D., 2009. Understanding race and human variation: why forensic anthropologists are good at identifying race. American Journal of Physical Anthropology 139, 68–76.

have belonged to in life. In the United States, races exist as socially defined groups which have been codified by the federal government. That these are official or bureaucratic races does not mean they have no biological meaning. Historically, race has played a large role in mating behavior, although how race has structured mating has changed over time and the interaction among America's groups is complex. Nevertheless, social races have different continental origins and different histories. Since a large majority of matings are within social race groups, preexisting variation is maintained and new variation can develop. It is critically important that forensic anthropologists understand the American population structure in order to make informed ancestry estimations.

Morphoscopic Traits Revisited

Morphoscopic traits were presented briefly in historical context. Their historical use has been based on the assumption that most or all of the members of a particular race will exhibit traits thought to characterize that race, and that variation within a race is minimal. There has been considerable progress on several fronts which promises to make these traits more useful. Problems to overcome in using them include (1) definition, scoring, and standardization; (2) appropriate statistical techniques; and (3) development of population-based data that can be used to investigate variation within and among populations. Traits may be scored as binary, that is, present or absent, and ordinal or ranked. Binary traits typically include the presence or absence of foramina such as parietal foramen, or accessory foramina such as accessory mental foramina, sutural bones such as ossicles in the lambdoid suture, or accessory tori such as the maxillary torus. Ordinal traits are scored into ordered categories, such as absent, small, medium, and large. Neither kind of trait is totally objective, so visual scoring inevitably leads to interobserver variation. Ordinal traits are usually continuously varying traits, which in principle could be measured but are not because measurement is difficult. A browridge, for example, varies continuously from a smooth surface to a large overhanging browridge, but can be arranged on an ordinal scale ranging from absent to large, with intermediate categories. Visual scoring has the advantage of being much faster.

Recent research has taken the first important steps in solving some of the problems mentioned above. Descriptions of traits have been developed to facilitate standardized scoring, and the process of assembling a database of traits is taking place. Examination of variation within and among populations has shown that traits said to characterize certain ancestral groups in lists such as those in **Table 1** occur in all major human groups, but in different frequencies. Postbregmatic depression, for example, is said to characterize African ancestry, but in African Americans, it is present in less than 50%, and occurs in almost 20% of individuals of European ancestry as well. The sharp inferior nasal border associated with Europeans also occurs in 20% of those of African ancestry.

Morphoscopic traits are similar to traditional measurements in many respects. Different populations exhibit overlapping distributions. They perform similarly in discriminating ancestry groups when traits are used in combination in multivariate analyses. They therefore have considerable potential to add another source of data to the difficult task of ancestry estimation, once suitable databases are in place and the software to analyze them developed. These examples make clear that the presence of a single trait will not be an indicator of ancestry.

Estimation from the Postcranial Skeleton

The postcranial skeleton has historically been considered less useful in ancestry estimation than the cranium. The main reason for this attitude is that the postcranial skeleton consists of a number of elements that do not provide a visual gestalt like the cranium does. Consequently, there has been far less research into the utility of the postcranial skeleton. There is, however, no a priori reason to believe that postcranial skeletal variation is less than that seen in the cranium, although one might expect the postcranial skeleton to reflect function to a greater extent than the cranium. Research has tended to focus on specific postcranial features associated with certain groups. Some of these are:

Anterior femoral curvature: There is a general progression in the amount of anterior curvature of the femoral diaphysis as follows: Native North Americans have pronounced anterior curvature, American Blacks the least, tending to very straight femora, and American Whites are intermediate.

Femur subtrochanteric shape: Subtrochanteric shape refers to the shape of the femur shaft just below the lesser trochanter, located on the proximal end. Subtrochanteric shape is normally assessed by means of the index of platymeria, defined as the anterior–posterior diameter divided by the mediolateral diameter, times 100. Low indices, less than 85, are defined as platymeric, meaning that the subtrochanteric region is relatively flat in the anterior–posterior direction. Native North American femora tend toward platymeria, while Whites and Blacks have higher indices. This tendency shows considerable consistency among Native Americans and is therefore often useful in distinguishing Native Americans from Blacks and Whites.

Intercondylar notch height: The distal end of the femur also shows some ancestry variation, at least as far as Blacks and Whites are concerned. A simple measurement that has been proposed is the height of the intercondylar notch with the femur lying on its dorsal surface. Blacks and Whites differ sufficiently to classify them correctly at a rate of about 80%.

General postcranial ancestry variation: The examples given above illustrate that certain specific elements of the postcranial

skeleton exhibit sufficient variation to be useful in ancestry estimation. Measurements of postcranial bones are also effective for discriminating ancestry groups in America. **Table 3** gives a preliminary comparison of Whites, Blacks, and Hispanics for cranial and postcranial measurements. It shows that postcranial discrimination serves almost as well as cranial discrimination.

Statistics and Probabilities

It is not our purpose to go into detail concerning statistical procedures utilized for ancestry estimation, but it is useful to outline their features in general terms. There are two types of probabilities that are useful in assessing whether an unknown individual could be a member of the group to which it is assigned. Both kinds are based on the Mahalanobis D^2. The posterior probability makes the assumption that the unknown individual belongs to one of the groups to which it is being compared. Therefore, the posterior probabilities must sum to 1.0. The question the posterior probability answers can be phrased as follows: Given that the unknown belongs to one of the groups to which it is being compared, which is the most likely? The highest posterior probability will always be associated with the group with the lowest Mahalanobis distance.

It may be the case that the unknown belongs to none of the groups to which it is being compared or is even similar to any of them, despite having a high posterior probability with one of them. The typicality probability does not assume any group membership and simply answers the question: Does the unknown fit within the range of variation of each group? Typicality probabilities are most commonly based on comparing Mahalanobis D^2 to the chi square distribution, with degrees of freedom equal to the number of variables. It is possible, and in fact happens frequently, that an unknown has a high posterior probability with one of the groups, but falls within the range of variation of several groups, making it impossible to completely exclude them from consideration.

Table 3 Comparison of cranial and postcranial discriminating efficiency of American Whites, Blacks, and Hispanics, based on nine variables for each data source

Group	Cranial % correct	Postcranial % correct
Blacks	79.4	73.5
Hispanics	67.8	61.9
Whites	77.9	74.9
Total	77.9	74.9

Source of data: Forensic Anthropology Data Bank, University of Tennessee, Knoxville.

Geometric Morphometry

Geometric morphometry analysis is based on the two- or three-dimensional (3D) coordinates obtained from skeletal landmarks, most commonly from the cranium. Geometric morphometry has been used mainly to address phylogenetic or population variation questions, but is being incorporated into forensic work as a more refined method to address questions of sex and ancestry estimation. Software has been developed exclusively for the purpose of estimating ancestry from coordinate data. Geomorphometric techniques offer some advantages, including visualizing variation, understanding more precisely what varies, and in separating size variation from shape variation. Those advantages are less clear when the objective is ancestry assessment of an individual cranium. A digitizer is required, not yet part of many forensic laboratories, and, at the present time at least, it is more cumbersome to enter coordinate data into the software. It has also not yet been demonstrated that classification accuracy is superior, although rigorous tests using comparable data have not yet been carried out.

Software

Statistical analyses such as those described above can be obtained using many of the software packages widely available, although one must provide the training sample data against which to compare the unknown skeleton. At least three software packages are available with built-in training samples and are specifically designed to analyze one case. Fordisc 3.1 provides two databases, one specifically designed for US applications, drawn from the forensic anthropology data bank, and one for worldwide applications, using the database of W.W. Howells. Fordisc 3.1 provides the user with many statistical choices, including posterior and typicality probabilities, stepwise selection of variables, analysis with raw, logged, or shape variables, as well as options for saving the analysis and incorporating it into forensic reports. It also provides graphical capabilities.

Cranid provides a more extensive worldwide database than Fordisc, incorporating Howells' plus 10 additional samples which fill in some of the gaps in Howells' coverage of the world. Cranid uses 29 variables and does not provide the user with a choice; all 29 must be present. Cranid provides classification by the usual linear discriminant function, as well as nearest-neighbor discriminant function, a useful alternative to linear discriminant function.

3D-id is currently the only software package that performs classification using coordinate data. It makes what would otherwise be a difficult and time-consuming task relatively easy, assuming one can obtain coordinates from the unknown skull. It will perform the analysis on whatever coordinates one obtains, and so is appropriate for fragmentary crania. The analysis can be performed on shape variables only, or one can restore size.

Conclusions and Future Directions

Estimating ancestry from skeletal remains is becoming an increasingly quantitative data-driven enterprise. In part, this is a natural evolution demanded by the increasing complexity of human populations and the questions forensic anthropologists seek to answer. In part, it is demanded by the increasing scientific rigor demanded by the courts, as seen in the Daubert decision, and by legislation following the National Academy of Science report on shortcomings in the quality of forensic science. It is no longer adequate for an expert witness to testify to ancestry based solely on his/her experience. It is now necessary for the procedures used to have gone through the peer-review process and have been published, and to have estimates of error rates. This can only be accomplished with procedures based on appropriate data and statistical procedures. Hence, future endeavors should be characterized by ever-broadening databases and new statistical methods. Data from modern skeletons from Europe, Asia, and Australia are badly needed if ancestry estimation is to reach its potential.

Ancestry estimation now demands the following:

1. It should be based on reference samples appropriate for the populations involved. These are likely to be specific to the country, or even part of the country involved.
2. It must also be based on time-appropriate reference samples. Individuals with twentieth-century birth years differ from those of earlier time periods, in some cases dramatically. Secular changes remain to be investigated in many regions of the world.
3. It should be arrived at using appropriate statistical procedures so that results can be stated in terms of probabilities. These should include both a posterior and typicality probability.
4. Procedures and methods should be fully described.

> See also: **Anthropology/Odontology:** Postmortem Interval; **Biology/DNA:** Ancestry Informative Markers.

Further Reading

Dirkmaat, D.C., Cabo, L.L., Ousley, S.D., 2008. New perspectives in forensic anthropology. Yearbook of Physical Anthropology 51, 33–52.

Hefner, J.T., 2009. Cranial nonmetric variation and estimating ancestry. Journal of Forensic Sciences 54 (5), 985–995.

Howells, W.W., 1995. Who's Who in Skulls: Ethnic Identification of Crania from Measurements, vol. 82. Peabody Museum of Archaeology and Ethnology, Harvard University, Cambridge, MA.

Komar, D.A., Buikstra, J.E., 2008. Forensic Anthropology: Contemporary Theory and Practice. Oxford University Press, New York.

L'Abbe, E.N., Van Rooyen, C., Nawrocki, S.P., Becker, P.J., 2011. An evaluation of non-metric cranial traits used to estimate ancestry in a South African sample. Forensic Science International 209 (1–3), 195 e191–197. 10.1016/j.forsciint.2011.04.002.

Ousley, S.D., Jantz, R.L., Freid, D., 2009. Understanding race and human variation: why forensic anthropologists are good at identifying race. American Journal of Physical Anthropology 139, 68–76.

Sauer, N.J., 1992. Forensic anthropology and the concept of race – if races don't exist, why are forensic anthropologists so good at identifying them. Social Science and Medicine 34 (2), 107–111.

Spradley, M.K., Jantz, R.L., Robinson, A., Peccerelli, F., 2008. Demographic change and forensic identification: problems in metric identification of hispanic skeletons. Journal of Forensic Sciences 53 (1), 21–28.

Wright, R., 2008. Detection of likely ancestry using CRANID [online]. In: Oxenham, M. (Ed.), Forensic Approaches to Death, Disaster and Abuse. Australian Academic Press, Bowen Hills, QLD, ISBN 9781875378906, pp. 111–122. Available at: http://search.informit.com.au/documentSummary; dn=804323190860089;res=IELHSS (cited September 02, 2011).

Relevant Websites

http://web.utk.edu—Jantz, R.L., Ousley, S.D. Fordisc 3.1.
http://www.3d-id.org—Slice, D.E., Ross, A., 2009. 3D-ID: Version 1 (accessed 16.01.10.).
http://www.box.net—Wright, Richard Cranid.

Ancestry/Race Websites

http://www.aaanet.org—American Anthropological Associate Statement of Race.
http://physanth.org—American Association of Physical Anthropologists Statement Lon Race.
http://dienekes.110mb.com—Model Based Clustering of Human Crania.
http://www.nature.com—Nature Genetics Special Issue on Race.

Data and Collection Websites

http://www.icpsr.umich.edu—Forensic Anthropology Data Bank.
http://konig.la.utk.edu/howells.htm or http://web.utk.edu—Howells Data.
http://skeletal.highfantastical.com—Skeletal Collections.

Forensic Age Estimation

A Schmeling, Institute of Legal Medicine, Münster, Germany

Introduction

Despite the alleged use of the eruption of second molars by the ancient Romans to evaluate readiness for military service, age diagnostics in living individuals is a relatively young branch of applied research within the forensic sciences. However, in recent years, its value and importance as an assessment tool has risen exponentially as the requirements for an informed opinion on the age of an individual have assumed increasing importance for the assessment of both legal and social categorization.

There are many areas in which the evaluation of age in the living have gained significant importance in recent years but the most prevalent concern issues pertaining to refugee and asylum seekers, suspects and delinquents, human trafficking, and child pornography. Age evaluation is also required for adoptive children from countries without birth registration. A further category which is on the rise is age evaluation in competitive sports to ensure that athletes are competing within an age-appropriate banding both for the sake of fairness and health protection. Parents have also been known to falsify the ages of their children, particularly of their sons, to obtain preferential educational opportunities. While it is undeniable that the majority of issues raised concerning age evaluation are predominantly within the juvenile aspect of the human age range, there are issues of legality in relation to the elderly, which tend to relate to matters of eligibility for state pension support or retirement law.

The first transregional scientific analysis of forensic age diagnostics in living individuals was conducted on the occasion of the 10th Lübeck Meeting of German Forensic Physicians in December 1999. At this meeting, it was suggested that a study group be set up, which would include forensic pathologists, dentists, radiologists, and anthropologists. They were tasked with producing recommendations for the issuing of expert opinions in order to standardize the hitherto common and partly varying procedure and to achieve quality assurance for expert opinions.

The international and interdisciplinary "Study Group on Forensic Age Diagnostics" was established in Berlin, Germany, on March 10, 2000. This study group has given recommendations for forensic age estimation in living individuals in criminal proceedings, in civil and asylum procedures, as well as in pension procedures. As an external quality control measure, the Study Group on Forensic Age Diagnostics annually organizes proficiency tests in which participants are sent the X-rays and physical examination results for a set of subjects and asked to estimate their ages.

Because of the explosive growth in knowledge over recent years, only qualified specialists in the field of forensic age diagnostics are capable of supplying expert opinions based on the current state of the sciences. A member list of the Study Group on Forensic Age Diagnostics can be downloaded from the Study Group's homepage. Successful participants in the Study Group's proficiency tests are also published on this homepage.

Outlined below are the methodological principles of forensic age diagnostics as applied to adolescents and young adults, child victims in child pornographic picture documents as well as to older adults for the purposes of clarifying pension entitlements.

Age Estimation in Adolescents and Young Adults

General Remarks

The persons to whom forensic examination is to be applied are foreigners without valid identity documents who are suspected of making false statements about their age and whose genuine age needs to be ascertained in the course of criminal, civil, or asylum proceedings. In many countries, the legally relevant age thresholds lie between 14 and 22 years of age.

According to the recommendations of the Study Group on Forensic Age Diagnostics for an age estimate, the following examinations should be performed in combination: physical examination with determination of anthropometric measures (body height and weight, constitutional type), inspection of signs of sexual maturation, as well as identification of any age-relevant developmental disorders.

- X-ray examination of the left hand
- Dental examination with determination of the dental status and X-ray examination of the dentition
- If the skeletal development of the hand is complete, an additional examination of the clavicles should be carried out, preferably by means of a conventional X-ray examination and/or a CT scan.

Guidelines for the use of ionizing radiation vary from country to country. When utilizing X-rays, the local regulations, statutes, or professional guidelines should be observed. As X-ray examinations for forensic age diagnostics take place without medical indications, the question should first be pursued as to whether the effective radiation doses given during the procedures used could be detrimental to the health of the persons examined.

Radiation Exposure in X-ray Examinations for the Purpose of Age Estimation

The effective dose from an X-ray examination of the hand is 0.1 microsievert (µSv), from an orthopantomogram (OPG) 26 µSv, from a conventional X-ray examination of the clavicles 220 µSv, and from a CT scan of the clavicles 600 µSv. According to the relatively high effective dose of the X-ray and CT examinations of the clavicles, their use should be restricted to individuals with completed hand ossification.

In order to assess the potential health risk of these X-ray examinations, the amounts of naturally occurring and civilizing radiation exposure are compared to amounts of radiation exposure from radiological procedures. The effective dose from naturally occurring radiation exposure in Germany is 2.1 mSv (millisievert) on average per year. Apart from the direct cosmic radiation of 0.3 mSv and the direct terrestrial radiation of 0.4 mSv, the ingestion of naturally occurring radioactive substances in the food contributes 0.3 mSv to the radiation exposure. For the inhalation of radon and its disintegration products, 1.1 mSv must be added. Compared to naturally occurring radiation exposure, one hand X-ray equals the naturally occurring radiation exposure of 25 min, one OPG is equivalent to 4.5 days, one X-ray of the clavicles is equal to 38 days, and one CT of the clavicles equals 104 days.

The radiation exposure from an intercontinental flight at an altitude of 12 000 m is 0.008 mSv per hour. It follows that the dose for a flight from Frankfurt to New York is 0.05 mSv. This means that the radiation exposure from two OPGs is equivalent to the radiation exposure from an intercontinental flight.

On the basis of this comparison, a relevant health risk as a result of X-ray examinations for forensic age estimations can be denied.

Concerning a possible health risk, the biological effect of X-rays needs to be discussed as well. In this case, a distinction between stochastic and nonstochastic radiation effects has to be made. Nonstochastic effects appear above 100 mSv and are therefore irrelevant to radiological diagnostics. DNA damage leading to mutations of the genotype and malign diseases is one of the stochastic effects. On the assumption that there is a linear dose–effect relation without a threshold between the risk of radiation exposure and the delivered radiation dose and thus that even X-rays in the low-dose region can cause a malign disease, cancer mortality risks can be calculated for adults and children. It has to be pointed out that the risk for children is twice the risk of adults. The German radiation

biologist Jung compared the mortality risk of X-ray examinations for age estimations with the mortality risk resulting from the participation in traffic. He came to the conclusion that the mortality risk of an OPG is comparable to the participation in traffic for 2.5 h. Thus the radiation risk of the X-ray examinations is as high as the risk the examined individual is exposed to on the way to the examination or the trial date. If the risk of an appointment for an age estimation seemed acceptable, this should also apply to the radiation risk of the X-ray examination.

It can be concluded that compared to other life risks, a relevant health risk of X-rays for the purpose of age estimation can be denied as well.

However, as long as the discussion about the biological radiation effect in the low-dose region is undecided, the so-called minimizing order remains valid without restrictions. It demands that any necessary examination is carried out with the minimum amount of radiation and without unnecessary exposure. Thus, no X-rays should be made beyond the examination range specified in scientific recommendations.

Physical Examination

The physical examination includes anthropometric measures such as body height, weight, and constitutional type, as well as visible signs of sexual maturity. In boys these are penile and testicular development, pubic hair, axillary hair, beard growth, and laryngeal prominence; in girls these are breast development, pubic hair, axillary hair, and shape of the hip.

Tanner's staging for sexual maturation is commonly used to determine the status of genital development, breast development, and pubic hair growth. Axillary hair growth, beard growth, and laryngeal development may be assessed using the four-stage classification of Neyzi et al.

Of the forensic methods recommended for age estimation, evaluating sexual maturity shows the largest range of variation and therefore should be used for age diagnostics only in conjunction with an evaluation of skeletal maturity and tooth development. However, the physical examination is indispensable to rule out any visible signs of age-related illness and to cross-check whether skeletal age and tooth age correspond to overall physical development.

Most diseases delay development and are thus conducive to underestimation of age. Such underestimation of age would not disadvantage the person concerned in terms of criminal prosecution. By contrast, overestimating age due to a disease that accelerates development should be avoided at all costs. Such diseases occur very rarely and include, above all, endocrinal disorders, which may affect not only the attainment of height and sexual development, but also skeletal development. Endocrinal diseases that may accelerate skeletal development include precocious puberty, adrenogenital syndrome, and hyperthyroidism.

The physical examination should look for symptoms of hormonal acceleration of development, such as gigantism, acromegaly, microplasia, virilization of girls, dissociated virilism of boys, goiter, or exophthalmos. If no abnormality is detected, it may be assumed that the probability of such a disease occurring is well below one per 1000. Another indication for a possible hormonal disease is a discrepancy between skeletal age and dental age, as dental development normally remains unaffected by endocrinal disorders.

X-Ray Examination of the Hand

Within the area of forensic age estimations in adolescents, skeletal maturation is a vital diagnostic pillar. In this connection, the hand skeleton is particularly suitable until the developmental processes are completed at the age of about 17–18 years. The maturity status of the hand may be considered to be representative for the entire skeletal system.

As agreed, an X-ray of the left hand is taken as, in all populations, the number of right-handers is higher, and, as a result, the right hand is more often exposed to traumata which can impair the skeletal development. However, there are no reported significant differences in the ossification rate of right and left hands.

Criteria for evaluating hand radiographs include the form and size of bone elements and the degree of epiphyseal ossification. To this effect, either a given X-ray image is compared with standard images of the relevant age and sex (radiographic atlas), or the degree of maturity or bone age is determined for selected bones (single bone method).

Various studies have demonstrated that although the single bone method requires more time, it does not necessarily yield more accurate results. Therefore, the two atlas methods developed by Greulich and Pyle as well as by Thiemann et al. seem to be appropriate for forensic age diagnostics.

Dental Examination

The main criteria for dental age estimation in adolescents and young adults are eruption and mineralization of the third molars.

Tooth eruption is a parameter of developmental morphology which, unlike tooth mineralization, can be determined in two ways: by clinical examination and/or by evaluation of dental X-rays. While "eruption" incorporates the entire journey of the tooth from its formation in the alveolar crypts to full occlusion, "emergence" is restricted to the time when any part of the tooth finally clears the gingival margin and becomes visible in the mouth until the stage when the tooth finally comes into occlusion with its partner tooth from the opposing jaw. Olze et al. defined a stage classification of third molar eruption based on evidence from conventional OPGs (**Figure 1**):

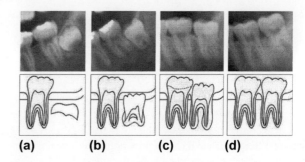

Figure 1   Stages of third molar eruption.

Stage A Occlusal plane covered with alveolar bone.
Stage B Alveolar emergence; complete resorption of alveolar bone over occlusal plane.
Stage C Gingival emergence; penetration of gingiva by at least one dental cusp.
Stage D Complete emergence in occlusal plane.

Various classifications have been devised for evaluating tooth mineralization. They differ with regard to the number of stages, the definition of each stage, and the presentation. To assess tooth mineralization, the classification of stages made by Demirjian et al (**Figure 2**). is the most suitable as the stages are defined by changes in form, independently of speculative estimates of length:

Stage A Cusp tips are mineralized but have not yet coalesced.
Stage B Mineralized cusps are united so the mature coronal morphology is well defined.

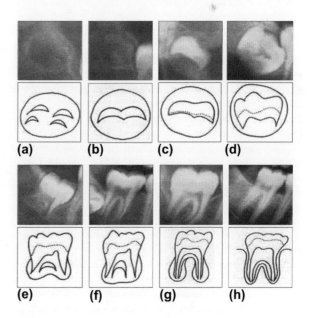

Figure 2   Demirjian's stages of third molar mineralization.

Stage C The crown is about half formed; the pulp chamber is evident and dentinal deposition is occurring.

Stage D Crown formation is complete to the dentoenamel junction. The pulp chamber has a trapezoidal form.

Stage E Formation of the interradicular bifurcation has begun. Root length is less than the crown length.

Stage F Root length is at least as great as crown length. Roots have funnel-shaped endings.

Stage G Root walls are parallel, but apices remain open.

Stage H Apical ends of the roots are completely closed, and the periodontal membrane has a uniform width around the root.

Both the eruption and the mineralization of third molars can be complete before the conclusion of the 18th year of life. Proof of completion of the 18th year of life may be provided by complete mineralization of the roots of impacted third molars as well as the lack of radiographic visibility of the root pulp or the periodontal ligament of the third molars.

Radiological Examination of the Clavicles

If the skeletal development of the hand is completed, an additional evaluation of the ossification status of the medial epiphysis of the clavicle should be performed, because all other examined developmental systems may already have completed their growth by that age.

Radiological methods to examine the medial clavicular epiphysis in living individuals are conventional radiography (CR), computed tomography (CT), as well as new approaches using magnet resonance imaging and ultrasound sonography.

While traditional classification systems differentiate between four stages of clavicle ossification (stage 1: ossification center not ossified; stage 2: ossification center ossified, epiphyseal plate not ossified; stage 3: epiphyseal plate partly ossified; stage 4: epiphyseal plate fully ossified), Schmeling et al. divided the stage of total epiphyseal fusion into two additional stages (stage 4: epiphyseal plate fully ossified, epiphyseal scar visible; stage 5: epiphyseal plate fully ossified, epiphyseal scar no longer visible). **Figure 3** shows the stages of clavicular ossification for CR and CT.

There is only one study referring to CR that meets the requirements of a reference study as stated by the Study Group on Forensic Age Diagnostics. In this study, the earliest age at which stage 3 was detected in either sex was 16 years. Stage 4 was first observed in women at 20 years and in men at 21 years. Stage 5 was first achieved by both sexes at age 26. It was concluded that plain chest radiographs can essentially provide a basis for assessing clavicular ossification. If overlap in posterior–anterior views impedes evaluation, additional oblique images should be taken to facilitate age estimation.

As the potential to assess CT images is dependent on slice thickness, slice thicknesses of a maximum of 1 mm should be in the practice of age estimation.

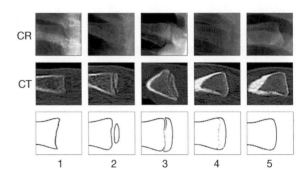

Figure 3 Stages of clavicular ossification (CR, conventional radiography; CT, computed tomography).

Recently, Kellinghaus et al. published data from a thin-slice CT study. In this study, stage 3 was first achieved by male individuals at age 17 and in females at age 16. The occurrence of stage 4 was first found in both sexes at the age of 21. In either sex, the earliest observation of stage 5 was at age 26.

A further improvement of age diagnostics based on clavicular ossification was the subdivision of stages 2 and 3 by Kellinghaus et al. Stage 3c first appeared at age 19 in both sexes. If stage 3c is found, it is therefore possible to substantiate that an individual has already reached the legally important age threshold of 18 years.

Comparative examinations showed that conventional X-rays and CT scans of the same clavicle can result in different ossification stages contingent on the method used. For the purposes of age estimation, this leads to the requirement to employ modality-specific reference studies.

Summarizing Age Diagnosis

The results of the physical examination, the radiographic examination of the hand, the dental examination, and the radiographic examination of the clavicles, as the case may be, should be compiled by the expert in charge of coordinating all contributions in a summarizing age diagnosis. The summarizing age estimate should include a discussion of the age-relevant variations resulting from application of the reference studies in an individual case, such as different ethnicity, different socioeconomic status, and their potential effect on the developmental status, or diseases that may affect the development of the individual examined, including their effect on the estimated age. If possible, a quantitative assessment of any such effect should be given.

The individual's most likely age is estimated on the basis of all partial diagnoses and a critical discussion of the individual case. If independent features are examined as part of an age diagnosis that combines several methods, it may be assumed that the margin of error for the combined age diagnosis is smaller than that for each individual feature. Combining methods makes it possible to identify statistical outliers, which should also reduce the scale of variation of the overall diagnosis to a certain nonquantifiable extent.

On the basis of the verification of age estimations carried out at the Berlin Institute of Legal Medicine (Charité), it may be assumed that the range of scatter of the summarizing age diagnosis lies at around ±12 months. Once development of the systems of characteristics examined is complete, only minimum age can be specified.

Influence of Ethnicity on the Development Systems Examined

As no forensically applicable reference studies are, as a rule, available for the regions of origin of the persons under examination, the question arises whether there are serious differences in development in diverse ethnic groups, which would prohibit the application of relevant age standards to members of ethnic groups other than the reference population.

Extensive studies of the relevant literature has demonstrated that defined stages of ossification, tooth development, and sexual maturation in the main ethnic groups relevant to forensic age estimation will proceed in the same fixed sequence so that the relevant reference studies can, in principle, be applied to other ethnic groups.

In the relevant age group, ethnicity evidently has no appreciable influence on skeletal maturation. The rate of ossification is primarily dependent on the socioeconomic status of a population. Comparatively, low socioeconomic status leads to a delay in development and thus to an underestimation of age. The application of the relevant reference studies to members of socioeconomically less-developed populations has no detrimental consequences for those affected as far as criminal proceedings are concerned—on the contrary.

With regard to the eruption and mineralization of the third molars, it has been ascertained that black Africans display an accelerated development in comparison with Europeans; by contrast, a relative retardation can be recorded in the case of Asians. For this reason, population-specific reference studies should be used to assess development of third molars in the practice of age estimation.

Methodology in Cases Where Legitimization of X-Ray Examinations Is Lacking

For age estimations without legitimization of X-ray examinations, the Study Group on Forensic Age Diagnostics recommends a physical examination covering anthropometric measurements, signs of sexual maturation, and potential age-related developmental disorders, as well as a dental examination with dental charting.

For legal reasons, findings from a radiological examination of the teeth or the hand skeleton, or other radiological characteristics of individual maturation may only be called upon if images with verified identity and known time of origin already exist.

It is to be expected that a considerable improvement in the reliability of such age estimations will be achieved in the near future by using radiation-free imaging techniques (ultrasound and magnetic resonance imaging).

Age Diagnostics in Child Victims in Child Pornographic Image Documents

In principle, age estimations in children in image documents too are made by evaluating outwardly visible growth and development processes. An evaluation of signs of sexual maturity, odontogenesis, and general proportions of the body and the face come into question.

In the evaluation of sexual maturation, the stagings commonly used in age estimations in living persons are applied. However, because of the wide variability of sexual maturation, it is only possible in exceptional cases to determine with the necessary probability that the individual portrayed is a child in the legal sense.

An assessment of dental development is a classic method of age diagnostics in children. When evaluating pictorial material, however, the examiner is reliant on sufficiently good visibility of the front teeth and on high picture quality. However, in exceptional cases where the milk teeth are well recognizable, important information on age can be gained.

Body proportions change in a characteristic way in the course of the individual development of infants into adults. Typical shifts in proportions are the result of different speeds of growth of the different regions of the body during certain phases of development. In particular, the proportional ratios between the trunk and the extremities and/or the trunk and the head, as well as the breadth and length ratios of each of the body segments can be used in age estimation. Although the assessment of body proportions alone only yields a rough age classification, it should always be included in the overall assessment.

The development of a child's face too is characterized by certain growth principles resulting in age-related facial proportions. In general, in the course of development from an infant to an adolescent and an adult, the neurocranium, which is very prominent in childhood, recedes with increasing age compared to the viscerocranium. The face itself undergoes ongoing extension, the mandible is emphasized, and as a whole, growth in height and depth as opposed to growth in breadth predominates in development. In a current pilot study, various measurements were surveyed on standardized facial photos of 373 persons in the age groups of 6, 10, 14, and 18 years. Using discriminant analysis, it was ascertained that it was possible to classify 60.3% of cases in the correct age group. Moreover, software is at present being developed within the scope of an EU project for automated age estimation on the basis of facial morphology.

Age Diagnostics in Older Adults for Clarification of Pension Entitlements

Age diagnostics in living persons for clarification of old-age pension entitlements must be carried out almost without exception on older adults (mostly from the fourth decade of life and upward). In this age range, age estimations using morphological procedures do not, as a rule, provide adequate exactitude. However, if radiological examinations of the teeth or appropriate sections of the skeleton were carried out in childhood, adolescence, or early adulthood for medical reasons and the relevant records are still available, these can be checked for suitability for morphological age estimation. In this process, it must be ensured that the records submitted really do come from the person in question. If the issue cannot be adequately resolved by means of this approach, biochemical age estimation on the basis of the degree of racemization of aspartic acid in the dentine can be discussed. In adulthood, determining the degree of racemization of aspartic acid in the dentine leads to significantly more accurate results than morphological methods.

To determine the degree of racemization of aspartic acid in the dentine, a tooth is necessary. The extraction of a tooth is, in principle, a bodily injury which is only justified in the event of appropriate medical indications and with the informed consent of the patient. In an identity assurance protocol to be signed by the dentist and the applicant, the identity of the applicant has to be determined as well as the fact that the tooth originated from the applicant. The examinations must be carried out in a competent laboratory with an adequate quality assurance system.

Conclusions

Forensic age diagnostics in living individuals has gained considerably in significance over recent years.

For the purposes of age estimation in adolescents and young adults, the Study Group on Forensic Age Diagnostics recommends a combination of a physical examination, an X-ray examination of the hand, a dental examination providing an OPG, as well as an additional radiological examination of the clavicles in cases where the hand skeleton is fully developed.

Where there is no legitimation for X-ray examinations, the range of methods is limited to a physical examination and dental charting. By using radiation-free imaging techniques, a significant improvement of the reliability of age estimations without legitimation of X-ray examinations may be expected.

The influence of ethnicity and socioeconomic status on the age characteristics examined must be taken into account in compiling a report.

Age estimation in child victims shown in child pornographic image documents is possible by means of assessment of signs of sexual maturity, dental development, general body proportions, and facial proportions. However, owing to wide variations in the characteristics available until now, it is only possible in individual cases to ascertain with the necessary probability that the legally relevant age limits have not been reached.

Age estimations in pension proceedings can be made on the basis of radiological records dating from childhood and adolescence insofar as identity is proven. If such records are not available, an ascertainment of the degree of racemization of aspartic acid in the dentine may be considered. The extraction of the tooth required for this method is only legitimized in the presence of a medical indication and with the informed consent of the person affected.

See also: **Digital Evidence:** Child Pornography; **Forensic Medicine/Clinical:** Identification.

Further Reading

Black, S., Aggrawal, A., Payne-James, J. (Eds.), 2010. Age Estimation in the Living: The Practitioner's Guide. Wiley-Blackwell, Hoboken.

Cattaneo, C., Obertová, Z., Ratnayake, M., et al., 2012. Can facial proportions taken from images be of use for ageing in cases of suspected child pornography? A pilot study. International Journal of Legal Medicine 126, 139–144.

Gabriel, P., Obertová, Z., Ratnayake, M., et al., 2011. Schätzung des Lebensalters kindlicher Opfer auf Bilddokumenten. Rechtliche Implikationen und Bedeutung im Ermittlungsverfahren. Rechtsmedizin 21, 7–11.

Greulich, W.W., Pyle, S.I., 1959. Radiographic Atlas of Skeletal Development of the Hand and Wrist. Stanford University Press, Stanford.

Kellinghaus, M., Schulz, R., Vieth, V., Schmidt, S., Pfeiffer, H., Schmeling, A., 2010. Enhanced possibilities to make statements on the ossification status of the medial clavicular epiphysis using an amplified staging scheme in evaluating thin-slice CT scans. International Journal of Legal Medicine 124, 321–325.

Kellinghaus, M., Schulz, R., Vieth, V., Schmidt, S., Schmeling, A., 2010. Forensic age estimation in living subjects based on the ossification status of the medial clavicular epiphysis as revealed by thin-slice multidetector computed tomography. International Journal of Legal Medicine 124, 149–154.

Lockemann, U., Fuhrmann, A., Püschel, K., Schmeling, A., Geserick, G., 2004. Empfehlungen für die Altersdiagnostik bei Jugendlichen und jungen Erwachsenen außerhalb des Strafverfahrens. Rechtsmedizin 14, 123–125.

Olze, A., Schmeling, A., Taniguchi, M., et al., 2004. Forensic age estimation in living subjects: the ethnic factor in wisdom tooth mineralization. International Journal of Legal Medicine 118, 170–173.

Olze, A., van Niekerk, P., Ishikawa, T., et al., 2007. Comparative study on the effect of ethnicity on wisdom tooth eruption. International Journal of Legal Medicine 121, 445–448.

Ritz-Timme, S., Kaatsch, H.-J., Marré, B., et al., 2002. Empfehlungen für die Altersdiagnostik bei Lebenden im Rentenverfahren. Rechtsmedizin 12, 193–194.

Schmeling, A., Schulz, R., Reisinger, W., Mühler, M., Wernecke, K.-D., Geserick, G., 2004. Studies on the time frame for ossification of medial clavicular epiphyseal cartilage in conventional radiography. International Journal of Legal Medicine 118, 5–8.

Schmeling, A., Schulz, R., Danner, B., Rösing, F.W., 2006. The impact of economic progress and modernization in medicine on the ossification of hand and wrist. International Journal of Legal Medicine 120, 121–126.

Schmeling, A., Grundmann, C., Fuhrmann, A., et al., 2008. Criteria for age estimation in living individuals. International Journal of Legal Medicine 122, 457–460.

Tanner, J.M., 1962. Growth at Adolescence. Blackwell, Oxford.

Thiemann, H.-H., Nitz, I., Schmeling, A. (Eds.), 2006. Röntgenatlas der normalen Hand im Kindesalter. Thieme, Stuttgart.

Key Terms

Adolescent, Adult, Age, Aging, Ancestry, Bilateral asymmetry, Body mass, Body parts, Body size, Bone histology, Child, Comparative anatomy, Craniometry, Discriminant functions, Diurnal variation, Estimate, Factors affecting stature estimation, Forensic anthropology, Forensic anthropology, Forensic data, Forensic odontology, Forensic radiology, Geometric morphometrics, Gross morphology, Historical development, Human osteology, Human remains, Human versus nonhuman diagnosis, Identity, Living, Long bones, Measurement error, Methods of stature estimation, Molecular anthropology, Morphology, Morphometrics, Morphoscopics, Osteometry, Population variation, Populations, Postcranial metrics, Race, Radiology, Secular change, Sexual dimorphism, Skeletal collections, Stature estimation, Stature in adults and adolescents, X-ray.

Review Questions

1. Why is determining human from nonhuman bone important legally?
2. How are human postcranial bones similar to those of other animals?
3. What does "plantigrade" mean?
4. How does fragmentation impede the determination of human/nonhuman?
5. How are nonhuman bones classified to species? What methods are used and which are most effective?
6. Why is estimation of sex important for forensic anthropology?
7. What is sexual dimorphism?
8. Which areas of the skeleton show more sexual dimorphism?
9. What factors can complicate estimation of sex? Why?
10. Can sex be reliably determined in subadults? Why or why not?
11. Why does a well-developed preauricular sulcus indicate "female"?
12. What is FORDISC? How is it used?
13. Why is estimating age in living subadults important forensically?
14. What methods work best at estimating age of subadults, living or deceased?
15. What methods work best at estimating age of adults, living or deceased?
16. Why is the clavicle important in estimating age?
17. What factors should be checked to determine if a fetus is full-term?
18. How could ethnic or socioeconomic status affect estimation of stature?
19. Which methods are most accurate for estimating stature?
20. What factors could influence the estimation of stature? Why and how can they be accounted for?

Discussion Questions

1. Describe the development of dentition and its relationship to estimating age. What factors could effect accuracy?
2. As Baccino and coauthors note, "Many published methods [of estimating age] have not been tested on diverse populations." Why would this be important, particularly in a forensic context?
3. Why has estimating the age of the living, adults and children, become of greater forensic concern?
4. Several anthropologists have suggested that "race" is a scientifically empty concept. Why? Is it still relevant in a forensic context? Why or why not?
5. How does linear regression apply to estimations of stature? Growth is a biological function: Is it truly linear and, if so, how?

Additional Readings

Albanese, J., Tuck, A., Gomes, J., Cardoso, H.F., 2016. An alternative approach for estimating stature from long bones that is not population-or group-specific. Forensic Science International 259, 59–68.

Algee-Hewitt, B.F., 2015. The Myth of Race. The Troubling Persistence of an Unscientific Idea. By Robert Wald Sussman. Harvard University Press, Cambridge, MA.

Boldsen, J.L., Milner, G.R., Boldsen, S.K., 2015. Sex estimation from modern American humeri and femora, accounting for sample variance structure. American Journal of Physical Anthropology 158 (4), 745–750.

Boyd, K.L., Villa, C., Lynnerup, N., 2015. The use of CT scans in estimating age at death by examining the extent of ectocranial suture closure. Journal of Forensic Sciences 60 (2), 363–369.

Franklin, D., Flavel, A., Noble, J., Swift, L., Karkhanis, S., 2015. Forensic age estimation in living individuals: methodological considerations in the context of medico-legal practice. Research and Reports in Forensic Medical Science 5, 53.

Krishan, K., Chatterjee, P.M., Kanchan, T., Kaur, S., Baryah, N., Singh, R.K., 2016. A review of sex estimation techniques during examination of skeletal remains in forensic anthropology casework. Forensic Science International 261 pp.165–e1.

Larsen, S.T., Thevissen, P., Lynnerup, N., Willems, G., Boldsen, J., 2015. Age estimation in the living. Forensic Science International 257.

Section 5. Pathology

Bone is a living system of the body, similar to the respiratory or digestive systems, but most people do not think of it that way. Bones appear static and firm; that they grow, remodel, heal, *live*, gets forgotten or ignored. Susceptible to disease like any other system of the body, bones have their own set of diseases as well as those that arise in other organs but affect the bone. Trauma also scars bone, leaving obvious and subtle clues visible only by radiograph or to the forensic anthropologist.

Bone Pathology and Antemortem Trauma

E Cunha, University of Coimbra, Coimbra, Portugal
J Pinheiro, Instituto Nacional de Medicina Legal, Coimbra, Portugal

Nomenclature

DISH	Diffuse idiopathic skeletal hyperostosis	OA	Osteoarthritis
FA	Forensic anthropology	SP	Spondyloarthropathy
FP	Forensic pathology	TB	Tuberculosis
ID	Identification		

Introduction

This chapter provides a summary of some bone pathologies that are useful for forensic anthropology (FA), focusing on aspects related to identification (ID). Antemortem trauma is also reviewed, with an emphasis on its benefits for FA, particularly in cases of child abuse or torture.

During the reconstructive phase of identification, forensic anthropologists—besides generating a biological profile of the victim—have to read the skeleton and/or body in order to identify factors of individualization. These factors make it possible to discriminate one individual from another; no two skeletons are alike.

Among the particularities of skeletons with the potential to discriminate, anthropologists must be particularly careful to distinguish between morphological and pathological traits. This is important because some of the so-called discrete traits—that is, nonmetric skeletal traits—can be misdiagnosed as lesions. Examples include sternal perforation or septal aperture in the humerus. The frontiers between morphology and pathology are fluid, and only solid determinations of anatomical variants can lead to reliable diagnoses.

Anthropologists also deal with paleopathology, which is the use of sources such as skeletons and iconography to study the history and evolution of diseases, although skeletons are the common elements between FA and paleopathology. However, while in FA one has the possibility to verify the diagnosis, this almost never occurs with past populations. The bridge between these two sciences is indeed important. Only with a strong background on reading and interpreting dry bones would one be able to recognize some pathologies.

Yet, in FA, the most important issue is not the diagnosis of the pathology itself, but more importantly the description of their consequences on the individual's life. A particular gait or an abnormal limb shape will be more easily recalled and/or confirmed by the relatives of the victim than the pathology itself. Spondyloarthropathy (SP) is a good example of this: although the family might not know the name of the disease, they may recognize the effects of this disorder on the limited mobility of the individual.

On the other hand, one has to bear in mind that forensic anthropologists can deal with cases where the bones are not dry. This means that a paleopathology background is not enough for reading the variety of bone lesions that can occur in FA.

A broader knowledge is necessary, namely an understanding of the whole reaction and healing process, including the bones, the vessels, muscles, ligaments, and skin. The interpretation of hemorrhagic signs, such as discoloration or other chromatic alterations and the recognition of ossified cartilages, can escape the attention of those who deal exclusively with dry bones.

While paleopathology is fundamental, reading lesions in FA is not a simple transposition of paleopathology techniques to more recent remains. Precisely because the bones are more recent, they may also preserve other tissues besides the hard ones; the main object of analysis can therefore be quite different between paleopathology and FA. Yet, some principles/rules are absolutely identical, the most important of which is that when trying to infer pathologies from the bone, the absence of evidence is not evidence of absence. Only some pathologies leave signs on the skeleton, which is one of the last systems of our body to respond to an aggression. (Aggression here refers to the action of any type of agent, physic or not, exterior to the body. Bacteria and virus are also examples of aggression agents.) Chronic diseases are much more likely to be visible postmortem; the exceptions are those diseases that initially focus on the bones themselves, such as a primary bone neoplasia. As a consequence, the majority of acute diseases will be imperceptible upon a simple visual examination and may thus escape the attention of the expert. Simultaneously, this implies that a majority of causes of death cannot be inferred from the skeleton.

It is important to recall that a lesion is not a pathology, but it is a conjunction of lesions in a skeleton, their pattern, distribution, and type which can eventually lead to the diagnosis of a pathology. Differential diagnosis, which is always mandatory, will be done on the basis of these lesion characteristics.

Bone Pathology

Types of Lesions and Bone Reaction

To interpret a lesion, one has to understand bone reaction as an aggression against the tissue. While alive, bone tissue will react by bone destruction (osteoclastic activity) and/or bone formation (osteoblastic formation). Pathognomonic reactions are very rare; that is, bone is monotonous in the way it reacts to external agents, which can limit the diagnosis of a specific disease, particularly when the skeleton is incomplete (common in forensic cases).

Keeping lesion description separate from lesion interpretation is a delicate balance. In any formal report, the description of the lesion should be detailed enough to permit a second opinion by another expert. An objective, descriptive approach is useful: location, size, type of lesion (e.g., lytic and exostosis), and pattern distribution within the skeleton (unifocal or symmetric, for instance) are obligatory (**Table 1**).

Table 1   Lesions' description

Lesions' location	Indicate the affected bone
	Specify the site on the bone related to the anatomical position: Shaft, epiphysis, metaphysis; anterior/posterior, medial/lateral aspects; superior/medium/inferior third, etc.
	Measure the distance (cm/mm) from lesion to reference anatomical points: Midclavicular line, nearest joint or epiphysis, etc.
Type of lesion	Lytic, hypertrofic, depressed, with cloaca, porosity, necrotic bone, etc.
Distribution pattern	Unifocal, symmetric, randomly distributed, diffuse widely distributed.
Size and shape of the lesion	Overall shape
	Pyramidal, elliptical, spherical,
	Size (cm/mm) according to shape
	Height and base, diameter, perimeter, width, etc.

In the eventuality that a missing person is known to suffer from a disease easily diagnosed by skeletal analysis (e.g., tuberculosis), the fact that the skeleton does not display any signs of that disease does not necessarily mean that the individual did not suffer from that illness. The developmental stage of the disease may be too early in the cycle to permit a full diagnosis: initial stages may be much less susceptible to affect bone and it will also depend upon the type of disease. For example, osseous TB will be more visible than a secondary bone lesion due to pulmonary TB.

The epidemiological data on the various disorders which affect the skeleton can be paramount to the forensic case by helping to clarify issues such as postmortem interval, sex, and age. A very advanced and therefore severe case of spondyloarthropathy will probably date before the use of corticoids; osteoporosis is more prevalent in women after the menopause; Paget's disease is more frequent in Europe than in Asia. The type of treatment, especially surgical intervention or a prosthesis, might also help a lot to assess the chronological context.

Pathologies Useful for FA

Among congenital and genetic conditions, while some are rare but obvious (as is the case of nanism and acromegalia), others, such as congenital fusions, supernumerary bones or their congenital absence, parietal foramina enlargement, and the failure of fusion of the neural arches, might require a differential diagnosis with other pathologies. Other conditions, such as cleft palate, craniosynostosis, or bone hypoplasia, which cause limb deficiencies, might be easily recognizable by their consequences on face physiognomy or gait, respectively, by both the expert and the victim's relatives.

Metabolic disorders, such as rickets (lack of vitamin D) and scurvy (lack of vitamin C), produce reactions in the bone which, in conjunction, can allow their diagnosis. While these disorders are very rare in developed countries, in the context of crimes against humanity, a forensic anthropologist has to be aware of the possibility of finding them in less-developed countries. Rickets is characterized by a deformity in the long bones, particularly those of the lower limbs, accompanied by bone porosity. In relation to scurvy, though it requires a prolonged deprivation of vitamin C and is therefore rare, when present, it attacks metaphyses which can easily fracture.

Osteoporosis is a well-known metabolic disease affecting in particular women past middle age. The loss of bone is perceptible by vertebral compression, or, in more severe cases, by vertebral fractures. Kyphosis is a symptom recognizable by relatives. In the appendicular skeleton, fractures of the forearm and the femoral neck are the pathognomonic signs. Bone densitometry and X-rays are valuable tools for the diagnosis which, in the case of preexisting antemortem elements of comparison, can facilitate positive ID. Furthermore, the fragility of the bones and their low weight can be good clues to this disease, although they can be confounded with taphonomical effects or even by other diseases, such as rheumatoid arthritis and spondyloarthropathy.

Concerning infectious diseases, bacterial infections are much more likely to lead to bone lesions than viral ones. Some infections may be identified, as with periostitis, where only the more external bone layer (the periosteum) is infected. In more severe cases, when the infection goes deeper into the medullar cavity of the bone, osteomyelitis results. This condition is more readily identifiable since necrotic bone, bone enlargement, and cloaca are almost unequivocal signs. Furthermore, it would be difficult for someone to suffer from osteomyelitis without a close relative knowing about it; moreover, the infection will typically be only in one bone and thus the pathology will be specific. Other infectious diseases which can be specifically diagnosed in the bone include tuberculosis, brucellosis, leprosy, and treponemostosis.

Mycobacterium tuberculosis (and also *Mycobacterium bovis*) mainly affects spongy bone, leading to the destruction of vertebral bodies (mainly adjoining thoracic ones), sometimes producing a kyphosis. The long-bone epiphyses can also be involved as well as the ribs.

Rhinomaxillary syndrome is one of the main features of leprosy: the loss of upper anterior dentition and destruction of the palate. Bones of the extremities, typically distal phalanges, are also affected. Physiognomic key traits will be noticed and remembered by the familiars of the persons who suffered from leprosy which will facilitate identification.

Congenital syphilis is a type of treponemal disease which leaves typical marks on the bones, in particular on the skull with characteristic aspects due to caries sicca. When the postcranial skeleton is implicated, normally it is one long bone such as the tibia, whose enlargement (the so-called saber shin, which is more common in yaws) will be observed in the absence of antibiotic treatment.

Finally, brucellosis appears in the skeleton with osteoarticular localizations typically in the superior anterior portion of the lumbar vertebrae. This very contagious disease might be confounded with TB. Its forensic relevance relies on the vector of contagious contact with animals and its higher prevalence in the Mediterranean countries.

Regarding degenerative disorders, osteoarthritis (OA) is the most common articular degenerative disease, affecting a significant percentage of individuals after the fourth decade of life. Osteophytes, porosity, and eburnation are the lesions which, particularly in conjunction, will allow the diagnosis of OA. Although the more common a disease is, the less chances it has to provide a positive ID; OA is nevertheless a paradigmatic example of the contrary. The fact that no two individuals can develop exactly the same osteophytes, of the same size, shape, and location, makes them valuable factors of identification, whenever antemortem X-rays are available to perform the mandatory comparison. The compatibility among at least four different points, among the ante- and postmortem X-rays, is considered to provide a positive identification.

Within nonarticular degenerative diseases, enthesopathies, now more appropriately designated as entheseal changes, play a major role in what FA is concerned. The lesions on the insertion sites of muscles, tendons, and ligaments can function as markers of occupational stress providing clues for the amount of physical effort done by certain individuals. Repetitive microtraumatisms on the sites of muscular insertions will provoke calcifications. Entheseal change on the tendon insertions of the Achilles, patella, or the calcification on the head of the ulna where triceps brachial inserts are some good examples. However, attention should be paid since some diseases, such as diffuse idiopathic skeletal hyperostosis (DISH) or SP, can cause these types of lesions; therefore, the diagnosis is not straightforward.

Moving now to rheumatic disorders, SP, with the typical sacro-iliac ankylosis and the ascending fusion of the vertebral column, when found would mean that the individuals under analysis were very limited in their motion; the bones will tend to be more fragile and light because of this. DISH is recognizable in the skeleton by a flowing right antero-lateral ligament ossification in the vertebral column. Symmetrical and evident entheseal changes in the appendicular skeleton are also key elements for the diagnosis. DISH is differentiated from SP because in DISH the vertebral bodies are not fused to each other and the intervertebral space is kept. This disorder, although asymptomatic, is associated with obesity and diabetes. Finally, a malignant neoplasia might have much more potential to provide ID, whereas benign lesions, such as button osteomas, can work as factors of identification in case there are antemortem examinations for comparison. Typically, the rarer a lesion is, the more chance it has to promote identity. Exuberant malignant neoplasms, with their destructive and irregular pattern, will be valuable tools to ID, especially because they are age dependent.

Further sources where bone pathologies that may help identification are discussed and listed in the Further Reading.

Antemortem Trauma

Besides a violent fracture, stress or fatigue fractures, which originate from the application of repeated forces of low magnitude over a period of time, can be frequent within gymnasts, athletes, ballet dancers, military recruits, and others who engage in repetitive physical activity. Stress fractures may assist with identity or with suggesting an occupation or hobby. Spondylolysis, which is a complete separation between the vertebral body and the corresponding arch of the vertebra, is the best-known type of stress fracture. Finally, pathological fractures have also to be taken into account, where a disease or condition, such as osteoporosis, rheumatoid arthritis, neoplasms, or others, weakens the bone and leads to a fracture.

For FA, a fundamental question remains concerning antemortem trauma: How long did the individual survive the lesion? Not only does this assist with the timing of the event and possible identification or elimination of the person in question, but also the forensic relevance of this issue is significant since it has serious legal repercussions.

Antemortem lesions do not have the same meaning in FA and in forensic pathology, as illustrated in **Figure 1**. In FA, antemortem trauma will be recognizable macroscopically or microscopically (the osteogenic response is able to be seen sooner by microscopic analysis). By a simple visual inspection, callus formation (gross enlargement of a portion of bone at the fracture site) (**Figure 2**) and periosteal reaction or the rounding of fracture margins will clearly indicate antemortem fracture. Yet, typical bone responses (osteoblastic, osteoclastic, line of demarcation, and sequestration) can only be seen through a microscope. It should be noted that distinguishing between postmortem and antemortem wounds with little survival time is still difficult to do histologically. It is indisputable that woven bone must be present (usually not visible before 2 weeks) to establish a specific antemortem period or even to determine an antemortem origin. It has to be emphasized that even radiology may miss fractures which histology, afterward, detects; histology always provides a more precise dating.

Figure 2   Misaligned, although treated, antemortem fracture of the femoral neck from an identified individual of a recent skeletal identified collection.

Recent studies have yielded important data on the important question of healing after trauma. After only 6 weeks, osteoclastic and osteoblastic activities were reported in healing cranial trauma. Interpretations of time elapsed since death evidence benefit from ongoing research on dry bone, such as in pilot studies on the detection of microscopic markers of hemorrhaging and wound age on dry bone. Whereas unequivocal signs of long-term survival can be reliably determined, short-term survival continues to be problematic. Recently identified skeletal collections are able to provide important data on this issue, since the hospitals still keep the patients' files concerning antemortem traumas (**Figure 2**).

Antemortem registration should be as complete and objective as possible (**Table 2**).

The value of antemortem trauma for FA can be systematized as follows:

- Identification
- A possible contribution to the determination of the cause of death
- Diagnosis of child abuse
- A tool to document human rights violation

The benefits for identification are obvious and well known since antemortem fractures are undoubtedly good factors of individualization. When treated with surgical intervention, the chances of ID are increased. Concerning the second advantage, although the signs of bone remodeling mean that the injuries did not cause the death, it is possible that subsequent complications might have caused it. The last two benefits of antemortem trauma for FA are discussed below.

Child Abuse

Skeletal damage in child abuse is a new and recent challenge in antemortem trauma. If cranial injuries are the most frequent

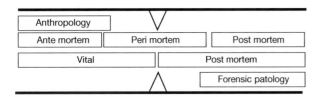

Figure 1   The different concepts of perimortem between pathology and anthropology.

Table 2   Antemortem trauma registration

Antemortem feature	Registration
Bone location	Indicate the affected bone See the same item in **Table 1**
Severity	Light, medium, severe
Trauma etiology	Blunt/sharp/perforated/mixed/ impossible to determine
Trauma mechanism	Tension/compression/twisting or torsion/bending, Angulating/ shearing/mixed/impossible to determine
Trauma classification according to severity of distortion	Simple fracture/comminuted fracture/compound open fracture/ refracture
Description of fracture	Complete/incomplete, direction, orientation, single line/irradiating/ "spider fracture"/"hinge" fracture, etc.
Callus formation	Yes or no If yes: weak, strong, exuberant
Periosteal reaction	Yes or no If yes: weak, strong, exuberant
Misalignment	Yes or no If yes: light, medium, severe
Pseudo-arthrosis	Yes or no If yes: light, medium, severe
Degree and success of repair	Yes or No
Estimation of time elapsed since the trauma occurrence	Possible/not possible
Microscopic analysis	Yes or no
Special cases	Amputation/surgical interventions/ prosthesis

cause of death in child abuse, it is the skeleton that brings the case to the health-care system and to a possible diagnosis with the antemortem lesions assuming a role of extreme relevance.

Forces that twist or create torsion in a bone can shear the periosteum from the bone, even without a fracture, and cause bleeding with new bone formation over the subperiosteal hematoma in 1–2 weeks. If it is incipient, it can be seen only in radiographs as a line parallel to the shaft of the cortical bone; if stronger forces are applied, the new bone growth can be observed in a visual examination.

Limb fractures, in the metaphysis or epiphyses, whether in the bone or in the periosteum, are often diagnosed in ossified tissues and are highly characteristic of child abuse. Forces of violent traction, or torsion of the limbs, are responsible for these injuries.

Epiphyseal–metaphyseal lesions, considered diagnostic of child abuse, because of the partial or complete dislocation of the epiphysis, the metaphysis, and a thin layer of metaphyseal reaction, can be seen in radiology. Because of the small size of the fragments, these are occasionally undetectable in a routine

analysis. An X-ray is crucial to identify these fragments and to orientate the FA examination. Diaphyseal injuries consisting of spiral fractures, caused by the twisting of the bone, and transverse fractures, caused by a direct blow or bending of the bone, are easier to observe than the epiphyseal–metaphyseal lesions. The range of healing stages, from the periosteal thickening to the callus, can be observed; the lack of treatment may be indicated by possible angulation or inappropriate consolidation of the fracture elements. Although a spiral fracture strongly suggests child abuse, it can be accidental.

The literature is controversial on cranial antemortem injuries in children. If present, they can be assumed as a putative sign of child abuse, as accidental trauma in these ages is extremely rare. Falls in domestic accidents, such as from a chair or from a bed, normally do not cause bone damage and, therefore, they rarely represent the primary cause of death in children. The parietal and temporal bones break more frequently; when severe enough, they may extend to the base of the skull.

Rib fractures in a child older than 6 months, if not a victim of a traffic accident or a major trauma and in the absence of any bone disease, strongly point to child abuse. Rib fractures can be multiple or bilateral, and of different ages, but are usually located in the posterior arch near the costo-vertebral junction. The classical aspect is the observation of a vertical line of sequential callus down one or both posterior rib arches, near the head of the ribs, having the appearance of a "string of beads" (**Figure 3**). This can be simply palpated and dissected in an autopsy or observed in an FA examination. In many forensic settings where radiologic facilities are not available, the direct observation of those calluses is sometimes the first alert for a child abuse case (**Figure 4**). Rib fractures are often better recognized after new bone formation than in recent conditions,

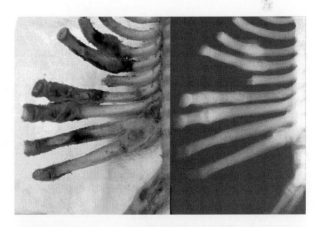

Figure 3   Radiograph of right ribs with "string of bead." None of the ribs has fusion between them, despite the large calluses. The bones are illustrated before final processing. Their condition stimulated concerns that ribs 6–7, 8–9, and 11–12 may have been conjoined. Radiographs confirm no fusion. Courtesy of Steve Symes.

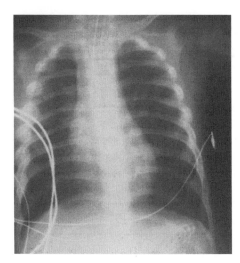

Figure 4 A child aged 2.5 months presented as a sudden infant death syndrome case, whose autopsy had diagnosed a shaken baby syndrome. The callus osseous observed in the posterior eighth left rib (first at autopsy and later in this RX), and a previous hospital internment when he was 1.5 months old, due to a bruise in the face consistent with a slap, both not explained by the parents, proved child abuse. A subdural hemorrhage and cerebral edema, in association with retinal hemorrhages, showed at histology not explained by the partum, helped in the diagnostic of the shaken baby syndrome.

either by radiology or at autopsy. A discrepancy between autopsy and radiology may eventually occur. Apart from the callus formation, refracture of the existing calluses may be observed (**Figure 5**). The posterior fractures may be due to squeezing or shaking the child, while lateral fractures will be due to antero-posterior compression.

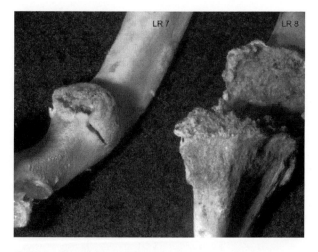

Figure 5 The calluses are large and suggest numerous episodes of refracture. Courtesy of Steve Symes.

A difficult question arises occasionally when these rib (consolidated) fractures are argued to be resuscitation injuries. In fact, fractures by chest compression are very uncommon in child because of the elasticity of the immature ribcage. Moreover, if properly applied, chest compression in a child is done with fingers and is unlikely to cause fractures. Normally, these fractures are observed in the anterior arch in the midclavicular line or sterno-condral junction, which is an important criterion for the differential diagnosis. However, the possibility of broken ribs in resuscitation situation should always be considered and diagnosed, carefully, on a case-by-case basis.

Fractures of the clavicle are relatively uncommon in children. However, those at the distal end may be caused by a sudden traction of the extremity. Fractures of the scapula (namely of the acromion) and sternum, although rare, can be related to child abuse, if other major trauma is excluded. Vertebrae, especially the lateral processes, should not be forgotten in an examination.

Wherever the site of the skeletal damage is observed, the characteristic pattern includes multiple traumas and variation in the age of the fractures. Accidental injuries usually produce single lesions, unless some bone disease, such as osteogenesis imperfecta (especially type V), infantile cortical hyperostosis, congenital syphilis, copper deficiency, or Menke's syndrome, can be proved.

In child abuse, bone damage must be related to any delay or absence of medical care, inconsistencies with developmental age, the history of injury changes over time, and to witness accounts.

Torture

Antemortem bone lesions may also be evidence of torture, as physical techniques are systematic or repetitive to force another person to yield information, to make confession or for any other reason. However, in cases of torture, the antemortem lesions coexist with recent perimortem fractures which would have probably caused the death of the victim. The issue will be to establish the right chronology of the injuries so that a reconstruction of the events may be possible. In order to achieve this objective, gross observations must be complemented by radiology and histological study. An excellent tool integrating the three perspectives (macroscopy, histology, and radiology) for the aging of fractures in human dry bones was published by Maat who compiled data from different sources in a single table. The authors made a previous approach to this issue providing a table with the time needed for the normal consolidation of fractures of the totality of human bones. CT and other new imaging techniques will ensure the accuracy of diagnostics in the near future.

Reports of torture revealed that 10% of the injuries were fractures in the following order: ribs, legs and pelvis, hands and wrists, spine, jaw, skull, and arms. Foreign bodies such as needles, wires, or wooden splinters can be found imbedded in the manual distal phalanxes after fingernail torture. Compression of the fingers and toes can result from minor bone injuries or even the loss of hands, fingers, or digits. Cutting off parts of extremities will show in the examination because of the missing parts of the bones and the smoothing of the bone borders with some remodeling if the subject lived long enough. Whenever more than one adjacent bone is involved (for example, the metacarpals) fusion between the distal superior surfaces may occur. Consolidation of fractures of the forearm (ulna and/or radius) is typical of the defense of the prisoner trying to protect, intentionally or by reflex, his head. Fracture of the anatomical neck of the humerus and dislocation of the gleno-humeral joint may be observed in postural torture by suspension of the body by the wrists or the arms. The healing of the fractures mentioned above, apart from the callus formation, is traduced by thickening of the bones, which is sometimes exuberant in extreme cases where there is a lack of treatment; positional abnormalities due to the dislocations of bones and pseudoarthrosis that result from the nonfusion of the bones often occur without treatment. Infectious complications, such as osteomyelitis, can appear secondarily to soft-tissue lacerations or exposed fractures.

Ossified fractures of the toes, metatarsals, tarsals, the ankle, amputations of distal phalanges, as well as ligamentous injuries and flatfoot deformations can be observed in the technique known as *falanga* or *falaca*. This technique consists of beating the feet, mainly but not exclusively on the sole, to avoid the recognition of bruises in soft tissues. Thickening of the plantar aponeurosis (apparent in adipocere bodies) suggests previous torture. Consequently, the impairment of blood circulation and the necrosis of muscles can extend to the bones, leading to the necrosis of metatarsal and proximal phalanges. Fractures may then occur and form exostoses. *Palmatoria*, a unique method used in Guinea-Bissau, consisting of repetitive blows to the shin, create a periosteal thickening of the tibia apart from endosteal and intramedular changes not visible in a classic examination (but seen radiologically) and can result in a fracture seen only in CT. Pellets and bullets may be found embedded in articulations, especially in the knees, a method known as kneecapping, which is also associated with fractures of the neighboring bones (legs and arms). The healing of these fractures, which may be splintered if high-velocity projectiles were used, is difficult and delayed; periostitis and osteomyelitis usually appear as complications. This method was used in North Ireland conflicts and also by American gangs that threaten to cripple the victim.

Healed fractures of the ribs and spine because of a beating in the thorax are common. Biomechanics of these fractures is complex and needs further research. Fractures by compression of the chest or pelvis are less known; they are difficult to interpret and occasionally are the object of undesirable speculation.

Although frequently mentioned in the literature, as a sign of manual or ligature strangulations, fracture of the hyoid bone seems to be very rare as a method of torture, because the time from torture to death is extremely narrow. Moreover, the real incidence of these fractures in all the compressions of the neck is much lower than previous reports in forensic textbooks which considered it as a classic sign of hanging or strangulation. In fact, case studies of fractures of the hyoid bone are scarce in the FA literature.

A healing butterfly fracture of the mandible may be extremely useful to identify beating on the face and possible torture, such as by the butt or the barrel of a firearm. But in cases of perimortem fractures in this location, when the victim has been shot to the head, this is a typical fracture; although it is theoretically consistent with blunt trauma, it is an artifact of high-velocity projectiles (so-called Kolusayin fractures) and should be interpreted with caution. The healing stage of the fracture will be crucial to distinguish between a simple execution and previous torture before the execution.

See also: **Anthropology/Odontology:** Biomechanics of Bone Trauma; Bone Trauma.

Further Reading

Barbian, L., Sledzik, P.S., 2008. Healing following cranial trauma. Journal of Forensic Sciences 53, 2.

Betz, P., Liebhardt, 1994. Rib fractures in children – resuscitation or child abuse? International Journal of Legal Medicine 106, 215–218.

Black, S., Ferguson, E. (Eds.), 2011. Forensic Anthropology 2000 to 2010. CRC, Boca Raton, FL.

Black, S., 2005. Bone pathology and antemortem trauma in forensic cases. In: Payne-James, J. (Ed.), Encyclopedia of Forensic and Legal Medicine. Elsevier, London.

Blau, S., Ubelaker, D. (Eds.), 2008. Handbook of Forensic Anthropology and Archaeology. Left Coast Press, Walnut Creek, CA.

Brodgon, B.G., Vogel, H., McDowell, J.D., 2003. A Radiologic Atlas of Abuse, Torture and Inflicted Trauma. CRC, Boca Raton, pp. 3–46.

Brodgon, B.G., 1998. Forensic Radiology. CRC, Boca Raton, pp. 281–315.

Bush, C.M., et al., 1996. Pediatric injuries from cardiopulmonary resuscitation. Annals of Emergency Medicine 28, 40–44.

Cattaneo, C., et al., 2010. The detection of microscopic markers of hemorrhaging and wound age on dry bone: a pilot study. American Journal Forensic Medicine and Pathology 31 (1), 22–26.

Cunha, E., Pinheiro, J., 2009. Ante-mortem trauma. In: Soren, B., Ubelaker, D. (Eds.), Handbook of Forensic Anthropology and Archaeology. Left Coast Press, Walnut Creek, CA.

Cunha, E., 2006. Pathology as a factor of personal identity in forensic anthropology. In: Schmitt, A., Cunha, E., Pinheiro, J. (Eds.), Forensic Anthropology and Medicine. Complementary Sciences from Recovery to Cause of Death. Humana, Tottowa, NJ, pp. 333–358.

Daegling, D., Warren, M., Hotzman, J., Casey, J., 2008. Self structural analysis of human rib fracture and implications for forensic interpretation. Journal of Forensic Sciences 53 (6).

Delabarde, T., 2008. Multiple healed rib fractures – timing of injuries in regard to death. In: Kimmerle, E.H., Baraybar, J.P. (Eds.), Skeletal Trauma: Identification of Injuries Resulting from Human Rights Abuse and Armed Conflict. CRC, Boca Raton, FL, pp. 236–244.

Helfer, R.E., Slovis, T.L., Black, M., 1977. Injuries resulting when small children fall out of bed. Pediatrics 60, 533–535.

Hoppenfield, S., Vasantha, L., 2000. Treatment and Rehabilitation of Fractures. Lippincott, Philadelphia.

Hougen, H.P., 2008. Torture sequels to the skeleton. In: Kimmerle, E.H., Baraybar, J.P. (Eds.), Skeletal Trauma: Identification of Injuries Resulting from Human Rights Abuse and Armed Conflict. CRC, Boca Raton, FL, pp. 234–235.

Jurmain, R., Villotte, S., 2010. Terminology. Entheses in medical literature and physical anthropology: a brief review (Online). In: Document Published Online in 4th February Following the Workshop in Musculoskeletal Stress Markers (MSM): Limitations and Achievements in the Reconstruction of Past Activity Patterns, University of Coimbra, Coimbra, 2–3 July 2009. CIAS – Centro de Investigação em Antropologia e Saúde. Available at: http://www.uc.pt/en/cia/msm/MSM_terminology3 (accessed 25.06.10.).

Kimmerlee, E., Barybar, J.P., 2008. Skeletal Trauma. Identification of Injuries Resulting from Human Rights Abuse and Armed Conflicts. CRC, Boca Raton, FL.

Klotzbach, H., Delling, G., Richter, E., Sperhake, J., Püschel, K., 2003. Post-mortem diagnosis and age estimation of infants' fractures. International Journal of Legal Medicine 117 (2), 82–89.

Love, J.C., Symes, S.A., 2004. Understanding rib fracture patterns: incomplete and buckle fractures. Journal of Forensic Sciences 49 (6), 1–6.

Maat, G.J.R., 2008. Dating of fractures in human dry bone tissues – the Berisha case. In: Kimmerle, E.H., Baraybar, J.P. (Eds.), Skeletal Trauma: Identification of Injuries Resulting from Human Rights Abuse and Armed Conflict. CRC, Boca Raton, FL, pp. 245–255.

Mays, S., Pinhasi, R., 2008. Advances in Human Paleopathology. Wiley, Chichester.

Merbs, C., 2004. Sagittal clefting of the body and other vertebral developmental errors in Canadian Inuit skeletons. American Journal of Physical Anthropology 133, 236–249.

Merten, D.F., Radkowski, M.A., Leonidas, J.C., 1983. The abused child: a radiological reappraisal. Radiology 146, 37–381.

Ortner, D., 2003. Identification of Pathological Conditions in Human Skeletal Remains, second ed. Academic Press, New York.

Pinheiro, J., Cunha, E., Cordeiro, C., Vieira, D., 2004. Bridging the gap between forensic anthropology and osteoarchaeology – a case of vascular pathology. International Journal of Osteoarchaeology 14, 137–144.

Pinheiro, J., Lyrio, A., Cunha, E., Symes, S., 2008. Cranial trauma: misleading injuries. In: Proceedings of the American Academy of Forensic Sciences. Annual Meeting, Washington, DC, p. 363.

Resnick, D., 2002. Diagnosis of Bone and Joint Disorders, fourth ed. Saunders, Philadelphia.

Roberts, C.A., Buikstra, J., 2003. The Bioarchaeology of Tuberculosis. A Global View on a Re-emerging Disease. University of Florida Press, Gainsville, FL.

Roberts, C., Manchester, K., 2005. The Archaeology of Disease. Sutton, Gloucester.

Saukko, P., Knight, B., 2004. Knight's Forensic Pathology, third ed. Arnold, London.

Schmidd, C., Symes, S., 2008. The Analysis of Burned Human Remains. Academic Press, London.

Forensic anthropology and medicine. In: Schmitt, A., Cunha, E., Pinheiro, J. (Eds.), 2006. Complementary Sciences from Recovery to Cause of Death. Humana, Tottowa, NJ.

Scott, A., Congram, D., Sweet, D., Fonseca, S., Skinner, M., 2010. Anthropological and radiographic comparison of antemortem surgical records for identification of skeletal remains. Journal of Forensic Sciences 55 (1).

The Society for Pediatric Radiology – National Association of Medical Examiners, 2004. Post-mortem radiography in the evaluation of unexpected death in children less than 2 years of age whose deaths suspicious for fatal abuse. Pediatric Radiology 34, 675–677.

Vogel, H., Schmitz-Engels, F., Grillo, C., 2007. Radiology of torture. European Journal of Radiology 63, 187–204.

Biomechanics of Bone Trauma

DJ Wescott, Texas State University, San Marcos, TX, USA

Glossary

Anisotropic A characteristic of a material that has different mechanical properties when loaded in different directions due to its directional structure.

Bending (angulation) A mode of loading such that the bone bends around its axis and experiences tension on the convex surface and compression on the opposite concave surface.

Brittle Characteristic of a material that readily breaks without plastic deformation when subjected to stress.

Buttressing Areas of struts or thickening of the bone.

Compliance A measure of the ease with which bone deforms or the inverse of stiffness.

Compression A mode of loading where the forces are acting in opposite directions along the longitudinal axis of the bone. Compression results in a decrease in length and an increase in width.

Ductility The ability of a material to deform under tensile stress.

Elastic deformation Deformation or strain in bone that is reversible when the stress is released.

Elastic modulus (Young's modulus) The ratio of stress to strain in the elastic region of deformation. Because of the anisotropic nature of bone, the moduli in compression and tension differ in bone or the slope of the stress–strain curve.

Plastic deformation Permanent strain that is unrecoverable when the bone is unstressed. Plastic deformation occurs between the yield point and the failure point.

Remodeling The removal and replacement of bone at a particular location by the coupled action of osteoclasts (bone-destructing cells) and osteoblasts (bone-building cells).

Stiffness (rigidity) The ability of a material to resist deformation or the load required to cause bone to deform a given amount. It is measured as the slope of the stress–strain curve and influenced by the relative proportion of collagen and hydroxyapatite crystals.

Strain The dimensional change in loaded bone. The principal strains are normal or shear.

Strength The ability of bone to withstand permanent deformation (the load at the yield point) or fracture (the load at failure point).

Stress The load per unit area of a bone, measured in pascal (Pa). The stress can be normal or shear.

Tension A mode of loading in which the forces act in opposite directions along the longitudinal axis of the bone. Tension results in an increase in length and decrease in width.

Yield point The point where bone begins to deform plastically.

Introduction

Biomechanics is the science of mechanical laws applied to biological tissue. Trauma is an extrinsic agent, force, or mechanism that causes injury or shock to a living tissue, usually due to violence or accident. Hence, the biomechanics of bone trauma is the application of mechanical laws to describe and interpret bone trauma and involves the examination of both the intrinsic (size, geometry, and material properties such as stiffness, elasticity, and density) and extrinsic (magnitude, duration, and direction of force) factors resulting in bone injury. Understanding the biomechanics of bone trauma allows forensic scientists to use the pattern of bone fractures to deduce the type and direction of loading that caused the bone to fail. This information then often can be used to determine proximate and ultimate cause of the injury.

Injuries to bone usually involve fracture (failure) or dislocation (displacement at a joint). The mechanisms of fractures are divided into direct, indirect, stress, or pathological. Fractures resulting from direct or indirect trauma are of greatest interest to forensic scientists. There are many direct and indirect agents that can cause trauma to bone including mechanical, thermal, electrical, and others. Most of the direct trauma of interest to forensic scientists results in injury at the point of impact due to blunt, sharp, or projectile forces. The differences among these agents are primarily determined by the size of the impact area and the magnitude and duration of the force. Indirect trauma results in injury at locations other than the point of impact or applied force. Stress and pathological injuries are associated with repetitive forces or disease processes, respectively, that weaken bone. This chapter primarily focuses on fractures or disruptions in the structural continuity of the bone due to direct mechanical trauma.

Goals of Trauma Analysis

The goals of trauma analysis in a medicolegal situation are to determine the proximate (i.e., immediate mechanism) and ultimate (e.g., manner of death) causes of the trauma. This is necessary to aid in determining the cause and manner of death by the medical examiner. In skeletonized or badly decomposed bodies, traumatic injuries of the bone may provide a major avenue for determining the cause and manner of death. However, even in fresh bodies, the direct observation of hard tissue should be conducted in all areas of suspected trauma because the gross examination of bone can provide valuable information that cannot always be obtained using other tissues or other visualizing methods (e.g., radiographs).

While the goals of trauma analysis are to determine the mechanism and ultimate cause of the trauma, the first step of trauma analysis is adequate description of the injury, its location, and pattern. Unfortunately, there can be considerable variation in the expression of injury due to the same mechanism as well as similarities in injuries caused by different mechanisms. Proper description of the injury morphology (i.e., size, shape, location, line of fracture propagation, segment relationships, and pattern) is the basis for determining the mechanism and aids in interpreting the ultimate cause. Interpreting the ultimate cause of the injury requires additional information such as the pattern of trauma in populations, the context of the human remains, and other sources of evidence.

Bone Structure and Material Properties

To lay the foundation for how fractures occur, it is important to first have an understanding of the structure of the bone and its material properties. These principles guide the analysis of bone trauma and provide a framework for interpreting the proximate cause of trauma.

Bone Structure

The overall strength of the bone is dependent on its material composition, organization, and overall geometry (amount and overall distribution of the bone). At the most basic level, bone is a composite material composed of an organic matrix with embedded mineral crystals. The organic component consists of collagen and other noncollagen fibers, while the inorganic component is primarily hydroxyapatite crystals. The organic components of bone are primarily responsible for tension properties (i.e., elasticity and toughness), while the inorganic components are responsible for compression properties (i.e., stiffness). In addition to collagen and hydroxyapatite, living bone also contains several types of cells (i.e., osteoblasts, osteoclasts, and osteocytes), blood vessels, nerves, and a significant amount of water. The water in bone increases its resistance to fracturing by absorbing large amounts of energy. Bone generally exists in woven or lamellar form. Woven bone is unorganized and laid down quickly. It is typically found in fast-growing bones or in the callus produced during fracture repair. Lamellar bone is highly organized bone laid down in layers with the orientation of the collagen fibers at different angles in each layer. There are also two primary types of bone based on density and porosity that have different biomechanical properties. Trabecular bone (also known as cancellous or spongy bone), commonly found in the interior of a bone near the ends of long bones and in cuboidal, irregular, and flat bones, has high porosity, low density, and is organized as laminated struts called trabeculae. Cortical bone (also known as compact bone) is the dense bone that forms the thick outer wall of long bones and the thin cortex of cuboidal, irregular, and flat bones. Cortical bone is composed of lamellar bone interspersed with osteons that allow for the incorporation of blood vessels and bone maintenance cells. Osteons can either be primary osteons or secondary (Haversian systems) depending on whether they are formed new or formed by the resorption and replacement of existing bone in a process known as remodeling. Cortical bone responds differently to loads depending on the number and size of osteons. Due to its structure, cortical bone is stronger along the longitudinal axis than along the transverse axis. Finally, the macrostructure of a bone is influenced by its cross-sectional shape, areas of buttressing (thickening), and differential density. During life, the architecture and material properties of a bone adapt to meet the functional demands it experiences.

Material Properties of a Bone

The strength of bone is generally defined as its ability to withstand loads (force or moment) without failing. Loads can be applied in tension (stretching), compression (compaction), bending (angulation), torsion (twisting), shear (sliding), or a combination of these basic components. These loads cause internal tensile, compressive, and shear stresses on the bone. The type of stress will vary with the direction of the force and the orientation of the bone. Bending loads produce tensile stress on one surface and compressive stress on the other, while torsion produces tension and compressive stress at an $\sim45°$ angle to the longitudinal axis and shear force in the transverse plane.

To understand how a bone behaves under loads, it is important to understand the relationship between stress and strain. Stress in its simplest definition is the intensity of load per unit area. Stress is generally measured on a small cube of bone to remove the effects of geometry. Strain, on the other hand, is the amount of dimensional change or deformation in shape that occurs due to an applied stress in one plane (**Figure 1**). Bone will fail when the strain becomes too great regardless of the level of stress. Strain can be either negative or positive depending on the type of load applied. For example, if the two ends of a cube of bone are pulled apart during tensile stress, the bone will undergo an increase in length (longitudinal strain) and a corresponding decrease in breadth (transverse strain). In this case, there is positive strain in length and negative strain in breadth. The ratio of transverse strain to the longitudinal strain is Poisson's ratio, which is ~0.3 for bone. If the load is applied in a manner that causes the angles of the bone cube sides to become distorted or slide, the bone is said to be undergoing shear strain.

To understand the relationship between stress and strain, imagine a cube of bone loaded in tension until it breaks. The load can be measured as a function of deformation to form a load-deformation curve (**Figure 2**). As bone is loaded, it will begin to deform. For a while, the deformation of bone is linearly proportional to the load placed on it. If the deformation is less than ~3%, the bone will return to its original shape once unloaded. However, as the load continues to the yield point, the curve begins to flatten. As can be seen in **Figure 2**, less loading is required to cause increasing deformation. If the load continues to increase, the bone will eventually reach a point of failure and will fracture. The load-deformation curve can be mathematically converted to a strain–stress curve to eliminate the effects of geometry. In the linear portion, the stress and strain are proportional to each other. The

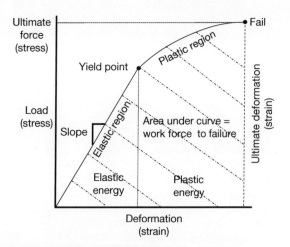

Figure 2 Idealized schematic illustrating the principles of load-deformation and stress–strain curves. The ultimate force (or stress) is denoted by the height of the curve, while the ultimate deformation (or strain) is denoted by the point of failure. The area under the curve represents the work to failure. The area between the origin and the vertical line dropping from the yield point equals the amount of energy absorbed elastically. The area between the two vertical lines (yield and ultimate strain) represents the amount of energy absorbed plastically. The slope in the elastic region of the curve represents the modulus of elasticity or stiffness. The yield point represents the point when bone stops behaving elastically and begins to behave plastically.

relationship of tensile stress to tensile strain is known as the modulus of elasticity or Young's modulus, while the ratio of shear stress to shear strain is known as the shear modulus. The greater the resistance of bone to stress (steepness of stress–strain curve slopes), the greater is its stiffness. If the bone is unloaded in the elastic region, the stress falls to zero when the strain returns to zero and the bone returns to its original shape. If the load is continued and deformation reaches the yield point, slippage occurs between layers of atoms and molecules at the cement lines, and the stress will return to zero but the strain will not. In this case, the bone is behaving plastically and will remain deformed without healing. If the load continues to increase, the bone will eventually reach its ultimate deformation or fracture point. Brittle bone will fracture under tension before or slightly after reaching the yield point and normally does not show any significant plastic deformation (**Figure 3**). Tough or ductile bone, on the other hand, will become plastically deformed before breaking under tension. Brittle bone is more resistant to compression stress, while ductile bone is more resistant to tensile stress. The energy absorbed by a bone per volume of area is equivalent to the area under the stress–strain curve and is sometimes referred to as the modulus of toughness. The area under the elastic region is the amount of energy absorbed elastically, while the area under the plastic region is equivalent to the energy absorbed plastically.

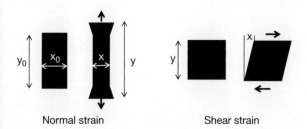

Figure 1 Schematic illustration of normal (tension) strain and shear strain. Strain is the fractional change in dimension of loaded material. Normal strain along the longitudinal axis is the difference between the deformed length (y) and the original length (y_0) divided by the original length (($y - y_0$)/y_0). The normal strain in the transverse axis is the deformed breadth (x) divided by the original breadth (x_0) divided by x_0. Poisson's ratio is the ratio of the transverse strain (x) to the longitudinal strain (y).

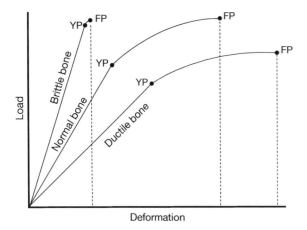

Figure 3 Idealized schematic illustrating the principles of a load-deformation curve for different bone conditions and quality. Brittle bone is stiffer and therefore has a steeper slope but fractures with little or no deformation in the plastic region and requires less work for failure than normal bone. Ductile bone undergoes greater deformation before failing and requires greater work for failure than normal bone. YP, yield point; FP, fracture point.

The stress–strain curve provides a basic understanding of the intrinsic nature of how bone responds to mechanical loads, but it must be kept in mind that bone is a dynamic composite tissue that exhibits anisotropic and viscoelastic characteristics and has a unique geometry. During life, the mechanical characteristics of bone must combine to meet the need for a stiffness and compliance while minimizing skeletal weight. Stiffness of bone reduces strain so it does not deform significantly under load and allows muscles to function more efficiently. Compliance, on the other hand, allows bone to absorb energy and deform to avoid failure during direct or indirect dynamic loading from a fall or blow. The anisotropic nature of bone causes it to behave differently depending on the direction of the force. As a result, the strain on bone is not necessarily the same as the direction of the applied force. That is, the value of the modulus in the stress–strain curve can be different depending on the orientation of the bone. The viscoelastic nature suggests that bone can deform like an elastic material. However, like a viscous material, bone will continue to deform or creep under constant pressure and its stiffness depends on the rate at which the load is applied. Bone becomes more brittle under rapid loading. Therefore, the ultimate or fracture strain is decreased. Also, as a result of its viscoelastic properties, bone is nearly twice as resistant to failure in compression as in tension. This is why bone will normally fail under tension before compression in adults.

The actual forces required to break a living bone are frequently different from the intrinsic strength of bone material, and numerous other factors can affect the force required to

fracture a living bone. In a living person, bone is protected from fracturing through energy-absorbing mechanisms including muscle contractions and deformation of soft tissues. During a fall, for example, muscles contract and reduce the bending of bones by lessening the tensile forces, and soft tissue will absorb much of the energy. However, if the energy-absorbing mechanisms that protect the bone are impaired by surprise, restriction, or incapacity, bones are more likely to fracture under less force. The size and geometry of bones also affect their ability to resist fracture. The geometry of bones allows them to effectively withstand normal loads while remaining light. Intuitively, large bones distribute forces over a larger area and are therefore more resistant to fracture than smaller bones of similar shape. Bones with a larger cross-sectional second moment of inertia and polar moment of inertia are also more resistant to bending and torsional fracture, respectively. Bone that is further from the neutral axis is more efficient at resisting strain. If two bones have the same cortical thickness, the bone with the larger diameter will have greater resistance to fracturing.

Effects of Age and Disease on Bone Material Properties

The age of the individual and some diseases may affect the quality and geometry of the bone, and therefore can significantly influence the fracture risk. Bone's resistance to fracturing can be influenced by any process that changes its material composition and geometry. The ratio of inorganic and organic components of bone (bone mineral density, BMD) affects stiffness (**Figure 3**). Highly mineralized bone is stiff but also brittle. As a result, less energy is required to break brittle bone than more compliant, less mineralized bone (**Figure 3**). Immature bone has a lower BMD than adult bone. As a result, immature bones have greater elasticity but less stiffness than adult bones and can absorb more energy and deformation before fracturing. This is why children are less likely to experience bone fractures from trauma than adults. Incomplete fractures are more common in the immature skeleton because the bone undergoes large deformation due to the ductile properties of the bone (**Figure 3**). In older adults, on the other hand, the bones become more mineralized, making them stiffer and more brittle. As a result, the bones of older individuals are stronger under compression loads, but less energy is required to cause them to break under tension. In addition, the strength of bone in older individuals may be reduced because of the greater number of secondary osteons, reduction of water content, and the loss of bone, especially trabeculae. Secondary osteons reduce bone density and increase cement lines, while the loss of water decreases the amount of energy that can be absorbed from trauma.

Similar to age, pathological changes in bone can affect its quality and geometry. Individuals with diseases such as osteoporosis, osteogenesis imperfecta, osteomyelitis, diabetes,

Paget's disease, Cushing's disease, rickets, scurvy, tumors, rheumatoid arthritis, and others may be at increased risk of bone fracture. Osteogenesis imperfecta, for example, reduces bone quality and causes long bone cortices to thin. Any apparent disease affecting bone should be noted and its role in the observed fractures should be discussed.

Fracture Propagation and Fracture Types

Fracture Propagation

When more energy is transferred to a bone than it can absorb, the bone will fracture because the strain will surpass the ultimate strain. Energy absorbed by a traumatic load builds up in the bone and is released by forming cracks. The greater the energy absorbed by the bone, the greater is the number of cracks that will form. As a result, high-energy trauma will cause bone to fragment, while low-energy loads will usually cause fracture without fragmentation. Bone is weakest in shear followed by tension and strongest in compression. Therefore, fractures will normally propagate in the bone along tension and shear planes. The shear planes run at ~45° angles from compressive and tensile stresses. Fractures also follow the path of least resistance. In the skull, for example, there are regions of buttressing (greater thickness) that impede horizontal bending of the skull bones. Therefore, fractures are more likely to occur between the areas of buttressing because the bone can be more easily bent. Fracture lines or cracks will often be diverted toward less-buttressed areas. Likewise, fractures may be terminated at suture lines or preexisting cracks since the energy is more efficiently dissipated through these structures.

Fracture Types

The type of fracture produced in bone depends on the amount and location of force applied and the area of impact. Proper description of bone injuries can provide information regarding the type and direction of forces and aid in the mechanism and ultimate cause of trauma. Unfortunately there is very little standardization in the procedures or terminology for documenting bone injuries. Furthermore, most bone trauma classifications are derived from the medical literature that are not necessarily appropriate for forensic scientists. Bone fractures are commonly classified based on general fracture types that occur in all bones, fractures that occur in specific bones, and fractures that cause soft tissue damage. Detailed descriptions of fracture types for each major bones of the body can be found in many references (see section "Further Reading"). The intent here is not to develop a standard system or provide an exhaustive list, but to give a biomechanical description of some of the fracture types commonly found in the forensic literature and typical forensic cases.

In all cases, bone injuries should be documented mentioning the bone or bones involved, specific location of injury on each bone, type of injury (fracture, dislocation, etc.), appearance of the injury, patterning of fracture lines, apparent direction of the force, length of the fractures, presence of deformation, evidence of the timing (antemortem, perimortem, postmortem) of the injury, and any evidence of complications. In addition, when possible, whether the fracture is open or closed, the percentage and direction of apposition (amount of contact between fragments in fresh or healed injuries), direction of rotation (internal or external rotation of the distal end), and degree and direction of angulation should be documented.

The first major distinction in fracture type is whether the break involves complete or incomplete discontinuity. These two classes of fractures are then subdivided based on the type of force, pattern of cracking, degree of fracturing, and bone type. Incomplete fracture types are commonly described as bow injuries (the force is dissipated between the yield and failure points), torus, greenstick, toddler, vertical, and depression fractures. Complete fractures are classified based on their shape and location and include transverse, oblique, spiral, comminuted, butterfly, segmental, and epiphyseal fractures. Cranial fractures include linear (simple linear, diastatic, and stellate), crush (depressed), and penetrating. While discussions of the type of fracture are useful for understanding the mechanism of force, the different types of fractures are not mutually exclusive. Linear fractures, for example, may arise from a depression fracture associated with blunt trauma or from a penetrating fracture associated with gunshot projectile trauma. In general, the type of fracture that occurs is often associated with the velocity and mass of the striking object and the area of the impact forces.

General Fracture Types

Transverse fractures result from forces applied perpendicular to the longitudinal axis of the bone, often as the result of bending forces on brittle bones and bones that are not under compression due to weight-bearing functions. When bent, the tensile stress is applied to the convex surface opposite the direction of force and compression stress on the concave surface forming a neutral axis (point at which the tensile and compressive stresses cancel each other out) near the center of the bone shaft. Since bone is more resistant to compression than tensile stress, the bone will fail on the tensile side. As the fracture propagates across the shaft toward the compression side, the cross-sectional area of the bone is reduced and the neutral axis shifts toward the compressive side until the fracture is complete. If the bone is under compressive forces as well, a transverse fracture will begin on the tensile side, but as the fracture crack moves toward the compression side, shear forces become greater and the fracture will begin to travel along the shear plane at approximately a 45° angle in one or both directions because bone is weaker in shear than in compression. If the fracture is propagated in both directions, it will result in a butterfly fracture characterized by a wedge-shaped fragment of bone, with its apex on the tension side and base on the compression side. Whether a butterfly fragment is produced probably depends on the duration and magnitude of the bending and compression loads. Bending forces may result in an incomplete transverse fracture (beginning on the tensile side), called a greensick fracture, that may or may not deviate at right angles. In greenstick fractures, the unfractured portion of the bone often remains permanently bent. Greenstick fractures are more common in immature bones that have greater compliance, but may also occur in adult bones such as the ribs. Under high loads, crushing or comminution of the bone may also occur. Avulsion fractures, which are usually of less forensic significance because they are self-inflicted, also result in a transverse fracture line. However, an avulsion fracture results when a muscle tendon, ligament, or joint capsule is pulled creating significant tensile stress that caused the bone to fracture.

Oblique fractures result from a combination of moderate bending and compressive forces or bending and torsion that cause the bone to break diagonally (often at a 45° angle) to the long axis. The angle of an oblique fracture depends on whether the compressive or bending force is greatest. If the compression forces are greater, the fracture will be more oblique. If the bending forces are greater, the fracture will be more transverse. Long oblique fractures, which are often difficult to differentiate from spiral fractures, occur when the predominant force is torsion. Oblique fractures often begin as transverse fractures but quickly follow the shear plane, resulting in a break with a short transverse section and a longer oblique section.

Spiral fractures occur due to torsion or twisting force that produces a fracture that circles or spirals around the shaft. When a long bone shaft is twisted, the compressive and tensile stresses are at approximately a 45° angle to the shaft. Tensile stresses produce a fracture that winds around the surface and breaks completely when a longitudinal fissure occurs or the beginning and ending edges of the crack connect. The fracture originates where the tension stress is greatest and follows the angle of rotation until the fracture ends are approximately parallel or above one another. The direction of the twisting can be determined by the direction of the spiral.

Comminuted fractures are those that result in more than two fragments, and often result from large direct or indirect forces with high-energy absorption. Indirect forces frequently result in a "T" or "Y" pattern fracture. Comminuted fractures may also result in direct blunt force trauma or penetration from a high-velocity projectile.

Crush fractures occur due to direct force to the bone, which results in depression (forces originating on one side) or compression (forces originating on two sides) fractures. Depression fractures can result in incomplete penetration of projectiles or blunt trauma produced by an object striking the bone. The degree of fracturing is affected by the size of the impact area and the velocity of the force. If the area of impact is small and the velocity is great, the resulting fracture may be a penetrating injury.

Torus, buckling, or impact fractures are due to compression force and occur when the ends of a long bone are driven toward each other. The resulting fracture is an outward displacement of the cortical bone around the circumference of the bone, usually near the end of the long bone shaft. Examples of how this type of fracture occurs include fracturing of the proximal humerus when falling onto outstretched upper limbs or fracturing of the metacarpals when punching or striking an object with the fist. Because the diaphysis is composed of thicker, denser cortical bone and the metaphysis is primarily trabecular bone surrounded by a thin layer of cortical bone, compression forces are more likely to result in buckling of the metaphysis than of the diaphysis. Buckling is also more likely to occur in immature bones than in adult bones.

Cranial fractures

Fractures of the skull can occur from direct or indirect trauma. Linear, crush, and penetrating fractures are common with direct trauma. As with more general fracture types, these fractures are not mutually exclusive. Under direct trauma, the skull behaves similar to a semielastic ball. The curve of the cranial vault at the impact site will flatten or bend internally while the surrounding bone will bend outward. Fracturing will occur on the tensile side in areas of bending. Whether the fracture will begin at the impact site and radiate away or begin away from the impact site and radiate in both directions probably depends on the elasticity of the skull, the size of the impact area, the size and shape of the object impacting the skull, the architecture of the skull at the impact area, the magnitude of the force, and other factors. Linear fractures often occur when the skull is struck or impacts an object of high mass. Low-velocity direct forces often result in linear or depressed (crush) fractures of the cranial vault. High-energy loads with a small impact area or pointed objects striking the skull will result in depression or penetrating injuries. Stellate or star-shaped fractures are formed by multiple linear fractures radiating from the point of impact. If the damage is more extensive, comminuted fractures may occur. Concentric fractures are produced when a blunt or penetrating object causes inward bending of the bone between radiating fractures. They generally circumscribe the impact area and are roughly perpendicular to the radiating fractures. As the plates of bone between radiating fractures bend inward, tensile stress occurs on the external surface of the outer table and progresses like transverse fractures from the outer to the inner table.

Bullet wounds are usually characterized by internally beveling entrance and externally beveling exit fractures. The shape of the wound depends on the angle at which the bullet strikes the bone. Because of the high energy and velocity associated with projectile force, the bone is unable to absorb the energy and fractures will commonly radiate from the initial perforating fracture. Concentric fracturing may also occur. However, unlike radiating and concentric fractures caused by blunt trauma, these fractures will initiate due to tension on the inner table of the vault due to intracranial pressure. In addition, trauma resulting from a gunshot will not display the inward deformation of the bone often seen in fractures occurring from blunt trauma.

See also: **Anthropology/Odontology:** Animal Effects on Bones; Archeology; Bone Pathology and Antemortem Trauma; Bone Trauma; History of Forensic Anthropology; Postmortem Interval.

Further Reading

Berryman, H.E., Symes, S.A., 1998. Recognizing gunshot and blunt cranial trauma through fracture interpretation. In: Reichs, K.J. (Ed.), Forensic Osteology: Advances in the Identification of Human Remains, second ed. Charles C. Thomas, Springfield, IL, pp. 333–352.

Bilo, R.A.C., Robben, S.G.F., Rijn, R.R., 2010. Forensic Aspects of Pediatric Fractures: Differentiating Accidental Trauma from Child Abuse. Springer, New York.

Currey, J.D., Butler, G., 1975. The mechanical properties of bone tissue in children. Journal of Bone and Joint Surgery 57A, 810–814.

Elstrom, J.A., Virkus, W.W., Pankovich, A., 2006. Handbook of Fractures, third ed. McGraw-Hill, New York.

Galloway, A. (Ed.), 1999. Broken Bones: Anthropological Analysis of Blunt Force Trauma. Charles C. Thomas, Springfield, IL.

Gurdjian, S., Webster, J.E., Lissner, H.R., 1950. The mechanism of skull fracture. Journal of Neurosurgery 7, 106–114.

Johnson, K.D., Tencer, A.F., 1994. Biomechanics in Orthopaedic Trauma: Bone Fracture and Fixation. Informa Healthcare, London.

Kimmerle, E.H., Baraybar, J.P., 2008. Skeletal Trauma: Identification of Injuries Resulting from Human Rights Abuse and Armed Conflict. CRC Press, Boca Raton, FL.

Lovell, N.C., 1997. Trauma analysis in paleopathology. Yearbook of Physical Anthropology 40, 139–170.

Moraitis, K., Spiliopoulou, C., 2006. Identification and differential diagnosis of perimortem blunt force trauma in tubular long bones. Forensic Science, Medicine, and Pathology 2, 221–229.

Pierce, M.C., Bertocci, G.E., Vogeley, E., Moreland, M.S., 2004. Evaluating long bone fractures in children: a biomechanical approach with illustrative cases. Child Abuse and Neglect 28, 505–524.

Spitz, W.U., Spitz, D.J., 2006. Medicolegal Investigation of Death: Guidelines for the Application of Pathology to Crime Investigation, fourth ed. Charles C. Thomas, Springfield, IL.

Turner, C.H., 2006. Bone strength: current concepts. Annuals of the New York Academy of Sciences 1068, 429–446.

Turner, C.H., Burr, D.B., 1993. Basic biomechanical measurements of bone: a tutorial. Bone 14, 595–608.

Wieberg, D.A.M., Wescott, D.J., 2008. Estimating the timing of long bone fractures: correlation between the postmortem interval, bone moisture content, and blunt force trauma fracture characteristics. Journal of Forensic Sciences 53, 1028–1034.

Relevant Websites

D.J. Wescott, http://www.txstate.edu—Texas State University.

Bone Trauma

G Quatrehomme and V Alunni, Université de Nice Sophia Antipolis, Nice, France

Glossary

Blunt Any weapon, tool, or object that is smooth without any pointed or sharp part.

Compression mechanism (skull) Generalized pressure exerted on the skull, leading to irreversible deformation of the pieces of bones.

Compression side of the bone The concave side when the bone sustains a force that deforms it.

Elastic deformation Reversible deformation of the pieces of bones.

Plastic deformation Irreversible deformation of the pieces of bones.

Sharp Any weapon, tool, or object that displays a beveled (cutting or stabbing) part.

Tension side of the bone The convex side when the bone sustains a force that deforms it.

Introduction

Forensic anthropology deals with identification of skeletons or bones, but also analysis of the bone lesions to attempt to find out the cause and manner of death, each time it is possible. Forensic anthropology copes with skeletons discovered in a forensic context, but also with altered bodies (mutilation, cremains, decomposition) in which analysis of bone lesions will bring up significant information. Each time there is an important alteration of soft tissues as in autopsy cases of severe putrefaction, bones may show the signs of assault or of various processes altering the bones. On the other hand, some bones may be absent, due to human or animal activity. This can be a very important issue, especially for some specific locations, such as the hyoid bone and thyroid cartilage (the bone and cartilage of strangulation), ribs (bones of assault injuries, among others), and metacarpals and phalanges of the hands (bones of defense wounds, among others). Furthermore, bones may suffer from taphonomic alterations that may lead to difficulties in understanding the perimortem wound process.

Analysis of bone lesions needs a thorough methodology. The first step is to know if the bone lesion is of ante-, peri-, or postmortem origin. The second step is to classify the wound and assess the mechanism. In the third step, we may make some hypotheses on the tool that may have caused the bone lesion.

Ante-, Peri-, or Postmortem Origin of the Bone Lesion

This is a main issue, because most of the lesions are post-mortem, and there is sometimes a great deal of controversy to ascertain a peri- or postmortem lesion, in front of courts. Briefly, *antemortem* lesions will be recognized when there is some healing of the bone, as a smoothing of the edges of the lesion, a production of bone around the lesion, an etched line parallel to and several millimeters from the actual fracture (periosteal uplifting). This needs 15 (in average) of evolution in adults (sometimes as little as 7 days), and less in children. If the death occurs before this 13- to 15-day span of time, it is usually impossible to state the antemortem feature of the lesion.

Postmortem lesions are very frequent and of various origins. They are due to the weather or the soil, but also result from botanic, animal, or even human activity. Weathering cracks are very well known and may deeply alter the bone. Alternance of sun and rain, and cycles of freezing–thawing are examples that will alter the bone. The bone tends to lose its main properties with the span of time, that is, elasticity, hydration, and stiffness. Therefore, dry bones (loss of collagen and water) will react differently in comparison with green bones. Unfortunately, green bone (at the time of death) becomes a dry bone after a span of time that differs from one case to another, because it is dramatically linked to the environment of the bone. It is usually impossible to differentiate between a postmortem fracture that occurred on a (still) green bone and a perimortem fracture. The hallmark of a postmortem fracture is probably the discoloration of the edges of the lesion. Unfortunately, this sign can be useful only when present, which demands probably months or even years to be clearly visible.

Eventually, *perimortem* lesions are very difficult to state with certainty. The issue comes from a period of uncertainty, as the antemortem lesion cannot be claimed (less than about 13 between the lesion and the occurrence of death) and the postmortem lesion as well (when the fracture or lesion occurs onto a green bone, and when there is no discoloration of the edges of the lesion). Greenstick fractures, joined skull fractures (the fragments are not totally separated along the margin of the lesion), depressed skull fractures, concentric and radiating fractures, and stellate fractures are observed in green (elastic) bones and therefore are usually of perimortem origin. As mentioned, the gradual loss of elasticity and water of the bone will lead to a brittle bone. The bone tends to shatter into smaller fragments. These differences may be difficult to ascertain, and, to tell the truth, the main hallmark of a perimortem fracture is when it is due to a sharp-force injury, or a gunshot wound. These kinds of mechanisms are nearly always of perimortem origin. It is quite unusual that a gunshot wound occurred postmortem and sharp force injuries as well. Chopping (blunt–sharp) and above all blunt trauma raise more uncertainty. We have dealt with several skeletons where a blunt or even sharp–blunt trauma was due to the fall of a rock on the skeletonized body.

Biomechanics

There are theoretically three subsequent phases when a bone sustains stress: (1) *Elastic phase.* In the beginning the load is relatively light and the bone will deform but this deformation is reversible: the bone is able to come back to its original shape (elastic deformation) as soon as the stress stops. In this first phase, the strain (the deformation) is proportional, in response, to the stress (the load); (2) *Plastic phase.* If the load is more important, the bone enters into a plastic deformation phase. After deforming in response to the stress, it is unable to come back to its original shape as the stress stops: there will be a permanent (plastic) deformation. During this phase, the stress–strain curve is not straight, because there is no proportionality any more between stress and strain; (3) *Fracture phase.* If the load is more important and exceeds the elastic and plastic components, the bone fractures.

Furthermore, we have to keep in mind that bone is a viscoelastic material, and is therefore twice stronger in compression than in tension. Thus, angulation of the bone will increase tensile forces on the convex side and compressive forces on the concave side. The bone will always yield first on the side of tension. The fracture begins under tension, keeps on toward the compression side, becoming more angulated, according to the shear forces that are generated. More about this is discussed elsewhere in this encyclopedia.

Classification of the Bone Lesions

Generally speaking, there are five kinds of lesions encountered in forensic anthropology: sharp-force injuries, blunt-force injuries, chopping wounds (blunt–sharp (if the blunt mechanism is predominant) or sharp–blunt (if the sharp mechanism is predominant) force injuries), gunshot wounds, and carbonization. An instrument is qualified as *sharp* when it presents a beveled part. It is very often a metal blade (e.g., a knife) which will act by cutting (when the blade moves more or less in the direction of the bone) or stabbing (when the tip of the blade acts perpendicularly or obliquely against the bone). But any beveled area of any instrument or element belonging to the environment may act like a blade or tip, under the condition that this part is beveled. The sharper the beveling, the easier the instrument will cut or stab. A *blunt* instrument is smooth, without sharp or pointed areas. An example of a blunt instrument is a bludgeon. The blunt instrument gives a pressure when it strikes the bone. The *sharp–blunt* or *blunt–sharp* instrument displays a sharp area, but also acts as a blunt tool, usually in reference to its weight or the violence of the blow (therefore, its kinetic energy). Thus, the blunt or sharp action is only a mechanism, and the element that has been able to produce it may be a weapon, a tool, an object, or any element of the environment. The main point is that the blunt element will lead to a blunt trauma, the sharp element will lead to a sharp trauma (a cutting or stabbing lesion), and the blunt–sharp element will lead to a blunt–sharp lesion, mixing both mechanisms. An axe is a good example of a sharp–blunt instrument, which acts by the sharp part of the blade, but also creates a blunt mechanism according to the weight of the instrument. Eventually, we will deal with the main aspects of the *gunshot wounds* to the bone. In this chapter, we will preclude carbonization of the bodies and the study of burned bones.

Sharp Injuries

Any sharp instrument will penetrate very easily into the bone, without any pressure exerted on it. The consequence is a very clear lesion, with regular edges of the wound. *Cutting* is due to the moving of the beveled area, for example, the blade of a knife, more or less in a parallel direction to the bone. The result is a linear or arciform (curved) lesion, often of small size. The arciform shape is explained by the displacement of the perpetrator or the victim during the cutting. This cutting lesion may be particularly seen on some specific locations of the body: the hands, the ribs. Concerning the hands, it is of paramount importance to examine all the metacarpals and phalanxes very carefully. These kinds of lesions are very frequent in sharp assaults and are called defense wounds. When there is an assault with a knife, the tendency of the victim is to protect himself or herself by putting the hand in front of the head. That is the reason why defense wounds are very frequent in this kind of foul play. Concerning the ribs, all 24 ribs (if available) must be examined with a great deal of attention. A cutting wound of an edge of a rib will be often of very small size, sometimes tiny, but of great importance. Occasionally there is a "mirror lesion," concerning two adjacent ribs. This double-sharp lesion occurs when the double blade penetrates between two adjacent ribs, leading to a cutting mark on both edges, or a cutting mark on one edge and a shaving pattern of the other edge. If it is a single blade, there is a sharp cutting wound on one rib, and a more or less blunt wound (chipping, irregular edges of the lesion) on the adjacent rib.

Stabbing is due to the percussion of the tip of the blade perpendicularly or obliquely to the surface of the bone. It may release a tiny mark on the bone or perforate it, passing through the bone. These stabbing wounds are usually seen on the sternum, scapula, ribs, skull, and sometimes on the long bones. Occasionally, the tip of the blade breaks and remains embedded within the bone.

The blade may penetrate through the thorax, giving a cutting lesion on one edge of the rib (and sometimes a mirror image) and then the blade moves on to the vertebra, giving a stabbing lesion on this last bone. Thus, two wounds may correspond to only one strike.

Stabbing wounds are sharp-force injuries and are typically very clear (clear shape, clear edges). But it is quite frequent that the perpetrator or the victim or the blade moved during the assault, so that some pressure is exerted to the bone, leading to some chipping of the lesion. Scanning electron microscopy has showed that the tip very often gives some pressure on the bone, especially when there is a tilt, and raises one side of the bone.

Blunt Injuries

Skull lesions
The methodology of analysis needs the study of three features: (1) the point of impact, (2) the associated fractures, and (3) the signs of compression.

Point of impact
A localized trauma leads to a localized deformation. Due to the elastic property of bones, the bone may return to its original shape. Therefore, the point of impact may be absent, and this is not a rare situation. A blow with a bludgeon is a good example of this possibility. The instrument is really blunt, and if the blow is not too violent, the deformation at the point of impact will be reversible, and there will be no visible lesion at the area of impact.

Sometimes the blow results in bone ecchymosis. This lesion does not display any sign on the external or internal table of the skull, but fine fractures and bleeding of the trabeculae of the diploe occur and explain the lesion. These bone ecchymoses have been described in old forensic literature when the diagnosis was made by transillumination (i.e., observing the skull through a source of light to see nonphysiologic discolorations of the skull) and by histopathology. More recently, bone ecchymoses have been confirmed by magnetic resonance imaging.

When the blow is more violent, there may be an indented fracture at the point of impact. The instrument produces an (incomplete) lesion of penetration or a (complete) perforation of the skull. In the case of a blunt instrument, as it cannot penetrate the bone because of its smooth shape, it will exert a lot of pressure on the bone. Therefore the point of impact, when it exists, will be unclear (the shape is vague and the edges are irregular).

Fractures
Fractures correspond to the dispersion of kinetic energy. They may be absent because the kinetic energy has been totally absorbed by the elastic deformation of the skull at the point of impact or by the indented lesion, when present. Fractures may be present, with or without any visible lesion at the point of impact.

Radiating or even concentric fractures may appear around the point of impact, which may be observable or not. The dispersion fractures of the skull vault are quite common. When they are caused by a blunt and quite light instrument, such as a bludgeon, and if the blow is not too violent, fractures may be visible without any point of impact. The same pattern is observed when the victim falls from his or her height on the flat ground: fractures of dispersion are observed, without any point of impact. According to some authors, the fractures do not always appear at the point of impact, this phenomenon being explained by the transmission of the forces at a distance but this statement is a source of controversy.

The fractures of the base of the skull are frequent and potentially very dangerous. They occur from impacts on the skull, the face, the mandible, or by compression. One can distinguish between (1) longitudinal fractures of the base, usually due to an impact on the front or on the back of the head and (2) transverse fractures of the base, which are usually due to lateral impacts of the vault. A quite common fracture is seen along the two petrous bones and is usually considered to be due to a lateral impact (but it is not always the case). Hinge fractures are transverse fractures that walk in front of the petrous bone through the sella turcica and are usually linked to lateral impacts to the head.

Compression of the skull
Compression of the skull is due to a generalized (and not a localized) pressure on the skull. The skull will decrease its size in the direction of the compression. On the first occasion, an elastic (and then reversible) deformation of the skull is observed; then a plastic (and then irreversible) deformation occurs, and the fractures appear in the direction of the force.

Compression is stated when there is a widening of the sutures and above all a widening of the fractures (termed "diastatic fractures"). This widening is explained by the permanent deformation of the pieces of bones which cannot perfectly come back to their original shape. The compression is seen when a "static loading" is applied to the skull. Theoretically, it rules out a high-speed projectile. It may occur with a slow-speed projectile and, above all, with a blunt trauma, where the stress is particularly slow.

The mechanism of compression is frequent in forensic pathology and anthropology: head rolled over by a vehicle, violent blow to the head, particularly when it is blocked against a wall or the ground, impact on the vertex of the head, fall from one's own height with head impact against the ground, fall from a height on the feet. All these situations tend to decrease the size of the skull in the direction of the force. To be sure, the fall from some height on the vertex leads to a very significant compression of the skull, with numerous and wide skull fractures, and a significant plastic deformation of the pieces of bone.

Ring fractures are very peculiar, occurring around the foramen magnum, sketching a ring pattern, associated with a diastasis (widening) of the mastoid suture and fissures of the petrous bone; they are usually attributed to a downward compression of the skull against the vertebral column (fall from a height on one's feet, violent vertical blow on the vertex), or a violent upward vertical blow on the chin (uppercut) or occiput. According to some authors, the downward force to the occiput should result in an internally directed beveling, while an upward force to the occiput should result in an externally directed beveling.

Chopping Injuries

In chopping wounds, both mechanisms (sharp and blunt) are associated with the injury. Thorough observation of the point of impact is required: it may be absent; if present, we have to observe the shape (clear or blurred) and the edges (clean or irregular). The presence or absence of dispersion fractures, and the presence or absence of signs of compression, are indispensible clues. This three-step analysis allows for the clear diagnosis of the mechanism. The sharper the instrument, the easier is the penetration, the less deformation exists at the point of impact, the less local pressure is exerted, and then the clearer is the shape of the impact lesion, the more regular are the edges of the lesion, and the less fractures of dispersion are observed. Conversely, when there is a violent blunt trauma, the instrument tries (but cannot) penetrate the skull, and therefore the lesion at the point of impact is unclear, the edges are irregular, and there are numerous associated fractures. As an example, with a blunt trauma by a hammer (**Figure 1**), the area of impact is unclear, and there are often impressive associated dispersion fractures. This can be explained by the huge pressure that is exerted onto the skull at the point of impact. Conversely, with a stabbing wound with a sharp pick (**Figure 2**), the perforation is very clear, the edges of the wound are very regular, and there are no associated fractures. In chopping (sharp–blunt) wounds, for example, with an axe, a hatchet (**Figure 3**), or a machete, the

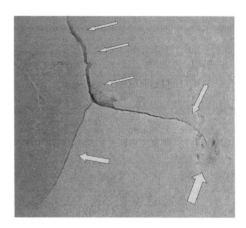

Figure 1 Blunt trauma with a hammer. The point of impact is very unclear ("ghostly" appearance, wide arrow). There are dispersion fractures (thin arrows) and compression mechanism as well (very thin arrows), with significant widening of the edges of the fractures.

Figure 2 Sharp trauma with a sharp, pointed pick. The point of impact is very clear, with clean and regular edges. There is no associated fracture. Small irregularities of the edges are visible, only with some magnification, demonstrating some pressure exerted while perforating the skull.

lesion mixes both features (blunt and sharp). Very often, the weight of the weapon and the violence of the blow explain the blunt component of the lesion (irregularities of the edges of the lesion and associated fractures). A wound due to an axe will show a straight regular edge with beveling and a blunt second edge with chipping off of bones and associated fractures of dispersion. Eventually, compression (**Figures 1 and 4**) is due to a generalized pressure exerted to the skull and leads to several or multiple wide fractures with permanent deformation of the pieces of bones. Compression may occur with blunt or blunt–sharp instruments.

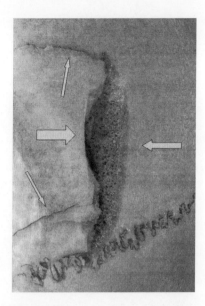

Figure 3 "Sharp–blunt" trauma by a hatchet (chopping wound). There is an irregular edge (wide arrow) and fractures (thin arrows), which represent the blunt part of the injury. The middle arrow points to a regular, beveled edge, which represents the sharp part of the injury.

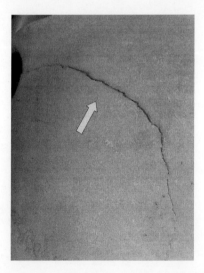

Figure 4 Compression mechanism. The fracture displays a widening (arrow) of its two edges. This is usually termed "diastatic fracture" and indicates an irreversible plastic deformation of the pieces of bones.

Long Bones

Sharp trauma of long bones is unusual, except in cases of postmortem dismemberment of the body. In this last case, the bones are of great value, showing specific injuries linked to the blade of a knife (sharp injury), the using of an axe or hatchet (sharp–blunt injury), and the using of a saw, which releases very valuable saw marks depending upon the type of saw. Basically, there are hand-powered saws and mechanical saws. The main features of a saw are the teeth per inch or points per inch and the presence of an alternating, racker, or wavy set. The clues left by a saw include the false start kerf (initial corners, kerf floor, floor corners) and the bone cross section (initial corners of the kerf, kerf walls, breakaway spur, and notch). We will not insist on the saw marks analysis and further information may be found in reference readings.

Except for dismembering, sharp wounds of long bones share the same features as the other locations (cutting or stabbing injuries). Chopping wounds of long bones are possible, for example, through an assault with an axe or a machete, leading to a sharp–blunt injury, as described earlier.

There are numerous basic mechanisms of blunt trauma of the long bones. Alms proposed to distinguish between (1) *traction* (leading to a transverse fracture); (2) *axial compression* (leading to an oblique fracture); (3) *bending* (leading to a transverse fracture); (4) *bending under axial compression* (leading to an oblique transverse fracture). The more the axial compression, the more vertical is the oblique part of the fracture. A butterfly fragment is often seen on the side of compression. This butterfly fragment is of great value, because it indicates without any ambiguity the side of tension and the side of compression, and therefore gives the direction of the blow; (5) *twisting* (leading to a spiral fracture); (6) *twisting associated with axial loading*; in real life, twisting is associated with axial loading. The more the axial compression force, the more nearly vertical is the plane of shear forces; and (7) *twisting with bending*; this mechanism looks like an angulation about an oblique axis. Usually this kind of fracture occurs at the junction between the middle and lower thirds of the tibia.

In short, transverse fractures result from angulation, oblique transverse fractures from an angulation with axial loading, spiral fractures from an axial twist with or without axial loading (the more the axial loading, the more vertical is the spiral), butterfly fractures from bending with axial loading, and oblique fractures from axial loading.

For the forensic assessment of the bone, a very important clue is the "direct" or "indirect" feature of the traumatism. Direct blows on the bone will lead to an angulation and therefore to transversal fractures. If both bones of the forearm are concerned, the fracture is at the same level on the two bones. If the blow strikes the inferior limb, there is very often an axial loading at the time of the blow (the inferior limb bearing the weight of the body), so that the fracture is often oblique transverse. In a forensic context, a transverse fracture of the superior limb and a transverse or oblique transverse fracture of the inferior limb may be possibly linked to an assault, with a direct impact on the forearm or the leg with a stick, for example. Conversely, spiral fractures of the limbs are in favor of a twist of the shaft, and then possibly an accident. A transverse fracture of the tibia with a butterfly fragment may be explained by a bending of the bone; therefore, it may be an accidental strike of the inferior limb by a car. For little children, spiral fractures may be due to child abuse with a violent torsion of the superior or inferior limb.

Other Locations

Blunt or sharp injuries of the *forearms* and *hands* are often defense wounds. That is the reason why the little bones of the hands are so important in forensic anthropology and have to be properly and thoroughly collected at the crime scene. Very often these lesions are tiny and the bones must be well prepared to be sure that there is no sharp lesion. Occasionally, suicide by phlebotomy with a blade used on the wrists may concern the forearm bones.

Blunt trauma of the *ribs* is frequent in cases of assaults or falls. Sharp injuries of ribs are of paramount importance. They are usually of small size (a simple tiny nick) and justify a serious preparation of the bone. It is impossible to see them if the ribs are not perfectly clean.

Blunt *facial injuries* by weapons like sticks or even fists are frequent and lead to anterior teeth fractures, nasal and zygomatic fractures, and blowout fracture of the orbit. The latter is seen when the eyeball is forced against the fragile orbital plate.

Hyoid bone, *cricoid*, and *thyroid cartilages* may show fracture or dislocation, resulting from strangulation. This is not always the case, because young victims display an important elasticity of the hyoid bone or thyroid cartilage, so that there is often no fracture, though strangulation really took place. Ossification increases with aging and leads to easier fractures by strangulation. Hanging leads to fractures or dislocations of the horns of the hyoid bone and the horns of the thyroid cartilage, but these fractures or dislocations are not compulsory.

Gunshot Wounds

Gunshot wounds cause peculiar blunt trauma due to projectiles shot by a firearm. The peculiarities come essentially from the velocity of the projectile, in comparison with a blunt trauma, which is very low in comparison, even if the blow is very violent. Analysis of gunshot wounds to bones needs to underline the entrance, the exit (when present), the direction of the shot, and the distance of the shot. We will only deal with gunshot wounds to the skull in this chapter.

Entrance Gunshot Wounds

The main features of a typical gunshot entrance wound to the skull are the circular or oval shape, the regularity, with sharp edges, a clear punched-out external appearance, and the *internal*

beveling of the wound, that is, the opening is beveled in the direction of the shot (**Figure 5**). This can be symbolized by a speaking tube (**Figure 6**), the widening of the tube indicating the direction of the bullet. This last feature is really the hallmark of the bony entrance wound, but may be partial (only a part of the circumference displays some beveling), very tiny (and difficult to assess), or even absent (especially when the bone is very thin, like in the orbital walls). When present, internal beveling is very useful (**Figure 5**), especially when the opening displays unusual shapes, is irregular, (occasionally) larger than the exit wound, or when the skull is fragmented. The explanations of internal beveling are quite unclear, but the pressure exerted by the bullet to the bone in the direction of and laterally to the pathway is probably a good explanation. It has to be pointed out that, though beveling is considered as the

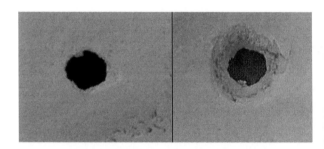

Figure 5 Typical skull entrance gunshot wound. The perforation is round, quite regular (though there is some chipping of the edge of the hole), and without beveling on the exocranial vault (left). Conversely, there is an obvious beveling of the same wound on the endocranial vault (right). The direction of the bullet is obvious from the outside to the inside of the skull.

Figure 6 This sketch emphasizes the direction of the bullet, that is, the enlargement of the perforation (beveling), like a speaking tube. Sketch by Benjamin Maes.

hallmark of gunshot injuries, it may exist with other kinds (e.g., sharp–blunt instruments) of perforations of the skull. It is said that the constitution of the skull vault with two layers of compact bone, separated by a layer of cancellous bone (the diploe), gives part of the explanation of the internal beveling of an entrance wound. But beveling in the direction of the shot does exist with other locations, like the edge of a long bone.

As for gunshot wounds to the skin, there can be very *atypical cases of gunshot entrance wounds* to bones. The shape may be triangular, rectangular, or irregular. These variable shapes may gain some explanation from several factors, as the yawing and tumbling of the bullet, its deformation against the bone, the slight width of the bone wall, or the presence of intermediate targets. Occasionally, the bullet digs a tunnel within the bone. This is rare because the high pressure associated with the pathway usually leads to a burst of the bone. But tunneling may be observed with small calibers, for example, in ribs or vertebrae.

External beveling of an entrance wound is very rare, usually involving handgun contact wounds and must be differentiated from chipping off of the edges of the opening, the latter being very plain. Usually, a more or less typical internal beveling is associated with the external beveling. Explanations of this inverted beveling of entrance wounds include the forceful return of gases in a contact shot and the blowback from pressure associated with temporary cavity formation. The twisting of the bullet while perforating the skull has been presented as an explanation, but must be ruled out because the twisting rifling is very slow in comparison with the velocity of the bullet.

Occasionally, as entry wounds to the skin, the bony entrance is larger than the exit wound. This phenomenon is well known and is usually dedicated to peculiar missiles like Brennekes.

Some gunshot entrance wounds may look like a blunt or a sharp–blunt (stabbing-blunt instrument) trauma. This may be explained by the fact that the bullet is blunt, but its tip may act as a pointed object, due to its velocity, especially when the bullet displays a pointed nose (and not a blunt nose or a wadcutter), when the bullet strikes perpendicularly to the bone, and when it is not destabilized before striking. Comparison of blunt trauma and gunshot trauma fractures show that plates of bone due to radiating fractures of the vault are levered out in gunshot wounds (the converse in blunt trauma). Concentric fractures will start under tension (in the inner table) and progress to the outer table, so that concentric fractures are beveled externally in gunshot wounds (the converse with blunt trauma).

But, most of all, shattering and fragmentation of the bone may lead to difficulties. In the context of forensic anthropology, it is not rare that some parts of bones are missing or destroyed. A semilunar defect must always draw attention and a gunshot wound must be suspected. The discovery of an internal beveling and the association with radiating or concentric fractures may help the diagnosis of a bullet perforation. X-rays may release some clues, when little particles of metallic density exist along the edges of a defect. Sometimes the presence of radiating or concentric fractures without any hole (missing or destroyed) allows for the suspicion of a gunshot wound.

A serious pitfall occurs when the bullet enters through a natural hole, like the foramen magnum, or the orbits (the orbit walls are often destroyed in a forensic anthropological context). In these cases, there is no visible skull entrance.

Exit Gunshot Wounds

Exit wounds are usually irregular, larger in size than the entrance, and also display an inward clean punched-out appearance and an external beveling (in the direction of the bullet). The increase in the size ratio is slight to very significant (ranging from 1.14 to 5.76 times in a series of 17 entrances per exit wounds). The explanation of the size increase is the instability (tumbling, loss of gyroscopic twisting) and the deformation of the projectile. This was stated by experimental studies of skin gunshot wounds in animals with nondeformable spheres as missiles. The shape of the exit wound is usually round or oval, but may also display a square, a rectangle, or a triangle shape. Often the shape is more irregular than the entrance wound. To be sure, an exit wound may be absent if the bullet has stayed inside the brain. As for the entrance, the bullet may also exit through a natural hole; in this situation, there is an entrance, but no exit and no bullet.

Again, external beveling is a hallmark of the exit wound, but, as for entrance wounds, may be partial, slight, or even absent, especially in thin bones. Internal beveling of an exit wound seems to be a very rare situation.

Fractures

Though fractures associated with gunshot entries and exits are really frequent, they are not compulsory. The perforation by the bullet is the primary fracture, the radiating fractures are the secondary fractures, and the concentric fractures are the tertiary fractures. Theoretically, concentric fractures occur if the kinetic energy is not dissipated by the hole and the radiating fractures. It has to be pointed out that the fractures of the entrance walk faster than the bullet, so that the fractures coming from the exit wound are stopped by the fractures coming from the entrance wound (crossing rule, also called Puppe's rule). (Puppe was German and he described his crossing rule in the German language as early as 1914 and was further quoted by Madea and Staak.) This may be of interest in order to state the area of the entrance and exit wounds when the skull is fragmented. This rule is also valuable when there are multiple shootings. The occurrence of fractures depends upon several factors, including the kinetic energy, the intrinsic behavior of the bullet (mushrooming, fragmentation), the destabilization of the bullet, the thinness or thickness of the bone, and the presence of an intermediate target.

Direction of the Shooting

In forensic cases, it is essential to give the direction of the shooting. The first assessment is to state the exact location of the entrance and exit wounds (when there is an exit wound). The features described earlier usually allow for this assessment. Then the direction of the shooting is straight between both holes. The angles have to be determined in reference to the horizontal, sagittal, and coronal planes; for the skull, the horizontal plane is the Frankfurt plane.

If there is no exit, the direction is stated between the entrance and a contralateral impact, when it exists (e.g., a bone ecchymosis or a little shattering of the inner table of the skull). Occasionally, the bullet or a fragment of it may be embedded inside the bone, and X-rays are of great value in these cases. If any of these signs is absent, one has to try to assess the direction of the bullet by observing the entrance hole: theoretically, if the hole is round, the bullet has struck perpendicularly to the bone; if the hole is oval, the bullet has struck with a tilt; and tangential wounds are very peculiar. Furthermore, it is said that beveling is elongated in the direction of shooting, but unfortunately this is not always the case.

Ricochet inside the skull is possible, but only occurs with small calibers when the bullet has lost nearly all of its kinetic energy. The deviation of the bullet after striking a bone is possible for the same reasons. Occasionally, the bullet has sufficient velocity to perforate a big vessel, and then is carried away in the blood circulation (this is termed "bullet embolus, embolization, or embolism"). It is said that a low kinetic energy bullet may pass around the skull under the scalp or around the thorax under the skin. We have never observed these last two situations.

Range of Shooting

Range of shooting is of paramount importance to reconstruct the death scene. Generally speaking, the intensity of fractures depends (among other factors) on the kinetic energy and then in part on the distance of shooting. High-speed projectiles produce multiple and intense fractures. But contact handgun shots, and above all contact shotgun shots, produce severe fractures often with bone loss and opening of the sutures. This is well explained by the massive increase of pressure inside the skull, due to gas entering from the weapon.

Caliber of the Bullet

The size of the defect does not reflect the size of the bullet. The intrinsic features of the bullet (shape, strength), the behavior of the bullet (tumbling, mushrooming, instability), and the intrinsic features of the bone (thickness, brittleness) are able to change the dimension of the hole.

Tangential Gunshot Wounds

Tangential gunshot wounds must be well known. Semilunar defects, grooves, gutter wounds, and keyhole defects have been described.

Semilunar defects are seen when the projectile strikes the very edge of a bone. It may be the edge of the orbit, the zygomatic process, a long bone, and even a vertebral plate, a rib, and so on, in fact, any bone whose edge is struck tangentially. The main feature of this tangential lesion is the presence of a beveling in the direction of shooting. Usually, this beveling is obvious in thick bones (like the edge of a femur or a humerus) but can be difficult to assess in thinner or slighter bones (e.g., ribs) that tend to burst.

Grooves may be dug up within bones, like the horizontal ramus of the mandible. We have also seen this kind of lesion in a strong mastoid. The bone must be strong enough and the shooting really tangential, so that the bone can support the track of the bullet without bursting.

LaGarde in the early twentieth century described *gutter wounds* to the skull. Three degrees were recognized by this author. In the first degree, only the outer table was fractured. In the second degree, the outer and the inner table were fractured (the latter by the waves of pressure). In the third degree, there was an actual perforation of the outer table, the diploe, and the inner table as well. Nevertheless, all these gutter wounds are tangential, according to the fact that the bullet strikes the skull but does not enter the braincase. The bullet will or will not keep the same angle (ricochet if the angle differs after having struck the skull). Even if the bullet does not penetrate the skull in these cases, the skull trauma is obvious and may lead to serious complications and even death, with or without fragments of bones penetrating the brain.

Keyhole defects have been described with handguns and shotguns as well. The bullet strikes the skull tangentially and then is fragmented. One of the two fragments enters the skull, giving a circular or oval defect with internal beveling that represents the initial impact and the entrance. And the other fragment immediately exits, creating an exit wound with external beveling, often more irregular than the entrance. Occasionally, the bullet does not split and no fragment enters the skull. The keyhole pattern (**Figure 7**) has to be well known by forensic pathologists and anthropologists, otherwise it is a great source of confusion. In forensic pathology, there are often two noncontiguous superficial holes in the skin, due to the bullet entering and immediately exiting. But in bone, the two holes are contiguous and termed keyhole defect or keyhole lesion. Keyhole defects of an exit wound are also reported on, but appear to be definitely exceptional.

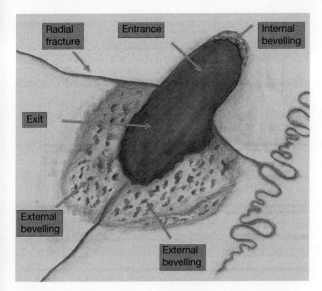

Labels on image: Radial fracture · Entrance · Internal bevelling · Exit · External bevelling · External bevelling

Figure 7 This sketch underlines a typical keyhole lesion. The bullet has struck the skull tangentially and has split. One of the two fragments penetrates the skull (no beveling on the exocranial vault, and we can guess that there is some internal beveling at the top right of the perforation). The second fragment exits immediately, creating an exit with external beveling. The entrance and exit are contiguous on the bone. Sketch by Benjamin Maes.

See also: **Anthropology/Odontology:** Animal Effects on Bones; Forensic Taphonomy; Postmortem Interval.

Further Reading

Alms, M., 1961. Fracture mechanics. Journal of Bone and Joint Surgery 43B (1), 162–166.

Alunni-Perret, V., Borg, C., Laugier, J.P., et al., 2010. Scanning electron microscopy analysis of experimental bone hacking trauma of the mandible. American Journal of Forensic Medicine and Pathology 31 (4), 326–329.

Alunni-Perret, V., Muller-Bolla, M., Laugier, J.P., et al., 2005. Scanning electron microscopy analysis of experimental bone hacking trauma. Journal of Forensic Sciences 50 (4), 796–801.

Baik, S.O., Uku, J.M., Sikirica, M., 1991. A case of external beveling with an entrance gunshot wound to the skull made by a small caliber rifle bullet. American Journal of Forensic Medicine and Pathology 12 (4), 334–336.

Berryman, H.E., Symes, S.A., 1998. Recognizing gunshot and blunt cranial trauma through fracture interpretation. In: Reichs, K.J. (Ed.), Forensic Osteology: Advances in the Identification of Human Remains, second ed. Charles C. Thomas, Springfield, IL, pp. 333–352.

Coe, J.I., 1982. External beveling of entrance wounds by handguns. American Journal of Forensic Medicine and Pathology 3 (3), 215–219.

Curry, J.D., 1970. The mechanical properties of bone. Clinical Orthopaedics 73, 210–231.

Di Maio, V.J.M., 1985. Gunshot Wounds: Practical Aspects of Firearms, Ballistics, and Forensic Techniques. CRC Press, Boca Raton, FL.

Dixon, D.S., 1982. Keyhole lesions in gunshot wounds of the skull and direction of fire. Journal of Forensic Sciences 27 (3), 555–566.

Dixon, D.S., 1984a. Pattern of intersecting fractures and direction of fire. Journal of Forensic Sciences 27, 555–566.

Dixon, D.S., 1984b. Exit keyhole lesions and direction of fire in gunshot wounds of the skull. Journal of Forensic Sciences 29, 336–339.

Evans, F.G., 1973. Mechanical Properties of Bone. Charles C. Thomas, Springfield, IL.

Haglund, W.D., Sorg, M.H., 2002. Advances in Forensic Taphonomy. Method, Theory and Archaeological Perspectives. CRC Press, Boca Raton, FL.

Harvey, F.H., Jones, A.M., 1980. Typical basal fracture of both petrous bones: an unreliable indicator of head impact site. Journal of Forensic Sciences 25, 280–286.

LaGarde, L., 1916. Gunshot Injuries. William Wood, New York.

Light, F.W.J., 1963. Gunshot wounds of entrance and exit in experimental animals. Journal of Trauma 3, 120–128.

Madea, B., Staak, M., 1988. Determination of the sequence of gunshot wounds to the skull. Journal of the Forensic Science Society 28, 321–328.

Mann, R.W., Owsley, D.W., 1992. Human osteology: key to the sequence of events in a postmortem shooting. Journal of Forensic Sciences 37 (5), 1386–1392.

Maples, W., 1986. Trauma analysis by the forensic anthropologist. In: Reichs, K.J. (Ed.), Forensic Osteology: Advances in the Identification of Human Remains. Charles C. Thomas, Springfield, IL, pp. 218–228.

Pavy, C., Lebreton, G., Sanchez, B., Roques, F., 2011. Aortic bullet embolization revealed by peripheral ischemia after a thoracic gunshot wound. Interactive Cardiovascular and Thoracic Surgery 12 (3), 520–522.

Quatrehomme, G., Alunni-Perret, V., 2006. Les lésions crâniennes tranchantes et contondantes en anthropologie médico-légale: étude préliminaire. Journal de Médecine Légale Droit Medical 49, 173–189.

Quatrehomme, G., Içscan, M.Y., 1997. Postmortem skeletal lesions. Forensic Science International 89, 155–165.

Quatrehomme, G., Içscan, M.Y., 1998a. Analysis of beveling in gunshot entrance wounds. Forensic Science International 93 (1), 45–60.

Quatrehomme, G., Içscan, M.Y., 1998b. Gunshot wounds to the skull: comparison of entries and exits. Forensic Science International 94 (1–2), 141–146.

Quatrehomme, G., Içscan, M.Y., 1999. Characteristics of gunshot wounds in the skull. Journal of Forensic Sciences 44 (3), 568–576.

Reichs, K.J., 1998. Postmortem dismemberment: recovery, analysis and interpretation. In: Reichs, K.J. (Ed.), Forensic Osteology. Advances in the Identification of Human Remains, second ed. Charles C. Thomas, Springfield, IL, pp. 353–388.

Simonin, C., 1962. Médecine légale judiciaire, 3 e édition (1955), 2 e tirage (1962). Librairie Maloine, Paris.

Sledzik, P.S., Kelly, M.A., 1998. The timing of injuries and manner of death: distinguishing among antemortem, perimortem and post-mortem trauma. In: Reichs, K.J. (Ed.), Forensic Osteology. Advances in the Identification of Human Remains, second ed. Charles C. Thomas, Springfield, IL, pp. 321–332 (quoted by Sauer, N.J.).

Spitz, W.U., 2006. Spitz and Fisher's Medicolegal Investigation of Death: Guidelines for the Application of Pathology to Crime Investigation. Charles C. Thomas, Springfield, IL.

Symes, S.A., Berryman, H.E., Smith, O.C., 1998. Saw marks in bone: introduction and examination of residual Kerf contour. In: Reichs, K.J. (Ed.), Forensic Osteology. Advances in the Identification of Human Remains, second ed. Charles C. Thomas, Springfield, IL, pp. 389–409.

Ubelaker, D.H., Adams, B.J., 1995. Differentiation of perimortem and postmortem trauma using taphonomic indicators. Journal of Forensic Sciences 40 (3), 509–512.

Blunt Injury

S Pollak, University of Freiburg, Freiburg, Germany
P Saukko, University of Turku, Turku, Finland

Glossary

Deceleration trauma When a body being in motion is forcibly stopped, the inner organs tend to continue the movement due to inertia so that the anatomical structures are subjected to tractive and shearing forces.

Fat embolism The term "fat embolism" indicates the presence of fat globules in the small vessels of the lungs and sometimes also in the systemic circulation, mostly as a consequence of major bone and/or soft tissue trauma.

Hemotympanum The term refers to the presence of blood in the tympanic cavity of the middle ear, often resulting from a basal skull fracture involving the petrous bone.

Lucid interval A temporary improvement after a head trauma followed by secondary deterioration (typically caused by a space-occupying intracranial hematoma).

Subarachnoid space This term describes the interval between the arachnoid membrane and the deeper pia mater (two meninges surrounding the brain and the spinal cord). The subarachnoid space normally contains the cerebrospinal fluid. In head injuries or as a consequence of a ruptured cerebral aneurysm, a hemorrhage may spread into the subarachnoid space leading to elevated intracranial pressure.

Introduction

The term "blunt trauma" can be defined as damage to the body due to mechanical force applied either by the impact of a moving blunt object or by movement of the body against a hard surface, both mechanisms resulting in the transfer of kinetic energy high enough to produce an injury (mainly by compression, traction, torsion, and shear stresses). Blunt-force injuries occur in criminal assaults (e.g., a blow with a blunt-edged instrument, a punch, or a kick), in physical child abuse, in traffic and industrial accidents, in suicides (a jump from a height), and in accidental falls brought about by the victims themselves.

Blunt Injuries to the Integument

Abrasions

Abrasions are superficial injuries to the skin characterized by a traumatic removal, detachment, or destruction of the epidermis, mostly caused by friction. In the so-called tangential or brush abrasions, a lateral rubbing action scrapes off the superficial layers of the skin (e.g., from the body's sliding across a rough surface) and leaves a denuded corium, which is initially covered with serosanguineous fluid. In fresh grazes, the direction of impact can often be determined by the abraded epidermal shreds that remain attached to the end of the scrape.

At a later time, the tissue fluid dries out and forms a brownish scab. If the lesion does not reach the dermis, it heals within several days without scarring. Infliction just before or after death results in a leathery ("parchment-like") appearance with a yellowish-brown discoloration (**Figure 1**).

Another type of abrasion is caused by a vertical impact to the skin (the so-called pressure or crushing abrasion). In such

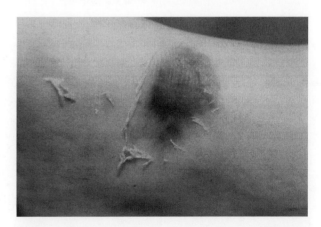

Figure 1 Tangential abrasion confined to the upper layers of the skin. The shreds of epidermis indicate the direction of impact. The central parts of the denuded corium show a parchment-like discoloration from drying.

cases, the injuring object may be reflected by the shape of the skin injury so that the patterned abrasion can be regarded as an imprint of the causative object.

Contusions

Contusions or bruises are extravasations of blood within the soft tissues originating from ruptured vessels as a result of blunt trauma. In this context, only the contusions that are visible externally are considered. Textbooks usually differentiate between intradermal and subcutaneous bruises. In the first-mentioned category, the hemorrhage is located directly under the epidermis, that is, in the corium. This kind of superficial hematoma is usually sharply defined and red, whereas the more common bruises of the deeper subcutaneous layer have blurred edges and, at least initially, a bluish-purple color.

Intradermal bruises may reflect the surface configuration of the impacting object (**Figure 2**). The skin that is squeezed into grooves will show intradermal bleeding, whereas the areas exposed to the elevated parts remain pale. Especially in falls from a height, the texture of the clothing may produce a pattern of intradermal bruises corresponding to the weaving structure. Patterned extravasations of this type are also seen in tire tread marks when an individual is run over by a wheel and in bruises from vertical stamping with ribbed soles.

Subcutaneous bruises are usually nonpatterned. Nevertheless, there may be bruising of special significance. If the body is struck by a stick, a broom handle, a pool cue, a rod, or any other elongated instrument, every blow leaves a double "tramline" bruise consisting of two parallel linear hematomas with an undamaged zone in between. Victims of blunt force violence often sustain contusions from self-defense, typically located on the ulnar aspects of the forearms and on the back of the hands. The upper arms may show groups of roundish bruises from fingertip pressure in cases of vigorous gripping. A periorbital hematoma ("black eye") is induced either by direct impact (e.g., a punch or a kick) or indirectly (due to seepage of blood from a fractured orbital roof, a fractured nasal bone, or from a neighboring scalp injury of the forehead; **Figure 3**).

In general, bruises are regarded as a sign of vitality indicating that the contusion was inflicted prior to death. During life, the blood from ruptured vessels is forced into the soft tissue by active extravasation. Nevertheless, to a limited extent, postmortem formation of contusions is possible due to passive ooze of blood. In surviving victims, a deep bruise may not become apparent on the skin until several hours or even days later because of the slow percolation of free blood from the original site to superficial tissue layers.

In a living person, the contusion undergoes a temporal series of color changes. Initially, most subcutaneous bruises appear purple-blue. As the hematoma resolves during the healing process, the hemoglobin released from the red blood cells is chemically degraded into other pigments such as hemosiderin, biliverdin, and bilirubin. The color changes—usually over the course of several days—to green and yellow before it finally disappears (**Figure 4**). However, the rate of change is quite variable and depends on numerous factors, above all, the extent of the bruise.

The size of an intradermal or subcutaneous hematoma is not always indicative of the intensity of the force applied to the affected area. Elderly people or patients suffering from bleeding diathesis may get bruises from slight knocks or for other minor

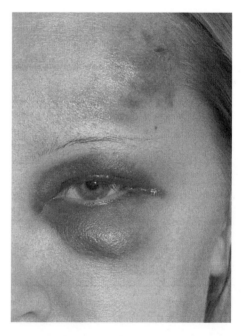

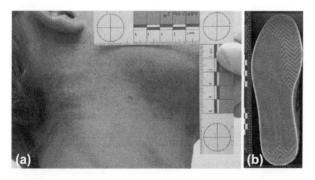

Figure 2   (a) Intradermal bruising corresponding to the ribbed sole pattern of the perpetrator's training shoes (b). The imprint was caused by stamping actions against the face and neck of the victim lying on the ground.

Figure 3   Periorbital hematoma of a live victim from a blow to the left frontal region. As a result of gravitational movement, the blood from the injured forehead spread to the eyelids within 1 day.

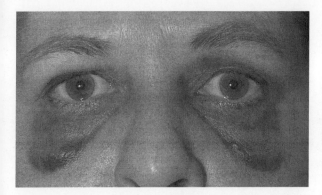

Figure 4 "Black eyes" inflicted by a single fist blow to the root of the nose (6 days before the photograph was taken). Note the yellow color on the periphery of the bruises.

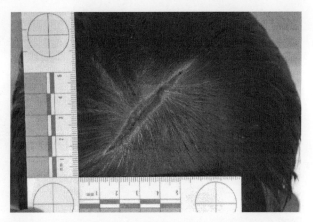

Figure 5 Occipital region of a 41-year-old man showing a slit-like laceration of the scalp surrounded by a reddish excoriation. The injury was caused by a fall on a concrete step when climbing over the balustrade of a balcony.

reasons. On the other hand, the absence of an externally visible injury does not necessarily mean that there was no relevant trauma. Subcutaneous bruises of surviving victims are often followed by gravity shifting of the hemorrhage leading to a secondary downward movement of the hematoma.

A special type of blunt injury to the soft tissues is frequently seen in pedestrians who have been struck or run over by motor vehicles. Both the skin and the subcutaneous layer may be avulsed from the underlying fascia or bones by shearing forces so that a blood-filled pocket is formed, typically in combination with a crush damage to the adjoining fatty tissue.

Lacerations

Lacerations are tears of the skin or of internal organs (see below). They may be caused by blows from blunt objects (such as a hammer, a whipped pistol, a rod, the toecaps of heavy footwear, or a fist); other lacerations are produced by impact from vehicles or by a fall to the ground. Lacerations occur most commonly in body regions where the integument directly overlies a firm bony base acting as support (scalp, face, back of the hand, and shins). When the force acts on the skin, the subcutaneous tissue is squeezed between the injuring object and the bony platform so that the integument is compressed and crushed until it tears and splits sideways (**Figures 5 and 6**).

Lacerations are characterized by abraded, bruised, and crushed wound margins. The edges of the tears are typically irregular and ragged with bridging tissue strands (vessels, nerves, and fibers) running from side to side. The wound slits may be linear (especially in blows with a narrow, edged instrument), Y-shaped, or star-like. If the impacting object hits the skin at an oblique angle, one of the edges will be ripped away resulting in unilateral undermining (undercutting and avulsion), which indicates the direction of the force. Sometimes foreign material from the causative instrument/surface is

deposited in the depth of the wound slit. The abrasion surrounding the tear may correspond to the shape and dimensions of the impacting blunt-surfaced instrument or—in the case of a fall to the ground—the area of contact.

Head Injuries

The head is a common target in assaults with blunt objects; other common causes of head injuries are traffic accidents, falls from a height, and falls from a standing position. The area of impact usually reveals injuries of the scalp or the facial skin, but it has to be stressed that severe and even lethal traumatization is not necessarily associated with scalp bruising, marked swelling, excoriation, and/or laceration. There may be no externally visible signs, especially in skin areas covered with hair and in cases of a fall onto a flat surface. An impact site on the vertex suggests that the head sustained a blow, whereas, in falls from standing positions, the scalp injuries are expected at the level of the brim of the hat.

Skull Fractures

These may involve the cranial vault, the base of the skull, and the facial skeleton. Although the presence of a skull fracture indicates severe traumatization, the fracture itself rarely threatens the victim's life. There are several types of skull fractures to be distinguished.

Single or multiple *linear fractures* are caused either by a blow with an object with a broad flat surface area or by a fall on the head so that the skull is deformed (flattening/indenting at the point of impact and outward bending/bulging in the periphery). The fracture lines originate where the bone is bent

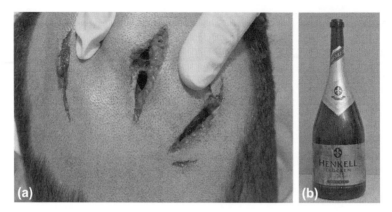

Figure 6   (a) Occipital region of a 27-year-old man, whose scalp had been shaved before autopsy, showing four lacerations from blows with an empty 3-L champagne bottle (b). Note the bridging tissue strand between the wound margins.

outward and therefore is exposed to traction forces exceeding the limits of the bone's elasticity; from these extruded parts of the skull, the fractures extend toward the area of impact, and also in the opposite direction. For this reason, either of the ends is often in congruity with the impact injury of the scalp. Several fracture lines may radiate outward from a central point of impact (**Figure 7(b)**) where the skull is often depressed and/or shattered to pieces forming a *spider's web* or mosaic pattern consisting of circular and radiating linear fractures (**Figure 8**). The sequence of skull injuries may be determined according to Puppe's rule: a later fracture does not cross a preexisting fracture line but terminates when reaching an earlier one.

Before fusion of the cranial sutures (i.e., in children and young adults), a fracture may travel along the seam resulting in diastasis (*diastatic fractures*). If a gaping fracture runs from one side of the cranial base to the other (mostly after lateral impact or side-to-side compression), this transverse type is called a *hinge fracture* because of the independent movement of the front and rear halves of the skull base.

Longitudinal fractures of the base of the skull often occur due to a fall on the occiput; in such instances, the linear fractures typically run through the posterior fossa either ending near the foramen magnum (**Figure 9**) or extending to the floor of the middle and anterior fossa. On the other hand,

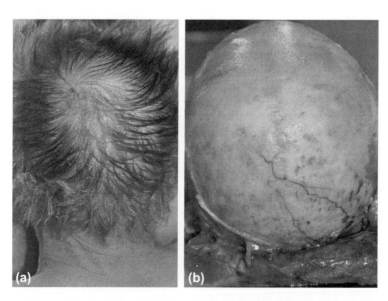

Figure 7   Fatal head trauma caused by a fall on the occiput. External examination of the scalp had only shown an inconspicuous skin abrasion and a shallow laceration (a). From this area of impact, linear fractures extended to the base of the skull (b).

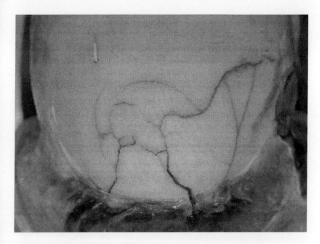

Figure 8 Frontal bone (squama) with linear fractures radiating outward from the area of impact and several additional circular fractures ("spider's web")—a 70-year-old car driver in a head-on collision.

longitudinal fractures of the base can also be produced by impaction of the frontal region.

Depending on its course and location, a *base fracture* may be followed by several *clinical signs:* bleeding from the ear (in fractures of the temporal bone with concomitant

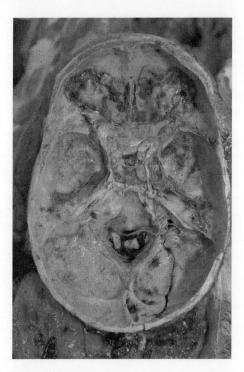

Figure 9 Base of the skull with linear fracture in the posterior fossa sustained in a fall on the occiput. Note the presence of secondary fractures in the anterior fossa floor.

hematotympanom and rupture of the eardrum); bleeding from the nose and mouth (in fractures involving paranasal sinuses, which provide a communication with the naso-pharynx); periorbital hematoma (from fractures of the orbital roofs); leakage of cerebrospinal fluid coming out of the nose or the ear (if the dura is injured along the fracture); and bacterial infection of the meninges (by spread from the nasal cavity, the paranasal sinuses, and the middle ear, especially when the fracture is accompanied by a tear of the dura).

Some special types of skull fractures can only be mentioned briefly. A *ring fracture* is located in the posterior fossa and encircles the foramen magnum. It occurs mostly in falls from a height onto the victim's feet or buttocks so that the cervical spine is driven into the skull. Another mechanism is seen in deceleration traumas, for instance, in head-on collisions, in passengers with fastened seat belts: Due to inertia, the nonre-strained head will continue to move forward exerting traction forces on the base of the skull.

Bone impressions and *depressed fractures* are always localized at the point of impact where the head is struck with an object having a relatively small surface area such as a hammer or a protruding corner of a piece of furniture. The outline of a clean-cut defect in the outer table may reproduce the shape and size of a sharp-edged instrument. If only limited force is applied, the depressed fracture can be restricted either to the outer or, less often, to the inner table of the skull (the latter with inward displacement of the bone fragments). A depressed fracture from a blow that struck the skullcap at an angle may be concentrically terraced. *Hole fractures* from bullets perforating a flat bone of the skull are mostly roundish and clean-cut at the site of entrance, but beveled out in a craterlike manner, at the exit site.

Blunt force applied to the occiput, mostly as a consequence of a fall on the back of the head, often causes independent fractures of the anterior cranial fossa such as cracks of the thin orbital roofs (*secondary fractures* at the site of the contrecoup; cf. **Figure 9**).

Intracranial Hemorrhages

A space-occupying bleeding into the brain membranes is fol-lowed by local displacement of the brain and raised intracra-nial pressure with concomitant flattening of the cerebral hemispheres. Intracranial hematomas as well as traumatic brain swelling, which often accompanies head injuries, may result in transtentorial (uncal) herniation (in cases of supra-tentorial mass lesion) and/or herniation of the cerebellar tonsils which are forced into the foramen magnum leading to compression of the brain stem with secondary damage and failure of the medullary respiratory centers.

From the clinical and forensic point of view, the possible occurrence of a so-called lucid or latent interval has to be mentioned. After initial unconsciousness (due to cerebral concussion), there may be a symptomless period of several hours or even days before the victim becomes comatose again because of the increased hemorrhage and, consequently, the raised intracranial pressure.

Epidural (extradural) hemorrhages are located between the skull and the underlying dura mater, which is stripped from the bone by bleeding from a torn vessel (**Figure 10**). Epidural hematomas have a typical disk- or lens-shaped appearance. The most common site is the temporal and the adjacent parietal region where the branches of the middle meningeal artery are easily lacerated in the course of a transecting fracture line. Since the well-adherent dura has to be avulsed from the bone, epidural hematomas more frequently originate from arterial bleeding than from venous bleeding (e.g., due to a torn dural sinus). In the great majority, an extradural hemorrhage is associated with a cranial fracture.

Subdural hematomas are intracranial bleedings located beneath the dura mater and above the arachnoid (**Figure 11**). Most often, the hemorrhage results from the tearing of over-stretched bridging veins that traverse the subdural space between the surface of the cerebral hemispheres and the superior sagittal sinus. Other possible sources of subdural bleeding are injuries to venous sinuses or to the cerebral parenchyma (such as cerebral contusions with concomitant laceration of the arachnoid). The subdural hemorrhage usually covers one cerebral hemisphere in a caplike manner from the parasagittal area via the lateral surface down to the basal fossas; on a horizontal section, it appears as a sickle-shaped accumulation of blood. In contrast to epidural hematomas, subdural hemorrhages are often not associated with skull fractures; additional damage to the brain tissue may also be absent. A high percentage of subdural bleedings are caused by acceleration or deceleration of the head, for instance, in falls when the head impacts a hard surface, and also in traffic accidents and

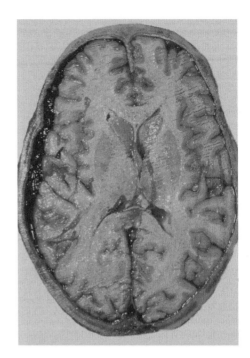

Figure 11 Acute subdural hemorrhage. The unilateral space-occupying lesion has slightly shifted the midline of the brain to the opposite side.

physical child abuse (battered child and shaken baby syndrome). Apart from acute and subacute subdural hemorrhages, there are prolonged cases of hematoma formation and organization, mainly in elderly people and sometimes without a history of previous traumatization. Such chronic subdural hematomas typically consist of brown and gelatinous blood accumulations adherent to the meninges and sometimes covered with a tough membrane.

Traumatic subarachnoid bleeding may result from damage to the cortex such as brain contusion (e.g., contrecoup lesions), from penetrating injuries to the brain, and as a consequence of vessel tears within the subarachnoid space. An extensive hemorrhage on the ventral surface and around the brain stem may arise from a laceration of an artery belonging to the circle of Willis or from another great vessel (such as a torn basilar and vertebral artery).

Cerebral Injuries

"Concussion of the brain" is a clinical diagnosis which means a disorder of cerebral function following immediately upon a (blunt) head injury. It is usually characterized by a transient loss of consciousness (initial coma) with subsequent amnesia from the actual moment of trauma; it is often combined with retrograde amnesia and vegetative signs such as nausea and

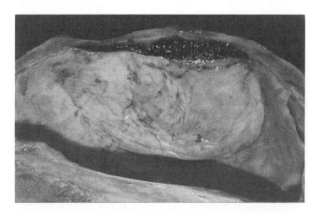

Figure 10 Extradural (epidural) hemorrhage in the parietotemporal area. The hematoma is located between the inner surface of the skull and the detached dura.

vomiting. In mere concussions, the unconsciousness lasts only for a relatively short time (<1 h) and the brain tissue does not show any evidence of structural damage. Nevertheless, even a simple cerebral concussion may be followed by the victim's death, if the head trauma is joined by interfering mechanisms (for instance, drowning or aspiration of gastric contents during unconsciousness).

Cerebral contusions are traumatic lesions of the brain frequently seen in the cortex and sometimes extending into the underlying white matter (**Figure 12**). Fresh contusion hemorrhages are mostly located on the crests of the gyri and composed of grouped streaklike or punctate blood extravasations (**Figure 13**). The cortical lesions are often covered with subarachnoid bleeding. In contrast to cerebral contusions, the term "laceration" means a major destruction of the anatomical context (for instance, mechanical separation of the tissue due to bone fragments or penetrating bullets). In the case of survival, the contusion hemorrhages are reabsorbed and assume a yellowish-brown appearance with softening and, finally, liquefaction of the affected areas.

Due to the injuring mechanism, most cerebral contusions occur in brain regions that are directly opposite to the point of

Figure 13 Close-up view of a contused brain region with characteristic streaklike, densely arranged hemorrhages in the cortex (cut surface).

impact. This contrecoup type of contusion is classically caused by a fall on the occiput, when the moving head is suddenly decelerated with the consequence that the inlying brain is damaged due to inertia. In falls on the back of the head, the contrecoup areas of the brain (poles and undersurfaces of the frontal and temporal lobes) are subjected to an ultrashort negative pressure ("cavitation") resulting in vessel ruptures and cortical hemorrhages (**Figure 14**). On the other hand, the so-called coup contusions arise at the area of impact due to the local deformation and compression of the brain. Even severe coup and contrecoup injuries are not necessarily associated with skull fractures. In victims with both coup and contrecoup lesions, the degree of contrecoup damage is usually more marked. Fracture contusions are localized in topographical correspondence to fracture lines and/or depressed fractures.

Diffuse axonal injury (DAI) is considered a consequence of shear and tensile strains from sudden acceleration/deceleration or rotational movements of the head. Overstretching of the nerve fibers in the white matter leads to axonal injury varying from temporary dysfunction to anatomical transection, the latter being followed by microscopically visible club-shaped retraction balls on the axons. The sites of predilection include the corpus callosum, the parasagittal white matter, the superior peduncles, and the upper brain stem. In the course of the repair process, microglial cells proliferate in the areas of axon damage. In victims of substantial head injuries, especially after traffic accidents, DAI may be responsible for prolonged coma and a fatal outcome even in the absence of an intracranial mass lesion.

Cerebral edema is a frequent finding in significant head injuries. The formation of edema is due to an increase in the fluid content of the brain, predominantly in the white matter. Posttraumatic edema may be generalized (diffuse) or related to focal tissue damage (e.g., adjacent to an area of cerebral

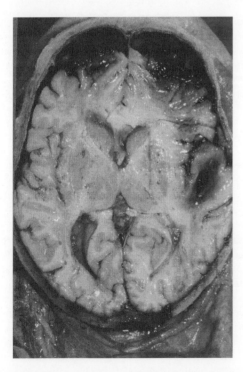

Figure 12 Contrecoup contusions of the frontal poles opposite to the point of impact (fall on the back of the head) with concomitant subarachnoid hematoma; traumatic intracerebral (subcortical) hematoma in the white matter of the right temporal lobe (in close vicinity to cerebral contusions in the overlying cortex).

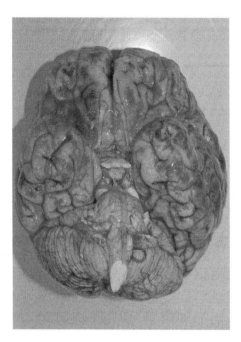

Figure 14   Contrecoup contusions on the undersurface of the frontal and temporal lobes (mostly located at the crests of the convolutions) with slight subarachnoid hemorrhage.

contusion or laceration). At autopsy, the weight of the brain is increased and the gyri are pale and flattened with shallow sulci in between. From the pathogenetic point of view, edema is attributed to a heightened vascular permeability which in turn may be worsened by additional hypoxia.

As with space-occupying lesions such as subdural or epidural hematomas, cerebral edema is a common cause of raised intracranial pressure. The enlarged volume of the edematous brain results in a displacement of cerebral tissue downward through the midbrain opening resulting in grooving of the unci and/or hippocampal herniation. Expansion of the subtentorial brain leads to herniation of the cerebellar tonsils which are forced into the foramen magnum. Herniation with concomitant compression of the brain stem may be followed by secondary hemorrhages (localized in the midbrain and pons) and finally by lethal dysfunction of the vital centers.

Injuries of the Chest

Nonpenetrating blunt force may damage the thoracic wall and/or the chest organs. *Rib fractures* are caused by either direct or indirect violence. In the first case, a localized force is applied and the underlying ribs are broken in the contact area; the other (indirect) type of rib fracture occurs away from the impact, mainly due to compression of the chest.

Rib fractures are frequently associated with *complications* that may be dangerous or even life threatening.

- If a victim sustains numerous fractures, the rib cage loses its rigidity so that the injured section of the chest wall will not participate in the expansion of the thorax during inspiration with the result of paradoxical respiration (*flail chest*) and concomitant hypoxia.
- Sharp, pointed ends of the rib fragments may penetrate the pleura and lacerate the lung and/or the intercostal blood vessels with consecutive bleeding into the chest cavity (*hemothorax*).
- A leak in the visceral pleura permits air to enter the pleural cavity (*pneumothorax*) so that the lung collapses, if it is not fixed to the chest wall by preexisting pleural adhesions. A valvelike leakage in the pleura leads to a so-called tension pneumothorax caused by an increasing pressure of trapped air in the pleural cavity and followed by a complete collapse of the affected lung and a shift of the mediastinum to the opposite side.
- The presence of air bubbles in the subcutis or in the mediastinum (*subcutaneous/mediastinal emphysema*) may derive from injuries of the trachea, the bronchi, the thoracic wall, or the lungs by air entering the adjacent soft tissues.

Blunt-force injuries to the *lung* are mainly encountered as contusions or lacerations. A contusion is typically caused by a substantial impact on the chest with consecutive inward bending of the thoracic cage. In young victims, contusions are not necessarily accompanied by fractures of the ribs or of the sternum because of the high pliability of the juvenile thoracic cage. From the morphological point of view, a contused lung shows bruising either as a subpleural suffusion or as an intrapulmonary hemorrhage. Lacerations of the lung can result when a severe compressive or crushing force is applied to the chest so that the pulmonary tissue bursts or tears. Another possible mechanism is inward displacement of a fractured rib which impales the lung (**Figure 15**).

Blunt traumatization of the *heart* manifests as concussion, contusion, or myocardial rupture. In most cases, the force is directly applied to the anterior chest, which compresses or crushes the heart between the sternum and the vertebral column. Bruises of the cardiac wall may be localized in the subepicardial fatty tissue (sometimes in combination with posttraumatic coronary occlusion) or within the myocardium, which then appears dark red from interstitial hemorrhage. Lacerations of the heart are most often seen in the relatively thin right ventricle or in the atria; they are less common in the left ventricle, the papillary muscles, the cardiac valves, the interatrial, and the interventricular septum. The risk of cardiac rupture is especially high during diastole when the heart chambers are filled with blood and therefore easily burst when they are exposed to a sudden compressive force. Such injuries usually have a fatal outcome either from massive blood loss and hemorrhagic shock (if the pericardial sac is torn and the

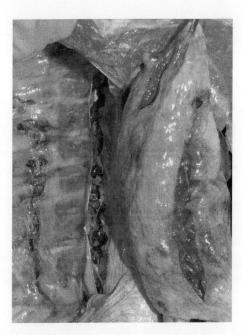

Figure 15 Serial rib fractures of the right hemithorax with concomitant laceration of the lung.

blood pours into a pleural cavity) or from cardiac tamponade (blood accumulation in the pericardial sac resulting in insufficient filling of the cardiac chambers and impaired forward circulation).

Traumatic aortic ruptures typically occur in vehicular accidents and in falls from a height. The most important mechanism is sudden deceleration, possibly in combination with compression and/or shearing. Traction forces tear the aorta transversely at two sites of predisposition: in the descending part of its arcus (near the attachment of the ligamentum arteriosum) (**Figure 16**) or immediately above the cusps of the aortic valve. Other locations (for instance, in association with a dislocated vertebral fracture) are rather rare. The laceration of the aorta may occur as either a complete or a partial transection. In the latter case, the outer layers of the vascular wall are not damaged; the intimal tears are often multiple, semicircular, and parallel (so-called ladder-rung tears). If the trauma is survived at least for a short time, a parietal thrombosis or a posttraumatic aneurysm may follow as a secondary complication.

Abdominal Injuries

Blunt-force injuries of the abdomen are frequently seen in traffic and work accidents, in child and spouse abuse, in other criminal assaults (with kicking, stamping, and punching), as well as in suicidal falls from heights. The abdominal organs

Figure 16 Transection of the aorta in the distal part of the arch (deceleration injury).

most vulnerable to blunt trauma are the solid liver and spleen on the one side and the mesentery on the other. Concomitant external signs of blunt traumatization such as contusions or abrasions are by no means obligatory. Substantial injuries to the liver, the spleen, and the mesentery have always to be regarded as life threatening and potentially fatal, especially in cases without rapid surgical treatment. The main reason is internal bleeding into the peritoneal cavity from lacerations (**Figures 17 and 18**). Ruptures of the liver and spleen can be classified as either transcapsular or subcapsular lacerations. In the first case, both capsule and parenchyma are injured so that the blood instantaneously pours into the peritoneal cavity. The second type of laceration is characterized by the initial formation of a subcapsular hematoma which expands continuously and possibly causes a delayed rupture when the covering capsule tears due to overstretching (mostly several hours or even days after the trauma).

The stomach and the intestine are less susceptible to blunt traumatization than the parenchymatous abdominal organs. The hollow viscera are more likely to rupture, if they are filled with food or fluid. Another reason why the intestine or stomach might be prone to damage is squeezing of the organs between the indented abdominal wall and the lumbar vertebrae. Fatal outcomes from contusions or lacerations of the gastrointestinal tract are usually due to diffuse peritonitis.

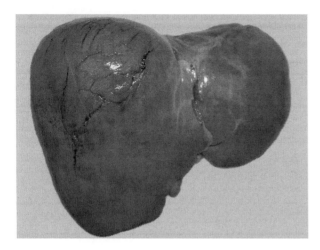

Figure 17   Multiple transcapsular lacerations of the liver.

Renal injuries are a relatively rare source of severe bleeding as the kidneys are located deep behind the peritoneum. Nevertheless, they can be ruptured by a heavy impact to the loin (for instance, in traffic accidents or assaults).

Although the empty urinary bladder is placed within the pelvis, when filled it moves upward and is therefore exposed to blunt traumatization of the lower abdomen. Consequently, rupture of the empty bladder is expected to be extraperitoneal and accompanied with pelvic fractures, whereas a bladder distended with urine may rupture into the peritoneal cavity.

Blunt traumatization of a pregnant uterus is a possible cause of fetal death, mostly due to separation or rupture of the placenta.

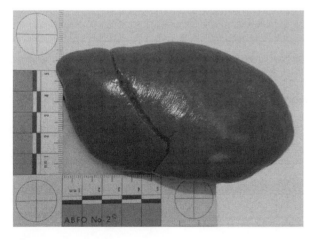

Figure 18   Laceration of the spleen.

Injuries to the Extremities

Besides injuries to the skin and the subcutaneous layer (see above), other anatomical structures such as the muscles, the bones, and the joints may be involved in blunt-force trauma. Extensive crushing of the soft tissues, the formation of blood-filled cavities, comminuted fractures, and severance of large vessels are common findings in victims of automobile–pedestrian accidents. Internal bleeding (from closed injuries) and external bleeding (from traumatic amputation, severe avulsive wounds, and compound fractures) are important factors contributing to hemorrhagic shock. Another sequel to blunt trauma is pulmonary and systemic fat embolism (caused by globules of fat, usually subsequent to fractures or damage of fatty tissues). In cases of prolonged survival, intercurrent infection and pulmonary embolism (originating from post-traumatic venous thrombosis) are dangerous and often fatal complications of an originally nonlethal injury.

See also: **Forensic Medicine/Causes of Death:** Systemic Response to Trauma; **Forensic Medicine/Clinical:** Child Abuse; Defense Wounds; **Forensic Medicine/Pathology:** Autopsy; Forensic Pathology – Principles and Overview.

Further Reading

Case, M., 2005. Head trauma: neuropathology. In: Payne-James, J., Byard, R.W., Corey, T.S., Henderson, C. (Eds.), Encyclopedia of Forensic and Legal Medicine, vol. 2. Elsevier Science, Amsterdam, pp. 472–480.

DiMaio, V.J., DiMaio, D., 2001. Forensic Pathology, second ed. CRC Press, Boca Raton, FL, pp. 92–185.

Hausmann, R., 2004. Timing of cortical contusions in human brain injury. In: Tsokos, M. (Ed.), Forensic Pathology Reviews, vol. 1. Humana Press, Totowa, NJ, pp. 53–75.

Henn, V., Lignitz, E., 2004. Kicking and trampling to death. In: Tsokos, M. (Ed.), Forensic Pathology Reviews, vol. 1. Humana Press, Totowa, NJ, pp. 31–50.

Kieser, J., Whittle, K., Wong, B., et al., 2008. Understanding craniofacial blunt force injury: a biomechanical perspective. In: Tsokos, M. (Ed.), Forensic Pathology Reviews, vol. 5. Humana Press, Totowa, NJ, pp. 39–51.

Lau, G., Teo, C.E.S., Chao, T., 2003. The pathology of trauma and death associated with fall from heights. In: Payne-James, J., Busuttil, A., Smock, W. (Eds.), Forensic Medicine: Clinical and Pathological Aspects. Greenwich Medical Media, London, pp. 321–335.

Marks, P., 2003. Head injury – fatal and nonfatal (and other neurologic causes of sudden death). In: Payne-James, J., Busuttil, A., Smock, W. (Eds.), Forensic Medicine: Clinical and Pathological Aspects. Greenwich Medical Media, London, pp. 321–335.

Marks, P., 2005. Deaths: trauma, head, and spine. In: Payne-James, J., Byard, R.W., Corey, T.S., Henderson, C. (Eds.), Encyclopedia of Forensic and Legal Medicine, vol. 2. Elsevier Science, Amsterdam, pp. 75–81.

Marks, P., 2005. Head trauma: pediatric and adult, clinical aspects. In: Payne-James, J., Byard, R.W., Corey, T.S., Henderson, C. (Eds.), Encyclopedia of Forensic and Legal Medicine, vol. 2. Elsevier Science, Amsterdam, pp. 461–472.

Oehmichen, M., Auer, R.N., König, H.G., 2006. Forensic Neuropathology and Associated Neurology. Springer, Berlin, Heidelberg, pp. 97–270.

Pollak, S., Saukko, P., 2003. Atlas of Forensic Medicine: CD-ROM. Chapter 5. Elsevier, Amsterdam.

Pollak, S., Saukko, P.J., 2009. Blunt force trauma. In: Jamieson, A., Moenssens, A. (Eds.), Wiley Encyclopedia of Forensic Science. Wiley, Chichester, pp. 396–441.

Saukko, P., Knight, B., 2004. Knight's Forensic Pathology, third ed. Arnold, London, pp. 136–221.

Spitz, W.U., 2006. Blunt force injury. In: Spitz, W.U. (Ed.), Spitz and Fisher's Medi-colegal Investigation of Death, fourth ed. Thomas, Springfield, IL, pp. 460–531.

Türk, E., 2008. Fatal falls from height. In: Tsokos, M. (Ed.), Forensic Pathology Reviews, vol. 5. Humana Press, Totowa, NJ, pp. 25–38.

Sharp Trauma

U Schmidt, Freiburg University Medical Center, Freiburg, Germany

Glossary

Epigastrium The part of the upper abdomen immediately over the stomach.
Fibrin Insoluble protein formed from fibrinogen during the clotting of blood; deposition of fibrin is also a response of different tissues to inflammation or injury.

Zygomatic bone The bone that forms the prominent part of the cheek and the outer side of the eye socket.

Introduction

Sharp-force injuries are the second most common cause of injury following trauma by blunt force. They are caused by sharp-pointed or keen-edged instruments, resulting in incised wounds, that is, cuts or slashes, stab wounds, or chop wounds, depending on the implement used and the manner of infliction.

Upon examination of sharp-force injuries, the forensic expert will be asked to differentiate between suicidal, homicidal, and accidental origins. Diagnostic findings, which are essential to make this distinction, include the following:

- kind of injury sustained by the victim (incised, stab, or chop wound);
- pattern of injuries, that is, their number and anatomical localization;
- characteristics of the instrument or weapon used;
- sequelae (e.g., from lesions to vessels and inner organs) or cause of death; and
- findings at the scene such as blood traces or bloodstain patterns.

Additional questions often raised in court are related to the level of force that had to be applied by the perpetrator, the chronological sequence of injuries inflicted to the victim, and the victim's capability of acting after traumatization.

Epidemiology

Partly owing to a restricted access to firearms, sharp force is the most frequent method of homicide in many European countries. Here, it accounts for about one-third of all killings, mostly by stabbing with knives. In the United States, killing by sharp force is second to gunfire. 80–90% of the perpetrators are male and aged between 20 and 40 years, which roughly corresponds to the general data contained in criminal statistics on homicides independent of how they were committed.

As regards the number of victims of sharp-force homicides, both sexes are almost evenly affected. As an exception, several studies from Scandinavian countries stated a considerably lower share of female victims (30% on average). Regarding bodily harm, male victims as well as male perpetrators are overrepresented, which is also in line with the circumstances generally known for acts of violence. As in other kinds of assault, a high percentage of offenders as well as victims are under the influence of alcohol and/or drugs of abuse.

Most frequently, sharp-force fatalities occur at the victim's home. This is especially the case when male perpetrators kill female victims, since homicides by sharp force often result from domestic conflicts between life partners. On the other hand, knife attacks involving a male perpetrator and a male victim often take place in the public space, as they frequently arise from personal disputes between (intoxicated) opponents.

According to the literature, sharp force accounts for 10.0–15.4% of attempted, but only for 2.0–3.1% of completed, suicides. Fatal injuries result more often from stabs to the chest (precordial region and epigastrium) and stabs/cuts to the neck than from cutting the wrists. The latter is frequently found in attempted suicides.

Accidental sharp-force fatalities are very rare. They account for ~2% of all sharp-force fatalities and for 0.3% of accidental deaths, respectively. In these cases, death is usually caused by exsanguination.

Self-inflicted injuries by sharp force are frequent in patients suffering from personality disorders, especially borderline personality, the majority of them being female adolescents. Apart from individuals with mental disorders, self-inflicted wounds are also seen in fictitious assaults and alleged sexual offenses. The wound morphology and the arrangement of the mostly superficial skin lesions often allow for a diagnosis on the spot.

Diagnosis is more difficult in cases of self-mutilation aiming at insurance fraud. Typical examples are chop wounds to the nondominant hand and fingers resulting in amputation of one or two digits, most often the thumb with the index finger ranking second.

Wound Morphology and Biomechanics

Blunt- and sharp-force injuries show some fundamental morphological differences allowing diagnostic differentiation. Contrary to injuries caused by blunt force, sharp-force injuries have cleanly severed wound edges, usually without concomitant abrasions or contusions. Tissue bridges between the wound edges, which are due to the unequal tear resistance of different types of tissues, are also absent in sharp-trauma injuries.

Incised Wounds: Cuts and Slashes

Cut wounds occur when a sharp-edged instrument moves in a direction tangential to the body surface. A cut formally describes an incision of the skin and the underlying soft tissue, whereas a slash implies cutting with a violent sweeping movement. Depending on its position in relation to the cleavage lines of the skin, the wound may gape more or less in a spindle-shaped way with the greatest depth in the middle decreasing toward the wound ends (**Figure 1**).

This is to be expected especially if the cut is localized on a curved part of the body surface, for example, in a longitudinal cut wound across the zygomatic bone or a transverse cut on the upper arm or calf. Both wound ends are pointed often forming a superficial "tail" or shallow incision. If the cutting edge is moved in an acute angle to the body surface, one of the wound edges is oblique, while the opposite one shows undermining. Sometimes, even a flap-like ablation of soft tissue can result. If cuts are located above bony structures (e.g., the skull), concomitant cut-like transection of the periosteum is occasionally seen (**Figure 2**). The only conclusion to be drawn from a cut wound is generally that it was caused by a sharp-edged instrument. The wound morphology alone usually does not provide hints as to characteristic features of the causative weapon/implement.

Stab Wounds

A stab wound is caused by a pointed object thrust into the body. In stabs to the trunk, the abdominal and/or thoracic cavities may be affected.

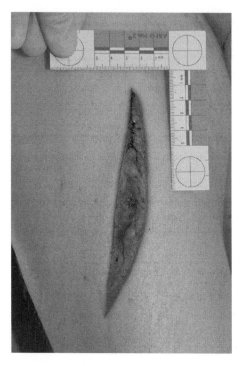

Figure 1 Cut wound on the right thigh of a 56-year-old man who was killed by sharp force and gunfire: clean-cut wound margins without any concomitant abrasions or hematomas. The wound shows its greatest depth in the middle decreasing toward the wound ends.

Under certain circumstances, some features of the stabbing instrument are reflected by the wound morphology. For example, a stab wound from a single-edged blade may show one sharply pointed end—corresponding to the cutting edge of the blade—and one rounded end on the side of the knife's back (**Figure 3**). As in incised wounds, the wound margins can be beveled or undermined when the blade enters the body at an oblique angle.

According to the dynamics of knife attacks, there is considerable relative movement between the assailant and the victim, and an irregular wound configuration is often found. When the knife has plunged into the body, turning of the victim or twisting of the blade before withdrawal causes L-, Y-, or V-shaped wounds (**Figure 4**).

Atypically shaped wounds can also result from stabs through skin folds or creases. "Incised stab wounds" result from a combination of cutting and stabbing movements. The wound may start as a cut, which terminates as a stab wound; on the other hand, some stab wounds turn into an incised wound as the knife is withdrawn at a shallow angle (**Figure 5**). Incised stab wounds are frequently found in victims of knife attacks.

Conclusions drawn from a stab wound on the properties of the stabbing instrument are subject to some uncertainties. Owing to the elasticity of the skin, the width of the blade can

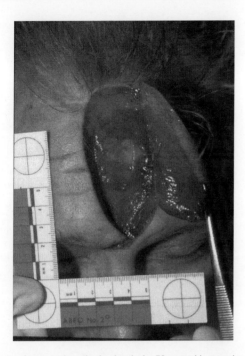

Figure 2 Cut wound on the forehead of a 59-year-old man who was killed by sharp force. The tangential movement of the knife led to flap-like ablation of the scalp. Also, the frontal bone's periosteum was severed.

only be roughly estimated even in the case of an orthogonal penetration without any additional cutting. Stab wounds associated with a hematoma or an imprint abrasion ("hilt mark") indicate that the blade was vigorously pushed in up to

Figure 3 Two stab wounds to the chest in a man killed by stabbing. As both wounds were inflicted with a single-edged foldable pocketknife, each of them shows a pointed wound end on the right side, and a more rounded end on the left side. The differing lengths of the skin wounds result from a differing depth of penetration and are related to the variable width of the tapered blade.

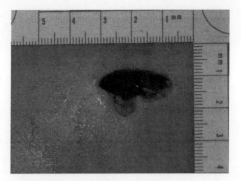

Figure 4 Abdominal stab wound in a young man who was involved in a fight between drunken opponents. The L-shape indicates that the blade was twisted in the body before withdrawal.

its end. The construction parts of the knife contacting the body surface may then be reflected by a patterned hilt mark (**Figure 6**). In this case, the length of the blade can be roughly estimated from the depth of the wound track, provided its end is clearly defined.

A vigorous stab up to the hilt can indent the soft tissues so that the depth of the wound track may exceed the length of the causative knife blade.

Where stable bony structures such as the spine are hit by a stab, the stabbing instrument may bend and occasionally parts of it (e.g., the tip) may break off and lodge in the wound track or quite often within the injured bone. Such fitting pieces found during autopsy help to identify the causative implement. When a knife is drawn over a bone or cartilage tangentially, the wound may reflect a serrated blade. The same applies to tangential movements across the skin in a transverse direction to the blade, which may produce parallel abrasions on the skin. Stab wounds perforating parenchymatous organs or muscles occasionally show parallel lines reflecting the teeth of a serrated blade.

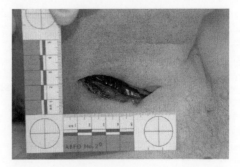

Figure 5 Incised stab wound on the neck of a 40-year-old man who was killed with a Swiss Army knife. Dissection of the wound track showed complete transection of the right common carotid artery and partial transection of the right internal jugular vein.

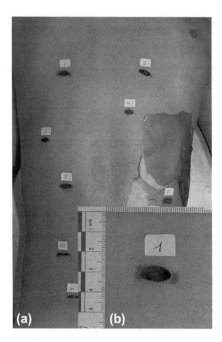

Figure 6 (a) Back of a young woman killed by multiple stab wounds (numbering does not refer to chronological sequence). The perpetrator tried to cover up the crime by arson, which led to superficial burns on the right side of the victim's body. The weapon involved was a single-edged butterfly knife. (b) Stab wound showing square skin abrasions on its ends. These "hilt marks" resulted from the knife's handle contacting the body surface when the knife was vigorously plunged into the body. Both wound ends are rounded due to the penetration of the ungrinded part of the blade ("ricasso," near the handle) into the body.

Stabbing instruments do not necessarily have to be edged, and there is a variety of pointed implements that are used to inflict stab wounds, for example, ice picks, forks, pens, scissors, and screwdrivers. When originating from such an implement, wound margins are often abraded. Wounds may show characteristic features, such as the flat Z-shaped injuries resulting from a closed pair of scissors or the four-point-star-shaped wounds caused by a Phillips screwdriver.

Chop Wounds

Chop wounds are caused by rather heavy objects with a sharp edge (e.g., axes, hatchets, cutlasses, and chopper knives) and/or very long blades (e.g., swords, sabers, and machetes). These objects sometimes cause injuries showing both sharp- and blunt-force elements, for example, additional fractures of the skullcap in blows to the head. Usually, heavy cutting weapons cause smooth-edged soft-tissue transections, although the wound margins may be abraded or contused when the penetrating object is wedge shaped as, for example, an axe. Of diagnostic significance is a smooth-edged skin and soft-tissue

lesion combined with a notch-like injury of the underlying bone; this constellation indicates a sharp-force injury and suggests that a heavy cutting weapon was used (**Figure 7**).

Injuries from Glass

Whenever broken bottles or pieces of glass are used for cutting or stabbing, the wound margins can show concomitant skin abrasions, notches, or hematomas (**Figure 8**). In 1929, Canuto described shallow epidermal transections on the wound ends that result from the keen breaking edges of the glass shards—so-called "Canuto's ends." Due to the three dimensionality of glass shards entering the body, two parallel epidermal transections can be found in many of these wounds (cf. **Figure 8(c)**). Another morphological feature is the displacement of body hair into the wound track that has also been attributed to the thickness of the glass shards' fracture surface. If stab-like injuries occur, splinters of glass may be found within the wound track as well, which facilitates the correct diagnosis. Valuable hints can often be derived from the findings at the scene, for example, broken glasses or bottles.

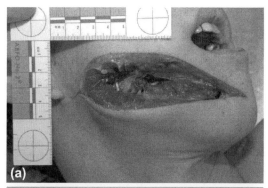

Figure 7 Young man killed by sharp force using a chopper knife. (a) Chop wound on the right mandible, which is also cleaved. (b) Several pieces of the chopper knife's thin-edged blade broke off during the attack and were recovered from several wounds upon autopsy.

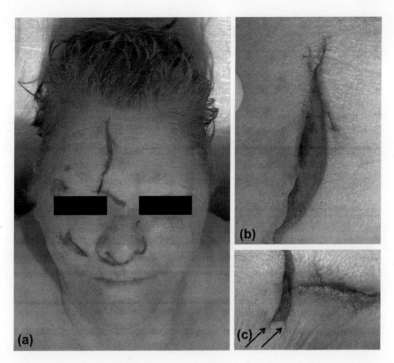

Figure 8 (a) Several injuries resulting from an accidental fall into a drinking glass, which splintered. The victim was a 64-year-old drunken woman. Fatal bleeding was conditioned by a preexisting coagulopathy due to liver cirrhosis. (b) The wounds show characteristics of a sharp-force injury, as well as concomitant abrasions, cuts, and hematomas (forehead). (c) Shallow epidermal cuts on the edges of an almost square wound end caused by a keen-edged glass shard (root of the nose/right eye).

If an intact drinking glass is thrown against an individual, the glass may splinter as it hits the head and resulting glass fragments or splinters can be found on the victim's clothing or hair. In addition, the glass fragments can cause superficial lesions of undraped skin in the head and neck regions. However, experiments show that these wounds hardly exceed a few millimeters in depth; deep, penetrating wounds of the neck are not to be expected. They can occur, however, when a drinking glass or bottle is broken before throwing it. This relates especially to vigorously thrown glass shards with spike-like protrusions. Systematic studies on the injuring potential of thrown (household) knives are still lacking.

The Physics and Dynamics of Stabbing

Numerous studies have been conducted to assess the thresholds of different physical parameters, which have to be passed to effect a stab wound on a victim's body. Many of these studies are based on specific questions related to the reconstruction of injuries, for example, whether it is possible to sustain a (fatal) stab wound by merely "running or falling" into a knife. Already in the nineteenth century, reports were published in the literature stating that it cannot be entirely ruled out that at least stabs penetrating only the soft tissue are of accidental origin.

For example, this may happen if the hand holding the knife is fixed in front of the trunk and no evasive movement is possible. The force or energy necessary for penetration not only depends on the stabbing impulse and velocity or the resistance of the different perforated structures (clothing, skin, soft tissue, internal organs, and bone), but also depends on the properties of the stabbing instrument used, especially the shape of the tip.

How far a stabbing object is able to penetrate essentially depends on the (elastic) resistance of the clothing and the skin, the presence of bony structures along the wound track, and also the reach of the arm holding the knife. Test stabs conducted by various authors showed that a mean force of 57–77 N was necessary to overcome the elastic resistance of uncovered skin. Additional layers of clothing increase these values by 62–112 N with tight-fitting clothes requiring a lower amount of force than loose-fitting clothes. Up to 200 N was necessary to perforate pigskin. The impact velocity measured ranged between 1–2 and 7 m s^{-1} for stabs subjectively regarded as weak or vigorous by the test persons.

Additional aspects to be considered are the weight of the knife used, the geometry of the blade tip, and the angle of the blade's point (**Figure 9**): stabbing with a "sheepsfoot" blade showing a straight cutting edge and curving back as in many bread knives will require higher penetrating forces than

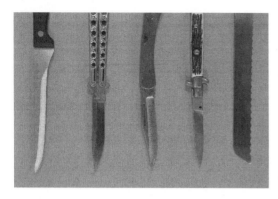

Figure 9 Examples of common blade tip geometries. From left: Boning knife with straight back and curved cutting edge ("back-point" blade); butterfly knife with slightly curved back ("drop-point" blade); foldable knife with concavely curved back at the tip ("clip-point" blade); slightly tapered foldable knife with the point lying on the blade's longitudinal centerline ("spear-point" blade); and bread knife with a curved back and a straight, serrated cutting edge ("sheepsfoot" blade).

stabbing with a symmetrically pointed "spear-point" blade or "needle-point" blade. The latter one is highly tapered, often twin-edged, showing a long and narrow point. It is commonly referred to as a "stiletto" or a "dagger." Household knives often show "back-point" blades ("straight-spine" blades) with a flat back and curved cutting edge or "drop-point" blades with a convexly formed back. "Clip-point" blades with a concavely formed back at the tip are often seen in Bowie, survival, and hunting knives as well as in pocket and other foldable knives. The smaller the angle of the blade's point, the lower are the forces required to induce a penetrating injury.

Depending on the structure of the bone, different amounts of force are necessary for perforation. Generally, one can assume that a submaximal stabbing impulse is sufficient to perforate thin bones such as the shoulder blade, the bones forming the eye sockets (especially the frontal and the zygomatic bone), and the temporal squama, as well as the ribs. Perforation of the temporal squama requires a force of about 250 N, parietal bone of about 500 N. However, in stabs effected with an elevated arm moving downwards ("overarm stabbing"), impact loading on the knife often approaches 1000 N; usual impact velocities range between 6 and 10 m s^{-1}.

An essential problem of the biomechanical investigation of stabbing processes is that there is still no validated model adequately simulating the mechanical properties of the skin of living human individuals.

Sequelae and Causes of Death

The predominant cause of death after sharp-force trauma is exsanguination. The pathological and anatomical diagnoses are made on the basis of sparse, inconspicuous hypostasis, pale internal organs with their characteristic color, a flaccid spleen with a wrinkled capsule, and the presence of striped subendocardial hemorrhages in the outflow channel of the left ventricle (the so-called exsanguinating hemorrhage).

Internal exsanguination is generally associated with a large accumulation of blood in the affected body cavities. The blood volume of an adult accounts for about 6–8% of his body weight. A loss of 1/3 of the blood volume is regarded as life threatening and of 2/3 as usually fatal. Other relevant factors are the speed of the blood loss, which depends on the type and the caliber of the severed vessel(s), and the localization of the injury. For example, if blood rapidly flows from a major arterial vessel into a preformed cavity, considerably smaller blood loss can already lead to death. In stab wounds of the abdominal region, the soft-tissue layers sometimes move in opposite directions after removal of the stabbing instrument so that no major external bleeding is seen. In spite of perforation of the abdominal wall and involvement of internal organs, the victim may retain the capability of acting until the clinical signs of blood volume deficiency become manifest, which may take several hours.

Cumulative surveys of the injuries found in criminal assaults and homicides with sharp-force trauma show that most injuries are localized on the chest and neck. This is attributed to the fact that a great number of offenses start with the victim and perpetrator initially facing each other in an upright position and that most stabs are effected with an elevated arm moving downwards. Consequently, lesions of the thoracic organs account for a large percentage of the potential sequelae and deaths. Stabs to the thorax may perforate the thoracic cavities and result in a pneumo- or hematothorax. A bilateral pneumothorax can be fatal because it restricts respiration. If the lungs are affected and blood seeps into the respiratory tract, blood aspiration is an important proof of vitality, but massive aspiration of blood can also be fatal in itself.

Stabs to the heart can cause cardiac tamponade. If 150–200 ml blood accumulates in the pericardial sac, blood influx during the diastole is so severely impaired that cardiac arrest results from the compression of the heart. Smaller ventricular lesions may cause successively increasing tamponades with volumes up to several 100 ml. Even then, the victim may retain the ability to act for some time.

If large veins in the proximity of the heart, for example, on the neck, are affected, a negative pressure in these vessels can cause air embolism. Especially in stab and cut wounds of the cervical region, one always has to check at autopsy whether the right cardiac ventricle contains air. Gas volumes of 70–150 ml are considered sufficient for fatal air embolism.

Injuries involving the central nervous system may occur, though they are rare. They include stabs to the cerebral skull (temporal squama and orbital) with direct damage to the brain or intracranial bleeding.

Homicide, Suicide, and Accident

Fatal sharp-force injuries are mainly found in homicides. In the literature, the relation of homicides versus suicides ranges between 4:1 and 5:2. As stated above, accidents with a lethal outcome are very rare. Several cases of fatal bleeding due to incision of major vessels, for example, by architectural glass, have been reported, and—despite its rarity—a "break, enter, and die syndrome" has been termed for such fatalities occurring during illegal break-ins. Thorough information about the situation at the scene is therefore indispensable to elucidate the course of an accident.

Various criteria have been tested for their significance and sensitivity as to diagnosing a homicide by sharp force and differentiating it from a suicidal act. Although the sensitivity of discriminating morphological criteria is not very high, some of them are satisfactorily specific. These are tentative or hesitation injuries in suicides and defense injuries in homicides. Tentative or hesitation injuries are mostly shallow cuts or minute stab wounds, which do not necessarily completely perforate the skin and can often be found adjacent to perforating injuries (**Figure 10**). Baring the injured area prior to cutting or stabbing suggests a suicidal act. It is important to realize that the reverse conclusion is not valid. As an example, less than half of the victims injured or killed by sharp force show defense injuries. So, the absence of defense injuries by no means excludes a homicidal act or an assault.

Relevant information can be derived from the pattern of injuries found on a victim's body. In suicides, injuries tend to be grouped in circumscribed body regions. They are preferably located in anatomical regions suggesting a fatal outcome. These include the precordial region; the epigastric angle where the apex beat—the cardiac impulse—can be felt; and regions where the pulse may be palpated, especially the wrists (radial artery) and neck (carotid artery), and also the cubital region (brachial artery), the hollow knee (popliteal artery), near the ankle joint (posterior tibial artery), and even the temporal region (temporal artery—**Figure 11**). Injuries to the trunk are predominantly localized on the front of the body. The suicide's handedness and the accessibility or reachability of the injured areas also have to be taken into account: thus right-handers tend to inflict wrist cuts predominantly on their left arm. If the suicide retains the ability to act for some time, the victim may be able to clean or remove the object used.

Some additional criteria are considered to be predictive of either homicide or suicide: bone and/or cartilage wounds are more frequently seen in homicides than in suicides; the longitudinal axes of stab wounds to the chest tend to be horizontal in suicides resulting from the blade being inserted through an intercostal space; and multiple sharp-force damage to the clothing corresponding to the victim's injuries is more often seen in homicides, whereas the large majority of suicides bares the target region before cutting or stabbing. However, suicides stabbing the precordial region without baring their chests are no unusual finding; in these cases, associations with psychiatric disorders or acute intoxication with alcohol or drugs of abuse has been stated.

Another feature that is rarely mentioned is the observation of suicides showing extensive blood traces on their palms, which is usually not the case in victims of homicides unless they sustained defense injuries on their hands.

Last but not least, the findings at the scene and—if present—biological trace evidence have to be considered. Although there are some criteria helping to correctly diagnose a homicide, suicide, or accident, the decision has to be made for each individual case considering as much information as possible.

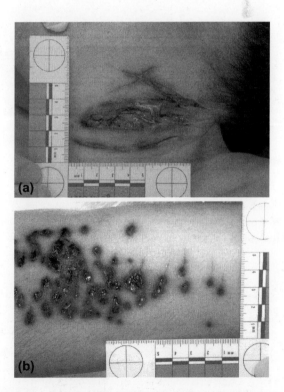

Figure 10 "Tentative" cuts and stabs in suicides. (a) Superficial cuts on the left side of a 53-year-old woman's neck, who used a scalpel to kill herself. Cause of death was exsanguination due to subtotal transection of the right internal jugular vein. (b) Multiple superficial stabs without any injury of great blood vessels in the left cubital region of a 39-year-old man.

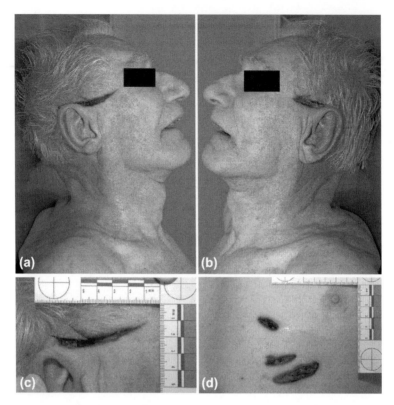

Figure 11   Suicide of an 86-year-old man by stabs to the chest. (a–c) Cuts in the left and right temporal regions. (d) Three stab wounds on the left side of the thorax with associated tentative injuries. Cause of death was a penetrating injury to the heart with pericardial tamponade and injury of the left lung with hematothorax.

Capability of Acting

For the reconstruction of an event, it is often necessary to assess whether the victim was still able to act after sustaining a stab or cut wound. In this respect, the capability of performing complex and targeted actions requiring full consciousness has to be distinguished from instinctive actions such as flight or defense reflexes. The decisive criterion of incapacitation is usually the onset of unconsciousness.

Immediate incapacitation after sustaining a stab or cut wound is relatively rare. This has been reported after injuries to the brainstem, for example, by a stab to the nape or through the posterior wall of the pharynx, after severance of both carotid arteries or after (almost complete) transection of the thoracic aorta with a sudden, significant fall in blood pressure. Lesions of the cerebrum or cerebellum by a penetrating pointed object need not necessarily lead to incapacitation. Essential factors for the rapid onset of unconsciousness are not only the size and anatomical localization of the affected brain area, but also whether major vessels are involved (especially the arteria cerebri media in stabs to the temporal region) associated with

intracranial bleeding and possible blunt traumatization of the skull.

After stabs and cuts to the cervical region, it is by no means impossible that the capability of acting is retained for several minutes. This depends on whether the relatively well-protected major arteries and veins of the neck are affected at all, whether the vessel has been completely severed and whether the blood can freely escape from the injured vessel. After suicidal cuts to the neck, considerable damage to the larynx and trachea but only minor vascular damage is quite often observed, which can also result in a prolonged ability to act. In some cases, the unsuccessful attempt to commit suicide by cuts to the neck may prompt the individual to inflict injuries to other body regions or to apply a second suicide method (e.g., jump from a height; complex suicide).

Even stabs to the heart are usually not associated with immediate incapacitation. Especially with short lesions of the left ventricle, the ability to act is often retained for several minutes. After 2- to 3-mm-long perforations of the endocardium, the ability to act was reported to continue for several hours due to slow loss of blood. Occasionally, histomorphological signs of wound healing such as deposition of fibrin and granulocytic infiltration along the track of the stab injury can be demonstrated.

Pulmonary or abdominal injuries normally do not result in immediate incapacitation.

See also: **Forensic Medicine/Causes of Death:** Blunt Injury; Systemic Response to Trauma; **Forensic Medicine/Clinical:** Defense Wounds; Self-Inflicted Injury; Suicide.

Further Reading

Bohnert, M., Hüttemann, H., Schmidt, U., 2006. Homicides by sharp force. In: Tsokos, M. (Ed.), Forensic Pathology Reviews, vol. 4. Humana Press, Totowa, NJ, pp. 65–89.

Buris, L., 1993. Forensic Medicine. Springer, Budapest, pp. 55–64.

Eisenmenger, W., 2004. Spitze, scharfe und halbscharfe Gewalt. In: Brinkmann, B., Madea, B. (Eds.), Handbuch gerichtliche Medizin. Springer, Berlin, Heidelberg, New York, pp. 571–591 (in German).

Gilchrist, M.D., Keenan, S., Curtis, M., Cassidy, M., Byrne, G., Destrade, M., 2008. Measuring knife stab penetration into skin simulant using a novel biaxial tension device. Forensic Science International 177, 52–65.

Jansen, E., Buster, M.C., Zuur, A.L., Das, C., 2009. Fatality of suicide attempts in Amsterdam 1996–2005. Crisis 30, 180–185.

Karger, B., Niemeyer, J., Brinkmann, B., 1999. Physical activity following fatal injury from sharp pointed weapons. International Journal of Legal Medicine 112, 188–191.

Lew, E., Matshes, E., 2005. Sharp force injuries. In: Dolniak, D., Matshes, E.W., Lew, E.O. (Eds.), Forensic Pathology – Principles and Practice. Elsevier Academic Press, Oxford, pp. 143–162.

Payne-James, J., Vanezis, P., 2005. Sharp and cutting-edge wounds. In: Byard, R.W., Corey, T.S., Henderson, C. (Eds.), Encyclopedia of Forensic and Legal Medicine, vol. 3. Elsevier Academic Press, Oxford, pp. 119–129.

Pollak, S., Saukko, P.J., 2003. Atlas of Forensic Medicine. CD-ROM. Chapter 6 (Sharp Trauma). Elsevier CD-ROM, Amsterdam.

Pollak, S., Saukko, P.J., 2008. Wounds, sharp injury. In: Jamieson, A., Moenssens, A. (Eds.), Wiley Encyclopedia of Forensic Science. John Wiley & Sons Ltd., Chichester, pp. 2646–2660.

Prokop, O., 1975. Einwirkung von scharfer Gewalt. In: Prokop, O., Göhler, W. (Eds.), Forensische Medizin, third ed. VEB Volk & Gesundheit, Berlin, pp. 166–179 (in German).

Schmidt, U., 2010. Sharp force injuries in 'clinical' forensic medicine. Forensic Science International 195, 1–5.

Spitz, W.U., 2006. Sharp force injury. In: Spitz, W.U. (Ed.), Spitz and Fisher's Medicolegal Investigation of Death, fourth ed. Thomas, Springfield, IL, pp. 252–309.

Vanezis, P., 2003. Sharp force trauma. In: Payne-James, J., Busuttil, A., Smock, W. (Eds.), Forensic Medicine: Clinical and Pathological Aspects. Greenwich Medical Media, London, pp. 307–319.

Gunshot Wounds

S Pollak, University of Freiburg, Freiburg, Germany
P Saukko, University of Turku, Turku, Finland

Parts of this chapter were published in the form of a book chapter in Wiley *Encyclopedia of Forensic Science* (A. Jamieson and A. Moenssens (Eds.)), volume 3, pp. 1380–1401, 2009. Reuse was kindly permitted by John Wiley & Sons Ltd.

Glossary

Bullet embolism Weak bullets or pellets may enter a blood vessel on one side without being able to perforate the opposite side so that they remain inside the vessel where they are transported along arteries or veins until they lodge in a more distal part of the systemic or pulmonary circulation (in body parts away from the wound channel).
Kinetic energy The kinetic energy of a moving object is equal to the mass multiplied by the square of the speed, multiplied by the constant 1/2. In SI units, the kinetic energy is measured in joules.
Simulant In the context of wound ballistics, simulants are materials that react to bullets in a manner similar to homogenous tissue as regards density, elasticity, capacity to absorb energy, etc. Therefore, they are suited for reproducible wound ballistic experiments. The most common simulants of soft tissues are gelatine and glycerine soap.

Introduction

Firearm injuries are regarded as a special form of blunt trauma. The damage to the organism is caused by the impact of a single projectile (or a multitude of pellets) propelled from a barrel by high-pressure combustion gases and striking the body at a high velocity. Gunshot wounds, in a broader sense, are also lesions caused by blank-cartridge weapons as well as injuries due to livestock stunners, stud guns used in the construction industry, and similar devices.

Wound Ballistics

Exterior ballistics deals with the behavior of the projectile after leaving the barrel (trajectory, velocity, etc.), while terminal ballistics covers the interaction between the projectile and the target. If the target is a human or animal body, one speaks of wound ballistics.

Fundamentals of the Wounding Capacity

The wounding capacity of a projectile is partly due to the direct destruction of anatomical structures along the bullet track by crushing, punching, and tearing. Another type of lesion is caused by changes in the pressure and displacement of tissue (with stretching and shearing) around the permanent wound channel. The extent of mechanical damage depends on the amount of kinetic energy (Ek) released in the tissue.

When a projectile penetrates the tissue, it is displaced laterally (radially)—that is, at right angles to the bullet path—thus forming a temporary wound cavity, whose diameter can be considerably larger than the bullet. The radially displaced tissue then moves back in the opposite direction toward the geometric bullet path.

The process just described is especially marked with high-energy projectiles, such as those fired from military and hunting rifles. In fluid-filled organs (e.g., heart, urinary bladder) or in the skull, the radial expansion may lead to a hydrodynamic effect with bursting of the encasing structures. Cases in which the brain is completely flung out of the cranial cavity are referred to as exenteration shots. Even a shot with a smaller transfer of Ek may cause indirect lesions away from the wound track, for example, skull fractures, cerebral contusions, and stretch mark-like tears of the facial skin.

The "permanent" wound channel represents the destructive passage of the bullet itself. The path is filled with blood and is surrounded by a more or less wide zone in which the tissue was temporarily stretched, thus suffering structural damage ("zone of extravasation").

By firing test shots at "simulants" such as gelatin or glycerin soap, the transfer of Ek in biological soft tissue can be visualized, as the density of these materials is similar to that of muscle. In contrast to elastic gelatin, soap shows an almost plastic deformation. The bullet path and the volume of the cavitation remaining after the firing of the shot are proportionate to the energy transferred.

A stable bullet with a low deformation potential (full-jacketed projectile, as used in military ammunition) produces a "narrow channel" in the simulant at first, which then opens into the larger temporary cavity as the projectile moves in a sideways position (when tumbling) and imparts more energy to the surrounding tissue. An expanding deformation of the projectile also increases the effect of the radial displacement and thus the volume of cavitation. In deformation projectiles (e.g., semi-jacketed hollow-point bullets as used in civilian hunting ammunition), the cavity starts forming immediately after penetration. A fragmentation of the projectile results in a multitude of wound tracks.

When projectiles of identical design, head configuration, and mass are fired, the transfer of energy in a dense medium and thus the extent of the temporary cavity essentially depend on the velocity of the bullet.

Wound Track

In gunshot injuries, the bullet may remain lodged in the body, or perforate it completely (through-and-through shot), or hit only the surface tangentially (graze wounds). In the first-mentioned type of gunshot wound, there is an entrance, but no exit wound. Rather often, projectiles traveling at a low velocity remain lodged under the tough and resilient skin on the side of the body opposite to the entrance wound, where their final position can be recognized by a hematoma and/or a palpable resistance. A radiological examination is advisable in any case to determine and document the localization of bullets and bullet fragments retained in the body.

For the determination of the angle of fire (in relation to the horizontal, sagittal, and frontal planes of the body), it is imperative that the length of the wound track and the localization of the entry and exit wounds or, in shots with the projectile retained inside the body, the final position (height from the plantar plane and the lateral distance from the median plane) of the bullet are exactly measured and recorded.

In most cases, the wound track in the body is linear. A full-jacketed rifle bullet, however, may produce a curved bullet path if its length in the body is longer than 20–30 cm. The deviation from the straight line begins when the projectile first moves into a lateral position, that is, in the region of the first cavitation, as the pressure gradient along the projectile becomes asymmetrical, thus creating a force component lateral to the direction of the movement.

Nonlinear bullet paths are often caused by internal ricochet. Inside the cranial cavity, such ricochets are seen in 10–25% of the cases and occur if the projectile is deflected from the internal table of the skull with a low residual energy. Bullets either ricochet back into the brain at an acute angle or pass along the inner surface of the skull producing a curved wound track in the underlying brain.

The latter type of ricochet occurs not only on the concave side of the cranium but also on other inner surfaces (e.g., ribs)

if a concave boundary surface continuously changes the direction of the bullet.

In a perforating shot, the projectile produces an exit wound as it leaves the body. Bullets with a low residual energy are sometimes no longer capable of perforating the clothing covering the exit wound. After having passed through one part of the body (e.g., the upper arm), the bullet may reenter another part (e.g., the thorax; **Figure 1**).

Graze shots produce groove-like lesions on the body surface, occasionally accompanied by short tears along the wound edges. If a projectile strikes the body with low residual energy, but does not penetrate, the affected skin may show an excoriation and/or a hematoma.

Intermediate Targets, Deflection of the Projectile

For the interpretation of a gunshot wound, it may be essential to know if the projectile struck the human body primarily or if it interacted with an intermediate object. For example, if the bullet first passes through an intermediate target, such as a door, the typical "ring of dirt" on the site where it entered the clothing or the body is missing, because the grayish-black depositions adhering to the bullet surface were already wiped off at the primary target.

When a bullet passes through the dense medium of an intermediate target, it loses its gyroscopic stability, resulting in a rotation around a lateral axis. If such a bullet then hits the body in an oblique or sideways position, the entrance wound is elongated and there is a higher loss of energy in the initial section of the wound track. Analogous effects may be seen when the bullet was already deformed at the primary target.

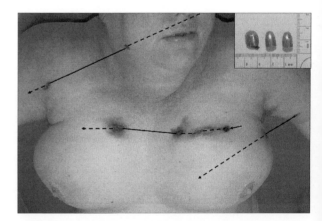

Figure 1 Forty-three-year-old homicide victim killed by three gunshots. The shots were fired from a 7.65-mm caliber pistol. Each of the bullets entered more than one body part (reentry shots). The full-jacketed bullets recovered at autopsy are shown in the right upper corner.

If a projectile is deflected by an intermediary target instead of penetrating it, one speaks of a ricochet. A change of direction may happen, for example, if the bullet strikes stone, concrete, or asphalt. In such cases, the bullet often shows a flattened, mirror-like surface. The deformation and/or fragmentation of the ricochet bullet may cause an atypical entrance wound with no, or an incomplete ring of dirt. Owing to the loss of velocity and the instability of the ricocheting projectile, its depth of penetration is less than in primary hits after an undisturbed trajectory.

Lethal Gunshot Injuries

According to statistical investigations, about 20% of gunshot injuries are primarily lethal, that is, the victims die before receiving medical care.

Generally, fatal consequences of a gunshot wound have also to be expected if weapons are used, which lay people would not consider very dangerous (e.g., air guns, blank-cartridge weapons, and 0.22 caliber rimfire rifles). For example, bullets fired from conventional air guns (with a common barrel diameter of 0.22 or 0.177 in, that is, 5.6 and 4.5 mm, respectively) may perforate the thin temporal squama or penetrate into the cranium via the orbital cavity. The gas jet of blank-cartridge guns has repeatedly caused penetrating skin lesions, bone fractures, and lethal injuries of vessels or organs, when fired from a very short distance. Of course, projectiles with a low energy fired from 0.22 caliber rimfire weapons may also produce fatal injuries if major organs or great vessels are hit along the bullet track.

In gunshot injuries with a fatal outcome, the direct lethal effect may be due to various causes. A special case is the gunshot-related "exenteration" of the brain from the skull. When the shot strikes the nape of the neck or the occipital region, it may directly destroy vital centers of the brain stem. More often, it is not the cerebral lesion as such, but the subsequent increase in the intracranial pressure (due to intracerebral, subarachnoidal, and subdural bleeding, sometimes associated with cerebral edema) that is responsible for the lethal outcome.

Gunshot fractures of the bony skull base are often followed by a hemorrhage into the nasopharynx; if the victim is unconscious, fatal aspiration of blood will result. Gunshot-related lacerations of the venous sinuses may act as entrance sites for air bubbles, possibly leading to death from venous air embolism.

Injuries to the heart, great vessels, or parenchymatous organs cause massive internal bleeding with consecutive hemorrhagic shock. Gunshots to the lung with traumatic pneumothorax are an acute threat because of the impaired respiration—especially if both sides are involved. Inflammatory complications are potential causes of delayed death.

Ability to Act

It is often wrongly believed that a gunshot to the head or the trunk always incapacitates the victim immediately. This opinion is disproved by a multitude of well-documented cases in which gunshot victims performed surprisingly differentiated actions even after severe traumatization of vital organs.

If a victim becomes unable to act, this is usually due to functional impairment of the central nervous system caused either directly by tissue lesions or indirectly by insufficient oxygen supply. Immediate incapacitation is to be expected if the bullet destroyed parts of the brain essential for physical activity—with exenteration of the entire organ in extreme cases. Targets of immediate incapacitation are the upper cervical spinal cord, the brain stem, the cerebellum, the basal ganglia, the motor areas of the cerebral cortex, and the large motor nerve tracts. The bullet need not necessarily pass through these cerebral regions directly, as the gunshot-related pressure and shearing forces can also damage nerve structures and impair functions away from the bullet path.

Cerebral hypoxia with consecutive unconsciousness following gunshots to the chest is mostly due to massive loss of blood. However, even if the bullet strikes the heart, the aorta, or other large arteries, blood circulation will hardly cease immediately, and even then the oxygen reserves left in the brain may be sufficient for simple and short actions. Consequently, rapid, but not immediate, incapacitation is to be expected after gunshot injuries of the heart, the aorta, and the pulmonary artery. On the other hand, victims will go down immediately if struck in the spinal cord.

The pathophysiological considerations just described have significant implications for the assessment of suicides in which several shots were fired. Continued ability to act after a cerebral gunshot injury is observed especially if low-energy ammunition was used and/or the bullet track did not involve the abovementioned structures of immediate incapacitation (upper cerebral spinal cord, brain stem, motor cortex areas, and large motor pathways). In most suicides with more than one shot to the head, only the frontal lobe(s) or one of the temporal lobes of the brain is involved. Multiple gunshots to the cardiac region are seen more often than multiple suicidal shots to the cerebral cranium.

Stopping Power

The term "stopping power" is used to characterize the potential biological effect of a projectile, in particular, its capacity to prevent a person from moving or attacking. Actually, the idea conveyed by movies and TV films that the impact of a bullet stops or even knocks down the affected person is not true in real situations. Bullets do not have the potential to throw people off their feet. Otherwise, the person who shoots the gun would be knocked over, as action and reaction are equal and opposite.

In fact, the effectiveness of the projectile depends on the amount of energy transferred to the body, leading to local displacement and destruction of tissue. In this context, the shape of the bullet is essential for its effectiveness: If the bullet head is blunt, deceleration and energy transfer are larger.

However, in real cases, the effect of a bullet not only results from its effectiveness but also to a large extent from the point of impact, that is, from the affected region and the relevant anatomical structures.

Embolism of Projectiles

The rarely seen transport of bullets or shot pellets within the vascular system is called embolization. Most of the embolized projectiles are of smaller caliber and low velocity, which is sufficient only to penetrate the artery or vein, but not to exit the vessel again, so that the foreign body, which is now localized inside the vessel, may be moved to a region of the body away from the bullet path, where it can be easily visualized by radiography.

Bullet and pellet embolization is mostly seen in the arterial system (entry via the heart or the aorta and transport, e.g., to the leg arteries). In rare cases, a projectile may enter a vein and travel from there to the (right) ventricle or to the branches of the pulmonary artery.

Delayed Effects

In survived gunshot injuries with retained bullets or pellets, the question arises as to whether this may cause chronic lead poisoning. Generally, the risk is assessed as being very low. Most cases reported in the literature refer to patients with projectiles lodged in the joints or bones. The latency period until an intoxication becomes manifest ranges from a few months to several decades.

Criminalistic Aspects

The purpose of clinical examination or autopsy of persons with gunshot injuries is to answer the following questions:

- Do the findings confirm the assumption of a gunshot injury?
- Number of hits?
- Did a striking projectile pass through the body or is it lodged in the body or did it produce a graze wound?
- What was the direction and angle of fire (trajectory)?
- Are there any clues as to the type of weapon and ammunition used?
- From what distance was the shot fired (contact shot, close-range shot, distant shot)?
- Do the wound characteristics in connection with the traces at the scene suggest self-infliction or involvement of another party?
- Did the gunshot injury result in immediate incapacitation?

Entrance and Exit Wounds

In order to determine the direction of fire, it is imperative that entrance and exit wounds are interpreted correctly.

Characteristics of Entrance Wounds

Typical features of an entrance wound in the skin include the following:

- punched-out hole (i.e., a central tissue substance defect that cannot be closed by approximation of its edges);
- marginal zone without epidermis (abrasion ring); and
- grayish-black ring of dirt (provided that the projectile did not pass through another target first).

When the shot was fired either with the muzzle in contact or at close/intermediate range, the respective signs can be regarded as further evidence of a bullet entry wound (**Figure 2(a)**).

Entrance Hole

The central entrance defect is roundish (if the projectile strikes at a right angle, **Figure 2(d)**) or oval (if it strikes at an oblique angle, **Figure 2(e)**). The diameter is usually smaller than that of the bullet.

The discrepancy between the caliber of the projectile and the diameter of the permanent entrance hole can be explained by the elastic behavior of the skin: On impact of the bullet head, the edges of the defect temporarily move centrifugally due to the radial forces causing a reversible widening of the bullet entrance hole. When the deformation forces cease, the elastic skin resumes its former shape so that the permanent entrance defect may be much smaller than the diameter of the bullet (this discrepancy is particularly marked on the palms of the hands and soles of the feet). The size of the skin wound, therefore, does not allow one to draw accurate conclusions as to the caliber of the projectile.

The reason for the skin defect remaining at the entrance site is essentially that the projectile transports tissue particles into the depth of the wound track. Moreover, at the moment of impact, small skin particles are flung back against the direction of fire.

Abrasion Collar (Abrasion Ring/Margin/Rim)

The central entrance hole is usually surrounded by a circumferential loss of epidermis (and its natural pigmentation), forming a moist, reddish margin when fresh and later assuming a brownish color due to the drying of the unprotected corium (**Figure 2(c) and (e)**).

With the help of high-speed photography, Sellier was able to prove already in 1967 that the epidermis-free margin of the entrance wound is not caused by any major indenting with consecutive overstretching and local friction. When the bullet head strikes the skin, backspatter of marginal tissue particles is induced by the pressure exerted on the entrance site. The former idea that the bullet head indents the skin before penetration, thus causing marginal abrasion, is not correct. It also does not result from the bullet being hot nor from its rotating movement.

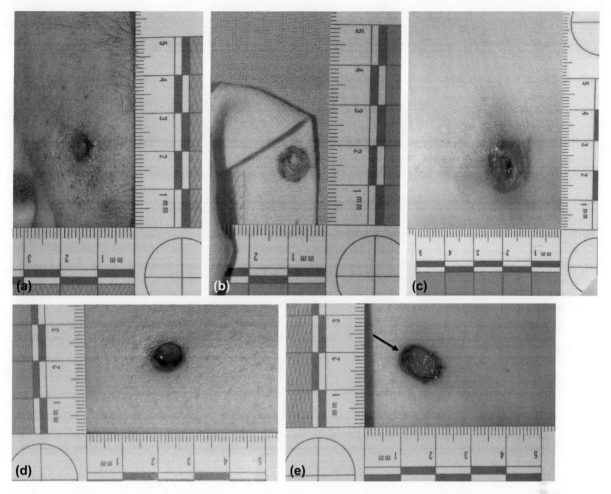

Figure 2 Bullet entrance sites. (a) Entry wound caused by a 0.22-LR projectile in front of the right ear showing a central tissue defect with a black ring of dirt covering the underlying abrasion collar. On the surrounding skin a zone of faint soot soiling and stippling can be seen (close-range shot). (b) Bullet hole in the uppermost layer of the clothing with a pronounced bullet wipe-off. (c) Bullet entrance wound in the chest (originally covered by clothing) with a wide abrasion ring but without a ring of dirt (round nose bullet, caliber 7.65 mm). (d) Entrance wound with punched-out skin defect and a remarkably narrow abrasion ring (9 × 19 mm police deployment cartridge QD PEP). (e) Angled shot (direction indicated by arrow).

In the peripheral parts of the abrasion collar, the epidermis is often torn and detached like wallpaper, so that parching can progress beyond the epidermis-free zone after prolonged exposure to air. When the bullet strikes at an oblique angle, the abrasion ring is elliptic and eccentric, being wider on the side from which the shot was fired. A unilateral widening of the abrasion collar thus gives an indication of the direction in which the bullet was traveling.

If the skin of the entrance region is under water, no abrasion ring is formed. The same is true for shots to the palms and soles. Entrance wounds from high-velocity centerfire rifles may lack a typical abrasion collar but show small splits radiating from the edges (the so-called microtears).

Bullet Wipe-Off ("Ring of Dirt," "Grease Ring")

The criminalistic importance of the bullet wipe is due to the fact that—at least on the primary target—this finding is a reliable sign of a bullet entrance.

The term bullet wipe refers to the mechanism of formation: when the projectile hits a skin region not covered by clothing, sooty remnants and other residues deposited on the bullet's head are transferred to the wound margin, so that a grayish-blackish ring (partly) overlies the abrasion collar (**Figure 2(a)**). More often, this ring of dirt is seen on the uppermost textile layer (**Figure 2(b)**), but not (or only vaguely) on the margin of the entrance wound. In oblique gunshots, the bullet wipe is eccentrically enlarged on the side from which the shot was fired. The bullet wipe is not a sign of a close-range or a contact shot, as it also occurs in distant shots.

Exit Wounds

The exit wound presents as a slit-like or stellate severance of tissue (**Figure 3**). In typical cases, there is—in contrast to the entry wound—no real hole, that is, no tissue defect. This means that the wound usually can be closed by bringing the edges into apposition. An exit wound produced by a bullet passing sideways through the skin may be slit-like and, therefore, mistaken for a stab wound.

Often, though not always, the size of the exit wound is larger than that of the entry wound. In practice, the uncritical application of this unreliable "rule" often leads to misinterpretations. Thus, contact shots fired to the head may show stellate entrance wounds with long radial tears; in such cases, the exit wound may be much smaller (**Figure 4**). In cases of splinter injuries (e.g., by fragments of explosive weapons), the entry wound is always larger than the corresponding exit. The differentiation between entrance and exit should never be made on the basis of simply comparing the wound dimensions.

The size of the exit wound mainly depends on the diameter of the temporary cavity at the site where the bullet leaves the body. In some cases, bone splinters carried along may also contribute to a larger exit hole. Many projectiles leave the body deformed and/or tumbling, which may also influence the shape of the exit wound.

It goes without saying that exit wounds cannot have a bullet wipe. Occasionally, the margins of the exit wound are abraded (shored) when a firm object (e.g., tight-fitting clothes, floor, wall, or back of a chair) is pressed against the body at the site of the exiting projectile (**Figure 3(c)**). Under such circumstances, the skin around the exit is abraded by the supporting surface. In contrast to the "original" abrasion ring around the entry wound, in "shored" or "supported" exits, the area of abrasion is not concentric, but irregular or lopsided and often disproportionately large.

Classification of Entrance Wounds in Relation to the Range from Muzzle to Target

To understand the different features of gunshot entry wounds, it is necessary to be familiar with the major processes occurring when a firearm is discharged. As the trigger is pulled, the firing pin is released and strikes the primer in the base of the cartridge case. The detonating primer ignites the propellant. The subsequent burning (deflagration) of the gunpowder generates a large amount of expanding gas, which is under high pressure

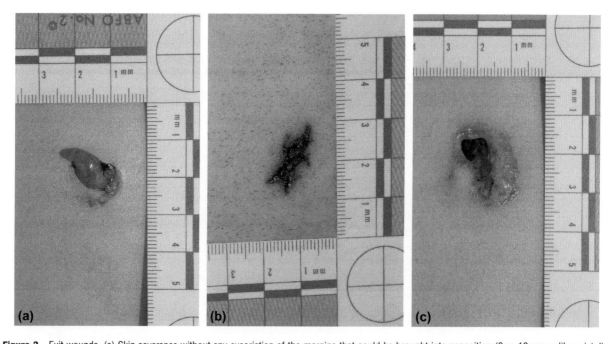

Figure 3   Exit wounds. (a) Skin severance without any excoriation of the margins that could be brought into apposition (9 × 19 mm caliber pistol). (b) Stellate exit wound of the cheek (caliber .30-06 hunting rifle). (c) Shared exit wound on the back (9 × 19 mm caliber pistol). At the moment of discharge, the exit region was in contact with the ground.

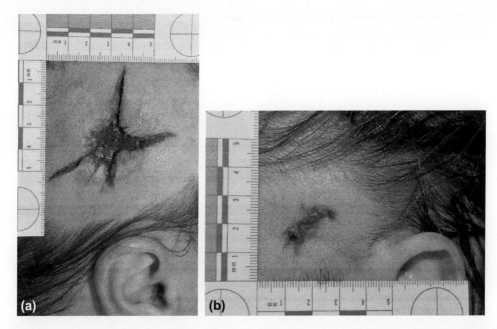

Figure 4 (a) Suicidal contact shot to the right temple with a caliber 9 × 19 mm pistol. The entrance wound shows a central defect and radial lacerations of different length. (b) Irregularly shaped exit wound close to the left ear. The maximum diameter of the exit wound is smaller than the larger splits at the entry site.

and propels the projectile down the barrel. The gas is composed of carbon monoxide, carbon dioxide, oxides of nitrogen, and other compounds. A small percentage of the powder grains remains unburned or only partly burned.

Already before the projectile leaves the barrel, a cloud of gunsmoke exits the muzzle. The term gunsmoke refers to the grayish-black combustion products of the powder that has not fully converted to gases. Essentially, gunsmoke consists of carbon in the form of soot.

Apart from the combustion gases and the finely dispersed soot, there are always unburned and partly burned powder grains expelled along with the projectile. The cloud of powder soot rapidly decelerates so that smoke soiling is to be expected only relatively close to the muzzle. The larger powder grains (having a diameter of at least several tenths of a millimeter) can also reach more distant targets.

The diameter of the spread and the density of soot and/or powder particles on a target are not only dependent on the range of fire but also on the cartridge type and the weapon (length of the barrel). Consequently, the range of discharge can only be evaluated by firing test shots with the respective weapon and ammunition.

In handguns, macroscopically visible traces of gunsmoke are to be expected up to a range of several centimeters. Depending on the weapon and ammunition, gunpowder grains may reach targets several decimeters away (in rifles also more than 1 m). The use of silencers strongly reduces the deposition of soot and powder particles, thus creating the false impression of a larger range of fire.

When a gun is discharged, two different light phenomena can be observed: first, the flame—a short, mostly dark red jet of fire caused by the not yet completely finished combustion of the powder particles; second, the muzzle flash—a glaring fire ball some distance away from the barrel end caused by the reaction of the incompletely oxidized combustion gases with the oxygen in the air.

With nitro powder, the extremely short impact of the muzzle flame is usually not sufficient to cause substantial burns on the clothing or skin. Sometimes, frizzing may be seen on the hair near the entry wound. Thermal damage is possible in shots with nitro ammunition fired from a very short distance (near contact), if textiles made of thermolabile synthetic fibers melt on the underlying skin. If black powder ammunition is used, close-range shots may cause impressively large burns.

In forensic medicine, three ranges of fire are distinguished according to morphological criteria:

- contact range;
- short/close and medium/intermediate range;
- long/distant range.

Contact Shots

The term "contact shot" means that the muzzle was held against the body surface at the time of discharge. In contact shots, soot-containing combustion gases are propelled into the depth of the entry wound. They expand beneath the skin and blacken the initial section of the wound track (pocket-like undermining, "powder cavity" containing soot and gunpowder particles). As the combustion gases have a high content of carbon monoxide (up to 50%), the surrounding tissue often assumes a bright cherry-red color (cf. **Figure 7(b)**). In tight (hard) contact shots, nearly all the combustion products enter the wound (**Figure 5**), whereas in loose, angled, or incomplete contacts, some soot may escape between the

muzzle and skin so that the adjacent surface is blackened (**Figures 6 and 7**).

The entrance region is bloated by the inrushing powder gases and balloons backward against the muzzle end of the weapon, which is imprinted on the skin causing a "muzzle abrasion" ("barrel marking," "muzzle contusion"). Mechanically, the muzzle imprint is mostly a patterned pressure abrasion with a tendency toward parching after exposure to air or—less frequently—an intradermal bruise (**Figure 5(a)**). Apart from the barrel end (or its contours), other

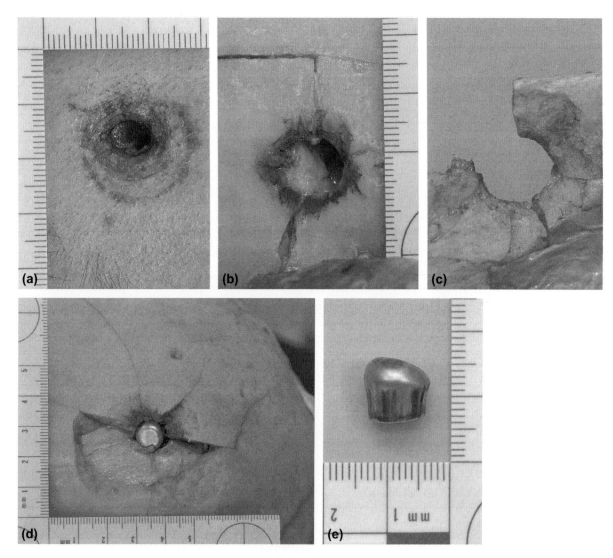

Figure 5   Hard-contact gunshot wound to the right temple (caliber 9 × 19 mm pistol). (a) Imprint mark mirroring the muzzle end of the weapon. (b) Entrance hole in the underlying skull surrounded by intense blackening from powder soot. (c) Inner surface of the skull showing a cone-shaped widening of the hole. (d) Final position of the flattened projectile (e) on the left side of the skullcap.

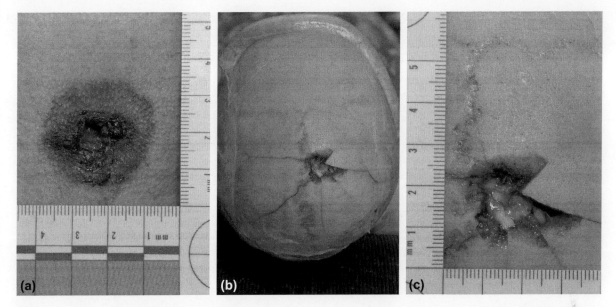

Figure 6 Suicide by a loose-contact shot to the submental region (caliber 9 × 19 mm pistol). (a) The entrance hole is surrounded by a concentric zone of intense powder soot blackening. (b) Exit site in the parietal region showing "outward bevelling" of the bone defect and radial fractures extending from the gunshot hole. (c) Close-up view of the exit in bone.

constructional parts situated near the muzzle, such as the front sight and/or the recoil spring guide may also be imprinted.

The muzzle contusion allows one to draw significant conclusions:

- The weapon was in contact with the skin at the instant of discharge.
- The configuration of the imprint mark corresponds with the constructional elements being in line with the muzzle or just behind. Therefore, the imprint mark can characterize the type of weapon used (e.g., revolver or pistol) or even a specific make or model.
- The imprint configuration may provide information as to the way in which the weapon was held at the moment of discharge. For example, an imprint of the front sight below the bullet entrance means that the weapon had been held upside down (i.e., with the handle pointing upward).

If the entrance wound is above a bony support (e.g., in the frontal and temporal regions), the subcutaneous expansion of the penetrating combustion gases may cause radial skin tears due to overstretching, resulting in a stellate wound of entrance (cf. **Figure 4**). This additional sign of a contact shot is facultative: Shots fired with low-energy ammunition such as 0.22 LR or 6.35 mm do not necessarily cause stellate lacerations even at sites having a bony support. Away from the entrance wound, stretch mark-like tears of the facial skin may occur, especially in shots to the forehead and the submental region.

Close- and Intermediate-Range Shots

In close-/intermediate-range shots, GSR (gunshot residues: soot and/or powder particles) are deposited around the entry wound. Usually, a distinction is made between close-range shots and medium (intermediate)-range shots.

Close-range shots are defined by the presence of a zone of powder soot soiling surrounding the bullet entrance (often associated with additional powder tattooing; **Figures 2(a) and 8**). The grayish-black soot leads to skin or textile discoloration of a cloudy structure, whose intensity decreases with growing firing distance. Shots fired at an oblique angle result in an asymmetrical soot pattern with unilateral extension on the side of the shooter or away from it (depending on the angle at which the shot was fired and the range of fire). Interfering objects, such as clothing or body parts (hand), may partially filter out the gunsmoke. Flash suppressors, which are often used in military rifles, have lateral smoke outlets, which may produce a flower-like pattern of soot with several radial petals corresponding to the number of slits. In revolvers, there is a gap between the cylinder and the barrel, which allows the combustion gases to emerge sideward. The soot and the powder grains escaping from the gap may produce a characteristic linear or L-shaped mark if the skin or a fabric is in close proximity at the time of discharge.

The term medium-range shot is used if no zone of powder soot blackening is discernible around the entry wound any

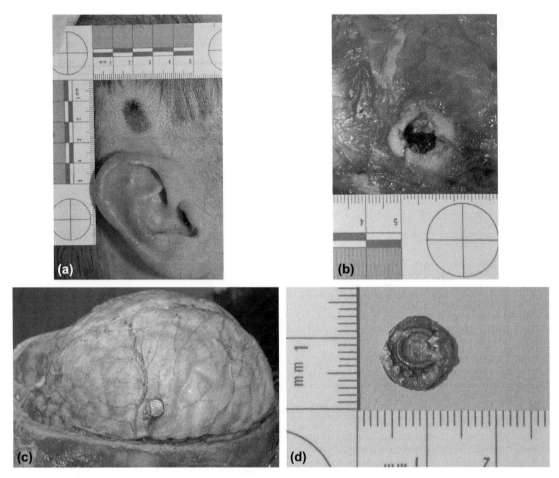

Figure 7 Angled contact shot to the right temple, 0.22-caliber rimfire rifle, suicide. (a) Entrance wound with eccentric soot blackening of the margins. (b) Entrance hole in skull surrounded by faint soot staining. The muscle tissue adhering to the bone has a cherry-red color due to the formation of carboxyhemoglobin and -myoglobin. (c) Left side of the cranial vault after removal of the skullcap; the mushroomed lead bullet (d) was lodged between dura and bone.

more, but there are unburned or partially burned gunpowder grains deposited on, or forced into, the skin or clothing. The penetrating capacity of the powder grains depends on the propellant (flake or ball powder, grain size), the weapon, the range of fire, and the surface properties of the target. At short shooting distances, grains may be driven through thin textiles and cause stippling on the underlying skin.

On the skin, the powder particles cause either superficial epidermal lesions (with subsequent drying) or—if deposited beneath the epithelium—petechial dermal hemorrhages. According to some authors, the term tattooing should be used to describe forceful in-driving, whereas the term stippling means the mere presence of impact markings.

The distribution pattern of powder tattooing/stippling varies according to the angle of fire: only perpendicular shots produce a radially symmetrical picture; in most other cases, the

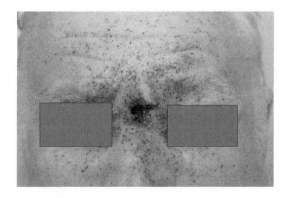

Figure 8 Homicidal close-range shot with a black powder gun (caliber 0.44 muzzle loading percussion pistol) showing soot soiling, pronounced stippling, and singeing of the eyebrows.

affected skin area is elliptic in shape. The entry wound may be localized outside the tattooing if the powder grains were partly filtered out by clothing or other primary targets. Pseudo-tattoo marks can be due to the fragments of an intermediate target, such as the window of a car. In such cases, fragments of glass may produce irregular stippling lesions on the person seated behind the perforated window.

Distant-Range Shots

In forensic usage, the term distant shot means that the weapon was discharged from such a distance that no soot and no powder grains could reach the body surface (skin or clothing in covered body regions). The minimum range for this type of gunshot wounds varies not only depending on the weapon and ammunition but also on the sensibility of the investigation method used.

The special methods of determining the range of fire cannot be discussed here. For securing and adequately preserving any GSR that may be present on the clothing or in the vicinity of entry wounds, close cooperation with the responsible experts is necessary. In any case, the relevant findings should be documented by photographs and also by X-rays, whenever possible.

Shotgun Injuries

Shotguns are hunting or sporting weapons intended to be fired from the shoulder. They are either single- or double-barreled, the barrels in the latter ones being arranged either side by side or "up and under." A so-called pump gun has a pipe magazine under the barrel, which can take up several cartridges. Usual shotgun shells with birdshot or buckshot contain a multitude of pellets, which first travel together for a short distance and then separate more and more. The increasing dispersal of the shot improves the hunter's chance of striking a moving target, such as a hare or a flying duck. The criminal use of shotguns on humans is common, and improvisations, such as sawn-off barrels, facilitate the handling and hiding of the weapon. Shortening the barrel results in an increased spread of the pellets in midrange and distant-range shotgun discharges. Shot pellets are made from lead, which is easily deformed when striking dense tissue (**Figure 9(d)**).

A shotgun contact wound is produced when the muzzle is placed tightly against the body surface. The entrance wound roughly corresponds to the gauge and is of circular shape in most body regions, but stellate over the bone (due to the expansion of the inrushing gases with consecutive backward ballooning of the skin). Sometimes, there is a clear imprint abrasion mark, for example, from the front sight or—in double-barreled weapons—from the nonfiring muzzle. The wound edges may be blackened, but most of the soot enters the body and is deposited in the depth of the wound. The surrounding muscle is often colored cherry-red due to carbon monoxide. An intraoral discharge or a contact wound to the head (forehead, temple, or under the jaw) leads to massive destruction of the skull (bursting of the head or shooting off of the face) and is occasionally associated with evisceration of the brain.

Even in cases with extreme splitting of the face and the scalp, careful approximation of the wound edges helps in finding the entrance site. Loose-contact discharge allows the escape of sooty combustion gases, staining the skin around the entrance hole. Intermediate-range shots are characterized by the presence of stippling/tattooing from unburned propellant (up to 1 m, depending on the type of powder). In close-distance discharges, additional smoke soiling is seen.

The injury pattern of shot ammunition is mainly influenced by the distance between the muzzle and the target: As the range increases, the initially circular entrance hole shows scalloping of the wound edge (nibbling or crenation); from a distance of approximately 2 m, peripheral pellets produce satellite-like holes outside the central entry defect (**Figure 9**). Ranges of several meters are characterized by a sieve-like wound pattern. If shots are fired from short distances, wads or plastic cups may either penetrate the body together with the shot or cause excoriations of characteristic shape on the victim's skin ("wad abrasion").

Shotgun slugs are large, single lead projectiles destined for smooth-bore shotguns and also for those having a choke at the end of the barrel. The hitting accuracy of shotgun slugs is considerably lower than that of rifle projectiles; as a consequence, they should not be used for distances beyond 35–50 m in hunting. Some shotgun slugs are designed according to the arrow principle (heavy front part and light rear part).

Internal Findings

The gunshot lesions of the inner organs can be discussed only briefly here. Special mention should be made, however, of bullet holes in the flat bones of the skull (cf. **Figures 5(b), (d), 6(b), (c), and 7(b)**). On the entrance side, the bone defect in the outer table is sharp edged and its minimum diameter roughly corresponds to the caliber of the projectile, whereas the inner table is beveled out in a cone-like manner. This characteristic widening on the exit side allows one to determine the direction of fire even in an isolated bone. For gunshot exit holes of the skull, the opposite is true: The outer table shows a crater-like defect (outward beveling). Projectiles striking at an acute angle produce keyhole-shaped entrance defects in flat bones with partial cratering of the outer table at the side away from the shooter. So the manner in which the bone breaks may indicate the inclination of the bullet path. Beveling is not restricted to the skullcap, as it is also seen in other flat bones, such as the sternum, the pelvis, and the ribs.

In contact shots to the cerebral cranium (e.g., the frontal, temporal, parietal, and occipital regions), soot deposits are found not only under the skin, but also around the bone defect

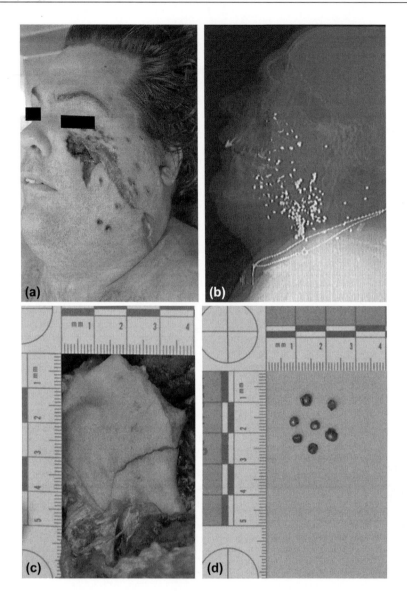

Figure 9   Homicide committed with a 16 G shotgun (diameter of the pellets 3.5 mm) from a distance of about 2 m. (a) The medial margin of the entrance wound is crenated whereas the lateral side is lacerated and surrounded by satellite holes from peripheral pellets and grazing pellet wounds. (b) Radiological documentation of the shot pattern. (c) Left ramus of the fragmented mandible with grayish lead debris from ricocheting pellets (d).

(cf. **Figures 5(b) and 7(b)**) and on the underside of the lifted-off periosteum, often even on the outer surface of the dura mater.

In many cases, radial fractures extend from gunshot holes of the skull (cf. **Figures 5(b), 6(b), and (c)**). According to Puppe's rule, a secondary fracture line will cease when it meets a preexisting fracture line, which may help one to determine the sequence of shots.

In soft tissue, the wound track collapses and/or is filled with blood. Postmortem probing of the bullet path involves the risk of causing artifacts and should therefore be avoided. Parenchymatous organs, such as the liver, the kidneys, and the spleen, may show large stellate wounds at the sites of entry and exit.

Whole projectiles or bullet fragments removed from the body by surgical intervention or during autopsy must be preserved for further laboratory investigation, including ballistic comparison. A recovered projectile provides information regarding the caliber, twist direction, number and width of lands and grooves as well as of the individual characteristics imparted by the inner surface of the barrel.

Blank firing pistols and revolvers are detailed facsimiles of real handguns. The blank cartridges destined for these weapons contain gunpowder, but no projectile. If the muzzle is held in close proximity to the body surface or even in contact with it, the gas jet from the blank gun is capable of penetrating the skin and causing potentially fatal injuries.

Forensic Examination and Documentation

In all firearm fatalities, careful documentation is of utmost importance. This includes taking photographs and close-up views of each wound using a scale. The clothing must be preserved, as the uppermost layer may exhibit the bullet wipe around entrance holes and depositions of soot and/or powder particles in close- and medium-range shots, respectively.

Whenever possible, X-rays should be taken before autopsy in two planes (anteroposterior as well as lateral views). They are not only useful for permanent and objective documentation but also helpful in exactly locating and characterizing all bullets and any metal fragments, including separated jackets. Radiographs are also a valuable tool to find projectiles lodged in body regions, which are hardly accessible during autopsy (e.g., within the vertebral column). In addition, X-rays provide evidence that a bullet might have been deflected or embolized.

All wounds have to be described exactly with regard to their location using fixed landmarks, such as the base of the heels, the midline, the height above the buttocks, and the distance from the top of the head. The documentation should also mention the size and shape of each wound, the features of the wound margins and their surroundings, the presence or absence of GSR such as soot or stippling on the clothing and/or skin, the total length of the wound tracks, and, of course, the injuries to the internal organs.

It is important to recover any bullets or major parts thereof from the body of the victim. Subsequent laboratory investigations may help in identifying the bullet type and assigning the fired bullet to a specific weapon.

Manner of Death

To classify a gunshot wound as suicidal, homicidal, or accidental, a synoptic evaluation of the scene and the circumstances of the case; the evidence obtained from the injuries; the victim's clothing; and the laboratory investigations concerning the weapon, ammunition, and the range of fire has to be made. Easy access to weapons due to permissive legislation is associated with increased rates of firearm homicide and suicide.

From the medicolegal point of view, the question has to be answered whether the entry wound is localized in a region typical for suicides: temple (cf. **Figures 4, 5, and 7**), mouth (**Figure 10**), cardiac region, forehead, and submental region (cf. **Figure 6(a)**). In almost all cases of suicide, the muzzle is held against the body or inserted into the oral cavity. In shots to the chest, the skin is seldom bared before. In more than 20% of the suicides committed with pistols or revolvers, the weapon is found clutched in the firing hand.

The examination of hands to detect GSR, especially lead, antimony, and barium originating from the primer, can be mentioned only briefly here. These residues escape mainly from the cylinder–barrel gap (in revolvers) or from the ejection

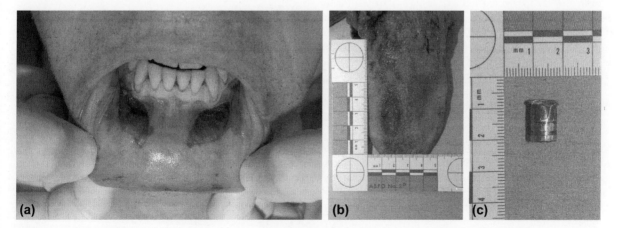

Figure 10 Intraoral shot from a 9 × 19 mm caliber pistol (suicide). (a) Symmetrical tears on the inner surface of the lower lip. (b) Dorsum of the tongue with soot deposition (near the apex) and tangential wound from the projectile (c).

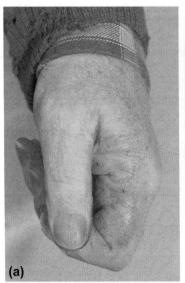 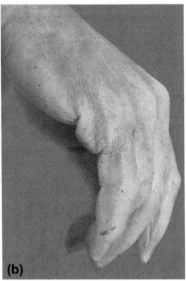

Figure 11   (a) Left hand used by a suicide to steady the barrel of a pistol: soot depositions on the radial aspect of the index finger. (b) Ulnar aspect of the right hand which had fired a pistol. The skin is spattered with a spray of blood.

port (in automatic pistols) and come to rest on the skin and/or clothing, where they can be collected for subsequent chemical analysis. The presence of GSR is detected by flameless atomic absorption spectroscopy or by scanning electron microscope–energy dispersive X-ray spectrometry.

Sometimes, clues suggesting suicide are found even on examination with the naked eye (**Figure 11**), for example, spray of blood or tissue deposits on the firing hand ("back-spatter" from the entry wound), traces of soot on thumb and index finger (if the muzzle end was held against the entrance site with one hand), or injuries from the edges of the recoiling slide. Direct and prolonged contact of the skin with the steel parts of the weapon in a moist environment promotes the formation of brownish rust stains. This phenomenon is found especially in suicides, although it is no proof that the shot was self-inflicted.

Injuries Caused by Explosives

In peacetime, injuries and fatalities owing to the detonation of explosives (letter or parcel bombs) are seen mainly in connection with politically motivated or terrorist attacks against persons, vehicles, and buildings. Accidents are mostly due to natural gas ignitions, chemical explosions, or improper handling of explosives, fireworks, etc. In countries without terrorist activities, suicides by explosives are rare and usually restricted to persons with a pertinent professional experience (**Figure 12**).

The injury pattern is typically characterized by a complex combination of different lesions. Mechanical tissue destruction up to traumatic amputation and evisceration is caused by blunt force (exploding device and other objects impacting the body, pressure wave), often associated with penetrating injuries from splinters, burning, and soot blackening of the skin. The internal examination may reveal organ and vascular damage, skeletal fractures, ruptured tympanic membranes, and acute pulmonary emphysema. A complete body X-ray examination should be performed whenever possible.

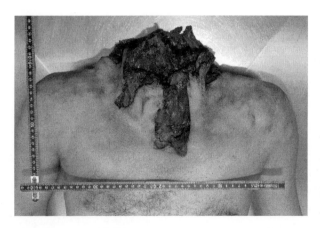

Figure 12   Occupation-related suicide of a blaster who had placed the explosive charge next to the back of his neck resulting in decapitation with concomitant soot soiling.

See also: **Pattern Evidence:** Shotgun Ammunition on a Target; **Pattern Evidence/Firearms:** Humane Killing Tools; Laboratory Analysis; Range; Residues.

Further Reading

Besant-Matthews, P.E., 2000. Examinations and interpretation of rifled firearm injuries. In: Mason, J.K., Purdue, B.N. (Eds.), The Pathology of Trauma, third ed. Arnold, London, pp. 47–60.

Bolliger, S.A., Kneubuhel, B.P., Thali, M.J., 2009. Gunshot. In: Thali, M.J., Dirnhofer, R., Vock, P. (Eds.), The Virtopsy Approach. CRC Press, Boca Raton, FL, pp. 318–331.

Cassidy, M., 2000. Smooth-bore firearm injuries. In: Mason, J.K., Purdue, B.N. (Eds.), The Pathology of Trauma. Arnold, London, pp. 61–74.

Crane, J., 2005. Explosive injury. In: Payne-James, J., Byard, R.W., Corey, T.S., Henderson, C. (Eds.), Encyclopedia of Forensic and Legal Medicine, vol. 3. Elsevier, Oxford, pp. 98–100.

Dana, S.E., DiMaio, V.J.M., 2003. Gunshot trauma. In: Payne-James, J., Busuttil, A., Smock, W. (Eds.), Forensic Medicine: Clinical and Pathological Aspects. Greenwich Medical Media, London, pp. 149–168.

DiMaio, V.J.M., 1999. Gunshot Wounds: Practical Aspects of Firearms, Ballistics, and Forensic Techniques, second ed. CRC Press, Boca Raton, FL.

Dodd, M.J., 2006. Terminal Ballistics: A Text and Atlas of Gunshot Wounds. CRC Press, Boca Raton, FL.

Grosse Perdekamp, M., Vennemann, B., Mattern, D., Serr, A., Pollak, S., 2005. Tissue defect at the gunshot entrance wound: what happens to the skin? International Journal of Legal Medicine 119 (4), 217–222.

Karger, B., 2008. Forensic ballistics. In: Tsokos, M. (Ed.), Forensic Pathology Reviews, vol. 5. Humana Press, Totowa, NJ, pp. 139–172.

Kirk, G.M., 2005. Firearm injuries. In: Payne-James, J., Byard, R.W., Corey, T.S., Henderson, C. (Eds.), Encyclopedia of Forensic and Legal Medicine, vol. 3. Elsevier, Oxford, pp. 110–118.

Lew, E., Dolinak, D., Matshes, E., 2005. Firearm injuries. In: Dolinak, D., Matshes, E.W., Lew, E.O. (Eds.), Forensic Pathology; Principles and Practice. Elsevier Academic Press, Burlington, MA, pp. 163–200.

Naidoo, S.R., 2005. Ballistic trauma, overview and statistics. In: Payne-James, J., Byard, R.W., Corey, T.S., Henderson, C. (Eds.), Encyclopedia of Forensic and Legal Medicine, vol. 1. Elsevier, Oxford, pp. 271–283.

Pollak, S., Rothschild, M.A., 2004. Gunshot injuries as a topic of medicolegal research in the German-speaking countries from the beginning of the 20th century up to the present time. Forensic Science International 144 (2–3), 201–210.

Pollak, S., Saukko, P., 2003. Injuries Due to Guns and Explosives. Atlas of Forensic Medicine (CD-ROM). Elsevier, Amsterdam (Chapter 7).

Saukko, P., Knight, B., 2004. Knight's Forensic Pathology, third ed. Arnold, London, pp. 245–280.

Sellier, K., 1969. Bullet entry studies of the skin. Beiträge zur Gerichtlichen Medizin 25, 265–270.

Sellier, K.G., Kneubuehl, B.P., 1994. Wound Ballistics and the Scientific Background. Elsevier, Amsterdam.

Smock, W.S., 2000. Evaluation of gunshot wounds. In: Siegel, J.A., Saukko, P.J., Knupfer, G.C. (Eds.), Encyclopedia of Forensic Sciences, vol. 1. Academic Press, London, pp. 378–384.

Spitz, W.U., 2006a. Injury by gunfire. In: Spitz, W.U. (Ed.), Spitz and Fisher's Medicolegal Investigation of Death, fourth ed. Thomas, Springfield, IL, pp. 607–746.

Spitz, W.U., 2006b. Medicolegal considerations of bomb explosions. In: Spitz, W.U. (Ed.), Spitz and Fisher's Medicolegal Investigation of Death, fourth ed. Thomas, Springfield, IL, pp. 777–782.

Torture

H Vogel, University Hospital Eppendorf, Hamburg, Germany

Introduction

The definition of torture varies depending on the source of the definition and the political or social agenda of the organization that created the definition. Encyclopedias, governments, international organizations, and nongovernment organizations (NGOs) commonly have different definitions for torture: for instance, the *Encyclopedia Britannica*, Wikipedia, the World Medical Association, Amnesty International (AI), and state governments may have strikingly different definitions of torture. In spite of the differences between these definitions, however, the existence of torture, and its coexistence with and dependence on violence are generally accepted facts. Torture is particularly dangerous because it is difficult to control: the application of physical or psychological violence for the purpose of torture often creates a dynamic of its own causing the procedure to gain its own momentum and separating the torture from the original intent. In other words, the torture will be committed for its own sake, rather than for the sake of eliciting information. Furthermore, torture is typically inflicted by, at the instigation of, or with the consent or acquiescence of, a public official or other person in authority. Therefore, perpetrators of torture are often attached to government bodies or to others who exercise power, such as organized criminal groups or insurgents. The association of torture with persons of authority may decrease the likelihood that the victims receive appropriate medical care in the aftermath of the torture, particularly in the acute phase. Because torture often requires the services of health professionals and legal professionals, it raises (additional) ethical conflicts.

Because intelligence is required to win wars, and torture is sometimes viewed as an acceptable and expeditious method for eliciting intelligence; torture may be practiced by governments and opposition groups, such as terrorist and insurgent groups, in times of war. Governments may also use torture to obtain information about planned or committed crimes; for example, in an attempt to prevent a terrorist attack. Government officials may argue that torture is justified when:

- Regulated by law
- The laws governing torture have been established by democratically elected officials
- The laws governing torture are applied by democratically elected governments

Waterboarding is a recent example of government use of a practice that is widely believed to be a torture technique. Waterboarding was considered acceptable and used by the administration of US President George W. Bush for the purpose of interrogating suspected al-Qaida members following the 9/11 attacks. Use of waterboarding has been condemned by many NGOs, including AI.

Torture is an age-old activity that has become more sophisticated with the passage of time. It is usually carried out clandestinely, and there is often a deliberate attempt to reduce any physical evidence of its practice. Therefore, documentation of such abuse is usually difficult to find; in the absence of physical evidence at the time of examination, accounts of torture are often based solely on historical reports. Typically, most torture is carried out in the early stages of the victims' confinement. If the torture is not initially fatal, the physical signs of torture have typically healed by the time the victim is released.

Victims who survive torture have usually been less-severely tortured than those who died. Victims who have escaped from torture and come to the attention of rehabilitation centers in Europe, America, and elsewhere are presumably less-severely tortured than those victims who were unable to escape. Torture that results in mutilation increases the probability that the victim will die. Victims who have been stabbed in the trunk (wounds that are oftentimes followed by pleurisy and peritonitis) survive less often than those who have been wounded only in their extremities.

Documentation of torture employs similar procedures, techniques, and modalities as are employed in the investigation of other forms of abuse. These procedures, and the equipment necessary to properly implement them, are usually scarce in countries where torture is common. This is the case in times of peace or war.

These circumstances influence any description of torture and the possibilities as well as opportunities to prove that torture has occurred.

Forms

The majority of torture methods have been in practice for many years. It is common for aggressors to invent new names for old procedures in order to make the torture technique seem less harmful, so that the technique is more acceptable to the public. Variations on existing methods and new methods have been developed in order to make it impossible to prove torture through physical examinations.

If physical findings of torture are present, the differential diagnosis must include other forms of physical damage, such as that caused by the following:

- abuse/maltreatment
- accidents, self-inflicted injuries
- initiation rites
- diseases

Torture methods may be used on all parts of the body, including the hand and arm, foot and leg, trunk (including genital organs), and head and neck. Special torture procedures are used on fingers, hands, and arms. Torture procedures include the following:

- Postural torture
- Stabbing and cutting of any part of the body
- Finger, hand, and arm
- Toe, foot, and leg
- Compression injuries
- Petite guillotine
- Water torture
  - Submersion
  - Deprivation
  - Forced ingestion
- Electric torture
- Psychological torture methods
- Noise, music, light, cold, etc.

Combinations of the techniques listed above are frequent.

Fingers

Torture involving the fingers is quite common and may produce reversible or permanent anatomical alterations. The effects of a variety of techniques can be seen in rehabilitation centers for torture victims.

Foreign bodies: When fingers are injured with needles or other sharp instruments, foreign bodies (pieces of those instruments) may become permanently lodged in the fingers. The introduction of needles, wires, or wooden splinters beneath the fingernails is widespread. These foreign bodies are often directed to the distal interphalangeal joint or even beyond. When retracted, splinters or other fragments may remain and be radiographically detectable (**Figure 1(a)–(c)**).

Fingernails: In South America and elsewhere, the extraction of fingernails has been practiced; this procedure, however, has reversible effects.

Loss of fingers and toes: Compression of digits by finger, thumb, and toe screws has been applied since medieval times. Bone damage may be minor (**Figure 3**) or major and lead to complete loss of a phalanx. Less-severe mechanical compression injuries are inflicted by stomping or striking with rifle butts or other objects. Fingers can also be lost (**Figure 2(a) and (b)**) or severely damaged by direct violence or by neurovascular loss as a result of squeezing. Squeezing can be accomplished by placing a stick between the fingers and then compressing them against each other in order to damage nerves and vessels without leaving visible traces.

Petite Guillotine: Using this device, the fingers, or parts of fingers, can be cut off in succession (**Figure 3**). The Petite Guillotine was developed in Iran during the times of the Shah and persists to present times.

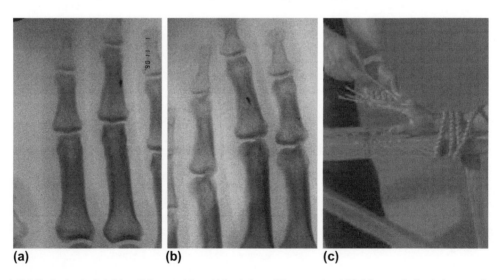

(a)   (b)   (c)

Figure 1   (a–c) Metallic foreign body left in soft tissues of the middle phalanx of the second and third fingers. During torture, needles or wires were introduced underneath the fingernails. Splinters remained after they were withdrawn.

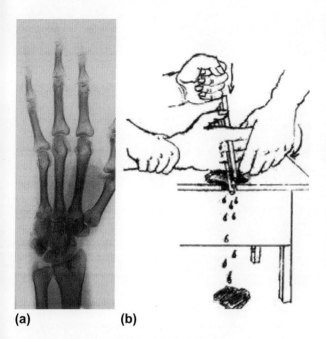

(a)   **(b)**

Figure 2   (a and b) Finger loss due to squeezing.

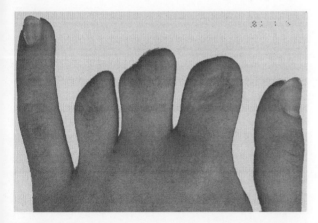

Figure 3   The guards of the Islamic Revolution imprisoned this 14-year-old girl. Parts of her fingers were cut off in the prison with the petite guillotine.

Suspension: Suspension on one or several fingers is reported from the Kurdish territories in the Arabic peninsula and in the neighboring countries. Suspension on fingers is an old method that has been in use since medieval times, for example, as punishment on sailing ships. It induces necrosis and loss of the finger. The thumb seems to be the preferred finger, perhaps for anatomical reasons (**Figure 4(a) and (b)**) and because of its major functional importance.

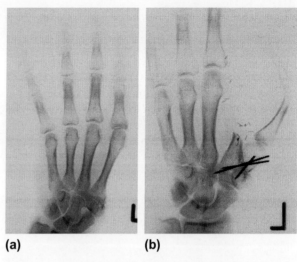

(a)   **(b)**

Figure 4   (a and b) Loss of thumb due to suspension (Kurd). This image from a hospital in Berlin shows how the fifth finger replaces the lost thumb.

Hands and Arms

Amputation: During the civil war in Sierra Leone, the hands of possible voters were cut off to prevent them from voting, as painting the fingers of individuals after they had voted controlled the national vote. Cutting off hands and feet of perpetrators of certain crimes is prescribed by Shari-ah, the law of the Koran. This punishment is applied in several Islamic countries where the Shari-ah is the official law.

Defensive fractures: The fracture of the forearm is a typical injury of defense. Persons instinctively or intentionally try to protect their head when under attack. A nightstick may fracture the ulna alone or the ulna together with the radius (**Figure 5**).

Mutilation: In Zaire, fractures of the hands and wrists are seen in journalists, writers, and artists (**Figure 6**). The aim is not only to hamper the victim's work, but also to cause functional injury by mutilating the part of the body that is the victim's main instrument of livelihood.

Fire: Scars from serious burns can cause contractures and deformation. Torture by fire has been reported in Africa.

Postural torture: This can be accomplished by requiring the victim to maintain a certain awkward (and even physiologic) posture for long periods of time, by binding the victim in various awkward and painful positions, or by suspension of the victim. Victims are sometimes suspended by the arms, which are bent backward with upward traction applied. Other forms bind the hands and feet together at the back (**Figure 7**).

Often, postural torture is applied with the intention to avoid evidence of the abuse. **Figure 8** depicts common forms of postural torture and suspension from South America.

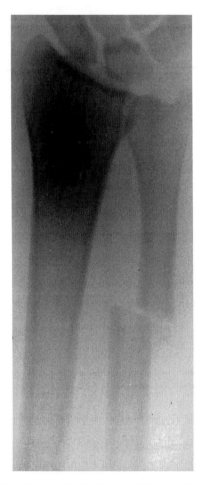

Figure 5 Fresh fracture (fending fracture) of the ulna. Defensive injuries sustained during beating.

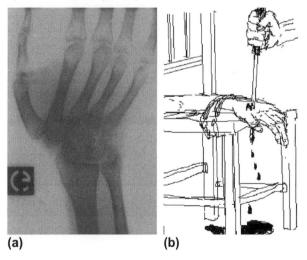

(a)   (b)

Figure 6 (a) Crushed wrist of a journalist (b) Stabbing the hand of a journalist.

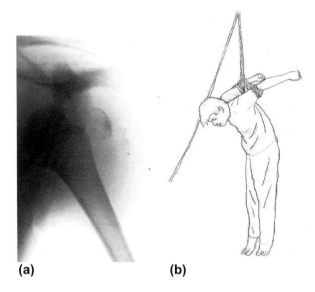

(a)   (b)

Figure 7 (a) Dislocation of the glenohumeral joint: glenoid process of scapula, humeral head, Hill–Sachs lesion in proximal humerus. (b) Suspension by the elbows, the arms bent backward. With such a suspension, dislocation of the shoulders is less common.

Having been imprisoned in a cage less high than the prisoner's height is reported from Kurds, Chinese, and Chileans. "Uncomfortable" positions can be easily enforced. Torture methods used in the "Abu Ghreib" prison in Iraq forced prisoners to maintain similar or identical positions, according to photographic evidence.

Foot and Leg

Feet and legs are common targets of torture; some techniques are fairly specific to geographic regions. Imaging may show typical or even characteristic findings; examples are falaka and palmatoria.

Falaka: Falaka is a widespread form of torture, sometimes known as falanga and in Spanish-speaking areas as bastinado. Falaka means beating the foot, primarily (but not exclusively) on the sole of the foot. Falaka is perpetrated in the Middle East (especially in Turkey and Iraq), in the Far East, and in some Spanish-speaking areas. Falaka produces edema; hematoma; fractures and injuries to the ligaments, tendons, fascia; and aponeurosis of the feet and ankle (**Figure 9(a)–(d)**). Shortly after torture, the clinical findings alone are usually diagnostic. Radiography can confirm or exclude fractures and allow estimation of the time interval since torture was applied.

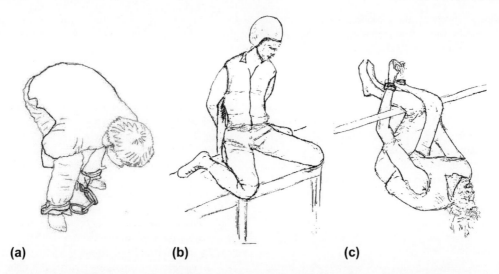

Figure 8 Common forms of postural torture (a), which hardly leave evidence, could be demonstrated by diagnostic imaging: "Il moto" (b) and "la barra" (c).

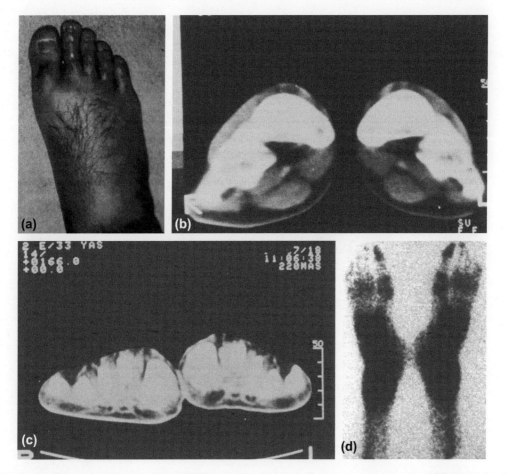

Figure 9 (a) Falaka. (b) Photograph of a foot after falaka. (c) CT, top: edema and hematoma, predominately plantar after falaka; below: chronic change after falaka, splay and flatfoot deformation due to relaxed ligaments and aponeurosis. (d) Scintigraphy: very high uptake in feet, several weeks after falaka.

In the author's experience, these beatings may fracture the toes, the metatarsals, the tarsals (especially the calcaneus), and occasionally the ankle. This is especially the case if the feet were fixed during the beating. Fractures of the lateral malleolus seem to be an exception; nevertheless, the lower leg near the ankle may be involved. Scintigraphy initially shows increased soft tissue activity after the beating (**Figure 9(d)**). Later, a generalized increased bony uptake with unusual degenerative changes may be found. When available, magnetic resonance imaging (MRI) is better than computed tomography (CT) in visualizing alterations of soft tissues including capsular thickening, atrophy, edema, and reparative changes. Later studies may prove earlier torture by demonstrating a thickened aponeurosis of the foot. MRI can also show bone bruises or edema.

Palmatoria: Palmatoria is an example of a method of localized torture that is virtually unique to a specific region—the small West African country of Guinea-Bissau. Palmatoria involves repetitive blows to the shin where the tibia lies closest to the skin. Radiographic examination may show periosteal reaction from subperiosteal hemorrhage and hematoma. Laminar or onionskin periostitis can persist for weeks or even years. Somewhat peculiar endosteal and medullary changes may be seen as well. Two case reports have shown that blows to this area of the tibia, using a rod, can produce a hidden endosteal fracture, which is likely to be undetected on plain films but obvious on CT. It is possible, and perhaps even likely, that some of the African cases would show similar findings, had more sophisticated imaging modality been applied.

Compression: Compression of digits by toe screws has been applied in Iran (**Figure 10(a) and (b)**). Bony damage can be of various degrees, and complete loss of a phalanx or an entire digit may occur. Mutilation is a possible consequence.

Foreign bodies: Corresponding to torture methods used on fingers and hands, foreign bodies are also introduced into the toes, often under the toenails (**Figure 15**) and into the feet. Radiography might find remaining splinters.

Toenails: Similar to fingernails, toenails may be extracted.

Extreme cold: Exposure to low temperatures may result in frostbite or even frozen-off toes.

Kneecapping: Kneecapping is a term originally used to describe a gunshot wound in the knee, usually by a handgun, in order to permanently maim or cripple the victim. In America, it has been mostly associated with gang warfare. In recent years, it has been seen during the civil strife in Northern Ireland. It is not certain as to which country is the importer and which the exporter. Kneecapping is no longer limited to the knee; other

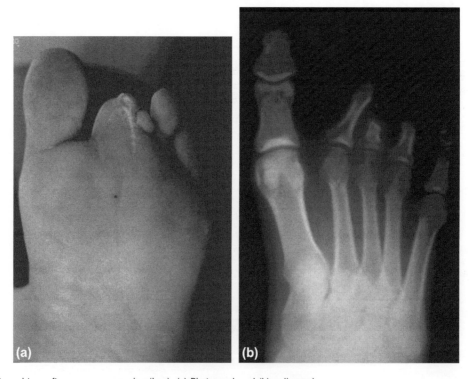

Figure 10   Destroyed toes after screw compression (Iran). (a) Photograph and (b) radiograph.

joints, particularly the ankle and elbow, are also targeted. In one known extreme case, both knees, both ankles, and both elbows were shot. Occasionally, other parts of the leg are involved. Radiographs can easily document the extent of injury and frequently disclose the bullet path, trajectory of fire, and location of the bullet. Bullets are frequently found in situ, as low-velocity weapons are often employed. Arterial damage is not uncommon, and angiography is frequently employed (**Figure 11(a)–(d)**).

Fire: Another famous incident of torture happened to Cuauhtémoc, the last king of the Aztecs, whose feet were burnt to mutilation on October 15, 1521, by Hernàn Cortés.

Head

Torture applied to the head is often fatal, a consequence that is usually accepted or even intended by the torturers when they use such techniques.

Stabbing: Only a few cases of this typically lethal wound have been documented (**Figure 12(a) and (b)**).

Beating: Beating the head may fracture the bones and cause intracranial bleeding. Teeth are often broken or dislocated during beating. These may be extracted or drilled as a form of pain induction. These injuries, of course, can be demonstrated by direct inspection as well as by radiography. In Chad, an uncommon form of torture involves a prisoner being beaten in the face producing fractures of the facial bones that can be demonstrated radiologically. Opacification of the maxillary sinuses is regularly seen due to bleeding, and subsequently sinusitis may develop.

Shaking: In the Middle East, the technique of violently shaking the suspect's upper torso is used. Occasionally, this may produce intracranial lesions much like those in the shaken baby syndrome. In Israel, the Supreme Court has outlawed this practice.

Neck

Strangulation: Strangulation as a special form of suffocation is employed worldwide, either for tormenting or for outright killing. Fracture of the larynx may be seen. Some European states have employed strangulation as one form of capital punishment. In Spain, the Garrotte was used for executions under Franco.

Trunk

Beating: Few specific injuries will be detected from generalized beating because, as pointed out, soft tissue and bony injury usually heal by the time the victim comes to

sympathetic medical attention. Residual deformities of rib and spinal fractures may be present, as may be deformities due to ligamentous tears or ruptures. Scintigraphy (**Figure 13**) shows increased bone metabolism up to 2 years after the beating, and may indicate a pattern of the beating.

Stabbing: Stabbing in the trunk carries a high risk of injury to vital organs, with a consequent high probability of a lethal infection. Therefore, this method is less seen and reported. In South Africa, gangs have been hunting young women to torture them by introducing bicycle spokes into the umbilicus. A variant of this was stabbing into the spine with intent to produce paraplegia. When stabbing occurs, fragments of the weapon or foreign bodies may remain and can be documented by a radiological method (**Figure 14**).

Injection: In former East Germany, a young man on his way to a discotheque was attacked by a gang and rendered unconscious. Upon being brought to the hospital, it was discovered that mercury had been injected into his chest wall.

Fractures: Rib fractures are common. Scintigraphically, they may be especially helpful to show the pattern of beating. Less known is the fracture due to compressing of chest or the pelvis.

Anus and genitals: Violence is often directed at genital organs (**Figure 15**). Hours after the abuse, scintigraphy may show an increased activity at the site of the injury. Diagnostic imaging can document some of the consequences, for example, remaining foreign bodies after sexual torture. Some injuries associated with perforation will often provoke death before diagnostic imaging is done. Stabbing into the anus is sometimes performed to make the victim suffer before death and/or to hide the killing from the public.

Sexual abuse of women, including female circumcision, is well known; however, violation of men is reported less often. A famous case is that of Mugabe, current president of Zimbabwe, who was violated in his youth. In Abu Ghraib, male prisoners were forced to perform sex acts on each other.

Electric Torture

Electricity as an instrument of torture can be used in multiple ways. In the Middle East, it is common to place the electrode between the toes, on the tongue, on the teeth, or on the penis. The location between the toes and on the tongue is chosen in order to hide the place of entrance of the electric current. The placement on the penis is selected not only to inflict pain but also to humiliate. In Africa, electrodes are placed on the teeth. In the Middle East, large electrodes are used on wet skin, and collarlike electrodes are placed on the neck. Electric current induces muscle contractions, which may result in outright bone fractures and/or soft tissue injuries, with subsequent later degenerative bone or joint changes. Electroshock may produce

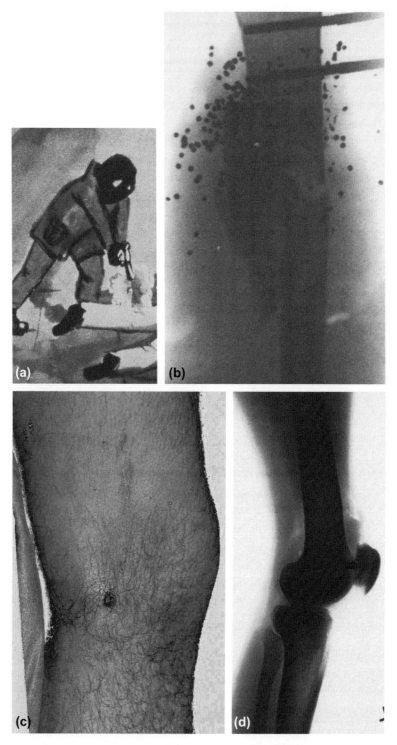

Figure 11   (a–d) Kneecapping, employing weapons. Shot into the upper leg with lead shot. Shot into the knee with a handgun. The projectile remains in the knee.

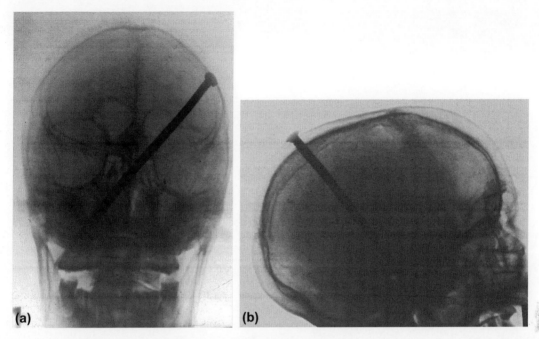

Figure 12   The original comment was "nail in head, witchcraft, deceased." The victim was said to be possessed by an evil spirit; the healer chose to liberate his patient from this evil by putting a nail into his head. The victim died after some days in hospital. Today, the author thinks this was a "medical killing" ("ritual murder") scheme, and that the killing was part of a magic procedure (Africa).

compression fractures of the vertebrae. Grand mal seizures may cause high thoracic vertebral fractures. Moreover, teeth can be lost and jaws broken.

For proving electric torture, local incision and microscopic evaluation may show characteristic necrosis, which is accepted as evidence by judges in Turkey. If the victims were immediately available, torture by electricity could probably be confirmed by MRI, such as the findings of high signal alterations on MRI examination of the chest in (normal, not tortured) patients undergoing cardioversion have indicated.

Water submersion: In submersion, often called "submarine," the victim's head is forced underwater until near drowning. The water is often polluted with excrement. Aspiration is virtually inevitable and the subsequent radiography changes may vary from pulmonary edema to extensive pneumonia. The latter may result in residual pulmonary scarring and adhesions. The findings are nonspecific, however.

Water deprivation: Deprivation of water can be an effective, even deadly, form of torture.

Water ingestion: Victims from Chad, Africa, have reported that they were bound with their arms behind them, then forced to ingest several liters of water within a very short time. Thereafter, they were thrown, or caused to fall, from a height of several meters to land on their anterior chest and abdomen,

with the aim of visceral rupture. One survivor was found to have a diaphragmatic hernia that might have been induced by this forced trauma.

Waterboarding: In this technique, a cloth or plastic wrap is placed over or in the person's mouth, and water is poured on to the person's head. In 2005, waterboarding was characterized as a "professional interrogation technique" by former CIA director Porter J. Goss; however, CIA officers who have subjected themselves to the technique lasted an average of 14 s before capitulating. There is a real risk of death from drowning, suffering a heart attack, or damage to the lungs from inhalation of water. Long-term effects include panic attacks, depression, and posttraumatic stress disorder.

Psychological Torture

Execution/Russian roulette/pretended execution: Victims of torture may be forced to assist in the execution and the torture of others. Not only do they see what they have to expect when it is their turn to be tortured, but they are often compelled to torture or kill a companion, friend, or relative. They may also be subjected to their own fake execution or forced to engage in Russian roulette.

Music/noise: Music may also be used for psychological torture. In nearly every German concentration camp, the SS forced

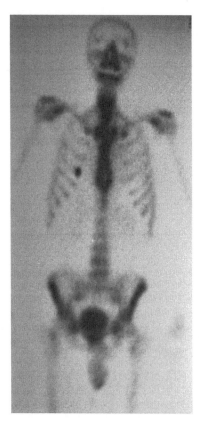

Figure 13 Beating. Scintigraphy. Increased bone metabolism in the anterior part of a rib on the right side of the victim due to beating.

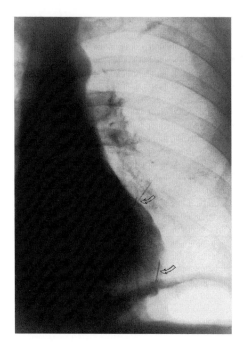

Figure 14 Needle fragments in the chest after stabbing with multiple needles.

victims to join orchestras that played military marches, folk songs, and popular songs, making the musicians feel as though they had joined forces with the SS; many of them committed suicide. Being exposed to loud or offensive music can break the victim's personality and give torturers absolute control.

Diagnosis and Differential Diagnosis

Torture can be classified as somatic, (bio)chemical (pharmacological), and psychological. However, multiple forms of somatic torture are designed and applied in a manner so as to avoid distinctive evidence by subsequent visual or radiologic inspection. Some techniques produce changes that can be depicted by imaging. In general, psychological and pharmacological torture does not lend itself to radiologic discovery; it seems possible, however, that, in the near future, functional MRI will be able to evidence findings which are characteristic for pharmacological torture and, in consequence will allow proving it. Diffusion tensor imaging (DTI) offers a promising approach: DTI can show damages of axons which are not visible on conventional MRI.

Physical and psychological examination is the basis of the investigation, and diagnostic imaging may contribute in certain cases. The findings have to be combined with the person's history and the cultural background of the case. There are regional differences in the design and infliction of torture and mistreatment throughout the world, and, unfortunately, new forms of torture are constantly being invented. The plausibility of the individual's history—specifically, the pattern of the inflicted physical and psychological violence—should be examined. These data are to be compared with what is known about the region, the time, and the forces/organizations which are said to have been involved in the torture. Diagnostic imaging sometimes allows visualizing a pattern and gives an approximation of the time passed. It is recommended to consider other causes of presumed torture trauma, such as accidents, crimes, local customs, and initiation rites, all of which may produce the same effects. Self-flagellation practiced by Shiites during the Ashura festival may serve as example: young men beat themselves on the back with multiple blades, resulting in bleeding, and the healing produces scars that should not be attributed to beating inflicted by others.

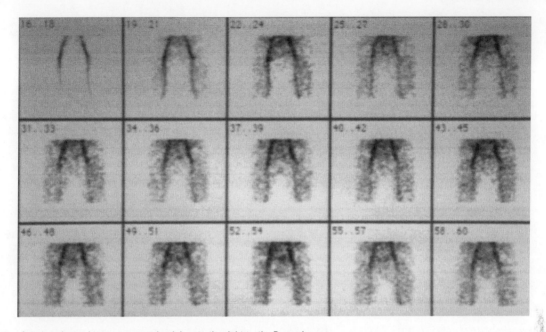

Figure 15 Scintigraphy to document squeezing injury to the right testis. Dynamic scan.

Ethics

Most medical organizations state that participating in torture is against medical ethics. However, physicians and other medical professions have been called upon to assist and/or supervise torture, provide expertise in rendering torture methods more effective, help in covering up consequences of torture, or modify (falsify) a forensic certificate. A conflict is also apparent when a physician is called upon to provide medical care for a person who has been tortured, remains in custody, and will be tortured again. Leopara and Millum, both activists with Médecins sans Frontières, discuss this problem and conclude: "If a tortured patient demands medical care, the physician should accept some form and degree of complicity in torture in order to assist the tortured patient. Three main factors should guide a doctor's decision in such circumstances: the expected consequences of the doctor's actions, the wishes of the patient, and the extent of the doctor's complicity with wrongdoing."

Conclusion

While objectivity is required, one must also constantly bear in mind that the case is not merely theoretical, but actually concerns a real human being. Much of the evidence comes from worldwide centers of rehabilitation for torture victims. Imaging sometimes depicts lesions so characteristic that they can be considered legal proof of previous torture and verify a presumed victim's claims.

Criteria that support claims of torture are as follows:

- Correlation between the type of torture and the findings derived from imaging procedures
- Correlation between the date of torture and the imaging appearance of the lesion
- Specific alterations, such as the periosteal reactions from palmatoria
- Correlating findings in a particular situation, such as imprisonment and nutritional deficiencies or sequelae from denial of treatment or surgery
- Patterns of beatings (proven by imaging) typical for a particular geographic location and corresponding with the victim's story

See also: **Forensic Medicine/Causes of Death:** Strangulation; **Forensic Medicine/Clinical:** Electrocution and Lightning Strike.

Further Reading

Aerzteblatt.de, 2011. Schädel-Hirn-trauma: Verbessertes MRT Zeigt Mehr Verletzungen. http://www.aerzteblatt.de/nachrichten/46118/ (retrieved 18.08.11; 18:06).
Bauer, J., 2011. Musik im Konzentrationslager Sachsenhausen. http://www.gedenkstaettenforum.de/nc/gedenkstaetten-rundbrief/rundbrief/news/juliane_brauer_musik_im_konzentrationslager_sachsenhausen/ (retrieved 18.08.11; 17:37).
Brogdon, B.G., 1998. Forensic Radiology. CRC Press, Boca Raton, FL. Chapter 17.
Brogdon, B.G., Crotty, J.M., 1999. The hidden divot: a new type of incomplete fracture? American Journal of Roentgenology 172, 789.

Bro-Rasmussen, F., Henriksen, O.B., Rasmussen, O., et al., 1982. Aseptic necrosis of bone following falanga torture. Ugeskrift for Laeger 144, 1165.

Leopara, C., Millum, J., 2011a. Should a Doctor Be Complicit with Torture. http://www.du.edu/korbel/news/2010/11/Chiara_Lepora_FSO.html (retrieved 11.08.11; 12:40).

Leopara, C., Millum, J., 2011b. The tortured patient. A medical dilemma. Hastings Center Report 41 (3), 38–47. http://www.medscape.com/viewarticle/742725.

Images. Falaka, 2012. http://www.google.de/search?tbm=isch&hl=de&source=hp& biw=729&bih=1240&q=abu+ghraib&gbv=2&oq=Abu&aq=5&aqi=g10&aql= &gs_sm=c&gs_upl=4427l5074l0l9340l3l3l0l0l0l0l159l349l2.1l3l0#hl=de& gbv=2&tbm=isch&sa=1&q=Falaka&pbx=1&oq=Falaka&aq=f&aqi=&aql= &gs_sm=e&gs_upl=267241l271063l0l273615l6l6l0l1l0l0l253l865l1.3.1l5l0 &bav=on.2,or.r_gc.r_pw. &fp=bfe0aa86fbc4cb55&biw=729&bih=1240 (retrieved 17.08.11; 14:24).

Forschergruppe: Musik, Konflikt und der Staat, 2011. http://www.uni-goettingen.de/ de/207622.html (retrieved 18.08.11; 16:55).

Forschergruppe: Musik, Konflikt und der Staat, 2011b. Newsletter Nr. 8 Vom 08.06.2011. http://www.uni-goettingen.de/de/217724.html (retrieved 18.08.11; 17:10).

Gaessner, S., Gurris, N., Pross, C. (Eds.), 2001. At the Side of Torture Survivors. Johns Hopkins University Press, Baltimore, MD.

Genefke, I.K., 1986. Torturen I Verden: Den Angar Os Alle. Hans Reizels Forlag, Copenhagen, pp. 1–27.

Images. Ghraib, 2012. http://www.google.de/search?tbm=isch&hl=de&source= hp&biw=729 &bih=1240&q=abu+ghraib&gbv=2&oq=Abu&aq=5&aqi=g10 &aql=&gs_sm=c&gs_upl=4427l5074l0l9340l3l3l0l0l0l0l159l349l2.1l3l0 (retrieved 17.08.11; 14:20).

Hayes, E., 1997. MRI illustrates history of torture. Diagnostic Imaging Europe 13, 17.

Hulverscheidt, M., 2011. Weibliche Genitalverstümmelung und ihre folgen. Konsequenzen für reisemedizinische Beratung. Flugmedizin ropenmedizin Reisemedizin 18 (4), 182–187.

Iacopino, V., Heiser, M., Pishever, S., Kirschner, R.H., 1996. Physician complicity in misrepresentation and omission of evidence of torture in postdetention medical examinations in Turkey. Journal of the American Medical Association 276, 396.

Jensen, T.S., Genefke, I.K., Hyldebrandt, N., Pedersen, H., Petersen, D., Weile, B., 1982. Cerebral atrophy in young torture victims. New England Journal of Medicine 307, 1334.

Lök, V., 1994. Oral Communication. International Torture Meeting, Istanbul.

Lök, V., Tunca, M., Kumanlioglu, K., Kapkin, E., Dirik, G., 1991. Bone scintigraphy as clue to previous torture. Lancet 337, 846.

Moreno, A., Grodin, M.A., 2000. The not-so-silent marks of torture. Journal of the American Medical Association 284, 538.

Özkalipci, Ö., Sahin, Ü., Baykal, T., et al., 2007. Iskence Atlasi – Iskencenin tibbi olarak belgelendirilmesinde muayene ve tanisal inceleme sonuclarinin kullanilmasi. Türkiye insan Haklari Vakfi.

Petrow, P., Page, P., Vanel, D., 2001. The hidden divot fracture: Brogdon's fracture, a new type of incomplete fracture. American Journal of Roentgenology 177, 946.

Sidel, V.W., 1996. Commentary: the social responsibilities of health professionals: lessons from their role in Nazi Germany. Journal of the American Medical Association 276, 1679.

Skylv, G., 1997. Falanga: diagnosis and treatment of late sequellae. Torture Supplement 1994.

Sonteg, D., September 9, 1991. A Strike against Brutality, Mobile Register.

Sternde, 2011. Musik als Folter. Die 'greatest Hits' von Guantanamo. http:// www.stern.de/politik/ausland/musik-als-folter-die-greatest-hits-von-guantanamo-648547.html (retrieved 18.07.11; 17:58).

Vogel, H., 2003. Torture. In: Brogdon, B.G., Vogel, H., McDowell, J.D. (Eds.), A Radiologic Atlas of Abuse, Torture, Terrorism, and Inflicted Trauma. CRC Press, Boca Raton, FL, pp. 105–124.

Wikipedia, 2011. List of Methods of Torture. http://en.wikipedia.org/wiki/List_of_torture_methods_and_devices (retrieved 24.06.11; 9:23).

Wikipedia, 2011. Female Genital Mutilation. http://en.wikipedia.org/wiki/Female_genital_mutilation.

Wikipedia, 2011. Waterborarding. http://en.wikipedia.org/wiki/Waterboarding (retrieved 24.06.11; 9:51).

World Medical Association, 1994. The Declaration of Tokyo, 1975. Ethical Codes and Declarations Relevant to the Health Professions. Amnesty International, New York, p. 9.

Key Terms

Abdominal injuries, Abrasion, Accidental injury, Antemortem trauma, Autopsy, Biomechanics, Blunt injury, Bone, Bone injury, Bone pathology, Bone trauma, Brittle, Bruise, Capability of acting, Cerebral contusion, Chop wound, Close-range shot, Computed tomography, Contact shot, Contusion, Cut, Death, Defense wound, Distant shot, Ductility, Elasticity, Electricity, Epidural hematoma, Falaka, Finger torture, Firearm injury, Forced position, Foreign bodies, Forensic anthropology, Fractures, Gunshot wounds, Hematoma, Homicide, Identification, Imaging, Incised wound, Initiation, Injuries to the extremities, Intracranial hemorrhage, Lacerations of inner organs, Nail torture, Plasticity, Radiographs, Range of fire, Rib fractures, Scintigraphy, Self-infliction, Sharp injury, Sharp force injury, Shotgun injury, Skeleton, Skin laceration, Skull fracture, Stab wound, Stabbing, Stiffness, Strain, Strangulation, Stress, Subdural hematoma, Suicide, Thoracic trauma, Torture, Trauma, Uncomfortable position, Water torture, Waterboarding, Wound ballistics

Review Questions

1. Why are the effects of a pathology on a person's life more important than the diagnosis of the pathology?
2. Why is reading pathologies in forensic anthropology not a "simple transposition" from paleopathology to forensic pathology?
3. What role does epidemiological data play in the diagnosis of bone pathologies in a forensic context?
4. Differentiate between congenital, metabolic, infectious, and traumatic pathologies.
5. How is antemortem trauma distinguished from postmortem trauma?
6. What patterns of trauma are suggested of child abuse and elder abuse? How do they differ?
7. What is *falanga* and what is its forensic implication?
8. What are the five ways by which loads can be applied to bone?

9. What is the relationship between stress and strain, and what are the implications for bone trauma?

10. List at least four types of bone fracture and how they occur?

11. Distinguish between contusions and lacerations in bone.

12. What is a hinge fracture?

13. What causes diffuse axonal injuries?

14. Sharp force trauma accounts for what percentage of attempted suicides? Completed suicides?

15. What is one characteristic of a sharp force trauma by a nonedged weapon such as a screwdriver?

16. What percentage of victims of sharp force attacks shows defensive wounds?

17. Do gunshot wounds to the head or trunk always incapacitate a victim immediately? What are the implications to crime scene reconstruction?

18. What is the "stopping power" of a firearm?

19. What are the characteristics of entrance wounds? Exit wounds?

20. What is an "abrasion collar"?

Discussion Questions

1. How can self-inflicted wounds be distinguished from those caused by an assault? Does the type of weapon (hammer, knife, firearm) matter? Why or why not?

2. Considering your answer to Discussion Question 1, how would handedness play a role in this distinction?

3. Do forensic anthropologists play a role in determining cause versus manner of death? Why or why not?

4. Given that forensic anthropologists typically deal only with hard tissues and that describing trauma is a type of diagnosis, what are the limitations of making determinations of abuse or torture for the profession? What are the ethical implications?

5. Do forensic anthropologists play a role in making determinations of pathology or trauma in the living? Why or why not?

Additional Readings

Berryman, H.E., Saul, T.B., 2015. Skeletal Evidence of Violent Sexual Assault in Remains with Excessive Evidence of Scavenging. Skeletal Trauma Analysis: Case Studies in Context. John Wiley & Sons, Ltd, New York, NY, pp. 118–129.

Blau, S., 2015. Working as a forensic archaeologist and/or anthropologist in post-conflict contexts: a consideration of professional responsibilities to the missing, the dead and their relatives. In: Ethics and the Archaeology of Violence. Springer, New York, pp. 215–228.

Blau, S., 2016. How traumatic: a review of the role of the forensic anthropologist in the examination and interpretation of skeletal trauma. Australian Journal of Forensic Sciences 1–20.

Christensen, A.M., Passalacqua, N.V., Schmunk, G.A., Fudenberg, J., Hartnett, K., Mitchell Jr., R.A., Love, J.C., deJong, J., Petaros, A., 2015. The value and availability of forensic anthropological consultation in medicolegal death investigations. Forensic Science, Medicine, and Pathology 11 (3), 438–441.

Corrieri, B., Márquez-Grant, N., 2015. What do bones tell us? The study of human skeletons from the perspective of forensic anthropology. Science Progress 98 (4), 391–402.

Pinheiro, J., Cunha, E., Symes, S., 2015. Over-interpretation of Bone Injuries and Implications for Cause and Manner of Death. Skeletal Trauma Analysis: Case Studies in Context. John Wiley and Sons, Ltd, New York, NY, pp. 27–41.

Steadman, D.W., Andersen, S.A., 2015. In: The Marty Miller Case: Introducing Forensic Anthropology. Hard Evidence: Case Studies in Forensic Anthropology, p. 8.

Section 6. Identification

For forensic anthropologists, "whoisit" is as important as "whodunnit." The goal of many, if not all, examinations is to determine who the individual presented is. Identification can be achieved and cross-referenced by a number of modes, including X-rays, prosthetics, dentition, and DNA. Whether it is the identification of hundreds, such as in a plane crash, or only one person, the work of the forensic anthropologist has significant influence on prosecutions, policy, and other legal issues, such as insurance or war crimes. The growth of forensic anthropology in this last area—the identification of those involved in or the victims of—armed conflict has solidified the profession into a necessary application of the study of the human body. Sadly, this seems to be a growth area for careers. With thousands of missing persons reported annually, forensic anthropology continues to be a crucial component to forensic investigations as well as bringing answers to those most in need by identifying their lost loved ones.

Identification of the Living

P Gabriel and W Huckenbeck, University Clinic Düsseldorf, Düsseldorf, Germany

Glossary

Comparison analysis Comparison of the features of a person shown on a reference image with the features of a suspect shown on a comparison image.

Comparison photo Photo showing a suspect in the same perspective as the perpetrator on surveillance material.

Feature analysis Analysis and description of individual features of a person shown on a reference image.

Reference photo or video Photo or video recorded by a surveillance camera showing the perpetrator.

Abbreviations

Alare (al)	The most lateral point on each alar contour
Cheilion (ch)	The point located at each labial commissure
Endocanthion (en)	The point at the inner commissure of the eye fissure. The soft endocanthion is located lateral to the bony landmark that is used in cephalometry
Exocanthion (ex)	The point at the outer commissure of the eye fissure. The soft exocanthion is slightly medial to the bony exocanthion
Gnathion (gn)	The lowest median landmark on the lower border of the mandible. It is identified by palpation and is identical to the bony gnathion
Gonion (go)	The most lateral point of the jawline at the mandibular angle
Postaureale (pa)	The most posterior point on the free margin of the ear
Preaureale (pra)	The most anterior point of the ear, located just in front of the helix attachment to the head
Pronasale (prn)	The furthest protruding point of the apex nasi, identified in a lateral view of the head in the rest position
Pupil (p)	Determined when the head is in the rest position and the eye is looking straight ahead

Sellion (se)	The deepest landmark located at the bottom of the nasofrontal angle		border of the nasal septum and the surface of the upper lip meet
Stomion (sto)	The point at the intersection of the MSP with the horizontal labial fissure between gently closed lips, with teeth shut in the natural position	**Superaureale (sa)**	The highest point on the free margin of the auricle
		Tragion (t)	The notch on the upper margin of the tragus
Subaureale (sba)	The lowest point on the free margin of the earlobe	**Trichion (tr)**	The point on the hairline (if present) in the MSP
Subnasale (sn)	The midpoint of the angle at the columellar base where the lower	**Zygion (zy)**	The most lateral point of the cheek region

Introduction

The study of recognition and identification processes probably has to do more with the cognitive sciences; however, in the forensic scenario, it is frequently necessary to identify people according to their somatic traits. In theory, each person can be distinguished from all others according to appearance. For this, the features must be closely examined. In daily life, one is sometimes mistaken by confusing a person with somebody else, but the actual existence of a real "look-alike" who displays the exact combination of features has not been scientifically proven. In fact, differences in certain features that are not noticed with a fleeting glance or when the person is not really well known to us (celebrity doubles) can always be found. Even identical (monozygotic) twins display differences in features that enable them to be differentiated.

In forensic practice, the degree of individualization is highly dependent on the quality of the images (photos and videos) and the frequency of the identifiable features/traits. Due to the hereditability of some features, close kinship can make the distinction of persons more difficult. Overall, a positive identification is very difficult to achieve and every feature has to be analyzed critically.

Established methods in forensic anthropology and classical criminology are used for the determination of individuality on the basis of facial and body appearances.

Despite the rapid advancement and increased practical application of DNA technology, the criminological importance of image analysis has not diminished, especially due to the fact that more and more areas of daily life are under video surveillance and can, in principle, be controlled. The increasing anonymization of business life (ATMs) and increasing mobility (forged identity documents) create further potential applications.

The general aspect of a person is important; nonetheless, initially, the study of single traits can be very useful, before proceeding to a unified comparison of the entire physiognomy. As a result, the general appearance of a person on a speed-camera image, surveillance photo, or video can initially be separated into traits or features.

As in all morphological contexts of identification, for a high level of confidence, a large number of corresponding and/or unique features are required. If, for example, extremely rare features (skin lesions such as scars, warts, tattoos, or birthmarks) are present on the reference photograph, a lower number of features may be sufficient. Exclusion of identity, on the other hand, can be reached by the difference in one trait, if its evaluation was objective and if the discordance cannot be explained by other reasons, for example, surgery and weight gain. On the other hand, in the case of a slight feature dissimilarity, the possibility of the dissimilarity being explained through lighting, image quality, contrast, masking, artifacts, etc., should be investigated.

The scientific methods of image identification were initially described in the German-speaking countries; this discipline has, however gained, in the past decades, a widespread diffusion in international literature, and actually represents a relevant field of application of forensic anthropology.

Facial Assessment

Checking for Suitability of Images

Initially, the examiner must view the available evidence material. In the case of video recordings, it is vital that he or she analyzes the material and produces suitable still images. Photomaterial should—whenever possible—be requested in digital form. After a successful digitalization of the evidence material, an attempt at an improvement in quality can be made. This must be limited to brightness, tone, and contrast; must be understandable; and must on no account lead to feature alterations. At this point, the assessor should decide whether the reference photograph/image material is suitable for an assessment or the maximum level of confidence that can be achieved in an identification. One should keep in mind that there is always the risk of image deformation, especially in digital images. A transformation of the image format can lead to a modification of image proportions. These deformations can sometimes only be corrected by specialists (e.g., engineers). Even image compression techniques that are very common in the storing of digital images can lead to feature alterations. For that reason, one should be very careful with images that show a high compression rate.

Feature Analysis: The Preliminary Step

It is recommended that the reference photograph/image be carefully analyzed. The individual areas of the head (head shape, face shape, facial proportions, hairline, forehead, eye, nasal, mouth, chin, lower jaw, cheek, ear region, and neck) can be analyzed, described, and classified usually according to specific references, such as Interpol atlases or more modern and complete ones such as the Department of Motor Vehicles (DMV) one (see Appendix). As far as the quality of the image material allows, an attempt is made in determining fine structures. Each feature complex is subdivided into numerous individual features. For instance, in the eye region these can be eyebrows, upper eyelid, distance between the eyes, eyelid axis, and lower eyelid.

Optical properties of the surveillance camera must be taken into account. In the case of surveillance cameras in ATMs, strong wide-angle lenses are often used to enable the capture of a wide area. Such "fish eye" lenses lead to image distortions: whereas the central portions appear squashed, the structures in the edge areas appear bent or stretched. Once again, specialists in such cases should be consulted in order to correct, if possible, dangerous image distortions.

Comparison Image

For the assessment, a comparison image whose perspective matches that of the reference photograph should be available. Ideally, the comparison image should be prepared by the examiner himself/herself. Only then can a safe, detailed, and reliable feature comparison be performed. Recordings from police identification records are standardized for their requirements and therefore often of limited use for an assessment. In addition, the dates when the reference and the comparison recordings were made must be taken into account, because alterations in the manifestations of features due to aging can have an effect to varying extents. Chronic illnesses can also change the appearance, whereby a relatively short time span between source and comparison photograph is required. Alterable features typically include hair style and beard style, and increase and decrease in weight. The possibility of previous surgery having taken place, as previously mentioned, must also be considered. In some cases, it may be necessary to record the comparison image with the same camera setup with which the evidence/reference photograph was made. In case an estimate of the height of the perpetrator is required, a reconstruction at the crime scene is required. The comparative images can also come from a 3D scan of the suspect, which would allow the examiner to virtually orient the 3D head and find the best-matching orientation subsequently on a computer. Feature analysis and classification can then be performed as mentioned for the reference photograph.

Comparison Analysis

After completion of the feature analysis of the reference photograph and of a suitable photograph of the suspect, a comparison can be performed. All the described features on the reference photograph are compared with all evaluated features and fine structures on the suspect's image. The similarities and dissimilarities are described and discussed according to set standards (e.g., DMV atlas). As far as single traits are concerned, the examiner can verify the existence of discordant traits or that of similar ones. This step therefore will give an idea of consistency of the two faces, that is, of how similar they are. Positive identification should not, however, be attempted at this point (and especially not on frequency and distribution of single traits among different populations).

Positive identification should be achieved once a global comparison of all traits and other more general features is performed. Different approaches exist. Some experts also use the superimposition of lines and general patterns on the images and verify the match. Another possibility is super-imposing the face in toto. However, this is extremely laborious and requires a lot of equipment. In addition, overlapping techniques may have a suggestive effect. Any examiner using such a method must be aware of this. The use of 3D techniques is becoming more and more important: 3D-comparison images of the suspect can be much more easily adjusted to the perpetrator's face on a reference image and the geometric comparison may be more objective. The influence of the focal length and the distortion of the objective lens can be eliminated by using 3D laser scanning and optical surface digitalization. On the other hand, 3D scans are much more time-consuming than conventional photography. However, in many practical cases, only a combination of different techniques will lead to reliable results.

At what point, however, can one say to have reached identification, or how should the expert express his or her judgment? Unlike geneticists, the morphologist cannot respond in a quantified manner for obvious reasons. Forensic experts who deal with facial identification often are reluctant to define from a numerical point of view the strength of their results. However, many courts and judges often require some understanding of the strength of their conclusions; in 2003, the Forensic Imagery Analysis Group (FIAG), born within BAHID (British Association for Human Identification), established a common procedure for describing the level of ascertainment of personal identification according to the degree of support (provided exclusion has not been achieved):

Level 0 Lends no support.
Level 1 Lends limited support.
Level 2 Lends moderate support.

Level 3 Lends support.
Level 4 Lends strong support.
Level 5 Lends powerful support.

Many other "classifications" exist. The problem still remains, however, just like with the anthropological or odontological identification of human remains, of what is enough for a positive identification beyond reasonable doubt.

Other Body Traits

Determining the height of the perpetrator

It has been mentioned above that the comparison of the stature of the perpetrator with that of the suspect can take place at the crime scene provided metric references exist on the reference photograph. Significant problems may arise concerning body posture, clothing, heels, etc., which must be taken into account. The procedure is, however, rather imprecise and therefore contains a large margin for error. For a negative identification in the case of an unusual height of the perpetrator, the procedure can be regarded as sufficiently secure. The most recent studies concerning this topic have highlighted that the reliability of height estimation in personal identification depends on the rarity of the estimated perpetrator's height and its closeness to the suspect's height. As in the preparation of comparison photographs, the question as to whether there has been any change in the camera equipment in the meantime must be investigated beforehand.

Another method for height estimation consists of using a virtual telecamera with the same characteristics of the video surveillance system with which the images were taken. The experimental data showed an average difference between estimated and real height of about 10 mm, together with a standard deviation of 10 mm. This procedure obviously requires that the individual be represented in his/her entire figure from the feet to the head.

Gait analysis

In video recordings, gait is recorded alongside the body size. In the case of an unusual gait, this can lead to narrowing down of the number of suspects or in the ideal case, to a positive identification of the perpetrator. The expert must, however, bear in mind that in a recreation of the sequence of events of the crime, the gait of the accused can intentionally be falsified. To prevent this, it has proven useful to film suspects when they believe that they are not being observed.

In addition, being systems based on the periodical nature of gait, they face clear limits when the subject is moving at a nonconstant speed and on a route which is nonlinear. Finally, these systems presuppose the analyses of sequences of gait, which usually cannot be defined by the few useful photograms of persons, taken during a generic walking phase. In addition, the entire methodology of gait analysis has not been standardized. Moreover, although gait can be considered an individualizing marker, the same individual can express different manners of walking according to different conditions (speed, mood, and environmental conditions). At the moment, gait analysis is a promising field of application, but still has to be standardized and thoroughly tested.

Age

The manifestation of facial features is, within certain limits, age dependent, although the modifications of facial features at different ages still need to be verified. During the growth phase, the main changes are in facial proportions from a child's to an adult's face; in addition, some measurements such as the ear length go on increasing after 18 years of age also. This may be used in the future to estimate the age of children and young people. In the last few years, increased attention has been given to the measurements of facial surfaces and volumes by the application of 3D image acquisition systems, which may be useful for the development of an age estimation method. However, further research is needed. Individual variability must, however, be taken into account. In adults, as the growth processes come to an end, facial modifications are due to natural aging, which, however is less predictable, and therefore less applicable to a possible age estimation method.

Further Features on the Skin, Hands, and Genitals

Occasionally, no facial features are visible on images but additional features that could lead to an identification are visible. In general, only features that are unusual should be described. These could, for instance, be scars on a part of the body, anatomical anomalies, anomalies after accidents or illnesses, tattoos, piercings, etc. The pattern of skin veins, for instance on the back of the hand, has also been shown to be highly individual.

In conclusion, in order to identify persons on the basis of features, these must be visible and should not be affected by strong environmental influences or rapid age changes. A prerequisite for objectivity in identification is the clear definition of the features and the description of the different manifestations of features. A general limitation of the examiner's evaluation lies in the quality of the reference photograph. Often, very individual features such as scars, birthmarks, warts, etc., cannot be evaluated due to graininess, lack of contrast, reflections, unsuitable perspective of the image, or artificial masking. The examiner must decide whether the number of features and their manifestation are sufficient for a positive or negative identification. **Figure 1** shows surveillance photos of the same driver (senior author). The number of facial features and therefore the reliability of a feature comparison vary widely from photo to photo.

Appendix: Morphological Assessment of Facial Features: The DMV Atlas

The following section shows the different areas of the human face, and deals briefly with the manifestations of the main

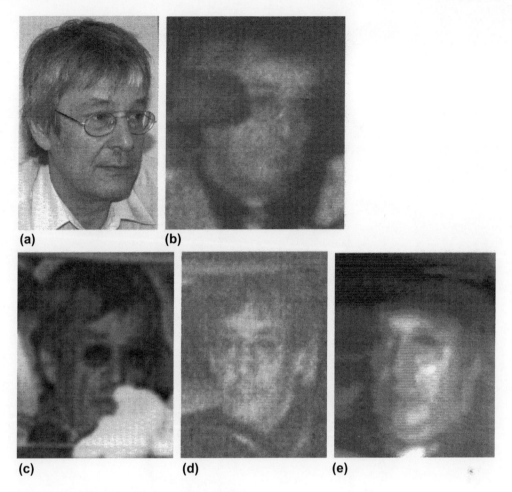

(a)　　　　　(b)

(c)　　　　　(d)　　　　　(e)

Figure 1　(a) Comparison photograph. (b–e) Traffic surveillance pictures.

features, included in the DMV atlas, one of the most recent amplifications of the traditional Interpol standards. Listing all fine structures is beyond the scope of this chapter. Nevertheless, this limited list shows that the subfeatures of the main areas—face shape, hairline, forehead, eye region, nose, mouth area, cheek area, chin, and ear—can be divided into different feature manifestations. The following sections therefore describe the manifestation of some main and subfeatures of the human face, which are included in the atlas for the evaluation of facial features. The atlas describes a total of 46 facial features that have been scientifically studied and the frequency of different manifestations determined. Special emphasis is placed on user-friendliness. Take as an example the face shape: In the atlas only six face shapes are examined, which are well distinguishable from one another. More than 20 different face shapes are found in older anthropological literature, some of which even experts find hard to distinguish between.

Face Shape

Face shapes are classified as rectangular, oval, round, pentagonal with pronounced mandible, wedge-shaped, and pentagonal with pronounced cheekbones. Examples are shown in **Figure 2**.

Forehead

The height of the forehead is classified relative to the height of the entire head (trichion–sellion). The breadth of the forehead is expressed in terms of the complete head. Possible descriptions for the frontal height are shown in **Figure 3**. Seen from the side, the forehead bias can be described.

Frontal Hairline

The shape of the hairline in frontal view can be described as shown in **Figure 4**.

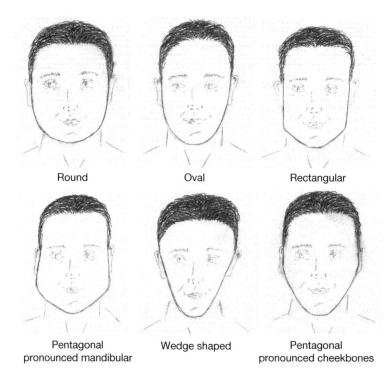

Round   Oval   Rectangular

Pentagonal   Wedge shaped   Pentagonal
pronounced mandibular   pronounced cheekbones

Figure 2 Face shape classifications.

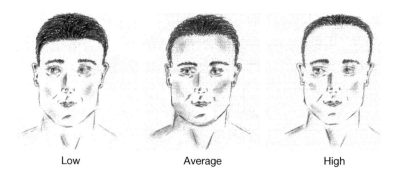

Low   Average   High

Figure 3 Forehead classifications.

Eye Region

The human eye region contains many features. Eyebrow height, eyebrow density, which can be medial or laterally pointed, and eyebrow shape can be described. There may be a mono-brow which is shown in **Figure 5**. The distance of upper eyelid–eyebrow in comparison to the complete face can be described as well as the lid axis, the size of the visible eye, and the distance between the eyes.

Nasal Region

The nasal region contains numerous subfeatures that can provide important information for positive or negative identification in the case of good-quality images.

The nose bridge length is defined as the distance between nasal root and nasal tip (sellion–pronasale) in comparison to the complete face. The breadth of the nasal bridge is described in comparison to the complete nose in frontal view. Nose

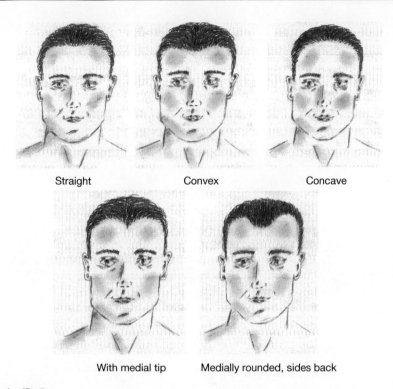

Straight   Convex   Concave

With medial tip   Medially rounded, sides back

Figure 4   Frontal hairline classification.

bridge process describes the run of the nasal bridge in frontal view. The nose profile must be estimated from a lateral view. The orientation of the nose tip is defined as the location from pronasale to subnasale in lateral/frontal view. In frontal view,

the nose tip shape can be specified. In lateral view, the nose protrusion (in comparison to the complete face) can be described (**Figure 6**). In frontal view, the nasal breadth is expressed as the degree of puffing of the alar wings (al–al). The

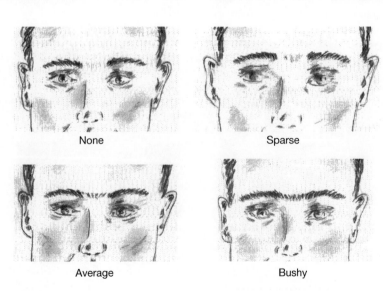

None   Sparse

Average   Bushy

Figure 5   Mono-brow classifications.

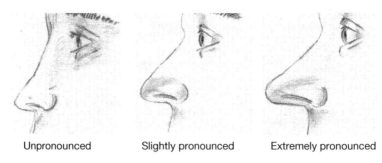

Unpronounced   Slightly pronounced   Extremely pronounced

Figure 6   Nose protrusion in lateral view.

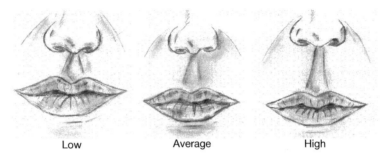

Low   Average   High

Figure 7   Classification of philtrum height.

length of the skinny alar wings in comparison to the complete nose in lateral view is called alar wing length. In lateral view, the nostrils can be specified.

Oral Region

The distance between upper vermillion and the nasal baseline (labiale superius–subnasale) is called the philtrum height (**Figure 7**). The degree of impression between lips and nose is called philtrum depth. Labial breadth is expressed as the distance between the corners of the mouth (cheilion–cheilion) in comparison to the complete face in frontal view. The shape of the upper rim of the vermillion (upper lip notch) can be described as well as the angle of the outer ends of the mouth slit.

Chin Shape

The form of the chin contour can be evaluated. The degree of transition from chin to the basis of the mandible can be described. In lateral view, the chin protrusion can be specified (**Figure 8**). Some individuals show a dimple in the chin. The height of the chin may also be differentiated.

Ear Region

In addition to the main features such as pinna and earlobe, the human ear contains a wide range of highly differentiated fine features, which can be very typical for an individual. Unfortunately, in practice, the quality of the reference photographs usually only allows an evaluation of the gross structures.

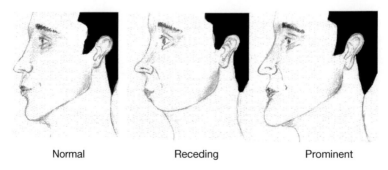

Normal   Receding   Prominent

Figure 8   Protrusion of the chin.

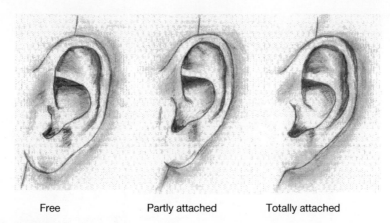

Free   Partly attached   Totally attached

Figure 9 Attachment of the earlobe.

The distance from the highest to the lowest point of the ear in lateral view (superaureale–subaureale) in comparison to the complete head is called ear height. The distance from the most anterior to the most posterior point of the ear (praeaureale–postaureale) can be described. The size of the earlobe is evaluated in comparison to the complete ear. The degree of attachment of the earlobe is shown in **Figure 9**. In frontal view, the degree to which the ears stick out (ear protrusion) can be judged.

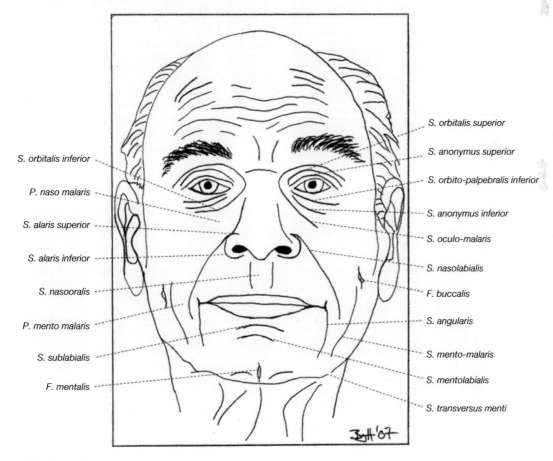

S. orbitalis inferior
P. naso malaris
S. alaris superior
S. alaris inferior
S. nasooralis
P. mento malaris
S. sublabialis
F. mentalis

S. orbitalis superior
S. anonymus superior
S. orbito-palpebralis inferior
S. anonymus inferior
S. oculo-malaris
S. nasolabialis
F. buccalis
S. angularis
S. mento-malaris
S. mentolabialis
S. transversus menti

Figure 10 Wrinkles and dimples.

Cheek and Throat Area

Depending on the subcutaneous fat tissue and bone structure, the cheek and throat area can be differently manifested. The cheek region can be extremely sunken (gaunt) or extensively to roundly padded. Flat depressions or "fleshy pockets" may be present. In the chin–throat area, a double or triple chin may be present. A depression below the cheekbones in frontal view may be visible.

Wrinkles and Dimples

As **Figure 10** shows, wrinkles and dimples can give the human face very individual, sometimes individual typical, traits. Precise definitions are required to describe these features, and these are also provided in **Figure 10**.

See also: **Anthropology/Odontology:** Aging the Dead and the Living; Facial Approximation; History of Forensic Anthropology; Personal Identification in Forensic Anthropology; **Digital Evidence:** Child Pornography; Digital Imaging: Enhancement and Authentication; **Forensic Medicine/Clinical:** Forensic Age Estimation; Identification; **Foundations:** Overview and Meaning of Identification/Individualization.

Further Reading

Bertillon, A., 1896. Signaletic Instructions Including the Theory and Practice of Anthropometrical Identification. National Library of Medicine, Chicago.

Brinker, H., 1985. Identifizieren und Wiedererkennen. Bemerkungen zum Unterschied und zur Beweisqualität. Archiv fur Kriminologie 176, 142–145.

Buck, U., Naether, S., Kreutz, K., Thali, M., 2011. Geometric facial comparison in speed-check photographs. International Journal of Legal Medicine 125, 785–790.

Cattaneo, C., Ritz-Timme, S., Gabriel, P., et al., 2009. The difficult issue of age assessment on pedo-pornographic material. Forensic Science International 183, 21–24.

Cattaneo, C., Cantatore, A., Ciaffi, R., et al., 2011. Personal identification by the comparison of facial profiles: testing the reliability of a high-resolution 3D–2D comparison model. Journal of Forensic Sciences 57, 182–187 [Epub ahead of print]. http://dx.doi.org/10.1111/j.1556-4029.2011.01944.x.

Cavanagh, D., Steyn, M., 2011. Facial reconstruction: soft tissue thickness values for South African black females. Forensic Science International 206 (1–3), 215.e1–215.e7.

De Angelis, D., Sala, R., Cantatore, A., et al., 2007. New method for height estimation of subjects represented in photograms taken from video surveillance systems. International Journal of Legal Medicine 121 (6), 489–492.

De Angelis, D., Sala, R., Cantatore, A., Grandi, M., Cattaneo, C., 2009. A new computer-assisted technique to aid personal identification. International Journal of Legal Medicine 123 (4), 351–356.

De Greef, S., Claes, P., Vandermeulen, D., Mollemans, W., Suetens, P., Willems, G., 1996. Morphological classification of facial features in adult Caucasian males based on an assessment of photographs of 50 subjects. Forensic Science 41 (5), 786–791.

Edler, R., Agarwal, P., Wertheim, D., Greenhill, D., 2006. The use of anthropometric proportion indices in the measurement of facial attractiveness. European Journal of Orthodontics 28 (3), 274–281.

Farkas, L.G., Katic, M.J., Forrest, C.R., 2007. Comparison of craniofacial measurements of young adult African-American and North American white males and females. Annals of Plastic Surgery 59, 692–775.

Ferrario, V.F., Sforza, C., Schmitz, J.H., Miani Jr., A., Taroni, G., 1995. Fourieranalyses of human soft tissue facial shape: sex differences in normal adults. Journal of Anatomy 187, 593–602.

Gabriel, P., Obertová, Z., Ratnayake, M., et al., 2010. Schätzung des Lebensalters kindlicher Opfer auf Bilddokumenten. Rechtsmedizin 21, 7–11.

Goos, M.I.M., Alberink, I.B., Ruifrok, A.C.C., 2005. 2D/3D image (facial) comparison using camera matching. Forensic Science International 163 (1–2), 10–17.

Hajnis, K., Farkas, L.G., Ngim, R.C.K., Lee, S.T., Venkatadri, G., 1994. Racial and ethnic morphometric differences in the craniofacial complex. In: Farkas, L.G. (Ed.), Anthropometry of the Head and Face, second ed. Raven Press, New York, pp. 201–217.

Halberstein, R.A., 2001. The application of anthropometric indices in forensic photography: three case studies. Journal of Forensic Sciences 46 (6), 1438–1441.

Heathcote, J., 1995. Why do old men have big ears? British Medical Journal 311, 1668.

Hirthammer, B.J., 2007. Die physiognomische Alterung des Menschen. Quantifizierung mittels 3DLaserscanners (Master Thesis). University of Ulm, Germany.

Iscan, M.Y., 1993. The introduction of techniques for photographic comparison: potential and problems. In: Iscan, M.Y., Helmer, R.P. (Eds.), Forensic Analyses of the Scull: Craniofacial Analyses, Reconstruction and Identification. Wiley-Liss, New York, pp. 57–70.

Kleinberg, K.F., Vanezis, P., 2007. Variation in proportion indices and angles between selected facial landmarks with rotation in the Frankfort plane. Medicine, Science, and the Law 47 (2), 107–116.

Kleinberg, K.F., Vanezis, P., Burton, A.M., 2007. Failure of anthropometry as a facial identification technique using high-quality photographs. Journal of Forensic Sciences 52 (4), 779–783.

Knussmann, R., 1983. Die vergleichende morphologische analyse als Identitätsnachweis. Strafverteidiger 3, 127–129.

Knussmann, R., 1988. Lehrbuch Anthropologie, vol. I/1. G. Fischer-Verlag, Stuttgart.

Knussmann, R., 1991. Zur Wahrscheinlichkeitsaussage im morphologischen Identitätsgutachten. NStZ 11 (4), 175–177.

Lynnerup, N., Andersen, M., Lauritsen, H.P., 2003. Facial image identification using Photomodeler^W. Legal Medicine 5, 156–160.

Macho, G.A., 1986. Cephalometric and craniometric age changes in adult humans. Annals of Human Biology 13 (1), 49–61.

Martin, R., Saller, K., 1957. Lehrbuch der Anthropologie in Systematischer Darstellung mit Besonderer Berücksichtigung der Anthropologischen Methoden. Gustav-Fischer-Verlag, Stuttgart.

Ohlrogge, S., Nohrden, D., Schmitt, R., Drabik, A., Gabriel, P., Ritz-Timme, S., 2008. Anthropologischer Atlas männlicher Gesichtsmerkmale – Anthropological Atlas of Male Facial Features. Verlag der Polizeiwissenschaften, Frankfurt/Main.

Ohlrogge, S., Arent, T., Huckenbeck, W., Gabriel, P., Ritz-Timme, S., 2009. Anthropologischer Atlas weiblicher Gesichtsmerkmale – Anthropological Atlas of Female Facial Features. Verlag der Polizeiwissenschaften, Frankfurt/Main.

Porter, G., Doran, G., 2000. An anatomical and photographic technique for forensic facial identification. Forensic Science International 114 (2), 97–105.

Ritz-Timme, S., Gabriel, P., Tutkuviene, J., et al., 2011a. Metric and morphological assessment of facial features: a study on three European populations. Forensic Science International 207, 239.e1–239.e8.

Ritz-Timme, S., Gabriel, P., Obertova, Z., et al., 2011b. A new atlas for the evaluation of facial features: advantages, limits, and applicability. International Journal of Legal Medicine 125, 301–306.

Roelofse, M.M., Steyn, M., Becker, P.J., 2008. Photo identification: facial metrical and morphological features in South African males. Forensic Science International 177 (2–3), 168–175.

Rösing, F.W., 2008. Morphologische identifikation von Personen. In: Buck, J., Krumbholz, H. (Eds.), Sachverständigenbeweis im Verkehrsrecht. Nomos-Verlag, Baden-Baden, pp. 201–219.

Shaner, D.J., Bamforth, S., Peterson, A.E., Beattie, O.B., 1998. Technical note: different techniques, different results – a comparison of photogrammetric and caliper-derived measurements. American Journal of Physical Anthropology 106, 547–552.

Thompson, T., Black, S., 2007. Forensic Human Identification – an Introduction. CRC Press, Boca Raton, FL.

Vanezis, P., Lu, D., Cockburn, J., et al., 1996. Morphological classification of facial features in adult Caucasian males based on an assessment of photographs of 50 subjects. Journal of Forensic Sciences 41, 786–791.

Ventura, F., Zacheo, A., Ventura, A., Pala, A., 2004. Computerized anthropomorphometric analyses of images: case report. Forensic Science International 146, 211–213.

Yoshino, M., Matsuda, H., Kubota, S., Imaizumi, K., Miyasaka, S., 2000. Computer-assisted facial image identification system using a 3-D physiognomic range finder. Forensic Science International 109, 225–237.

Facial Approximation

CN Stephan, Central Identification Laboratory, HI, USA

Glossary

Anterior The front of the body or a direction toward it.

Exophthalmometer An instrument used to measure anterior positioning of the eyeballs in the skull.

Flower's point The point where the posterior lacrimal crest meets the frontal bone.

Frankfurt horizontal The posture of the head when the two porion (superior most points of the external auditory meatus on each side) and the left orbitale (lowest point of the left eye socket) lie in the same horizontal plane, parallel to the floor.

Freeway space The gap that is present between the upper and lower teeth when the mandible is in its physiologic rest position.

Lateral The side of the body or a direction toward it.

Median plane The section running vertically through the body that bisects it into two equal parts.

Natural head position The posture of the head when an individual is standing with their visual axis horizontal (i.e., parallel to the floor). This plane differs from the Frankfurt Horizontal by ~5°.

Posterior The back of the body or a direction toward it.

Supine Position of the body, lying down, but face up.

Introduction

In cases where skeletons prove difficult to identify using DNA, dental record comparison, and/or nondental radiographic comparison, and where a skull is present, attempts may be made to predict the facial appearance from the skull (**Figure 1**). Such procedures are termed "facial approximation" and are undertaken on the assumption that the skull typography closely relates to the overlying soft tissue of the face. The predicted face is then advertised in the mass media (alongside other case details) with calls for anyone who recognizes the face, or has further information, to contact the appropriate authorities.

In the forensic context, the value of the method is derived from the media release and two possible successful outcomes. First, the facial approximation may help draw public attention to the case amplifying case exposure and maximizing leads that contribute to case resolution. Second, the predicted face may directly promote recognitions of the deceased individual. The latter outcome is the mainstream aim of facial approximation, but whether or not the method reliably fulfills it is contentious (see the section Anatomical Legitimacy and Accuracy of Methods). Irrespective of its scientific accuracy, facial approximation is justified in a forensic investigation context because it can contribute meaningfully to the investigation, even when the predicted face does not specifically produce recognition.

Note here that any recognition of a facial approximation is not grounds for identification. The recognition can only be regarded as tentative, and identification can only be established or denied after further tests with other, more reliable, methods. Facial approximation, therefore, acts as a vehicle for an identification to be made, but it is not an identification method in and of itself.

Until recently, face prediction from the skull was popularly known as facial reconstruction or facial reproduction—terms that are increasingly being abandoned because they overemphasize the scientific basis and accuracy of the methods. Consequently, these terms are also avoided here.

Method History

The first published attempt at facial approximation was made in 1898 by Kollmann and Büchly. In the early 1900s, the method was regarded to communicate only the broad characteristics of a person's face; in particular, the race. This changed to a capability for portrait reconstruction (approximation so close to the appearance of a living person that an unknown individual could be identified) in the 1950s with the Russian anthropologist Gerasimov, and it has since remained the mainstream aim of modern facial approximation methods. The first documented success of the method, in its medicolegal context, was in 1918 concerning a 1916 homicide case from New York (USA), where the method was used to help identify a skeleton as Dominick La Rosa.

For most of its life, facial approximation has been manually executed by sculpting in clay or some other modeling mastic on the skull or a skull cast. However, computerized approaches have emerged over the last 20 years and major revisions of core face prediction protocols have simultaneously taken place. While computer methods have radically changed the way in which methods are performed, the software is not typically commercially or widely available, so manual (sculpting or drawing) methods remain widely employed. Given the methods' high dependency on anatomy and practitioner dexterity, anatomists, anthropologists, and artists have commonly collaborated to undertake the protocols.

Since the late 1990s, facial approximation methods have been classified into one of three categories: anatomical, soft tissue depth, or combination methods (otherwise termed the morphoscopic/morphometric/combination methods; or the Russian/American/combination methods). The "anatomical" category was designated to concern only those methods that required the construction of the facial muscles (to the exclusion of mean soft tissue depth values). The "soft tissue depth" category, as the name suggests, was meant to concern only those methods using mean soft tissue depths, and the "combination" category was meant to represent methods that blended the two aforementioned approaches. This

system is now recognized to be defunct because mean soft tissue depths underpin all facial approximation methods (even the Russian/morphoscopic/anatomical methods) and because Gerasimov (the recognized founder of Russian methods) actively avoided the construction of the muscles of facial expression. Facial approximation methods, whether executed manually or by computers are, therefore, best described as varying along a continuum: with "mean soft tissue depths" at one extreme and "individualized face anatomy" at the other.

Contemporary Methods

Skull Preparation

For manual methods, the skull is normally duplicated in plaster, acrylic, or some other material so that the original can be spared of any damage and so that it can be used as a reference during the face prediction process. For most computerized approaches, the skull will be scanned using a three-dimensional (3D) scanner, so it can be used within the electronic environment. In all cases, the mandible should be attached to the skull with an ~3–4 mm spacer at the glenoid fossa, to simulate the articular disc of the temporomandibular joint. The anterior teeth of the maxilla and mandible should also be separated by ~2–3 mm to simulate the physiologic freeway space present in the living subject at rest.

Figure 1   An example of a three-dimensional (3D) manual facial approximation, with the corresponding face. Reproduced from Stephan, C.N., Henneberg, M., 2006. Recognition by facial approximation: case specific examples and empirical tests. Forensic Science International 156, 182–191, with permission from Elsevier.

Soft Tissue Depths

Except for some computerized approaches that use deformations of existing 3D face meshes to create the new faces, all contemporary manual methods depend on mean facial soft tissue depths (MFSTD). This includes computer approaches that rely on virtual sculpting.

Soft tissue depths are used to quantify the distance from the skull surface to the facial surface and their means represent average values. Typically the soft depths have been collected for males and females of different ages and ancestral groups and they are represented on the skull so that the practitioner has a rough estimate of how far the soft tissues should extend from the skull surface. The soft tissue depths of many different subjects have been studied over facial approximation's life span (including embalmed cadavers, fresh cadavers, supine living subjects, and upright living subjects) and a variety of different measurement protocols have also been employed (e.g., needle puncture, B-mode ultrasound, A-mode ultrasound, lateral cephalographs, magnetic resonance imaging, and computed tomography (CT) scans—including cone beam CT).

The small differences that are found between different groups of subjects and studies are often used to justify their separate data logging; however, the practical meaning of these differences are difficult to evaluate because the data are confounded by numerous types of errors (sampling error, observer error, and error inherent to the type of measurement technique employed). Consequently, the small differences between studies and/or their samples may not accurately reflect the real differences between the population groups or the studies.

Table 1 Landmark definitions for the tallied mean soft tissue depths illustrated in **Figure 2** and reported in **Table 2**

Skeletal landmarks	Definitions
Opisthocranion (op)	Midline ectocranial point at farthest chord length from glabella
Vertex (v)	Highest midline ectocranial point
Glabella (g)	Most anterior midline point on the frontal bone
Nasion (n)	Midline point on the nasofrontal suture
Mid-nasal (mn)	Point on internasal suture midway between nasion and rhinion
Rhinion (rhi)	Midline point at the inferior free end of the internasal suture
Subnasale (sn)	Midline point just below the anterior nasal spine (soft tissue equivalent = midline point of the angle at the columella base where the septum and upper lip join)
Mid-philtrum (mp)	Midline point midway between the base of the nasal spine and prosthion on the anterior edge of the maxillae (soft tissue equivalent = midline point midway between soft tissue subnasale and the vermilion border of the upper lip in the groove of the philtrum)
Labrale superius (ls)	Midline landmark at the most anterior edge of the superior alveolar ridge of maxillae (soft tissue equivalent = midline soft tissue point at the vermilion border of upper lip)
Labrale inferius (li)	Midline point at the most anterior edge on the inferior alveolar ridge of the maxillae (soft tissue equivalent = midline soft tissue point at the vermilion border of lower lip)
Mentolabial sulcus (mls)	Deepest midline point in the groove superior to the mental eminence
Pogonion (pg)	Most anterior midline point on the mental eminence of the mandible
Gnathion (gn)	Midline point half way between the angle and the most anterior and inferior points on the bony chin
Menton (m)	Most inferior midline point at the mental symphysis of the mandible
Mid-supra orbital (mso)	Point on the supraorbital rim at the midsagittal plane of the orbit
Mid-infra orbital (mio)	Point on the infraorbital rim at the midsagittal plane of the orbit
Alare curvature point (acp)	Point $\sim$3 mm lateral to the border of the nasal aperture (soft tissue equivalent = point indicating the most lateral insertion of the nasal wing base into the face)
Gonion (go)	Point on the lateral aspect of the border of mandibular angle where a tangent bisects the angle formed by the posterior ramus border and the inferior corpus border
Zygion (zy)	Most lateral extent of the lateral surface of the zygomatic arch
Supra canine (sC)	Point on superior alveolar ridge superior to the maxillary canine(s)
Infra canine (iC)	Point on inferior alveolar ridge inferior to the mandibular canine(s)
Supra M^2 (sM^2)	Point on superior alveolar ridge superior to the maxillary 2 nd M(s)
Infra M_2 (iM_2)	Point on inferior alveolar ridge inferior to the mandibular 2 nd M(s)
Mid-ramus (mr)	Point at the center of the mandibular ramus
Mid-mandibular border (mmb)	Point on the inferior border of the corpus of the mandible midway between pogonion and gonion

Landmarks are positioned assuming that the skull is in the Frankfurt horizontal. The soft tissue equivalents overlay the hard tissue positions except where otherwise stated.
Source: Reproduced from Stephan, C.N., Simpson, E.K., 2008. Facial soft tissue depths in craniofacial identification (part I): An analytical review of the published adult data. Journal of Forensic Sciences 53, 1257–1272, with permission from Wiley-Blackwell.

To date, none of the mechanisms for MFSTD error have been adequately addressed in the facial approximation literature nor has the degree of application error been fully elucidated. Moreover, means have been unanimously employed for what are almost certainly skewed data (measurements can be extremely large but never extremely small or negative), whose central tendencies are better represented by other statistics. These limitations have recently prompted the pooling of data in efforts to provide values that are as comprehensive and accurate as possible, while other central tendency indicators are calculated. These tallied soft tissue depth tables have been calculated across essentially all studies published in the literature and represent the largest sampled standards currently available (see **Table 1** for landmark definitions, **Figure 2** for positions on the skull, and **Table 2** for the tallied soft tissue depths). These mean data hold the advantage that groups are not tenuously categorized, sample sizes are large, and real soft tissue depth values are triangulated upon by averaging data across different measurement protocols.

Noncomputerized Manual Methods

When drawing the predicted face, using soft modeling mastic (such as clay) to sculpt it, or constructing the muscles of facial expression as part of the facial approximation process, it is helpful to attach soft tissue depth pegs to the duplicate skull for reasons described above. If the modeling mastic is much stiffer (as for wax/rosin composites) and the muscles of facial expression are not built, the mastic itself can be used to indicate the depth, removing the need for indicator pegs (**Figure 3**). Once mean soft tissue depths are represented on the duplicate skull, the temporalis and masseter muscles are modeled according to the bony markings that indicate their general locations. Other anatomical structures, such as the superficial temporal fat pad, can also be added according to known anatomical relationships (**Figure 3**). In areas where mean soft tissue depths are not available, the depth of the tissue should be interpolated using the neighboring soft tissue depth markers and the practitioner's knowledge of human anatomy. This underscores the importance for practitioners to possess an extensive knowledge of the subject (human anatomy), and preferably, to hold tertiary qualifications in it.

The facial features are then added and generally their order of construction is not important; so long as the deeper structures are represented prior to other overlying, more superficial, components. To replicate typical anatomical positions, the eyeball should be located in the eye socket closer to the orbital roof and lateral orbital wall (each by 2–3 mm). An exophthalmometer should also be used to position the corneal apex ~16 mm anterior to the lateral orbital wall (**Figure 4**).

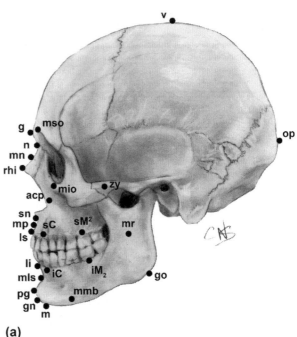

(a)

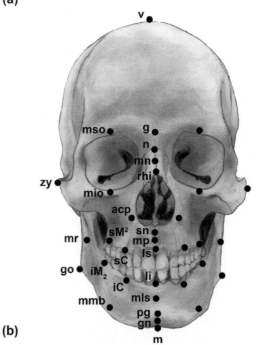

(b)

Figure 2 Soft tissue depth measurement sites: (a) lateral view, and (b) frontal view. See **Table 1** for definitions of landmarks. Reproduced from Stephan, C.N., Simpson, E.K., 2008. Facial soft tissue depths in craniofacial identification (part I): An analytical review of the published adult data. Journal of Forensic Sciences 53, 1257–1272, with permission from Wiley-Blackwell.

Table 2 Tallied facial soft tissue depths for adults and subadults

Soft tissue depths	Individuals ≤11 years			Individuals 12–17 years			Individuals ≥18 years		
	Mean	s	n	Mean	s	N	Mean	s	n
Median points									
op	–	–	–	–	–	–	6.5	2.5	990
v	–	–	–	–	–	–	5.0	1.0	785
g	5.0	1.0	2098	5.5	1.0	1539	5.5	1.0	4542
n	7.0	1.5	2102	7.5	1.5	1751	6.0	1.5	4417
mn	4.0	1.0	415	4.0	1.0	454	4.0	1.0	919
rhi	2.5	1.0	1046	2.5	1.0	700	3.0	1.0	4307
sn	9.5	2.0	1247	12.0	2.0	993	12.5	3.0	1170
mp	12.0	2.5	1703	14.5	3.0	1500	11.0	2.5	3955
ls	13.5	2.0	1475	14.5	2.5	1558	11.5	3.0	4216
Li	14.5	2.5	1293	15.5	2.5	1399	13.0	2.5	4017
mls	10.0	2.0	1666	11.0	2.0	1428	11.0	2.0	4497
pg	10.5	2.5	2099	12.0	2.5	1777	11.0	2.5	4891
gn	6.5	2.0	1044	7.5	2.0	660	8.5	3.0	381
m	9.0	3.0	160	9.0	2.5	103	7.0	2.5	3795
Bilateral points									
mso	5.0	1.0	469	6.0	1.0	245	6.0	1.5	1838
mio	6.0	1.5	521	7.0	1.5	250	7.0	3.5	1910
acp	7.5	2.0	410	7.5	2.0	103	9.5	2.0	1361
go	13.0	3.5	575	17.0	3.5	108	10.0	6.0	3320
zy	7.5	1.5	110	8.0	2.0	147	6.0	1.0	3545
sC	–	–	–	11.0	2.5	103	9.5	2.0	3113
iC	–	–	–	10.5	2.5	103	10.5	2.0	1157
sM^2	–	–	–	27.0	4.0	103	26.0	5.5	1212
iM$_2$	–	–	–	23.0	4.0	103	19.5	4.5	1151
mr	18.0	4.0	108	19.5	4.5	142	17.5	4.0	2637
mmb	10.5	3.5	411	12.5	3.5	103	10.5	4.5	548

Source: Data reproduced from Stephan, C.N., Simpson, E.K., 2008. Facial soft tissue depths in craniofacial identification (part I): An analytical review of the published adult data. Journal of Forensic Sciences 53, 1257–1272; Stephan, C.N., Simpson, E.K., 2008. Facial soft tissue depths in craniofacial identification (part II): An analytical review of the published sub-adult data. Journal of Forensic Sciences 53, 1273–1279, with permission from Wiley-Blackwell.

The muscles of facial expression (see Further Reading) can then be added but most of their construction is based on intuitive speculation in accordance with stereotypical patterns. An alternate approach is to use strips of clay to join the soft tissue depth markers together in a meshlike scaffold over the skull, removing the need to subjectively speculate on the facial expression muscles (**Figure 3**).

The medial canthus (inner corner of the eye fissure) should be placed ~5 mm lateral to the medial orbital wall and lateral canthus ~4.5 mm medial to the lateral orbital wall. The malar tubercle can be used to position both the medial and lateral canthal ligaments on either side, if it is present, since both canthi roughly fall at the same height and at the malar tubercle level. If a malar tubercle is not present, it can be estimated reliably 10 mm below the frontozygomatic suture. The width of the nose is established by the width of the nasal aperture (= 167% of its distance) and the height of the alar wings by the crista conchalis on the inner margins of the bony

nose. The projection of the nasal tip and its height can be estimated within several millimeters using various regression equations derived from the skull. The mouth width is equal to 133% of the intercanine distance measured from the lateral aspects of the teeth. The height of the lips approximate the height of the enamel of the front teeth and the lip closure line, in the median plane, sits at about one-third of the way up the central incisors. If any unusual anatomy exists on the skull, it should be clearly represented in the face since it may provide a trigger for recognition. In the same way, any unusual dental features should be exhibited, so constructing the face in smiling posture may be necessary.

At this point, the skull should be positioned in the natural head position—but note that this does not prevent reference to the Frankfurt horizontal if it is needed for facial feature prediction. Blocking in around the muscles of facial expression will be required, especially when softer modeling materials are used, so that they do not collapse at later face

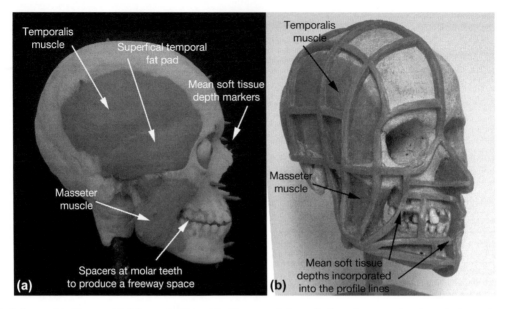

Figure 3   Partially complete 3D manual facial approximations: (a) with mean soft tissue depth markers, muscles of mastication, and superficial temporal fat pat; (b) with profile lines to connect mean soft tissue depth values over the muscles of mastication. Figure (a) modified from Stephan, C.N., Devine, M., 2009. The superficial temporal fat pad and its ramifications for temporalis muscle construction in facial approximation. Forensic Science International 191, 70–79, with permission from Elsevier.

construction stages. If the muscles of facial expression were constructed, sheets of modeling mastic ~4-mm thick are placed over the muscles to simulate the skin and subcutaneous tissues (**Figure 5**). The thicknesses of these sheets need to be adjusted to the various face regions to reflect realistic depths. It should not be applied around the eyes, for example, where the skin is extremely thin and the orbicularis oculi muscles are close to the surface. The neck and ears are then added and should be modeled with special attention to the age and sex of the individual. The ear is positioned on the head using the external auditory meatus as a guide—the bony meatus falls ~5–6 mm more anterior and inferior to the soft tissue opening. The ear lobe morphology (attached or free) should be represented in accordance with the most prevalent frequency/type for the ancestral group of the skull in question. Hair can be modeled after its length and texture and form (wavy, straight, etc.), if a sample is recovered from the body disposal site. The final facial approximation should be photographed in black and white so as to downplay color that cannot be predicted from the skull (e.g., color of the irises).

Computerized Methods

The most basic computerized facial approximation methods are 2D and require facial feature images to be selected from

a library according to the skull's morphology, and assembled to produce a face. 3D manual facial approximation methods have also been computerized using hap tic feedback devices, so that modeling takes place virtually, over a scanned skull using virtual sculpting tools that exert resistance on hand-held devices at the user interface. Although offering some features that manual methods cannot (e.g., X-ray like views of the skull encased in the soft tissue), these methods are largely plagued by the same weakness as their noncomputerized manual counterparts (practitioner subjectivity). Yet another approach is to produce a 3D manually sculpted face first, photograph it, and then enhance it by digitally adding or refining features on the computer.

Higher level computer methods are underpinned by more rigorous statistical procedures and are typically more automated and objective. A common approach is to scan the skull in question (skull 1) and search a library of skull/face pairs (also called surface references) for an individual with similar skull morphology (skull 2). This surface reference is then deformed to fit the skull in question (skull 2 warped to fit skull 1) and the same or similar algorithm applied to the facial surface map to produce the facial approximation. A modification of this approach is to use a library of skull/face averages for searches, rather than skull/face pairs that represent single individuals, or to deform all reference surfaces of individuals and merge them. A variety of statistical

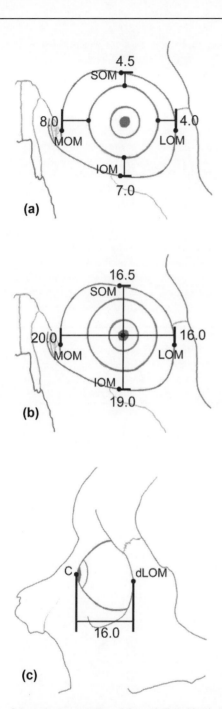

(a)

(b)

(c)

Figure 4 Schematic representation of the eyeball position in the orbit according to anatomical relationships and mean measurements (mm): (a) distance of eyeball edge to orbit; (b) distance of pupil center to orbit; and (c) distance of corneal apex to lateral orbital rim. SOM, midpoint of the supraorbital margin; IOM, midpoint of the infero-orbital margin; LOM, the lateral most point of the lateral orbital margin; MOM, Flower's point; C, corneal apex; dLOM, deepest (or most posterior) point of the lateral orbital margin.

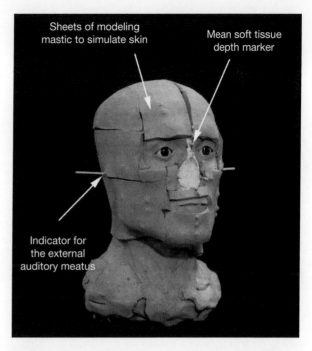

Figure 5 Partially complete 3D manual facial approximation illustrating the sheets of mastic overlaid on the deeper face structures and muscles of facial expression to approximate facial contours. Nose, ears, and lips are yet to be added to this approximation and the facial surface refined so that the join lines are not visible.

approaches exist for undertaking the deformation and generating the facial approximation (including regression on principal components and latent variables regression). These computer methods offer great potential for quantification and standardization; however, they currently suffer from two primary disadvantages: (1) few validation results have been published so their accuracy has largely not been documented as far as facial recognition is concerned; and (2) the software is often custom designed so it is not widely available, for example, for commercial purchase. These circumstances may change in the near future.

Media Release

Once constructed, the facial approximation should be advertised on a "slow" media day to ensure that it receives maximum coverage. Advertisement release on days (or weeks) where other major news events will detract from the article should be avoided. Use of multiple media outlets and formats is recommended and, where possible, the facial approximation practitioner should retain control over what images are used and have input into how they are presented to maximize opportunities for success.

Anatomical Legitimacy and Accuracy of Methods

Facial approximation methods have commonly been portrayed in the prior literature as highly tuned, accurate, and anatomically legitimate techniques. Over the last 10 years, however, there has been an avalanche of studies that have demonstrated major gaps and shown that many traditional soft tissue prediction guidelines have no underlying anatomical justification and/or are erroneous. Space does not permit for a description of these inaccurate guidelines; however, further information can be found in the recommended reading. Much work remains to be done in the future to cross-check other unverified guidelines and to produce new improved soft tissue prediction rules.

No consensus currently exists on the ability for facial approximation methods to generate purposeful and correct recognitions; however, the repeatability of 3D manual methods is unanimously acknowledged to be problematic. Casework success with the method is reported to be high by some practitioners within the field (60 to ~100%), but there are as many studies showing poor recognition rates of facial approximations as there are studies showing higher rates (see Further Reading). Recognition performance of the facial approximation depicted in **Figure 1** is provided in **Figure 6** as an example of what can be expected under controlled scientific tests. In evaluating the published literature, readers should be mindful

that greater motivators exist for practitioners to share their successful results in this applied field than to publicly disclose their failures.

The subjective nature of large components of the facial approximation method largely restricts its use to cases where tested and more objective methods cannot be used (such as DNA, dental comparison, and nondental radiographic comparison). Consequently, the challenge remains to produce a verified face prediction method that warrants classification as "scientific," and which reliably produces correct facial recognitions in the hands of any practitioner. Irrespectively, the power that current facial approximation holds to focus community attention on a case justifies its use in many circumstances and numerous prior successes of the method in forensic investigations demonstrate the method's value. Under no circumstances should facial approximation methods be used as a single line of evidence for a formal identification: where a facial approximation is recognized, an indicator for an identity is obtained, and this must be confirmed or denied using other methods.

See also: **Anthropology/Odontology:** Forensic Anthropology: An Introduction; History of Forensic Anthropology; Odontology; Personal Identification in Forensic Anthropology; **Forensic Medicine/Clinical:** Identification; **Foundations:** Overview and Meaning of Identification/Individualization.

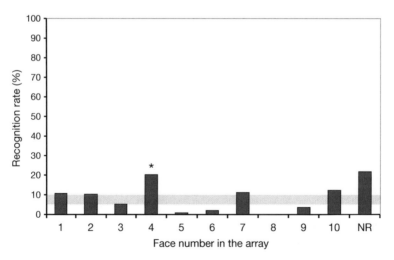

Figure 6   Recognition performance of the facial approximation presented in **Figure 1** using 259 assessors. The facial approximation was presented in an array of nine other faces, all shown simultaneously to the assessors. The assessors were asked to decide if the individual representing the facial approximation was, or was not, present in the array; and in the case of the former, which sequence number. The correctly corresponding face was #4 and was recognized above chance rates (5–10%) at statistically significant levels using a Chi-square test ($p < .05\%$ as indicated by *). NR, no recognition made. Adapted from Stephan, C.N., Cicolini, J., 2010. The reproducibility of facial approximation accuracy results generated from photospread tests. Forensic Science International 201, 133–137, with permission from Elsevier.

Further Reading

De Greef, S., Willems, G., 2005. Three-dimensional cranio-facial reconstruction in forensic identification: latest progress and new tendencies in the 21st century. Journal of Forensic Sciences 50, 12–17.

Gerasimov, M.M., 1955. Vosstanovlenie lica po cerepu. Izdat. Akademii Nauk SSSR, Moskva.

i$can, M.Y., Helmer, R., 1993. Forensic Analysis of the Skull. Wiley-Liss, New York.

Jordanov, J., 2003. Head Reconstruction by the Skull. Marin Drinov Academic Publishing House, Sofia.

Prag, J., Neave, R., 1997. Making Faces: Using Forensic and Archaeological Evidence. British Museum Press, London.

Snow, C.C., Gatliff, B.P., McWilliams, K.R., 1970. Reconstruction of facial features from the skull: an evaluation of its usefulness in forensic anthropology. American Journal of Physical Anthropology 33, 221–228.

Stephan, C.N., 2009a. Craniofacial identification: techniques of facial approximation and craniofacial superimposition. In: Blau, S., Ubelaker, D.H. (Eds.), Handbook of Forensic Anthropology and Archaeology. Left Coast Press, Walnut Creek, pp. 304–321.

Stephan, C.N., 2009b. The accuracy of facial 'reconstruction': a review of the published data and their interpretive value. Minerva Medicolegale 129, 47–60.

Stephan, C.N., Henneberg, M., 2001. Building faces from dry skulls: are they recognized above chance rates? Journal of Forensic Sciences 46, 432–440.

Stephan, C.N., Simpson, E.K., 2008. Facial soft tissue depths in craniofacial identification (part I): an analytical review of the published adult data. Journal of Forensic Sciences 53, 1257–1272.

Taylor, K.T., 2001. Forensic Art and Illustration. CRC Press, Boca Raton, FL.

Taylor, R.G., Angel, C., 1998. Facial reconstruction and approximation. In: Clement, J.G., Ranson, D.L. (Eds.), Craniofacial Identification in Forensic Medicine. Oxford University Press, New York, pp. 177–185.

Tyrrell, A.J., Evison, M.P., Chamberlain, A.T., Green, M.A., 1997. Forensic three-dimensional facial reconstruction: Historical review and contemporary developments. Journal of Forensic Sciences 42, 653–661.

Wilkinson, C., 2004. Forensic Facial Reconstruction. Cambridge University Press, Cambridge.

Wilkinson, C., 2005. Computerized forensic facial reconstruction. Forensic Science, Medicine, and Pathology 1, 173–177.

Relevant Websites

http://www.craniofacialidentification.com/ — Craniofacial Identification.
http://www.askaforensicartist.com/ — Forensic Art.

Personal Identification in Forensic Anthropology

CV Hurst, Michigan State University, East Lansing, MI, USA
A Soler, Pima County Office of the Medical Examiner, Tucson, AZ, USA
TW Fenton, Michigan State University, East Lansing, MI, USA

Glossary

Antemortem Events, materials, or records occurring or collected before death.

Comparative radiography The direct, point-by-point comparison of antemortem radiographs (X-rays) of a missing person with those obtained from the remains.

Decedent The deceased person.

Exclusion A conclusion based on sufficient evidence to determine that the known identity and the decedent are not the same individual.

Failure to exclude A conclusion based on sufficient evidence to determine that the known identity and the decedent may be the same individual but lacking information to make a personal identification.

Insufficient evidence A conclusion that the available evidence is lacking to the degree that no determination of inclusion or exclusion can be made.

Lot number A number assigned to identify a particular group, shipment, or lot of material from a manufacturer.

Morphology The overall shape or structure of the bone.

Multiple corresponding factors The matching of a number of nonscientific physical characteristics and contextual evidence between a known individual and a set of remains.

Personal identification The matching of a set of remains to a known individual.

Positive identification See scientific identification.

Postmortem Events, materials, or records occurring or collected after death.

Scientific identification The matching of antemortem and postmortem records to sufficient detail in a scientific systematic point-by-point comparison to conclude that they are from one individual to the exclusion of all other reasonable matches.

Serial number A unique set of numbers assigned for the identification of a specific item.

Tentative identification A potential match of a known person to the decedent.

Trabecular bone Also known as cancellous bone or spongy bone, the light and porous bony structure that is found at the end of long bones and within vertebrae.

Visual recognition The identification of a known person by a family member or friend who views the remains of the decedent.

Introduction

Identification of human remains is one of the foremost goals in a medicolegal death investigation. An expedient and accurate identification is imperative to serve both the family of the decedent and the medicolegal system. A personal identification can provide a sense of closure to the bereaved, allows for the release of the body, and is necessary to file an accurate death certificate for the distribution of benefits and to initiate an investigation in cases of homicide or suspicious deaths. Medicolegal death investigation is the responsibility of the medical examiner or coroner, and it is ultimately these medicolegal authorities that must decide whether there is sufficient evidence to establish a personal identification and authorize a death certificate. Therefore, the degree to which a forensic anthropologist is involved in a case is at the discretion of the medical examiner or coroner. As such, it is the duty of the forensic anthropologist to utilize his or her expertise to fulfill these requests.

Personal Identification

Personal identification is the matching of a set of remains to a known individual and it is the ultimate goal in a forensic investigation. Positive identification is a term that has long been used in medicolegal investigations to indicate an identification based on the scientific methods of fingerprint analysis, comparative dental or medical radiography, and nuclear DNA assessments. However, this terminology is problematic because it implies that a legal personal identification based on methods not considered "positive" is a weaker form of identification. Thus, in this work, the term "scientific identification" is utilized to describe an identification that is accomplished through the matching of antemortem and postmortem records to sufficient detail in a scientific point-by-point comparison to conclude that one individual is represented to the exclusion of all other reasonable matches. However, a personal identification can be established via a variety of different processes, including scientific identification, visual recognition of a cadaver, and multiple corresponding factors where there is a preponderance of evidence that matches between the decedent and the missing person. Each of these techniques represents a different level of identification; however, all are considered personal identification and ultimately lead to the release of the remains from the medical examiner's office.

In a majority of cases, someone who knew the decedent can identify the person through visual recognition of the face. This type of identification is a common process in many medical examiners' offices, especially in cases of recent deaths. Either people who knew the decedent are asked to view the physical remains or driver's license photographs are consulted to visually confirm the identification. This form of personal identification is outside the purview of forensic osteology, however, and is not discussed in detail in this chapter. In cases where visual recognition is not possible, including those with severe trauma, burning, decomposition, or skeletonization, medical examiners or coroners may consult with a forensic anthropologist to aid in the identification process. Forensic anthropologists can assist in either establishing a scientific identification or contributing to an identification with information from skeletal analyses to limit potential matches to the decedent. Before the discussion of forensic anthropological methods, levels of personal identification must first be defined and addressed.

Types of Personal Identification

Scientific Identification

Scientific identification is a classification that systematically compares known antemortem information of a missing person with postmortem information of the deceased to ensure that they represent one and the same individual. A scientific identification is accomplished when biological antemortem and postmortem information match, with no unexplainable differences, and in sufficient detail to conclude that they represent the same individual to the exclusion of all other individuals. Examples of scientific identification methods include comparisons of nuclear DNA, fingerprints, and dental and medical radiography. Each of these techniques has

demonstrated utility in scientifically identifying individuals by focusing on unique aspects of the human body.

A common question from medicolegal investigators, judges, and juries is, "how many points of similarity are necessary to reach a scientific identification?" Currently, no minimum number of consistent morphologies required for a scientific identification has been established. What this means is that a single point of consistency can represent a scientific identification if considered individualizing. However, practitioners of comparative radiographic methods strive to use multiple morphologies in their analyses.

Although a scientific identification can be considered an optimal method for identifying human remains, it is not always possible or practical. A major impediment to scientific identifications is access to the appropriate resources—the absence of either finances or properly trained forensic experts. A medical examiner or coroner may not have access to forensic professionals trained in methods suitable for scientific identifications. In other cases, financial constraints may prevent medical examiners/coroners from utilizing such consultants or laboratory analyses. Lack of time to process such cases may also preclude a scientific identification. Both families and funeral homes can apply significant pressure to medicolegal investigators for the release of the decedent, and many scientific identification techniques can take time to complete.

A final limitation that may prohibit a scientific identification is lack of appropriate or adequate antemortem records. Although dental and medical radiographs seem commonplace, there remains a large segment of the population that has never had a radiograph taken. In other cases, the antemortem radiographs may be difficult or impossible to locate or the quality of radiographs may be too poor to be useful. As a result of these potential barriers, many medical examiner's or coroner's offices rely on more expedient and cost-effective methods to personally identify human remains.

Multiple Corresponding Factors

In cases where there is no scientific antemortem information available for comparison between the missing person and decedent, medical examiners or coroners may rely on multiple corresponding factors to support a potential identification. This approach utilizes contextual evidence in conjunction with a number of physical features to arrive at an identification. Contextual evidence may refer to the location where the decedent was found and personal effects associated with the remains, whereas physical features may include the biological profile, tattoos, piercings, dental characteristics, surgical alterations, and mitochondrial DNA. These identifications are made by a preponderance of matching nonscientific or nonunique characteristics and vary in strength depending on the number and the quality of factors contributing to the identification. Furthermore, it is the combination of distinctive physical features and contextual evidence that makes an identification via multiple corresponding factors a personal identification. For instance, if the remains of an edentulous female in her mid-80s with a hysterectomy and evidence of a healing hip fracture were found in the secured home of an elderly woman of that same description, there would be multiple physical and contextual characteristics to indicate that the decedent and the woman who lived in the home were the same person. This identification by multiple corresponding factors is much stronger than an identification of a young woman found in a public location and identified through visual comparison to a driver's license or passport found with the remains.

Methods of Scientific Identification

Personal identifications, as outlined above, can be made at several levels of confidence, with a scientific identification being the gold standard. Although there are a number of methods that forensic anthropologists can utilize to contribute to the identification process, comparative medical and dental radiography are the only scientific techniques that can establish a scientific identification.

Comparative Radiography

Comparative radiography is the point-by-point comparison of antemortem radiographs of a missing person with the corresponding postmortem films of the decedent. To control for differences caused by radiographic imaging, it is essential that the postmortem radiographs simulate the antemortem films as closely as possible in both scope and angulation, making sure to highlight the same skeletal features. This can be particularly challenging in cases where remains are in a state of decomposition or skeletonization that make them more difficult to appropriately position. This may require the anthropologist to take many sets of postmortem films, but without such efforts a radiographic comparison is not possible.

Dental radiographic comparisons

Radiographic comparisons fall into two broad categories—dental and medical. With annual dental examinations becoming the standard of care, the likelihood of an individual having antemortem dental radiographs is quite high. Additionally, the mineral composition of teeth makes them extremely resilient to postmortem damage, decomposition, temperature extremes, and fire destruction. Thus, both ante-mortem and postmortem dental information are likely to be available for comparison. Furthermore, the variety of dental structures and dental treatments provides numerous features that, when taken in combination, can offer an individualizing suite of characteristics. Features of dental radiographs that can be used in forensic identifications include crown and root morphology, tooth angulation, bone trabecular patterns, maxillary sinus morphology, the location and morphology of dental restorations, cavities or other dental pathologies, and missing teeth (**Figure 1**). Beyond the tooth structures visible in dental radiographs, other anatomical landmarks are also used to corroborate an identification. The increasing use of panoramic radiographs provides even more features for comparison, including the nasal aperture, the nasal septum, nasal conchae, inferior and lateral borders of the eye orbits, and mandibular morphology (**Figure 2**).

Medical radiographic comparisons

Although dentition is the most common feature used for positive identification, any area of the body documented in antemortem radiographs could potentially be employed for such purposes. In medical radiographic images, overall morphology of the bone, anatomical landmarks, trabecular patterns, orientation, placement of foreign materials including bullets or shrapnel and surgical implements, skeletal anomalies, pathological conditions, and evidence of traumatic injury can be used. Relatively common areas for radiographs to be taken during life include the head, chest, and limbs.

An antemortem radiograph of the head can be extremely helpful for a forensic anthropologist attempting to make an identification. Beyond the potential of using the dental information contained within such a radiograph, it has been demonstrated that the frontal sinus is a structure that has a unique morphology in all individuals (**Figure 3**). Located above the eye orbits in a person's forehead, the bilateral frontal sinus is a hollow air cavity that is commonly asymmetrical and highly variable between individuals. Thus, it is an ideal structure to be used in a scientific identification. In the case of young individuals, however, the frontal sinus may not be fully developed and may not be available for comparison.

The chest is another common anatomical region for comparative radiography. While antemortem radiographs are often taken to visualize the lungs or other organs, skeletal features may be visible and useful for comparative purposes. Studies have shown that features of the vertebral column are individualizing and can be used for scientific identifications. Similar to dental comparisons, it is the suite of features of the vertebral column that makes it personalizing (**Figure 4**). Areas that are visible on radiographs and can be used in a point-by-point comparison include the shape of the vertebral bodies, the spinous processes, the transverse processes, the pedicles, intervertebral disc space, and any arthritic lipping or other degenerative changes. Studies have shown that features of the vertebral column outlined above are consistent in radiographs that have been taken decades apart and prove the utility of such radiographs for use in scientific identifications.

An interesting application for the use of anterior–posterior chest radiographs is the identification of missing American soldiers from past military operations at The Joint POW/MIA

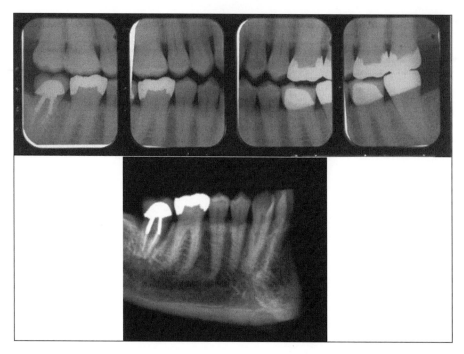

Figure 1   The postmortem (bottom) dental radiographs highlight the same dental restorations and simulate the antemortem (top) radiographs for a scientific identification.

Accounting Command Central Identification Laboratory (JPAC-CIL). Owing to tuberculosis concerns, chest radiographs became a routine procedure across the United States Armed Forces in 1942, unknowingly creating an archive of antemortem radiographs for American soldiers. Thus, forensic anthropologists are utilizing these archives to help identify the remains of soldiers that went missing during the Korean War.

In many skeletal radiographs, the details of the trabecular bone can be seen and used in the comparison. As bone is a living tissue that is constantly remodeling, the consistency of such structures through the passage of time may be considered a concern. If the trabecular bone structure changes over time, an

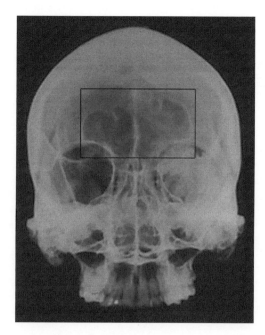

Figure 3   An anterior–posterior radiograph of the cranium with the unique morphology of the frontal sinus highlighted in the red box (dark in print versions).

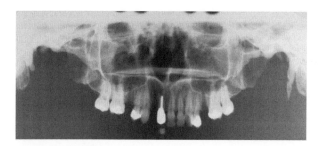

Figure 2   A panoramic radiograph showing maxillary dentition, nasal aperture, septum, conchae, and eye orbits.

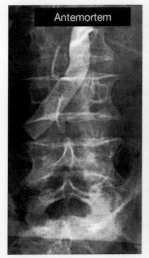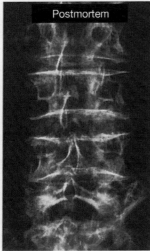

Figure 4 Antemortem and postmortem radiographs demonstrating consistency in shape and location of spinous processes, pedicles, and centra.

individual could be wrongfully excluded. However, studies of trabecular patterns have shown that the morphology is maintained over time and through subsequent remodeling events. It has now been demonstrated that even with age-related bone loss, trabecular bone patterns can provide individualizing information to aid in identification.

The role of experience

While forensic anthropologists can provide important contributions to personal identifications using comparative radiography, it is of utmost importance that the individual has been trained in comparative radiographic comparisons and is aware of the limitations of the method and their experience in making identifications. A number of studies have demonstrated that the interpreter's experience level directly affects his or her ability to make a correct identification. To the untrained eye, standard anatomical landmarks may be identified as consistencies between antemortem and postmortem radiographs. In reality, however, these features are relatively consistent between most individuals and are not always individualizing. Forensic anthropologists with training and experience are able to differentiate the distinctive skeletal features that will be useful for a personal identification from those that are commonplace. This underscores the importance of appropriate forensic training and experience for practitioners to accurately make scientific identifications.

Validation studies

Historically, scientific identifications have been admissible in the court of law; however, new standards for expert testimony

have encouraged the publication of validation studies for various types of dental and medical radiographs for scientific identification purposes. Therefore, many validation studies have either been published or are forthcoming. To test the utility of various skeletal structures, researchers investigate its uniqueness within a sample population or practitioners' ability to utilize the structure to match simulated antemortem and postmortem radiographs. By establishing known error rates and statistical probabilities of the antemortem and postmortem radiographs originating from a single person, forensic anthropologists can confidently report on the accuracy of their methods in the court of law.

Possible Conclusions in a Scientific Identification

In every scientific identification consultation, the forensic anthropologist may reach one of three possible conclusions—a personal identification, an exclusion, or an insufficiency of evidence for determination.

Identification

To establish a scientific identification, a forensic anthropologist must perform a systematic detailed comparison with the goal of finding consistency in the overall skeletal morphology and in unique or identifying features. If a significant amount of time has passed since the antemortem radiograph was taken, there may be noticeable differences between the two sets of radiographs. Such time discrepancies must be taken into account. Alternatively, any noticeable differences between radiographs must be explainable by the passage of time or slight differences in angulation of the image. If one of these explanations cannot be used to describe a discrepancy between sets of radiographs, the antemortem and postmortem records are likely not from the same individual, and the potential match may be excluded.

Exclusion

In the case of an exclusion, sufficient evidence is available from the antemortem records to conclude that the presumptive individual and the decedent could not possibly represent the same individual. This results when disparities between antemortem and postmortem records cannot be explained by the passage of time, by differences in radiographic angulation, or for any other reasonable cause. The exclusion of a missing person means they are eliminated from the list of potential matches and it is necessary for new potential matches to be located and tested. Although the exclusion of a potential identification may send medicolegal investigators back to the field to gather more information, it is an important contribution toward the proper identification of the deceased, as it narrows down the list of possible matches.

Insufficient Evidence

At times, antemortem records are unavailable, too generalized, of poor quality, or too far removed in time to be useful. In such cases, a forensic anthropologist is unable to determine whether the antemortem and postmortem records originated from the same individual. This includes situations where the available antemortem information is consistent with the postmortem evidence from the decedent; however, the consistent features are not individualizing to the extent required to make a personal identification. Essentially, the forensic anthropologist is unable to exclude the owner of the antemortem records from the list of possible identities of the decedent but cannot definitively make a match. As an example, if no antemortem medical or dental records are available, the forensic anthropologist may only be able to comment on whether the biological profile of the skeletal remains is consistent with those of the potential decedent.

In cases where the antemortem data simply do not exist, or are of poor quality, the forensic anthropologist may be unable to either support or reject the hypothesis that the decedent and the remains represent the same individual. At this point in an analysis, a forensic anthropologist cannot contribute any further until investigative work is able to locate more complete or better quality antemortem records that may be used to retest the hypothesis that the missing person and the decedent represent the same individual.

Methods Contributing to Identification

While comparative radiographic techniques are the only anthropological methods that can directly identify a decedent, there are a number of analytical techniques a forensic anthropologist can employ to contribute to the identification process. These efforts generally help by limiting the list of potential matches to the decedent, moving the investigation closer to a personal identification.

Biological Profile

Acquiring antemortem records is a critical first step toward making an identification; however, this requires some idea of the identity of the deceased. This would be a person or a list of reported missing persons who are potential matches to the decedent. Therefore, the forensic anthropologist may be consulted to assess the biological profile of the remains in order to narrow the list of potential matches. Once a short list of possible matches has been compiled, antemortem records and other identifying information may be gathered for these

individuals. A biological profile consists of the sex, age, ancestry, and living stature of an individual. In cases where soft tissue is unavailable for visual determination of these characteristics, a forensic anthropologist can assess particular skeletal morphologies to estimate each feature of the biological profile. A report of the biological profile and any unique skeletal features of the individual may help investigators identify potential missing person matches to the decedent. Once a possible identity is ascertained, a forensic anthropologist may be asked to employ the techniques outlined above to obtain a personal identification.

Skeletal Pathologies and Anomalies

In cases where antemortem radiographs are not available, photos or descriptions of individualizing features may lead to an identification through multiple corresponding factors. Similar to comparative radiography, this requires a possible missing person match and cooperation with those that knew the decedent to obtain information on potentially identifying features. Although medical records may not contain radiographs for comparison, they can still be used for information on dental procedures, such as extractions and root canals, or medical intervention, including fracture stabilization or surgeries that may be reflected in the skeletal remains. Additionally, skeletal anomalies, such as a cleft palate or scoliosis, can also be used as identifying features. If soft tissue is still present on the decedent, distinctive freckles, birthmarks, or tattoos may also be used to corroborate a potential identity. If one of these features is particularly rare or unique, it may serve as strong evidence of a decedent's identity. In most cases, however, a forensic anthropologist must be cautious in relying on such characteristics for identifications because any single characteristic may not be unique in isolation.

Surgical Implants

Beyond biological features of an individual, identifications may result from the analyses of objects found within a person. As previously discussed, dental restorations in the form of fillings, root canals, and crowns can display a unique morphology useful in comparative radiography. Other foreign objects within the body can serve a similar purpose. The placement of metal plates, screws, or rods for bone stability after traumatic injury or the persistence of a bullet or shrapnel can help individualize a decedent (**Figure 5**). Sternotomy wires used to suture the sternum after open-heart surgery are especially useful. Unlike other surgical implants that have a particular shape and often standardized placement within the body, sternotomy wires are pliable and are hand twisted making a series of wires entirely unique (**Figure 6**). If antemortem medical radiographs exist of such structures, a radiographic

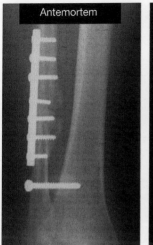
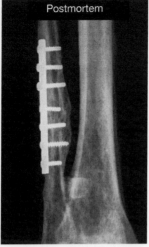

Figure 5 The antemortem (left) and postmortem (right) radiographs of a surgical plate and screws used to stabilize a fibula after injury.

comparison may be possible leading to a scientific identification.

An additional benefit to surgical implants is the potential for obtaining individualizing information to reach a tentative identification. Many surgical implants are etched with the company's logo in addition to a serial or lot number (**Figure 7**). In some cases, these serial numbers are unique and can be traced to the individual in which the implement was placed. In cases where only a lot number is present, it may be possible to track that number to a batch of implants, time period, and the hospitals to which they were sent. Through collaborative efforts by the forensic anthropologist, surgical supply companies, and hospitals, it may be possible to produce a list of potential patients who received the medical implant in question. The forensic anthropologist is often responsible for the careful removal of the surgical implement to minimize damage to both the bone and the implant, and to retrieve the important information.

Photographic Imaging Techniques

Although they are not often considered a form of identification, techniques that utilize photographic images can be used to either exclude a possible identification or support its continued inclusion in a list of potential matches. Skull–photo superimposition is a method in which an electronic mixer is used to superimpose the photo of a known individual onto the skeletal remains of the decedent (**Figure 8**). These two images are expertly manipulated and scaled to align relevant physical features and assess facial proportionality (**Figure 9**). Features that can be aligned between the fleshed face and the

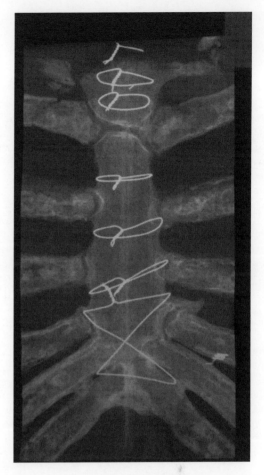

Figure 6 A postmortem radiograph of an individualizing series of sternotomy wires.

skeletonized cranium include the teeth, the outer edge of the eye orbits, the bottom margin of the nasal aperture, the midpoint of the chin, and the openings for the ear canals. If these points can all be brought into alignment, effectively superimposing the photograph onto the cranium, the two remain a potential match. Alternatively, if the features cannot be aligned, the presumptive identification may either be excluded or a conclusion of insufficient evidence made if the images lack clarity.

The use of photographic superimposition may also be applied to cases of living individuals. Specially trained forensic anthropologists use photo–photo or photo–video superimpositions to compare images of a perpetrator and a suspect to determine if they could represent the same person. A methodology similar to skull–photo superimposition is employed, where the two images are aligned to compare facial proportions; eye shape and spacing; nose size and shape; ear location,

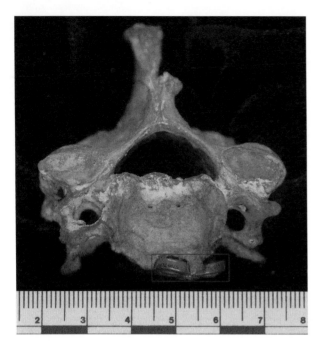

Figure 7   A cervical vertebra with a surgical plate displaying a lot number.

size, and shape; lip morphology; and any additional unique features such as freckles, moles, or scars.

Conclusion

Medical examiners and coroners are charged with the important responsibility of legally identifying a deceased individual. This may require consultation with forensic specialists in other fields of study who have expertise in various methods of personal identification. As specialists in skeletal biology and human variation, forensic anthropologists are experts in the assessment of a biological profile and are proficient in distinguishing atypical or unique skeletal features that can be used in an identification. Furthermore, those experts with additional training in comparative dental and medical radiography can utilize scientific methods to affect a scientific identification. In every case, a forensic anthropologist should employ all of their education and experience to ensure that a proper personal identification is made. This also means that forensic anthropologists must know the boundaries of their own knowledge and the limitations of the methods they are employing. As personal identification legally confirms a person's death and is necessary for the execution of a death certificate and the resulting distribution of benefits, a nonidentification is always superior to a misidentification. Thus, it is of great importance that forensic anthropologists pursue thoughtful and thorough consideration in every case.

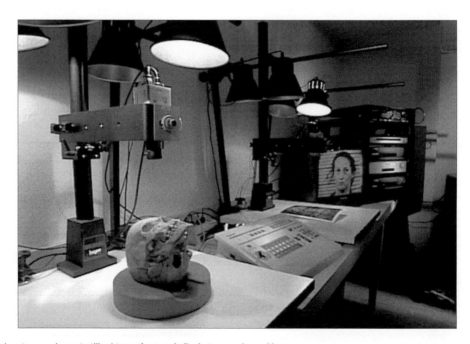

Figure 8   The laboratory equipment utilized to perform a skull–photo superimposition.

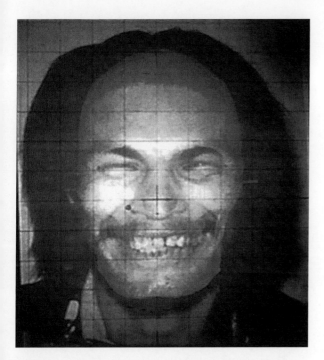

Figure 9 A successful skull–photo superimposition showing the matching of skeletal structures to facial features, including the missing left central maxillary incisor.

See also: **Anthropology/Odontology:** Aging the Dead and the Living; Ancestry; Identification of the Living; Odontology; Sexing; Stature and Build; **Biology/DNA:** Disaster Victim Identification; The National Missing and Unidentified Persons System (NamUs); **Forensic Medicine/Clinical:** Forensic Age Estimation; Identification; **Legal:** Expert Witness Qualifications and Testimony.

Further Reading

Anderson, B.E., 2008. Identifying the dead: methods utilized by the Pima County (Arizona) office of the medical examiner for undocumented border crossers: 2001–2006. Journal of Forensic Sciences 53 (1), 8–15.

Brogden, B.G., 1998. Radiological identification of individual remains. In: Brogden, B.G. (Ed.), Forensic Radiology. CRC Press, New York, pp. 149–187.

Christensen, A.M., 2005. Testing the reliability of frontal sinuses in positive identification. Journal of Forensic Sciences 50 (1), 8–22.

Dix, J., Graham, M., 2000. Time of Death, Decomposition, and Identification: An Atlas. CRC Press, Boca Raton, FL.

Fenton, T.W., Heard, A.N., Sauer, N.J., 2008. Skull-photo superimposition and border deaths: identification through exclusion and the failure to exclude. Journal of Forensic Sciences 53 (1), 34–40.

Fierro, M.F., 1993. Identification of human remains. In: Fisher, W.U. (Ed.), Medicolegal Investigation of Death. Charles C Thomas, Springfield, IL, pp. 71–117.

Hogge, J.P., Messmer, J.M., Doan, Q.N., 1994. Radiographic identification of unknown human remains and interpreter experience level. Journal of Forensic Sciences 39 (2), 373–377.

Jablonski, N.G., Shum, B.S., 1989. Identification of unknown human remains by comparison of antemortem and postmortem radiographs. Forensic Science International 42 (3), 221–230.

Kahana, T., Hiss, J., Smith, P., 1998. Quantitative assessment of trabecular bone pattern identification. Journal of Forensic Sciences 43 (6), 1144–1147.

Koot, M.G., Sauer, N.J., Fenton, T.W., 2005. Radiographic human identification using bones of the hand. Journal of Forensic Sciences 50 (2), 263–268.

Kuehn, C.M., Taylor, K.M., Mann, F.A., Wilson, A.J., Harruff, R.C., 2002. Validation of chest x-ray comparisons for unknown decedent identification. Journal of Forensic Sciences 47 (4), 1–5.

Lundy, J.K., 1986. Physical anthropology in forensic medicine. Anthropology Today 2 (5), 14–17.

Maclean, D.F., Kogon, S.L., Stitt, L.W., 1994. Validation of dental radiographs for human identification. Journal of Forensic Sciences 39 (5), 1195–1200.

Mann, R.W., 1998. Use of bone trabeculae to establish positive identification. Forensic Science International 98 (1–2), 91–99.

Messman, J.M., 1986. Radiographic identification. In: Fierro, M.F. (Ed.), CAP Handbook for Postmortem Examination of Unidentified Remains: Developing Identifications of Well-Preserved, Decomposed, Burned, and Skeletonized Remains. College of American Pathologists, Skokie, IL.

Rathbun, T.A., Buikstra, J.E. (Eds.), 1998. Human Identification: Case Studies in Forensic Anthropology. Charles C Thomas, Springfield, IL.

Richmond, R., Pretty, I.A., 2010. Identification of the edentulous individual: an investigation into the accuracy of radiographic identifications. Journal of Forensic Sciences 55 (4), 984–987.

Rogers, T.L., Allard, T.T., 2004. Expert testimony and positive identification of human remains through cranial suture patterns. Journal of Forensic Sciences 49 (2), 1–5.

Sauer, N.J., Brantley, R.E., Barondess, D.A., 1988. The effects of aging on the comparability of antemortem and postmortem radiographs. Journal of Forensic Sciences 33 (5), 1223–1230.

Sholl, S.A., Moody, G.H., 2001. Evaluation of dental radiographic identification: an experimental study. Forensic Science International 115, 165–169.

Soomer, H., Lincoln, M.J., Ranta, H., Penttila, A., Leibur, E., 2003. Dentists' qualifications affect the accuracy of radiographic identification. Journal of Forensic Sciences 48 (5), 1–6.

Steadman, D.W., Konigsberg, L.W., 2003. Multiple points of similarity. In: Steadman, D.W. (Ed.), Hard Evidence: Case Studies in Forensic Anthropology. Prentice Hall, Upper Saddle River, NJ.

Stephan, C.N., Winburn, A.P., Christensen, A.F., Tyrrell, A.J., 2011. Skeletal identification by radiographic comparison: blind tests of a morphoscopic method using antemortem chest radiographs. J. Forensic Sci. 56 (2), 320–332.

Scientific Working Group for Forensic Anthropology (SWGANTH). 2010. Personal Identification Issue Date: 6/30/2010. Revision: 0. [Online]. Available at: www.swganth.org.

Ubelaker, D.H., Jacobs, C.H., 1995. Identification of orthopedic device manufacturers. Journal of Forensic Sciences 40 (2), 168–170.

Valenzuela, A., 1997. Radiographic comparison of the lumbar spine for positive identification of human remains. The American Journal of Forensic Medicine and Pathology 18 (1), 40–44.

Wilson, R.J., Bethard, J.D., DiGangi, E.A., 2011. The use of orthopedic surgical devices for forensic identification. Journal of Forensic Sciences 56 (2), 460–469.

Relevant Websites

http://www.theiai.org/—The International Association for Identification.

http://www.swgdvi.org/—The Scientific Working Group for Disaster Victim Identification.

www.swganth.org—The Scientific Working Group for Forensic Anthropology.

Odontology

JG Clement, The University of Melbourne, Melbourne, VIC, Australia

Glossary

Cementum A bonelike tissue covering the roots of teeth providing anchorage for a periodontal ligament, which is inserted into the bone of the jaws to attach the teeth.
Dental enamel The hard translucent covering of the crowns of the teeth comprising 96% by weight skeletal mineral.
Dentine The tissue forming the bulk of the tooth containing within it a soft-tissue pulp upon which this tissue relies for its nutrition and its capacity for repair in the face of environmental challenge.

Orthopantomogram A type of radiographic image used widely in dentistry to provide a panoramic radiographic image of a person's upper and lower jaws and teeth simultaneously.
Radiograph The correct term for an image produced by X-rays on some form of recording medium, often photographic film.

Definitions

In the context of this encyclopedia, "odontology" is synonymous with "forensic dentistry" and "forensic odontostomatology." None of the terms is really adequate for what is today one of the fastest-emerging microspecialties within the broader subject of dental science. Nevertheless, as all of the somewhat limited definitions imply, a forensic odontologist is someone who understands the significance of the conjunction of the law and dentistry and can therefore explain the complexities and subtleties of dental evidence to the courts. This capacity to report on findings and then progress to express an opinion relies upon the courts affording expert status to the witness. In the adversarial systems of justice, this may require the expertise to be established on each occasion to the satisfaction of the judge from the outset. In a practical sense, it is the combination of education, training, and experience appropriate to the case currently before the court that is scrutinized, and so track record has a major part to play in the decision.

The forensic odontologist has to be not only an experienced licensed or registered practitioner of clinical dentistry but someone who is also able to observe, record, gather, preserve, and interpret dental evidence, and who is then able to make it meaningful within a legal context. In common with all good expert witnesses, this requires special skills, such as the ability to communicate clearly and simply by word and in written reports.

The Nature of the Work

In Victoria, Australia, a state of approximately 5.5 million people, the casework is roughly typical of that encountered in many modern, technologically advanced, prosperous, urbanized, industrialized societies. While tens of thousands of coronial autopsies are conducted every decade, only a few hundred cases (~2.5% of all autopsies) need forensic dental expertise to assist the investigations. Of these, ~90% require the corroboration of a putative identity by comparison with existing antemortem dental records or the establishment of broad indicators of identity when no antemortem records exist or can be located. In most cases, the injuries to, or decay of, the body precludes visual identification. Incineration of remains is the most common cause of disfigurement followed by decomposition, severe trauma, and skeletonization.

Therefore, while forensic odontology increasingly encompasses cases dealing with issues of causation of injuries and assessments for the quantum of damage where compensation is sought by a victim of assault or injury, relating to claims of negligence or malpractice by dentists and related professionals, the main thrust of day-to-day casework still remains primarily that of the corroboration of identity of deceased persons. Historically, there are numerous accounts of famous persons being identified postmortem by recognition of certain peculiarities within their dentitions. In more recent times, in the aftermath of major catastrophes, both natural and artificial, including the aftermath of civil conflict and war, the use of forensic dental expertise in disaster victim-identification teams has been shown to be extremely effective and much less expensive and time-consuming than other methods. The involvement of forensic odontological expertise in the investigation of state-sponsored violence and acts of genocide against populations and acts of genocide has focused sharply on the ethic and moral foundations that underpin the work of all health-care professionals who identify the dead for the sake of the living and provide irrefutable evidence for the historical record.

Why Is Dental Evidence So Good for Corroborating Identity?

Everyone has teeth. When they do not, it is common for people to wear prostheses. If they have never developed teeth, this is, in itself, so unusual as to be highly individualizing and may be only one manifestation of a syndrome with other, more obvious, physical signs.

The form of teeth and the detail of their arrangement in the dental arches provide a body of information that is probably unique to the individual. Even in identical twins, the slight variations in tooth form and position can enable the twins to be separated on the basis of their dentitions.

Add to the above criteria, the almost infinite variation that can be added to the dentition by way of dental treatments (extractions, unique handmade dental restorations, and different use of restorative materials, prostheses, and orthodontic appliances) and the dentition is certainly as individual as a fingerprint.

One great advantage over fingerprint evidence for the corroboration of identity arises from the resistance of the oral structures to fire or putrefaction. Teeth and bone can be heated to temperatures approaching the melting point of skeletal mineral (>1600 °C) without appreciable loss of microstructure or tertiary architecture. Furthermore, the teeth represent the only part of the skeleton that normally protrudes from the soft tissues of the body and is therefore available for examination and recording by photography or dental impressions before death.

This accessibility is the second advantage of dental evidence over fingerprints, particularly in societies where the taking and retention of fingerprints from persons is strictly limited to those with an existing criminal record. Similarly, much medical treatment returns the patient to full health with no residual indicators of a temporary disease permanently expressed; a sore throat is a transient event that leaves no scar and therefore nothing permanent and tangible with which postmortem comparisons can be made. Conversely, when some medical procedures, such as orthopedic surgery for a prosthetic hip replacement, are performed, the resulting records in all their forms are excellent for identification purposes (**Figure 1**).

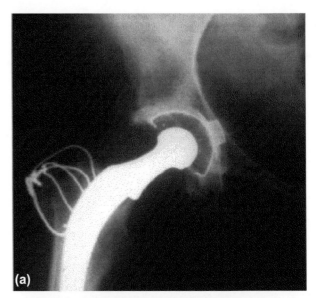

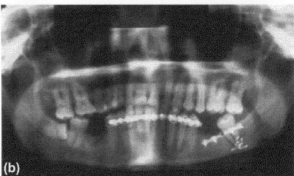

Figure 1   (a) Postoperative radiograph of a prosthetic hip joint. When such permanent evidence of medical treatment exists, it is excellent for corroborating the identity of a body even where there has been no putative identity developed. The type and unique serial number of prosthesis can lead to an immediate identification when national registers exist to monitor all joint replacements, as is the case of Australia. Similarly, the gauge of the wire, the number and nature of the turns, twists, and loops in it, taken together are a signature of the operating surgeon and provide a unique image for comparative purposes. Such images are not as commonplace as dental records and X-rays. (b) This is the oro-dental equivalent of (a). A panoramic antemortem radiograph that reveals internal fixation of a reduced mandibular fracture. None of this metallic surgical material was seen at dissection, being completely internalized within the jaw after a long period of healing.

Unfortunately, for identification purposes, such treatments are still not commonplace but their placement in an aging population is certain to increase.

By comparison with such still relatively uncommon surgical treatment, almost everyone in the developed world has had to attend a dentist for a dental checkup or treatment at some time in his or her life. The attendance at the dentist inevitably results in the production of records. All are potentially valuable. These may be in the form of written clinical notes and odontograms (dental charts), plaster casts of the dentition or radiographs ("X-rays"), or, less usefully, even just an itemized bill for payment. Worldwide, the standards of record keeping are highly variable. Broadly speaking, the more prosperous and developed the society, the better are the standards of record keeping, but there are exceptions. In the absence of comprehensive written or graphical records, the contribution of "dental X-rays" to the process of corroborating identification can hardly be overstated.

Even when no treatment has been carried out in the form of dental restorations or "fillings," X-rays may have been taken to check for the presence of tooth decay at hidden and inaccessible sites such as the contact points between adjacent teeth at the back of the mouth, or to monitor the progress of periodontal diseases. In addition to the specific clinical need to take the X-ray, the resulting radiograph conveniently records many, normally inconsequential, features of the dentition and jaws. These characteristics include the size and shapes of tooth roots, dental restorations, and the pulp chambers within the teeth. The internal architecture of the bones of the jaws is often clearly revealed and may show the internal struts of bone, called trabeculae, the presence of healing tooth sockets postextraction, the retained roots of teeth, or the crypts containing developing teeth (**Figure 2**). In larger radiographs, such as those depicting panoramic views of the jaws (orthopantomograms—OPGs or more strictly OPTs in dentists' jargon), the details may be less clear but there is a compensating increase in the number of structures imaged. These include the maxillary sinuses of the skeletal complex of the upper jaw. The paranasal sinuses are air-filled spaces or pneumatizations of the skull, all in communication with the upper respiratory tract, which increase in size during early life but then stabilize in adulthood (**Figure 3**).

Similarly, when X-rays are taken of the whole head, other sinuses that have formed within the bones of the forehead (the frontal sinuses) may be displayed. The size and shape of sinuses are very variable. Furthermore, they are often partially divided internally by walls or septa whose position is also stable and which are clearly visible on X-ray. The combination of these two features means that X-ray images of the sinuses can be excellent for comparison with postmortem findings, when the sinuses can be repeatedly X-rayed in slightly differing orientations until direct visual comparison of similarities and differences validates a "match." To achieve a valid match, and therefore a "positive identification," all the features of interest must coincide simultaneously with all other features depicted on both radiographs. This requirement is an important check and a good internal standard to ensure that a match of important features has not been unwittingly created. The process of comparison can be done by eye by directly overlaying antemortem and postmortem radiographs, or digitally by subtracting one image from the other when all that remains is that which is different between the two views.

Sometimes, the radiographs to be compared may look quite different from each other and yet yield evidence of a match of certain features. A good example might be if some teeth were present in the antemortem clinical X-ray image, yet missing in the corresponding postmortem view (perhaps lost per mortem as a result of trauma or putrefaction). Supposing the feature to be compared was the shape and form of the sinuses, then, provided the tooth socket outlines still matched in size, shape, and position, the missing teeth would not matter nor would it invalidate the match.

Another potential complication can arise from the passage of considerable time between the taking of the antemortem X-ray and the taking of corresponding views postmortem. This is particularly the case if the antemortem record has been taken when deciduous (baby) teeth are still present, but the

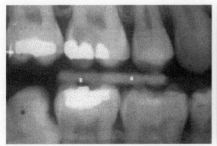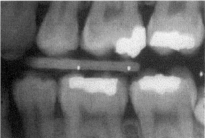

Figure 2 A pair of intraoral "bitewing" radiographs. These are the most common radiological views of the mouth, routinely taken by dentists to check for tooth decay or the presence or progress of degenerative disease in the supporting tissues of the teeth. Such images also serendipitously reveal the state of dental maturity in the young and summarize much of the restorative dental treatment experienced by the individual throughout the life. In these particular radiographs, the crowns of the as-yet-unerupted wisdom teeth can just be seen. The form of the other teeth, specifically the shapes of their roots in their sockets and the internal pulp chambers, is clearly seen. This patient has had eight dental amalgam restorations. Each restoration has a unique silhouette for any given geometric/radiographic projection.

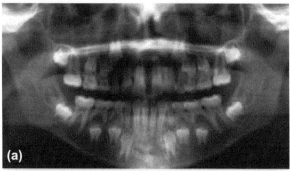

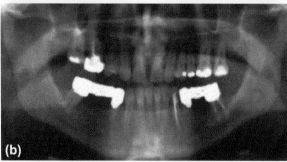

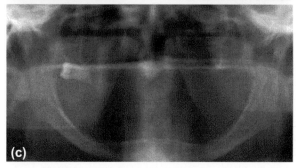

Figure 3 Three panoramic radiographs (orthopantomograms, OPGs). (a) Radiograph from a child aged about 8 years. It shows a mixture of deciduous and permanent teeth erupted and functional within the oral cavity. Beneath them, within the jaws, there are many successional teeth developing in crypts. Knowledge of the chronology of tooth development and emergence sequence for the dentition allows age estimation to be undertaken with reasonable certainty during the first two decades of a person's life. (b) Radiograph from a middle-aged person aged 50 years. The patient has had multiple root canal treatments, during which finely tapered gutta percha points have been cemented into the root canals of several teeth. This style of treatment is now rather outdated. The combination of many dental restorations and root fillings has produced a unique pattern of features that is invaluable for identification purposes. (c) A radiograph from an elderly person aged 80 years. The natural teeth have all been extracted many years ago and full dentures have been worn ever since. This OPG reveals the presence of a single, completely formed tooth unerupted in the right maxilla. This tooth, previously undiscovered, has been buried within the jaws since the time of its initial formation over 60 years ago. The presence, form,

postmortem views are not taken until those deciduous teeth have been shed and replaced by permanent successors.

This serves as a good example of why an expert opinion is necessary to explain to laypeople, which includes lawyers within the legal system, that, although the images look different, they are really of the same person, but just taken at different stages of their life, which is explicable if the chronology of dental development is understood and explained clearly (**Figure 4**).

When No Antemortem Records Exist

So far, the assumption has been made that antemortem records exist and, once located, can be used for comparison with postmortem findings. However, records are not always traceable or retained. In about one-third of cases in Victoria, Australia (a state with high immigration), no records are available for the odontologist to use as a basis for comparison. In such cases, what inferences can be made?

Teeth develop in a predictable sequence, which enables age to be estimated during their formation with reasonable accuracy. This period extends from midfetal life until the attainment of physical adulthood in the early part of the third decade. In the absence of birth records, the eruption of second permanent molars formed the basis upon which children were deemed old enough to work in factories during the industrial revolution in Britain in the early 1800s—a nationwide forensic application of dental knowledge affecting the lives of millions. During adulthood, the teeth and their supporting tissues undergo progressive changes. These can be greatly influenced by diet, habits, customs, and lifestyle. In this context, the frontline task confronting the forensic odontologist differs little from any discipline concerned with reconstructing past events from incomplete evidence and the interpretation of their significance. In archeology, paleontology, and biological anthropology, there is inevitably an imposed reliance upon inference and comparison with accumulated knowledge rather than a direct "concrete" comparison between records and findings. The results of such inferences need to be carefully presented to avoid the impression of unwarranted certainty. Comprehensive accounts of the determination of ancestry, gender, and age from the orofacial structures have been published (**Figure 5**).

For example, in the 1960s, Gustafson consolidated many of the age-related changes of teeth into a unifying series of age-predictive regression equations. He scored the progressive infilling of the dental pulp chambers by secondary dentine, attrition caused by tooth-to-tooth contact under the influence of the diet, compensatory cementum deposition on tooth

and position of the unerupted tooth, taken together with the myriad of other anatomical features depicted simultaneously, are unique.

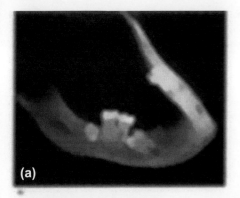

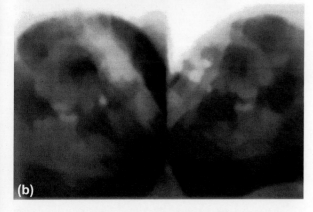

Figure 4 A homicide case where the mandible is the only part of the skull to have been retrieved after prolonged immersion of the body. (a) The lateral oblique view of the recovered skeletalized mandible shows a very unusual developmental malpositioning of the mandibular premolars. The malformation was bilateral. (b) Two lateral oblique views (left and right) of the same person taken during life by the school dental service. The misplaced premolars can clearly be seen on both sides of the jaw. More teeth are present in these earlier clinical radiographs, but the difference between (a) and (b) is explicable when the intervening period is taken.

roots, the migration of soft-tissue gingival attachments, and increasing translucency of dentine due to increased peritubular (strictly, intratubular) dentine deposition. Several other researchers have critically revisited and revised all or part of Gustafson's method, introducing minor modifications from time to time (**Figure 6**). In essence, Gustafson's method was probably successful at that time because of the homogeneity of his Swedish sample in terms of ancestry, genes, social and lifestyle factors, and diet. The methods are of much less use in countries such as Australia, where there has been recent, large-scale immigration from many different places by peoples of different ancestry, each with their own cultural overlay of past diet, habits, and customs.

Of all the age-related factors described above, the increasing translucency of dentine with age is probably the most physiologically related and hence the least affected by environmental influence.

In common with other products of complex epithelial/mesenchymal interactions, such as fingerprints, the teeth also reveal evidence of heritability in some of their features. This results in ancestral differences of "ethnic traits" in the dentition, which can be of forensic importance. Anthropologists who study populations rather than individuals for evidence of individual identity tend to use large numbers of physical measurements to investigate "ethnic traits." This metric approach has spawned many studies on tooth crown dimensions, often from plaster casts obtained in the field or directly from living individuals over a period of time. The results are of limited forensic value where there is a much greater emphasis on individuality and unique identifiers.

Interactions with Other Professionals

For the majority of cases, it is expected that the odontologist will form part of a team of investigators. Such teams may comprise a pathologist; police investigators and scene of crime personnel; mortuary staff; photographers; sculptors; artists; and other experts, such as entomologists, molecular biologists, or accident investigators. In cases where living victims of assault have to be examined and treated, the composition of the team will differ but is likely to include hospital doctors, nurses, and the staff of the local government social services department.

Whatever the composition of the group, clear lines of responsibility and reporting need to be understood by all involved from the outset. The coordinator/facilitator/leader (usually the most senior police officer) has to have a clear overview of the evidential requirements for the entire investigation and to be aware of the sometimes conflicting requirements of the investigators. For example, it would be a catastrophe for the forensic odontologist to adopt the policy of slavishly resecting the jaws of deceased victims, just in order to make examination of the dentition easier, if the only available evidence that would have corroborated identity required the facial skeleton to be kept intact. While on this point, it is also important to note that such a procedure should only ever be undertaken if disfigurement of the face is already so extreme that viewing of remains by next of kin would be advised against, or where a truly expert dissection and reflection of facial tissues can be done and then replaced over the skeleton after the dental procedures have been completed. This may take the form of inspection of the teeth and jaws in situ, an inspection of the teeth and jaws after excision, followed by their replacement or the permanent removal of the jaws. The structure and form of the face are then restored by the insertion of prosthesis. Groups that comprise experts who understand each other's skills, perhaps because they have worked together on numerous occasions in the past, undertake the best

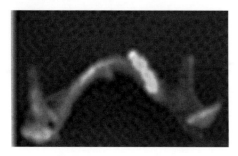

Figure 5   An archeological specimen. This mandible was found on the Chatham Islands east of New Zealand. The specimen carries a history of a fracture that at one time split the body of the mandible lengthways. Teeth were lost in the fracture line, either at the time of the injury or during subsequent infection before eventual healing. The bony fragments are misunited because the fracture was never reduced by a doctor prior to bony repair. As a consequence of the loss of teeth, the man was obliged to chew on one side of the jaw only. Those teeth show heavy attrition. Taken together, these derangements have almost certainly led to the osteoarthritic degeneration of the jaw joint on one side. From the above observations and inferences, it would be highly unlikely that this person would have lived in the last 100 years. The find is therefore of little interest in a coronial context.

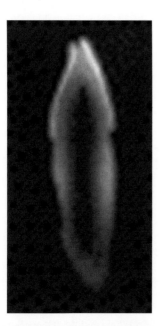

Figure 6   Age changes to the teeth. This longitudinal section through a tooth has been X-rayed to produce a microradiograph. The tooth came from a middle-aged person. It shows attrition through the enamel to dentine, and the vital reactionary changes in the underlying dentine. The cervical margin (neck) of the tooth reveals cervical abrasion after gingival recession has taken place. To compensate for the loss of enamel from the crown due to wear, more cementum (a bone-like substance) has been deposited at the tip of the root. These and other changes were those quantified by Gustafson.

investigations, but in all cases, it is important for each expert to know what is required of him or her. A case conference at the outset of a multidisciplinary investigation quickly repays the time and energy expended by assuring efficiencies and precision later on. Sometimes, what was initially seen as an apparently uncomplicated "deceased person identification," undertaken on behalf of the coroner, can later be discovered to really be an event requiring a full homicide investigation. In many jurisdictions, the evidential requirements for different courts differ in their rigor. In the UK system of justice, and many of its derivatives around the world, the coroner requires proof of identification only "on the balance of probability," whereas a higher court which may have to try an accused person facing a charge of murder requires identification to be established more stringently "beyond reasonable doubt." It is therefore important for the forensic odontologist to anticipate where every case may lead and to conduct their investigation with the final forum for their deliberations clearly in mind.

Bite Marks, Bruising, and Other Injuries to Skin

Forensic odontologists are frequently called to look at people, both dead and alive, or objects which may retain "tool marks" left by an interaction with the teeth of a person or an animal or animals (or something which closely resembles such marks). The circumstances range from excellent, clearly identifiable, bite marks left by an individual in a dimensionally stable substrate such as hard cheese or chocolate, to the badly mauled, barely recognizable remains of a deceased person killed by a large carnivore or carnivores (**Figure 7**). The situation can be even more difficult if the case is one involving postmortem animal predation of the corpse, where scattering of the remains and superimposed decomposition add complexity. Where a person has been mauled to death and the animal thought to have caused the injuries can be caught or killed, it is relatively simple, by the use of emetics or dissection, respectively, to prove the involvement of the animal. In instances where humans bite other persons, it is uncommon for large pieces of tissue to be removed. The marks remaining from the bite may range from an excellent silhouette of the dental arches and individual teeth to something very diffuse and indistinct; the latter case is unfortunately the far more common circumstance, especially if there has been a delay prior to the collection of photographic evidence.

The poor fidelity of human skin as a recording medium, its deformability and elasticity, its capacity to heal, and the curved nature of the external surface of the body, added to the complex form of the dental arches and the many possible movements of the jaws during biting, combine to make scientific analysis of bite mark injuries very problematic. While there are a growing number of noncontact, three-dimensional surface scanners that can accurately record curved three-dimensional shapes and

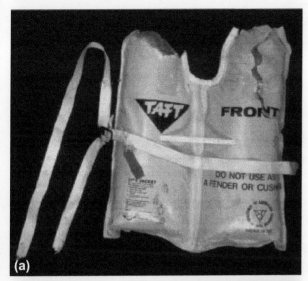

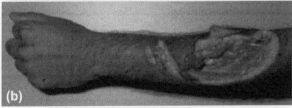

Figure 7 Shark bites. (a) A life jacket recovered after a yacht was lost. The jacket carries serrated bite marks left by a large shark. (b) (See color plate XYZ) A postmortem shark bite on the remains of someone who had already drowned. The arcing lacerations with regular spacing are quite typical of a medium-sized shark.

skin color and texture for analysis that are being introduced into clinical environments, they are not yet widely available. As current police procedure requires many possible bite marks to be investigated on living victims, some very distressed, in the technologically restricted environment of a hospital accident department or, worse, in a police station, the use of sophisticated technology is not possible. The odontologist then has to try to interpret much less informative primary sources of information such as two-dimensional photographs of what are always three-dimensional injuries. It is this constraint which has led to some conspicuous errors of interpretation that in turn have led to wrongful convictions, some only overturned years after the event on the basis of a later DNA analysis of evidence originally collected from the crime scene. Where the injuries are less severe and/or more diffuse, photography may still be the only practical method for documenting the injuries. Ultraviolet or infrared light beyond the visible spectrum can be used to produce images that reveal bruising, which may be undetectable using visible light. Exactly what histological or chemical changes to the skin enable these images of old and/or

"latent" bruising to be made still have to be determined and again interpretation can be controversial, particularly as it may be impossible to separate tissue changes induced by both recent and past injuries to the same part of the body.

Without the foundations of fundamental scientific knowledge about the biology and chemistry of bruising, and the ability to model accurately the actions of the teeth and jaws interacting with the soft tissues of the body in a realistic, dynamic way, the presentation of bite mark evidence to the courts will remain problematic.

Where some topography in the form of indentations, cuts, abrasions, or exudates can be found on the victim, the recording of bite marks is customarily done by means of dental impression materials and swabs for biological analyses. Impressions taken from such injuries are used to make rigid models in plaster or dental stone. These models can then be used for comparison with the dentition or models of the dentition of the suspected assailant (or victim if a self-inflicted injury is possible). Photographs usually augment the use of such models.

In Australia, bite mark evidence has become so discredited in the wake of two prominent cases that drew heavily upon the opinion of foreign experts, and in which it was later judged that some of the experts must have misinterpreted their observations despite coming to the same conclusions, that in a subsequent protocol established for the taking of "intimate samples," bite mark evidence was considered to be of little value. This unfortunate extrapolation overlooks the great exculpatory value of bite marks to an investigation and the justice system. By way of contrast, in South Africa, a country suffering from high rates of interpersonal violence, bite mark interpretation is carried out routinely and the courts accept the evidence proffered by the odontologists.

Other Skills

Implied in the previous section is a requirement for the forensic odontologist to have a comprehensive knowledge of comparative dental anatomy. At its most obvious, there is a common need to be able to sort animal remains from those of human beings. While some anthropologists and archeologists are experts in this, very few understand the dentition as well as their dental colleagues, particularly where only particulate remains or fragments of skeletal material are found and a study of microstructure is required. An expert knowledge of the differences in microscopic tooth tissue structure between different genera is particularly important in forensic cases where a consumer alleges contamination of foodstuffs. Further, in those countries where people are still killed by wild animals, it is important to be able to recognize the characteristic pattern of injuries inflicted by the local predators.

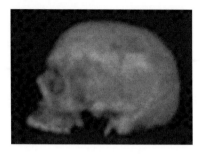

Figure 8 An anatomical replica in methylmethacrylate made with dental techniques for use in a courtroom demonstration by the pathologist years after the interment or cremation of the remains. Three-dimensional replicas are much more successful than two-dimensional photographs for displaying osseous injuries, such as hatchet wounds or bullet trajectories. Courtesy of RW Taylor, Melbourne Dental School.

Summary

At this time, forensic odontology remains one of the most reliable, cheapest, and quickest means of corroborating human identity (**Figure 8**), especially in the wake of mass disasters for victim identification. By its very tangible nature, it is easily presented to, and understood by, juries. Twenty-five years ago, anticipating many of the identification tasks would be more likely to be answered by advances in molecular biology, and realizing that DNA evidence would become more reliable and, more importantly, less controversial in court, it was widely assumed that the future of forensic odontology would be very limited. This has not occurred. For a variety of reasons including poor crime scene and continuity of evidence management, technical difficulties with contaminated or degraded samples, and difficulty of obtaining reliable reference samples for comparison, DNA analysis is still of much less practical value than dental comparisons for corroboration of identity in disaster victim-identification situations. Forensic odontological methods are quick and cheap by comparison, which is an additional advantage. Age-at-death determination from predictable and progressive changes to the organic matrices of hard tissues is a technique that has not yet become widespread, despite important ongoing studies showing its feasibility in the hands of a very small number of exponents.

However, while much of what is done today may still be in the ascendancy, other aspects of the work of the forensic odontologist may soon become redundant. Forensic sculpting to recreate an approximation of the facial features of the deceased utilizing remnant skull evidence, a once popular technique of last resort, has a limited future for several reasons. There have now been numerous studies and practical examples of the wide divergence in the results obtained by different practitioners when multiple reconstructions have been made

from the same skull and contextual information. These results sit uneasily with the evermore rigorous scientific scrutiny demanded of most forensic activities by the courts. However, perhaps the greater challenge to the validity of facial sculpting will come from modern mathematics and engineering where statistical approaches derived from combined data sets of surface scanning of facial features integrated with computed tomography (CT) images of the underlying skeleton will permit the automated generation of the most plausible face to fit upon any CT or laser topographic scan of an unknown skull projected into the statistical framework. There is a large degree of overlap between these morphometric approaches and psychological research into facial distinctiveness, memorability, and recognition, with all its cultural and same race/other race overtones.

The very precise anatomical modeling of human skeletal remains, to be used as aides-mémoires for the pathologist and as court exhibits long after the interment or cremation of the deceased, has its basis in dental materials and technology. These skills will only remain in high demand until the rapidly emerging technology of three-dimensional printing becomes commonplace and thereby inexpensive. This trend has begun and the landscape will be transformed very rapidly.

However, to return to our fundamentals, the forensic odontologist is a person with dental qualifications and clinical expertise who also has considerable experience of the law and courts and issues relating to the ethics and the conduct of the dental profession at large. It is commonplace for police faced with allegations of professional misconduct or charges of physical or sexual assault at the hands of a dentist in a clinical setting to consult the forensic odontologist. Investigators see him or her as a sound, balanced, and broadly experienced professional peer, who understands what is deemed to be acceptable contemporary clinical behavior in dentistry before considering whether a prima facie case exists that warrants further investigation and a possible prosecution.

The investigation of illegal, unregistered practitioners, and the premises from which they operate, rightly involves the forensic odontologist, who is able to advise on health and safety aspects for the on-scene investigators and the legal status of prescription medicines recovered at the scene. These are but two examples, but other important issues pertaining to consent to treatment, confidentiality, access to records, malpractice, litigation, risk minimization, and evidence-based practice are subjects to which much more prominence has been devoted in newer medical school curricula where departments of legal medicine have been newly established. These developments are now being mirrored in dentistry, and consequently the forensic odontologist will rightly be in the vanguard of such advances and the benefits they bring to our society.

See also: Anthropology; Archeology; Child Sexual Assault; Human Remains and Identity; Mass Grave Investigation; Radiology; Pattern Evidence; Aging the Dead and the Living; Facial Approximation; Personal Identification; Identification of the Living; Disaster Victim Identification; Identification and Comparison; Clinical Forensic Medicine; Child Abuse; Forensic Age Estimation; Airplane Crashes and Other Mass Disasters; Recovery of Human Remains; Innocence Project; International Courts and Forensic Science; Identification and Classification.

Further Reading

Arany, S., Ohtani, S., 2010. Age estimation by racemization method in teeth: application of aspartic acid, glutamate and alanine. Journal of Forensic Sciences 55 (3), 701–705.

Blackwell, S.A., Taylor, R.V., Gordon, I., et al., 2006. 3-D imaging and quantitative comparison of human dentitions and simulated bite marks. International Journal of Legal Medicine 4, 1–9.

Bush, M.A., Bush, P.J., Sheets, D.H., 2011a. A study of multiple bite marks inflicted in human skin by a single dentition using geometric morphometric analysis. Forensic Science International 211, 1–8.

Bush, M.A., Bush, P.J., Sheets, D.H., 2011b. Statistical evidence for the similarity of the human dentition. Journal of Forensic Sciences 56 (1), 118–123.

Claes, P., Vandermeulen, D., De Greef, S., Willems, G., Suetens, P., 2006. Craniofacial reconstruction using a combined statistical model of face shape and soft tissue-depths: methodology and validation. Forensic Science International 159 (Suppl. 1), S147–S158.

Clement, J.G., Bassed, R.B., Graham, J.P., 2010. Forensic odontology. In: Selby, H., Freckleton, I. (Eds.), Expert Evidence Practice and Advocacy. Law Book Company, Sydney (Chapter 34).

Clement, J.G., 1998. Dental identification. In: Clement, J.G., Ranson, D.L. (Eds.), Craniofacial Identification in Forensic Medicine. Arnold, London, pp. 63–81.

Clement, J.G., 2011. Bite marks. In: Gall, J., Payne-James, J. (Eds.), Current Practice in Forensic Medicine. John Wiley and Sons, London, pp. 291–308 (Chapter 11).

Gustafson, G., 1950. Age determination on teeth. The Journal of the American Dental Association 41, 45–54.

Hill, H., Claes, P., Corcoran, M., Walters, M., Johnston, A., Clement, J.G., 2011. How different is different? Criterion and sensitivity in face-space. Frontiers in Perception Science. (Online) http://dx.doi.org/10.3389/fpsyg.2011.00041.

Kraus, Jordan, 1965. The Human Dentition before Birth. Lea and Febiger, Philadelphia.

Liversidge, H.M., Lyons, F., Hector, M.P., 2003. The accuracy of three methods of age estimation using radiographic measurements of developing teeth. Forensic Science International 131 (1), 22–29.

Logan, W.H.G., Kronfeld, R., 1933. Development of the human jaws and surrounding structures from birth until the age of fifteen years. The Journal of the American Dental Association 20, 379–427.

Ogino, T., Ogino, N., Nagy, B., 1985. Application of aspartic acid racemisation to forensic odontology: postmortem designation of age at death. Forensic Science International 29, 259–267.

Page, M., Taylor, J., Blenkin, M., 2011a. Forensic identification science evidence since Daubert: Part 1 – a quantitative analysis of the exclusion of forensic identification science evidence. Journal of Forensic Sciences 56, 1180–1184. http://dx.doi.org/10.1111/j.1556-4029.2011.01777.x.

Page, M., Taylor, J., Blenkin, M., 2011b. Forensic identification science evidence since Daubert: Part 2 – judicial reasoning in decisions to exclude forensic identification evidence on the grounds of reliability. Journal of Forensic Sciences 56 (4), 913–917.

Saunders, E., 1837. The Teeth as a Test of Age, Considered with Reference to the Factory Children: Addressed to the Members of Both Houses of Parliament. Renshaw, London.

Shields, L.B.E., Bernstein, M.L., Hunsaker, J.C., Stewart, D.M., 2009. Dog bite-related fatalities. A 15 year review of Kentucky Medical Examiner cases. The American Journal of Forensic Medicine and Pathology 30 (3), 223–230.

Disaster Victim Identification

WH Goodwin and T Simmons, University of Central Lancashire, Preston, UK

Abbreviations

AM	Antemortem	PM	Postmortem
DVI	Disaster victim identification	STR	Short-tandem repeat
ICRC	International Committee of the Red Cross	VNTR	Variable number tandem repeat

Introduction

In every disaster or conflict, the need to recover and identify the deceased is a matter of urgency, foremost on behalf of the psychological needs of relatives of those missing; the right to know the fate of one's missing relatives is a fundamental right and should be respected and enacted—this principle holds regardless of the circumstances that have led to the death. Alongside humanitarian needs, disaster victim identification (DVI) also addresses legal concerns regarding everything from civil suits concerning liability in an aviation, train, or ferry disaster, the need to provide death certificates for purposes of inheritance and remarriage, through to the prosecution of perpetrators of war crimes.

The scope of DVI operations has evolved significantly since the mid-1990s, when most instances centered on transport accidents involving up to a few hundred victims. Advances have been driven in part technically by developments, particularly in DNA analysis, that have increased the circumstances in which identification of human remains is possible. Politically, the response to several events of international importance in the late-twentieth and early twenty-first centuries, such as conflicts in the Balkans (1991–99), the World Trade Center attack (2001), and the pan-Asian Tsunamis (2004), focused a large amount of resource to the identification of the victims. This led to logistical and technical advances in DVI and also to higher expectations for forensic science to be used for human identification following disasters and conflicts, even when there are thousands of victims.

Disaster Classification

A disaster can be defined as an unexpected event causing death or injury to many people. Traditional considerations for activating a DVI response related to "mass disasters," where external assistance was required following a catastrophic event that overwhelmed the resources of an affected community and rendered it unable to respond adequately acting alone. There are many different types of disaster that can necessitate DVI including traffic accidents, natural disasters, technical/industrial accidents, terrorist attacks, and events that occur during conflict, both within and between countries.

In addition to the type of disaster, an important aspect when considering DVI is whether it is open or closed. Closed disasters, such as aircraft crashes, are those in which the identities of the victims are known through crew and passenger manifests (although these may not be entirely accurate in all cases); in such instances, the task of the DVI team is largely to match the identity of the remains to individuals known to be missing. In many of these cases, access to relevant antemortem (AM) information necessary for matching is also facilitated by the relative ease of locating kin, medical and dental records, and DNA samples. Open disasters are those in which the identity and even the number of the victims are unknown. Establishing who was indeed a victim can be quite complicated even in a thoroughly modern society where it may take several days or weeks, even years to resolve in a situation of limited fatalities; in the case of a natural disaster involving multiple countries or locations within a country and thousands to tens of thousands of victims of multiple nationalities, it can take years to resolve. For victims of conflict, where the number and identity of victims are unknown, individuals disappeared over several years (or decades), the location of graves has been obscured, AM records are scant or lacking in their entirety and political will and monetary resources are slim, identification, when possible, can take decades. It should also be noted that it is possible to have a classification of combined, for example, when a plane crashes on a populated area killing people of the ground as well as those in the plane.

Management of DVI

Interpol recommends that each member state should establish a permanent DVI team, with preplanning and training for disasters. In planning for and following a disaster multiple facets of the DVI operation have to be considered, for example, initial assessment of the scope of the disaster, mapping and searching of the affected area, estimating the number of victims and degree of fragmentation, methodology to recover and transport the corpses, methodology to be used for identification, and identifying the individuals/medicolegal institutes that are to be involved in the identification process. The criteria that must be met before identifications are made must also be agreed upon prior to bodies being released to families—this becomes increasingly important with increasing numbers of victims as this augments the probability of incorrect identifications.

Another important decision is the scope of the identification process, that is, with fragmented remains what will the operation aim to identify—whole bodies only, recognizable body parts, body parts of a specific size? In cases of extreme fragmentation (e.g., plane crashes) or disruption of primary burials into secondary and even tertiary mass burials (e.g., Bosnia), it is also necessary to have a policy in place regarding how relatives of the missing will be informed when a portion of their missing person has been identified. Through this policy, relatives of the missing may, for example, elect to be notified when (1) the entire identification process has been completed and all the remains identified of the individual are collected and returned at a single time; (2) the first body part has been identified; or (3) every time a body part has been identified. This allows the relatives of the missing to assert some control over their relationship to the identification process and also decide at which point they wish to hold memorial and/or funeral services.

Principles of Identification

Identification of individuals killed in mass disasters and conflicts should be held to the same standards as identification of individuals killed (or found dead) under any other circumstance. The processes used in identifying individuals must be robust and the families of the missing must have confidence in the identification process. Decisions regarding the methods of identification to be employed are influenced by the condition of the victims, personnel involved in the identification, resources, and technology, as well as by the availability of AM comparatives. There are four widely recognized means of positive identification, whereby a single method alone can be used to make an identification; all others must be regarded as a means of presumptive identification, which can be used to support identification or generate further leads to identity, but may not in themselves "make" an identification.

Fingerprints, dental/medical records (including radiographs), nuclear DNA, and unique medical identifiers are all means of primary positive identification. Visual recognition (of tattoos, facial features, birth marks, scars, etc.), a matching biological profile generated by forensic anthropologists (age, sex, race, stature, and AM trauma/pathology), matching medical conditions identified by pathologists, facial superimposition, matching personal effects and clothing, matching identification documents, exclusion (when, for example, there is only one child among the victims) and/or matching mitochondrial DNA (mtDNA) profiles are secondary means of identification, ideally for use in support of the primary methods (**Figure 1**).

Methods of Identification

Objective Methods

Objective methods, sometimes referred to as scientific methods, if applied appropriately, can give unambiguous identifications.

Fingerprints

Identification of individuals through fingerprints is a well-established scientific method, and is routinely used worldwide. In humans, the palms and fingers are covered in skin that is thickened with ridges that helps to grip surfaces (friction ridge skin); the soles of the feet and toes are also covered with friction ridge skin. Friction ridge skin is considered to be unique and over the last 100 years of application, with millions of fingerprints used for forensic identification, only a handful of issues of misidentification have been reported, making fingerprints a powerful means of identification; importantly fingerprints remain unchanged throughout life, other than through scarring.

Several systems have been developed to classify fingerprints, all of which are based on categorization of the overall pattern, that is loops, arches, and whorls, and then identification of distinct combinations of features within the pattern, such as bifurcations, lakes, and ridge endings. Its utility to DVI identification varies from case to case. The remains have to be fleshed and in a state of preservation that allows for prints to be taken—this may be possible even with partially decomposed and even burned remains, as fingers curl inward when exposed to fire, thus preserving the ridge details.

As with all other forms of identification, AM records also need to exist for comparison. Whether extensive AM records are available varies depending on the country or countries involved; many countries collect fingerprints from all of its citizens once they reach adulthood and this information is typically held in a national computer, which allows rapid searching—in other countries legislation may prevent the storage of fingerprints, or restrict it to those arrested in connection to a criminal offense. If no AM records are available, it may be possible to recover AM

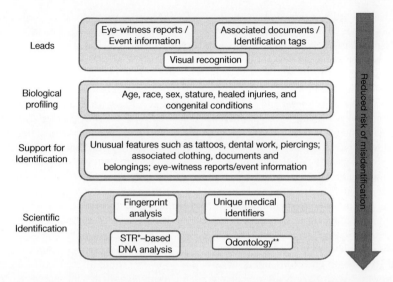

Figure 1 Identifications obtained using visual recognition or other customary means are, where possible, supported by comparing antemortem and postmortem data to allow biological profiling and collection of additional evidence to support the identification. Ideally, identifications should be supported by at least one form of scientific identification, which greatly reduces the possibility of misidentification. *, SNP-based DNA analysis could also provide scientific identification but is not widely used; **, scientific identification using odontology would normally require comparison of dental radiographs or other features that would be considered to be unique. SNP, single-nucleotide polymorphism.

prints from the personal possessions of the missing person(s), assuming there is reliable information on who is actually missing. With a computer-based search using an automated fingerprint identification system, a list of candidate matches can be produced in seconds; however, the algorithms are not sufficiently refined to produce exact matches and computer-generated matches have to be examined manually by an expert to establish a confirmed match.

Dental radiographs

The identification of individuals based on a comparison of AM and postmortem (PM) radiographs is, arguably, a somewhat subjective process, but one which is nonetheless recognized as a scientific means by which a positive identification may be made. While in the past, radiographic equipment may not have been available in situ and radiographers were forced to ship bulky equipment and improvise darkrooms in which to develop the films, this is no longer an obstacle. Portable digital radiographic equipment—some even hand held—is widely available, and rapidly becoming cost-effective. If not available in the country in which the disaster or conflict has occurred, this equipment is so portable that it can be carried as hand luggage in the passenger compartment of aircraft deploying individuals to the scene.

The AM-PM matching of radiographs for identification is more widely accepted in forensic dentistry than in forensic anthropology, where the former is most often based on radiographic images of dental restorations and/or implants,

which evince the unique characteristics of both the morphology of the lesion and that of the dentist's individual technique and thus afford multiple surfaces for examination (**Figure 2**), the latter relies upon matching frontal sinus, cranial sutures, vertebral morphology, and even bone trabecular patterns, not just the orthopedic equivalent of implants,

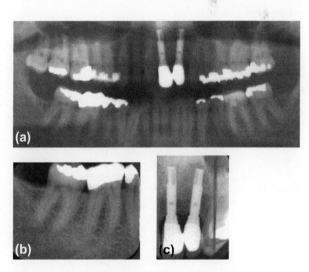

Figure 2 (a) Antemortem orthopantogram, (b) postmortem mandibular, and (c) maxillary radiographs from the same individual. Radiographs courtesy of Dr John Robson.

fixators, pins, plates, screws, and artificial joints. Although the angle at which an AM radiograph is taken may cause distortion, elongation, and superimposition of features in a dental radiograph, the problem is often compounded in an orthopedic image by additional factors such as age-related changes in joint surfaces and trabecular realignment caused by the application of differing stresses due to activity level and type with age. In all radiographic comparisons, the years elapsed between when the AM image was made and the individual's death must be taken into consideration. Superimposition of the AM-PM images of restorations is a frequently used technique in conjunction with the correspondence of measurements. Again, there is somewhat better correspondence within dental images than even within internal fixators used in fracture repair, as remodeling of bone due to weightbearing contributes to the movement of implanted devices over time. Dental records themselves (e.g., notations of teeth treated, condition of teeth, etc.) are not definitive in DVI as both omissions and mistakes in recording do occur, however, such records are potentially useful when comparing large numbers of AM and PM records to establish possible matches and in providing additional support for an identification; in some contexts dental records are used when radiographs are not available.

The utility of dental radiographs tends to be limited to developed countries where individuals typically visit the dentist and radiography is commonly used as part of routine examinations or following any major dental work. The dentist normally keeps either the developed radiographs themselves, microfilm of those radiographs, or stores digital radiographic images in the patient's electronic file. When disaster victims have not been subjected to trauma that has resulted in disruption of the dentition and AM records are available, forensic odontology is a powerful means of achieving identifications.

Nuclear DNA

Since its introduction into forensic science in 1985, DNA profiling has become commonplace in forensic laboratories worldwide. Its primary forensic use is for the identification material recovered from scenes of crimes; however, it is also widely used in the identification of human remains, particularly following on from transport disasters, such as plane crashes.

By the early to mid-1990s, the analysis of short tandem repeats (STRs) had replaced variable number tandem repeat

(VNTR)-based analysis. STRs had several advantages: they could be analyzed using polymerase chain reaction (PCR)-based methods, which made them much more sensitive; the alleles of STR loci are also much shorter, making the analysis of degraded material easier; several STR loci could be analyzed in one reaction and analyzed together using capillary electrophoresis (CE), which greatly reduced the time taken to carry out the analysis; and the profiles could be broken down into a series of numbers corresponding to the number of core repeats present in each allele, which allows comparisons to be made between DNA profiles generated within a laboratory and also to compare profiles generated in different laboratories.

STRs are found throughout the genome and they are composed of short blocks of sequence that are repeated in tandem—the STRs commonly used for forensic analysis have blocks of sequence that are four or five base pairs long (**Figure 3**). While there are numerous STR loci in the human genome that could be used as forensic markers, around 20–25 are commonly used. These have been selected for being highly discriminating (typically having a large number of variants (alleles) that differ in the number core repeats) and for being easy to analyze using PCR-based technology. Using current methodology DNA profiles can, in principle, be generated within a few hours and produce a profile that is extremely rare, if not unique (**Figure 4**).

Because of the limited discrimination capacity of the early profiling systems, it was not until 1991 that DNA profiling was successfully employed in the identification of human remains—in this case, a murder victim in the UK. It has since been successfully applied to cases that range from the identification of individual bodies to more complex scenarios with multiple victims following, for example, air crashes, fires and explosions, terrorist attacks, natural disasters, and conflicts. A distinct advantage of DNA analysis in DVI is that all tissues contain DNA, and therefore the method will work on highly fragmented remains and enable fragments of bodies to be reassociated.

As with the other forms of identification, the use of DNA analysis in DVI will vary from context to context. Whether DNA can be recovered from the human remains depends on the degree of environmental insult, for example, if the remains have been subjected to high temperatures in excess of 200 °C or there has been a long delay in locating and recovering the remains the DNA can be highly degraded, and it may not be possible to generate a profile. AM data are required for

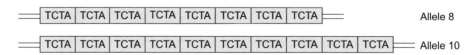

Figure 3 The structure of a short tandem repeat. This example shows the structure of two alleles from the locus D8S1179. The DNA either side of the core repeats is called flanking DNA. The alleles are named according to the number of repeats that they contain—hence alleles 8 and 10.

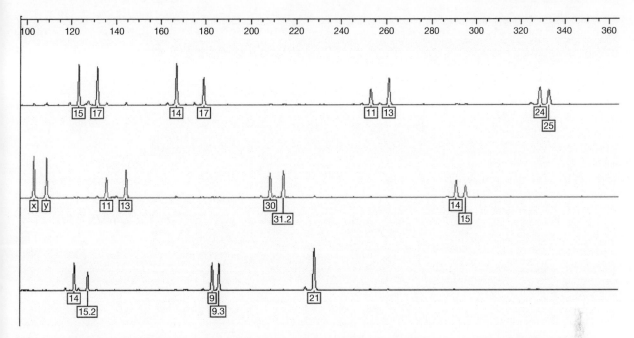

Figure 4 A DNA profile is represented by a series of peaks that can be broken down into a numerical code—the numbers correspond to the number of core repeats in each short tandem repeat (STR) allele. The profile above contains the information on 10 STR loci and the amelogenin locus, which differentiates between the X and Y chromosomes—in this profile, labeled X and Y (showing that this DNA sample is from a male).

comparison: this can be in the form of a direct comparison if a biological sample from the missing person is available, or more commonly by comparison to biological relatives of the missing person.

Unique medical identifiers

On occasions, PM analysis of human remains may happen upon a medical implant; typical examples are artificial joints and pacemakers. These medical devices come with a unique serial number and can allow for unambiguous identification as long as the relevant information can be located. Needless to say, identifications through this method are not common.

Data Collection

Data collection, both PM and AM, is a critical component of the DVI operation. Several agencies, both national and international, have developed forms that facilitate the systematic collection of data that can be used in the identification process. The most commonly employed system for DVI work uses the Interpol forms—these have been specifically developed for DVI work. The International Committee of the Red Cross has also developed AM and PM forms, which have been designed for use in postconflict scenarios (**Figure 5**). Both these systems can be computerized with the data entered into a relational database, allowing AM and PM data to be cross-searched. National

authorities have also developed their own systems, for example, in the US, the Disaster Mortuary Operational Response Team has its own set of recording forms and database recording similar information. Obviously, the more victims and the greater the fragmentation of those individuals, the more imperative it is to computerize PM and AM records. Searching by hand through records for matches, especially when the personnel who originally recorded PM details are no longer available and memory is lacking, is a frustrating exercise.

Postmortem

The cooperation and teamwork of experts, sharing of information, and agreement concerning and adherence to criteria by which an identification will be made, are critical to the management and effective performance of any DVI team. The work flow in the morgue, and hence floor plan, should be arranged to facilitate the processing of remains as well as the communication among the various teams of experts. The technical experts involved in the collection of data will vary depending on the state of the human remains; typically teams will comprise some or all of a pathologist, who will undertake a PM examination; an anthropologist to examine skeletal material; an odontologist to take radiographs and examine the teeth; a radiographer to take whole body X-rays; a fingerprint expert; and a biologist to take samples for DNA analysis. Other individuals, for example police officers and crime scene

Dental treatment:
Has the missing person received any dental treatment such as

- Crowns, such as gold-capped teeth
- Color: gold, silver, white
- Fillings (incl. color if known)
- False teeth (dentures)- upper, lower
- Bridge or other special dental treatment
- Extraction

Also indicate wherever there is uncertainty (for example, the family member may know that an upper left front tooth is misssing, but is unsure which one).

If possible, use a drawing, and/or indicate the described features in the chart below

If the missing person is a child, please indicate which baby teeth have erupted, which have fallen out and which permanent teeth have erupted and use the chart below

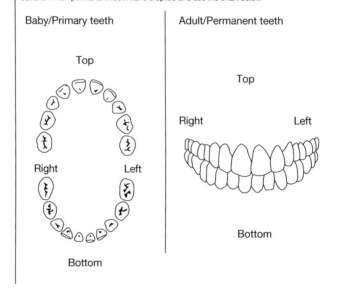

Figure 5   A section of the antemortem data collection form developed by the International Committee of the Red Cross.

investigators, will also be involved carrying out tasks such as documenting personal belongings, clothing, taking photographs, and ensuring chain of custody for any evidential items.

Antemortem

A prerequisite to the application of any of these methods is the existence of relevant, reliable AM data. Following a mass disaster, an AM data collection interview is typically conducted with relatives of the missing. The collection of AM data is as much a specialized process as conducting a PM examination, and interviews of relatives of the missing should be performed only by trained personnel. Interviews are best performed by native speakers of the language, so in-country training of personnel should be planned. During the interview, information

concerning the individual's physical description, a description of the clothing the individual was wearing, and any personal effects that were with the individual are recorded on an AM data form—this form should be compatible with the PM form to allow searching of comparable fields of information. A photograph of the missing person is collected and the existence and whereabouts of medical and dental records for that individual are noted so that these can be requested from doctors and dentists at a later date. Photographs of the victim's smiling can also be useful as the teeth may have distinguishing morphology or features such as spots caused by hypoplasia. During this interview, if possible, DNA samples are taken and latent fingerprints are enhanced and collected from the home of the missing person. DNA samples may be direct reference samples (e.g., from the missing person's toothbrush or hair-brush) or indirect reference samples, preferably from their immediate kin (father, mother, children).

The above methods work very well in developed countries and the process above describes the situation in a country with well-developed infrastructure. However, the infrastructure of many less-developed countries does not facilitate the collection, maintenance, and storage of such relevant records that drive the DVI process for the citizenry of developed countries. In postconflict situations, even where such records may have existed at one time, they may have been destroyed during the conflict or its aftermath or have become unavailable due to political and boundary shifts. In natural or other mass disasters in less-developed countries, the same may be true regarding destruction of extant records or the lack of relevant records. Furthermore, subsequent to mass disasters and conflicts many individuals are frequently displaced internally or have become refugees in neighboring countries. This makes locating relevant kin of the missing difficult, and organizing and conducting AM interviews challenging. Whenever possible, it is recommended to avoid retraumatizing the relatives of the missing by repeated visits and questions, as these doubtless reopen wounds, doubts, and raise anxiety.

Selection of Methods for Identification

In any mass disaster, the method that can be employed successfully will be dictated according to the condition of the remains, the composition of experts in the DVI team, the technical and financial resources available, and the choices made by the team's leadership during the course of its operational mandate.

Prior to DNA analysis, comparison of dental records was the most widely used method to achieve identifications. Analysis of five disasters in the UK between 1985 and 1989 which comprised three air disasters, a capsized ferry, and a fire on an oil platform, identified that dental records had been used to identify, on average, over 80% of the recovered bodies. In more recent large-scale disasters, for example, in the World Trade Center investigations, DNA was the first choice for identification and generated the majority of identifications by a single modality (86%), dental and fingerprints combined only yielding an additional 10% of identifications. Similarly, since the inception of the International Commission for Missing Person's DNA laboratory in Tuzla (Bosnia), identifications from the 1992 to 1995 Bosnian conflict have been DNA-led, with secondary means of identification used, where possible, to support the DNA-based identification—as of mid-2011, over 13 000 individuals in Bosnia and Herzegovina had been identified and returned to their families. In contrast, although DNA was initially a method of first choice in the Asian Tsunami identifications in Thailand, 11 months after the tsunami 80% of foreign victims had been identified using dental

comparisons—dental analysis with local victims identified 55% of Thai victims, lower than with foreign victims due to the lack of AM records in many cases. Overall, in the 15 months following the disaster, identifications had been made using dental alone, 1105; dental plus others, 1451; fingerprints alone, 670; fingerprints plus others 927; DNA alone, 27; DNA plus others 459.

There are reasons for the success ratios of the identification methods in each of the above examples. In the World Trade Center, victim fragmentation was extreme and the goal was set to identify every piece of tissue greater than or equal to 5 cm^3, thus necessitating the use of DNA. In Bosnia, lack of AM medical and dental records, commingling in secondary mass graves, and time elapsed since the deaths of the victims are but a few of the factors that dictated the reliance on DNA rather than other primary identifiers. In Thailand, important factors included that dental-based identifications could be made for many of the foreign victims relatively rapidly; many bodies were not fragmented, removing the requirement for DNA-based reassociation; fingerprint analysis was successful with many Thai victims; limited in-country facilities were capable of handling the volume of DNA samples from the disaster; and decomposition of tissue was rapid in the tropical environment, making DNA analysis difficult.

Evaluation of Identification Data

The exact procedures used in the identification process vary from country to country and from scenario to scenario. Typically, identifications are made through an organization that acts as an identification commission or board; this would typically include an expert from the main disciplines involved in making identifications—investigators/crime scene investigators, fingerprint examiners, odontologists, pathologists, anthropologists, and DNA analysts—and should be presided over by the legal authority charged with issuing death certificates. In this manner, all the evidence contributing to the identification of an individual in a mass disaster is reviewed a final time by everyone who has contributed to that process, and a legal decision concerning the establishment of positive identity and repatriation of the remains to kin can be completed.

Evaluating the identification is a complex task, especially as the number of victims increases—this heightens the possibility of coincidental matches, which, if not detected, can lead to misidentifications. An often cited example where this occurred is the identification of a fire officer recovered from the World Trade Center following 9/11, who was misidentified on the basis of his clothing that identified him as a fire officer from a particular unit coupled with a rare congenital anomaly in spinal vertebra. The identification was not confirmed by any of the recognized objective methods of identification and DNA analysis later exposed the misidentification, but only after the remains had been returned to the wrong family—the rare medical condition had been shared by one of his colleagues in his unit. Such seemingly remote coincidences become more likely as the number of victims increases.

Conclusions

The requirement for governments and indeed the international community to be able to mount an effective DVI response following disasters and conflicts is widely accepted. Recent technological advances in terms of DNA analysis, portable radiographic equipment, and sophisticated computer databases that allow comparison of AM and PM data have increased the number of cases where the identification of human remains is possible. There will always be limitations as to what is possible; for example, following the World Trade Center identifications, even with an enormous effort expended, no identification could be made for over 40% of the victims, which should not distract from the success in identifying over 1500 victims. With continued improvements in technology, preparedness, and infrastructure to deal with a large number of samples in a timely fashion, there is the potential to have a greater proportion of victims identified and returned to their families following future disasters and conflicts.

See also: **Anthropology/Odontology:** History of Forensic Anthropology; Odontology; Personal Identification in Forensic Anthropology; **Biology/DNA:** DNA Extraction and Quantification; MiniSTRs; Mitochondrial DNA; Short Tandem Repeats; Single-Nucleotide Polymorphisms; The National Missing and Unidentified Persons System (NamUs); **Forensic Medicine/Clinical:** Airplane Crashes and Other Mass Disasters; **Forensic Medicine/Pathology:** Autopsy.

Further Reading

Ballantyne, J., 1997. Mass disaster genetics. Nature Genetics 15, 329–331.

Biesecker, L.G., Bailey-Wilson, J.E., Ballantyne, J., et al., 2005. Epidemiology – DNA identifications after the 9/11 World Trade Center attack. Science 310, 1122–1123.

Bowers, C.M., 2004. Forensic Dental Evidence: An Investigator's Handbook. Elsevier, Amsterdam.

Brenner, C.H., 2006. Some mathematical problems in the DNA identification of victims in the 2004 tsunami and similar mass fatalities. Forensic Science International 157, 172–180.

Dolan, S.M., Saraiya, D.S., Donkervoort, S., Rogel, K., Lieber, C., Sozer, A., 2009. The emerging role of genetics professionals in forensic kinship DNA identification after a mass fatality: lessons learned from Hurricane Katrina volunteers. Genetics in Medicine 11, 414–417.

Donkervoort, S., Dolan, S.M., Beckwith, M., Northrup, T.P., Sozer, A., 2008. Enhancing accurate data collection in mass fatality kinship identifications: lessons learned from Hurricane Katrina. Forensic Science International Genetics 2, 354–362.

Huffine, E., Crews, J., Kennedy, B., Bomberger, K., Zinbo, A., 2001. Mass identification of persons missing from the break-up of the former Yugoslavia: structure, function, and role of the International Commission on Missing Persons. Croatian Medical Journal 42, 271–275.

International Committee of the Red Cross, 2004. The Missing and Their Families – Documents of Reference. ICRC, Geneva.

International Committee of the Red Cross, 2009. Missing People, DNA Analysis and Identification of Human Remains. ICRC, Geneva.

Interpol, 2009. Disaster Victim Identification Guide. Interpol, Lyon.

Keough, M.E., Simmons, T., Samuels, M., 2004. Missing persons in post-conflict settings: best practices for integrating psychosocial and scientific approaches. The Journal of the Royal Society for the Promotion of Health 124, 271–275.

Morgan, O.W., Sribanditmongkol, P., Perera, C., Sulasmi, Y., Van Alphen, D., Sondorp, E., 2006. Mass fatality management following the South Asian tsunami disaster: case studies in Thailand, Indonesia, and Sri Lanka. PLoS Medicine 3, e195.

National Institute of Justice, 2005. Lessons Learned from 9/11: DNA Identification in Mass Fatality Incidents. US Department of Justice, Washington, DC.

Prinz, M., Carracedo, A., Mayr, W.R., et al., 2007. DNA Commission of the International Society for Forensic Genetics (ISFG): recommendations regarding the role of forensic genetics for disaster victim identification (DVI). Forensic Science International Genetics 1, 3–12.

Schuller-Gotzburg, P., Suchanek, J., 2007. Forensic odontologists successfully identify tsunami victims in Phuket, Thailand. Forensic Science International 171, 204–207.

Ubelaker, D.H., Jacobs, C., 1995. Identification of orthopedic device manufacturer. Journal of Forensic Sciences 40, 168–170.

The National Missing and Unidentified Persons System (NamUs)

MM Houck, Consolidated Forensic Laboratory, Washington, DC, USA

Introduction

It has been estimated that there are approximately 40 000 unidentified human remains in the offices of the nation's medical examiners and coroners or were buried or cremated before being identified. In June 2007, Office of Justice Program's Bureau of Justice Statistics (BJS) confirmed that, in a typical year, medical examiners and coroners handle approximately 4400 unidentified human decedent cases, 1000 of which remain unidentified after one year. BJS further identified the need to improve record-retention policies. As of 2004, more than half (51%) of the nation's medical examiners' offices had no policy for retaining records—such as X-rays, DNA, or fingerprints—on unidentified human decedents. BJS also noted, however, that more than 90% of offices servicing large jurisdictions did have such a policy. Cases of missing persons 18 years old and younger must be reported, but reporting adult missing persons is voluntary. Only a few states have laws that require law enforcement agencies to prepare missing person reports on adults. Overall, there is a low rate of reporting these cases through National Crime Information Center.

The National Missing and Unidentified Persons System (NamUs) is a national centralized repository and resource center for missing persons and unidentified decedent records. NamUs is a free online system that can be searched by medical examiners, coroners, law enforcement officials, and the general public from all over the country in the hope of resolving these cases. The Missing Persons Database contains information about missing persons, which can be entered by anyone; however, before it appears as a case on NamUs, the information is verified. NamUs provides a user with a variety of resources, including the ability to print missing persons' posters and receive free biometric collection and testing assistance. Other resources include links to state clearinghouses, medical examiners and coroners' offices, law enforcement agencies, victim assistance groups, and pertinent legislation.

The Unidentified Persons Database contains information entered by medical examiners and coroners. Unidentified persons are people who have died and whose bodies have not been identified. Anyone can search this database using characteristics such as sex, race, distinct body features, and even dental information.

The newly added UnClaimed Persons database (UCP) contains information about deceased persons who have been identified by name but for whom no next of kin or family member has been identified or located to claim the body for burial or other disposition. Only medical examiners and coroners may enter cases in the UCP database. However, the database is searchable by the public using a missing person's name and year of birth.

When a new missing person or unidentified decedent case is entered into NamUs, the system automatically performs cross matching comparisons between the databases, searching for matches or similarities between cases. NamUs provides free DNA testing and other forensic services, such as anthropology and odontology assistance. NamUs' Missing Persons Database and Unidentified Persons Database are now available in Spanish.

Acknowledgment

Material provided by OJP from Website http://www.namus.gov.

See also: **Biology/DNA:** DNA Databases; **Investigations:** Fingerprints; **Pattern Evidence/Fingerprints (Dactyloscopy):** Identification and Classification.

Further Reading

Ritter, N., 2007. Missing persons and unidentified remains: the nation's silent mass disaster. NIJ Journal 256, 2–7. http://www.nij.gov.

Identification

C Cattaneo and D Gibelli, Università degli Studi di Milano, Milano, Italy

Introduction

Personal identification is one of the most relevant issues in forensic pathology. In all countries with a structured legal system, cadavers must be formally identified. The reasons behind such obligations are certainly moral and also concern aspects of criminal and civil procedures: in fact, without knowing who the victim of a crime is, it is very difficult to begin investigating and without appropriate identification of the deceased, civil matters such as insurance policies and questions concerning inheritance cannot be concluded. As to what each specific legal system implies as reliable identification, this is another matter. If the body is well preserved, it is frequently sufficient to have family or acquaintances formally, and responsibly, identify the body. But in the case of decomposed cadavers or remains, this cannot or must not be the case, although some judges would like to conclude identification issues (saving on expenses is usually the issue) relying on personal belongings, clothing, or other nonbiological evidence. It is clear that this is incorrect and that biological identification, when possible, should always be sought in order to avoid serious mistakes: Interpol protocols, for one, to stress this point.

How to identify a cadaver or human remains is another issue. In this age of DNA, usually, identification is relatively, quickly, and cheaply achieved by genetic testing. Nonetheless, particularly in the case of severely decomposed human remains, many other methods can be as reliable but quicker and cheaper, such as odontology. In many cases, as will be discussed later, particularly in cases of vagrants or when neither antemortem DNA or relatives nor clinical dental or medical data are available, judges and pathologists should be aware that other methods exist.

A final preliminary comment that must be made concerns the degree of confidence and reliability of a specific identification method or rationale. Many different schools exist as to how to classify levels of identification: the two extremes are exclusion and positive (certain) identification. In between, there are a series of nuances that can be summed up as different degrees of compatibility, for example, no elements allowing for exclusion but concordant characters are very general, or several and specific characters with a high identification potential but not sufficient to reach positive identification. The question is how much is enough for positive identification? Unfortunately, there is no real answer. Some methods, such as DNA and fingerprinting, have managed to quantify the degree of correspondence of two biological samples (e.g., the cadaver and the toothbrush of the person whom the cadaver was thought to "belong to" in life). In other words, a statistical analysis of the frequency of discrete characters (alleles, minutiae) can lead the expert to express the probability of these two samples belonging to the same person as a number (e.g., 98%). Obviously, any method of this sort will be very popular among judges as it has a known error and neatly complies with Daubert and Kumho rules. Other methods, particularly those based on the comparison of morphology (e.g., odontological and radiological/osteological ones), have more difficulty in quantifying their response. For example, how can an odontologist say what the probability of two different persons sharing the same asset of dental features is? Dental assets change in time and discrete characters are difficult to standardize and study worldwide (although some authors have approached this issue). Or, more simply, what is the probability that two individuals share the same two scars and three tattoos? The answer depends on the types of scars and tattoos, of course, and also on a large deal of subjectivity. Nonetheless, most pathologists will (correctly) continue to identify with morphological and clinical features; one should, however, bear in mind the limits and issues that can be raised with such methods.

The following is a brief survey of identification approaches. The authors wish to stress, however, how the world of identification concerns not only positive identification, that is, matching antemortem with postmortem data (when there already is a possible match), but also cases where there is no clue as to who the body belongs to. This is a frequently underestimated issue, and in these cases, the pathologist must use as many disciplines as necessary to build a biological profile of the cadaver or human remains that should be automatically matched with missing persons databases (when these exist, and hoping the person has been reported missing by someone) and give maximum circulation of the biological profile on newspapers, television, and so on. Thus, the article is divided into two parts: the first dealing with unidentified cadavers and the second with positive identification.

Part I. Unidentified Cadavers

The issue of unidentified decedents is a large and underestimated one, also because of the lack of knowledge concerning the frequency of unknown decedents in different geographical contexts. Very few countries have a database for the comparison of missing persons and unidentified decedents, which is surprising, given the increase in legal and illegal immigration and a society with looser family and social ties and obligations. Hanzlick et al. published epidemiological data from Fulton County (Georgia) and created one of the first Web sites with information and demographical data on unidentified decedents.

Very few indications are available in Europe, and in different countries, the precise number of unknown decedents is not recorded or still partially known; a recent study from Italy (a high immigration rate country) reported that at least 800 individuals are recorded as unidentified in medicolegal institutes. Similar orders of magnitude have been given for France by the press but official numbers do not exist. However, the real frequency of unknown decedents is likely to be higher than reported, due to the occurrence of unrecorded immigrants and the lack of precise information on unidentified bodies in different institutes of legal medicine and morgues.

Identification in every case requires a comparison between antemortem information from the "suspect" (the person who the remains may belong to) and postmortem data from the corpse; however, this comparison can be performed between profiles only if a possible match has been reached. And the possible match(es) is selected because it shows compatible characters, for example, such as sex, race, age, and stature, with those of the cadaver. Building up general data from remains is called "general identification," and the biological data extrapolated from the cadaver or human remains are the so-called "biological profile."

The biological profile consists of general characteristics of sex, age, race, and height of the individual and all individual markers that can be useful for identification (tattoos, scars, bone calluses, dental work, etc.). When the cadaver is in good condition, the pathologist can be independent in extrapolating all relevant information (although a toxicologist may be useful for detecting the presence of helpful (identification-wise) substances or medication in the blood or tissues). If the remains are badly preserved or skeletonized, then an anthropologist and odontologist may be useful. Most of the steps and diagnoses these disciplines, particularly anthropology, go through are discussed in the relevant articles. Briefly, when genitalia are not recognizable, sex can be easily defined by the analysis of the pelvis, and especially of the pubis, whereas cranial characteristics are less reliable; an accurate diagnosis can exceed 98% with the pelvis. In addition, the cranial features may suffer important modifications with time, as shown by masculinization usually reported in the crania of old females. On the other hand, osteological diagnosis of sex is difficult or even impossible to reach in case of subadults, where DNA must come in.

On the contrary, age estimation is easier in subadults than in adults, where it can be performed from the analysis of skeletal and dental development. The error of age estimation increases with age. In adults, age estimation can be linked only to degeneration processes. The main methods are Suchey–Brooks' method on the pubic symphysis, Iscan's method on the fourth rib's osteochondral surface, and Lovejoy's method on the auricular surface of the ilium. Most commonly applied dental methods are Lamendin's and Kvaal–Solheim's methods. Ancestry determination in decomposed corpses can rely on the histological analysis of residual skin and hair, which show decisive differences between the main races. In skeletonized remains, the diagnosis of ancestry may be reached by morphological and metrical assessments of the cranium and postcranial bones. In addition, race determination may be performed by Fordisc software®, based on different cranial and postcranial measurements taken in American samples from different ancestries, although its adherence to the main racial groups is questionable. Stature is related to the length of long bones and can be determined also from fragmented bones by specific formulae, but in this case, the inaccuracy is high. A complete X-ray analysis is obligatory in order to verify the presence of bone traits (e.g., Harris lines, calluses) as well as dental traits (e.g., restorations), which can be useful. Finally, facial reconstruction should be performed provided investigators have the final "identikit" circulate with the appropriate precautions: facial reproductions may remind observers of a person who has been missing, but it may not necessarily bear a close resemblance.

Once the biological profile is complete, the obtained identikit should be compared with missing persons and/or circulate as much as possible in the hope that someone (investigators or the general public) may come up with a possible match for identity.

Part II. Personal Identification: Comparison Between Antemortem and Postmortem Data

Once circumstantial evidence, comparison with missing persons or other investigative activities, has led to a suspicion of identity, personal identification is then based on the analysis of the specific and individualizing characteristics observed in the unknown decedent and their comparison with similar data from the matching "suspect": every type of identification requires a comparison that must be founded on biological features. Positive identification may be reached by different methods. The first and most immediate for well-preserved cadavers is visual recognition of facial characteristics (e.g., with a photograph). The comparison may also be performed through fingerprints or genetic comparison if an adequate antemortem reference sample is available. In addition, since dental and skeletal features are unique, odontological and radiological methods may be applied with success if consistent antemortem material from the identity suspect can be obtained. Finally, superimposition methods (craniofacial and dental superimpositions) can be used when other procedures cannot be applied, although the significance of results is questionable and their importance is limited to specific cases.

Individual Markers

Specific descriptors such as tattoos, prostheses, nevi, and scars may be useful for identification and, therefore, should be described and photographed. For this reason, with decomposed and burnt remains, specific care must be taken to clean the skin surface, at times by scraping off the initial epidermal layer, in order to visualize scars, moles, and tattoos that may be hidden underneath soot and superficially burnt skin.

As for most morphological methods of comparison between antemortem and postmortem material, there is no consensus concerning how many descriptors are needed in order to reach a positive identification; literature recently has attempted at standardizing the frequency of specific human descriptors among the general population. This may give the first impulse for statistical evaluation of bodily markers. However, one should consider that every descriptor from a morphological point of view is unique, although it may be found in other individuals. For example, a surgical scar is likely to be useful for personal identification; however, other persons may have a similar marker in the same bodily area. Most markers are highly individualizing, since their morphology is unique; for example, a thoracotomy follows a standard procedure, but the profile of the cut mark, the sutures, and manner of bone remodeling lead to a unique profile of the marker, which is different among individuals.

The following is a list of more specialized identification procedures that go beyond the pathologist's competence.

Facial Identification

In different countries, the main identification procedure consists of showing the corpse to the relatives or acquaintances who are requested to give a positive identification, although visual recognition is often influenced by the emotional status of the observers, who are perhaps often more prone to identify the corpse by clothes and personal belongings. At times, however, even though the cadaver is easily identifiable visually, no acquaintances seem to exist or can be contacted. At this point, comparison of facial traits with identity papers such as drivers' licenses can be requested.

Indeed, facial features may be of some help for personal identification through a scientific process, although their reliability still needs to be verified. How can two faces (antemortem photograph and the cadaver) be proven as belonging to the same person? In cases of personal identification of the living from video surveillance systems, for example, comparison and superimposition of facial features is commonly used. In these cases, the morphological features of two facial profiles are compared in order to point out possible differences that may lead to an exclusion or similarities that may justify an identification. However, many limits still affect such procedures, particularly the lack of a standardized manner of comparison between two images. Therefore, at the moment, the comparison of facial features may be useful only for an exclusion of identity, if gross and otherwise inexplicable discordances between the two facial profiles are found. In addition, one should consider that these methods have been tested for personal identification in the living, whereas at the moment there are no experimental studies concerning this topic in case of unknown decedents (**Figure 1**). A similar rationale can be used for other parts of the body, for example, venous and mole patterns, with the limitations stated above.

Figure 1 Example of superimposition between a 3-D scan of the cadaver [in yellow (light gray in print versions)] and the 2D image of the antemortem photograph.

Fingerprint Analysis

Fingerprints are among the most individualizing features, since they are also different in homozygous twins and are usually recorded by qualified police personnel: in addition, literature shows that even in corpses radically compromised by decomposition or charring processes, they can be recorded and used for identification, provided antemortem prints are available. In many counties, however, this is limited to individuals who have a criminal record. Databases such as automated fingerprint identification system (AFIS) have proven to be efficient for this purpose worldwide. The problem concerning the pathologist or forensic expert in general may be in extracting prints from dead bodies that have already undergone decomposition.

According to the specific alterations, fingerprints can be recovered by different procedures and treatments: when hands are mummified or charred, which implies a loss of liquids, fingerprints have to be softened and reinflated, for example, by alternate incubation in alcohol and sodium hydroxide solutions. Once the fingerprints are softened, they may be inflated by injection of saline solution. In case of carbonized hands, the fists are often clenched and, therefore, are better preserved from the heat; in this case, they should be accurately preserved and cleaned avoiding any further damage; then, the application of specific types of latex can be useful in recovering a print (**Figure 2**).

In case of putrefaction, the first procedure consists of stopping any further modification, which can be reached by hardening the skin in ethanol for a time between a few minutes and 1–2 h. Saponification causes flattening of the papillary crests, so before inking the fingerprints should be reinflated.

Several methods have been published for recovering prints from decomposed human remains. It is important to realize that even in a cadaver that seems badly preserved and beyond fingerprinting, these methods can give useful fingerprints.

DNA Testing

Genetic analysis is usually considered the main method of identification in the cases of unknown decedents and is undoubtedly the most popular one. In countries with DNA databases, this may be, indeed, the best way to a quick and reliable identification. Comparison of the DNA postmortem asset from the cadaver or human remains with the antemortem asset of a "suspect" implies obtaining biological material that certainly contains DNA of that specific person from, for example, a toothbrush, a razor, or other personal belongings. It must be certain that they are not contaminated. DNA from close relatives can also be useful and easily obtained with a mouth swab.

Nonetheless, sometimes the recovery of antemortem material may not be possible, for example, in cases where relatives are not present (this may occur for mass graves where the bodies are discovered decades after the massacre or in cases of vagrants or illegal immigrants). On the other hand, some postmortem substrates such as calcined tissues or dry bone may still be challenging for the geneticist since DNA extraction may not be banal. Furthermore, sometimes DNA testing may be longer and more expensive than other methods, for example, dental comparison.

Odontological Methods

Teeth are highly individualizing markers, thanks to anatomical uniqueness and modifications that may derive from therapeutical and pathological variables; these factors contribute to creating a unique profile, different from one individual to the other. In addition, teeth are resistant to many taphonomical agents and carbonization and can be easily analyzed for personal identification.

Antemortem data usually come from the dentist who treated the person in life and may provide descriptions, casts

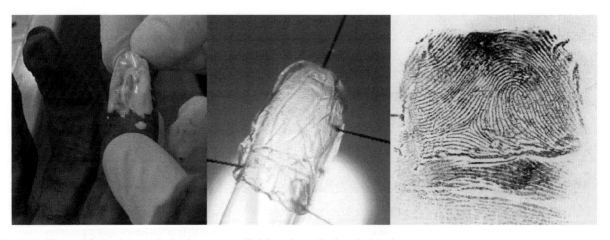

Figure 2   Phases of fingerprint reproduction from a mummified finger by application of a latex layer.

and orthopantomographs, and other dental radiographs (**Figure 3**). In collecting antemortem material, one should always keep in mind that the dental asset may vary with time; therefore, clinical data sometimes may not be reliable, according to time lapse and treatment between when the data were created and death. This explains the difficulties encountered in cases of personal identification of subadults, who often undergo frequent odontological treatments and are affected by growth, with consequent progressive modification of the odontological profile.

Teeth individualizing markers are not only in the oral cavity but also in the palatal rugae. Palatal rugae are irregular ridges of connective tissue across the front portion of the palate and are highly variable and stable with time, regardless of odontological treatment. Recent articles also show that radical modifications of the palate caused, for example, by rapid maxillary expansion do not appreciably modify the profile, which can still be used for identification. In addition, comparison of the palatal profile does not require specific skills, since the results do not seem to vary between observers with and without odontological experience. The only condition for applying this method is the availability of an antemortem cast of the upper arch, which is usually taken before many odontological treatments.

Radiological Methods: Comparison of Bone Profiles

The morphology of bones can also be extremely useful, usually from antemortem radiological analyses; in addition, some radiological examinations are frequently performed on the general population, for example, chest X-rays, and the bones visible on these exams can be useful for identification. However, this osteological approach is based on the morphological assessment of bone structures; this means that the results will not be easily quantifiable, with clear limits in expressing the probability of positive identification. In fact, while most physiological, surgical, and pathological bone features seem to be quite common as proven by the first studies concerning the analysis of frequencies of specific markers within the general population, the morphology of every bone is

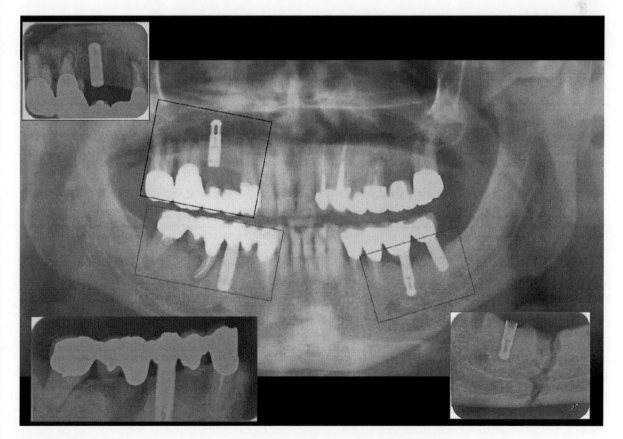

Figure 3 Odontological comparison by postmortem intraoral X-rays (defined by a colored line) and antemortem ortopantomography in the background.

unique although difficult to fit in a numerical perspective. At the moment, very few bone districts have reached an adequate standardization from a statistical point of view and precise algorithms by which to identify; the comparison of frontal sinuses is the most reliable method of identification, since they are different even in homozygous twins, and their applicability is limited only by the low frequency of this cranial radiograph in the general population (**Figure 4**). Other attempts at the standardization of the comparison of other districts such as the thoracic vertebral margin are still experimental and need further studies.

Some authors have attempted at determining a minimum criteria for identification, which are stated in one to four unique analogous features without discrepancies, but a general agreement concerning this topic actually does not exist. There is no univocal and valid definition for the term "unique"; therefore, the main difficulty consists of determining which feature may be considered unique and how many features are needed to reach an identification. In addition, since the comparison is based on a morphological evaluation, the matches and mismatches between the two profiles are often subjective and left to the personal opinion of the observer.

Superimposition Methods

When none of the previously cited methods can be used, a last possibility lies in the superimposition of photos from the identity suspect and images of the cranium of the unknown decedent. This procedure, called craniofacial superimposition, cannot be used alone to reach a positive identification because of its low reliability. The main reasons consist of the difference between the two compared profiles (soft tissues and hard tissues); in addition, the results and success of this method of identification are highly variable according to different authors. At the moment, the only reliable use consists of excluding identity if gross incompatibilities are observed (**Figure 5**).

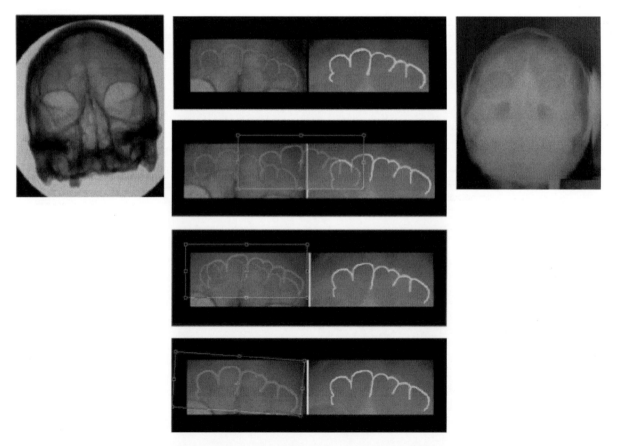

Figure 4 Example of superimposition of frontal sinuses between antemortem X-rays from the identity suspect (on the right) and the unknown decedent (on the left); frontal sinuses in the antemortem are in yellow (white in print versions) and the postmortem in red (gray in print versions); the results of the superimposition in orange (light gray in print versions).

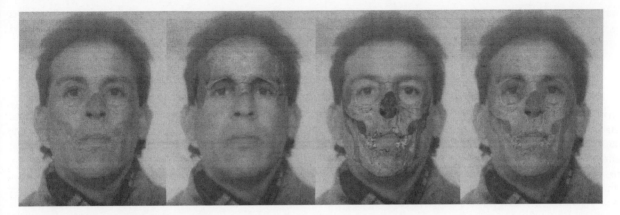

Figure 5 Example of craniofacial superimposition.

A similar procedure can be applied to dental profiles: if antemortem photos of the missing individual when smiling and showing his or her front teeth are available, a comparison can be performed by a superimposition of the dental elements visible in the photograph and those visible in a photograph of the cadaver or of a dental cast of the remains. In this case, the identification potential is greater because the method compares the same structures (teeth): one should only pay extreme caution to obtaining the same orientation and verifying that gross alterations of the teeth did not occur after the picture was taken.

Conclusions

An unidentified body may come in different conditions, ranging from well preserved to skeletonized or burnt. For this reason, the expert should be familiar with most methods of identification in order to choose the most reliable, cheapest, and fastest one for that specific case.

This survey is concluded with an outline summarizing, at present, possible solutions for performing positive identification of human remains by comparing antemortem and post-mortem data, with the relative advantages and disadvantages.

Well-Preserved Body

It should be stressed that it may be more difficult to compare a dead face with the picture of a living face in the attempt to declare that it is the same person. This is confirmed by the difficulties encountered by anthropologists dealing with the identification of living individuals on photographic material (e.g., on video surveillance recordings of bank robberies, etc.). In these cases, it is necessary to compare the physiognomic traits of the person represented on tape or a photograph with the face of the suspected thief or assailant. While this appears to be a banal and intuitively simple activity, it is anything but simple. Comparing the morphological and metric traits of two images for the purpose of arriving at a definite identification of the subject is still complex: this is due to the differences in orientation of the two images and to the lack of standardization of such procedures. In the same manner, in the case of a well-preserved cadaver to be compared with a photograph of a living person, serious problems in determining the traits that may be crucial for identification can turn up. It is for this reason that it is important to support a mere resemblance with specific descriptors such as scars, tattoos, moles, and so on.

Identification can obviously be performed by the methods suggested below.

Putrefied, Burnt, Partly, or Completely Skeletonized Human Remains

For this type of material, depending on which districts are better preserved, the following methods should be applied:

Significant descriptors: This is the case of putrefied bodies presenting countermarks (or features) so singular as that they may be used for identification purposes. Examples of these identification instruments are residues of tattoos, scars, bone prostheses or anomalies, unusual mutilations, and surgical operations.

Fingerprinting (dactyloscopy): It is always worth while trying to restore the papillary crests in order to be able to obtain sufficient dactyloscopic data for the comparison of fingerprints. This, however, presumes that the subject's prints were taken during his lifetime and that antemortem fingerprints of the subject are available.

Odontology: If a detailed antemortem dental chart, dental radiographs, or other clinical dental data exist, they can be used for comparison with the dentition of the human remains. Such data, however, must be available and the dentition of the remains fairly well preserved. The advantages of this method are its rapidity and low costs. One disadvantage, compared to DNA analysis, could be the nonquantifiability of the result. For example, it is almost impossible to provide a judge with the numerical probability that two different individuals may share the same dentition. Many odontologists, however, feel that quantification of the result would be useless and that morphological methods are based on the operator's experience and common sense.

DNA: This is the most popular method and most expensive. It is necessary, nevertheless, to be able to extract the DNA from the remains, and in the case of dry bone, this can be difficult for the presence of polymerase chain reaction (PCR) inhibitors and degradation. Furthermore, there may exist no adequate relatives for DNA comparison or objects such as toothbrushes and combs from which to extract the individual's antemortem DNA may not be retrievable, as in the case of vagrants and illegal immigrants. The advantages of this method consist in being able to supply a quantitative result, owing to the studies on the distribution of the alleles of specific loci within a certain population, which makes it possible to provide the probability that another person shares the same genetic asset. Other possible setbacks may be that it is more expensive and requires more time.

Anthropology–Osteology: Image superimposition: These methods are used when the above-described methods are not applicable. Superimposition can be dental or craniofacial. As already mentioned, dental superimposition requires the existence of a decent-quality photograph of the living subject, smiling, in order to be able to compare his or her dental profile with that of the human remains. Craniofacial superimposition, where craniometric points of the soft tissues are compared with craniometric points of the remains, is less reliable. These investigations require good quality photographs. In the case of dental superimposition, the methodology, although incapable of quantifying the error, at least compares the same structures.

Radiological comparison of frontal sinus shape or the morphological correspondence between the shape of any bone (e.g., vertebra) can be a valid method of identification, although one must be very cautious in matching the orientation of the antemortem and postmortem radiographs and in looking for sufficient corresponding traits.

In conclusion, results always need to be carefully examined by an experienced observer. Personal identification has to be carried out with a set of data, after having carefully evaluated the limits and the possible sources of error of each method.

See also: **Anthropology/Odontology:** Aging the Dead and the Living; Ancestry; Facial Approximation; Odontology; Personal Identification in Forensic Anthropology; Sexing; Stature and Build.

Further Reading

Besana, J.L., Rogers, T.L., 2010. Personal identification using the frontal sinus. Journal of Forensic Sciences 55 (3), 584–589.

Brooks, S.T., Suchey, J.M., 1990. Skeletal age determination based on the os pubis: a comparison of the Acsadi-Nemeskèri and Suchey-Brooks methods. Human Evolution 5, 227–238.

Brooks, S.T., 1955. Skeletal age at death: the reliability of cranial and pubic age indicators. American Journal of Physical Anthropology 13, 567–597.

Cattaneo, C., Ritz-Timme, S., Schutz, H.W., et al., 2000. Unidentified cadavers and human remains in the EU: an unknown issue. International Journal of Legal Medicine 113 (3), N1–N3.

Cattaneo, C., Porta, D., De Angelis, D., Gibelli, D., Poppa, P., Grandi, M., 2010. Unidentified bodies and human remains: an Italian glimpse through a European problem. Forensic Science International 195, 167 e1–6.

Christensen, A.M., 2005. Testing the reliability of frontal sinuses in positive identification. Journal of Forensic Sciences 50, 18–22.

Ciaffi, R., Gibelli, D., Cattaneo, C., 2011. Forensic radiology and personal identification of unidentified bodies: a review. La Radiologia Medica 116, 960–968.

Daubert v. Merrell Dow Pharmaceuticals. 1993. 509 U.S. 579, 92–102.

De Angelis, D., Riboli, F., Gibelli, D., Cappella, A., Cattaneo, C., September 2012. Palatal rugae as an individualising marker: reliability for forensic odontology and personal identification. Science and Justice 52 (3), 181–184.

Fenton, T.W., Heard, A.N., Sauer, N.J., 2008. Skull-photo superimposition and border deaths: identification through exclusion and the failure to exclude. Journal of Forensic Sciences 53 (1), 34–40.

Fischman, S.L., 1985. The use of medical and dental radiographs in identification. International Dental Journal 35, 301–306.

Ghosh, A.K., Sinha, P., 2001. An economised craniofacial identification system. Forensic Science International 117, 109–119.

Giles, E., Elliot, O., 1963. Sex determination by discriminant function analysis of crania. American Journal of Physical Anthropology 21, 53–68.

Grivas, C.R., Komar, D.A., 2008. Kumho, Daubert, and the nature of scientific inquiry: implications for forensic anthropology. Journal of Forensic Sciences 53 (4), 771–776.

Hanzlick, R., Clark, S., 2008. The unidentified decedent reporting system – a model national website registry for the unidentified deceased. The American Journal of Forensic Medicine and Pathology 29, 106–113.

Hanzlick, R., Smith, G.P., 2006. Identification of unidentified deceased – turnaround times, methods and demographics in Fulton County, Georgia. The American Journal of Forensic Medicine and Pathology 27, 79–84.

Hanzlick, R., 2006. Identification of unidentified deceased and locating next of kin. The American Journal of Forensic Medicine and Pathology 27, 126–128.

Iscan, M.Y., Loth, S.R., Wright, R.K., 1984. Age estimation from the rib by phase analysis: white males. Journal of Forensic Sciences 29, 1094–1104.

Iscan, M.Y., Loth, S.R., Wright, R.K., 1985. Age estimation from the rib by phase analysis: white females. Journal of Forensic Sciences 30, 853–863.

Ishii, M., Yayama, K., Motani, H., et al., 2011. Application of superimposition-based personal identification using skull computed tomography images. Journal of Forensic Sciences 56 (4), 960–966.

Italian Department of the Interior, June 2010. Extraordinary Commissioner for missing People, V Semestral Report.

Kahana, Y., Grande, A., Tancredi, D.M., Penalver, J., Hiss, J., 2001. Fingerprinting the deceased: traditional and new techniques. Journal of Forensic Sciences 46, 908–912.

Kahana, T., Goldin, L., Hiss, J., 2002. Personal identification based on radiographic vertebral features. The American Journal of Forensic Medicine and Pathology 23 (1), 36–41.

Kumho Tire Co. v. Carmichael. 1999. 526 U.S. 137.

Kvaal, S.I., Kolltveit, K.M., Thomsen, I.O., Solheim, T., 1995. Age estimation of adults from dental radiographs. Forensic Science International 74 (3), 175–185.

Lamendin, H., Baccino, E., Humbert, J.F., Tavernier, J.C., Nossintchouk, R.M., Zerillia, A., 1992. A simple technique for age estimation in adult corpses: the two criteria dental method. Journal of Forensic Sciences 37, 1373–1379.

Lovejoy, C.O., Meindle, R.S., Mensforth, R.P., Barton, T.J., 1985. Multifactorial determination of skeletal age at death: a method and blind tests of its accuracy. American Journal of Physical Anthropology 68, 1–14.

Meindl, R.S., Lovejoy, C.O., Mensforth, R.P., Don Carlos, L., 1985. Accuracy and direction of error in the sexing of the skeleton implications for palaeodemography. American Journal of Physical Anthropology 68, 79–85.

Muthusubramanian, M., Limson, K.S., Julian, R., 2005. Analysis of rugae in burn victims and cadavers to simulate rugae identification in cases of incineration and decomposition. The Journal of Forensic Odonto-Stomatology 23, 26–29.

Ohtani, M., Nishida, N., Chiba, T., Fukuda, M., Miyamoto, Y., Yoshioka, N., 2008. Indication and limitations of using palatal rugae for personal identification in edentuolous cases. Forensic Science International 176, 178–182.

Ousley, S.D., Jantz, R.L., 1996. Fordisc 2.0: Personal Computer Forensic Discriminant Function. The University of Tennessee, Knoxville.

Page, M., Taylor, J., Blenkin, M., 2011. Forensic identification science evidence since Daubert: Part I – a quantitative analysis of the exclusion of forensic identification science evidence. Journal of Forensic Sciences 56 (5), 1180–1184.

Paulozzi, J., Cox, C.S., Williams, D.D., Nolte, K.B., 2008. John and Jane Doe: the epidemiology of unidentified decedents. Journal of Forensic Sciences 53 (4), 1–6.

Phenice, T.W., 1969. A newly developed visual method of sexing os pubis. American Journal of Physical Anthropology 30, 297–302.

Prince, D.A., Ubelaker, D., 2002. Application of Lamendin's adult dental aging technique to a diverse skeletal sample. Journal of Forensic Sciences 47, 107–116.

Quatrehomme, G., Fronty, P., Sapanet, M., Grevin, G., Bailet, P., Ollier, A., 1996. Identification by frontal sinus patterns in forensic anthropology. Forensic Science International 83, 147–153.

Ramenzoni, L.L., Line, S.R.P., 2006. Automated biometrics-based personal identification of the Hunter-Schreger bands of dental enamel. Proceedings of the Royal Society B 273, 1155–1158.

Saukko, P., Knight, B., 2005. Forensic Pathology, third ed. Arnold Ed., London.

Scheuer, L., Black, S., 2000. Developmental Juvenile Osteology. Academic Press, New York.

Schmitt, A., Cunha, E., Pinheiro, J., 2006. Forensic Anthropology and Medicine – Complementary Sciences from Recovery to Cause of Death. Humana Press, Totowa, NJ.

Shepherd, K.L., Wlash-Haney, H., Coburn, M.U., 2010. Surgical sutures as a means of identifying human remains. Journal of Forensic Sciences 55 (1), 237–240.

Smith, V.A., Christensen, A.M., Myers, S.W., 2010. The reliability of visually comparing small frontal sinuses. Journal of Forensic Sciences 55 (6), 1413–1415.

Stephan, C.N., Winburn, A.P., Christensen, A.F., Tyrrell, A.J., 2011. Skeletal identification by radiographic comparison: blind tests of a morphoscopic method using antemortem chest radiographs. Journal of Forensic Sciences 56 (2), 320–332.

Trotter, M., Gleser, G., 1952. Estimation of stature from long bones of American Whites and Negroes. American Journal of Physical Anthropology 10, 463–514.

Trotter, M., Gleser, G., 1958. A re-evaluation of estimation of stature based on measurements of stature taken during life and of long bones after death. American Journal of Physical Anthropology 8, 79–123.

Ubelaker, D.H., 1999. Human Skeletal Remains: Excavation, Analysis, Interpretation, third ed. Taraxacum, Washington, DC.

Watamaniuk, L., Rogers, T., 2010. Positive personal identification of human remains based on thoracic vertebral margin morphology. Journal of Forensic Sciences 55 (5), 1162–1170.

Williams, B.A., Rogers, T.L., 2006. Evaluating the accuracy and precision of cranial morphological traits for sex determination. Journal of Forensic Sciences 51 (4), 729–735.

Wilson, R.J., Bethard, J.D., DiGangi, E.A., 2011. The use of orthopaedic surgical devices for forensic identification. Journal of Forensic Sciences 56 (2), 460–469.

Yoshino, M., Miyasaka, S., Sato, H., Seta, S., 1998. Classification system of frontal sinus patterns. Journal of the Canadian Society of Forensic Science 22, 135–146.

Key Terms

3-D techniques, Age estimation, Anatomical replicas, Anatomy, Animal bites, Biological profile, Bite marks, Body height determination, Child abuse, Comparative radiography, Comparison analysis, Comparison photo, Computer modeling, Craniofacial analysis, Dentistry, Disaster victim identification, DNA, Evidence, Face, Face prediction, Facial approximation, Facial features, Facial recognition, Facial reconstruction, Facial reproduction, Facial soft tissue depths, Feature analysis, Fingerprint analysis, Fingerprints, Forensic anthropology, Forensic art, Forensic dentistry, Forensic odontology, Forensic radiology, Gait analysis, Identification, Litigation, Malpractice, Mass disasters, Medicolegal investigation, Missing persons, Multiple corresponding factors, Orofacial trauma, Personal identification, Positive identification, Probability of identification, Radiography, Reference photo, Scientific identification, Sexual assault, Short tandem repeats, Skeleton, Skull, Skull–photo superimposition, Surgical implants, Surveillance photo, Surveillance video.

Review Questions

1. In identifying someone by an image, why does the suitability of the image need to be checked first? How is this done?
2. Why should the dates when images were taken be considered?
3. Why is gait analysis not suitable for identification?
4. What is the DMV Atlas? Why is it important in identification?
5. What is the philtrum? What is the vermilion?
6. Who is Gerasimov?
7. When was the first successful forensic facial approximation?
8. What are the two broad categories of facial approximation?
9. What is the success rate of facial approximations in casework? Why do you think this is?
10. Why can't facial approximations be used for positive identifications?
11. What are the impediments to forensic identification? Why would these impediments exist?

12. Why would antemortem dental records be difficult to obtain?
13. What is the difference between personal identification and scientific identification?
14. What anatomical characteristics can be compared in dental radiographs?
15. What are the three outcomes of attempting a scientific identification?
16. What information can be obtained from surgical implants?
17. Give two examples each of closed disasters and open disasters.
18. What is DMORT?
19. What does DVI stand for?
20. What is NameUS?

Discussion Questions

1. Gabriel and Huckenbeck say, "In theory, each person can be distinguished from all others according to appearance." Why do they add "in theory"? What are the practical implications for forensic identification? On what is this theory based?
2. Review Houck on the comparative method. Why does inclusion for identity require some number of traits in concordance but exclusion only one? If traits have a range of value for strength of inclusion, do traits for exclusion have ranges of value as well? That is, do any traits exist that only "might" exclude someone?
3. In facial approximations, which is more important—art or science? How does the computerization of the process affect your discussion?
4. In a disaster victim identification situation, what do you think would be the best order of methods to attempt identification? Why wouldn't you collect DNA from every victim and wait for the results?
5. Consider Goodwin and Simmons' anecdote about the misidentified 9/11 firefighter. Why do the chances of coincidental features increase as the number of victims increase? How could a misidentification like this, with such a compelling feature, be avoided?

Additional Readings

Bassed, R., Bott, E., 2015. Application of Post-mortem Computed Tomography to Forensic Odontology. Forensic Odontology: Principles and Practice, pp. 419–437.

Briggs, C.A., Buck, A.M., 2016. The Role of the Anthropologist in Disaster Victim Identification: The Bali Incidents of 2002 and 2004. Handbook of Forensic Anthropology and Archaeology. Left Coast Press, 2009, pp. 407–415.

Brough, A.L., Morgan, B., Rutty, G.N., 2015. The basics of disaster victim identification. Journal of Forensic Radiology and Imaging 3 (1), 29–37.

Merli, C., Buck, T., 2015. Forensic identification and identity politics in 2004 post-tsunami Thailand: negotiating dissolving boundaries. Human Remains and Violence: An Interdisciplinary Journal 1 (1), 3–22.

Sledzik, P.S., Bryson, S.W., 2016. Mass Fatality Management. Koenig and Schultz's Disaster Medicine: Comprehensive Principles and Practices, p. 361.

Toom, V., 2016. Whose body is it? Technolegal materialization of victims' bodies and remains after the World Trade Center terrorist attacks. Science, Technology & Human Values 41 (4), 686–708.

Section 7. Statistics and Interpretation

Forensic anthropology has a long history of metrics and statistics, placing it well within the umbrella of validated sciences. Populations of study, scant, and scarce historically, have grown larger, more available, and digital, making research and checking results much easier. Explaining those statistics to a layperson, however, is no mean feat and requires specialized training that few scientists get. Anthropologists would do well to use their understanding of people and culture to learn "better practices" on educating complex statistics—and then help the rest of forensic science with this critical and tricky problem.

The Frequentist Approach to Forensic Evidence Interpretation

JM Curran, University of Auckland, Auckland, New Zealand

Glossary

Probability A quantity between 0 and 1 that represents the chance of an event occurring. Probabilities may sometimes be expressed as percentages, or as odds, without loss of information. A probability may also be used to express a degree of belief that an event will occur. Such probabilities are often referred to as "subjective."

Probability (density) function A probability function describes the probabilities associated with the values of a discrete random variable. When the random variable is a continuous measurement, such as time or length, then a probability density function describes the density associated with a particular outcome. Density refers to the height of the curve. For a continuous random variable, the probability of an event is given by the area under the probability density curve.

Random experiment A situation where the outcome is not known in advance. One may know what the possible outcomes are but the exact outcome is not known until the experiment is conducted.

Random variable A variable that measures the outcome of a random experiment. One may know the range of possible values that a random variable may take on, but not the actual value until the experiment has been conducted.

Sample The word sample in the statistical sense means a set, or group, of objects or measurements taken from a larger population. In this chapter, sample means a set of (representative) objects taken from the crime scene source or recovered from a suspect.

Specimen The word specimen is used to avoid confusion with the word sample. A specimen in this chapter means a smaller part, or subsample, of some evidential source. For example, one may refer to a specimen of paint from the scene. This embodies the fact that one does not have a choice when selecting a specimen, and therefore one cannot be sure that the specimen is representative of the source.

Common questions in forensic science are "did this evidence come from this crime scene?" or "does this blood come from that man?" The answers to these questions become probabilistic when the circumstances become less than certain. Statistical inference provides the tools and the framework in which probability can be addressed. Questions like those above are often called questions of common source and have been addressed with a variety of statistical frequentist techniques. These techniques are best illustrated with an example.

Example

The following example is taken from the field of forensic glass evidence interpretation.

A window is broken during the commission of a crime. Several hours later, a suspect is apprehended. Six small fragments of glass are recovered in a search of the suspect's clothing, footwear, and headgear. Random samples of six fragments of glass are taken from the crime scene window. The glass recovered from the suspect is called the recovered (or questioned) sample (or specimen), and the glass taken from the scene is called the control sample. The refractive indices (RIs) of each fragment in each sample were determined and are given in **Table 1**.

In the ensuing sections, some summary statistics derived from the data in **Table 1** will be useful.

Range Tests

Range tests broadly describe a class of methods that compare measurements made on evidence recovered from a suspect to the range of the control source. The range of a set of measurements is defined at the interval from the minimum observed value to the maximum observed value. The range can be expressed as an interval, for example, or as a length given by the difference of the maximum and the minimum, for example, 0.000112. The interval definition is used in this chapter.

The simplest range test compares the recovered measurements in sequence to the control sample range. If a measurement falls outside of the control range, then it is deemed not to have originated from the control source. In the glass example, the smallest recovered RI measurement (1.529049) falls below the smallest control measurement; therefore, this fragment is deemed not to have come from the scene. The minimum observed in the control sample above and the maximum observed in the control sample below are the remainder of the recovered measurements; therefore, these fragments are deemed to have come from the control source. That is, in this example, five of the six recovered fragments found on the suspect are said to have come from the crime scene.

The choice of language in this example is deliberately simple to illustrate the technique rather than provide a comprehensive statement about the strength of the evidence. A weaker statement might be that the control and recovered fragments have common physical characteristics.

This type of range test is easily extended to the multivariate situation. The need for this extension arises in situations where multiple measurements are made on different attributes of the same object. For example, elemental analysis techniques are commonly used in forensic science. These techniques simultaneously measure the concentrations of a number of chemical elements in a specimen. The criterion for making a statement of common source, or of similar characteristics, is that all of the measurements made on the recovered specimen must fall within the range observed in the control sample. An example is shown in **Table 2**. The recovered sample measurement for zirconium (99) falls outside the range observed in the control sample; therefore, this measurement would be said not to have come from the control source.

Range tests such as those described above are very simple to carry out, and require no sophisticated computation of any sort. However, they are very susceptible to outliers. Outliers, in the statistical sense, are measurements which are considerably different from the bulk of the measurements. Outliers may arise from true measurement error, misclassification, contamination, or simply by chance.

Most statisticians do not use the range as an estimate of the spread or variability of a set of measurements in any other context than simple description. Most formal statistical procedures which require a measure of variability use the sample standard deviation. This idea motivates a set of improved range tests which are sometimes called two-sigma (2σ) or three-sigma (3σ) rules.

In the simple range test, the recovered measurements are compared to an interval defined by the minimum and maximum observed values in the control sample. A 2σ rule is used to modify the control interval to the interval defined by the control mean plus or minus twice the control standard deviation, that is, $(\bar{x}_c - 2s_c, \bar{x}_c + 2s_c)$, where $\bar{x}_c$ and s_c are the mean and standard deviation of the control sample. If a 3σ rule is used, then the interval is defined by $\bar{x}_c \pm 3s_c$. Using the summary statistics in **Table 3**, the 2σ control interval is

$$\bar{x}_c \pm 2s_c = (1.529077 - 2 \times 4.04 \times 10^{-5}, \ 1.529077$$

$$+ 2 \times 4.04 \times 10^5) = (1.529042, \ 1.529204)$$

Table 1 The refractive indices of a control and recovered sample of glass

Control	Recovered
1.529077	1.529049
1.529085	1.529108
1.52912	1.529118
1.529133	1.529141
1.529135	1.529146
1.529189	1.529153

Table 2 An example of a range test with elemental concentration data

	Fe	Mn	Ba	Sr	Zr	Cr
Control minimum	1978	53	166	143	70	1494
Control maximum	2322	62	200	169	90	1771
Recovered	2320	62	192	166	99	1766

Table 3 Summary statistics for the control and recovered measurements

Statistic	Control	Recovered
Minimum	1.529077	1.529049
Mean $(\overline{X})$	1.529123	1.529119
Maximum	1.529189	1.529153
Standard deviation (s)	4.04×10^{-5}	3.84×10^{-5}

The choice of two or three is motivated by what is known in statistics as the 68-95-99.7, $\sigma - 2\sigma - 3\sigma$, or the empirical rule, which states that for normally distributed data, approximately 68% of the observations lie within one standard deviation of the mean, approximately 95% of the observations lie within two standard deviations of the mean, and approximately 99.7% of the observations lie within three standard deviation of the mean. In the forensic glass example, all of the observations lie within two standard deviations of the mean, that is, within the 2σ interval. While 2σ rules have better statistical properties, the sequential comparison of the recovered measurements to the control intervals has an unacceptably high false exclusion rate, where the probability of declaring at least one measurement in a set of n_r measurements to be from a different source when they are indeed from the same source is given by

$$P = 1 - (1 - \alpha)^{n_r}$$

The value of α is 0.05 or 0.003 depending on whether a 2σ or 3σ rule is being used. This issue is known as a multiple comparison problem and occurs in many situations in statistics. Several practitioners claim that false inclusions rather than false exclusions are the more serious problem. That is, if a recovered item is said to have a common source with the control measurements when it is truly from a different source, then the evidence may implicate the defendant in a crime he or she did not commit. In theory, the more different the control and recovered measurements, the lower is the chance of a false inclusion. However, in practice, small sample sizes, which are common in forensic science, can badly affect the statistical properties of all approaches. In statistical terms, such tests are said to have low power. This means they have a poor probability of detecting a true difference when one exists. Both arguments have some validity, but neither is important because the frequentist approach does not consider the evidence with respect to the alternative hypothesis.

2σ rules may be used with multivariate data. The idea is easily extended by calculating 2σ or 3σ intervals for each variable measured in the control sample. If a measurement made on the recovered sample falls outside of any of the control sample intervals, then a statement of common source is not made. The extra comparisons, incurred by the extra measurements made on each item, compound the multiple comparison problem. Theoretically, this could be overcome by calculating a confidence ellipsoid for the control which is the multivariate equivalent of the interval. However, in practice, this is almost never done.

The shortcomings of range tests may be addressed by using summary statistics on the samples, such as the sample means, rather than the individual measurements. This approach has the advantage that it is less susceptible to outliers, it is less susceptible (but not immune) to multiple comparison problems, and it uses as much information as possible from the data in a single step. Such approaches usually fall into the framework of formal statistical hypothesis tests.

Formal Hypothesis Tests

The frequentist hypothesis-testing framework is commonly used in the scientific literature. It has been used in a number of forensic disciplines to statistically address the issue of common source. This approach typically revolves around the comparison of the two sample means with respect to the observed variation in the samples.

However, most statistical hypothesis tests follow the same general steps:

1. Ask a question.
2. Formulate your question statistically—that is, find a statistic you think might answer your question.
3. Propose a null hypothesis.
4. Propose an alternative hypothesis.
5. Calculate your test statistic.
6. Calculate the P-value.
7. Interpret the P-value.

These steps use terms which need a brief definition. The null hypothesis is generally the hypothesis of no difference or no change. It means that any difference or change could easily be explained by random chance alone. It is a hypothesis that represents the statement "these measurements are (statistically) indistinguishable" or "these measurements come from the same source." It is important to note that the second statement is not accurately reflected by the null hypothesis. The alternative hypothesis, although not formally included in the computation, is the hypothesis of difference or change. The test statistic is a summary number that may be calculated from the observed data. The P-value is defined in words as "the probability of observing a test statistic as large as, or larger than, the one observed if the null hypothesis is true." If X is any test statistic and X_0 is the value of an observed statistic in a particular case, then the P-value can be written statistically as

$$P = \Pr(X \geq X_0 | H_0 \text{ true})$$

If the *P*-value is small, then the correct interpretation is that the test statistic is unlikely to have occurred by random chance alone if the null hypothesis is true. In this situation, it is common to say that "the null hypothesis is rejected." If the *P*-value is small, it is incorrect to assume that the result would be more likely if the alternative hypothesis were true. It is incorrect to make this assumption because no part of the calculation makes any reference to the alternative hypothesis, and, therefore, the result might be equally unlikely under the alternative hypothesis. If the *P*-value is large, then the correct interpretation is that the test statistic is likely to have occurred by random chance alone if the null hypothesis were true. Again, any interpretation which then infers that the result is unlikely under the alternative hypothesis is incorrect. The *P*-value is not the probability that the null hypothesis is true.

Significance Levels and Small or Big Values

The definition of what constitutes a small or large value is arbitrary, but is related to the acceptable risk of rejecting the null hypothesis when it really is true. This type of mistake is called a type I error. In practice, if the *P*-value is less than 0.05, or 0.01, then it is deemed to be small. The choice of these numbers is arbitrary, but they can be crudely interpreted as being "less than 1 chance in 20 (or 1 chance in 100)" of making an incorrect decision (on average, if the null hypothesis is true). The caveats in the brackets in the previous sentence are quite important and are often overlooked.

The critical values 0.05, 0.01, etc. are called the significance of the test in the Neyman–Pearson orthodoxy and is usually denoted as α. The significance is, specifically, the probability of making a type I error that the user is prepared to accept. Acceptance of this probability is not dictated by the test, but by the cost associated with making an incorrect decision. In science, $\alpha = 0.05$ is typically used. In legal situations, however, it may be preferable to use $\alpha \leq 0.01$. This is often viewed as complying with Blackstone's ratio. English jurist William Blackstone said "[It is] better that ten guilty persons escape than that one innocent suffer," although if $\alpha = 0.01$, then the ratio is 100:1 rather than Blackstone's 10:1. Decreasing the value of α, however, is not without consequence. The smaller the value of α, the harder it becomes to reject the null hypothesis when it is false or, equivalently, to detect a difference when one truly exists. That is, the significance of a test α has a complementary relationship with the probability of making a type II error, β. β is the probability of a false acceptance, or the probability of deciding that the null hypothesis is true when in fact the alternative is true. The quantity $1 - \beta$ is called the power of a test. As α decreases, β increases and, correspondingly, the power of the test is reduced.

The significance of a test is often stated in a number of different ways. People alternatively use α, $1 - \alpha$, $100 \times \alpha\%$, and $100 \times (1 - \alpha)\%$. That is, statements such as "the test was significant at the 0.05%, 0.95%, 5%, and 95% level" all occur frequently in the scientific literature. The original Neyman–Pearson framework defined α as the significance level; however, the intention of the alternatives given above is usually understood. If a *P*-value is smaller than the significance level (α), then the test is often said to be significant at the α level. Correspondingly, if the *P*-value is greater than the significance level, then the test is said to be not significant at the α level.

Hypothesis tests are more easily understood when referring to specific tests rather than in general terms. The two-sample *t*-test has a long tradition in scientific literature and has been used in forensic science. It is discussed in the next section.

The Two-Sample *t*-Test

The two-sample *t*-test is often used to test the hypothesis that the control sample and the recovered sample come from distributions with the same mean and variance. The inference in this situation is that if the fragments do come from distributions with the same mean and variance, then they are indistinguishable and therefore may have a common source. This is often incorrectly interpreted as "the recovered fragments come from the crime scene."

The two-sample *t*-test compares the difference in the sample means to the difference that one would expect by random variation, or chance, alone. The idea is to make a probability statement about the difference in the true, but unknown, means of the sources that the samples come from. If the means are the same, then one can say that "the recovered sample cannot be distinguished from the control scene."

Formally, let the n_c measurements on the control sample be denoted x_i, $i = 1, \ldots, n_c$, and the n_r measurements on the recovered sample be denoted y_j, $j = 1, \ldots, n_r$. The control sample is assumed to have come from a normal distribution with mean μ_c and standard deviation σ_c. Similarly, the recovered sample is assumed to have come from a normal distribution with mean μ_r and standard deviation σ_r. This is expressed as $x_i \sim N(\mu_c, \sigma_c)$ and $y_j \sim N(\mu_r, \sigma_r)$. The traditional (pooled) two-sample *t*-test formally tests the null hypothesis that the distribution means are the same under the explicit assumption that $\sigma_c = \sigma_r = \sigma$ (and therefore that the sample standard deviations are each an estimate of the common standard deviation σ):

$$H_0 : \mu_c = \mu_r \text{ or equivalently } H_0 : \mu_c - \mu_r = 0$$

The alternative hypothesis is that the distribution means are different:

$$H_1 : \mu_c \neq \mu_r \text{ or equivalently } H_0 : \mu_c - \mu_r \neq 0$$

To test the null hypothesis, a test statistic is compared to the distribution of values one would expect to observe if the null hypothesis is true. For the two-sample t-test, the test statistic is given by

$$T_0 = \frac{\bar{x} - \bar{y}}{\sqrt{\left(\dfrac{1}{n_c} + \dfrac{1}{n_r}\right)\dfrac{(n_c - 1)s_c^2 + (n_r - 1)s_r^2}{n_c + n_r - 2}}}$$

where $\bar{x}, \bar{y}, s_c$, and s_r are the sample means and sample standard deviations of the control and recovered samples, respectively. The significance of the test is evaluated by comparing the observed value of T_0 to the distribution of values one would observe if the null hypothesis is true, or the null distribution. For the two-sample t-test, this is student's t-distribution and is parameterized by its degrees of freedom. The degrees of freedom, $df = n_c + n_r - 2$, reflect the sample size, and in some sense, the amount of information that is available. The comparison of the observed test statistic to the null distribution is summarized by the P-value.

For the two-sample t-test this becomes

$$P = \Pr(T \geq T_0 | H_0 \text{ true})$$

The absolute value of the test statistic is used here because it makes no difference whether the recovered mean is smaller or larger than the control mean, merely the fact that it is different. It is important to note that the equal variance assumption can be relaxed. There are occasional circumstances where this is a sensible option. This version of the t-test is known as Welch's t-test. The formula for the test statistic has a different denominator, and the formula for the degrees of freedom is much more complicated, but bounded by $\min(n_c, n_r) - 1$ and $n_c + n_r - 2$.

The pooled two-sample t-test can be illustrated using the glass example. The observed test statistic is

$$T_0 = \frac{\bar{x} - \bar{y}}{\sqrt{\left(\dfrac{1}{n_c} + \dfrac{1}{n_r}\right)\dfrac{(n_c - 1)s_c^2 + (n_r - 1)s_r^2}{n_c + n_r - 2}}}$$

$$= \frac{1.529123 - 1.529119}{\sqrt{\left(\dfrac{1}{6} + \dfrac{1}{6}\right)\dfrac{(6 - 1)\left(4.04 \times 10^{-5}\right)^2 + (6 - 1)\left(3.84 \times 10^{-5}\right)^2}{6 + 6 - 2}}}$$

$$= \frac{4 \times 10^{-6}}{2.278 \times 10^{-5}} = 0.1756$$

H_0, the P-value, is calculated using a t-distribution with $n_c + n_r - 2 = 6 + 6 - 2 = 10$ degrees of freedom. This is easily done in Microsoft Excel using the TDIST function, or in R using the pt function. The resulting P-value is 0.86. This is a large P-value, and "on average one would expect a result like this approximately 86 times in 100 by random chance alone." That is, this result is extremely likely to have occurred by random

chance alone, hence H_0 cannot be rejected. Note that, unlike the range test, this procedure does not omit the smallest recovered RI value. This information is included in both the recovered mean and, more importantly, in the recovered standard deviation. The inclusion of this fragment will increase the recovered variability and make it (slightly) harder to reject the null hypothesis. Some practitioners are bothered by this and use range-like tests to exclude observations from the evidence evaluation. Such practice can lead to dangerously misleading conclusions if no account is taken of the omitted information.

It is not entirely necessary to calculate a P-value in this example because this test statistic can be interpreted as "the observed difference is approximately 0.18 standard deviations away from the mean when the null hypothesis is true. If the observed difference was more than 2 standard deviations away from the mean, then we would start to suspect that it was unlikely to have occurred by random chance alone. Given that 0.18 is much smaller than 2, we would intuit that the observed difference can be attributed to random variation."

The two-sample t-test has a multivariate analogue known as Hotelling's T^2. This test has been used in forensic science, but it is relatively uncommon. It is more common to perform tests on each variable. This approach is subject to the multiple testing problems discussed earlier. Hotelling's T^2 avoids such issues, and also takes into account the potential correlations between measurements. It does, however, have large sample size requirements, which traditionally have been problematic.

Confidence Intervals

Hypothesis tests have a very rigid interpretation in that the user makes a decision to either accept or reject the null hypothesis based on the P-value. Such an approach leads to what Ken Smalldon called the "fall-off-the-cliff effect." Consider a situation where the P-value is 0.049, and the criterion for rejection is 0.05. In this case, the scientist would reject the null hypothesis. However, if the P-value were 0.051, then the scientist would accept the null hypothesis. That is, a tiny change in the numbers leads to a complete reversal of the decision. Such logic is extremely hard to justify to the court. In some situations, an alternative is to present a confidence interval.

To form a confidence interval, the scientist must choose a confidence level. The confidence level is directly analogous to the significance level for a (two-tailed) hypothesis test. The confidence level is usually stated as a percentage of the form $100 \times (1 - \alpha)\%$. For example, if $\alpha = 0.05$, then this is referred to as 95% confidence level, and the resulting interval as a 95% confidence interval. Confidence intervals also have a confidence statement attached to them. That is, the scientist may state that they are $100 \times (1 - \alpha)\%$ confident that the interval contains the true value of interest. Note that this is not a statement of probability. Confidence refers to the ideas of repeated sampling or infinite populations that are the foundation of the frequentist philosophy of statistics. The confidence level refers to the random nature of the interval rather than the behavior of a specific interval.

In general, confidence intervals take the form

$$\hat{\theta} \pm z_\alpha^* \text{se}\left(\hat{\theta}\right)$$

The quantity θ is referred to as the quantity of interest. It may be a mean, a difference in means, a proportion, a difference in proportions, an odds ratio, or even a likelihood ratio. It is not a restrictive list, and it is application specific. The quantity $\text{se}\left(\hat{\theta}\right)$ is called the standard error of the estimate. It is the estimated standard deviation of the quantity of interest. The value Z_α^* is a multiplier chosen from an application-specific statistical distribution which reflects the confidence level. In general, the smaller the value of α, the larger the value of Z_α^* will be. Confidence intervals for many standard situations can be found in most undergraduate statistics texts.

A confidence interval for the glass example is given here for illustration. In general, a $100 \times (1 - \alpha)\%$ confidence interval for the difference in the two means is given by

$$\bar{x} - \bar{y} \pm t_{df}^*(1 - \alpha/2)\text{se}(\bar{x} - \bar{y})$$

Under the assumption that the samples come from populations with the same variance, the standard error of the difference in the means is given by

$$\text{se}(\bar{x} - \bar{y}) = \sqrt{\left(\frac{1}{n_c} + \frac{1}{n_r}\right)\frac{(n_c - 1)s_c^2 + (n_r - 1)s_r^2}{n_c + n_r - 2}}$$

which is the denominator of the test statistic in the two-sample t-test. This makes sense when one considers that the hypothesis essentially compares the observed difference to the estimated variability in the difference. This formula is considerably simpler when the assumption of equal variances is dropped:

$$\text{se}(\bar{x} - \bar{y}) = \sqrt{\frac{s_c^2}{n_c} + \frac{s_r^2}{n_r}}$$

However, the formula for the degrees of freedom, given by Welch's approximation, is more complicated (and not given here). The critical value is the $100(1 - \alpha/2)$ percentile of Student's t-distribution with $n_c + n_r - 2$ degrees of freedom (assuming equal variances for both populations). This can be calculated using a handbook of statistical tables, the Microsoft Excel function TINV, or the R function qt.

Therefore, a 95% confidence interval for the glass example is given by

$$4 \times 10^{-6} \pm 2.228 \times 2.277 \times 10^{-5}$$
$$= \left(-4.7 \times 10^{-5}, \ 5.5 \times 10^{-5}\right)$$

The confidence interval contains 0, which is the hypothesized difference (recall H_0: $\mu_c - \mu = 0$). This means that if a P-value were calculated, then it would be greater than 0.05. In general, if a $100 \times (1 - \alpha)\%$ confidence interval contains the hypothesized value of interest, then the associated P-value from a hypothesis test will be greater than α (for a two-tailed test), and if the interval does not contain the hypothesized value of interest, then the P-value will be less than α (for a two-tailed test).

Controversies and Issues

There has been considerable criticism in the forensic science and legal literature over the last 30 years regarding the appropriateness of frequentist approaches to the interpretation of evidence, and the relevance of frequentist methods in legal proceedings. Such discussion would seem to be at odds with the last 100 or so years in many fields of science, where frequentist methods are on the whole the accepted standard for judging experimental success.

Most of the controversy is summarized by a statement given by Robertson and Vignaux, which says that a significant hypothesis test does not answer the question the court is interested in. The court wants to know "how much more (or less) likely does this piece of evidence make it that the accused is guilty?" A significance test on the other hand tells the court "what is the probability that I would observe this result (match) by chance alone?" Robertson and Vignaux succinctly called this "the right answer to the wrong question." Proponents of the Bayesian approach, also known as the likelihood ratio approach, or the logical approach, believe that the evidence must be evaluated with respect to at least two competing hypotheses. Such a belief is not actually at odds with the Neyman–Pearson school of hypothesis testing, but in the Bayesian approach, the alternative hypothesis explicitly enters the probability calculations.

There are also more fundamental criticisms which stem from the definitions of probability. Within the field of statistics there are two schools of inference which are known as Bayesian and frequentist. These names of these schools relate, in general, to the frequentist and Bayesian definitions of probability.

The frequentist definition of probability, as the name suggests, depends on the long-term frequency of an event.

In the frequentist approach to inference, the inference relies on the concept of either an infinite population or repeated sampling. Additionally, the parameters of a model, or values about which the scientist wishes to make an inference, are generally regarded as fixed but unknown. The data are regarded as random. This means that statements are made about the random nature of the data rather than the unknown parameters. The practical consequence of this is that it should prevent the scientist from making statements about the probability of a hypothesis being true, or about a confidence interval containing the true value with a certain probability. In practice, however, such statements are still made.

By contrast, the Bayesian definition of probability is that it is a measure of belief.

In Bayesian inference, the parameters of interest are regarded as random and unknowable and the data as fixed. In the Bayesian framework, assumptions about the unknown parameters are represented by prior probabilities or beliefs, and these are updated with additional information—the data to yield posterior probabilities. This means that a scientist using Bayesian techniques can make statements about the probability of hypotheses, or probability about credible intervals containing the true value. Credible intervals are the Bayesian equivalent of confidence intervals.

It may be of some interest that it is not completely necessary to accept the Bayesian definition of probability to use the Bayesian approach.

See also: **Foundations:** Statistical Interpretation of Evidence: Bayesian Analysis.

Further Reading

Aitken, C.G.G., Taroni, F., 2004. Statistics and the Evaluation of Evidence for Forensic Scientists, second ed. Wiley, Chichester.

Balding, D.J., 2005. Weight-of-Evidence for Forensic DNA Profiles. Wiley, Hoboken, NJ.

Curran, J.M., 2010. Introduction to Data Analysis with R for Forensic Scientists. CRC Press, Boca Raton, FL.

Curran, J.M., Hicks, T.N., Buckleton, J.S., 2000. Forensic Interpretation of Glass Evidence. CRC Press, Boca Raton, FL.

Evett, I.W., Weir, B.S., 1998. Interpreting DNA Evidence: Statistical Genetics for Forensic Scientists. Sinauer Associates, Sunderland, MA.

Hair, J.F., Black, W.C., Babin, B.J., Anderson, R.E., 2009. Multivariate Data Analysis, seventh ed. Pearson Prentice Hall, Upper Saddle River, NJ.

Lucy, D., 2005. Introduction to Statistics for Forensic Scientists. Wiley, Chichester.

Moore, D.S., McCabe, G.P., 2006. Introduction to the Practice of Statistics, fifth ed. W.H. Freeman, New York.

Robertson, B., Vignaux, G.A., 1995. Interpreting Evidence: Evaluating Forensic Science in the Court Room. Wiley, Chichester.

Wild, C.J., Seber, G.A.F., 2000. Chance Encounters: A First Course in Data Analysis and Inference. Wiley, New York.

Statistical Interpretation of Evidence: Bayesian Analysis

CGG Aitken, The University of Edinburgh, Edinburgh, United Kingdom
F Taroni and A Biedermann, The University of Lausanne, Lausanne-Dorigny, Switzerland

Glossary

Bayes' theorem Bayes' theorem is a consequence of the basic laws of probabilities and can be applied for revising beliefs about uncertain propositions in the light of new evidence. In judicial contexts, reasoning according to Bayes' theorem is used in order to examine whether particular evidence strengthens or weakens a case. More generally, Bayes' theorem provides a standard for logically correct reasoning under uncertainty.

Likelihood ratio A likelihood ratio is defined by a ratio of two conditional probabilities: the probability of the evidence given each of two mutually exclusive and competing propositions. In forensic science applications, the likelihood ratio is used as an expression for the meaning of scientific evidence and as a measure for its probative value.

Probability Probability is a measurement device for uncertainty. In one of its most widespread interpretations, it serves the purpose of expressing an individual's personal degrees of beliefs about uncertain propositions. Probability is governed by several axiomatic laws that constitute a fundamental framework for inductive logic.

Introduction

Bruno de Finetti, a pioneering subjective probabilist, considered that the role of probability theory in inductive logic is to show how the evaluations of probabilities of future events are to be modified in the light of observed events, and that this translates, in the mathematical formulation of induction, the meaning of the phrase "to learn from experience." Forensic scientists, as an illustrative example, routinely face inductive reasoning when they seek to evaluate or interpret the meaning of items of scientific evidence. This directs attention to Bayes' theorem, which, in essence, formalizes induction.

In Bayesian analysis, all available information is used in order to reduce the extent of uncertainty associated with an inferential problem. As new information is obtained, it is combined with any previous information, and this forms the basis for statistical procedures. The formal mechanism used to combine new information with previously available information is generally known as Bayes' theorem. Bayes' theorem involves the use of probabilities because probability can be thought of as the coherent language of uncertainty. At any given point in time, the scientist's state of information about some uncertain event (or quantity) can be represented by a set of probabilities. When new information is obtained, these probabilities are revised in order that they may represent all the available information. The idea of "revising" probabilities is not one that should be interpreted as a "correction." An updated probability is not a correction or a better evaluation of an initial probability, but solely a different probability, because it is conditioned by a new (extended) state of information.

The statistical evaluation and interpretation of evidence thus relies on a rule that relates the dependencies among uncertain events through conditional probabilities. This rule enables one to specify the value of evidence in the sense of the effect that evidence has on beliefs in an issue, such as the guilt or innocence of a defendant. The underlying ideas can be applied to categorical and continuous data. They can also be applied to situations in which there are no, or limited, data but in which there are subjective opinions. They are used to ensure a logical and coherent structure to the evaluation of items of evidence.

Bayes' Rule

The Bayesian approach is named after the Reverend Thomas Bayes, a nonconformist preacher of the eighteenth century. To him is attributed an important rule that shows how uncertainty about an event, say R, can be changed by the knowledge of another event, say S:

$$\Pr(R|S) = \Pr(S|R)\Pr(R)/\Pr(S)$$

where Pr denotes probability and the bar | denotes the conditioning. Thus, $\Pr(R|S)$ is the probability that R occurs, given that S has occurred. Probabilities are values between 0 and 1. The value 0 corresponds to an event that is impossible to happen, and 1 to an event that is certain to happen. Probabilities are most appropriately interpreted as subjective—in the sense of "personal"—expressions of degrees of belief held by an individual. As such they reflect the degree of imperfection of an individual's knowledge. Such belief is graduated: as evidence accumulates, one can believe in the truth of an event more or less than before, one can believe more in the truth of a given event than in the truth of another event, etc. The fundamental principle in this interpretation is that the degrees of belief of a rational individual obey the rules of probability. Therefore, probability represents the quantified judgment of a particular individual. Because a probability is a measure of a degree of belief rather than a long-run frequency (as suggested by other interpretations of probability), it is perfectly reasonable to assign probability to an event that involves a nonrepetitive situation. This makes the interpretation of probability, based on measures of belief, particularly useful for judicial contexts.

An alternative version of the Bayes' rule is its odds form, where $\overline{R}$ denotes the complement of R so that $\Pr(\overline{R}) = 1 - \Pr(R)$. Then the odds in favor of R are $\Pr(R)/\Pr(\overline{R})$, denoted $O(R)$ and the odds in favor of R given that S has occurred are denoted $O(R|S)$. The odds form of Bayes' rule is then:

$$O(R|S) = \frac{\Pr(S|R)}{\Pr(S|\overline{R})} \times O(R)$$

In forensic science, S, R, and $\overline{R}$ are generally replaced in the odds form of Bayes' rule by E, H_p, and H_d where E is the scientific evidence, H_p is the hypothesis proposed by the prosecution, and H_d is the hypothesis proposed by the defense. Thus, one has:

$$O(H_p|E) = \frac{\Pr(E|H_p)}{\Pr(E|H_d)} \times O(H_p)$$

The left-hand side of the equation is the odds in favor of the prosecution hypothesis after the scientific evidence has been presented. This is known as the *posterior odds*. The odds $O(H_p)$ are the prior odds (i.e., odds prior to the presentation of the evidence). The factor that converts prior odds to posterior odds is the fraction

$$\frac{\Pr(E|H_p)}{\Pr(E|H_d)}$$

known as the *Bayes' factor*. In forensic contexts, it is regularly termed "likelihood ratio" and abbreviated by V, short for "value." It can take values between 0 and ∞. A value greater than one provides support to the prosecution's hypothesis H_p and a value less than one favors the defense's hypothesis H_d. Evidence for which the value is one is neutral in that the evidence is not relevant for discriminating between the two hypotheses of interest. Note that if logarithms are used, the

relationship becomes additive. This has a very pleasing intuitive interpretation of weighing evidence in the scales of justice and the logarithm of the Bayes' factor is known, after the works of the statistician I.J. Good, as the "weight of evidence." It is not necessary for the propositions in the terms denoted $O(R)$ and $O(R|S)$ above to be complementary; the rule still holds. Thus, the prosecution and defense hypotheses do not need to be complementary.

The probative value of scientific evidence is assessed by determining a value for the Bayes' factor. The proper task of forensic scientists is the determination of that value. The role of judge and jury will be that of assessing the prior and posterior odds. Scientists can inform recipients of expert information on how their prior odds are altered by the evidence, but scientists cannot by themselves assign a value to the prior or posterior odds. In order to assign such a value, all the other evidence in a case has to be considered.

The terms "evaluation" and "interpretation" are sometimes considered synonyms, but it is helpful to conceive of a distinction. "Evaluation" is the determination of a value for the Bayes' factor. "Interpretation" refers to the meaning attached to their value.

The Value of Evidence

The evaluation of scientific evidence may be thought of as the assessment of a comparison. This comparison is between qualities (such as genetic traits) or results of measurements (such as refractive indices of glass fragments) of crime-related (recovered) material and of control (potential source) material. For the assessment of scientific evidence, it is widely accepted that the forensic scientist should consider at least a pair of competing hypotheses, in the context habitually denoted H_p and H_d, to illustrate their description of the fact under examination. These hypotheses are formalized representations of the framework of circumstances. Their formulation is a crucial basis for a logical approach to the evaluation of evidence. A classification developed mainly by researchers in the United Kingdom during the late 1990s, referred to as a "hierarchy of propositions," considers three main categories or levels. It involves the so-called "source," the "activity," and the "crime" level.

Categorical Data and Discrete Hypotheses

Source Level Evaluation

The assessment at source level depends on analyses and measurements on the recovered (of unknown origin) and control (of known origin) samples. The value of a trace (or a stain) under source level propositions, such as "Mr. X's pullover is the source of the recovered fibers" and "Mr. X's pullover is not the source of the recovered fibers" (so that another clothing is the source of the trace), does not need to take account of anything other than the analytical information obtained during laboratory examination. The probability of the evidence under the first hypothesis (numerator of the Bayes' factor) is considered from a comparison between two samples (the recovered and the control) assuming they have come from the same source. The probability of the evidence under the second hypothesis (denominator of the Bayes' factor) is considered by comparison of the characteristics of the control and recovered samples in the context of a relevant population of alternative sources. The population from which the source may be thought to have come is called relevant population.

Consider a scenario in which n textile fibers have been left at the scene of the crime by the person who committed the crime. A suspect has been arrested and it is desired to establish the strength of the link between the suspect and the crime. A comparison between the results of measurements of the physical/chemical characteristics of the questioned fibers and those of a sample taken from the suspect's pullover is made by a forensic scientist. The two hypotheses of interest are H_p, the fibers recovered from the suspect's pullover, and H_d, the fibers recovered from some garment other than that of the suspect. The evidence E has two parts: y, the characteristic, Γ, say, of the recovered fibers, and x, the characteristic Γ, say, of the defendant's pullover. If the recovered fibers and the defendant's pullover have different (incompatible) characteristics, then the suspect's pullover would not be investigated in further detail.

Let I denote the background information. This could include (eyewitness) evidence concerning the type of garment worn by the criminal, for example. The value of the evidence is then

$$\frac{\Pr(E|H_p, I)}{\Pr(E|H_d, I)} = \frac{\Pr(x, y|H_p, I)}{\Pr(x, y|H_d, I)} = \frac{\Pr(y|x, H_p, I)}{\Pr(y|x, H_d, I)} \times \frac{\Pr(x|H_p, I)}{\Pr(x|H_d, I)}$$

Consider two assumptions:

The characteristics of the defendant's pullover are independent of whether his pullover is the source of the recovered fibers (H_p) or not (H_d) and thus $\Pr(x|H_p, I) = \Pr(x|H_d, I)$.

If the defendant's pullover was not the source of the recovered fibers (H_d), then the evidence about the fibers at the crime scene (y) is independent of the evidence (x) about the characteristics of the defendant's pullover and thus $\Pr(y|x, H_p, I) = \Pr(y|H_d, I)$.

Hence

$$V = \frac{\Pr(y|x, H_p, I)}{\Pr(y|H_d, I)}$$

The scientist knows, in addition, from data previously collected (population studies) that fiber type Γ occurs in 100γ % of some relevant population, say Ψ.

Assuming that the defendant's pullover is the source of the recovered fibers, the probability that the recovered fibers are of characteristic Γ, given the defendant's pullover is the source and is of characteristic Γ, is 1. Thus, the numerator of V is 1. Alternatively, it is assumed that the suspect's pullover was not the source of the recovered fibers. The relevant population is deemed to be Ψ. The true donor of the recovered fibers is an unknown member of Ψ. Evidence y is to the effect that the crime fibers are of characteristic Γ. This is to say that an unknown member of Ψ is Γ. The probability of this is the probability that a fiber donor drawn at random from Ψ has characteristic Γ, which is γ. Thus

$$V = \frac{1}{\gamma}$$

This value, $1/\gamma$, is the value of the evidence of the characteristics of the recovered fibers when the garment donor is a member of Ψ. Given that γ is a value between 0 and 1, the Bayes' factor is greater than 1, so the evidence is said to be a value $1/\gamma$ times more likely if the suspect's pullover was the source of the recovered fibers than if it were not. Qualitative scales have been proposed and they are intended to make it easier to convey the meaning of the numerical value of the evidence. However, there is ongoing discussion about the degree to which this target has been achieved.

Activity Level Evaluation

The hierarchical level relates to an activity. It requires that the definition of the hypotheses of interest include an action. Such hypotheses could be for example, "Mr. X sat on the car driver's seat," and "Mr. X never sat on the car driver's seat." The consequence of this activity—the sitting on a driver's seat—is a contact between the driver and the seat of the car. Consequently, a transfer of material (i.e., fibers in this example) may be expected. Therefore, the scientist needs to consider more detailed information about the case under examination. It relates to the transfer and persistence of fibers on the car driver's seat. This demonstrates that activity level hypotheses cannot be addressed without a framework of circumstances.

Consider, for the sake of illustration, the following scenario. A crime has been committed during which the blood of a victim has been shed. A suspect has been arrested. A single blood stain of genotype Γ has been found on an item of the suspect's clothing. The suspect's genotype is not Γ. The victim's genotype is Γ. There are two possibilities:

T_0: the blood stain came from some background source;
T_1: the blood stain was transferred during the commission of the crime.

As before, there are two hypotheses to consider:

H_p: the suspect assaulted the victim;

H_d: the suspect did not assault the victim (for example, but taken to mean he is not involved in any way whatsoever with the victim).

The evidence E to be considered is that a single blood stain has been found on the suspect's clothing and that it is of genotype Γ. The information that the victim's genotype is Γ is considered as part of the relevant background information I. A general expression of the value of the evidence then is $V = \Pr(E|H_p, I)/\Pr(E|H_d, I)$.

Consider the numerator first and event T_0 initially. This supposes "a contact" between the suspect and the victim, but no blood transfer to the suspect. This is an event with probability $\Pr(T_0/H_p, I)$. Also, a stain of genotype Γ must have been transferred by some other means, an event with probability $\Pr(B, \Gamma)$ where B refers to the event of a transfer of a stain from a source (i.e., a background source) other than the crime scene (here the victim).

Next, consider T_1, the event of blood transfer to the suspect, an event with probability $\Pr(T_1|H_p, I)$. Given T_1, H_p, and the genotype Γ of the victim, it is certain that the transferred stain is Γ. This assumes also that no blood has been transferred from a background source.

Let $t_0 = \Pr(T_0|H_p, I)$ and $t_1 = \Pr(T_1|H_p, I)$ denote the probabilities of no stain or one stain being transferred during the course of the crime. Let b_0 and b_1, respectively, denote the probabilities that a person from the relevant population will have zero blood stains or one blood stain on clothing. Let γ denote the probability that a stain acquired innocently on the clothing of a person from the relevant population will be of genotype Γ. This probability may be different from the proportion of individuals in the general population which are of type Γ. Then $\Pr(B, \Gamma) = \gamma b_1$ and the numerator can be written as $t_0\gamma b_1 + t_1 b_0$. This expresses that the presence of a stain of type Γ depends on the probability of there being no transfer (t_0), times there being such a stain as background ($b_1\gamma$), plus the probability of transfer of such a stain (t_1), times the probability of there being no such stain beforehand (b_0).

Now consider the denominator where it is supposed that the suspect and the victim were not "in contact." The presence of the stain is then explained by chance alone. The denominator then takes the value $\Pr(B, \Gamma)$ which equals γb_1.

In summary, the value of the evidence is thus

$$V = \frac{t_0\gamma b_1 + t_1 b_0}{\gamma b_1}$$

Extensions to cases involving transfer in the other direction (from perpetrator to scene/victim rather than from scene/victim to perpetrator), for example, or generalizations involving n stains and k groups are available in the specialized literature on the topic.

Crime Level Evaluation

At the "crime level," hypotheses are closest to those of interest to the jury. A formal development of the likelihood ratio under "crime level" hypotheses shows that two additional parameters are of interest: (1) one concerns material that may be "relevant," meaning that it came from the offender (it is relevant to the consideration of the suspect as a possible offender) and (2) the other concerns the recognition that if the material is not relevant to the case, then it may have arrived at the scene from the suspect for innocent reasons.

Consider the following two hypotheses of interest:

H_p: the suspect is the offender;
H_d: the suspect is not the offender.

Notice the difference between these hypotheses and those of the previous sections on source or activity level. At source level, the hypotheses referred to the suspect being, or not being, the donor of the recovered trace found at the crime scene. Now, the hypotheses are stronger, because they specify the suspect as a possible offender.

In the formal development of the likelihood ratio, a link is needed between what is observed (i.e., the stain at the crime scene) and the hypotheses according to which the suspect is or is not the offender. The connection is made in two steps. The first is the consideration of a hypothesis that the crime stain came from the offender and the alternative hypothesis that the crime stain did not come from the offender. If it is assumed that the crime stain came from the offender, the second step is the consideration of a hypothesis that the crime stain came from the suspect and the alternative that the crime stain did not come from the suspect.

Developing the likelihood ratio in view of these two pairs of hypotheses introduces the concepts of (1) "relevance probability," usually denoted r, and (2) "innocent acquisition probability," usually denoted as a. The resulting expression of the value of the evidence takes the following form:

$$V = \frac{r + \gamma'(1-r)}{\gamma r[a + (1-a)\gamma'](1-r)}$$

Note the difference between two possible expressions γ and γ' of the rarity of the corresponding characteristic. In fact, γ' is the probability that the crime stain would be of a given type, if it had been left by an unknown person who was unconnected with the crime. The population of people who may have left the stain is not necessarily the same as the population from which the criminal is assumed to have come. For DNA evidence, however, it may be acceptable to assume $\gamma = \gamma'$.

Continuous Data and Discrete Hypotheses

A seminal paper in 1977 by Dennis Lindley showed how the Bayes' factor could be used to evaluate evidence given by continuous data in the form of measurements. The measurements used by Lindley by way of illustration were those of the refractive index of glass. There were two sources of variation in such measurements, the variation within a window and the variation between different windows. Lindley showed how these two sources of variation could be accounted for in a single statistic. He was also able to account for the two factors that are of importance to a forensic scientist: (1) the similarity between the recovered and control sample and (2) the typicality of any perceived similarity. When the data are in the form of continuous measurements, the Bayes' factor is a ratio of probability density functions rather than a ratio of probabilities.

Consider a set x of control measurements and another set y of recovered measurements of a particular characteristic, such as the refractive index of glass. For this example, x would be a set of measurements of refractive indices on fragments of a broken window at the crime scene and y a set of measurements of refractive indices on fragments of glass found on a suspect. If the suspect was at the crime scene then the fragments found on him could have come from the window at the crime scene. If he was not there then the fragments have come from some other, unknown, source.

The quantitative part of the evidence concerning the glass fragments in this case can be denoted by $E = (x, y)$. The Bayes' factor is then written as follows:

$$V = \frac{f(x, y|H_p, I)}{f(x, y|H_d, I)}$$

Bayes' theorem and the rules of conditional probability apply to probability density functions $f(\cdot)$ as well as to probabilities. The value of the evidence V of the evidence may be rewritten—following the argument presented in the section on discrete data—as

$$V = \frac{f(y|x, H_p, I)}{f(y|H_d, I)}$$

This formulation of the expression for V shows that for the numerator the distribution of the recovered measurements, conditional on the control measurements as well as I, is considered. For the denominator, the distribution of the recovered measurements is considered over the distribution of the whole of the relevant population. The denominator is called the "marginal distribution" of the recovered measurements in the relevant population.

In a Bayesian approach, the characteristic of interest is parameterized, for example by the mean. Denote the parameter by θ. This parameter may vary from source (window) to source (another window).

Consider the two propositions to be compared are

H_p: the recovered sample is from the same source as the control sample;

H_d: the recovered sample is from a different source than the control sample.

The measurements x are from a distribution with parameter θ_1, say, and the measurements y are from a distribution with parameter θ_2, say. If x and y come from the same source, then $\theta_1 = \theta_2$, otherwise $\theta_1 \neq \theta_2$. In practice, the parameter θ is not known and the analysis is done with the marginal probability densities of x and y. The above equation for V can be rewritten as:

$$V = \frac{\int f(y|\theta)f(x|\theta)\pi(\theta)d\theta}{\int f(x|\theta)\pi(\theta)d\theta \int f(y|\theta)\pi(\theta)d\theta}$$

For those unfamiliar with these kinds of manipulations, Bayes' theorem applied to conditional probability distributions is used to write $f(\theta|x)$ as $\int f(x|\theta)\pi(\theta)/f(x)$. The law of total probability with integration replacing summation is used to write $f(x)$ as $\int f(x|\theta)\pi(\theta)d\theta$. Note that $\pi(\theta)$ represents the prior distribution on the unknown parameter. Therefore, the Bayes' factor does not depend only upon the sample data. It is the ratio of two weighted likelihoods.

Often, the distributions of $(x|\theta)$ and $(y|\theta)$ are assumed to be normal, with θ representing the mean, varying from source to source, and the variance is assumed to be constant from source to source. Those assumptions can be relaxed and (1) various possibilities can been assumed for the distribution of $(x|\theta)$, $(y|\theta)$, and θ and (2) a three-level hierarchical model (variance assumed not constant) can be considered. Moreover, developments for multivariate data are also possible.

Principles of Evidence Evaluation

Three principles arise from the application of the ideas outlined so far.

First, the evaluation is meaningful only when at least one alternative hypothesis is addressed. So, the distribution of the data has to be considered under (at least) two hypotheses, typically that of the prosecution and that of the defense.

The second principle is that evaluation is based on consideration of probabilities of the evidence, given a particular issue is assumed true, $Pr(E|H_p)$ and $Pr(E|H_d)$.

The third principle is that the evaluation and interpretation of the evidence is carried out within a framework of circumstances. It has to be conditioned on the background information I.

The application of those principles guarantees some desiderata in the scientist's attitude in evaluating and offering evidence, such as balance, transparency, robustness, and added value. The degree to which the scientist succeeds in meeting these criteria depends crucially on the chosen inferential framework which may be judged by the criteria of flexibility and logic.

Interpretation

Continuous Data and Continuous Hypothesis

So far the outline focused on categorical (or continuous) data and discrete hypotheses, but Bayesian analysis also deals with situations involving continuous hypotheses. In particular, it may happen that scientists encounter continuous propositions. A typical instance of this is the situation where a parameter, such as a mean, needs to be estimated. As an example, suppose that a random sample, $x = (x_1, ..., x_n)$, is available. For example, this may be the case in which a scientist is interested in blood alcohol concentration on the basis of a series of n measurements taken from a given individual arrested by traffic police.

Suppose further that the data follow a Normal distribution with unknown mean, θ, and known variance, σ^2. Suppose also that there is some background information available so that some values of θ seem more likely a priori. Then, assuming a conjugate Normal prior distribution for the parameter of interest, that is the mean θ, having a mean μ and a variance τ^2, it can be shown that the posterior density is still normal distributed, $N(\mu(x), \tau^2(x))$, with

$$\text{mean } \mu(x) = \frac{\frac{\sigma^2}{n}}{\frac{\sigma^2}{n} + \tau^2}\mu + \frac{\tau^2}{\frac{\sigma^2}{n} + \tau^2}\bar{x} \text{ and variance } \tau^2(x)$$

$$= \frac{\frac{\sigma^2}{n}\tau^2}{\frac{\sigma^2}{n} + \tau^2}$$

The posterior mean is a weighted average of the prior mean μ and the sample mean $\bar{x}$, with weights proportional to the variances corresponding to the prior distribution and the sampling distribution. Comparable lines of reasoning can be invoked to approach situations involving unknown variances, alternative distributions, and data distributions.

Pitfalls of Intuition

The Bayesian approach to the interpretation of evidence enables various errors and fallacies to be exposed. The most well known of these are the prosecutor's and defender's fallacies. As an example, consider a crime where a blood stain is found at the scene and it is established that it has come from the criminal. Only for sake of illustration, consider that the stain has a profile which is present in only 1% of the population. It is also supposed that the size of the relevant population is 200 000. A suspect is identified by other means and his blood is found to be of the same profile as that found at the crime scene.

The prosecutor argues that, because the blood profile is present in only 1% of the population, there is only a 1% chance that the suspect is innocent. There is a 99% chance that he is guilty. The defense attorney argues that, because 1% of 200 000 is 2000, the suspect is only one person in 2000. There is a probability of 1/2000 that he is guilty. This is then used to argue that the blood group is, therefore, of little probative value and not very helpful in the case.

Consideration of the odds form of Bayes' rule explains these fallacies. Denote the blood evidence by E and let the two competing hypotheses be H_p, the suspect is guilty, and H_d, the suspect is innocent. Then the odds form of Bayes' rule is that (omitting I from notation)

$$\frac{\Pr(H_p|E)}{\Pr(H_d|E)} = \frac{\Pr(E|H_p)}{\Pr(E|H_d)} \times \frac{\Pr(H_p)}{\Pr(H_d)}$$

The Bayes' factor is $\Pr(E|H_p)/\Pr(E/H_d) = 1/0.01 = 100$. The posterior odds are increased by a factor of 100.

Consider the prosecutor's statement. It claims that the probability of guilt, after presentation of the evidence, is 0.99. In formal terms, this corresponds to $\Pr(H_p|E) = 0.99$ and, hence, $\Pr(H_d|E) = 0.01$. The posterior odds are 99, which is approximately 100. V is also 100. Thus, the prior odds are 1 and $\Pr(H_p) = \Pr(H_d) = 0.5$. For the prosecutor's fallacy to be correct the prior belief is that the suspect is just as likely to be guilty as innocent.

The defense argues that the posterior probability of guilt $\Pr(H_p|E)$ equals 1/2000 and, hence, $\Pr(H_d|E)$ equals 1999/2000. The posterior odds are 1/1999, which is approximately 1/2000. Since the posterior odds are bigger by a factor of 100 than the prior odds, the prior odds are 1/200 000, or the reciprocal of the population size. The defense is arguing that the prior belief in guilt is approximately 1/200 000. This could be expressed as a belief that the suspect is just as likely to be guilty as anyone else in the relevant population. The fallacy arises because the defense then argues that the evidence is not relevant. However, before the evidence was led, the suspect was one of 200 000 people, after the evidence was led he is only one of 2000 people. Evidence which reduces the size of the pool of potential criminals by a factor of 100 is surely relevant.

Other errors have been identified. The "ultimate issue error" is another name for the prosecutor's fallacy. It confuses the probability of the evidence if a defendant is innocent with the probability he is innocent, given the evidence. The ultimate issue is the issue proposed by the prosecution of which it is asking the court to find in favor. The "source probability error" is to claim the defendant is the source of the evidence. This would place the defendant at the scene of the crime but would not, in itself, be enough to show that he was guilty. The "probability (another match) error" consists of equating the rarity of a characteristic with the probability that another person has this characteristic. The "numerical conversion error" equates the reciprocal of rarity of the corresponding characteristic to the number of people that have to be examined before another person with the same characteristic is found.

More generally, high values for the evidence provide strong support for the prosecution's case. They are not, however, sufficient in themselves to declare a defendant guilty. The prior odds have to be considered as well. Very high values for the evidence, when combined with very small values for prior odds, may produce small values for the posterior odds. This may be the case when the suspect has been selected as a result of a database search and when there is little or no other evidence against the suspect.

> *See also:* **Biology/DNA:** Bayesian Networks; DNA – Statistical Probability; **Foundations:** Overview and Meaning of Identification/Individualization.

Further Reading

Aitken, C.G.G., Lucy, D., 2004. Evaluation of trace evidence in the form of multivariate data. Journal of the Royal Statistical Society: Series C (Applied Statistics) 53, 109–122.

Aitken, C.G.G., Taroni, F., 2004. Statistics and the Evaluation of Evidence for Forensic Scientists. John Wiley & Sons, Chichester.

Bozza, S., Taroni, F., Raymond, R., Schmittbuhl, M., 2008. Probabilistic evaluation of handwriting evidence: likelihood ratio for authorship. Journal of the Royal Statistical Society: Series C (Applied Statistics) 57 (3), 329–341.

Evett, I.W., 1984. A quantitative theory for interpreting transfer evidence in criminal cases. Journal of the Royal Statistical Society: Series C (Applied Statistics) 33, 25–32.

Evett, I.W., 1987. Bayesian inference and forensic science: problems and perspectives. The Statistician 36, 99–105.

Evett, I.W., Lambert, J.A., Buckleton, J.S., 1998. A Bayesian approach to interpreting footwear marks in forensic casework. Science & Justice 38, 241–247.

Evett, I.W., Weir, B.S., 1998. Interpreting DNA Evidence. Sinauer, Sunderland, MA.

Good, I.J., 1991. Weight of evidence and the Bayesian likelihood ratio. In: Aitken, C.G.G., Stoney, D.A. (Eds.), The Use of Statistics in Forensic Science. John Wiley & Sons, Chichester, pp. 85–106.

Koehler, J.J., Chia, A., Lindsey, S., 1995. The random match probability in DNA evidence: irrelevant and prejudicial? Jurimetrics Journal 35, 201–219.

Lindley, D.V., 1997. A problem in forensic science. Biometrika 64, 207–213.

Robertson, B., Vignaux, G.A., 1995. Interpreting Evidence: Evaluating Forensic Science in the Courtroom. John Wiley & Sons, Chichester.

Schum, D.A., 2001. Evidential Foundations of Probabilistic Reasoning. Northwestern University Press, Evanston.

Taroni, F., Bozza, S., Biedermann, A., Garbolino, P., Aitken, C.G.G., 2010. Data Analysis in Forensic Science: A Bayesian Decision Perspective. John Wiley & Sons, Chichester.

Taroni, F., Champod, C., Margot, P., 1998. Forerunners of Bayesianism in early forensic science. Jurimetrics Journal 38, 183–200.

Thompson, W.C., Schumann, E.L., 1987. Interpretation of statistical evidence in criminal trials: the prosecutor's fallacy and the defence attorney's fallacy. Law and Human Behaviour 11, 167–187.

Thompson, W.C., Taroni, F., Aitken, C.G.G., 2003. How the probability of a false positive affects the value of DNA evidence. Journal of Forensic Sciences 38, 47–54.

Forensic Intelligence

O Ribaux and P Margot, University of Lausanne, Lausanne, Switzerland
R Julian and SF Kelty, University of Tasmania, Hobart, TAS, Australia

Glossary

Forensic intelligence The accurate, timely, and useful product of logically processing forensic case data for crime investigation and crime analysis purposes.

Trace The remnant of a presence or an action. Pattern, signal, or object, the "trace" is an apparent sign, which is sometimes latent.

Introduction

Forensic science plays an ever-increasing and critical role in the justice system. It operates generally in supporting criminal and civil investigations and/or providing expert opinion and "scientific" information to assist courts in their decisions.

Forensic intelligence encompasses and goes beyond assisting in investigations and court decisions. It does this through the interpretation of forensic case data (i.e., marks or traces of various types left behind or made by a person or his/her accessories during the commission of an unlawful act) that contribute to decision making in a variety of ways. When forensic science is integrated in policing contexts, it can operate as a silent witness helping to support strategic decisions, police operations, or crime prevention without involving a court case. For instance, forensic science frequently provides leads to investigators before a person is arrested (e.g., major crime inquiries). It can also assist in a more proactive style of policing (e.g., intelligence-led policing) and to crime analysis functions through the potential to link persons, crimes, and crime scenes. Forensic intelligence has demonstrated promising capabilities and is still developing in many directions.

Currently, within forensic science there is a debate about what role it should take and what contribution it should make. In the context of this debate, the concept of forensic intelligence has created some tensions. Some practitioners adopt the position that forensic science should be strictly justice oriented in a traditional paradigm, whereas many practitioners who work within policing environments adopt a position that broadens the role of forensic science into the security system. Both systems overlap without a clear integration. Therefore, in attempting to clarify its practical contribution, forensic science does not escape the very old debate about how justice and security are configured.

Traces as Forensic Case Data, Sign, Information, Evidence, and Intelligence

Forensic science is the study and analysis of traces. Traces can be defined as the remnant of a presence (a person or object located at a certain place at a certain time) or of an action. Whether it be a pattern, a signal, or an object, a "trace" is an apparent sign of presence or actions. Traces can also sometimes be latent.

There are several essential characteristics of traces, which are listed below:

- A trace has a reality that exists independently of any meaning that can be attributed to it.
- It comes from the past and cannot be reproduced.
- It can be fragmentary, incomplete, imperfect (remnant).
- It is not usual within a given environment; it is the effect of an unusual activity at a place at a given time which has disrupted the usual equilibrium of the environment.
- A pertinent trace has generally been transferred unknowingly by the person who committed the action (a planted trace may be indicative of deception).
- It contains a sign which is information on its source (who, with what).
- It contains information about the action which has produced it (how, when, where, what, why).

One of the many consequences of these essential characteristics is that the trace allows the measurement of its physical, chemical, and biological elements. These measurements can be compared with other data or information, independently of any meaning. The trace becomes meaningful only after analysis when the results have been interpreted within a context; for example, when the trace is connected with an event of interest. In forensic science, an event becomes an event of interest when it breaches criminal or civil codes and other laws or rules.

Of importance is the process through which a trace, the material element, becomes an explanation of the circumstances of its presence, which affects its subsequent use. The trace becomes a sign that conveys information about what has occurred. Traces only become evidence after the court has considered the relevance of the trace to the case in order to assist the court in its decision. At this point, forensic intelligence broadens the scope of forensic science through the many other ways of interpreting traces. Here, "evidence" generalizes to "intelligence." Intelligence can be defined as *the interpretation of forensic case data to support a variety of different decisions in the interconnected web of processes crossing each policing system*.

Within forensic intelligence, it is argued that any discipline interested in unlawful events where traces are generated should consider the integration of forensic case data as a primary piece of information. Can we realistically talk about violent criminal behavior without considering the physical exchanges that took place? Or of illicit drug trafficking without studying the substances in question, their manufacturing process, and their effects on people? Or of fire and arson without considering the mechanisms of combustion? Or of counterfeiting without understanding the manufacturing processes and the marks they produce? Or of environmental problems without considering the chemical analysis of suspected specimens? From this perspective, forensic intelligence combines certain approaches in criminology with forensic science.

The potential value of forensic intelligence within contemporary policing models is clear, and it can be coherently integrated into policing at strategic, operational, and/or tactical levels.

Intelligence-Led Policing

Forensic intelligence operates within police environments. There are many models of policing, all of which recognize the fluidity of information and the rigor of its treatment as critical aspects contributing to efficacy and efficiency.

One of these models is intelligence-led policing. This model promotes a systematic analysis of available information that allows decisions to be made at the strategic, operational, and/or tactical level. This type of policing, where an analytical capacity is developed and utilized, provides a mechanism for achieving a greater understanding of security challenges and addressing them in a proactive way. Crime and criminal intelligence analysis is the term given to the organization of collected data that has been collated and analyzed. This knowledge is then disseminated and becomes "intelligence" that can be used by decision makers.

One of the key challenges is to determine how forensic case data can be processed and integrated into intelligence-led policing models. At the very least, decision making in such models can be informed by logically processed information arising from an organized memory of traces, presented in

a timely and usable form according to the decision to be taken. This form of intelligence can be invaluable in making informed decisions.

Intelligence-Led Systems and Examples of Forensic Intelligence Activities

In an intelligence-led policing system, the variety of forms that forensic intelligence could take has not yet been fully explored or formalized. In order to illustrate its contributions, some components of the system and their interactions are presented in the simplified model (**Figure 1**).

Of importance is the overlap between criminal justice and security systems. More often than not, this overlap is not clearly defined. We now turn to describe how forensic intelligence covers four main categories or functions.

Tactical Intelligence and Investigative Leads

According to Kind, the judicial process operates in three chapters: first, the problem to find; second, the decision to charge; and last, the trial process. Each chapter has its own logic, beginning with the facts, interpreting the facts, then potentially discovering a profile of the person and of his/her activity. This leads to a structuring of information which makes the process more deductive and involves assessing the consequences if the person participated in the activity. Finally, there is the trial itself with a more general focus on justice and an interest in forensic science. The implementation of the process depends heavily on the judicial context and its procedures: competencies for making decisions are distributed in very different ways in different jurisdictions. However, whatever the organization, at many points, the interpretation and intelligence provided by forensic case data support decision making. For instance, forensic intelligence can occur in a tactical context when:

- Pointing to a suspect (e.g., through a database) or a set of persons (when partial DNA is compared to a database) in order to direct the investigation;
- Eliminating persons previously of interest through DNA sweeps;
- Analyzing a substance seized on a person in order to help establish the crime (e.g., confirming an illicit substance or determining the quantity). Further, to check if the substance can be linked with other seizures that will indicate if this should be treated as a separate case or as elements of organized trafficking. In addition, presenting this information as intelligence may support a decision about detaining a person/s;
- Detecting serial offenses carried out by the same person through crime scene linking (e.g., the comparison of footmarks, DNA, and earmarks). On this basis, analyzing the

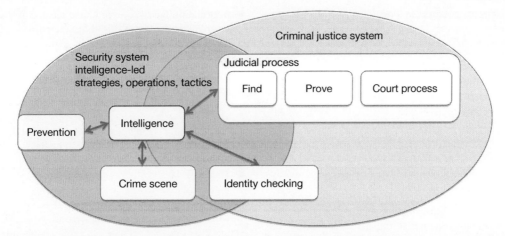

Figure 1 A very simplified and limited model showing the overlap between security and the criminal justice systems. It illustrates the central role of intelligence that should drive most functions. The particular components that are displayed are interconnected. They can partly or significantly rely upon forensic intelligence. Investigations, divided into three chapters in the judicial process, according to Kind, overlap with the policing environment. This is a source of tensions that are addressed further.

series and suggesting lines of inquiry or proactive operational procedures (e.g., surveillance or decoy);
- Understanding a modus operandi through the analysis of a crime scene that can help devise a profile of the perpetrator, and subsequent lines of inquiry.

Operational Intelligence through Sustained Crime Analysis

The sustained collection, collation, and analysis of specific forensic case data can improve many crime analysis processes and subsequently support decisions of all kinds.

One of the most elementary and systematic police tasks is to check and establish the identity of a person or persons. This frequently occurs in the street or at particular checkpoints. Many methods exist for checking identities, the most applicable depending largely on the context in which it occurs (time, availability of techniques, light). A basic operational field task in many countries is the careful examination of identity documents. Field officers carry out this task and must be informed and trained about the relevant features to check in a document. However, a variety of evolving techniques are being used by different counterfeiters to deceive document examiners. This knowledge and the real-time determination of the best method for checking documents must be systematically updated and disseminated to field officers.

For this purpose, a forensic intelligence process can be delineated. It consists of collecting fraudulent documents and observations from field officers. The documents and the observations are then collated, compared, and analyzed to extract relevant characteristics resulting from the current manufacturing processes used by criminals. How these characteristics can be detected as simply as possible is determined and eventually this knowledge is disseminated and used as intelligence for supporting decisions made when checking documents in the field.

This process can be generalized to tackle a variety of counterfeiting problems faced by authorities. The continuous analysis and monitoring of potentially counterfeited watches, drugs, and other objects and materials can benefit from the implementation of such specific forensic intelligence processes.

Forensic intelligence is not limited to this specific case; the approach can be generalized in relation to different types of crime activities or problems. High-volume crimes, violent crimes, the use of guns, and other repetitive problems such as arson and fire or even graffiti may benefit from the integration of forensic case data with other more traditional data used for this purpose (geographical information, chronologies, modus operandi). This list can be extended to include other national security themes relating to terrorism.

Currently, the management of these problems focuses on traditional sources of information and does not make use of forensic intelligence except when dealing with specific cases. These traditional methods do not take advantage of the strengths and potential value of the information obtained through forensic science. The current approach is not coherent and it misses one of the richest sources of information since repetitive crimes are more firmly linked through forensic comparisons than by other more fragile methods, such as hunches or psychological profiles. How to build the best (simple, flexible, adaptive, cost-effective, respectful to privacy, rapid, selective) architecture for the sustained analysis of crime problems is a real challenge and the basis of intensive research.

Strategic Intelligence through the Integration and Analysis of Forensic Links

Linking crimes through forensic case data provides information on the size, the extent, and the evolution of criminal phenomena. This inductive process leads to a model that may add value to knowledge gained through other criminological studies. For instance, the systematic detection of links through illicit drug profiling provides intelligence that eventually influences strategic decisions at a political level or informs prevention programs (e.g., detecting products that pose a risk to population health, or detecting the routes used to traffic illicit substances). DNA linking creates potentially relevant information about the structure of certain forms of criminality (how repetitive), the mobility of criminals (how each criminal travels), or even about criminal careers. Nevertheless, the strategic use of forensic case data is still very rare despite its advantages; typically, policing organizations offer no rational explanations other than following routine and the lack of training and education.

Forensic Science Performance

In an intelligence-led style of policing, systematically assessing the efficiency of each forensic intelligence function is a fundamental attitude. This leads to a focus on the cost–benefit ratio of the activity depending on the objectives that relate to various strategies. In this model, performance indicators often focus on crime detection or conviction in order to perceive how forensic science contributes to the justice system. These can be valid indicators when forensic science is considered from a traditional perspective. However, forensic intelligence cannot be evaluated in this way because its added value resides in how it supports decision making in policing, not in directly solving crime.

Limits of Forensic Intelligence and Requirements

The nature of traces limits the extent and types of inferences that can be made. Traces come from the past, and the course of time is not reversible. Singular events cannot be reproduced; they must be imagined through abduction (what are the possible or reasonable causes of the observed effects?). Moreover, traces can be fragmentary and incomplete, and their relevance uncertain. In addition, incompleteness is a characteristic of crime scene processing: there is no established procedure guaranteeing that the material associated with the investigated activity will be found; absence of traces does not mean that no trace exists.

These considerations highlight some of the logical difficulties that go beyond techniques and methods. A number of significant consequences follow:

- Information is lost forever. Crime scene examination aims to optimize the quantity and quality of material collected. This means that crime scene examination cannot be restricted to the systematic application of standard operating procedures and techniques. It necessitates the adoption of a scientific attitude (in a broad sense) at the scene through the logical processing of what is observed.

- The types of reasoning that rely on traces are said to be "approximate" and "nonmonotonic," that is, each new piece of information may provoke the revision of what was inferred.

- The trace does not tell the whole history, only a part of it that may be substantial (or not) according to the problem at hand and the recovered material. It is frequently useless when used in isolation. The trace must be integrated within a framework that collates and interprets the many sources available, thereby limiting any breaks in the reasoning process that result from arbitrary inferences being made in separate disciplines.

Challenges and Tensions

These fundamental limitations explain why traditional forensic organizations experience many difficulties in dealing with intelligence issues and integration.

First, delivering forensic intelligence "services" and evaluating their efficiency according to a formalized relationship between a client and a customer is very hard, if not an intractable task. For instance, in the course of a major inquiry, relevant operational decisions depend strongly on the case itself as well as the reasoning capacity of the team that is in charge; they cannot be defined in routine terms. An investigation calls for transversal, fluid, and hard-to-formalize reasoning that uses general forensic science and other knowledge; for example, crime analysts, behavioral scientists, pathologists, investigators, and forensic scientists are more frequently required to work in an integrated way in major inquiries nowadays. However, this is not the case in most forensic science laboratories where activities are separated according to traditional branches of the hard sciences (e.g., chemistry, biology, physics) or more modern disciplines (e.g., computer science, life sciences). This is exemplified by the influential NAS report (2009) that does not identify the richness of the information content that may be obtained through integration and formal analysis. There is a need to develop specialist support knowledge; however, it is well known that specialized (and separated) organizations privilege their own objectives according to their vertical structures. They tend to adopt a negative view of horizontal processes that involve the sharing of knowledge across agencies, in part due to concerns related to accountability; at the very least, they do not prioritize such processes. Specialist organizations have therefore had dramatic and negative effects on the development of forensic intelligence.

The previous argument should lead to a reformulation of the process from a policing perspective. A change of culture is needed in many policing organizations for a better integration of forensic case data. Crime analysis units also need to be aware of the benefits of integrating forensic intelligence.

Finally, forensic policy and its efficiency cannot be entirely evaluated according to justice concerns. A better general question is how does forensic science contribute to crime reduction? Of course, this is a complex question that is difficult to address through the application of valid experimental methods. However, other less-ambitious but related questions can be answered. For instance, what is the performance of forensic case data (and their combination) in linking crimes and thus supporting crime analysis functions? What is the quality and quantity of traces collected, and what do they contribute to intelligence processes? And how can forensic science boost other activities? However, the assessment framework for addressing these questions is still in its infancy.

The integrative form of problem solving inherent in forensic intelligence is useful for examining both specific cases and the evolution of criminality more generally. Importantly, however, it is at odds with recent propositions that call for more standard operating procedures, and the separation of forensic science activities from law enforcement environments. Actually, what lies behind this tension is a very old dilemma about the information needed to interpret traces. Do we favor the use of contextual information for driving the reasoning pattern and selecting relevant actions, or do we avoid it because it may influence judgment and possibly lead to miscarriages of justice? Or can we combine both?

Forensic science suffers from some confusion. It often remains confined inside arbitrary barriers erected by some police organizations, other agencies in the justice system, or the logic of the market. This is a result of the environment in which forensic science developed and which has governed its growth and activities historically. Whether it can now capture how security and justice paradigms may coexist to produce forensic intelligence tasks remains to be seen. This point can be illustrated by, for example, the decision to increase the proportion of cases attended by crime scene examiners in high-volume crime. Two possible intentions may direct this decision: it is a decision in response to a demand from the public who are concerned that no crime scene examiner is engaged when they are victimized, implying that the police do not consider their case seriously; it is a decision that logically fits within a strategy of providing the many investigative, intelligence, and justice processes with a greater quantity of information. In the first situation, the policing strategy targets the improvement of the image of police work independently of the quality and quantity of information collected and its contribution to the treatment of crime problems. This strategy is often adopted for political

benefit or to address the community policing objective of reassuring the public, rather than as a response to crime phenomena. The second option may be more difficult and demanding intellectually but is the only logical and ethical policy.

In such uncertain environments, contradictions arise that place forensic scientists in a less than advantageous position where procedures are to be followed in a routine manner. This prevents them from going beyond or thinking "out of the box" when solving forensic problems which are, by their very nature, singular.

Conclusion

Forensic intelligence calls for a return to the very fundamental object studied by forensic science: the trace. It comprises methods, techniques, and inferential activities that all combine to bring information to decision makers in policing at all levels (strategic, operational, and tactical) within a systematic and integrated framework.

Forensic science should therefore be seen as an autonomous discipline. Its major contribution should be to bring support to decisions in many environments, rather than exclusively to serve the justice system and court processes.

Nevertheless, progress is slow because of a traditional resistance to innovation and the expectations from justice agencies that drive the outcomes of police organizations and forensic laboratories. Intelligence-led strategies develop slowly and with difficulty, which in turn hampers the progress of forensic intelligence. Moreover, even when an intelligence culture develops within an organization, an awareness of the potential for traces to support decision-making remains low. A change of paradigm is needed in which the trace left by an offender is considered as a basic element of the crime puzzle, like corners and edges, on which to build the overall picture.

See also: **Behavioral:** Modus Operandi; Serial Killing; **Biology/DNA:** DNA Databases; Significance; **Chemistry/Trace/Forensic Geosciences:** Crime Scene Considerations; **Foundations:** History of Forensic Sciences; Principles of Forensic Science; Semiotics, Heuristics, and Inferences Used by Forensic Scientists; **Investigations:** Crime Scene to Court; Forensic Intelligence Analysis.

Further Reading

Barclay, D., 2009. Using forensic science in major crime inquiries. In: Fraser, J., Williams, R. (Eds.), Handbook of Forensic Science. Willan, Cullompton, pp. 337–358.
Birkett, J., 1989. Scientific scene linking. Journal of the Forensic Science Society 29, 271–284.

Bradbury, S.-A., Feist, A., 2005. The Use of Forensic Science in Volume Crime Investigations: A Review of the Research Literature. Home Office, London.

Braga, A.A., Pierce, G.L., 2004. Linking crime guns: the impact of ballistics imaging technology on the productivity of the Boston Police Department's Ballistics Units. Journal of Forensic Sciences 49 (4), 1–6.

Brodeur, J.-P., Shearing, C., 2005. Configuring security and justice. European Journal of Criminology 2 (4), 379–406.

Buzzini, P., Massonnet, G., 2004. A market study of green spray by Fourier transform infrared (FTIR) and Raman spectroscopy. Science and Justice 44 (3), 123–131.

Cole, S., 2011. Acculturating forensic science: what is scientific culture and how can forensic science adopt it? The Fordham Urban Law Journal 38, 435–472.

Crispino, F., Ribaux, O., Houck, M., Margot, P., 2011. Forensic science – a true science? Australian Journal of Forensic Sciences 43, 157–176.

Crispino, F., 2008. Nature and place of crime scene management within forensic sciences. Science and Justice 1, 24–28.

Kind, S.S., 1987. The Scientific Investigation of Crime. Forensic Science Services, Harrogate.

Kind, S.S., 1994. Crime investigation and the criminal trial: a three chapter paradigm of evidence. Journal of the Forensic Science Society 34 (3), 155–164.

Lawless, C., 2010. A Curious Reconstruction? the Shaping of 'Marketized' Forensic Science. The London School of Economics and Political Science, Centre for Analysis of Risk and Regulation, London.

Margot, P., 2011. Forensic science on trial – what is the law of the land? Autralian Journal of Forensic Science 43, 83–97.

Milne, R., 2001. Operation bigfoot, a volume crime database project. Science and Justice 41 (3), 215–217.

Napier, T.J., 2002. Scene linking using footwear mark database. Science and Justice 42 (1), 39–43.

National Academy of Sciences, 2009. Strengthening Forensic Science in the United States: A Path Forward. National Academy of Sciences/National Academies Press, Washington, DC.

Papilloud, J., 2004. L'incendie volontaire, méthodes et outils d'investigation – Analyses stratégiques et opérationnelles (Doctoral thesis). University of Lausanne.

Ratcliffe, J., 2008. Intelligence-Led Policing. Willan, Cullompton, UK.

Ribaux, O., Margot, P., 1999. Inference structures for crime analysis and intelligence using forensic science data: the example of burglary. Forensic Science International 100, 193–210.

Ribaux, O., Margot, P., 2003. Case-based reasoning in criminal intelligence using forensic case data. Science and Justice 43 (3), 135–143.

Ribaux, O., Girod, A., Walsh, S., Margot, P., Mizrahi, S., Clivaz, V., 2003. Forensic intelligence and crime analysis. Probability, Law and Risk 2 (2), 47–60.

Ribaux, O., Walsh, S.J., Margot, P., 2006. The contribution of forensic science to crime analysis and investigation: forensic intelligence. Forensic Science International 156, 171–181.

Ribaux, O., Baylon, A., Roux, C., et al., 2010a. Intelligence-led crime scene processing. Part I: forensic intelligence. Forensic Science International 195 (1), 10–16.

Ribaux, O., Baylon, A., Lock, E., et al., 2010b. Intelligence-led crime scene processing. Part II: intelligence and crime scene examination. Forensic Science International 199, 63–71.

Roman, J.K., Reid, S., Reid, J., Chalfin, A., Adams, W., Knight, C., 2008. The DNA Field Experiment: Cost-Effectiveness Analysis of the Use of DNA in the Investigation of High-Volume Crimes. Urban Institute, Justice Policy Center NCJ 222318, Washington, DC.

Saks, M.J., 1994. Implications of the Daubert test for forensic identification science. Shepard's Expert and Scientific Evidence 1 (3), 427–434.

Schuliar, Y., 2009. La coordination scientifique dans les investigations criminelles. Proposition d'organisation, aspects éthiques ou de la nécessité d'un nouveau métier (Ph.D. thesis). Université Paris 5 – Descartes and University of Lausanne.

Sheptycki, J., 2004. Organizational pathologies in police intelligence: some contributions to the lexicon of intelligence-led policing. European Journal of Criminology 1 (3), 307–332.

Tilley, N., Townsley, M., 2009. Forensic science in UK policing: strategies, tactics and effectiveness. In: Fraser, J., Williams, R. (Eds.), Handbook of Forensic Science. Willan, Cullompton, pp. 359–379.

Relevant Websites

www.ceps.edu.au/—ARC Centre of Excellence in Policing and Security (last accessed 06.05.12.).

http://www.popcenter.org/—Center for Problem Oriented Policing (last accessed 06.05.12.).

http://www.iaca.net/—International Association of Crime Analysts (last accessed 06.05.12.).

http://jratcliffe.net/—Jerry Ratcliffe's Home Page (last accessed 06.05.12.).

http://www.ucl.ac.uk/jdi/—Jill Dando Institute of Security and Crime Science (last accessed 06.05.12.).

Forensic Intelligence Analysis

LR Rockwell, Forensic and Intelligence Services, LLC, Alexandria, VA, USA

Glossary

Forensic intelligence analysis The process of analyzing forensic problems in the most accurate manner possible in order to create logical, unbiased analyses concerning probable past events.
Intelligence analysis The process of analyzing national security and intelligence problems in the most accurate manner possible.

Mental models Simplified information processing strategies that are inherent in the human brain.
Structured analytic techniques Logical, proven structures for critical thinking.

Intelligence Analysis and Forensic Science

Forensic scientists and national security intelligence analysts have similar occupations: on a daily basis, practitioners in both groups must answer questions that require them to know the unknowable. For intelligence analysts, knowing the unknowable helps them forecast future events that may impact national security. For forensic scientists, knowing the unknowable helps them better understand the past in order to help solve crimes. The information that forensic scientists and intelligence analysts need to perform their vital roles effectively is unknowable for many reasons. Crimes, like threats to national security, occur as part of complex social situations that are often difficult for scientists and analysts to discern. Necessary information is often unavailable, sometimes because it is kept secret by criminals or intelligence targets. Moreover, these practitioners' ability to apply logical, critical thinking to these questions is negatively affected by biases inherent in human thought processes. The intelligence community has developed analytic tools and techniques to help analysts answer national security questions more effectively in light of these difficulties; in essence, to help them better "know the unknowable." Forensic scientists can use these same critical thinking and reasoning tools to help them answer questions about crimes more effectively and accurately.

What Is Forensic Intelligence Analysis?

The proven processes used by intelligence analysts—whose work shares many similarities with forensic practitioners'—should be the basis for a definition forensic intelligence analysis, or forensic analysis. The analytic processes developed and used by the intelligence community can provide substantial benefits to forensic practitioners and will be examined first.

Intelligence analysis can be defined as the process of analyzing national security and intelligence problems in the most accurate manner possible. The result of this process is logical, unbiased intelligence concerning potential future events and probable past events. The process requires the appropriate use of structured analytic tools and techniques, which are used to analyze facts gathered through the traditional research process. The facts used in an analytic project should be drawn from as many data sources as is feasible and appropriate, given the project's time and information constraints. This analysis is particularly valuable to intelligence consumers because it facilitates the production of judgments and assessments which are based on, but provided in addition to, the facts gathered during the research process. These judgments and assessments are typically the most important part of any intelligence product and are often referred to as the "value added" to the final product. Thus, the value of the analytic product far exceeds the facts on which it is based. Because of this, the intelligence analysis process is often described to those who are unfamiliar with the profession as "adding two plus two and getting a total greater than four."

Analysis produced using structured analytic techniques is significantly more likely to be accurate than analysis produced without the aid of such techniques; however, even intelligence produced by the analysis process described above cannot always accurately predict future events or recreate past events. Intelligence analysis has limitations; namely, it cannot accurately reveal future or past events in their entirety as would a fortune teller, medium, or wizard in a story. Instead, the intelligence that results from this process consists of predictions and judgments that vary in confidence (the perceived likelihood of accuracy) based on the quality and quantity of information available to the analyst at the time of analysis. Regardless of the confidence level of intelligence created using structured analytic techniques, this intelligence will almost always be more accurate than intelligence created without the benefit of the intelligence analysis process and its attendant tools, techniques, and practices.

Although forensic intelligence and forensic intelligence analysis are inseparable, forensic intelligence has received the bulk of the forensic community's attention. Forensic intelligence, which is the end result of the forensic intelligence analysis process, can be used on its own or reanalyzed in conjunction with other pieces of evidence to develop more new forensic intelligence. Examples of forensic intelligence include but are not limited to analytic opinions such as a fingerprint "match," the exclusion of a suspect based on DNA evidence, or the determination that a knife in evidence is consistent with the knife used to stab a specific crime victim. Forensic intelligence can be used to develop investigative leads, to show trends and patterns within and between crimes and jurisdictions, to help strategic decision makers determine the best possible use of resources or course of action for a laboratory or police department, and to inform national security analyses. In part because each subsequent analysis has the potential to compound errors in the original forensic analysis, a greater focus on forensic intelligence analysis is necessary to ensure that initial and subsequent forensic intelligence products are as accurate as possible.

Establishing a process for conducting analysis in the forensic science discipline will improve the products that forensic scientists provide to citizens, investigators, prosecutors, and defense attorneys, such as reports or testimony. The process necessary to ensure that forensic analysis is logical and unbiased can be successfully borrowed from the analytic process already in use by the intelligence community. Using these existing techniques will not only help improve the quality of forensic intelligence analysis, but it will allow the forensic science discipline to avoid duplicating research, which has already been conducted in the fields of psychology and intelligence analysis, that is relevant to improving the quality of analysis. The tools necessary to improve the quality of forensic analysis are conspicuously absent from this relatively young discipline's toolkit and could be easily added by borrowing the preformed concepts from the intelligence community. The structured analytic techniques used by the intelligence community should be among the most used of the forensic community's tools. With regular use, these tools could resolve many of the issues of analytic accuracy that have raised questions about the validity of the forensic science and the forensic community.

Forensic intelligence analysis, therefore, can be defined as the process of analyzing forensic problems in the most accurate manner possible in order to create logical, unbiased analyses concerning probable past events. The process requires the appropriate use of structured analytic tools and techniques, in conjunction with the use of multiple data sources whenever feasible and appropriate. Forensic intelligence analysis also provides "value added" to its customers by taking raw facts, such as a shell casing, blood, or a fingerprint, analyzing those facts and providing the resultant judgments and assessments to forensic customers. Investigators, prosecutors, and defense attorneys would have little use for forensic evidence if all they received was the evidence itself.

Similarities between Forensic Science and Intelligence Analysis

The tools and methods used by intelligence analysts can be applied to forensic science because the work of intelligence analysts and forensic practitioners is very similar. As was mentioned earlier, practitioners in both groups must know the unknowable. This task is understandably difficult, whether performed by an intelligence analyst who typically needs to understand how future events may unfold, or by a forensic scientist who needs to understand how past events may have unfolded. Intelligence analysts typically answer questions which may impact national security, such as "Will a terrorist attack occur in Washington DC in the next 6 months?" "Will dictator X declare war on country Y within the next 2 weeks?" or "Will the outbreak of flu in country Z spread to the United States?" Forensic practitioners, on the other hand, typically ask crime-related questions that focus on past events, such as "Is the DNA found on victim A consistent with the DNA of suspect B?" "Could the fibers found at the crime scene have come from the shirt owned by suspect C?" or "Could this knife be the knife that was used to stab victim D?"

When answering questions like these, both intelligence analysts and forensic practitioners must provide sound analysis to their customers. To do this successfully, practitioners in both groups must do the following:

- Make sound, unbiased judgments about probable past or future events.
- Employ logical argumentation.
- Provide objective judgments and insights.
- Use critical thinking skills and structured analytic techniques. This helps prevent bias and ensure logical reasoning, thereby increasing the odds that judgments will be objective, logical, and unbiased.
- Uncover trends and show explicit connections between related events, persons, places, etc.
- Interpret information, rather than simply describing information.
- Incorporate alternative analysis (additional explanations of how events may unfold or may have unfolded) when appropriate.

- Exhibit consistency of analysis over time, or highlight the changes in the analysis and explain the reasons (new information became available, etc.) for those changes.
- Evaluate the quality and reliability of information that may be used in analysis in order to ensure that each piece of information receives appropriate consideration in the analysis. High-quality information from highly reliable sources should have more weight in the analytic process than low-quality information or information from unreliable sources.
- Distinguish between underlying facts and the practitioner's assumptions and judgments. This must be done so that the customer can clearly and easily distinguish between what is true and what might be true, in order to prevent future analytic errors caused by analysis predicated on analytic assumptions—which may later prove to be false—instead of facts.
- Provide the best analysis possible.

Both groups must perform these tasks while limited by unfavorable conditions. Specifically, both intelligence analysts and forensic practitioners will frequently find that they have neither enough time nor enough information to perform these tasks as well or as completely as they would like to. Forensic practitioners and intelligence analysts must both:

- *Deal with limited or incomplete information.* Crime scenes rarely contain all of the information necessary to solve a crime. Intelligence analysts researching specific issues know that most situations are too complex to understand in their entirety. This is complicated by the fact that, in almost all situations, 100% of the information pertaining to that topic simply is not available. Analysts who work on topics related to potential future events know that unanticipated developments can skew analysis.
- *Deal with unreliable, conflicting, or ambiguous information.*
- *Deal with denial and deception.* Suspects, witnesses, and intelligence targets may intentionally or unintentionally withhold important information or lie in order to mislead investigators and analysts.
- *Deal with information in the context of volatile and unknowable social situations.* Analysts cannot always be aware of the cultural and social forces acting on intelligence targets, victims, witnesses, or criminals. Without awareness of these factors, it can be difficult for practitioners to understand the motivations of these actors, which can skew analysis.
- *Work within limited time frames.* The time available to process a crime scene or research an issue is limited. Some types of evidence degrade over time. Other types of evidence, such as the temperature of an object, are time sensitive.
- *Collect appropriate information.* Both analysts and forensic practitioners can collect too much information, thereby gathering irrelevant information that makes it more difficult to conduct analysis. Analysts researching an issue may find that their searches have gotten off topic, or find that they are collecting deceptive information supplied by the intelligence target.

- *Identify information gaps.* Identifying what is not known is vital to both groups, in order that they can do their best to find the missing information to do analysis with the most complete picture. Crime scenes rarely contain all of the information necessary to solve a crime. Gaps, once identified, must be filled through other means, such as interviews and traditional investigation.

Intelligence Failures

When intelligence analysts fail to meet the criteria described in the previous section, and thus to properly forecast future events, the result is what the intelligence community calls an "intelligence failure." Some of the most infamous intelligence failures include the intelligence community's failure to predict the 1941 attack on Pearl Harbor; the 1973 Yom Kippur War; the 1990 invasion of Kuwait; the 1998 Indian nuclear tests; the 2001 Al Qaeda attacks in New York City, Virginia, and Pennsylvania; and the 2003 declaration that Iraq was in possession of weapons of mass destruction.

The forensic science discipline has had its own intelligence failures, which will be called "forensic failures" for the purpose of this chapter. Several of these have been well publicized by the media, such as the 2002 Washington DC sniper case, in which forensic profiling techniques predicted that the sniper was a middle-aged white male with military training who was acting alone and driving a white van. The sniper was actually two black men acting in concert and driving a blue Chevrolet Caprice; only one of the men was middle aged and had been trained in the military, the other was a teenager. The Madrid train bombing case, in which the Federal Bureau of Investigation (FBI) aggressively pursued false leads, is another example of a forensic failure. In this case, the FBI matched a fingerprint found on a bag containing detonating devices to a US citizen, Mr. Brandon Mayfield, who was subsequently arrested. The FBI, which claimed that the fingerprint was "100% verified" as belonging to Mr. Mayfield, refused to concede that the fingerprint may not have belonged to Mr. Mayfield long after Spanish police presented compelling evidence that the fingerprint had actually been left by an Algerian national with a criminal record and a Spanish residency permit. Research also has shown that forensic failures occur in fingerprint analysis: when told that investigators believe that the suspect is "definitely" guilty, that the suspect committed a violent crime, or that the print and suspect were previously matched, fingerprint examiners are much more likely to declare matches where there are none.

The roots of intelligence failures and forensic failures can almost always be traced to simplified—and often faulty—information processing strategies that are inherent in the human brain. These simplified information processing strategies cause errors in thinking, known as cognitive biases, which are compounded by other factors commonly at work in forensic and intelligence analyses, such as lack of information, the presence of disinformation, lack of time to conduct additional analysis or further research, and so forth. These biases are purely functions of human information processing strategies and are not motivated by emotional or intellectual predispositions toward certain judgments.

These simplified information processing strategies are known as mental models. The thought processes that result from mental models are consistent, predictable, subconscious, and—in spite of the previous paragraph's evidence to the contrary—extremely helpful to the species. Mental models are part of the evolutionary process and allow humans to process otherwise incomprehensible volumes of information. By helping humans deal more effectively with ambiguity and complexity, these mental models have also helped the species to survive and thrive.

The cognitive biases that result from these mental models are also detrimental: they commonly cause humans to jump to conclusions, miss the obvious, and simply draw inaccurate conclusions. Cognitive biases interfere with logical thinking in a number of ways. First, these biases cause people to perceive what they expect to perceive, which often occurs even if evidence initially exists that should discredit the person's perception. Adding to this, these mind-sets, whether based on accurately or inaccurately perceived information, form very quickly but tend to resist change for a prolonged period of time. When new information becomes available, it is most often assimilated into the existing mindset. If the new information conflicts with or refutes this mindset, it is frequently dismissed as unreliable or simply ignored. Simply, humans' initial mind-sets—which, in this case, would be well thought of as hypotheses—will frequently interfere with accurate analysis even after better, more complete information becomes available.

The forensic failure associated with the FBI's handling of the Madrid train bombing case is an excellent example of how mental models can interfere with logical thinking and, therefore, with good forensic science. Prior to the train bombing, the FBI had identified Mr. Mayfield, who converted to Islam after marrying an Egyptian woman, as a potential Islamic extremist. Based on the volume of surveillance dedicated to Mr. Mayfield and his family, it is likely that agents had become convinced that Mr. Mayfield was, in fact, a terrorist. When Mr. Mayfield's fingerprint came back as one of 20 others that was a possible match for the print found on the bag containing the detonators, this information—which should have been viewed with caution—was instead used to proclaim that the print had been "100% verified" as belonging to Mr. Mayfield, and was thus assimilated into the agents' existing mindset. When the Spanish police examined the prints and found them to be inconsistent with Mr. Mayfield's prints, this evidence was ignored. It was not until the Spanish police matched the prints to the Algerian criminal and a warrant was issued for his arrest that the FBI recognized and conceded its mistake. The US District Court judge who presided over a subsequent lawsuit found that the FBI had "fabricated and concocted" evidence against Mr. Mayfield, which is consistent with the FBI assimilating new evidence into its existing mindset, and dismissing evidence which did not fit that mindset.

Cognitive biases are extremely difficult to overcome. Even when one is aware of them, it is rarely possible to stop or diminish their effects, as the mental models that cause them are "hard-wired" into human brains. It is likely that the FBI analysts who worked the Madrid train bombing case had at least heard of them, and it is all but certain that the Central Intelligence Agency (CIA) analysts who contributed to the Iraqi weapons of mass destruction intelligence failure had learned about cognitive biases as well as techniques used to overcome their effects during basic analytic training at CIA.

The Benefits of Structured Analytic Techniques

Structured analytic techniques, which are logical, proven structures for critical thinking, can help intelligence analysts and forensic practitioners overcome the effects of cognitive biases and deal more effectively with bad, limited, or false information. There are many structured analytic techniques, each of which can be used at a different stage of an analytic problem to ensure the logic of the analysis. Although not every technique is appropriate for every analytic problem, every analytic problem will benefit from the use of appropriate structured analytic techniques. Structured analytic techniques are commonly used in business to ensure that corporations and other organizations make the best possible decisions.

ructured analytic techniques help critical thinkers overcome cognitive biases in many ways. These techniques help allow the imposition of analytic will and logic on the subconscious mind, thus overcoming the effects of flawed mental models. They also help thinkers focus their analysis, and increase the accuracy and efficiency of human thought processes. In the process, they help the mind make sense of complex problems, allow the mind to focus on only one element of the problem at a time, and compare those elements against each other. This is far different from trying to solve a complex problem "in one's head," which often makes it difficult to clearly see the scope of the problem, let alone identify, isolate, and compare each element of the issue. Structured analytic techniques also facilitate visual analysis, which harnesses more effective brainpower in addition to doing all of the above.

Structured analysis is very different from the intuitive analysis that is commonly used by persons writing college-level papers and reasoning their way through everyday events. It is common for persons who use intuitive analysis to arrive at incorrect conclusions. This process is driven by the mental models described in the previous section. Intuitive analysis starts when the individual identifies one potential hypothesis or explanation for events. Because of the effects of mental models, it then becomes very difficult for that individual to consider alternative hypotheses or explanations. The chosen hypothesis typically appears to mesh with the evidence the individual has observed to that point, even if the individual has done very little research about and has very little understanding of the issue at hand. When the individual accumulates new evidence and compares it to the hypothesis to see if the evidence fits, or supports, the chosen hypothesis, mental models come into play again and evidence that does not support the hypothesis may be dismissed or ignored. Additional supporting evidence will be identified and used to create a strong argument for the chosen hypothesis, even if evidence which should have discredited the hypothesis has been discovered.

Structured analysis is much more likely to produce accurate conclusions than intuitive analysis. This broad process is supplemented along the way by a variety of structured analytic techniques designed to ensure the step-by-step integrity of the process. Unlike intuitive analysis, this process begins with the identification of the widest possible array of explanations, often called a "full set of alternative hypotheses," for the observed activity. At this stage, structured analytic techniques will be used to help identify this range of hypotheses and identify underlying (and possibly incorrect) assumptions. Next, research will begin, and the analyst will identify evidence with diagnostic value. Structured analytic techniques designed to determine the quality and reliability of evidence will be used at this stage. The collected and analyzed evidence will then be compared to the available hypotheses and used to discredit, rather than support, the hypotheses. The structured analytic techniques used in this process prevent analysts from falling prey to the effects of mental models that occur in the intuitive analysis process.

The use of structured analytic techniques can have enormous benefits for forensic practitioners. Not only do these techniques help practitioners overcome cognitive biases, they also clarify practitioners' thought processes and help them identify fallacies, information gaps, and errors in logic. These techniques also help practitioners deal more effectively with limited time and resources, and limited or ambiguous information. The use of structured analytic techniques also improves group work, increases consistency among practitioners, provides records of the analytic process, and makes it possible for one practitioner to pick up the analytic process where another left off. By forcing practitioners to order their thoughts logically, the use of structured analytic techniques also helps them to communicate more effectively and express facts clearly. Altogether, use of these techniques improves the accuracy of the practitioners' analysis and communication, making the final product more useful for investigators, prosecutors, and defense attorneys who rely on forensic practitioners' services.

See also: **Behavioral:** Investigative Psychology; **Foundations:** Forensic Intelligence; Semiotics, Heuristics, and Inferences Used by Forensic Scientists; **Professional:** Education and Accreditation in Forensic Science; Ethics.

Further Reading

Central Intelligence Agency, 2009. A Tradecraft Primer. Central Intelligence Agency, McLean, VA. https://www.cia.gov/library/center-for-the-study-of-intelligence/csi-publications/books-and-monographs/Tradecraft%20Primer-apr09.pdf.

Heuer, R., 1999. The Psychology of Intelligence Analysis. Central Intelligence Agency, McLean, VA. https://www.cia.gov/library/center-for-the-study-of-intelligence/csi-publications/books-and-monographs/psychology-of-intelligence- analysis/PsychofIntelNew.pdf.

Heuer, R., Pherson, R., 2011. Structured Analytic Techniques for Intelligence Analysis. CQ Press, Washington, DC.

Jones, M.D., 1998. The Thinker's Toolkit: Fourteen Powerful Techniques for Problem Solving. Times Business, New York.

Kahneman, D., 2011. Thinking, Fast and Slow. Farrar, Straus & Giroux, New York.

Ratcliffe, J.H. (Ed.), 2009. Strategic Thinking in Criminal Intelligence. The Federation Press, New South Wales, Australia.

Relevant Website

https://www.cia.gov—Central Intelligence Agency, CSI, Psychology of Intelligence Analysis; A Tradecraft Primer: Structured Analytic Techniques for Improving Intelligence Analysis.

Intuitive analysis	Structured analysis
Quickly choose one hypothesis that seems to fit available evidence.	Start with a full set of alternative hypotheses.
Accumulate evidence and see how that evidence fits the chosen hypothesis.	Identify and emphasize evidence with diagnostic value.
Seek additional evidence to support the hypothesis, with the aim of presenting a strong argument.	Seek evidence to refute hypotheses, rather than seeking evidence to support hypotheses.

Standard Methods

J Brandi and L Wilson-Wilde, National Institute of Forensic Science, ANZPAA, Melbourne, VIC, Australia

Glossary

ANZPAA Australia New Zealand Police Advisory Agency
ASCLD American Society of Crime Laboratory Directors
DIS Draft International Standard
DNA Deoxyribonucleic acid
ENFSI European Network of Forensic Science Institutes
EU European Union
FAD Field Application Document
IEC International Electrotechnical Commission

ISO International Organization for Standardization
NATA National Association of Testing Authorities
NIFS National Institute of Forensic Science
PAS Publicly Available Specification
SMANZFL Senior Managers of Australia and New Zealand Forensic Laboratories
UKAS United Kingdom Accreditation Service

Introduction

Forensic science has made a significant contribution to the investigation of crime and the administration of justice and is well established within these processes. Additionally, in recent years, popular media have substantially increased the profile of the field. Reliance on forensic science for the purposes of identification has also been highlighted globally by its application in the aftermath of mass disasters and terrorist acts, with forensic technologies being widely applied to the identification of victims and, in the case of terrorist attacks, identification of the perpetrators.

While the contribution that forensic science makes to reliable justice outcomes is undeniable, its application requires a thorough understanding of the discipline being applied and its potential pitfalls. Similar to any tool in the investigator's kit, without the requisite expertise and relevant support systems, forensic results may be misapplied or results misinterpreted.

In order to minimize the risk of errors, forensic facilities have developed a quality assurance program for all forensic processes. The relationship between the forensic process (the application of scientific methodology within a laboratory) and quality assurance processes (accreditation, certification, and standardization) is demonstrated in **Figure 1**.

Forensic laboratories seek accreditation from testing authorities to ensure compliance with national or international standards for laboratory practice. As part of this compliance, laboratories have documented practices and procedures (methods) that specify the conditions under which examinations shall be applied, conducted, interpreted, and reported.

These methods should be based on published peer-reviewed research and subject to in-house validation or verification.

Forensic practitioners themselves require some form of certification, either through authorization by their facility to carry out specific classes of examination and analysis

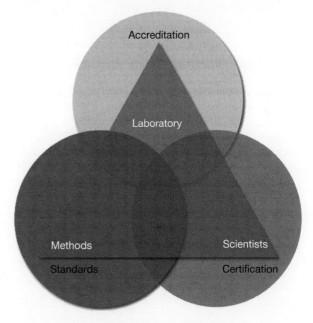

Figure 1 Relationships between the forensic process and quality assurance program, outlining the role of standards.

(the methods) or through qualified membership to a group or society. Certification schemes usually require ongoing assessment of the practitioners' performance within their areas of expertise.

Although each laboratory maintains a quality assurance program, variations in practices and procedures are not uncommon. In addition, in circumstances where a particular specialized expertise not available through an accredited forensic facility is required to assist in an investigation, investigators may seek the services of experts from other service providers such as a university, museum, or private forensic service provider. Such services may fall outside the established quality controls that exist in forensic facilities, and therefore, may be unlikely to be covered by accreditation or certification. This may also result in variations in practice.

Such variations may impact on the results obtained from an examination, or the way a result is interpreted and reported to an investigator or a court of law. The ramifications of variations may be significant: a perpetrator may escape justice or an innocent person may be unjustly punished.

The increased exchange of forensic evidence and information between states and nations highlights the role of common standards for forensic service providers in order to avoid uncertainty regarding the way in which an item has been handled, the methods that have been used, and how the results have been interpreted. The use of standards ensures the continuing reliability and quality of forensic science at an international level.

Why Standards Are Required?

Unreliable justice outcomes damage public faith in the legal system and may also lead to legal challenges as to the accuracy of forensic evidence. In the following case studies, the focus is on cases involving DNA evidence; however, the implications of the cases with respect to the lack of national or international standards are more generally applicable to forensic science practice and procedures. A review of these cases illustrates that the failings have generally been the result of breakdowns in processes or procedures, and not of failures of the scientific technique.

Case Study 1

Over a 7-year period, millions of Euros and hundreds of thousands of police hours were spent searching for a female suspected serial killer in Europe. The suspect was linked through DNA matches between a series of 40 crime scenes in Germany, Austria, and France. The DNA was linked to the murder of a female church warden in 1993, the murder of a 22-year-old policewoman in 2007, and the execution-style killings of three Georgian car dealers. Suspicions regarding the possibility of contamination arose when the number and diversity of linked crimes increased. Many of the cases were solved, but no female suspect with a matching DNA profile could be located. The initial doubts were confirmed when the same DNA profile was found during an investigation into the identity of a burned body in France that was thought to belong to an asylum seeker who had disappeared in 2002. Using swabs (pooled together) of the missing man's collected fingerprints, the DNA was extracted to produce a profile that was found to match the female suspect's DNA profile from the linked cases. Investigators began to suspect that batches of cotton swabs had been contaminated with DNA from an unknown source during the manufacturing process. Further products have since been identified as having contaminations resulting from the manufacturing process. The supposedly uncontaminated sterile swabs are used by police forces in several European countries.

Case Study 2

In 2006, a 48-year-old woman fell unconscious in a nightclub in Melbourne (Australia). Although she had no memory of being sexually assaulted, there were concerns that she may have been drugged and assaulted. Vaginal swabs were collected from the alleged victim at a designated facility in a hospital. When analyzed at a forensic laboratory, a DNA match was reported that linked biological material on the alleged victim's sample to the reference DNA profile from an earlier incident involving a 19-year-old male (although this earlier incident was determined as no offense having occurred). Police investigating the matter became concerned that there was no supporting evidence to link the male suspect to the alleged victim and queried the laboratory about the possibility of cross-contamination between the two cases. The forensic facility discounted the possibility on the basis of the two samples being examined by different technicians, at different times, and in different areas of the laboratory, and of their being processed in different batches. At the trial, the young male was convicted of the sexual assault and sentenced to 6 years imprisonment. The case was appealed. The prosecution investigation, in preparation for the retrial, revealed that the DNA samples relating to the earlier case were collected approximately 28 h before the alleged victim's vaginal swabs were collected, and by the same doctor in the same examination room within the same designated facility. It was at this point that the high possibility of contamination of the alleged victim's vaginal swab was realized and a subsequent inquiry found that contamination at the point of sample collection in the hospital was the most likely explanation. When the matter came before the court in 2009, it was accepted that a miscarriage of justice had occurred and a verdict of not guilty was entered.

The cases above provide examples where compliance with national or international forensic standards could have a role in minimizing the avoidable waste of investigational resources and poor justice outcomes. While there may be variations in practices across jurisdictions based on the legal environment and technical application, the scientific basis for the methodologies and procedures that are utilized is universal. This universal approach should apply to the entire forensic process, from the identification and collection of items and samples, including packaging and sample integrity, through to analysis, interpretation of results, and reporting. This is where defined forensic standards can provide guidance in acceptable practice for scientists, and confidence in the expert opinions provided for the judicial process.

The United States National Academy of Sciences Report 2009

The report published by The National Academy of Sciences (NAS) in 2009, (under a direction from US Congress) *Strengthening Forensic Science in the United States: A Path Forward* (the "NAS Report"), highlighted problems that existed in the field of forensic science within the United States and called for the establishment of a National Institute of Forensic Science (NIFS) to develop forensic science standards to address the identified problems.

Although the NAS Report focused on the situation with respect to forensic science practice in the United States, it is obvious that the issues identified and recommendations provided apply globally and have implications for all forensic practitioners.

In particular, the NAS Report stated that operational principles and procedures for many forensic science disciplines were not standardized, either between or within jurisdictions. Furthermore, where protocols aimed at facilitating consensus are in place, such as Scientific Working Group standards, they are not intended to be enforceable. This is seen to pose a threat to the quality of forensic science practice, reinforcing the need for systematic changes, including establishing enforceable standards, to promote best practice, ensure consistent outcomes, and reliability of forensic science as a whole. Many disciplines have already taken steps to identify where improvements in their fields can be made.

The Purpose of Standards

Standards provide guidance and set out specifications and procedures that ensure that products, services, and systems are reliable and perform consistently to an expected level and that confidence can be placed on their outcomes. They are regularly reviewed to ensure that they keep pace with new technologies.

As voluntary consensus documents the application of standards is by choice unless their use is mandated by government or specified by a contract. Standards may also be applied by means of a voluntary industry code or by quasi-regulation such as a standard endorsed by government.

Standards are intended to be practical. While they may exceed the minimum expectations of performance or practice, they are not intended to be difficult to comply with, based as they are on sound scientific principles, the experience of practitioners, and the expectations of the end user.

Standards define the level of expectations for a quality service. In the case of forensic standards, the end users are usually law enforcement agencies and the justice system, but the outcome of any investigation or trial impacts on society, either as a whole or as individuals. Society has an expectation that services and products comply with national or international standards; forensic science laboratories should not be exempt from the same expectations.

Advantages of Recognized Forensic Standards

Forensic science standards provide the following benefits:

- consistency of practice within laboratories;
- consistency in procedures across laboratories and agencies;
- defined standards of reliability and quality for all forensic practitioners;
- standard practices that private practitioners, smaller agencies, and institutions will be able to refer to in order to ensure that their work meets the required standard for acceptance in a judicial setting; and
- judicial confidence in forensic science laboratory output.

Compliance to a platform of relevant standards for forensic science disciplines ensures that methodologies are robust, repeatable, and validated, and that training as well as experience across laboratories is consistent. This has a direct bearing on the quality of scientific evidence presented in the courts and reduces the risk of poor justice outcomes, such as exemplified in the case studies mentioned previously. Consistent and accepted forensic standards will benefit all users of the judicial system, including members of the public as well as investigators, legal practitioners, and forensic scientists.

Recognized standards facilitate professional mobility. This is a direct consequence of standards and standardization. Professional mobility has many advantages in times when a rapid response is required to scenes of major crime or disaster, which is beyond the means and capabilities of any one laboratory (e.g., multiagency responses to mass disasters or terrorist acts). Besides reducing resource requirements, this also enhances forensic capacity and capability, and the development of individuals and forensic disciplines.

The existence of forensic science standards benefits smaller specialized forensic service providers and individual practitioners who provide niche forensic services to the public and the judicial system. These service providers are often unable to meet the cost of external accreditation and are looking for guidance in developing procedures and protocols that would ensure legal acceptability and consumer confidence, within the constraints of their environment. Forensic science standards provide the guidance in developing practices and procedures that specialized service providers require.

Forensic science standards reduce the risk of miscarriage of justice and, therefore, have the potential for significant savings to society with respect to the costs of retrials or other litigious processes. Additionally, standards reduce the duplication of effort that occurs in establishing concurrent methodologies.

Global Standard Environment

International Standards

Accreditation helps establish trust in the validity of the basic analytic methods used in forensic laboratories by offering evidence that laboratory activities are performed in accordance with relevant standards and applicable guidelines. Most accredited forensic laboratories are assessed against ISO/IEC 17025 "General requirements for the competence of testing and calibration laboratories," published by the International Organization for Standardization (ISO). The objective of this Standard is to specify the general requirements for the competence of a laboratory to carry out tests and calibrations, including sampling, performed using standard, nonstandard, and laboratory-developed methods. Although specific in parts, the requirements of ISO/IEC 17025 are generally at an organizational level and specify laboratory management requirements, with an emphasis on policy and documentation. As such, ISO/IEC 17025 does not address the requirements for sampling and testing in a forensic laboratory that serves the justice system. To address this gap, some accreditation bodies have developed field application guides that provide specific guidance to forensic laboratories; however, the focus of such guides is on laboratory procedures rather than crime scene procedures. The International Laboratory Accreditation Cooperation (ILAC) is an international cooperation of accreditation bodies, which promotes and harmonizes laboratory and inspection accreditation practices. ILAC also publishes guidelines for forensic science laboratories in the application of ISO/IEC 17025.

In the absence of any specific standard covering the collection and examination of material for forensic purposes, the United Kingdom Accreditation Service (UKAS) is developing accreditation for the scene of crime investigation against the international standard ISO/IEC 17020—General criteria for the operation of various types of inspection bodies performing inspection. The use of ISO/IEC 17020 for forensic accreditation takes the relevant aspects of the Standard and applies it to crime scene investigations. However, although ISO/IEC 17020 may be generally applicable to crime scene examination, it is unlikely that it can be extended to forensic laboratories as it is aimed at criteria for inspection bodies in the examination of "materials, products, installations, plant, processes, work procedures, or services" to provide certification.

ISO/IEC DIS 27037: Information technology—Security techniques—Guidelines for identification, collection, acquisition, and preservation of digital evidence.

In 2008, the ISO/IEC Joint Technical Committee commenced the development of a standard for "Evidence Acquisition Procedure for Digital Forensics," which will provide detailed guidance on the acquisition of electronic evidence and subsequent maintenance of its integrity. It will define and describe the process of recognition and identification of the evidence, documentation of the crime scene, collection and preservation of the evidence, and the packaging and transportation of the evidence. The aim of the standard is to provide guidance to law enforcement and digital (computer) forensic scientists to maintain the integrity of electronic evidence required for extradition between law enforcement agencies across national borders. The standard will also provide guidance to private companies that have to preserve electronic evidence to assist criminal investigations by law enforcement agencies.

North America

In the United States, over 385 crime laboratories are accredited by the American Society of Crime Laboratory Directors/Laboratory Accreditation Board (ASCLD/LAB), including federal laboratories, state and local agency laboratories, as well as private laboratories. Since 2004, ASCLD/LAB has provided accreditation under the ASCLD/LAB-International Accreditation Program that is based on ISO/IEC 17025, supplemented by forensic specific requirements. Since 2009, all new applications for accreditation are assessed against ISO/IEC 17025 although approximately half of the accredited laboratories continue to be assessed against a legacy system.

ASCLD/LAB also accredits forensic facilities outside the United States, including facilities in Canada, Hong Kong, Malaysia, New Zealand, and Singapore.

ASTM International (formerly known as the American Society for Testing and Materials—ASTM) publishes a range of forensic standards. ASTM is currently harmonizing their standards with ISO. The ASTM approach to forensic standards (through the work of the Committee E-30) has produced widely recognized documents as guidelines for practice or specific forensic methods. As guidelines, ASTM standards do not necessarily hold the same authority as a standard and can be quite prescriptive regarding specific processes or application. In addition, numerous ASTM forensic standards include processes that are common to many forensic disciplines (such as exhibit collection, storage, analysis, and reporting results) and, therefore, the scope and procedures covered often overlap to a significant extent.

United Kingdom

The UKAS is the sole national accreditation body recognized by the UK government to assess, against internationally agreed standards, organizations that provide certification, testing, inspection, and calibration services. Forensic laboratories in the United Kingdom are accredited by UKAS against ISO/IEC 17025.

British Standards Institution, the National Standards Body of the United Kingdom, released a Publicly Available Specification (PAS) for forensic kits in 2012. PAS 377: Consumables used in the collection, preservation, and processing of material for forensic analysis—specification for performance, manufacturing, and forensic kit assembly.

The Forensic Science Regulator sets quality standards for forensic science used in the criminal justice system in England and Wales. The Regulator continues to publish quality guides for forensic science although the guides are not published as Standards and, therefore, do not hold the same authority.

Manual of Regulation Part One: Policy and Principles (published for consultation) sets out the high-level principles proposed by the regulator and the methods by which the regulator intends to set and monitor quality standards in the delivery of forensic science evidence to the criminal justice system.

Codes of Practice and Conduct for forensic science providers and practitioners in the Criminal Justice System: the code of practice and conduct is based on the good practice that accredited providers are already required to demonstrate under ISO/IEC 17025.

Developing a Quality Standard for Fingerprint Examination: This position paper sets out the initial views of the fingerprint quality standards specialist group, indicates that quality standards must be developed for fingerprint examination to address the known risk of human error in this cognitive discipline.

Europe

In 2009, in order to step up cooperation in combating terrorism and cross-border crime, the European Union adopted an Act under the EU Treaty on accreditation of forensic service providers carrying out laboratory activities to ensure that forensic service providers carrying out laboratory activities are accredited by a national accreditation body as complying with ISO/IEC 17025. This Act provides a legally binding instrument on the accreditation of all forensic service providers carrying out laboratory activities for the analysis of scientific evidence.

The European Network of Forensic Science Institutes (ENFSI) is recognized as an expert group in the field of forensic sciences, which aims to ensure the quality of forensic science throughout Europe and publishes best practice manuals and glossaries of forensic terms. ENFSI encourages laboratories to comply with best practice and international standards for quality and competence assurance.

Australia

The National Association of Testing Authorities (NATA) accredits all government laboratories against ISO/IEC 17025. To support ISO/IEC 17025, NATA developed a Field Application Document (FAD) for forensic science laboratories. The FAD provides guidance to forensic laboratories in the application of ISO/IEC 17025 but does not address the standardization of specific processes and procedures. Specific requirements, such as sample recognition and collection at a scene, appropriate sample packaging and labeling, transport of forensic samples, sample continuity, examination and interpretation of results, reporting evidence of fact or opinion evidence, are not specifically covered in either ISO/IEC 17025 or the FAD.

Owing to a number of inadequate justice outcomes that impacted negatively on the perception of the field of forensic science, the Senior Managers of Australia and New Zealand Forensic Laboratories (SMANZFL) recognized the need for a suite of agreed national forensic standards. SMANZFL, working with the Australia New Zealand policing Advisory Agency National Institute of Forensic Science (ANZPAA NIFS), developed a framework for forensic science standards via Standards Australia.

Standards Australia is recognized by the Australian Government as the peak nongovernment Standards body in Australia, develops internationally aligned standards, and is a participating member of ISO and IEC.

The Standards Australia Forensic Analysis Committee (CH-041) was established by Standards Australia in 2009. It comprises representatives from stakeholder organizations: law enforcement, forensic facilities, judicial representatives, ANZPAA NIFS representatives, educators, and testing facilities from around Australia.

The core forensic standards provide a comprehensive framework of forensic science standards that are applicable to the majority of forensic science disciplines:

- AS 5388.1 Forensic Analysis Part 1: Recognition, recording, recovery, transport, and storage of material;
- AS 5388.2 Forensic Analysis Part 2: Analysis and examination of material;
- AS 5388.3 Forensic Analysis Part 3: Interpretation; and
- AS 5388.4 Forensic Analysis Part 4: Reporting.

The core standards can then be supported by the development of discipline-specific forensic science standards in the future, referencing the core standards for the more universal aspects of forensic science practice such as collection of forensic

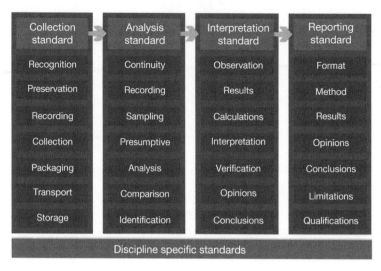

Collection standard	Analysis standard	Interpretation standard	Reporting standard
Recognition	Continuity	Observation	Format
Preservation	Recording	Results	Method
Recording	Sampling	Calculations	Results
Collection	Presumptive	Interpretation	Opinions
Packaging	Analysis	Verification	Conclusions
Transport	Comparison	Opinions	Limitations
Storage	Identification	Conclusions	Qualifications

Discipline specific standards

Figure 2   The "core" forensic standards cover the universal aspects of forensic science practice.

material, examination techniques, interpretation of analytical results, and reporting of findings (see **Figure 2**).

Challenges in Developing Standards

Standards are not designed to replace procedure documents, laboratory methods, or facility policies. Therefore, the challenge is to produce standards that are not prescriptive with respect to methodology but recognize the existing accepted practice and define the expectations of reliability and consistency of the results that are obtained and reported.

In the forensic environment, this can be achieved by defining:

- the requirements for protecting the integrity of forensic material from its recognition and collection, and through subsequent analysis stages;
- the appropriate recommended practices and procedures that may be applied to the examination and analysis of forensic material;
- the required performance parameters for analytical techniques;
- the way various analysis and examination results shall be interpreted; and
- the appropriate wording to use when reporting results, conclusions, and opinions.

By not specifying detailed analytical methodology or examination procedures, standards allow practitioners to determine the appropriate method to apply to a particular forensic process, according to the practice and procedure documents approved by their facility, while still fulfilling the requirements of a standard for reliability and consistency.

Agreed standards ensure robust, reliable, and consistent results and are an important part of the quality system globally. The development of forensic standards ensures the continuing reliability and quality of forensic science and the continued confidence of investigators and the courts.

Acknowledgment

The authors wish to acknowledge the assistance provided by Nancy Bakker, Marketing and Communications Officer, Australia New Zealand Policing Advisory Agency in creating the diagrams used in this chapter.

See also: **Legal:** DNA Exonerations; Legal Aspects of Forensic Science; The Innocence Project; When Science Changes, How Does Law Respond; **Management/Quality in Forensic Science:** Accreditation; Certification; Principles of Quality Assurance; Risk Management.

Further Reading

Acts Adopted under the EU Treaty, December 9, 2009. Council framework Decision 2009/905/JHA of 30 November 2009 on Accreditation of forensic service providers carrying out laboratory activities. Official Journal of the European Union L322 52, 14–15.

Fraser, J., Buckleton, J., Gill, P., 2010. Review of DNA Reporting Practices by Victoria Police Forensic Services Division. http://www.vicpolicenews.com.au/images/stories/news/feature_story/victoria%20police%20forensic%20services%20review%20%20report%20%20april%20202010.pdf.

Gill, P., Rowlands, D., Tully, G., Bastisch, I., Staples, T., Scott, P., 2010. Letter to the editor: manufacturer contamination of disposable plastic-ware and other reagents – an agreed position statement by ENFSI, SWGDAM and BSAG. Forensic Science International. Genetics 4, 269–270.

ISO/IEC 17020, 2000. General Criteria for the Operation of Various Types of Bodies Performing Inspection.

ISO/IEC 17025, 2005. General Requirements for the Competence of Testing and Calibration Laboratories.

Committee on Identifying the Needs of the Forensic Sciences Community, National Research Council, 2009. Strengthening Forensic Science in the United States: A Path Forward. The National Academies Press, Washington, DC.

Neuhuber, F., Dunkelmann, B., Höckner, G., Kiesslich, J., Klausriegler, E., Radacher, M., 2009. Female criminals – It's not always the offender! Forensic Science International Genetics 2 (1), 145–146.

Vincent, F.H.R., 2010. Inquiry into the Circumstances that Led to the Conviction of Mr Farah Abdulkadir Jama. Victorian Government Printer.

Relevant Websites

www.astm.org—ASTM International, formerly known as the American Society for Testing and Materials (ASTM).

www.bsigroup.com—British Standards Institution (BSI).

www.homeoffice.gov.uk—Forensic Science Regulator (FSR).

www.iso.org—International Organization for Standardization (ISO).

www.nata.com.au—National Association of Testing Authorities (NATA).

www.nifs.com.au—National Institute of Forensic Science (NIFS).

www.standards.org.au—Standards Australia.

Measurement Uncertainty

T Vosk, Criminal Defense Law Firm, Kirkland, WA, USA

Glossary

Bias The quantitative characterization of systematic error.

Combined uncertainty The standard uncertainty associated with the final measurement result determined by "adding" up the standard uncertainties associated with each of the individual sources of uncertainty.

Coverage factor A positive, real number that when multiplied by a measurement's combined uncertainty yields the expanded uncertainty. The coverage factor determines the level of confidence associated with a coverage interval.

Coverage interval An interval about the best estimate of a measurand's "true" value that will contain those values believed to be attributable to the measurand with a specified level of confidence.

Expended uncertainty Measure of uncertainty obtained by multiplying a measurement's combined uncertainty by a coverage factor. It defines the half width of a coverage interval.

Level of confidence The probability, defined as a degree of belief, that the "true" value of a measurand lies within the range defined by a coverage interval.

Measurand The quantity whose value is sought to be determined by a measurement.

Measurement function A function that describes the relationship between the measurand value and those quantities required to determine it.

Quantity Physical properties subject to measurement, such as length, time, weight, and concentration.

Random error The inherent unpredictable fluctuation in measured values under fixed conditions.

Sensitivity coefficients The partial derivatives of a measurement function that describe how the measurand's value varies with changes in the values of the input quantities.

Standard uncertainty Measurement uncertainty expressed as the standard deviation of a frequency- or belief-based probability distribution.

Systematic error The tendency of a set of measurements to consistently (on average) underestimate or overestimate the "true" value of a measurand by a given value or percentage.

Uncertainty The quantitative characterization of the dispersion of values that, based on one's universe of information concerning a measurement, are believed to be reasonably attributable to a measurand.

Nomenclature

b_{ias}	Bia
$\overline{\gamma}_c$	Bias corrected mean measured value
Y_b	Best estimate of "true" measurand value
μ_c	Combined uncertainty
k	Coverage factor
U	Expanded uncertainty
X	Input quantities
ε_m	Maximum total error
$\overline{\gamma}$	Mean measured value
$f(X_1,X_2,...,X_N)$	Measurement function
ε	Measurement error
γ	Measured value
$Y_{99\%}$	Measurand value with 99% level of confidence
ε_{ran}	Random error
μ_r	Relative standard uncertainty
$\partial f/\partial x_i$	Sensitivity coefficients
σ	Standard deviation
μ	Standard uncertainty
ε_{sys}	Systematic error
Y	"True" measurand value
$\boxplus$	Unspecified method for combining ε_{sys} and ε_{ran}

Measurement

Measurement constitutes a specific category of scientific investigation. It is an empirical process whereby a researcher seeks to determine the numerical magnitude attributable to some physical/phenomenological quantity of interest referred to as the "measurand." Many naively consider measurement to be a mechanical process whereby the quantity of interest is sensed/probed by a measuring instrument yielding directly the value attributable to the measurand. This mechanical activity is simply one step in the overall measurement process, however. Alone, it does not tell us what we want to know about the value(s) attributable to a measurand. Rather than a passively mechanical process of probing and discovery, measurement is more completely understood as an empirically grounded, information-based inference requiring active input from the researcher before any value can be attributed to a measurand. Measurement uncertainty identifies in an explicit, quantitatively rigorous manner the limitations governing the rational inferences that can be made concerning the value(s) attributable to a measurand based on the results of measurement.

Measurement to Meaning

Measurement Error and Error Analysis

What does a measurement result mean? In other words, given a measured value γ, what value(s) can actually be attributed to a measurand? Laypeople often interpret the value reported by a measurement as representing the singular "true" value attributable to a measurand (**Figure 1**):

$$Y = \gamma \qquad [1]$$

Science has long realized, however, that "error" is an inherent characteristic of measurement distinguishing

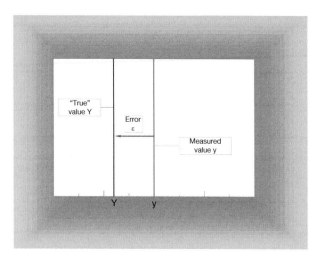

Figure 2   Measurement in reality inherent error.

measured values from the "true" quantity values sought to be determined (**Figure 2**).

Error analysis is the traditional approach to the interpretation of measurement results. It is based on the premise that if the error associated with a measurement can be determined then a measurand's "true" value can also be determined:

$$Y = \gamma - \varepsilon \qquad [2]$$

There are two types of errors associated with every measurement: random and systematic. Systematic error is the tendency of a method/instrument to yield values that are consistently (on average) artificially inflated or depressed with respect to the "true" values of the quantities being measured. It is quantitatively characterized as bias (**Figure 3**).

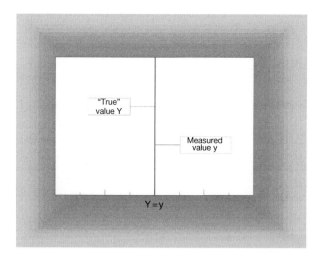

Figure 1   Measurement as singular "True" value.

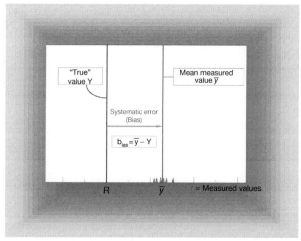

Figure 3   Systematic error and bias.

The identification of systematic error can be one of the most difficult aspects of the measurement process. The reason is that if one is measuring an unknown quantity, the measured values themselves provide no basis for concluding that they are systematically offset from the measurand's "true" value. Thus, one can never know whether all systematic errors associated with a measurement have been identified. Some sources of systematic error can be identified and quantified through measurement of reference materials. Even when rigorously determined in this manner, however, the magnitude of the bias can never be exactly known.

Random error is the unpredictable/random fluctuation in measured values under fixed conditions. It introduces inherent variability into the measurement process placing a fundamental limitation on the repeatability of measured results. For many common situations, the random variation in a measurement's results can be approximately characterized by a Gaussian (normal) distribution (**Figure 4**).

Random error is quantitatively characterized by a set of measurement's standard deviation:

$$\sigma_\gamma = \sqrt{\frac{\sum_{i=1}^n (\gamma_i - \overline{\gamma})^2}{n-1}} \qquad [3]$$

The standard deviation provides a measure of the variability of individually measured values about their mean. If there is significant variability, the standard deviation will be large. If variability is slight, the standard deviation will be small.

Systematic and random errors describe aspects of the *physical state of a measurement*. It is not always clear whether an error should be categorized as systematic or random, and the determination may be context dependent. Taken together, they constitute what is formally known as "measurement error" (**Figure 5**).

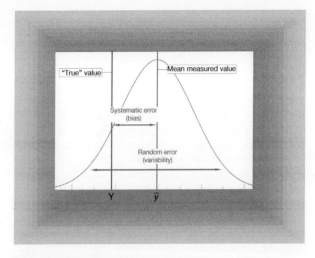

Figure 5 Measurement error.

The total error associated with a measurement can never be absolutely determined, that is, it is unknowable. As a result, error analysis can never supply a measurand's "true" value. Instead, the goal of error analysis is to identify, minimize, and eliminate *as best as possible* all identifiable sources of error so as to provide an estimate of a measurand's value that is *as close as possible* to its "true" value (**Figure 6**).

This requires some method for combining systematic and random components of error to obtain a characterization of a measurement's total error:

$$\varepsilon = \varepsilon_{sys} \boxplus \varepsilon_{ran} \qquad [4]$$

To understand where this leads, one must have an idea of the mathematical underpinnings of error analysis. Error

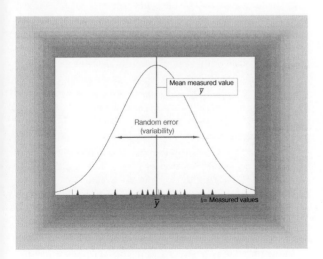

Figure 4 Random error and variability.

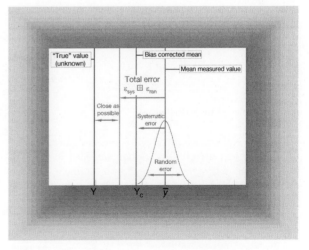

Figure 6 Error analysis estimate as close as possible.

analysis is ground in frequentist statistical theory. Frequentist theory defines probability in terms of relative frequency of occurrence. This means that the probability that a particular condition will be found to exist is determined by how frequently it occurs within the universe of all possible events. Although these probabilities can seldom be known because the universe of all possible events can seldom be completely known, they can be "objectively" estimated as the relative frequency of occurrence over sample data sets. What is critical is that in error analysis, the estimation of probabilities is "objectively" based solely on statistical sampling according to the frequentist paradigm.

The analysis of random error fits well within the frequentist paradigm. On the other hand, except in limited circumstances, the evaluation of systematic error does not. Because systematic and random errors are different in nature, each requires distinct treatment. There is no rigorously justifiable manner within the frequentist paradigm by which systematic and random errors can be combined to yield a statistically meaningful estimate of a measurement's total error.

Due to the frequentist underpinnings of error analysis, the best it can provide is an upper limit on a measurement's total error. This bounded error is often expressed as some linear combination of the bias and standard deviation associated with a measurement:

$$\varepsilon_m = b_{ias} + 3\sigma \qquad [5]$$

This places a bound on the maximum separation expected between a measured and "true" value. It does not, however, denote how close together the two values are *actually* expected to lie. In other words, it tells us the worst a measurement result could be without any indication of how good it actually is. Moreover, the meaning of this bounded error is vague, as it fails to tell us how probable it is that a measured value lies within the prescribed range of the measurand's "true" value. Given a measured value y, the best error analysis provides is an incompletely defined estimate of the maximum separation between a measured value and a "true" value. It cannot tell us the values that are likely to be attributable to the measurand given a particular measured value.

The Meaning of Meaning

A significant epistemological question surrounds any scientific proposition: Is a scientific proposition intended to describe some physical state of the universe itself or simply to describe our state of knowledge about such a physical state? If it is the former, the direct object of the proposition is an external fully independent reality. If it is the latter, the direct object of the proposition is an internal cognitive position that is information-dependent. Many claim that if scientific propositions are to be objectively meaningful, they must fall into the first

category. Others counter that regardless of the objective content of scientific propositions, they necessarily reside in the second category as all we can ever actually claim to know is our internal cognitive state, not some independent external reality.

Although seemingly esoteric, the position adopted can have practical implications. It may change not only the interpretation of scientific statements but also the manner in which they can be investigated. And so it is with scientific measurement. When a measurement result is reported, is it to be interpreted as a statement about the physical state of a measurand? Or, is it simply an expression of our state of knowledge about the measurand's physical state? And what are the practical implications of the choice made?

Measurement error is an aspect of the *physical state* of a measurement. It is related to a measurand through error analysis that purports to convey the bounds of its actual *physical state* through the determination of a bounded error. Where a precise estimate of a measurand's actual value is not critical, the bounded error may provide a result with sufficient meaning to be useful. Where a measurand's actual value is important, however, this level of meaning may be inadequate. If possible, one would like to understand the meaning of a measured value in terms of how it maps into those values that are *likely* to be attributable to the measurand.

Measurement Uncertainty

The New Paradigm

Measurement uncertainty addresses the shortcomings of error analysis by fundamentally redefining the way measurement is interpreted and providing a quantitative metric for mapping measured values into those believed to be reasonably attributable to a measurand. In this new paradigm, error is replaced as the focus of analysis by a new entity: uncertainty. This is not a matter of mere semantics. Uncertainty and error are completely distinct concepts. While measurement error concerns the actual *physical state of* a measurand, measurement uncertainty relates to the *state of knowledge about* the measurand.

This does not mean that those phenomena formerly understood as systematic and random errors are ignored. To the contrary, they are fully encompassed within the uncertainty framework. What they represent, however, has been reconceptualized to overcome the limitations inherent in frequentist philosophy. Central to the uncertainty paradigm is the alternative Bayesian notion of probability as a degree of belief. That is, probability is defined by how strongly one believes a given proposition. This formulation permits consideration of information about a measurand beyond that cognizable in frequentist theory and provides a common basis for its analysis whether statistically or nonstatistically based.

In the uncertainty paradigm, as in error analysis, a measurand's "true" value is unknowable. However, this is not due to the physical phenomenon of irreducible error, but due to the impossibility of our ever possessing perfect knowledge concerning a measurand's state. Uncertainty focuses on this limitation interpreting a measurement result as a probability distribution that characterizes one's state of knowledge about a measurand's value. While measurement error as a physical phenomenon is as unknowable as a measurand's "true" value, the characterization of a result as a probability distribution in this manner permits a result's uncertainty to be rigorously determined.

When a measurement is performed, it always takes place against a backdrop of existing information about the measurement to be made and the measurand itself. Some of this information may be in the form of statistically obtained data, while some may be based on other sources such as general knowledge of the behavior and properties of relevant materials, methods, and instruments. When a measurement is performed, the discrete value obtained adds to our universe of information and updates our state of knowledge concerning the measurand. Because our information is necessarily incomplete, our knowledge concerning the measurand remains fuzzy. Given the information possessed, the discrete value obtained represents a packet of values dispersed about the measured result, all of which are believed to be attributable to the measurand with relative degrees of conviction (**Figure 7**).

It is the identification of probabilities as degrees of belief that transforms this packet of values into a probability distribution. In this context, the meaning of a measured value corresponds to a probability distribution characterizing the relative likelihood of the values believed to be attributable to a measurand based on the totality of currently available information (**Figure 8**).

This distribution completely specifies our state of knowledge concerning the values attributable to a measurand.

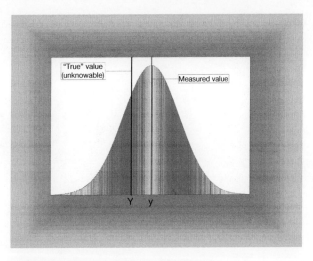

Figure 8 Measurement as probability distribution.

Moreover, it delineates in a mathematically rigorous manner how a measured value, y, maps into those values believed to be attributable to a measurand. By doing so, it also determines the inferences that can be made concerning a measurand's value based on the values measured.

As an example, given a measured value, the distribution permits one to determine the probability that a measurand's value lies within any given range of values. In this context, one can think of the probability associated with the distribution as being equal to the area under the curve representing it. The probability that a measurand's value lies within a specified range is given by the proportion of the area under the curve spanning the range in question to the total area under the curve (**Figure 9**).

Given a measured value, y, the question of what values can *reasonably* be attributed to a measurand involves two competing considerations. First, we want to exclude values that, although possible, are highly improbable. Second, we need to include enough values so that there is a significant probability that the measurand's value is actually among those considered. The measurement's probability distribution provides a conceptually straightforward way of accomplishing this. Simply slice off the tails of the distribution while including enough of its

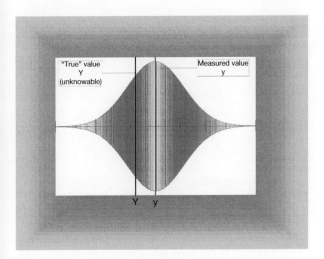

Figure 7 Measurement as packet of values.

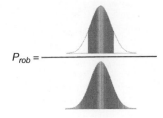

$$P_{rob} = $$

Figure 9 Probability = ratio of areas under curve.

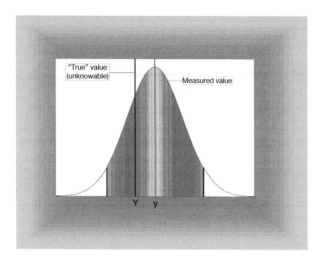

Figure 10 Values reasonably attributable to measurand.

middle so that the area of the remaining region represents a significant probability that the measurand's value lies within it (**Figure 10**).

From this, we can obtain a range of values reasonably attributable to a measurand, along with an associated probability that the value of the measurand lies within it. This defines the uncertainty of a measurement. Measurement uncertainty is the quantitative characterization of the dispersion of values that, based on the universe of information concerning a measurement, are believed to be *reasonably* attributable to a measurand. The half-width of this range of values is known as a result's expanded uncertainty, U (**Figure 11**).

The expanded uncertainty defines what is known as a "coverage interval" about a measured value. The coverage interval conveys the set of quantity values reasonably attributed to the measurand along with the specific probability that its "true" value actually lies within this range. The probability is referred to as the interval's associated "level of confidence." Coverage intervals having an associated level of confidence between 95% and 99.7% are typically selected (**Figure 12**):

$$\text{Coverge intervel}$$
$$\gamma - U < Y_{99\%} < \gamma + U \qquad [6]$$

Coverage Interval versus Confidence Interval

Coverage intervals and confidence intervals are distinct tools and should not be confused. A coverage interval is a metrological concept based on Bayesian analysis. In this framework, parameters of interest can be treated as random variables so that they can be the subject of probabilistic statements without logical inconsistency. The level of confidence associated with a coverage interval refers to the probability, understood as a degree of belief, that a measurand's value lies within the interval.

A confidence interval is a statistical concept based on frequentist methodology. In this framework, the stochastic nature of the investigation lies entirely in the sampling process, not the parameter value. Accordingly, the level of confidence associated with a confidence interval does not associate a probability with the measurand value. Rather, its object is the interval itself. If one were to conduct multiple sets of measurements and generate a confidence interval for each set, the level of confidence tells you the proportion of these intervals that would be expected to cover/overlap a measurand's value (**Figure 13**).

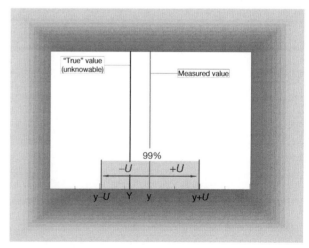

Figure 12 Coverage interval.

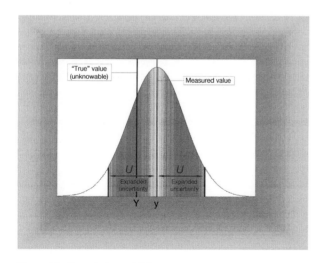

Figure 11 Expanded uncertainty.

There are two types of uncertainties: type A and type B. Unlike the two types of errors, type A and type B uncertainties are not distinguished by the nature of their source. Instead, they are defined by the manner in which they are determined. Type

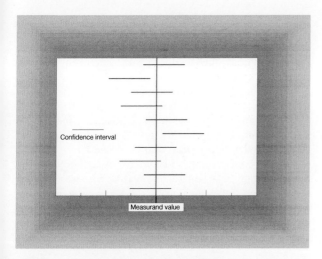

Figure 13 Interpretation of a confidence interval.

A uncertainty refers to the uncertainty that has been determined by statistical (frequentist) methods utilizing observed frequency distributions. Type B uncertainty refers to the uncertainty that has been determined by nonstatistical means relying on knowledge, experience, and judgment to create belief-based a priori distributions.

Type A evaluations are often referred to as "objective" and type B as "subjective." However, this does not mean that type B evaluations are any less real or valid than type A. Both evaluations rely on accepted notions of probability. Nor is one approach necessarily superior to the other. Whether type A or type B analysis yields better results is context dependent.

Regardless of the approach employed to determine them, a foundational tenant of this paradigm is that the uncertainties themselves do not differ in nature. Once determined, all distributions are interpreted in the Bayesian manner, representing models of our state of knowledge quantified according to degree of belief. This permits type A and type B uncertainties to be treated on equal footing as standard deviations of the distributions they are based on, providing rigorous justification for their combination into a "combined uncertainty" using traditional methods of analysis.

The importance of this lies in the fact that a measurement's uncertainty is usually made up of the combination of uncertainties from several distinct sources. To understand the significance, recall the inability of error analysis to combine systematic and random errors in a rigorously justifiable manner to determine a measurement's total error. To avoid confusion, in the context of uncertainty, systematic errors are referred to as "systematic effects." For pedagogical purposes, systematic effects were not included in the above discussion. Nonetheless, the determination of uncertainty assumes that every measurement has been corrected for significant systematic effects.

What the uncertainty paradigm permits us to do, regardless of the nature of a systematic effect or how it has been quantified, is to treat it as a probability distribution. When this is done, the distribution's expectation yields the required systematic correction (hereinafter referred to as bias) and its standard deviation characterizes the uncertainty associated with the bias. Treated in this manner, systematic effects and their associated uncertainties are placed on equal footing with measured values and their associated uncertainties, so that those phenomena formerly understood as systematic and random errors can now be combined in a logically consistent and rigorously justifiable manner. In general, the evaluation of the uncertainty arising from systematic effects may be either type A or type B.

Returning to the above discussion, it can now be seen that the uncertainty paradigm naturally incorporates systematic effects into the mapping of measured values to those believed to be attributable to a measurand (**Figure 14**).

The correction shifts the position of the probability distribution along the axis of values while the uncertainty associated with the correction will modify the shape of the distribution. As would be expected, this will shift the coverage interval in the direction of the correction as well.

Something that must be considered at this point is that given the inherent variability of measured values, it is seldom acceptable to base the determination of a measurand's value on a single measurement. Good practice requires acquisition of multiple measured values combined to determine their mean. The *best estimate* of a measurand's "true" value is then given by the *bias corrected mean* of the measured values:

$$\text{Best estimate} = \text{bias corrected mean}$$
$$Y_b = \overline{Y}_c \qquad [7]$$

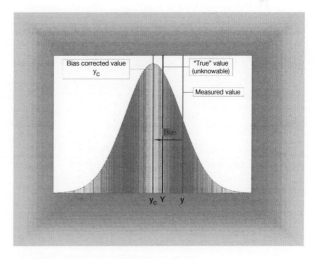

Figure 14 Mapping measurement to "reality."

It is a fundamental principle of measurement that where the actual value of a measurand is important, a result is not complete and cannot be properly interpreted unless it has been corrected for bias and is accompanied by a quantitative statement of its uncertainty. Accordingly, a complete measurement result consists of the best estimate of the measurand's "true" value accompanied by its uncertainty:

$$\text{Measurement result} = \text{best estimate} \pm \text{uncertainty}$$
$$Y_{99\%} = Y_b \pm U \qquad [8]$$

$$\text{Coverage interval}$$
$$Y_b - U < Y_{99\%} < Y_b + U \qquad [9]$$

Measurement Uncertainty: A Forensic Example

The value of a measurand can be critical to the determination of certain criminal matters. For example, some states define the offense of driving under the influence of alcohol (DUI) by an individual's "true" breath alcohol concentration (BrAC). The measurement of BrAC, like any other scientific measurement, is accompanied by uncertainty. Thus, by themselves, the values reported by a breath test machine tell us little about an individual's "true" BrAC and whether they have actually committed a crime. Consider tests administered to two different individuals on different instruments in a state where DUI is defined by a BrAC of 0.08 g/210 L (**Figures 15 and 16**).

Each test reports identical BrAC values in excess of the state's per se limit with a mean value of 0.0825 g/210 L. Without more, these "breath test tickets" clearly seem to indicate that the BrACs in question exceed the legal limit. Moreover, given that

Blank test	.000
Internal standard	Verified
Subject sample	.084
Blank test	.000
External standard	.082
Blank test	.000
Subject sample	.081
Blank test	.000

Figure 15   Identical measurement results different measurement meaning: Breath analysis.

Blank test	.000
Internal standard	Verified
Subject sample	.084
Blank test	.000
External standard	.079
Blank test	.000
Subject sample	.081
Blank test	.000

Figure 16   Breath analysis.

the external standard readings are both reading true, there is actually no way to distinguish between these two tests.

The two tests' uncertainties reveal a different picture though. Despite identically measured values, the uncertainty of each, expressed as coverage intervals, is different (**Figures 17 and 18**).

Clearly, the computed uncertainty associated with test 1 is greater than that associated with test 2. Moreover, further examination reveals that the likelihood that each individual's BrAC is actually less than 0.08 g/210 L is nearly 20% and 10% for tests 1 and 2, respectively (**Figures 19 and 20**).

Thus, not only do these "identical" tests not have identical meanings, but each represents a sizable likelihood in the context of reasonable doubt that the BrACs in question are less than the relevant limit. Proper interpretation of these results clearly requires knowledge of their uncertainty.

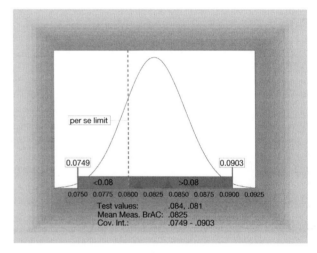

Figure 17   Breath alcohol concentration test 1.

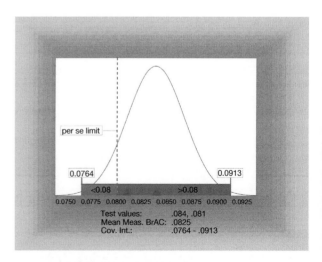

Figure 18   Breath alcohol concentration test 2.

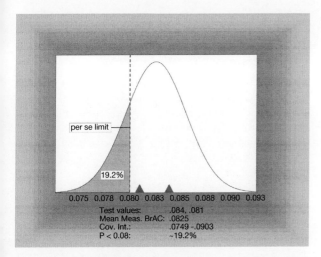

Figure 19 Breath alcohol concentration test 1.

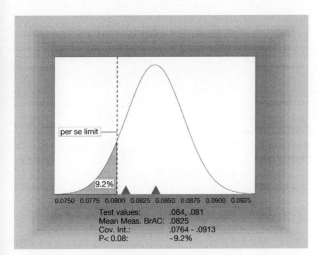

Figure 20 Breath alcohol concentration test 2.

Determining Measurement Uncertainty

There are several different methods for determining a measurement's uncertainty. The first step in each is to identify and quantify all systematic effects and appropriately correct for each.

The second step is typically the identification of relevant sources of uncertainty. A common way to document these is through a cause and effect diagram, which depicts each source of uncertainty and their relationship to each other and the final result (**Figure 21**).

When all the quantities on which a measured value depends can be varied simultaneously, a result's uncertainty can be determined, directly using statistical methods. Except for simple measurements, however, this approach is typically not practical.

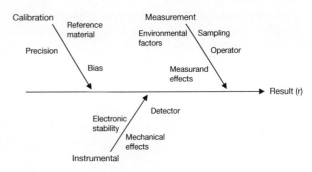

Figure 21 Cause and effect diagram.

Generally, then, the next step is to determine the magnitude of each of the relevant uncertainties. Each is quantified as a standard deviation and referred to as a "standard uncertainty":

$$\text{Standard uncertainty} \quad [10]$$
$$\mu \equiv \sigma$$

The relative standard uncertainty is the ratio of the standard uncertainty to the best estimate of the measurand value. It can be useful when combining or comparing uncertainties of separate measurements:

$$\text{Relative stsndard uncertainty} \quad [11]$$
$$\mu_{r_\gamma} = \frac{\mu_\gamma}{|Y_b|}$$

For some measurements, each source of uncertainty may be associated with the measurement as a whole and manifest itself independently as a direct effect on the final result. Such is the case with direct measurements. In these circumstances, a result's "combined uncertainty," μ_c, is given by the root sum square (rss) of the standard uncertainties:

$$\mu_c = \sqrt{\sum_{i=1}^{n} \mu_i^2} \quad [12]$$

Most measurements are indirect in nature, determining a measurand's value through its relationship to other measured quantities. The most common method of determining uncertainty in these circumstances is discussed in the *Guide to the Expression of Uncertainty in Measurement* (the *GUM*). Application of the *GUM* requires that a measurement be modeled as a mathematical function, referred to as the measurement function:

$$\text{Measurement funtion} \quad [13]$$
$$Y = f(X_1, X_2, \ldots, X_N)$$

This function describes the relationship between the measurand value and those quantities required to determine it. For example, if the measurand is the volume of a cylinder, the measurement function might be given as

$$V(r, h) = \pi r^2 h \quad [14]$$

The combined uncertainty of the measurand is determined by "adding" up the individual standard uncertainties using the method of *propagation of uncertainty*:

$$\mu_c = \sqrt{\sum_{i=1}^{N} \left(\frac{\partial f}{\partial x_i} \cdot \mu_{x_i} \right)^2 + 2 \sum_{i=1}^{N-1} \sum_{j=i+1}^{N} \frac{\partial f}{\partial x_i} \cdot \frac{\partial f}{\partial x_i} \cdot \mu_{x_i x_j}} \quad [15]$$

If each of the input quantities is independent, the expression simplifies to

$$\mu_c = \sqrt{\sum_{i=1}^{N} \left(\frac{\partial f}{\partial x_i} \cdot \mu_{x_i} \right)^2} \quad [16]$$

For the volume of a cylinder, the combined uncertainty would be given by the expression

$$\mu_{cv} = \sqrt{(2\pi r h \mu_r)^2 + (\pi r^2 \mu_h)^2} \quad [17]$$

Propagation of Uncertainty: Applied to Measurement Functions with Independent Input Quantities

1. Measurement function:

$$Y = a \cdot X \quad [18]$$

$$Y_b = a \cdot x_b \quad [19]$$

$$\mu_Y = a \cdot \mu_x \quad [20]$$

2. Measurement function:

$$Y = X^n \quad [21]$$

$$Y_b = x_b^n \quad [22]$$

$$\mu_{r_Y} = \frac{\mu_Y}{|Y_b|} = |n| = \frac{\mu_x}{|x_b|} \quad [23]$$

3. Measurement function:

$$Y = X - W + \cdots + Z \quad [24]$$

$$Y_b = x_b - w_b + \cdots + z_b \quad [25]$$

$$\mu_Y = \sqrt{\mu_x^2 + \mu_w^2 + \cdots + \mu_z^2} \quad [26]$$

4. Measurement function:

$$Y = \frac{X \times \cdots \times W}{Z \times \cdots \times Q} \quad [27]$$

$$Y_b = \frac{x_b \times \cdots \times w_b}{z_b \times \cdots \times q_b} \quad [28]$$

$$\mu_{r_Y} = \frac{\mu_Y}{|Y_b|}$$
$$= \sqrt{\left(\frac{\mu_x}{x_b} \right)^2 + \left(\frac{\mu_w}{w_b} \right)^2 + \cdots + \left(\frac{\mu_z}{z_b} \right)^2 + \left(\frac{\mu_q}{q_b} \right)^2} \quad [29]$$

The expanded uncertainty is obtained by multiplying the combined uncertainty by a coverage factor, k:

$$\text{Expanded uncertainty}$$
$$U = k_{\mu_c} \quad [30]$$

The coverage factor determines the coverage interval's level of confidence. It is commonly based on a t-distribution. Where a measurement's degrees of freedom are sufficiently large, the level of confidence bestowed by a given coverage factor is approximately that associated with a Gaussian distribution (**Figure 22**).

The coverage factor is typically chosen to yield a level of confidence of 95% or greater. For the volume of a cylinder, the expanded uncertainty yielding a 99% level of confidence would be given by the expression

$$U = 2.576 \sqrt{(2\pi r h \mu_r)^2 + (\pi r^2 \mu_h)^2} \quad [31]$$

For the GUM to apply, the distribution characterizing a final result must not depart appreciably from normality. Where this is not the case, or where a measurement function is complicated or unknown, a more general approach to the determination of uncertainty is based on the *propagation of distributions*. Instead of determining the standard uncertainty of each input quantity and combining them, the distributions characterizing the quantity value of each input quantity are directly combined to construct the distribution characterizing our state of knowledge of the measurand's value (**Figure 23**).

The standard deviation of the final distribution yields a result's standard uncertainty. It should be noted that the resultant distribution and, hence, its uncertainty (coverage interval) need not be symmetric about the mean. The Monte Carlo method, a computer-based iterative simulation process, is an example of this approach.

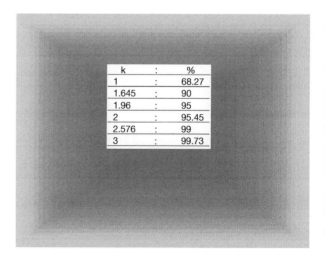

k	:	%
1	:	68.27
1.645	:	90
1.96	:	95
2	:	95.45
2.576	:	99
3	:	99.73

Figure 22 Coverage factors and levels of confidence: Gaussian distribution.

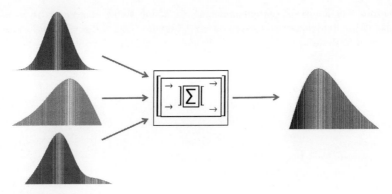

Figure 23 Propagation of distributions.

A final approach to the determination of uncertainty is the top-down method, so-called because it focuses on the measurement process as a whole instead of its detailed breakdown into distinct sources of uncertainty. It utilizes overall reproducibility estimates, based on measurement trials, as a direct estimate of the uncertainty associated with a measurement method. This approach is often utilized where a measurement function is complicated or unknown. Although each has its advantages, in certain circumstances, the *GUM* and top-down approaches can be used together to determine the uncertainty of a measurement where desirable.

Meaning Requires Uncertainty

Scientific measurement provides a powerful tool for investigating physical phenomena. No matter how good a measurement is, we can never know the "true" value of the quantity of interest. Error analysis focuses on the measurand itself, with the intent of providing a value that is as close as possible to its "true" value. What it actually provides is an ill-defined upper limit on a measurement's total error, revealing the worst a measured value might be without conveying how good it actually is. Uncertainty analysis focuses on our state of knowledge about a measurand, providing a quantitative mapping of measured values into those values believed to be actually and reasonably attributable to the quantity of interest. This conveys the meaning of a result by rigorously defining and constraining the inferences that can be drawn from it. Accordingly, where the actual value of a measurand is important, a result is not complete and cannot be properly interpreted unless it is accompanied by a quantitative statement of its uncertainty.

See also: **Foundations:** Statistical Interpretation of Evidence: Bayesian Analysis; The Frequentist Approach to Forensic Evidence Interpretation; **Legal:** Legal Aspects of Forensic Science; **Methods:** Chemometrics; **Toxicology:** Interpretation of Results; **Toxicology/Alcohol:** Breath Alcohol.

Further Reading

Ehrlich, C., Dybkaer, R., Wöger, W., 2007. Evolution of philosophy and description of measurement. Accreditation and Quality Assurance 12, 201–218.

Estler, W.T., 1999. Measurement as inference: fundamental ideas. CIRP Annals 48 (2), 611–631.

EURACHEM, 2000. Quantifying Uncertainty in Analytical Measurement. QUAM:2000.1.

EURACHEM, 2007. Measurement Uncertainty Arising from Sampling: A Guide to Methods and Approaches.

ISO, 2004. Guidance for the Use of Repeatability, Reproducibility and Trueness Estimates in Measurement Uncertainty Estimation. ISO/TS 21748.

JCGM, 2008. Evaluation of measurement data – guide to the expression of uncertainty in measurement (GUM). JCGM 100, 2008.

JCGM, 2008. Evaluation of measurement data – Supplement 1 to the 'guide to the expression of uncertainty in measurement' – propagation of distributions using a Monte Carlo method. JCGM 101, 2008.

JCGM, 2008. International vocabulary of metrology – basic and general concepts and associated terms (VIM). JCGM 200, 2008.

JCGM, 2009. Evaluation of measurement data – an introduction to the 'guide to the expression of uncertainty in measurement' and related documents. JCGM 104, 2009.

Kacker, R., Sommer, K., Kessel, R., 2007. Evolution of modern approaches to express uncertainty in measurement. Metrologia 44, 513–529.

Kirkup, L., Frenkel, B., 2006. An Introduction to Uncertainty in Measurement: Using the GUM (Guide to the Expression of Uncertainty in Measurement). Cambridge University Press, New York.

NIST, 1994. Guidelines for Evaluating and Expressing the Uncertainty of NIST Measurement Results. NIST 1297.

Vosk, T., 2010. Trial by numbers: uncertainty in the quest for truth and justice. NACDL Champion 56, 48–56 (reprinted with permission in The Voice for the Defense 40 (3), 24–33(2011)).

Key Terms

Accreditation, Analysis, Bayes' factor, Bayes' rule, Bayesian, Bayesian inference, Bias, Categorical data, Code, Cognitive bias, Confidence intervals, Consensus, Continuous data, Coverage interval, Crime analysis, Crime investigation, Crime scene, Criminal analysis, Criminal intelligence analysis, Decision making, Degree of belief, Evidence evaluation, Examination, Fallacy, Forensic analysis, Forensic intelligence, Frequentist inference, Frequentist, Guideline, GUM, Handbook, Hypothesis testing, Intelligence analysis, Intelligence-led policing, Interpretation, Likelihood ratio, Measurement, Measurement error, Mental models, Method, National security, Posterior probability, Practice, Prior probability, Probability distribution, Probability theory, Probability, Procedure, Propagation of distributions, Propagation of uncertainty, Quality, Random error, Range tests, Serial crime, Sign, Specification, Standard, Structured analytic techniques, Subjective probability, Systematic error, Trace, Type A uncertainty, Type B uncertainty, Uncertainty.

Review Questions

1. What is "frequentist inference"?
2. What is a range test? How is it used? What is "the cliff problem"?
3. What is the empirical rule? When is it used? When can it **not** be used?
4. When does the value of α (alpha) vary? How is this determined?
5. What is the null hypothesis? What is the alternate hypothesis?
6. What can be said if the P-value is low? What cannot be said? Why?
7. What are some of the problems using the two-sample T test? If Hotelling's T^2 avoids these issues, why is not it used more often in forensic science?
8. What is U? What part does it play in confidence intervals?
9. What is Bayes' rule? What is based upon?
10. If Bayes' rule is based on "subjective—in the sense of 'personal'—expression of degrees of belief held by an individual," is it appropriate for use in science? Why or why not?
11. What are likelihood ratios? How do they differ from Bayes' rule?
12. If background population frequencies are not known, can likelihood ratios still be used?
13. What are prior odds? What are posterior odds?
14. What is the "prosecutor's fallacy"? What is the "defender's fallacy"? How do these relate to the work of a forensic scientist?
15. What is forensic intelligence? What role can forensic anthropology play in it?
16. What is a measurand? Give three examples in forensic anthropology.
17. What is cluster analysis? What does it do?
18. What is principle component analysis? How is it visually represented?
19. How does discriminate analysis work? Does it work in conjunction with principle component analysis? Why or why not?
20. What is measurement uncertainty? What are the types of uncertainty? How are they different than "errors"?

Discussion Questions

1. Forensic anthropology depends upon measurements and statistics. This provides it with a seemingly objective scientific perspective. Yet bias does have an effect on analyses and results (see Nakhaeizadeh and coauthors articles in Additional Readings). How could forensic anthropology continue with its proven methods but avoid bias?
2. How would you explain the frequentist approach to a jury? How would you explain the bayesian approach to the same jury? What about regression analysis?
3. Which approach is best for forensic anthropology: frequentist or bayesian? Why? How are they different?
4. Assume you examine a skeleton but have no tools or instruments for measurement. What could you say about the remains? How certain would you be? How would you convey your certainty to a jury? To another anthropologist?
5. What does "error" mean to laypeople? What does it mean in statistics? What does it mean in forensic science? How can you reconcile these definitions?

Additional Readings

Christensen, A.M., Crowder, C.M., Ousley, S.D., Houck, M.M., 2014. Error and its meaning in forensic science. Journal of Forensic Sciences 59 (1), 123–126.

Ferrante, L., Skrami, E., Gesuita, R., Cameriere, R., 2015. Bayesian calibration for forensic age estimation. Statistics in Medicine 34 (10), 1779–1790.

Found, B., 2015. Deciphering the human condition: the rise of cognitive forensics. Australian Journal of Forensic Sciences 47 (4), 386–401.

MacLean, C.L., Dror, I.E., 2016. A Primer on the Psychology of Cognitive Bias. Blinding as a Solution to Bias: Strengthening Biomedical Science, Forensic Science, and Law, p. 13.

Nakhaeizadeh, S., Hanson, I., Dozzi, N., 2014. The power of contextual effects in forensic anthropology: a study of bias ability in the visual interpretations of trauma analysis on skeletal remains. Journal of Forensic Sciences 59 (5), 1177–1183.

Nakhaeizadeh, S., Dror, I.E., Morgan, R.M., 2015. Emergence of cognitive bias in forensic science and criminal investigations. The British Journal of American Legal Studies 4, 527.

Shirley, N.R., Ramirez Montes, P.A., 2015. Age estimation in forensic anthropology: quantification of observer error in phase versus component-based methods. Journal of Forensic Sciences 60 (1), 107–111.

Section 8. Professional Topics

Few forensic anthropologists work full time in laboratories or even in groups of more than one or two professionals. Nevertheless, they face the same professional issues as any other forensic scientist, more so because of their intersection with human bodies and native peoples: Finding a skeleton does not mean it is a recent case and many archaeological finds start out as forensic (and vice versa). Testifying in court can be daunting if it is not done frequently; like any other skill, practice makes "perfect." Forensic anthropologists tend not to testify that often but when they do, their evidence tends to be central to the case and of utmost significance. Along with forensic pathologists, forensic anthropologists face more health and safety issues than the average forensic scientist because of their close contact with biological materials and decomposed remains.

Crime Scene to Court

K Ramsey and E Burton, Greater Manchester Police Forensic Services Branch, Manchester, UK

Glossary

CBRN Chemical, biological, radiation, and nuclear incidents.

CCTV Closed circuit television (cameras or evidence from).

CPD Continuous professional development.

CPS Crown Prosecution Service (UK).

HTCU Hi-tech crime unit (examination of hardware/software/data/images from any system or device).

L2 Level 2 investigations, specific skills required for, e.g., covert operations, deployment and substitution of items, and forensic markers.

LCH Local Clearing House (firearms).

NaBIS National Ballistic Intelligence Service (UK).

NCA National Crime Agency (UK).

NOS National occupational standards.

T1/2/3 CSI Skill tiers defined for crime scene investigation officers, with 1 being the most basic level of training (usually volume crime offenses only), 2 being the range of volume, serious and major crime investigations, and 3 being trained in crime scene management/the coordination of complex investigations.

VSC/ESDA Video spectral comparison—the analysis of inks, primarily in fraudulent documents; electro static detection analysis—the examination of (writing) indentations on paper.

Introduction

A multitude of disciplines evolved within forensic science during the twentieth century, resulting in highly specialized fields of evidential opportunities to support criminal investigations. Many of the more traditional disciplines, for example, footwear analysis and blood pattern interpretation, now have well-established principles and methodologies that have been proven in a criminal justice context; developments in these areas are largely confined to technical support systems and information sharing through databases. The very rapid rate of development of DNA profiling techniques during the 1980s and 1990s led to the emergence of national and international DNA databases; however, the pace of change has now significantly reduced. Conversely, the end of the twentieth century and the early part of the twenty-first century have seen an explosion of new forensic evidence types that are less established in court—disciplines such as CCTV, mobile phone, computer analysis, and the use of digital images and social media are collectively referred to as e-forensics.

Owing to the highly specialized nature of each forensic discipline and the varied rate of evolution, forensic science effectively represents a composite of interrelated, and often distinct, opportunities to support criminal investigations.

Most current models of forensic service delivery, especially where part of a wider organization, for example, police forces and enforcement agencies, have arisen over time by bolting on additional elements and clustering together within related fields. If the current capability of forensic science were to be designed from scratch as an effective entity, it is certain that a more integrated, and hence effective, structure would be proposed.

In addition, there has been a professionalization of forensic science in the workplace and increasing requirements for regulation; as recently as the 1980s, crime scene investigation, for example, was widely undertaken by police officers and was largely restricted to recording/recovering visible evidence; this was used in a limited capacity to support that particular investigation without scope for wider intelligence development. Now, crime scene investigation is predominantly undertaken by specialist staff employed to exclusively undertake these duties.

To practice in a forensic discipline, specialized training, qualifications, and competency levels are required. The range of evidence types that have potential to support investigations has widened considerably. Some disciplines lend themselves to cross-skilling.

Public expectations of what forensic science can deliver have been heightened by highly popular mainstream television programs, both documentary and fictional. Often, the expectation of what can be delivered exceeds what is either possible or financially sensible. This leads to a requirement on service providers and users to make informed (evidential and financial) decisions regarding the best use of forensic evidence in support of investigations.

This article considers options to optimize the use of forensic evidence types recovered from crime scenes in the context of the different models available to criminal justice systems; the concept of integrated case management is outlined and discussed.

Task

To bring together all potential forensic evidential opportunities, holistically review their significance to the investigation, prioritize the progression of work, deliver the best evidence to the court for testing (complying with all continuity, integrity, and quality requirements), and ensure the best value for money when determining spend on forensic evidence.

Internationally, there are variable constraints and opportunities due both to the different criminal justice models and the commercial market situation at state/regional and country levels.

Models

1. All forensic evidence sourced within a law enforcement agency, for example, a police laboratory.
2. All forensic evidence provided by external specialists contracted to a law enforcement agency.
3. Composite of (1) and (2).

Forensic Strategies

The recovery of evidence from the crime scene is only the start of the forensic process. Once the evidence has been collected, packaged, and preserved, it needs to be analyzed in order to provide meaningful information to the investigation and subsequently the courts.

Forensic examinations are carried out in order to implicate or eliminate individuals and also in order to establish what has occurred during the commission of an offense or incident.

Deciding what analysis is required can be a complex process. Some of the issues for consideration include the following:

● Is it necessary to examine all the evidence that is recovered?
● Should every possible test be carried out?

In an ideal world, it would be preferable to carry out every possible analysis; however, in reality, it is likely that this will be neither practicable nor financially viable. In addition, carrying out every possible analysis would overload forensic laboratories.

When making decisions about what forensic analysis should be carried out, it is vitally important that consideration is given to both the potential prosecution and defense cases. An impartial approach must be taken to assessing examination requirements. It is often not necessary to carry out an examination of every item of evidence recovered, but examinations should be directed to where value could potentially be added to an investigation.

A forensic strategy should be developed around every case where forensic evidence plays a part and may relate to an overall case or to an individual item of evidence. A forensic strategy should be developed in a holistic manner taking into account all potential evidence types and should direct and coordinate the forensic examinations/analyses that are required.

Forensic strategies can be developed in different ways by one or more of the following:

● Investigating officer
● Crime scene investigator (CSI) or crime scene manager
● Forensic scientist/forensic specialist
● Forensic submissions officer (forensic submissions officer is a role that can be variably named; this role relates to an informed individual within a police force or law

enforcement agency who uses knowledge and expertise to advise on forensic analysis and who has decision-making authority and control of the budgetary spend; may also be known as forensic advisor, scientific support manager, etc.)

- Legal representative
- Pathologist

Forensic strategies are generally initially developed and applied by individuals involved in the prosecution aspects of a crime. Although this is the case, it is vitally important that a balanced and unbiased approach is taken to the development of a strategy and consideration given to information that may support the defense case as well as the prosecution case. Examinations that are likely to add value or provide information to an investigation (irrespective of whether it will support or weaken the prosecution case) should be carried out and all results must be disclosed to the defense team. Defense should also be given the opportunity to carry out any review of strategies, examination processes, and/or results that they require and be provided with access to any items of evidence that they want to examine themselves in order to build the defense case.

In order to develop the forensic strategy and make appropriate decisions about which forensic examinations will be of value to the investigation, the following are necessary:

- To be able to gather as much information as possible about the circumstances of the case
  - ○ circumstances of evidence recovery
  - ○ accounts given by victim(s), witnesses, suspect(s), etc.
- To have an understanding and knowledge of forensic science and its application to investigations

A forensic strategy meeting is a useful way of ensuring that all relevant parties are aware of the full circumstances of the case and enables a "multiagency" discussion about the processing of all exhibits to optimize evidential potential in a comprehensive and coordinated manner.

It can often be the case that police officers do not have a full understanding or knowledge of forensic science, likewise forensic scientists historically have had a relatively poor understanding of police and investigative processes; this can lead to miscommunication and confusion in relation to the application of forensic science to meet investigative needs. A joint approach to the development of forensic strategies helps to improve the communication and understanding on a case-by-case basis.

A formal forensic strategy meeting is often required only in more serious cases; however, the general approach can be applied to any investigation. Even in the most simple of cases, it is often beneficial for discussions to take place among the investigating officer, the CSI, the forensic advisor/budget holder/decision maker, and the prosecutor. Alternatively, generic strategies can be implemented, for example, for a particular crime type or modus operandi.

When making an assessment regarding the potential examination of a particular item and the development of a forensic strategy, the requirements of the investigation are the primary concern and consideration should be given to the following issues:

- The type and nature of the item/exhibit
- The context of the item
  - ○ Exactly where and when it was recovered
  - ○ Condition of the item, that is, wet, damaged, etc.
- The integrity of the item
  - ○ Has it been appropriately recovered, handled, packaged, and preserved?
  - ○ Is the security and continuity of the item intact?
- The potential evidence that may be obtained from the item, for example, DNA, fingerprints, fibers, footwear marks
- The information these evidence types may provide to the investigation
- Whether this potential information is likely to add value to the investigation
  - ○ Is it possible that new information will be provided?
  - ○ Is it possible that an account given by a witness, victim, or suspect will be supported or refuted?
  - ○ Will the information help to establish what has occurred?
- Whether there is a conflict among potential evidence types, and if so, which evidence type will be of most value under the circumstances
  - ○ For example, swabbing/taping for DNA may damage fingerprints, but where the DNA is likely to be at low levels and requires specialized low-template DNA analysis, the presence of DNA may not necessarily prove contact with an item, whereas fingerprints will always prove that contact has occurred
- The chances of success, that is, obtaining a result/information of value to the investigation (this may be inclusive or exclusive)

Much work has historically been completed in relation to developing and understanding the success rates relating to DNA profiling; however, relatively little work has been undertaken to fully understand the success rates associated with other forensic evidence. This is largely due to the fact that other evidence types, such as fibers, gunshot residue, footwear marks, etc., are generally more complex to interpret than DNA. In relation to DNA profiling, success rates are generally based on the chances of obtaining a DNA profile; however, with the other evidence types, the value of the outcome is very much dependent on the circumstances of the investigation. For example, when searching an item of clothing taken from a suspect for glass, the absence of glass or the presence of glass could both be of value to the investigation depending on the circumstances. The presence of glass on the clothing that matches control sample(s) from the crime scene is only of value if its presence cannot be accounted for in any legitimate way; conversely, the absence of glass on the item of clothing may lead to a conclusion that the suspect was not involved in the offense, depending on the circumstances of the offense and arrest.

In addition to being able to understand and evaluate the chances of being able to obtain a meaningful result, it is also vital that the value of the overall contribution to the entire case is understood. This involves being able to understand the value and contribution of the forensic examination to the detection of the offense as well as the outcome of the court process. This is an even more difficult issue to evaluate and understand than the chances of being able to obtain a forensic test result.

Because the value of forensic evidence is so dependent on the individual case circumstances, decisions about examinations must be made on an individual case basis. There have been recent developments in some agencies/forces to better understand the chances of success of different types of forensic evidence and the value to investigations; this will help to better inform decisions about evidential potential and examination viability as well as assist in achieving value for money. This approach is best described as *forensic effectiveness*.

The forensic strategy should also take into account the timescales associated with the investigative process and the criminal justice system, and it should be ensured that forensic analysis can meet the requirements of the criminal justice process, including court dates and any requirements to disclose appropriate information to the defense team(s).

Each police force/law enforcement agency will have its own approach to the submission of exhibits for forensic examination/analysis; irrespective of whether the analysis is carried out in an internal police laboratory, external commercial company, or government-owned laboratory, these approaches can be applied to all examinations and all evidence types.

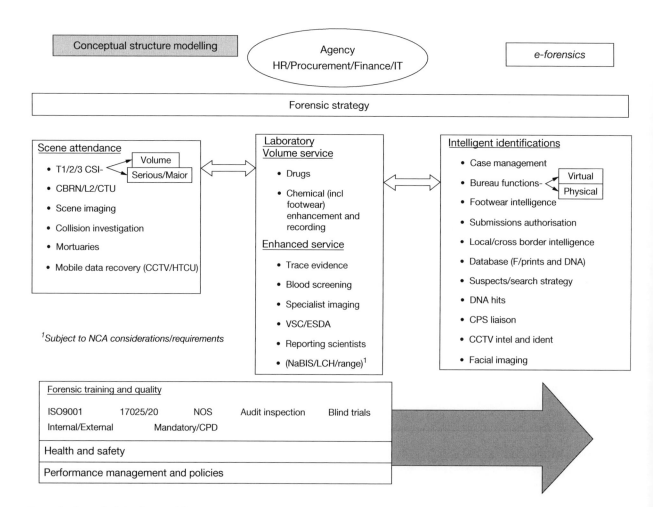

Figure 1   Conceptual structure modeling.

These approaches help to ensure that decisions are made based on scientific knowledge, viability, and evidential value taking into account all aspects of the investigation. They will help to ensure that the best evidence is obtained while considering value for money and that it can be applied to any investigation irrespective of the seriousness of the offense or the scale of the investigation.

Integrated Case Management

The concept and use of forensic strategies in directing investigations are not new but are often limited by the evolved structure of forensic disciplines within investigative agencies. Classically, DNA and fingerprint evidence from volume crimes will be independently submitted at the same time by different routes and this often results in wasted effort/spends and duplicated results. The development and use of forensic intelligence has been variable. Emerging thinking includes organizational redesign of forensics to better integrate with related functions such as intelligence collection, targeted deployment of resources, and prioritized forensic submissions.

The concept of integrated case management draws together informed operational deployment (e.g., of crime scene investigators) followed by a more holistic approach to submissions for testing. The strategy takes greater account of supporting intelligence and desired outcomes. Regular reviews and trigger points are included for the staged submission of potential evidence, and communication with investigators is enhanced so allowing for a more responsive and directed investigation.

Ultimately, the production of *intelligent identifications* can be better achieved by having an integrated process that links the enforcement priorities, available resources, potential forensic evidence, intelligence, and prosecutor requirements; this model provides flexibility to respond to changing demands and gives an increased likelihood of efficient and effective spend on forensic support to investigations. There is no single way to achieve this, but an illustration of how to rethink some of the traditional silo-based forensic disciplines is provided in **Figure 1**.

Summary

The single biggest challenge to the forensic science community during the twenty-first century is to modernize delivery of integrated services in support of investigations. This must

- build on the previous development of each discipline;
- accommodate the new and emerging technological disciplines;
- meet the regulatory requirements;
- reflect the changing workforce and skills; and
- deliver the best evidence to courts in support of investigations.

See also: **Foundations:** Forensic Intelligence; History of Forensic Sciences; Principles of Forensic Science.

Further Reading

Faigman, D.L., et al., 2006. Modern Scientific Evidence: The Law and Science of Expert Testimony.

Fisher, B.A.J., Fisher, D.R., 2012. Techniques of Crime Scene Investigation, eighth ed. CRC, Boca Raton, FL.

Houck, M., Crispino, F., McAdam, T., 2013. The Science of Crime Scenes. Elsevier.

Innocence Project, 2011. http://www.innocenceproject.org/Content/Facts_on_PostConviction_DNA_Exonerations.php (accessed 10.03.11.).

Kirk, P.L., 1974. In: Thornton, J.L. (Ed.), Crime Investigation, second ed. Wiley, New York. (1985 reprint ed., Krieger Publishing Company, Malabar, FL).

NAS, 2009. Strengthening Forensic Science in the United States: A Path Forward. NAS Report: Committee on Identifying the Needs of the Forensic Sciences Community. National Academies Press, Washington, DC.

White, P., 2010. Crime Scene to Court: The Essentials of Forensic Science. Royal Society of Chemistry, Cambridge, ISBN 978-1-84755-882-4.

Expert Witness Qualifications and Testimony

C Henderson, Stetson University College of Law, Gulfport, FL, USA
KW Lenz, Saint Petersburg, FL, USA

Introduction

The field of scientific interpretation of evidence and its portrayal in popular media has progressed to the point that expert testimony at trial is not only commonly accepted by judge and jury, but also expected. This chapter addresses the factors that influence the selection of an expert, including the importance of investigating the expert's credentials and making an informed assessment of the credibility that the expert's qualifications will project to a judge and jurors.

Although this chapter is written from a US perspective, many of the issues discussed here are applicable to expert witness testimony worldwide. This chapter will not, however, address the legal standards for the admissibility of expert testimony or attorneys' ethics in dealing with experts.

Selecting an Expert

Many variables should be considered in selecting an expert witness, including the expert's availability, cost, experience, and reputation. When an expert serves as a consultant or in the pretrial phases of litigation, the criteria for selecting that expert may be limited to the expert's competency in the field. As a trial witness, however, the expert's integrity, charisma, and overall effectiveness as a witness must also be considered.

Thus, consideration should be given not only to the expert's formal training but also to the expert's personality; demeanor; and capacity to organize, express, and interpret complex concepts for the jury. The weight accorded to the expert's opinion by the judge or jury will be determined in large part by the expert's perceived character, objectivity, and impartiality.

Of course, the quality of the expert's credentials remains an important factor to consider as well. A thorough evaluation of an expert should take into account matters such as (1) the membership requirements of the associations to which the expert belongs, (2) how the expert's credentials compare to those of the opposing expert, (3) whether the journals in which the expert's articles appear are held in high regard in the field, and (4) whether the conclusions in those articles were subject to peer review. Studies of jurors' perceptions of experts can be particularly helpful in guiding this evaluation.

Care should always be taken to verify the credentials of one's own expert, as well as those of an adversary's expert, for although it is unlikely that an expert has faked credentials, it has occurred. Indeed, experts have come under increased scrutiny in recent years for fabricating or inflating their qualifications.

Qualifications

The court must determine whether a proffered witness is qualified to testify as an expert, and that determination will not be overturned except for an abuse of discretion (*Kumho Tire Co. Ltd. v. Carmichael*); but see, for example, *Radlein v. Holiday Inns, Inc.* (holding that the trial court's decision will not be reversed unless there is a clear showing of error). Federal Rule of Evidence 702 states that a witness may qualify as an expert on the basis of knowledge, skill, training, experience, or education. An expert witness must possess only one of these traits for the judge to find the expert qualified to give an opinion. In making this evaluation, the judge may consider the expert's educational background, work experience, publications, awards, teaching, speaking, or other professional engagements, prior expert–witness testimony, and membership in professional associations.

Often, the expert may have to educate the attorney proffering the expert regarding the significance of particular experience, achievements, and certifications to ensure that they are appropriately presented to the judge. An expert must be prepared to explain board certification and licensure requirements to the judge in detail.

Experience as an Expert Witness

Experience and training are often more significant than academic background and are accorded more weight by jurors, according to at least one study evaluating juror perceptions of fingerprint experts. However, experience as an expert witness, standing alone, does not qualify someone as an expert in later cases. One court rejected the opinion of a witness who had testified as an expert 126 times (*Bogosian v. Mercedes-Benz of North America Inc.*). Another court noted that, "it would be absurd to conclude that one can become an expert by accumulating experience in testifying" (*Thomas J. Kline, Inc. v. Lonillard, Inc.*). Conversely, a lack of previous experience as an expert witness does not disqualify one from testifying as an expert, because "even the most qualified expert must have his first day in court" (*US v. Locascio*).

Education and Training

An expert may be qualified on the basis of academic credentials, including the expert's undergraduate, graduate, and postgraduate work. An expert's academic credentials should only be issued by accredited educational institutions and programs, because the proliferation of the Internet, while laudable for so many reasons, has also rekindled the old-fashioned diploma mill. One such business, Diplomas 4U, once provided bachelor's, master's, MBA, or PhD degrees in its customers' field of choice; advertisements assured that no one would be turned down and that there would be no bothersome tests, classes, books, or interviews. After studying this issue, the National Academy of Sciences has concluded that it is crucially important to improve undergraduate and graduate forensic science programs with, among other things, attractive scholarship and fellowship offerings, and funding for research programs to attract research universities and students in fields relevant to forensic science.

An expert should continuously perform research and publish in the expert's field, preferably in peer-reviewed publications. Teaching experience is another of the qualifications that judges will evaluate: all forms of teaching—regular, specialty, guest lecturing, visiting professorships, continuing education, and short courses—weigh in as credentials. An expert should also be up to date with developments in his or her field of expertise by reading the current literature, enrolling in continuing education seminars, joining professional societies, and attending professional meetings.

Membership in Professional Associations

A study published by the US Department of Justice in 1987 found that jurors perceived those fingerprint experts who belonged to professional associations to be more credible than other experts, and presumed experts would belong to such groups (Illsley, *supra*). It is therefore important for an expert to remain active and participate in professional societies; the expert's credibility is diminished if the expert has not recently attended a professional meeting. Professional associations that only require annual dues payment to become a member are not as prestigious as associations that are joined by special invitation only, by approval of special referees, or by passing an examination.

Thus, an expert should be selective about which professional associations to join. The NAS Report calls for

standardized accreditation and/or certification, as well as a uniform code of ethics:

> Although some areas of the forensic science disciplines have made notable efforts to achieve standardization and best practices, most disciplines still lack any consistent structure for the enforcement of "better practices," operating standards, and certification and accreditation programs.... Accreditation is required in only three states ... [and] [i]n other states, accreditation is voluntary, as is individual certification.... NAS Report at 213.

Thus, the NAS Report calls for the creation of a federal agency to develop tools to advance reliability in forensic science, to ensure standards that reflect best practices, and serve as accreditation tools for laboratories and as guides for the education, training, and certification of professionals (NAS Report at 214).

Increased Scrutiny of Experts

Experts have come under increased scrutiny for either fabricating or inflating their qualifications. In Florida, in 1998, a person who had been testifying as an expert in toxicology for 3 years for both the prosecution and defense in criminal cases was prosecuted for perjury for testifying with fraudulent credentials. The expert claimed to possess masters and doctorate degrees from Florida Atlantic University, but when a prosecutor sought to confirm the claims, he discovered that the registrar's office had no record of the expert attending or receiving a degree from the university.

In another case, a Harvard medical professor was sued for trademark infringement for falsely claiming to be board certified by the American Board of Psychiatry and Neurology (ABPN) in five trials (*ABPN v. Johnson–Powell*). The board sought to seize the expert's witness fees and treble damages, but the court denied that relief because it believed the expert was unlikely to infringe in the future.

In 2007, a court granted the plaintiff a new trial in her product liability action when it was discovered that the pharmaceutical company's cardiology expert had misrepresented his credentials by testifying that he was board certified in internal medicine and cardiovascular disease when in fact those certifications had expired (*In re Vioxx Products*).

In addition to perjury prosecutions for false qualifications, some jurisdictions also prosecute for academic fraud. For example, in Florida, a person who misrepresents association with, or academic standing at, a postsecondary educational institution is guilty of a first-degree misdemeanor (Fla. Stat. § 817.566).

Courts have also overturned convictions where the experts testified outside their field of expertise. Instances include a medical examiner testifying to shoe-pattern analysis and an evidence technician with no ballistics expertise giving testimony about bullet trajectory (see *Gilliam v. State*; *Kelvin v. State*).

There is evidence to suggest that, since the Supreme Court's decisions in *Daubert v. Merrell Dow Pharmaceuticals, Inc.*, and Kuhmo Tire Co., courts have been more willing to exclude expert testimony. The Federal Judicial Center compared a 1998 survey of 303 federal judges with a 1991 survey. In 1998, 41% of the judges claimed to have excluded expert testimony, whereas only 25% of the judges did so in 1991. A 2001 RAND study similarly concluded that judges were becoming more vigilant gatekeepers; for example, in the US Third Circuit Court of Appeals, the exclusion rate in products liability cases rose from 53% to 70%. This contradicts most of the reported case law following *Daubert*, which seems to indicate that the exclusion of expert testimony remains the exception, not the rule (see Fed. R. Evid. 702).

Weight of the Evidence

Once a judge decides that an expert may testify, the jury must then decide the weight to accord the expert's opinion. Jurors have become familiar with the role of the expert witness at trial through the coverage of high-profile cases in the popular media and fictional television depictions such as "CSI." Studies have shown that jurors have increased expectations for scientific evidence, and that in cases based on circumstantial evidence, jurors are more likely to acquit a defendant if the government did not provide some form of scientific evidence. Expert witnesses and attorneys should be aware of studies regarding jurors' perceptions of expert witnesses and how those perceptions have evolved over time.

For example, a 1994 study revealed that the characteristics of experts that were most important to jurors in determining the experts' credibility were (1) the expert's willingness to draw firm conclusions and (2) the expert's ability to convey technical information in plain language that a layperson could understand. Another study concluded that an expert's believability is linked to the expert's qualifications, familiarity with the facts of the case, good reasoning, and perceived impartiality. Jurors were also influenced by independent research that corresponded with the expert's opinion.

A 1998 study exposed jurors as a more skeptical, cynical group. Among the findings, the study concluded that 50% of those surveyed thought that expert witnesses say only what they are paid to say; 33% did not believe police testimony; and 75% said they would set aside what a judge says the law requires and reach a verdict the jurors felt was right. Yet another study concluded that using expert testimony to counter the prosecution's expert in criminal cases caused jurors to be skeptical of all expert testimony, rather than simply sensitizing them to flaws in the prosecution expert's testimony. In fact, jurors rendered more guilty verdicts when they heard defense expert testimony than when they did not. This study throws into question the Supreme Court's assumption in *Daubert* that opposing expert testimony effectively safeguards against "junk" science in the courtroom.

Increasing awareness of errant experts and exonerations of the wrongly accused has influenced how jurors perceive scientific evidence. For example, background beliefs about the possibility of laboratory errors and intentional tampering affect the weight jurors afford a DNA report, and jurors with such beliefs gave probability estimates less weight. A separate poll regarding forensic fraud and its impact on potential jurors found that 32% think wrongful convictions happen frequently and 23% said that wrongful convictions are rarely an accident.

Experts must understand that effective communication with jurors requires organized content, and the effective use of visual presentation techniques including, whenever possible, demonstrative exhibits that incorporate large, user-friendly data presentation monitors and systems for use both by the court and by individual jurors, as well as interactive electronic timelines and e-documents that allow jurors to feel they are in control of and have access to all information regarding the facts of the trial. Data also suggest that when testifying to jurors, experts should attempt to associate themselves with a more collaborative, personalized role such as a teacher, rather than a more hierarchal and impersonal profession such as a scientist. Surveys confirm these conclusions distinguishing jurors from generations X and Y from past generations. For example, while 64% of jurors overall believe that the police tell the truth when they testify, only 51% of jurors aged 18–24 years old share that belief; 60% overall and 72% of those aged 18–25 viewed presentations using videos, simulations, and computers positively.

Conclusion

Expert testimony will continue to play an important role in the future. Expert witnesses have been facing increased scrutiny in the US and worldwide. For more effective expert testimony, lawyers and experts must be aware of the factors that the courts will evaluate in order to determine whether an expert is qualified or not, as well as jurors' changing perceptions of experts.

Further Reading

ABPN v. Johnson-Powell, 129F.3d 1 (1st Cir. 1997).

Aronson, P., November 2, 1998. Jurors: a biased, independent lot. National Law Journal A1.

Bogosian v. Mercedes-Benz of North America Inc., 104F.3d 472, 477 (1st Cir. 1997).

Committee on Identifying the Needs of the Forensic Sciences Community, National Research Council, August 2009. Strengthening Forensic Science in the United States: A Path Forward. The "NAS Report". National Academy of Sciences, pp. 238–239.

Daubert v. Merrell Dow Pharmaceuticals, Inc., 509 U.S. 579 (1993).

Dixon, L., Gill, B., 2001. Changes in the Standards in Admitting Expert Evidence in Federal Civil Cases since Daubert Decision. RAND Monograph.

Fed. R. Evid. 702, Adv. Cmte. Note to the 2000 Amendment (2000).

Fitzgerald Jr., H., Dec. 1, 1998. Phony "expert" Jailed for 3 Years. Ft. Lauderdale Sun-Sentinel 3D.

Fla. Stat. } 817.566 (2004).

Gilliam v. State, 514 So. 2d 1098 (Fla. 1987); Kelvin v. State, 610 So. 2d 1359 (Fla. App. 1 Dist. 1992).

Godfrey, E., May 27, 2001. Poll shows Oklahomans distrust system. The Daily Oklahoman A1.

Hamlin, S., 2000. Who are today's jurors and how do you reach them? Litigation 9 (Spring).

Illsley, C., July 1987. Juries, fingerprints, and the expert fingerprint witness. In: Presentation at the International Symposium on Latent Prints at the FBI Academy.

In re Vioxx Products, 489F. Supp. 2d 587 (E.D. La. 2007).

Kim, Y.S., Barak, G., Shelton, D.E., 2009. Examining the 'CSI-effect' in the cases of circumstantial evidence and eyewitness testimony: multivariate and path analyses. Journal of Criminal Justice 37, 452.

Thomas J. Kline, Inc. v. Lonillard, Inc., 878F.2d 791, 800 (4th Cir. 1989); cert. denied, 493 U.S. 1073 (1990).

Kumho Tire Co. Ltd. v. Carmichael, 526 U.S. 137, 143 (1999).

Levett, L.M., Kovera, M.B., 2007. The effectiveness of opposing expert witnesses for educating jurors about unreliable expert evidence. Law and Human Behavior 32 (4), 363–374 (Pub. online October 17, 2007).

National Clearinghouse for Science, Technology and the Law at Stetson University College of Law, Bibliography of Resources Related to the CSI Effect. http://www.ncstl.org/education/CSI%20Effect%20Bibliography (accessed 24.07.11.).

Radlein v. Holiday Inns, Inc., 971 So.2d 1200 (La. App. 4 Cir. 2007).

Schklar, J., Seidman, S., 1999. Juror reactions to DNA evidence: errors and expectancies. Law and Human Behavior 23, 159.

Shelton, D.E., Kim, Y.S., Barak, G., 2009. An indirect-effects model of mediated adjudication: the CSI myth, the tech effect, and metropolitan jurors' expectations for scientific evidence. Vanderbilt Journal of Entertainment and Technology Law 12, 1.

Shuman, D.W., et al., 1994. An empirical examination of the use of expert witnesses in the courts – Part II: a three city study. Jurimetrics 35, 193.

Shuman, D.W., et al., 1996. Assessing the believability of expert witnesses: science in the jurybox. Jurimetrics 37, 23.

The Technical Working Group on Education and Training in Forensic Science, June 2004. Education and Training in Forensic Science: A Guide for Forensic Science Laboratories, Educational Institutions and Students. National Institutes of Justice Special Report.

U.S. v. Locascio, 6F.3d 924, 937 (2d Cir. 1993) ("even the most qualified expert must have his first day in court"), cert. denied, 511 U.S. 1070 (1994).

Voris, B.V., October 23, 2000. Jurors to lawyers: dare to be dull. The National Law Journal A1.

Forensic Laboratory Reports

J Epstein, Widener University School of Law, Wilmington, DE, USA

There is no precise formula, dictated by law or science, as to what a forensic laboratory report must contain when it reports test results or analysis outcomes. Its content may be determined by the individual examiner's predilections, internal laboratory policy, the law of the jurisdiction, accreditation organization standards, or the reason(s) for its production. What can be said with certainty is that by understanding the current criticism of the practice of producing forensic laboratory reports and trends in standards for reports, and by considering the use to which the report may be put in the court process and the legal and ethical commands regarding reporting and, more generally, the duties of the forensic scientist, a model for forensic laboratory reports can be identified.

Before discussing these factors, it bears mention that the term "report" itself lacks clarity, as it may refer to the complete case file documenting the examination or just to the compilation of results. For this chapter, the term "report" denotes the latter—the document prepared for the consumer [the investigator, counsel, or court official who directed that the examination and testing be conducted]. Even this report may vary in degree of detail, as there can be the summary report advising the requesting party of the outcome; a more formal report prepared for disclosure to the court or opposing counsel as part of pretrial discovery; an amplification of the initial discovery-generated report when it is determined that the expert will in fact testify; and a report that will be presented in lieu of actual testimony. Additional documentation may include an administrative or dispositional report detailing the receipt or return of the item(s) sent for analysis.

What must also be acknowledged is that the expert's role in the adjudicative process is in some ways defined by whether the system is adversarial, with the expert being called by the party seeking to establish a point, as in the United States; or "inquisitorial/common law," where the expert is a court witness, presumed to be neutral, and without allegiance to a particular party, as in France, Belgium, and Germany. These demarcations are not always adhered to, as American law permits a trial judge to appoint and take testimony from a "court" expert under Federal Rule of Evidence 706, and in some cases involving offenses of fraud and falsification, France permits competing experts. These differing roles, however, do not alter the necessary components of a forensic laboratory report (and, as is detailed below), both ethical and legal considerations as well as a commitment to the role of science

may require the report to be neutral and to acknowledge any limitations and/or weaknesses.

Contents of a Report—A "Science" Standard

At least in the United States, there has been substantial criticism of forensic laboratory reporting. This is found in *Strengthening Forensic Science: A Path Forward*, the 2009 report of the National Research Council of the National Academy of Sciences. After reporting that forensic laboratory reports lack precise terminology, it concluded that most laboratory reports do not meet the standard it proposed: As a general matter, laboratory reports generated as the result of a scientific analysis should be complete and thorough. They should describe, at a minimum, methods and materials, procedures, results, and conclusions, and they should identify, as appropriate, the sources of uncertainty in the procedures and conclusions along with estimates of their scale (to indicate the level of confidence in the results). Although it is not appropriate and practicable to provide as much detail as might be expected in a research paper, sufficient content should be provided to allow the nonscientist reader to understand what has been done and permit informed and unbiased scrutiny of the conclusion.

This criticism does not stand in isolation. A 2011 British court decision also expressed concern over the sufficiency of detail and documentation in a forensic [latent print] prosecution. After noting the failure of the examiner to contemporaneously record "detailed notes of his examination and the reasons for his conclusions[,]" the court added that [t]he quality of the reports provided by the Nottinghamshire Fingerprint Bureau for the trial reflected standards that existed in other areas of forensic science some years ago, and not the vastly improved standards expected in contemporary forensic science.

The NRC standard is more detailed than that of various forensic organizations. ASCLD/LAB, for example, requires that only written reports be generated for "all analytical work" and must contain conclusions and opinions and a clear communication of "the significance of associations made...."

Other standards address the need for full documentation, but do not distinguish between a laboratory's bench notes and the final product. For example, International Organization for Standardization's ISO/IEC Standard 5.10.5 requires that "the laboratory shall document the basis upon which the opinions and interpretations have been made" without specifying where that information is to be recorded. Similar language is used for ballistics reports, as recommended by the Scientific Working Group for firearms and toolmarks requiring that "[w]hen opinions and interpretations are included, the laboratory shall document the basis upon which the opinions and interpretations have been made. Opinions and interpretations shall be clearly marked as such in the test report."

Yet, the more detailed mandate urged by the NRC report is not unique. Scholars and agencies have articulated similar or at least substantial standards. A publication of *The Royal Society of Chemistry* in 2004, suggested the following information as appropriate for inclusion in an expert report:

- A summary of the event to contextualize the scientific test(s);
- An outline of the scientific work conducted;
- A listing of items examined;
- Description of the work performed;
- A statement interpreting the findings; and
- An overall conclusion.

The RSC text also urges that the report identify the assistants in the testing and the role each played and include appendices with tables or similar displays of test results.

For DNA analysis, the Federal Bureau of Investigation's standards for DNA laboratories require reports to include a description of the evidence examined and of the technology, results and/or conclusions, and a "quantitative or qualitative interpretative statement."

One final scientific issue regarding the contents of a report is the concern over bias. Research has shown that information received by the analyst might affect his/her judgment, as when the examiner receives domain-irrelevant information such as the fact that the suspect whose fingerprints are being examined "confessed to the crime" or when the verification is not "blind." Documentation of such information in a laboratory report (or the bench notes) is one responsive action, as is an internal laboratory policy to reduce analyst or verifier exposure to potentially biasing information.

Contents of Report: Legal Standards

That which science requires is to some extent mirrored in legal requirements for expert reports. These vary from nation to nation, and within nations when states or regions have their own authority to legislate criminal practice.

In the United Kingdom, Rule 33.3, Criminal Procedure Rules 2010 mandates contents of a full report, that is, one for submission in court, as follows:

1. the findings on which they have relied in making the report or statement;
2. details of which of the findings stated in the report or statement are within their own knowledge, which were obtained as a result of examinations, measurements, tests, etc. carried out by another person and whether or not those examinations, measurements, tests, etc. were carried out under the expert's supervision;
3. the identity, qualifications, relevant experience, and any certification of the person who carried out the examination, measurement, test, etc.;
4. details of any statements of fact, literature, or other information upon which they have relied, either to identify the examination or test requirements, or which are material to the opinions expressed in the report or statement or upon which those opinions are based;
5. a summary of the conclusions and opinions reached and a rationale for these;
6. a statement that if any of the information on which their conclusions or opinions are based changes then the conclusions or opinions will have to be reviewed;
7. where there is a range of opinion on the matters dealt with in the report or statement, a summary of the range of opinion, and reasons for the expert's own opinion;
8. any information that may cast doubt on their interpretation or opinion; and
9. if the expert is not able to give an opinion without qualification, what the qualification is.

Much less specific is the legislated mandate for federal criminal prosecutions in the United States. Under Federal Rule of Criminal Procedure 16, the Government must permit the defense to inspect and to copy or photograph the results or reports of any scientific test or experiment and must produce before trial a written summary of any proposed expert testimony that describes the witness' opinions, the bases and reasons for those opinions, and the witness' qualifications. Defense counsel in criminal cases has a reciprocal disclosure requirement. Despite the seeming generality of these terms, American courts have at times interpreted them to require some greater detail in the reports, such as underlying documentation.

In the United States, an additional requirement derived from the Constitution's guarantee of Due Process of Law may affect what must be included in a laboratory report issued by a police or other government agency. The prosecution must disclose information that is "favorable to the accused" and "material either to guilt or to punishment" as well as "evidence that the defense might have used to impeach the Government's witnesses by showing bias or interest." This extends to "evidence affecting credibility[.]" This information is generally denominated "Brady material."

The applicability of these rules to official [police or state] laboratories is settled. The US Supreme Court has held that the disclosure obligation extends to police agencies working with the prosecution, and this has been extended to forensic examiners. Hence, in a report or some other communication, a forensic examiner in government employ must ensure that "Brady material" is disclosed.

What remains to be defined are the terms "exculpatory" or "impeachment" information. The core of each is easily described. Evidence is "exculpatory" if it tends to reduce the degree of guilt or question proof of culpability; "impeachment" information is proof of a bias or interest, or otherwise information that could be used to contradict or attack the credibility of the analyst or report. This type of disclosure parallels that of forensic laboratory reports imposed by the United Kingdom's evidence code. The code requires inclusion in the report of "a summary of the range of opinion and reasons for the expert's own opinion; [] any information that may cast doubt on their interpretation or opinion; and if the expert is not able to give an opinion without qualification, what the qualification is."

Reports: Stand-Alone Evidence or Support for a Testifying Expert

Whether a laboratory report may stand on its own as evidence in a trial, or instead must be accompanied by testimony of the forensic analyst, is a function of the law of the jurisdiction in which the case is tried. In the United States, a prosecution expert's report may not be admitted on its own, as this is deemed to violate the defendant's right to confront adverse witnesses. The Supreme Court in Melendez-Diaz versus Massachusetts held that a certificate of analysis fell within the core class of testimonial statements because it was a solemn "declaration or affirmation made for the purpose of establishing or proving some fact." In the 2011 follow-up of the Melendez-Diaz decision, the Court further held that another lab analyst may not come in to testify to the report's contents, at least where the other analyst neither supervised nor observed the initial testing. [This applies only to prosecution expert reports, as in the United States only the defendant has a guarantee of the right to confront witnesses. Admissibility of a defense forensic report without examiner testimony would be determined by the state's rules of evidence, but is generally unheard of.]

At the same time, the confrontation right does not mean that the analyst must testify. A state may create a notice and demand statute under which the prosecution notifies the defendant of its intent to use an analyst's report as evidence at trial, after which the defendant has a specified period of time in which to demand the expert's live testimony. A defendant's failure to "demand" waives the need for the analyst's presence and allows use of the report. As well, an accused may always agree to stipulate to the report's content, eliminating the need for any live testimony.

The Melendez-Diaz approach is not followed uniformly on an international basis. Canada permits proof by means of an expert report, without live testimony, where the proponent of the report has provided it to the opposing party and the trial court recognizes the author as a legitimate expert. The court retains discretion to mandate the expert's appearance for cross-examination. Australia's Evidence Act of 1995 similarly authorizes expert proof by certificate, but the opposing party may require the offering side to "call the person who signed the certificate to give evidence." In the United Kingdom, expert reports are themselves admissible as evidence, subject to the judge's discretion in requiring the analyst or examiner to appear.

Ethical Considerations and Forensic Reports

The decision of what to include in a forensic laboratory report, beyond that required by law or by science, may be informed by ethical considerations. Forensic organizations often have ethical codes, but they may be silent as to the particulars of report writing. Illustrative is the Code of the American Board of Criminalistics, which only asserts general obligations such as "[e]nsure that a full and complete disclosure of the findings is made to the submitting agency[.]" Other codes may not mention reporting at all but instead address only the delivery of information without distinguishing between the written report and a courtroom presentation of evidence. An exception is that of the Australian and New Zealand Forensic Science Society, Inc., which requires that a report be nonpartisan when results are ambiguous. "Where test results or conclusions are capable of being interpreted to the advantage of either side in a legal proceeding, each result or conclusion should be given weight according to its merit."

Ethical considerations may also be imposed by law. In the United Kingdom, the expert is deemed to hold only one allegiance, that to the court, regardless of the party who retained the individual. Specific ethical obligations are imposed for written reports. First, where there is a range of opinion, the expert must summarize the various positions. Second, if the opinion rendered cannot be given without qualification, the expert must disclose that and state the qualifying aspects or concerns.

Conclusion

Within and across nations, there is no clear standard for forensic reports intended for court use, except where prescribed by law. What should be manifest is that the more detailed the report, and thus the more it is capable of rigorous assessment by an independent expert evaluator, the more credibility will be attributed to both the results and the examiner.

See also: **Legal:** History of the Law's Reception of Forensic Science; Legal Aspects of Forensic Science; Legal Systems: Adversarial and Inquisitorial; **Management/Quality in Forensic Science:** *Sequential Unmasking.* Minimizing Observer Effects in Forensic Science; **Professional:** Ethics.

Further Reading

Codes of Practice and Conduct for Forensic Science Providers and Practitioners in the Criminal Justice System, pp. 44–45 (United Kingdom). http://www.homeoffice.gov.uk/publications/police/forensic-science-regulator1/quality-standards-codes-practice?view=Binary.

Dror, I.E., Cole, S., 2010. The vision in 'blind' justice: expert perception, judgment and visual cognition in forensic pattern recognition. Psychonomic Bulletin and Review 17 (2), 161–167.

Dror, I.E., Rosenthal, R., 2008. Meta-analytically quantifying the reliability and bias ability of forensic experts. Journal of Forensic Sciences 53 (4), 900–903.

National Research Council, 2009. Strengthening Forensic Science in the United States: A Path Forward. National Academies Press, Washington, DC. http://www.ncjrs.gov/pdffiles1/nij/grants/228091.pdf.

Quality Assurance Standards for Forensic DNA Testing Laboratories, Standard 11.2. http://www.cstl.nist.gov/strbase/QAS/Final-FBI-Director-Forensic-Standards.pdf.

Reviewing Historical Practices of Forensic Science Laboratories, September 29, 2010. http://www.ascld.org/.

Rothwell, T., 2004. Presentation of expert forensic evidence. In: White, P. (Ed.), Crime Scene to Court: The Essentials of Forensic Science, second ed. RSC, Cambridge, pp. 430–432 (Chapter 15).

Spencer, J.R., 2002. Evidence. European Criminal Procedures. Cambridge University Press, New York, pp. 632–635 (Chapter 15).

Relevant Websites

http://www.afte.org/AssociationInfo/a_codeofethics.htm—Association of Firearms and Toolmarks Examiners, AFTE Code of Ethics.

http://www.anzfss.org.au/code_of_ethics.htm—Australian and New Zealand Forensic Science Society.

http://www.ascld.org/—The American Society of Crime Laboratory Directors.

http://www.ascld-lab.org/—The American Society of Crime Laboratory Directors Laboratory Accreditation Board.

http://www.criminalistics.com/ethics.cfm—American Board of Criminalistics, Rules of Professional Conduct.

http://www.forensicdna.com/Media/Bias_FS.htm—(An extended list of articles on the issue of bias in forensic examinations).

http://www.iso.org/iso/home.html—International Organization for Standardization.

http://www.swggun.org/swg/index.php?option=com_content&view=article&id=25:transition-from-ascldlab-legacy-to-isoiec-17025&catid=10:guidelines-adopted&Itemid=6—SWGGUN, Transition from ASCLD/LAB Legacy to ISO/IEC 17025.

http://webarchive.nationalarchives.gov.uk/+/; http://www.justice.gov.uk/criminal/procrules_fin/contents/rules/part_33.htm—United Kingdom, Criminal Procedure Rules 2010.

Legal Aspects of Forensic Science

G Edmond, The University of New South Wales, Sydney, NSW, Australia
SA Cole, University of California, Irvine, CA, USA

Glossary

Facts in issue Facts contested at trial.
Trier of fact (also tribunal of fact or fact-finder)
Responsible for factual determinations (i.e., guilt or
liability) at trial. Conventionally the jury, though in judge-
only trials the judge is also responsible for fact finding.

Voir dire A hearing to determine an admissibility issue
before or during trial. The jury is usually absent to prevent
them hearing, and being influenced by, evidence that may
be deemed inadmissible and excluded.

Introduction

In legal institutions, the primary role of forensic science is to
assist with proof. It provides evidence that assists the trier of
fact (usually a jury) to determine guilt (criminal)—beyond
reasonable doubt—or liability in civil proceedings—on the
balance of probability. Mostly, this involves routine analytical
and comparative processes that lead to reports that help with
investigations and the production of guilty pleas. In a small
proportion of criminal cases, accusations are contested,
through trials, and on these occasions expert witnesses are
often required to present their evidence (or testimony) orally in
the form, usually, of incriminating opinions.

The stakes involved, especially in criminal proceedings,
place a premium on the need for reliable forensic science
evidence. Historically, judges have been inclined to allow
forensic scientists and other investigators to testify, and sometimes speculate, regardless of underlying research. The past two
decades have seen increasing interest in formal admissibility
rules across civil justice and criminal justice systems, though
the application of such rules to forensic science has been
inconsistent, with courts preferring to rely on trial processes to
expose questionable evidence.

Chain of Custody: Collection, Transport, Handling, and Storage of Samples

Most jurisdictions have legislation, or guidelines, regulating the
collection and handling of samples that might be used for
forensic purposes. Where the samples are taken from persons
or their property, these tend to be conditioned by privacy
concerns linked to constitutions and bills of rights.

Many of the problems associated with the collection,
transportation, and handling of samples and materials have
been substantially reduced, if not eliminated, through administrative solutions including enhanced labeling, tamper-proof
bags, bar codes, and restricted access. While chain of custody,
the continuity of exhibits and contamination all continue to
raise problems, in recent years the primary epistemic challenges
to forensic science evidence have focused upon validity and
reliability, interpretations and expression of evidence, and the
weight to assign expert opinions.

Admissibility of Forensic Science

To be admissible in criminal (and most civil) proceedings,
forensic science evidence must be relevant and satisfy jurisdictional requirements for exception to the general rule pro-
hibiting opinion evidence. In most jurisdictions, the party
adducing the evidence, especially the state, must give notice of
the expert evidence to opposing parties in order for them to
take the evidence into account and provide an opportunity
to take advice or obtain an alternative expert opinion. Failure to
comply with formal rules, such as improperly obtaining
samples or conducting an illegal search, for example, may lead
to exclusion or require formal approval by a trial judge before
any resulting evidence is admissible.

Challenges to forensic science evidence are usually focused
on admissibility and weight. Admissibility governs what expert
evidence can be presented to the trier of fact during the trial.
The trier of fact can base their decision only upon admissible
evidence. The weight of the evidence is the value of the
evidence assigned by the trier of fact. It is shaped by
the assumptions and prejudices they bring to the trial as well as

the way opinions fare in response to direct and redirect (examination and reexamination), cross-examination, rebuttal opinions, and other evidence, opening and closing addresses, and any directions or warnings from the trial judge.

Admissibility Standards

Most forensic science evidence is classified as opinion evidence (as opposed to fact). Opinions are ordinarily inadmissible, though all jurisdictions maintain formal exceptions for the opinions of experts, such as forensic scientists. Historically, scientists and other expert witnesses were also prevented from expressing views directly on the issue to be determined by the trier of fact (e.g., murder, insanity, or negligence). Largely in abeyance, this (ultimate issue) rule was intended to prevent the expert from usurping the prerogative of the trier of fact.

Formal qualifications or experience, the existence of a "field of knowledge" and evidence of "acceptance" among relevant experts once grounded the admissibility of expert opinions. These standards prevail in the United Kingdom, New Zealand, and some United States and Australian states, although there is a gradual trend toward the formal adoption of admissibility standards incorporating concern with the reliability of expert techniques and derivative opinions. This trend, most conspicuous in the United States and Canada, is often traced to an influential civil decision by the United States Supreme Court.

Daubert v. Merrell Dow Pharmaceuticals, Inc. (1993) explained that for admission of scientific opinion evidence should be not only relevant but also reliable. *Daubert* included several criteria that might assist trial judges with admissibility determinations. In *Kumho Tire Co v. Carmichael* (1999) the Supreme Court effectively extended the application of these criteria to nonscientific forms of expert opinion evidence, though both cases reinforce the need for flexible gatekeeping. Interestingly, the International Association of Arson Investigators filed a brief in *Kumho* arguing that arson investigators were not "scientific experts" and should not be subject to the *Daubert* standard.

In jurisdictions beyond the United States, there is often considerable interest in the availability and admissibility of facts (or data) underlying expert opinion evidence. These technical legal concerns, about the basis of opinions, may influence admissibility determinations, but increasingly are associated with the probative value (or weight) to assign to the evidence. Basis rules are intended to enable opposing parties to test the foundations of an opinion and put the trier of fact in a position to evaluate the process and any conclusion.

Admissibility decisions are often made after a *voir dire* (or *Daubert* hearing). They usually take place in court in the absence of the jury, though they are sometimes resolved through written submissions. Because the purpose of admissibility hearings is to screen out "charlatan" experts who may dupe naive lay jurors, where trial judges sit without juries (i.e., summarily), admissibility standards and discretions tend to be relaxed. The law presumes that a judge can and will properly value (or weigh) evidence and is capable of disregarding unreliable and prejudicial forms of incriminating expert opinion when determining liability or guilt.

In most jurisdictions, judges have a demonstrated tendency to admit incriminating opinion evidence and—based on submissions and objections—are more likely to scrutinize expert opinion evidence adduced by criminal defendants (and plaintiffs).

Mandatory and Discretionary Exclusions

In addition to formal admissibility standards, most jurisdictions confer powers, usually in the form of a discretion (e.g., United States Federal Rules of Evidence R403) to exclude otherwise admissible evidence—including expert opinion evidence. In some jurisdictions (e.g., many Australian states), this assumes the form of an obligation. Where otherwise admissible, if the probative value of expert evidence—that is, its ability to rationally influence the assessment of facts in issue—is outweighed by the risk of unfair prejudice to the accused or by the risk of misleading or confusing the jury, the judge may exclude the evidence. This discretion/obligation is intended to prevent weak and potentially unfairly prejudicial evidence from contaminating criminal proceedings by distracting the trier of fact or wasting time and resources.

Admissibility Practice

The National Academy of Sciences (NAS) report, public inquiries, empirical and comparative studies cast doubt on both the effectiveness and distinctiveness of admissibility standards, including those associated with reliability. The various studies and reviews suggest that unreliable forensic science and forensic science of unknown reliability is routinely admitted in criminal proceedings.

In practice, courts in most jurisdictions prefer to admit forensic science testimony and leave questions about the value of the evidence to be contested in trial and determined by the trier of fact. Where the admissibility of evidence and concerns about unfair prejudice are raised, they are more likely to lead to caveats and qualifications to the expression of opinions than exclusion per se.

Courts in the adversarial tradition maintain considerable confidence in the ability of the trial and trial safeguards to identify, expose, and effectively convey problems with expert opinion evidence.

Expert Evidence at Trial

Once admitted, the probative value or weight of expert evidence may be contested during the trial.

Most expert evidence is presented orally, by a legally qualified expert witness, during the trial. Some jurisdictions have certification procedures that facilitate the admission of expert reports. Where, however, the evidence is contested, most jurisdictions require the analyst who performed the tests, or developed the conclusions, to testify in person. This requirement was recently emphatically restated in *Melendez-Diaz v. Massachusetts* (2009), where the United States Supreme Court rejected the contention that laboratory reports were admissible without the ability to cross-examine the forensic scientist. Ordinarily, the state leads incriminating oral evidence from the forensic scientist through a state-employed prosecutor. Then the defendant may, usually via counsel provided through public funds, cross-examine the witness. Thereafter, the prosecution may repair or clarify any issues raised during cross-examination through redirect (or reexamination).

The state usually presents its entire case before the defense makes some kind of insufficient evidence submission (e.g., no case to answer) or responds to the accusation with its own evidence. The defense has no formal obligation to prove anything, and any reasonable doubts pertaining to the defendant's guilt should result in acquittal.

The defense may also call and examine witnesses, including expert witnesses, who may, in turn, be cross-examined by the prosecutor (and any codefendants). Subject to resources and the availability of legally acceptable expert witnesses, the defense may adduce original expert evidence inconsistent with guilt or rebuttal evidence that challenges the incriminating forensic science called by the state.

Examination-in-Chief (or Direct)

The party calling the witness normally adduces evidence by questioning its witness with nonleading questions. The rule against leading questions is often relaxed for expert witnesses, and in some jurisdictions (or where the judge is the trier of fact) the expert's report or conclusions might be substituted for examination-in-chief.

Cross-examination

The primary means for identifying and exposing limitations with expert evidence and (not unrelated) the credibility of expert witnesses is through cross-examination. During cross-examination, lawyers are entitled to ask leading questions and to explore issues relevant to the evidence and underlying techniques, as well as the abilities, experience, and qualifications of the expert witness, including prior opinions and performances, in detail.

Cross-examination may be confrontational and aggressive or the examiner might seek to calmly elicit information and concessions that raise doubt or positively support a defense raised by the accused.

Reexamination (or Redirect)

Following cross-examination, the party that called the witness may reexamine (i.e., redirect) to clarify or repair issues raised during cross-examination. Ordinarily, a party cannot cross-examine its own expert witness, though all other parties, including codefendants, may cross-examine witnesses called by another defendant.

Rebuttal (and Defense) Experts

At trial, the accused may adduce expert evidence to provide an opinion or interpretation that is inconsistent with the case advanced by the prosecution (defense expert), or may call an expert witness to challenge the scientific evidence led by the state (a rebuttal expert). Rebuttal experts may retest samples and exhibits though usually, constrained by resources, their roles are restricted to criticisms of methods, interpretations, and conclusions. Since the state, in many instances, maintains a near monopoly on forensic science expertise, almost all of the expert witnesses called by defendants are retired forensic scientists, though some are academics.

One of the major problems for both the defense and the state is the availability and cost of experts (and testing). Necessarily, public funding for defense experts is much more constrained than expenditure on investigations and prosecutions. The state is far more likely to adduce forensic science evidence than the accused and the likelihood of expert challenge tends to be low, though particularly low in much of the United States. Tightening of resources and increasing privatization of forensic science services makes testing, including testing that may produce results consistent with nonguilt, more difficult to justify.

Expression of Opinions

The manner in which experts express their opinions has become a source of increasing controversy. In recent years, especially in the aftermath of the NAS report, the Goudge Inquiry, and the English Court of Appeal decision in *R v. T* (2010), it has become reasonably common for judges to regulate the manner in which an expert may express his or her opinion in court. Such efforts are intended to facilitate admission while preventing expert opinions extending beyond what experimental evidence can support.

Rather than exclude forensic science evidence, lawyers and judges often facilitate an admissibility compromise by tempering (i.e., negotiating) the strength of the conclusion—almost always represented as conservative. That is, judges may require or approve weaker expressions (such as describing similarities rather than positively identifying a source) than those proffered by the proponent of the evidence.

Judicial Guidance to Jurors

In many jurisdictions, the judge is either required (e.g., most Australian jurisdictions) or retains a discretion (e.g., England and Wales) to caution the jury about types of evidence that are considered to be unreliable or problematic. The basis for these might be statutory or drawn from the collective experience of judges. Expert evidence, particularly forms of evidence used for comparison or identification (such as probabilistic DNA evidence), is usually included within the types of evidence that receive judicial comment. Judges often instruct juries about dangers with expert evidence and expert disagreement. Jurors are sometimes instructed that they might reject an expert's opinion, though jurisprudence is divided on whether juries can simply reject the uncontested opinion of a formally qualified expert.

Ultimately, decisions about the weight to attach to expert evidence are matters for the trier of fact. In practice, the jury is entitled to accept the opinion of a forensic scientist, even if the testimony is speculative and based on techniques that have not been thoroughly tested or were obtained in circumstances that dramatically increased the possibility of error.

Appellate Review and Postconviction

Concerns about the conduct of the trial, such as the admission or exclusion of expert evidence, or the way in which an opinion was expressed, often manifest postconviction. Few, if any, jurisdictions allow interlocutory appeals on the admissibility of expert opinion evidence. Consequently, appellate courts normally consider appeals pertaining to expert opinion evidence in the context of a review of the entire case. Issues relating to the value of expert opinion may be considered alongside other incriminating evidence, such as admissions or other forensic science evidence, and in conjunction with knowledge about prior convictions and sentence. Furthermore, failure to object to forensic science evidence in preliminary hearings or at trial, even where there was no public funding for expert assistance, may limit the ability to raise the issue on appeal. Failure to take timely objection, whatever the explanation, is often treated as a bar to subsequent review.

Ordinarily, though especially where the case against an accused appears to be compelling, there needs to be some nontrivial oversight or problem for success on appeal. On review, an appellate court may uphold the conviction notwithstanding errors associated with the admission or, as is more likely, expression of expert opinions. In such circumstances, the strength of the overall case is considered to be sufficient to sustain the conviction. In such circumstances, procedural errors or limitations may be characterized as harmless. Successful appeals usually lead to retrials—where mistakes identified on appeal should be addressed.

Separate from courts of appeal, several jurisdictions (such as England and Wales and Scotland) have established Criminal Cases Review Commissions—statutory bodies empowered to undertake independent reviews of questioned convictions. Such commissions are usually empowered to review convictions and refer questionable cases to appellate courts. Only appellate courts (and, in some jurisdictions politicians), however, can formally quash convictions (or order retrials). In addition, many jurisdictions have facilities for Royal Commissions, public inquiries and independent reviews following miscarriages of justice associated with serious or endemic problems with criminal justice practice (e.g., the Runciman Royal Commission, Goudge Inquiry, and various state forensic science commissions).

Legal Safeguards in Practice

Historically, admissibility standards, exclusionary discretions, the ability to cross-examine, adduce rebuttal expert evidence, and give warnings with the authority of the judicial office/bench were, along with appellate review (and prosecutorial restraint), conceived to provide a robust and fair response to the presentation, assessment, and review of incriminating expert opinions, the need for fairness and the risk of wrongful conviction. Recent empirical studies, however, have raised questions about the ability of the (adversarial) trial and appeal to adequately explore, convey, and expose problems with forensic science and medicine evidence.

The frailty of trial safeguards, revelations about the problematic empirical foundations of many forensic sciences (see NAS), in conjunction with the synergistic effects of forensic science and nonscientific evidence, means that the rigorous enforcement of admissibility standards and the exclusion of insufficiently reliable expert opinion is probably more important than previously appreciated.

Lay Assessment of Forensic Science

Trials and appeals place decision-making responsibility—for admissibility, probative value (or weight) and the strength of the overall case—upon persons usually without scientific or technical training. This approach made sense historically because the vast majority of the evidence presented at trial was of a nontechnical kind—for example, witness testimony. The use of expert witnesses and reliance on forms of specialized knowledge has increased dramatically in recent decades. This not only affects the manner in which evidence is presented but may also impair the ability of lay participants to recognize limitations and regulate expert opinion at trial and on appeal.

The technical ability of jurors and judges remains the subject of ongoing controversy. Research, primarily from the United States, suggests that many judges do not perform much better than juries when assessing scientific and technical evidence and that judges have difficulty understanding and applying reliability criteria, such as those associated with *Daubert*. Questions about lay legal participants (lawyers, judges, and jurors), particularly their ability to consistently and adequately understand scientific and technical evidence, remain unanswered.

Judges, for example, have not developed demanding admissibility standards or strictly enforced those admissibility standards indexed to the reliability of forensic science evidence. Rather, judges have tended to trust the state's investigative institutions, the trial and its safeguards.

CSI Effects

It has become increasingly common for lawyers, forensic scientists, academic commentators, and media outlets to claim that juries are susceptible to what is called the "CSI effect." The term derives from the popular American television program CSI (Crime Scene Investigation), which commenced broadcasting in 2000, became the most popular television in the country for a time, spawned several spin-offs and imitators, and achieved global distribution and popularity. The program is usually structured so that forensic evidence definitively and unambiguously resolves the unknown facts about each case. It has been criticized for this tendency, as well as for exaggerating the capacity and resources available in forensic laboratories, for taking dramatic license with the job descriptions of forensic scientists (e.g., depicting them carrying weapons and making arrests), and for occasionally fabricating nonexistent forensic techniques. Because of these features, many have claimed that the television program has an effect, the "CSI effect," on the behavior of those participating in the criminal justice system. Some articulations of the "CSI effect" merely claim that attorneys have adjusted trial tactics by, for example, explaining why the failure to recover a particular forensic trace from an individual does not necessarily prove that individual was not present. Others advance the more troubling claim that jurors are acquitting defendants in cases where forensic evidence is absent, cases in which they would have convicted had the television program *CSI* never existed. At present, the evidence that juror behavior has changed in this manner is weak. In addition, it is important to distinguish the "CSI effect" from what has been called the "Tech effect"—that is, more appropriate recalibrations of juror expectations in response to actual advances in forensic science and technology.

Plea Bargains and Interrogations

The vast majority of resolved criminal cases are settled through plea bargains. Forensic science evidence is a very regular feature of plea bargains with some types of forensic evidence (e.g., DNA and fingerprint "matches") likely to lead defense lawyers to advise their clients to plead guilty. Indeed, it may reasonably be argued that the primary role of forensic evidence in some legal systems is to serve as a form of leverage in plea negotiations. Another role for forensic evidence is to serve a similar role in police interrogations. Persuading a suspect that forensic science implies his/her guilt is a common interrogation tactic. While reliable forensic science results provide a legitimate basis for questioning, in the United States, for example, lying to a suspect about the existence or results of forensic testing does not render any consequential admission or plea inadmissible.

The failure to enforce reliability standards rigorously, in conjunction with the weakness of trial and appellate safeguards and the likelihood of conviction at trial, means that innocent individuals may sometimes plead guilty in order to avoid the risk of dramatically longer (or lethal) sentences if convicted after contesting an accusation at trial. To the extent that forensic sciences are not demonstrably reliable, they presumably contribute to some pragmatic compromises by innocent persons.

Duties of an Expert Witness and Expert Reports

Experts have always testified under oath or affirmation to tell the truth.

Largely in response to controversies (and parallel civil justice reforms), many jurisdictions have begun to impose a range of formal duties and obligations, sometimes codified (e.g., United Kingdom and Australia) on expert witnesses. These codes, particularly statutory codes and rules of court, tend to reinforce the duties of an expert witness: to act impartially (as a servant of the court rather than a party); to disclose conflicting opinions and bodies of thought; to readily concede limitations and critical literature. English and Australian rules tend to require disclosure and transparency in expert reports and testimony. In addition, societies of forensic scientists and other professional organizations often maintain their own codes of conduct or ethical prescriptions for members.

There is, however, little evidence that the expansion of formal codes has led to improved expert performances, greater circumspection in testimony, or higher quality expert reports. With a few conspicuous exceptions (e.g., Michael West and Sir Roy Meadow), forensic scientists are infrequently prevented from testifying because of formal breaches and, even in the aftermath of scandal and judicial censure, forensic scientists are rarely disciplined by professional bodies.

Wrongful Convictions

Recent reviews of wrongful convictions in the United States, typically cases exposed by Innocence Projects where individuals were exonerated by DNA evidence, suggest that in a large proportion of these cases flawed or misleading forensic science testimony was admitted. These cases suggest that, for a variety of reasons, forensic science failed to correct investigators' beliefs in the guilt of innocent persons which had been formed on the basis of other forms of incriminating, though mistaken, evidence—such as eyewitness testimony and false confessions. Thus, forensic science has both contributed and exposed wrongful convictions.

Wrongful convictions also reinforce how traditional legal safeguards and appellate review may struggle to identify and expose weaknesses in forensic science and other kinds of evidence (e.g., eyewitness identification) or overcome their synergistic effects even when they are mistaken.

Expert Witness Immunity

Historically, forensic scientists have been immune from suit for negligence. However, recent developments in England and Wales, following *Jones v. Kaney* (2011), suggest that in some circumstances immunity may be lost, thereby potentially exposing expert witnesses to liability for mistakes caused through negligence, inadvertence, and incompetence.

See also: **Foundations:** Evidence/Classification; Overview and Meaning of Identification/Individualization; Statistical Interpretation of Evidence: Bayesian Analysis; The Frequentist Approach to Forensic Evidence Interpretation; **Legal:** DNA Exonerations; Expert Witness Qualifications and Testimony; Forensic Laboratory Reports; History of the Law's Reception of Forensic Science; Legal Systems: Adversarial and Inquisitorial; The Innocence Project; When Science Changes, How Does Law Respond; **Management/Quality in Forensic Science:** *Sequential Unmasking*: Minimizing Observer Effects in Forensic Science; **Pattern Evidence/Fingerprints (Dactyloscopy):** Friction Ridge Skin Impression Evidence – Standards of Proof; **Professional:** National Academy of Sciences (NAS).

Further Reading

Edmond, G., Roach, K., 2011. A contextual approach to the admissibility of the state's forensic science and medical evidence. University of Toronto Law Journal 61, 343–409.

Faigman, D., Saks, M., Sanders, J., Cheng, E., 2008. Modern Scientific Evidence. West/Thompson Publishing, St. Paul, MN.

Freckelton, I., Selby, H., 2009. Expert Evidence. Lawbook, Sydney.

Garrett, B., 2011. Convicting the Innocent. Harvard University Press, Cambridge, MA.

Gatowski, S., Dobbin, S., Richardson, J., 2001. Asking the gatekeepers: a national survey of judges on judging expert evidence in a post-*Daubert* world. Law and Human Behavior 25, 433–458.

Giannelli, P., 2004. *Ake v. Oklahoma*: the right to expert assistance in a post-*Daubert*, post-DNA world. Cornell Law Review 89, 1305–1419.

Goudge, S., 2008. Inquiry into Pediatric Forensic Pathology in Ontario. Government Printer, Ontario.

Groscup, J., Penrod, S., Studebaker, C., Huss, M., O'Neil, K., 2002. The effects of *Daubert* on the admissibility of expert testimony in state and federal criminal cases. Psychology, Public Policy, and Law 8, 339–372.

Jasanoff, S., 1995. Science at the Bar. Harvard University Press, Cambridge, MA.

Law Commission, 2011. Expert Evidence in Criminal Proceedings in England and Wales. HMSO, London.

Ligertwood, A., Edmond, G., 2010. Australian Evidence, fifth ed. LexisNexis, Sydney.

McQuiston-Surrett, D., Saks, M., 2009. The testimony of forensic identification science: what expert witnesses say and what fact finders hear. Law and Human Behavior 33, 436–453.

Roberts, P., Zuckerman, A., 2010. Criminal Evidence, second ed. Oxford University Press, Oxford.

Saks, M.J., Faigman, D.L., 2008. Failed forensics: how forensic science lost its way and how it might yet find it. Annual Review of Law and Social Science 4, 149–171.

Shelton, D.E., Kim, Y.S., Barak, G., 2009. An indirect-effects model of mediated adjudication: the CSI myth, the tech effect, and metropolitan Jurors' expectations for scientific evidence. Vanderbilt Journal of Entertainment and Technology Law 12, 1–43.

Health and Safety

N Scudder and B Saw, Australian Federal Police, Canberra, ACT, Australia

Glossary

Clandestine laboratory ("Clan labs") Setting up of equipment or supplies for the manufacture of illegal compounds such as drugs or explosives.

Confined space An enclosed or partially enclosed space that is not intended or designed primarily for human occupancy, within which there is a risk of one or more of the following: (1) an oxygen concentration outside the safe oxygen range. (2) A concentration of airborne contaminant that may cause impairment, loss of consciousness, or asphyxiation. (3) A concentration of flammable airborne contaminant that may cause injury from fire or explosion. (4) Engulfment in a stored free-flowing solid or a rising level of liquid that may cause suffocation or drowning.

Dynamic risk management The continuous assessment of risk in the rapidly changing circumstances of an operational incident, in order to implement the control measures necessary to ensure an acceptable level of safety.

Hazard The potential for a substance to cause adverse effects.

Hierarchy of control measures Ranking of measures taken to prevent or reduce hazard exposure according to effectiveness, from the most effective measures that eliminate hazards to the least effective that achieve only limited protection.

OHS policy A policy document indicating an organization's commitment to OHS, its intentions, objectives, and priorities and identifying roles and responsibilities.

Risk The likelihood of injury or illness arising from exposure to any hazard(s) and the magnitude of the adverse effect.

Occupational Health and Safety Policy

The legislation in many countries places the onus of responsibility on employers to provide a healthy and safe working environment under occupational health and safety (OHS) legislation and common law. Employers should ensure that all managers, supervisors, and staff are aware of their OHS responsibilities. Management leadership can positively influence OHS outcomes for an organization.

Workplace health and safety is an ongoing process. Subject to the legislative requirements of each jurisdiction, in most instances, a documented OHS policy is required. The development of such a policy requires the commitment of both staff and management. Once commitment has been achieved, the OHS policy should be developed with involvement from all stakeholders and promulgated.

The OHS policy should:

- articulate the organization's commitment to OHS;
- indicate that sufficient resources (both financial and personnel) will be provided to promote and maintain OHS standards and meet OHS requirements;
- outline the organization's intentions, objectives, and priorities OHS;
- describe in broad terms the means by which the objectives will be met;
- identify the roles and responsibilities of management, supervisors, and staff in meeting OHS requirements; and
- be signed off by the most senior manager of the organization, reflecting the importance of the policy.

The OHS policy should be reviewed periodically to ensure its currency.

The OHS policy is, however, only one part of an appropriate OHS strategy for a forensic organization. The OHS policy must be underpinned by risk assessments and incident/accident reports that enable the organization to assess its OHS exposure, to meet legislative requirements such as reporting obligations, and to respond to risks appropriately.

An organization can develop a list of the main hazards that its staff are likely to be exposed to in the course of their duties, utilizing OHS reports, incident/accident reports, and previous risk assessments. Prioritizing the main health and safety issues allows the organization to develop appropriate action plans to meet the objectives of its OHS policy.

Forensic organizations may consider integration of some OHS requirements with their quality assurance system. Many laboratories effectively use their quality system to embed OHS requirements in their documented procedures, to review OHS hazards as part of a periodic audit program, or to manage elements of their OHS action plans through their corrective action system. OHS, similar to quality, can then be viewed as an important yet integrated component of an effective management system.

Risk Assessments

Once potential OHS hazards have been identified, forensic organizations should evaluate the likelihood of injury from the interaction to the hazard and the magnitude of the adverse effect. The process of risk assessment will be very useful for managing potential OHS hazards within the facility and the expected external work environment. The purpose of the risk assessment process is to ensure that all workplace hazards have been identified, recorded, assessed, controlled, and reviewed. The desired outcome of this process is to eliminate, as far as practicable, the risk of injury or illness to personnel, damage to property, and damage to the environment. The process of developing risk assessment is often better suited to the known work environment. An OHS assessment of an office or laboratory can quickly identify specific hazards that may require attention. Obviously, this works well for the office and laboratory environment within one's control; however, each external scene will be different.

It is important that the range of potential hazards in external crime scenes and work environments is considered. While some risks can be grouped and managed collectively, the specific hazard and risk mitigation and control will vary from scene to scene given the circumstances. Given this, forensic practitioners should have an ability to undertake dynamic risk assessments, or "risk on the run" as it is known in some jurisdictions.

Dynamic Risk Management

Dynamic risk assessments are conducted by a forensic practitioner as part of the attendance and examination process. In some instances, such as attendance at a clan lab, a person may be designated as the Site Safety Officer and have carriage of this as well as health and safety for all personnel at the site. Practitioners should be trained to assess the risk given the circumstances at the time, considering the actual hazards present at a crime scene.

A designated forensic practitioner or Site Safety Officer should undertake a quick reconnaissance of the crime scene to ensure the safety of forensic practitioners and others working at the scene. A review of the scene should be repeated whenever the situation at the scene changes. This could involve a visual inspection without entering the crime scene and asking a number of questions. For example:

- Does the crime scene involve structures that are now unstable?
- Has confirmation been obtained from the fire brigade or other emergency responders that power, gas, and water to the site have been turned off?
- Is there adequate shelter so that practitioners can rest without succumbing to environmental stressors such as heat, cold, wind, or rain?

It is important to close the loop, and incorporate any strategic elements of each dynamic risk assessment in OHS policy and planning. After each incident, any relevant information obtained during the dynamic risk assessment should be recorded and collated for strategic analysis.

Hierarchy of Control Measures

Within OHS, there is a "hierarchy of control" designed to mitigate or resolve a risk deemed unacceptably high.

The hierarchy of control is a sequence of options which offer a number of ways to approach the hazard control process. Various control options may be available. It is important to choose the control that most effectively eliminates the hazard or minimizes the risk in the circumstances. This may involve a single control measure or a combination of different controls that together provide the highest level of protection that is reasonably practicable.

1. Eliminate the hazard. If this is not practical, then:
2. Substitute the hazard with a lesser risk. If this is not practical, then:
3. Isolate the hazard. If this is not practical, then:
4. Use engineering controls. If this is not practical, then:
5. Use administrative controls, such as safe work practices, instruction, and training. If this is not practical, then:
6. Use personal protective equipment (PPE), such as gloves, eye protection, boots, and respirators.

It is important that management and staff discuss and consult, where possible, during all phases of the hazard identification, risk assessment, and risk control process.

Examples

1. If an organization is considering purchasing a piece of analytical equipment, and two products have the same capabilities but substantially different noise levels during operation, the organization may consider the noise level of the equipment during procurement, and opt for the quieter system. This example demonstrates the principle of eliminating the hazard at source, which is the most effective

control measure, when compared to training and provision of PPE such as hearing protection.

2. In the case of a fire scene of a building, applying a hierarchy of control approach, it is first necessary to consider the elimination or substitution of hazards. In a fire scene, this is not possible. It is, however, possible to isolate the scene to prevent danger to the public and to maintain the integrity of the scene. Power, water, and gas to a building should be disconnected prior to entering the site. A structural engineer's opinion may be necessary prior to entry to the building. Safe entry and exit to the site can be established. Other administrative controls, such as briefing practitioners and maintaining records of the entry and exit of personnel, may be applied. Finally, practitioners can be prevented from entering the fire scene unless utilizing the appropriate PPE.

Specific Laboratory Hazards

The likely hazards within a laboratory environment include the following.

Chemicals

Chemical exposure may occur through inhalation, skin absorption, or direct ingestion and, once absorbed are stored in a particular organ or tissue, metabolized, or excreted. The effect of a chemical on a person is dependent on a number of factors such as duration and frequency of exposure, concentration of the chemical, and an individual's metabolism. A synergistic effect may occur when the undesirable effects of one substance are intensified if exposure has occurred to another substance.

Some nanomaterials exhibit different chemical properties compared to what they exhibit on a macroscale. As this is a relatively new field, there is insufficient knowledge regarding the hazards posed by nanomaterials. The potential hazards associated with nanomaterials may include increased reactivity because of their increased surface-area-to-volume ratio, the ability to cross some of the body's protective mechanism, and the lack of the body's immunity against such small particles. Because of this lack of knowledge, the suggested control strategy to be used when working with nanomaterials should be "as low as reasonably achievable" approach to reduce exposure.

The effects of chemicals on the body may be categorized:

- poisonous or toxic chemicals are absorbed into the body and exert either an acute or short-term effect, such as headache, nausea, or loss of consciousness, or a long-term effect such as liver or kidney damage, cancer, or chronic lung disease;
- corrosive chemicals burn the skin, eyes, or respiratory tract;
- irritants can inflame the skin or lungs, causing conditions such as dermatitis or bronchitis;

- sensitizers may exert long-term effects, especially to the skin (such as contact dermatitis) and to the respiratory tract (such as occupational asthma) by inducing an allergic reaction; and
- explosive or flammable substances pose immediate danger of fire and explosion, causing damage to the body through direct burning, or through inhalation of toxic fumes emitted during combustion.

Safety data sheets (SDS), also known as material safety data sheets (MSDS), are designed to provide relevant information regarding the identity, physical characteristics, safe storage, use, disposal, first-aid treatment, and spill management of substances that are handled in the workplace. The information includes whether the substance is deemed to be a hazardous and/or a dangerous goods item. At a minimum, the SDS should be consulted before the first use of a chemical or other substance within a laboratory, or if practitioners are unfamiliar with the product. Copies of SDS should be retained according to legislative requirements. In some jurisdictions, electronic SDS management systems can allow an efficient way of accessing up-to-date SDS information.

Sharps

Sharps are objects that have sharp edges or points that have the potential to cut, scratch, or puncture the skin. Sharps can cause physical injury and have the potential to introduce infectious and toxic agents through the wounds created in the skin. Examples include hypodermic syringes and needles, knives, or broken glassware.

All forensic practitioners have a responsibility to handle and package sharps safely. Particular care should be given to ensuring that sharps are appropriately labeled when packaged. Sharps such as knives could, for example, be packaged in clear plastic tubes, making it easier for a person opening the item to identify the contents and the direction the sharp items is facing. Forensic labs should be encouraged to develop policies that encourage forensic practitioners and others that submit items to develop safe-packaging procedures.

Biological Material

Examples of "biological material" commonly encountered in forensic examinations include body tissue, blood, and body fluids (urine, saliva, vomit, pus, seminal fluid, vaginal fluid, and feces). Biological material is potentially hazardous as it may contain infectious agents such as viruses, bacteria, fungi, and parasites that cause a variety of communicable diseases.

Hair, fur, and items of clothing that have been in close contact with humans or animals may also harbor parasites such as fleas or nits.

When examining plant material, such as cannabis, consideration should be given to the presence of *Aspergillus* sp. mold. If the *Aspergillus* spores are inhaled into the lungs, a serious, chronic respiratory or sinus infection can result. If mold is visible, the cannabis should be treated as a biological and respiratory hazard.

It is impossible to determine the prevalence of infectious or communicable diseases in the environment in which forensic practitioners work. Consequently, practitioners should adhere to recommended procedures for handling biological material and adopt an approach known as the "standard precautions." This approach requires practitioners to assume that all biological materials are a potential source of infection, independent of diagnosis or perceived level of underlying risk.

Vaccinations should be offered for practitioners. The types of vaccinations given may depend on whether work is confined to the laboratory or whether work is performed in the field, as well as whether forensic practitioners are likely to be deployed overseas where other diseases may be more prevalent.

Firearms

Forensic practitioners may retrieve firearms from crime scenes. All personnel who may be required to handle firearms, either in the field, in the laboratory, or in support roles such as property or exhibit stores should be trained in how to render a firearm safe. As with the "standard precautions," it is important to consider all firearms as potentially loaded, and adopt the practice of never pointing a firearm in the direction of another person, even after it has been rendered safe.

Firearms examiners, who undertake firearms investigations including test firing and bullet recovery, will be exposed to hazards such as noise and lead. They should have their hearing and blood lead levels monitored on a regular basis, to ensure that hearing protection is being worn and is functioning correctly, and any exposure to lead from the firearms is quickly identified and addressed.

Computer Forensics Laboratory

Computer forensic examiners specialize in obtaining, analyzing, and reporting on electronic evidence stored on computers and other electronic devices. Crimes involving a computer can range across the spectrum of criminal activity, from child pornography to theft of personal data to destruction of intellectual property. Potential hazards involve static postures, occupational overuse, and stress from viewing graphic images.

Some suggestions to minimize the stress from viewing graphic images are as follows:

- psychological assessment before and after viewing graphic material, and periodically;

- exposure to only one medium, for example, visual material only, rather than examining both sound and visual material simultaneously;
- specifying limits as to the amount of time spent examining explicit material in a day, and
- ceasing any examination of explicit material at the end of their shift, to allow themselves time to refocus attention away from this stressor.

Electrical/Machinery

Forensic laboratories use a wide range of electrical equipment and machinery. Practitioners need to ensure that any inherent risk from electric shock is mitigated. The use of residual current devices (safety switches) is an appropriate strategy, as is visual inspection and periodic testing and tagging of power cords, to detect obvious damage, wear and other conditions which might render it unsafe by a person qualified to do so under the legislation in effect in the jurisdiction.

Fume Cupboards

Fume cupboards are integral to minimizing the risk of exposure to chemical and biological hazards. Not all fume cupboards are suitable for all hazards. Fume cupboards should be maintained and inspected periodically. During maintenance, attention should be given to the following:

- the fume cupboard itself, including flow rates and replacement of absorbents or filters;
- in the case of externally vented fume cupboards, the ductwork and location of external vents. This is particularly important during any building maintenance or refurbishment.

Fume cupboards must be used for all operations that have the potential to release hazardous fumes, mists, or dusts.

- Before commencement of work, ensure that the fume cupboard is clean and free from contamination.
- Ensure the minimum of equipment is stored in the fume cupboard and is placed toward the back of the cupboard to reduce disturbance to the air flowing into the fume cupboard.
- Lower the sash as far as practicable during use to improve fume containment.

Recirculating fume cabinets rely on filtration or absorption to remove airborne contaminants released in the fume cabinet before the exhaust air is discharged back into the laboratory. They are suitable for light to moderate use with a known range of substances. The range of substances for which each cabinet can be used is limited by the need for compatibility with the chemicals in use as well as with the particular type of absorbent or filter fitted to the cabinet.

Robotics

The introduction of automated robotic platforms has significantly enhanced the efficiency of forensic analysis. The use of robotics is becoming more common and is very useful for a range of repetitive laboratory tasks. Besides saving time, robotics overcomes the need for repetitive work involved in pipetting, eliminating musculo-skeletal injuries.

Hazards associated with robotics include the risk of exposure to the chemicals used in the work, electrocution, and cutting, stabbing, or shearing from the moveable parts of the robot. The interlocks on the robots should not be bypassed.

X-rays

X-rays are used in analytical and imaging instrumentation. Potential exposure to X-rays is generally localized to specific parts of the body, usually the hands or fingers. Depending on the X-ray energies delivered, effects may range from erythema (redness) at point of exposure, blood changes, cancer through to death. Depending on the legislative requirement in each country, practitioners working with X-ray equipment may be required to use dosimeters to assess radiation dose.

Lasers

Lasers span the visible and nonvisible electromagnetic spectrum and have many applications in forensic science, including Raman spectroscopy. Lasers are generally classified according to the level of risk they represent. Damage from laser beams can be thermal or photochemical. The primary sites of damage are the eyes and skin. Hazards associated with laser work may include the following:

- fire,
- explosion,
- electrocution, and
- inhalation of contaminants from laser interactions.

Precautions for use of lasers include the following:

- Display the class of laser in use.
- Appropriate protective eye wear with side protection and appropriate attenuation for the wavelength(s) in use must be worn.
- Interlocks on the laser should not be bypassed.
- Keep the laser beam path away from eye level whether one is seated or standing.

High-Intensity Light Sources

High-intensity light sources such as the Polilight® provide a range of colored light bands and white light for forensic work.

- Care should be taken that high-intensity white light is not directed onto any object at short distances from the end of

the light guide, as this can cause severe heat damage to the object, and may result in a fire.
- The light beam should never be directed at eyes as the light can cause permanent damage.

Manual Handling

Manual handling refers to any activity that involves lifting, lowering, carrying, pushing, pulling, holding, restraining, or the application of force. Only a very small number of manual handling injuries are caused by the lifting of heavy weights alone. Actions such as reaching, twisting, bending, or maintaining static postures contribute to injury affecting the muscle or skeletal systems of the body. These musculo-skeletal injuries predominantly involve the neck, back or shoulder or arm muscle, tendon, ligament, or joints.

Injuries may be caused from activities such as maintaining static postures while working at fume cupboards, repetitive keyboard and mouse work, pipetting, prolonged use of comparison microscopes.

Some preventative strategies include the following:

- Seeking further assistance to have the activities assessed to minimize the manual handling risks inherent in the activity.
- Planning tasks so that rest breaks are scheduled.
- Choosing the best tools for the tasks.
- Alternate hands while using a mouse, if possible.

There is a move to make instruments smaller and more portable for use at crime scenes. While this has significant benefits, including potentially reducing the number of exhibits collected, moving equipment can also raise manual handling concerns.

General Laboratory Management

Housekeeping is important in laboratories. It is important to maintain clear passageways, have proper labeling of chemicals, clean and uncluttered work areas and appropriate storage. The handling of powders is a potentially hazardous operation and good housekeeping can help minimize airborne contamination from spilled materials. Having a planned preventative maintenance program and regular inspections of the workplace, plant, and equipment are essential for the smooth running of the laboratory.

Handling of Exhibits in Court

Each evidential item must be appropriately packaged and sealed, if this is not already the case, before it is exhibited in court. Items such as clothing which are normally stored in paper may need to be repackaged in clear plastic allowing the item to remain sealed, and minimizing the risk of cross-contamination when handled in court. Caution should be exercised against opening exhibits in court, in case any hazards such as mold or irritant fumes are released.

Hazards in the Field

Forensic practitioners are often required to work or train in the field. Consideration should be given to managing hazards which may affect practitioners, including the following:

- environmental hazards such as heat, cold, humidity or wet weather, the terrain, and fauna or flora at the scene;
- the type of operation, for example, working in a clandestine laboratory often involves quite specific hazards;
- the possible presence of offenders or other security risks such as booby traps at a scene; and
- the availability of first aid and emergency response domestically and overseas.

The risks from these hazards should be considered within the scope of the exercise or operation. Some possible responses to hazards, which may be considered in a dynamic risk assessment, include the following:

- Designating a location for emergency equipment, such as a crime scene vehicle, and ensuring that disinfectants, antiseptics, and a first aid kit are easily accessible;
- Planning an emergency exit from the scene and ensuring that this is communicated to all personnel present;
- Establishing a decontamination point if there is exposure to chemical or biological material;
- The use of appropriate PPE including sunglasses, sunscreen, and hats when working outdoors;
- Depending on the external temperature, work activity, duration, and PPE worn, practitioners should have access to shade for rest and adequate fluids if required during hot weather to prevent heat stress. The wearing of PPE including chemical suits and respirators requires longer and more frequent periods of rest break for recovery in hot temperatures and humid environment;
- In cold weather, provision should be made to have adequate warm clothing and a sheltered area;
- The risk of animal or dog bites while attending a crime scene should not be discounted. If practitioners are searching in vegetated areas, the risk of snake or tick bites should be considered, along with possible exposure to plants such as poison ivy or stinging nettles.

Confined Spaces

Forensic practitioners may have to enter confined spaces. Due to the high risks associated with entering the confined space, many jurisdictions mandate that entry into a confined space must not be made until a confined-space permit has been issued. Practitioners must receive specific training before work or entry into confined spaces.

Chemical Biological and Radiological and Nuclear Incidents

Forensic practitioners may be required to attend a chemical biological and radiological and nuclear (CBRN) incident. CBRN incidents where forensic practitioners may attend and conduct examinations include the following:

- chemical (warfare agent, toxic industrial chemical);
- biological (weaponized agent, natural disease);
- radiological (discrete, or wide area contamination); and
- nuclear.

Depending on the response agency protocol in place, forensic practitioners may be working closely with the fire brigade and other emergency first responders. Entry must not be made into the "warm" or "hot" zone of the scene without consultation with the other emergency first responders.

Clan Labs

Clan labs pose a significant threat to the health and safety of police officers, forensic practitioners, the general public, and the environment. There are many hazards associated with clan labs including the following:

- flammable materials and/or explosive atmosphere;
- acutely toxic atmospheres;
- leaking or damaged compressed gas cylinders; and
- traps and hazards deliberately set to cause injury or death to police and other responders.

As a result of the frequency at which clan labs are encountered and the severe and variable risks associated with the investigation, many jurisdictions have developed specific policies and procedures concerning clan lab investigations.

For forensic practitioners to deal with clan labs requires a high level of fitness as well as technical expertise. Practitioners have to understand the following:

- illicit drug chemistry;
- how to neutralize the risks of explosions, fires, chemical burns, and toxic fumes;
- how to handle, store, and dispose of hazardous materials; and
- how to treat medical conditions caused by exposure.

Practitioners must also wear full protective equipment including respirators and may be required to move equipment at the clan lab in the process of collecting evidence. The storage and handling of unknown chemicals from clandestine laboratories or seizures should also be considered. Preliminary identification should take place, before its storage or disposal.

When unknowns such as "white powders," chemicals (in liquid, solid, or gas state) or biological materials are encountered in the field, it is prudent to be cautious and obtain up-to-date intelligence to shed more light on what is at the scene. It may be an explosive material or contain anthrax spores or ricin or something as innocuous as talc.

Some precautions include the following:

- wearing the appropriate level of protective clothing/equipment for the activity;
- avoiding direct contact with the substance, even if only in small quantities;
- not smelling or tasting anything from the scene;
- noting physical characteristics such as color, form, and consistency;
- where it is safe to do so, looking for hazard symbols on packaging or labels if available; and
- seeking specialist advice if unable to identify the substance.

Potential Hazards during an Overseas Deployment

Forensic practitioners can be required to work overseas to assist with large-scale disasters. An example was the Thailand Tsunami Victim Identification process involving forensic practitioners from 30 countries working to recover and identify bodies. Forensic practitioners need to be mindful of hazards likely to be encountered during an overseas deployment depending on the location, magnitude of the operation, and how many practitioners are deployed. Some hazards to be considered include the following:

- climatic demands;
- remote and sometimes dangerous terrain;
- different cultural sensitivities;
- security requirements;
- different levels of infrastructure support at the locality;
- logistics, including the transport of large quantities of equipment, manual handling, setting up, and packing up;
- different hygiene levels;
- diseases that can be transmitted by insect and or animal vectors;
- the possibility of infectious diseases; and
- asbestos and other hazards in buildings.

Work-Related Stress

Practitioners at work may experience work-related stress. There are some specific stressors unique within forensic work. Forensic practitioners may experience workplace-related stress due to their attendances at morgues, violent crime scenes, Disaster Victim Identification or from requirements to view explicit or graphic material or images.

Indicators of stress include changes in eating habits, tiredness due to changes in sleep patterns, frequent absences from work, reduced productivity, concentration, motivation, and morale. Physical symptoms may include headaches, abdominal pains, diarrhea, constipation, high blood pressure, insomnia, anxiety state, and depression.

Many organizations offer programs to provide assistance to employees, including counseling to help practitioners to deal with work-related stress or resilience training to manage work–life balance.

See also: **Management/Quality in Forensic Science:** Principles of Quality Assurance; Risk Management; Principles of Laboratory Organization.

Further Reading

Clancy, D., Billinghurst, A., Cater, H., 2009. Hazard identification and risk assessment – understanding the transition from the documented plan to assessing dynamic risk in bio security emergencies. In: World Conference on Disaster Management, Sydney, Australia. http://www.humansafety.com.au/getattachment/da338cb7-29b0-4d3a-8a06-d7dc0b569a87/C20.aspx.

Furr, K., 2000. Handbook of Laboratory Safety, fifth ed. CRC Press, Florida.

Green-McKenzie, J., Watkins, M., 2005. Occupational hazards: law enforcement officers are at risk of body fluid exposure. Here's what to expect if it happens to you. Law Enforcement Magazine 29 (9), 52–54, 56, 58.

Hanson, D., 2007. Hazardous duty training officers to tackle hazmat emergencies. Law Enforcement Technology 34 (4), 80–85.

Haski, R., Cardilini, G., Bartolo, W., 2011. Laboratory Safety Manual. CCH Australia Ltd, Sydney.

Horswell, J., 2000. The Practice of Crime Scene Investigation. CRC Press, Florida.

Jackel, G., 2004. The High Cost of Stress, vol. 1. AUSPOL: The Official Publication of the Australian Federal Police Association and ALAJA, 4–37.

Mayhew, C., 2001a. Occupational health and safety risks faced by police officers. Australian Institute of Criminology. Trends and Issues in Crime and Criminal Justice 196, 1–6.

Mayhew, C., 2001b. Protecting the occupational health and safety of police officers. Australian Institute of Criminology. Trends and Issues in Crime and Criminal Justice 197, 1–6.

Rothernbaum, D., 2010. Exposed: an officer's story. Clan Lab Safety Alert 7 (2), 1–2.

Smith, D., 2005. Psychosocial occupational health issues in contemporary police work: a review of research evidence. Journal of Occupational Health and Safety, Australia and New Zealand 21 (3), 217–228.

Tillman, C., 2007. Principles of Occupational Health and Hygiene: An Introduction. Allen & Unwin, Crows Nest.

Whitman, M., Smith, C., 2005. The culture of safety: no one gets hurt today. Police Chief LXXII (11), 20–24, 26–27.

Winder, C., 2011. Hazard Alert: Managing Workplace Hazardous Substances. CCH Australia Ltd, Sydney.

Witter, R., Martyny, J., Mueller, K., Gottschall, B., Newman, L., 2007. Symptoms experienced by law enforcement personnel during methamphetamine lab investigation. Journal of Occupational and Environmental Hygiene 4, 895–902.

Relevant Websites

http://www.ccohs.ca/oshanswers/occup_workplace/labtech.html—Canadian Centre for Occupational Health and Safety (CCOHS).

http://www.cdc.gov/niosh/—Centers for Disease Control and Prevention (CDC).

http://www.forensic.gov.uk/html/company/foi/publication-scheme/health-and-safety/—Forensic Science Service, Health and Safety.

http://www.hse.gov.uk/services/police/index.htm—Health and Safety Executive (HSE).

http://www.police.qld.gov.au/Resources/Internet/rti/policies/documents/QPSForensicServicesHealth_SafetyManual.pdf—Health and Safety Manual, Police Forensic Services, Queensland Police.

http://www.londonhealthandsafetygroup.org/archive.html—London Health and Safety Group.

http://www.osha.gov/—Occupational Safety & Health Administration.

http://www.ccohs.ca/oshanswers/occup_workplace/police.html—What Do Police Do?.

Ethics

R Weinstock, University of California, Los Angeles, CA, USA; West Los Angeles Veterans Affairs Medical Center, Los Angeles, CA, USA
GB Leong, Center for Forensic Services, Western State Hospital, Tacoma, WA, USA
JA Silva, VA Outpatient Clinic, San Jose, CA, USA

Introduction

Ethics in the forensic sciences is complex and challenging, as a result of functioning at the interface of science and law—two major disciplines with differing methods, values, and goals. The law needs to obtain definitive answers in order to resolve disputes promptly and render justice. In contrast, science reaches tentative conclusions, subject to change with further evidence. Forensic science applies science to legal issues, but many differences exist between legal ethics and either scientific or professional ethics. There are specific ethical requirements for each scientific discipline with additional ethical requirements whenever scientific skills are applied to legal matters. Frequently, the two ethical requirements supplement each other. Many scientific disciplines facilitate forensic ethics by addressing the ethical aspects of the application of that discipline to legal issues, but not all disciplines do so. Whenever these requirements conflict, ethical dilemmas are created. Although there are many potential ethical problems in forensic science, most problems can be resolved by following codes of ethics or standards of good forensic practice.

Forensic Science Ethics and Personal Ethics

Forensic science ethics is the ethics of applying science to law. Many ethical facets in forensic science are controversial. Some forensic scientists attempt to resolve ethical disputes by making an apparently arbitrary distinction between "ethics" and "morals." However, these terms have been used interchangeably in philosophy for many years. The arbitrary distinction between "ethics" and "morals" enables those forensic scientists to avoid many ethical dilemmas by labeling certain ethical problems as only personal moral issues. Such ethical matters and dilemmas are thereby excluded from scientific and professional ethics discourse and consideration. The more appropriate distinction would be between personal ethics or morals, current professional and scientific ethics, and the practitioner's view of what should be professional and scientific ethical behavior. Most issues can be considered from either a personal or a scientific and professional ethical perspective, even though complex ethical problems may not lead to a consensus.

In the personal sphere, "ethics" or "morals" refer to the concerns forensic scientists have that are based on personal ethical (moral) or religious considerations not derived from their professional and scientific roles. In the professional and scientific spheres, "ethics" is the term traditionally used. "Ethics" in this context refers to fundamental foundational rules or guidelines regulating conduct in scientific and professional disciplines or forensic science organizations. In contrast, rules of conduct or matters of etiquette are less fundamental matters that should be distinguished from ethics.

Organizational Forensic Science Ethics

For various reasons, not all professional and scientific organizations have ethical requirements or methods of enforcing them. When an organization does enforce its ethics, due process or procedures are required both ethically and legally, in which accused members have an opportunity to hear the charges against them and present a defense. The advantage of ethics enforcement by a forensic science organization is that knowledgeable peers oversee one another. Otherwise such oversight may be taken over by outsiders, who may be insufficiently familiar with the discipline or profession to be able to be fair and effective.

Ethical requirements ideally should be enforceable. They should address minimally acceptable professional and scientific behavior. Behavior below these standards should result in a finding of an ethical violation with appropriate punitive sanctions. Sanctions can range from warnings and reprimands, to suspension and expulsion from an organization. A limitation on the ability of organizations to enforce ethical standards is that they cannot enforce ethical standards and requirements on nonmembers or on individuals who withdraw from membership. However, some organizations publish the fact that a member resigned from the organization while under an ethics investigation, in disciplines in which licensing boards have authority, licenses could be suspended or revoked.

Although it is essential to meet basic minimal ethical requirements, the attainment of only a minimal threshold of ethical practice does not necessarily indicate good forensic practice. Failure to find an ethical violation is far from meaning that the professional or scientist necessarily is displaying impeccable ethics. Like the "not guilty" adjudication in legal proceedings, it may mean only that there is an insufficient basis to prove that a practitioner has violated forensic science ethics.

Basic Minimal Ethics and Aspirational Ethics

Some organizations distinguish between ethical requirements representing basic minimal requirements and aspirational standards or standards of good forensic science practice. Although many organizations confuse these two types of ethical standards, a clear distinction is important so that forensic scientists can determine which provisions represent basic minimal standards that must never be violated, and which represent a higher ideal threshold of desirable and exemplary conduct. The aspirational provisions represent desirable standards toward which forensic practitioners should strive. "Good" forensic scientists will do so. In contrast to minimal standards, failure to achieve aspirational standards should not lead to sanctions. Sometimes, there could be an acceptable reason for not meeting the standards of good forensic practice.

An aspirational standard may sometimes be unenforceable because an assessment of the intent of the forensic scientist may be necessary in order to evaluate the behavior. Since intent is subjective, its determination may be difficult, if not impossible, to ascertain. Nonetheless, a good forensic scientist will try to meet the aspirational standard. Alternatively, a standard may be potentially enforceable, but may not be a minimal standard meriting sanction. Instead it might represent more a matter of desirable or good forensic practice.

Poor forensic practice does not necessarily mean unethical practice. Some inadequate forensic evaluations might represent lack of knowledge or failure to keep up to date in a forensic science discipline. The appropriate action in such instances might involve education rather than a punitive sanction. Other inadequate evaluations may result from time pressure and/or overwork that may contribute to overlooking some important aspects of a case. Although an evaluation may be inadequate, the negligence might not be of sufficient gravity to violate a basic minimal ethics requirement.

Codes of Ethics in Forensic Science Practice

Organizations such as the American Academy of Forensic Sciences have developed a code of ethics and conduct that the organization enforces. The ethics code states that members "shall refrain from providing any material misrepresentation of education, training, experience or area of expertise." It also requires members to "refrain from providing any misrepresentation of data upon which an expert opinion or conclusion is based." Additional provisions are part of the code of conduct. They are designed to prevent members from falsely claiming to represent an organization and from engaging in conduct, adverse to the best interests and purposes of the organization. Such transgressions of a code of conduct may violate the rules of the organization but may not represent violations of fundamental forensic scientific ethics. The code of ethics and conduct also has provisions describing due process or procedures.

When enforcing a code of ethics, the following questions, as enumerated by Rosner, should be answered:

1. What provision is the member accused of violating?
2. What are the criteria for that provision?
3. What are the relevant data?
4. What is the reasoning by which it is determined that the member has or has not violated the specific provision?

It is important to write ethics provisions clearly in order to prevent ambiguity that could result in an ethics hearing degenerating into a popularity contest. For example, in the absence of clear guidelines, there is a danger that a verdict could primarily become dependent on whether a hearing panel likes an accused individual, whether the accused person's views on a controversial issue are popular, or whether the accused is part of the "in" group. As a result, the actual seriousness of the ethics offense would become much less relevant, with less effort expended toward determining exactly what happened and for what reason, thus obscuring the stated goal of the hearing.

If there are sections of the code that potentially are unclear to a reader, clarifying interpretations should be disseminated to the organization's membership. It is essential for members to have information in advance about the specific types of conduct that are prohibited (minimal standards), with a clear distinction from those that are encouraged (aspirational standards). If there is any potential ambiguity, a way must be found to provide the necessary clarification. One possible means is to print an explanation of the issue in the organization's newsletter.

Standards for Good Forensic Practice

Aspirational standards are standards of good practice or even excellence. Good forensic practitioners should strive to attain these standards despite the fact that only minimal basic ethical standards are subject to enforcement. The American Academy of Forensic Sciences' Committee on Good Forensic Practice has developed the following Standards for Good Forensic Practice.

1. Forensic scientists generally should follow the standards of their respective disciplines. They should apply with care any assessment methods, technical skills, scientific, and other areas of specialized knowledge, to legal issues and questions. They should always strive to do high quality work.

2. Forensic scientists should strive to keep current and maintain competence in their scientific disciplines. Although competence at minimum should be a goal, forensic scientists should strive for excellence.

3. Forensic scientists should demonstrate honesty and should strive for objectivity, by examining scientific questions from all reasonable perspectives and by actively seeking all relevant obtainable data that could distinguish between plausible alternative possibilities.

4. Forensic scientists should strive to be free from any conflict of interest. They should possess an independence that would protect their objectivity. Any potential conflict of interest should be disclosed. Work on relevant cases should be avoided or discontinued if objectivity may be compromised.

5. Forensic scientists should undertake cases and give opinion only in their areas of expertise, attained through education, training, and experience.

6. Forensic scientists should attempt to identify, deter, and help eliminate unethical behavior by other forensic scientists through methods such as discussion with a colleague, education, and if unsuccessful, by filing an ethics complaint.

7. It is essential to recognize that honest differences of opinion exist and do not imply unethical behavior by either expert. The legal adversary system includes opposing attorneys seeking out experts with favorable opinions. Forensic scientists should not be blamed unfairly for unpopular verdicts, honest differences of opinion, or the vagaries of the legal system.

8. Passions against an opposing disagreeing expert, or personal animosity, should not constitute the basis for an ethics complaint. Ethics complaints must be made in good faith. If based on passion alone, such ethics complaints themselves are inappropriate.

9. Forensic scientists should present their opinions to the trier of fact in concise understandable language, but care must be taken since such efforts can result in over-simplification and loss of some precision. In their efforts to communicate effectively, forensic scientists should strive to be as accurate as possible and avoid distortion. Every reasonable effort should be made to ensure that others (including attorneys) do not distort the forensic scientist's opinion.

10. Forensic scientists should strive to instill the highest ethical and scientific standards in their students and colleagues through such means as teaching, supervision, setting a good example, publications, and presentations at meetings.

11. Forensic scientists should strive for excellence and the highest degree of integrity. Forensic opinions should not be based on undisciplined bias, personal advantage, or a desire to please an employer or an attorney.

12. When forensic scientists are asked to express opinion on a legal issue, they should make every effort to become familiar with the applicable legal criteria in the pertinent jurisdiction. They should take care to reach only those legal conclusions that result from proper application of the data to that legal issue.

13. Unlike attorneys, forensic scientists are not adversaries. They take an oath in court to tell the whole truth. They should make every effort to uphold that oath.

14. When a forensic scientist accepts any privileged information from an attorney, care should be taken to ensure that all such information is kept confidential and does not reach the opposing side. After accepting such information, forensic scientists should not provide their services to the opposing side unless legally ordered to do so. Forensic scientists should alert attorneys not to make payment or provide privileged information, if they wish to retain the option to be employed by the opposing side.

Ethical Problems in the Forensic Sciences

Some forensic scientists confuse their role with that of an attorney. The attorney's role is to present the best one-sided case for his/her client, the only exception being not to argue for anything, the attorney knows to be untrue. Unlike an expert witness, attorneys take no oath in court. In contrast, forensic scientists take an oath "to tell the truth, the whole truth, and nothing but the truth." If forensic scientists assume the attorney's total advocacy role and present the best one-sided case for the retaining attorney regardless of the "truth" and the oath taken, the forensic experts may be perceived as "hired guns." They thereby vilify not only their own reputation, but also taint that of the entire field. Many forensic scientists consider the "hired gun" problem the most serious ethical problem in forensic science.

A "hired gun" can establish a track record of testifying for both the plaintiff (prosecution) and defense depending on the side that hires the expert. An effective "hired gun" can appear impartial and objective by giving one-sided misleading persuasive explanations for whichever side hires him/her for a particular case. "Hired guns" not only always make the best case for the side hiring them, but alternatively they could also do so for a side for which they have a personal bias, regardless of which side they actually believe is right. In contrast, it is possible to have a bias and preferentially work for one side, yet refuse to take on a case unless the forensic scientist honestly believes an opinion is true with the greatest objectivity possible. The distinction between a hired gun and an expert with an idiosyncratic opinion is not always clear-cut without knowing what is in the mind of the expert. Even if experts firmly believe an opinion because of personal bias so that they honestly may be telling what they believe to be true, others frequently might incorrectly view the opinion as a dishonest distortion of the truth. Sometimes, the problem is an insufficient effort by the expert to be objective, or an honest difference of opinion between forensic scientists.

Honest differences of opinion do exist as they do in every science and profession including law, and it is unfair to blame forensic scientists and forensic science for the battle of the "experts." Additionally, once a forensic scientist reaches an honest objective opinion, the pressures of our adversary system encourage experts to advocate for their opinion. It is difficult to remain totally objective when defending an opinion. Subtle pressures can also bias an expert, such as the wish to please an attorney or an employer. An honest expert should make every effort to form opinion based on the evidence, even if contrary to the wishes of the hiring person or institution. There are also questions about what it means to tell the truth, the whole truth, and nothing but the truth. Does it mean the expert should try to offer the whole truth and not a misleading part of the truth to the degree that the attorneys and the court will permit? Or is it enough to present only that part of the truth that will help the case and rely on good cross-examination (which may not happen especially if the case is settled before trial) to bring out the rest of the truth? Or should some portions of the truth that may lead to conclusions contrary to the expert's opinion be presented solely as a tactical maneuver to make a preemptive strike so that those aspects can be debunked before the other side has a chance to present them?

Should a forensic scientist try to participate in the legal system only in ways that further justice or should the forensic scientist solely answer the questions asked and trust the adversarial system to usually achieve justice? The adversarial approach exists in those countries such as the United States that base their system on English common law. Should forensic scientists lend their expertise to sides trying to achieve an "unjust" outcome? Is it presumptuous for forensic scientists to try to further only what they see as justice or what is consistent with their professional scientific or personal values? Answers to these questions presently lack a consensus and a resolution does not seem likely in the foreseeable future.

Foundations of Ethics

Are ethical guidelines arbitrary rules, or are they based on something more basic and fundamental? Ethical codes address "important" issues, and seem to represent more than codes of conduct or codes of etiquette. Sometimes codes confuse etiquette (such as not criticizing another scientist or professional or not hurting an organization) with fundamental ethical issues. There are questions whether any ethical truth is objectively right or wrong, or whether all ethics is subjective and one code is as good as another. Some, who view ethics as subjective, see it as solely dependent on the mores of a specific culture or scientific discipline. They believe that what is considered ethical is only what is morally right to individuals, in that culture or group.

Some consider that the only foundation for ethics and morals is religion. However, religion itself lacks objectivity not only within the confines of a single religion, but also because there would be no consensus as to which of the many different religions should be the standard bearer. Some religions in the past have advocated human sacrifice. Did that make it "right" for them? There is a long tradition of secular ethics independent of religion in Western democratic countries. Although religion can be a basis for ethics, many religiously observant people can be unethical and do "wrong" things despite engaging in religious practice. Atheists can be very ethical and committed to philosophical study to determine what is "right." Although religion can undoubtedly motivate many people to do what is "right," by no means is religion a necessary foundation for ethics and morals.

Two primary schools of thought exist regarding the basis for ethics. One is consequentialist and proposes that the ethical thing is whatever leads to the best consequences, such as the most good or happiness for the most people. A subset of this position is utilitarianism, insofar as what is most useful is ethical. Another school is deontological and bases ethics on an intrinsic duty. Actions are intrinsically right or wrong regardless of consequences. An example of the latter is the philosopher Immanuel Kant's categorical imperative—to do what you believe any ethical person in your position should do, such that the maxim you are following should be a universal principle for all to follow.

There can be problems with following any of these positions too rigidly. You might consider justice an intrinsic deontological duty, much as Kant did. Does that mean though that every crime no matter how small should be investigated until the perpetrator is punished? It takes consequentialist considerations to balance this duty with the desirability of spending government money on other things that might be more important for society's welfare. Investigating every crime thoroughly until the criminal is caught would use up all our society's resources. No funds would be left for other desirable purposes. Additionally, if deontological considerations were primary, two deontological duties might conflict without any principle to resolve the conflict.

Similarly, following only consequentialist considerations result in problems. For example, it might decrease crime in society if it were perceived that every criminal was always swiftly caught and punished and no criminal ever got away with a crime. To achieve this end it might help to choose individuals from an unpopular group such as prior offenders, try them in secret, find them guilty, and execute them quickly and publicly. Such a procedure might in fact have some deterrent value and decrease crime especially if it were used for white-collar crimes like embezzling money or income tax fraud. However, deontological considerations of justice convince us that there is something wrong with this procedure. There are even contrary consequentialist considerations. Government could become very powerful, and any of us could be arbitrarily tried, convicted, and executed even if we were innocent. All of us would be at potential risk. Thus, a purely consequentialist foundation for ethics would also provide no way to decide between these competing consequences to determine the right action.

The best approach requires a consideration of both types of ethical foundations, but there is no higher order rule to help us in balancing these considerations. The theoretical approach to resolving ethical dilemmas essentially uses universal ethical principles as "axioms" from which particular ethical judgments are deduced as "theorems." A solution to a problem in a particular case is deduced from the ethical principle. However, there usually is no higher order ethical rule or principle to help us decide among competing ethical principles.

In contrast, the practical approach, known philosophically as "casuistry," does not involve universal theoretical principles and rules but require us to consider the issues from the perspective of a particular case. General ethical principles and rules essentially are "maxims" that can be fully understood only in terms of paradigmatic cases that define their meaning and force. However, there can be and often are, differences of opinion about which facets of a case should be overriding, with no ethical guidance to help us in weighing and balancing competing ethical maxims.

In both instances, deontological and consequential considerations can assist us in determining what is "right." However, when ethical rules and principles conflict, there generally is no rule, principle, or maxim to help us resolve the conflict. Therefore, it is essential that forensic scientists are able and prepared to think through and resolve ethical dilemmas themselves. In difficult situations, more than one solution usually should be considered acceptable, and ethics committees should not place sanctions on forensic scientists for following either course. In order to help reach the "best" solution in such cases, consultation should often be obtained from experienced forensic scientists, knowledgeable about ethics issues.

Ethical Dilemmas

Ethical dilemmas often defy consensus solutions. When ethical responsibilities conflict, some forensic scientists always give the legal needs, a priority. The majority, however, usually give the legal needs, a priority, but make exceptions if the law desires an action that violates serious aspects of the values and ethics of their own scientific discipline or profession. In such situations, their professional or scientific values, ethics, and responsibilities may outweigh the desires of the legal system, and preclude their involvement in that aspect of a legal case. Personal ethics and morals can also preclude such involvement. Although the legal system can establish legal ethics, only scientific, professional, and forensic science disciplines and organizations can establish forensic science ethics. The law cannot determine what is ethical in forensic science; it only can determine what is legal.

Ethical dilemmas occur when there are conflicting ethical duties. An example of such a conflict occurs in forensic psychiatry, in circumstances in which a practitioner might sometimes believe that the most accurate and truthful assessment would be attained by misleading the person being evaluated. Such deception is often legal, but it violates forensic psychiatric ethics as promulgated by the American Academy of Psychiatry and the Law. Most forensic psychiatrists follow the guideline of the forensic psychiatric profession, regardless of the frequent legality of such deception. In another instance, many consider the presentation of aggravating circumstances in a death penalty phase of a trial, a violation of medical ethics, even if such aggravating circumstances are true and such testimony in the United States violates no current ethical requirement. The same is true if individuals incompetent to be executed are treated to make them competent. These problems occur when medical or psychological skills are used to evaluate an individual for forensic purposes.

The specter of ethical conflict, however, is by no means limited to forensic psychiatry and psychology or other branches of forensic medicine, but it occurs in all forensic sciences. The use of DNA evidence in the courtroom, although seemingly based on sophisticated modern scientific techniques, with unusually high levels of reliability and certainty, is another example of a highly controversial area. Problems in other aspects such as data collection can be questioned. In many ways it seems counterintuitive that there can be such divergence in professional opinion when accurate data such as DNA evidence are introduced. Nonetheless, controversy does exist about the interpretation of DNA data among highly respected forensic scientists, such as in the widely publicized criminal trial of O.J. Simpson. Does that necessarily mean that one side is unethical or is it possible for honest forensic scientists to hold strong opposing views? One possible explanation is that the highly accurate nature of DNA evidence has made many problems more significant. Potential ethical and data collection problems that had been readily ignored when identification methods were less accurate, suddenly have begun to loom in importance. Many such controversies exist in all forensic science disciplines.

Conclusion

Although the ethical course of action is clear in the majority of situations, it is essential for the "good" forensic scientist to be knowledgeable about ethics in order to be able to resolve ethical dilemmas when difficult situations arise. It is essential to know the minimal requirements in a code of ethics in order to stay out of trouble and avoid sanctions. However, such codes do not and cannot address all contingencies since differing requirements as well as aspirational standards may conflict. Generally, there is no higher order rule telling us how to resolve such a conflict. In such instances, sometimes with knowledgeable help, forensic scientists must work out their own ethical solutions. Such dilemmas are likely to occur when different disciplines with differing ethics and values intersect, such as science and law, in forensic science practice.

Various organizations address different issues in their codes. Two minimal standards for forensic scientists are the need to be clear and truthful, and not to distort credentials and data. However, the good forensic scientist should strive for more than just staying out of trouble and meeting minimum standards. "Good" forensic scientists should strive for excellence, both in their ethics and in their forensic science work.

Ethical complexity in the forensic sciences is not a reason to avoid forensic practice. Forensic scientists should accept the challenge, but should be prepared to confront and assess potential ethical conflicts. Myriad problems beset all disciplines, especially those that interface with two very different disciplines such as science and law. Forensic science is an interesting, stimulating, and productive vital occupation, but it is necessary to become informed about as many facets as possible in order to become a good ethical practitioner. In most cases, despite the potential ethical dilemmas that have been enumerated, the forensic science codes of ethics provide the required minimal ethics solutions. Those wishing to be good forensic science practitioners, who strive for excellence, generally can find guidance in standards of good forensic practice. It is only in relatively rare cases that ethical standards conflict or there are conflicts between provisions in the standards of good forensic practice. In such instances, forensic scientists should be prepared, perhaps with consultation, to perform their own ethical analyses.

See also: **Foundations:** Principles of Forensic Science; **Legal:** Legal Aspects of Forensic Science.

Further Reading

AAFS Committee on Good Forensic Practice, 1999. Advisory opinion. Academy News 20, 24.

American Academy of Forensic Sciences, 1998. Code of Ethics and Conduct. American Academy of Forensic Sciences, Colorado Springs.

American Academy of Psychiatry and the Law, 1998. Ethical Guidelines for the Practice of Forensic Psychiatry. American Academy of Psychiatry and the Law, Bloomfield, CT.

Appelbaum, P.S., 1997. A theory of ethics in forensic psychiatry. Bulletin of the American Academy of Psychiatry and the Law 25, 233–247.

Beauchamp, T.L., 1982. Philosophical Ethics: An Introduction to Moral Philosophy. McGraw Hill, New York.

Beauchamp, T.L., Childress, J.F., 1994. Principles of Biomedical Ethics, fourth ed. Oxford University Press, New York.

Callahan, J.C., 1988. Ethical Issues in Professional Life. Oxford University Press, New York.

Code of Ethics for the Academy Editorial, 1986. Journal of Forensic Science 31, 798–799.

Diamond, B.L., 1992. The forensic psychiatrist: consultant vs. activist in legal doctrine. Bulletin of the American Academy of Psychiatry and the Law 20, 119–132.

Diamond, B.L., 1994. The fallacy of the impartial expert. In: Quen, J. (Ed.), Selected Papers of Bernard L. Diamond. Analytic Press, Hillside, NJ.

Dyer, A.R., 1988. Ethics and Psychiatry. American Psychiatric Press, Washington, DC.

Hundert, E.M., 1987. A model for ethical problem solving in medicine with practical applications. American Journal of Psychiatry 144, 839–846.

Jasinoff, S., 1995. Science at the Bar: Law Science and Technology in America. Harvard University Press, Cambridge.

Jonsen, A.R., Toulman, S., 1988. The Abuse of Casuistry. University of California Press, Berkeley, CA.

Katz, J., 1992. 'The fallacy of the impartial expert' revisited. Bulletin of the American Academy of Psychiatry and the Law 23, 141–152.

Mills, D.H., 1997. Comments from the perspective of the AAFS ethics committee. Journal of Forensic Science 42, 1207–1208.

Murphy, J., Coleman, J.L., 1990. Philosophy of Law: An Introduction to Jurisprudence, revised ed. Westview Press Co, Boulder, CO.

Nordby, J.J., 1997. A member of the Roy Rogers Riders Club is expected to follow the rules. Journal of Forensic Science 42, 1195–1197.

Rachels, J., 1993. The Elements of Moral Philosophy, second ed. McGraw-Hill, New York.

Rosner, R., 1994. Principles and Practice of Forensic Psychiatry. Chapman & Hall, New York.

Rosner, R., 1997. Foundations of ethical practice in the forensic sciences. Journal of Forensic Science 42, 1191–1194.

Rosner, R., Weinstock, R., 1990. Ethical Practice in Psychiatry and the Law. Plenum Press, New York.

Stone, A.A., 1984. Law, Psychiatry and Morality. American Psychiatric Press, Washington, DC.

Weinstock, R., 1997. Ethical practice in the forensic sciences – an introduction. Journal of Forensic Science 42, 1189–1190.

Weinstock, R., 1998. Letter to the editor. Journal of the American Academy of Psychiatry and the Law 26, 151–155.

Weinstock, R., Leong, G.B., Silva, J.A., 1991. Opinions expressed by AAPL forensic psychiatrists on controversial ethical guidelines: a survey. Bulletin of the American Academy of Psychiatry and the Law 19, 237–248. Erratum 19:393.

Key Terms

Admissibility, Admissible, Appeals, Best evidence, Bias, Brady material, Chain of custody, Conflict, Confrontation, Cross-examination, CSI effect, Daubert, Defense expert, Discovery, Ethical considerations, Ethics, Evidence, Expert evidence, Expert immunity, Expert witness, Expert, Forensic laboratory report, Forensic, Frye, Hazard, Health, Holistic approach, Innocence projects,

Integrated case management, Investigations, Judicial discretion, Juror, Jury instructions, Kuhmo, Law, Occupational health and safety (OHS), Opinion evidence, Plea bargain, Risk, Safety, Science, Strategy, Submissions, Testimony, Trial safeguards, Trial, Witness, Wrongful convictions.

Review Questions

1. Are the models offered for forensic service provision suggested by Ramsey and Burton the only ones available? What other models might there be?
2. What' is a "forensic strategy"? What questions are part of developing one? Why is it important to a case and to a laboratory?
3. Why is integration of forensic cases "the single biggest challenge to the forensic science community"?
4. What is currently in forensic reports? How do these differ from other scientific reports? How do they differ from published articles in peer-reviewed journals? What *should* be in forensic reports? Make a table listing each component and compare.
5. Who is the "audience" of forensic reports? The police using the technical information to investigate the case or other scientists who must review the technical information? Is it both? How does this affect the content of forensic reports? Should it?
6. How do the legal requirements of the contents of a forensic report differ between the UK and the US?
7. Can forensic reports stand on their own (that is, without an expert's testimony)? What determines this?
8. Are there ethical obligations to the format and content of a forensic report? If so, what are they?
9. What is "Brady material"?
10. What is "OHS"? What should this policy articulate?
11. What is a risk, in OHS terms? How is it prevented or mitigated? What is the hierarchy of control measures?
12. List some specific forensic anthropology hazards. What are their risks, how are they managed? Do they differ between the field and the laboratory? Why?
13. Why is good housekeeping important in a forensic laboratory?
14. Why is stress a health and safety issue? What types of analysis are particularly prone to mental or stress issues?
15. Many forensic anthropologists are primarily employed by universities and assist law enforcement "on the side." What ethical issues arise because of this part-time status?
16. Review Question 15. What *legal* issues arise from forensic anthropologists' part-time status? For example, what about discovery?
17. What does it mean to void dire an expert?
18. What is direct testimony? What is cross-examination? How do they differ? Who asks which questions?
19. Who is the "trier of fact"?
20. How is the wording of a report different from the wording of testimony? Should it differ? If so, how?

Discussion Questions

1. How should forensic examinations and analyses be "integrated"? With laboratory specialization, how can cases move through a forensic laboratory in an integrated fashion? What are the benefits to doing this? What are the problems?
2. Why are forensic reports formatted the way they are? Is there a better way to present this information? Who are they written for and who *should* they be written for?
3. Are some types of forensic science more prone to hazards and health risks than others? If so, list them and explain why they are; if not, why not?
4. Does good general laboratory practice hold true for a forensic anthropology facility or are there reasons to go above and beyond those precautions?
5. How does one provide quality and safety when operating in the field, say, at the site of an aircraft crash in the middle of a wooded area?

Additional Readings

Blau, S., 2015. Working as a forensic archaeologist and/or anthropologist in post-conflict contexts: a consideration of professional responsibilities to the missing, the dead and their relatives. In: Ethics and the Archaeology of Violence. Springer, New York, pp. 215–228.

González-Ruibal, A., Moshenska, G., 2015. Ethics and the Archaeology of Violence. Springer Science + Business Media, New York.

Roberts, L.G., Dabbs, G.R., Spencer, J.R., 2016. An update on the hazards and risks of forensic anthropology, Part I: human remains. Journal of Forensic Sciences 61 (S1).

Roberts, L.G., Dabbs, G.R., Spencer, J.R., 2016. An update on the hazards and risks of forensic anthropology, Part II: field and laboratory considerations. Journal of Forensic Sciences 61 (S1).

Robben, A.C., 2016. Digging for the disappeared: forensic science after Atrocity by Adam Rosenblatt (review). Human Rights Quarterly 38 (1), 224–228.

Sledzik, P.S., Bryson, S.W., 2016. Mass Fatality Management. Koenig and Schultz's Disaster Medicine: Comprehensive Principles and Practices, p. 361.

INDEX

'*Note*: Page numbers followed by "f" indicate figures, "t" indicate tables and "b" indicate boxes.'

A

Printed and bound by CPI Group (UK) Ltd, Croydon, CR0 4YY

11/06/2025

01899189-0015